World War II

World War II
Policy and Strategy
Selected Documents with Commentary

Hans-Adolf Jacobsen and Arthur L. Smith, Jr.

Clio Books

Santa Barbara, California
Oxford, England

Library of Congress Cataloging in Publication Data
Main entry under title:
World War II, policy and strategy.
    Includes bibliographical references and index.
    1. World War, 1939–1945—Sources. I. Jacobsen, Hans
Adolf, 1925– II. Smith, Arthur Lee, 1927–
D735.W65   940.53'1   79-11507
ISBN 0-87436-291-1

American Bibliographical Center—Clio Press
2040 Alameda Padre Serra, Box 4397
Santa Barbara, California 93103

Clio Press, Ltd.
Woodside House, Hinksey Hill
Oxford, OX1 5BE, England

Manufactured in the United States of America

Contents

Preface

Current interest in World War II appears to have reached universal proportions. Television, newspapers, novels, and nonfiction alike are unceasing with their flow of "war stories." No doubt much of this is due to the postwar generation's desire to know more of the events that have shaped their lives. However, the continued release of war documents of every description kindles the interest of older generations as well.

The intent of the present volume is to provide a meaningful and comprehensive view of World War II through the presentation of the most important documents (although a few may be more interesting than important). Major events are viewed from a global perspective, providing a basis for judgment and interpretation that is not single-nation oriented. It is felt that the organization, with introductions, documents, and chronology, succeeds in that purpose. The study should serve the student, scholar, and lay reader alike.

We gratefully acknowledge permission to quote from the following sources: Hans-Adolf Jacobsen, ed., *Generaloberst Halder,* III (Stuttgart: W. Kohlhammer Verlag, 1964); *The War Reports of General of the Army George C. Marshall, General of the Army H. H. Arnold, Admiral Ernest J. King* (New York: J. B. Lippincott Co., 1947); Arthur Bryant, *The Turn of the Tide* (London: William Collins, 1957); B. L. Montgomery, *The Memoirs of Field Marshal, The Viscount Montgomery,* 1958 ed., reprinted by permission of Thomas Y. Crowell; Albert Speer, *Inside the Third Reich* (New York: Macmillan Publishing Co., Inc., 1970); Louis Snyder, *The War: A Concise History,* 1960 ed., reprinted by permission of Simon and Schuster; *The Rommel Papers,* ed. and copyright 1953, B. H. Liddell Hart, reprinted by permission of Harcourt Brace Jovanovich, Inc.; "Report to the Secretary of War . . . June 1945," reprinted by permission of the *Bulletin of the Atomic Scientists,* copyright 1946 by the Educational Foundation for Nuclear Science; and *Sukarno: An Autobiography As Told to Cindy Adams* (New York: The Bobbs-Merrill Co., Inc., 1965).

HANS-ADOLF JACOBSEN
Bonn

ARTHUR L. SMITH, JR.
Los Angeles

*An Introduction to World War II as an Historical
Phenomenon*

It is many years since the Second World War ended; however, the fateful events of that short span of time between 1939 and 1945 continue to shape and influence the world. The results of that great conflict set into motion a continuing and worldwide struggle that divided nations, changed the age-old balance of power in Europe, Asia, and Africa, and the end is still not in sight. The basic question of just how this happened remains a challenge.

One important advantage has come with the passage of time and that is the availability of the documentation necessary to fully examine the events. Thus, much has been done to clarify the motives and decisions that surrounded many important happenings. It is now possible to write much more objectively about World War II than it was in the decade immediately following war's end. However, the very materials that the historian hoped for have come in such an unending stream that no single individual is capable of evaluating it all.[1] The task then becomes one of following the essential lines of development and eliminating extraneous excursions into less important byways.

Of course, many general studies have properly focused certain events and clearly developed a large variety of aspects of the war from strategic planning to victory and/or defeat. Despite the many surveys, however, there remain important questions still to be answered. The following discussion will attempt to illustrate some of the complexities in identifying a number of these fundamental problems which require more thorough research and clarification. Generally, these problems may be separated into several broad areas for purposes of discussion: 1) Placing the war in an historical context; 2) War as "the continuation of politics by the intervention of other means;"[2] and 3) The image of war.

1) *Placing the war in an historical context.* The difficulty in defining the place in world history that World War II occupies rests upon the inability of modern scholarship to draw exact perimeters. The reason for this is the absence of any real general analysis of the large movements and events

that comprise the causes of the war. The sheer magnitude of modern imperialism, national struggles for independence, revolution, dictatorship, and world wars represents a formidable barrier to any easy or quick understanding. However, this has not prevented historical production on the subject of World War II; quite the contrary! Despite the vast number of books and studies published about the war those attempting a general analysis fall into five broad categories (or some combination thereof). These are military, national, regional, global, and ideological.

The military approach, concentrating upon the details of the battles between opposing forces, remains the most popular. Here, the goal is described as overpowering the enemy at all costs. Victory is the aim without regard to resources spent or losses suffered. All the facts necessary to gain a knowledge of war on that level, both quantitative and qualitative, are supplied. This means extensive descriptions of war weapons, military training, economic potentials, and manpower requirements. The emphasis is upon battle, however, and in the extensive writing devoted to preparations, execution, and conclusions, care is taken to give every due to the variety of military arms involved from infantry to air force to navy and marines. The respective opponents are diligently scrutinized as to strengths and weaknesses in organization, command structure, and smoothness of operation.[3]

Once the mass of detail and analysis has been properly assembled the fundamental questions of exactly which ingredients turned the tide of battle toward defeat or victory are answered. How important was the overall defensive or offensive strategy employed? What were the advantages and disadvantages of a single front war as compared to two or more fronts? (Obviously, war on all fronts, as Germany ultimately experienced, becomes impossible to sustain indefinitely.) Just how successfully all of this can be clearly conveyed to the reader depends on the historians. In order to adequately collate all conceivable elements that contributed to either defeat or victory on the battlefield everything that can be weighed in the balance must be considered, from psychological warfare to partisan and underground resistance.[4]

This approach to understanding war provides certain obvious insights, although it is already dated. The error is to ignore the influence of politics upon military events. A war in modern times does not occur in a vacuum, and herein lies the major weakness in the military interpretation. Inevitably the range of vision is narrowed and this in turn reduces the number of factors that can and must be considered for final evaluation. An example of this sort of shortcoming can be found with Erich von Manstein's *Lost Victories*[5] (the very title suggests the approach discussed above). Here, the military power is viewed as having moved into its own orbit separate from and with little or no relationship to the original political forces that prompted it. Any grasp of the important links between the flow of politics and the war fronts is obscured and with it all chance of understanding the meaning of the war.

The national approach. When the study of war is approached from the national or state standpoint the predominant emphasis is placed upon the singular history of one state or another. Military data is utilized here too, since approaches often overlap; however, the purpose is to relate the military aspects to the political and social lives of a nation. The immediate advantage of such an approach is to provide a structure that connects political objectives (to force one's political will upon the enemy), military priorities, and general overall planning.[6] This allows us to measure and judge the influences of a belligerent nation's political and social structure upon its military complex. Only this approach illuminates the interrelationship of homefront with war's front wherein the extent of coordinating all available resources to support the war effort is seen. In this manner the forces that stand behind a government are shown in clearer relief as well.[7] In addition, such an approach goes far toward explaining the ethical importance of these events and therefore has been used widely in the writings on national history and war.[8]

Most historians who have used the national approach have been fully aware of its limitation; namely, it is a partial interpretation because of having been developed primarily from the viewpoint of a single country. This means that many factors that may well have been deciding ones in any conflict are omitted or treated only partially since they remain beyond the scope of such a treatment. The mere fact that a war involving many nations is written about in a unilateral fashion precludes basic comparisons that come with evidence drawn from several societies. Last, but by no means least, a national approach greatly exaggerates the role of an individual state and imbues it with an importance that is distorted.

Some of these obvious shortcomings are solved with a *regional approach,* which discards the idea of using a single state as a starting point and embraces a region instead. The political, social, and cultural characteristics determined by the geography and history of Europe or Eastern Asia, for instance, allow for a focus within the regional framework. This is a more comprehensive approach than that of the nation-state since a much larger picture is gained. It is possible to identify many more elements than would be visible in a national study, such as power blocs, areas of differences, and common interests among several nations. The regional study provides a perspective that permits a look at the basic feature of wars of all kinds in the 20th century. That is, that the aim of war is no longer just the seizing of territories or the securing of strategic positions; it is to displace one system of values with another as in total revolution. The victor must impress his system with a domination that is absolute. This has brought either loyalties (collaborators) or opposition (resistance fighters). To many of the conquered it becomes a choice between either freedom or submission to totalitarianism.[9] Despite the broader approach with regionalism, however, the European experience has illustrated the inability of regional forces to exert decisive influence on the international political scene.

The entrance of the United States, for example, into World War I proved the importance of intervention by an outside force, for it shifted the balance of power and produced a winning side. The same was true during World War II in Asia when the United States became involved there.[10]

The fourth approach in the problem of placing the war in an historical perspective is *global.* Since this is an attempt at providing a total view of events on a worldwide scale it obviously requires an heroic effort by both historian and reader. If a balanced result is to be achieved there can be no compromise with the documentation, for a failure to deal with the fact of global interdependence—rather than the matter of a divided Germany, Vietnam, or Korea—would be to miss the major theme of world history since 1941.

The global involvement can easily be seen in the United States' transition from a nonbelligerent nation in 1940 to its extensive world commitments by 1942–43. In 1944, American overseas military forces were distributed from the European theater (some 50%), to the Mediterranean (17%), to the Pacific (26%), Africa, China, India, the Middle East, Burma, and the Caribbean (the remaining 7%).[11] Meanwhile, America had reached mammoth proportions as a functioning war machine fulfilling massive requirements of supply, communications, and industrial production at an ever increasing rate.

A fifth approach may be termed *ideological,* and applies basically to that area of the world dominated by Communism (this includes forms of Communism outside the Soviet orbit such as Maoism or Titoism). History is interpreted here in terms of class structure and there is little room for a consideration of other forces in arriving at evaluations. This can quickly be determined by a reading of Communist produced histories.[12]

A problem that is fairly common to all of the approaches that have been discussed is *periodization,* or labeling units of time in a selected chronology of the war. This stems from the influence of the military approach with its strong reliance upon following the course of events one after the other in what appears to be an inevitable unfolding. This seemingly fixed sequence depends, of course, on which side is supplying the historical account. While Anglo-American writers might choose to separate war periods into descriptions like "years of isolation or appeasement," "prelude to disaster," "standing alone," "forming the Grand Alliance," "turn of the tide," and "the final victory," the German version would begin with "victory in the east and west," "a German occupied Europe," "apex of power," "military reversals," and "the final collapse." There is also the "period" treatment which simply divides the war into periods of success and failure and uses this formula for all situations, national and international.[13]

This dated military approach has been widely used, however, and separates the war into five broad areas: origins; the war in Europe, Africa, and the Near East; Sino-Japanese War; the war in the Pacific; and the war at sea. Add a conclusion and everything has been covered. Within the broad areas are more than a dozen subdivisions detailing somewhat smaller subjects in careful chronological order. This starts with the German campaign in Poland in 1939, and ends with the final phase of the war against Japan in 1945.[14] Occasionally, this approach may attempt some balance by including materials on economics and politics in wartime or even sections of a specialized nature such as resistance movements, Jewish persecution, or occupation problems.[15]

Soviet historians do not utilize the technique of periodization, but instead differentiate between war periods as being detrimental or helpful to socialist goals. Thus, Soviet writings view the Anglo-French alliance in 1939–40 as part of the larger imperialist struggle and not a crusade against Hitler. The war only became a "just" one in Soviet eyes when opposition began to grow against German occupation authority and Russia entered the conflict. At this stage even the capitalist powers became acceptable partners linked in a common cause to destroy fascism.

2) *War as "the continuation of politics by the intervention of other means."* It is now clear that to comprehend a world at war means to assess and understand every element that contributes to the total process. However, if we accept Clausewitz's definition of war as "the continuation of politics by other means," valid until the end of World War II (and the appearance of new weaponry), then it would be wrong to view 1939 to 1945 simply as a series of battlefield defeats and/or victories. In pursuing our study we must not lose sight of the war aims of the more powerful nations, for it is here and only here that the insights are secured into how larger policy emerges, how war is conducted, and what forces direct and shape the overall course. This is not to say that we reduce the importance of the military action, the development of weapons, efforts of the industrial and economic complexes, or discard the value in examining war from the regional and global perspectives. In fact, all of these areas are, when integrated into the whole, absolutely vital to completing a history of World War II that rises above the large number of works that have been written from the narrower viewpoints. This will provide a truthful record and at the same time allow the historian to make fair judgments in a highly important task that has now become possible.

AN ALTERNATE SOLUTION

We have discussed the lack of conventional World War II histories to accomplish the job of producing any real, complete analysis of that conflict. We also briefly pointed out reasons for this failure. It is time to suggest that a history of World War II can be written that would avoid these pitfalls and incorporate findings and judgments that would succeed in presenting the reader with a full picture.

Beginning with the title "The 'New Order' in Europe and the Establishment of the 'Greater East Asia Co-Prosperity Sphere,' 1939–1943," such an approach would first deal with the aims and politics of Germany, Italy, and Japan. These were the nations that began their respective drives toward global power and conquest in the 1930s.[16]

Although these nations had similar goals with their expansionist policies, their individual systems contained some fundamental differences. Actions were primarily of a unilateral nature, with little or no coordination in advance; therefore, one cannot view them in the light of a planned conspiracy to destroy world peace. It should be noted also that the individual policies followed had different sources of support in the various nations; in Europe the dictatorships remained oblivious to the cautionary pleadings of their military staffs, while in Japan the generals ignored all warnings and rejected any civilian restraint.

Research on the question of early war responsibility—1939 to 1941—has led to the assumption by some historians that this conflict did not come into being because of the uncontrolled ambitions of one state only.[17] The shares of responsibility quite obviously vary, but all of the major powers had in some manner been instrumental in the promotion of fascism. In their desperation to preserve peace the European states sought to appease Mussolini and Hitler, while the Soviet Union looked to its own methods by a non-aggression pact with Germany. Even the United States must carry some of the burden with its isolationist position that only encouraged expansionist-minded nations. However, the major responsibility belongs to the Hitler regime with its determination to obtain objectives regardless of the price in human suffering.

German, Italian, and Japanese objectives were pursued with a certain amount of commonality. That is, each nation's political philosophy contained the premise that there was an historical right due it; each too regarded forceful conquest as an acceptable means of achieving the desired objectives (land, labor, resources, and ideological control). Perhaps one of the strongest features that Japanese imperialism had in common with that of Germany and Italy was the fact that their power politics was rooted more in impoverishment and crisis than in a largess of capital and goods as was characteristic of the classical imperialist nations.[18] It might be noted, however, that the kind of late imperialism practiced by the Nazis featured conscious long-range planning quite characteristic of the leading ideologies of our century. This occurred despite the fact that the German geographic base was limited to its highest point of expansion by 1943.

The underlying theme of the introductory text would be the constant monitoring of the methods of these late imperialist powers as they set about accomplishing their long-range goals. This would include relevant data on the alliances that were formed, the degree of resistance encountered, and in the brief periods of victory, how they governed their subject peoples. The military measures taken by Great Britain and the Soviet Union during this same period play an insignificant role, for these nations were struggling for their very existence.

In this suggested approach both temporary and long-range political planning must have designations that properly indicate their importance. This would force the writers to abandon the treatment of battle to battle. In other words, the heretofore importance and space given these campaigns would now be devoted to the victor's plans for the conquered and how they were implemented. This explains the *reasons* for the war and must always be kept in view; Germany fought to create an economic and military climate that furthered the plans for a Greater Reich; Italy struggled to make her own Mediterranean empire; and Japan wanted to construct an Asian sphere under her domination.[19]

If this principle of always searching for the basic motivations behind the war is followed consistently, then the entire project will result in a logical and meaningful history of World War II. The emphasis upon the importance of the main stream of politics will provide an explanation that is not obscured by particularism and confusion.

The introduction would properly conclude with a detailed description of the three empires created by Germany, Italy, and Japan, and this would include a critical appraisal of the war policies of those nations. Some attention should be given as well to the beginnings of significant opposition within their respective states to the continued leadership of Mussolini and Hitler.

By approaching the problem this way students could begin to form a complete image of the size and shape of Japanese and Axis expansion. They would also begin to see why the Axis powers could not have won the war, for peoples everywhere (including those in their own nations) were starting to exhibit an outrage toward the inhuman system of totalitarianism and militarism.

A few words should be added here on the subject of planning and warfare, beginning perhaps with Clausewitz's warning that a war should not be started without knowing in advance the reason and the ultimate objective. Everything that follows is determined by this down to the smallest details. It is impossible to measure the resources needed without knowing the size of purpose. This does not rest entirely upon one's own capabilities but upon having fairly complete knowledge of the capacities of one's enemies as well. The human and industrial resources of the enemy must be studied as closely as your own.[20]

It is rather ironic that the works of 19th-century military strategists such as Clausewitz were generally ignored by the German military during World War II, while the United States issued a special military edition of *The Living Thoughts of Clausewitz*[21] in 1943. Following a completely senseless path of destruction aimed at the political and social systems of her enemies, Germany in particular attempted to substitute totalitarianism based upon a foundation created from untruths. Ignoring the advice of Clausewitz that the strength of the enemies must be studied and accurately measured, Hitler and the German High Command—as well as all of the German people—were to pay dearly for underestimating the power potentials of Great Britain, Russia, and the United States. In retrospect, this appears to be such an obvious and colossal blunder that one is prone to conclude that the war was lost before it had begun, and thus there were really never any so-called missed opportunities.[22]

The concluding portion of a revised text must focus clearly on the politics of the major powers who opposed Hitler, and the policies and strategies they developed (with due attention to the resistance and independence movements occurring on a worldwide scale). This anti-Hitler coalition (primarily Britain, the U. S., and the U. S. S. R.) had already begun to take the offensive during 1942–43 on virtually all fighting fronts and to force the course of action. Just as German-Italian-Japanese actions dominated at the beginning of the war, with Allied efforts at defense remaining background activity, the position is reversed: Axis and Japanese defensive campaigns are not as important as the unfolding of the "Grand Strategy" developed by Britain and the United States, nor the push of Russian power toward Eastern and Central Europe. The concluding text could be properly titled "1943–1945: The Annihilation of the Axis Powers and the Beginnings of a Future Peace Structure."

The Allies had perhaps little serious disagreement on how the war was to be conducted or in arriving at the larger goals; the "beat Germany first" principle had been unanimously endorsed. This is not to minimize the importance of keeping in mind the many factors that are intermingled into the broad panorama of war that have already been noted.

The final determination of the Allies to carry out a program aimed at creating new political and social foundations in the defeated nations in such a manner to preclude wars of the future was guaranteed by treaty. This meant the establishment of a system of collective security that found its origins in the creation of the Atlantic Charter in 1941.[23]

It would be incorrect to imply, however, that the anti-Hitler coalition entered the war for the sole purpose of establishing a new security system, for obviously individual nation's motives differed widely. Even in the closest of alliances, that of Great Britain and the United States, there was considerable difference of opinion on the solutions to many common problems; part of this stemmed from divided aims. In other areas, such as France, the Low Countries, Norway, Denmark, Greece, and Czechoslovakia, all intended to reestablish themselves as democratic nations, while India and Southeast Asia looked to full independence from their former colonial rulers. China was already beginning to encounter the problems of revolution. However, the air was full of hope and the western Allies with their Atlantic Charter pronouncement and continued enunciation of the principles for world peace inspired the support of most peoples whether in Europe, Asia, or Africa.[24]

On the issue of post-war independence for all colonial peoples there were fundamental historical differences between the United States and Great Britain. The U.S. regarded the liquidation of colonial empires as a major goal to be achieved in world affairs while Great Britain, as a long-time colonial power, was opposed. The coming to power of the British Labour Party in 1945 and the economic and military inability to continue in the pre-war manner brought a change in policy for England.

The creation of a new collective security system was compatible with the Soviet Union's desire for providing a bulwark against future aggressions; however, the Soviet leadership did not interpret any such instrument as the Atlantic Charter or wartime agreements as committing them to policies contrary to Communist doctrine.[25] It should not be forgotten that ever since the Soviet Union had taken the offensive she had followed a policy of Communist domination over the so-called liberated territories.

In conclusion the revised text might delve into the question of just how a successful wartime alliance of the western Allies and Russia combined to defeat the European Axis and Japan and then, instead of creating a new world, descended into a conflict so far-reaching in its complexities and ramifications that it consumed the next generation. This Cold War or East-West struggle, or Free versus the Slave world, or whatever designation fits the time and place found its immediate origins in World War II.[26] Somewhere the powerful World War II alliances began to weaken and fall apart; trust and confidence were replaced by suspicion and hostility. The broad differences of opinion that had been buried under the exigencies of war now surfaced as the most important problems in the world. The fact that the Soviet Union assumed they could do as they pleased with liberated territories without regard to the wishes of the inhabitants or the governments that had been in exile now created a widening gulf with the western Allies that grew increasingly dangerous.[27]

The situation was somewhat different in Asia, however, for here the decolonization process was in its death throes and could not be delayed or halted. It is important to note that the leadership in this long-awaited move to independence had been primarily Communist-led. Nor should the fact be ignored that the process had contributed to Japan's ultimate defeat as the strength of these new forces emerged.

It would be wrong to judge all of these historical events as purely background to the Cold War as many United States' historians are prone to do, for the reasons are many and varied and are not linked exclusively to the growing East-West conflict.[28]

In all fairness only an historical study which takes into account the true conditions of a time will ever be able to reflect it accurately. Only when this analysis is used in the widest of frameworks will an understanding of the great changes wrought by World War II be possible. As an historical problem it has had no parallel.

It is perhaps appropriate here to comment upon some aspects of war policy after 1942. Very importantly, the preponderance of favorable factors were on the side of the western Allies and Russia. For example, the Allied coalition brought together over two-thirds of all the material and human resources in the world. The Allies also enjoyed vast geographical advantages which gave them the superior strategic position. While both the western Allies and Soviet Russia combined represented a force that nothing could withstand, it is important to recognize that none of the powers alone could have brought about the same kind of victory. Just which of the major powers contributed the most to that victory is difficult to say although the Soviet version leaves little doubt for Communist readers.[29]

When the war's immediate aftermath is considered it becomes clear that the Soviet Union pursued a direct and consistent course during the latter part of the war, and that was to win as much territory as possible for Communism. The Soviet leaders never forgot their political purpose of advancing the doctrines of Marx and Lenin, and the unprecedented opportunity was presented them to advance right to the heart of Germany. They took advantage of the immense goodwill that flowed toward them as liberators from the Nazi domination, and quickly established puppet states in their own image in Central and Eastern Europe. China too was soon on the path to Communism under the powerful leadership of Mao Tse-tung.[30]

The western Allies, meanwhile, had failed to develop a unity of purpose toward political reconstruction that was in accord with their democratic principles. The cliché that they had won the war but lost the peace unfortunately proved true. Toward the end of the war, when the decisions and choices had to be made, they—and especially the United States—refused to place clearly enunciated political considerations ahead of lesser concerns (certain national aims, for example). A lack of awareness of the political climate that was growing at war's end proved a major blunder that was never recouped.

During the war many slogans and words were utilized in an attempt to bridge the communications gap between the western Allies and Russia, and what exact meanings were conveyed by words like "freedom," "democracy," and "peace" is impossible to say. The words came from the historical and political experience of each individual nation and had meaning within that framework, and none seemed to question whether or not there could be different meanings. As western leaders, Franklin Roosevelt and Winston Churchill must share some of the burden for the assumptions that persisted and created the illusion that the Soviets were being slowly but surely persuaded of the wisdom of democratic ways.[31] Since the British Prime Minister had a record of expressed reservations vis-à-vis the Communist system he has not had to bear the same historical criticism often associated with Roosevelt's role. The strong belief of the American president that he and Stalin enjoyed a relationship of mutual trust and understanding was rudely shattered shortly before the European war ended.[32]

Of course, judgment is far easier to pass after the results of the event are known and it should be kept in mind that leaders dealing with current events rarely have all the facts necessary for definitive decision. Wartime is a far more aggravated situation than any other time and all the more complex for it. This is especially true of World War II for it had no past parallel in terms of magnitude. Considering the global aspects of the war during the period 1943–45, it is quite difficult to imagine the western Allies taking any different course and risking a rupture in the alliance with Russia.[33] By the very act of joining against a common enemy the western Allies had endorsed Soviet aims in Eastern and Central Europe. They did not have the right nor the power to shape the political destiny of Europe until they opened their own front with Operation "Overlord" in June of 1944.[34]

Finally, before concluding, the following special topics should be mentioned and briefly discussed:

3) *The image of war.* This subject requires a far more extensive treatment than it has received to date. It is important to know just how changing views and images of war influenced major political decisions both before war's outbreak and during the war. How could war be allowed to start despite the many international treaties and systems of security that had been erected, and particularly after the experience of World War I? Some of the answer is that the experience of war, no matter how bloody and disastrous, does not dissuade nations from believing that they can successfully gain their political ends by this means. The leaders calculate the terrible costs in human life and materials as the price that must be paid and obviously decide that it is worth it. The history of warfare before 1914 had allowed the dubious value of such calculations, but the First World War had shown the full face of total involvement to the degree that it proved many times uncontrollable. Total war was a new experience and it began to develop and unleash forces that defied restraint. By the time of World War I this trend was characterized by the most radical of policies.

Since this is the case that was amply demonstrated by World War II, it then becomes clear that acts of warfare alone will not bring victory and such factors as civilian morale, home front economy, supplies of all variety, ingenuity in meeting war's demands in technology and production became the decisive ones. Modern war, as World War II proved, cannot be sustained without the integral support of a functioning and corresponding economy that can carry on without interruption.[35]

It was not until the turn of the century that military planners began the departure from the former practice of providing their initial forces with all necessary supplies and equipment at war's outbreak. Now, the thinking of the military became more expansive and plans included virtually anything a nation could produce and store that served an army's needs. However, despite the enormous producing capacity of modern nations in World War II there was an equally enormous demand and use of war materiel of every kind. Nations had to constantly develop and introduce new economies that would help to prolong the resources. As Germany's war requirements increased apace she never hesitated to exploit those states under Nazi control, but by 1943 the production capacity of the western Allies and

Russia had begun to inexorably reverse the ratio of the earlier war years. The gigantic quantities of war materiel that the United States began to deliver by 1944 under the Lend-Lease agreements with Great Britain and Russia soon started to eclipse everything else.[36]

All of this played a major role in the defeat of the Axis powers and Japan and greatly aided the ability of the western Allies and Russia to employ blockades, take the air offensive, and, in general, smash the enemies on all fronts. In addition, they gained superiority in military technology, and the United States in particular soon reached a pinnacle of power with the atomic bomb and a new world of weaponry was opened.[37]

A further note is the sheer size of human participation in both world wars of the 20th century which was, of course, related to the enormous population increase of the time. Total war during the 1914–18 period witnessed the deaths of over 9 million soldiers out of a combat pool of some 60 million. This compared to World War II figures of 110 million soldiers in combat and 27 million of them killed (with an almost equal figure for civilian casualties). The major loss of life was suffered in both wars by the same two nations, Germany and Russia. The statistics on damage to properties are absolutely staggering.[38]

Revisionism and World War II. Revisionism in history is to correct, to change or amend, and hopefully the search to find the "real" truth of the past goes on indefinitely. Sometimes this leads to rather fundamental changes in just how history is viewed from one generation to the next. In establishing the responsibility for World War I, for example, historians working in the post-war era produced a totally different version from that held by the victorious powers in 1919. Much of the credit enabling historians to develop the full and corrected history of the causes of World War I was due to the availability of proper documentation. The era of secrecy in international relations was ending, and with the Bolshevik Revolution and Germany's defeat subsequent efforts at "revealing all"[39] prompted work upon a reconstruction of the war's causes. An important school of revisionist historians from many nations thrived for the next two decades.[40] There has been no comparable movement in revisionist research and writing on the Second World War.[41] This has not been due to lack of documentation; in fact, despite the absence of substantial French and Russian materials the quantity of records available is overwhelming.[42] The obvious reason is that the mass of documentation does not support fundamental revisions of the causes of World War II.

By and large the victorious nations in World War II regarded their struggles against the Axis powers and Japan as absolutely necessary. Then and now that conflict continues to be viewed as a "just war." Many misconceptions and corrections concerning the actual course of the war have been revealed by the continued examination of the wartime records. However, these items fall much more into the category of such things as breaking an enemy code or reevaluating an opponent's armament efforts rather than any basic alteration of the causes of the war.[43] Most of the questions that historians examine in relation to gaining greater insight into causes of the war are subject to long-range evaluations and in some instances are almost the results of changing attitudes rather than the uncovering of new evidence.

Chapter I
The Predominance of Germany
on the Continent, 1939—1940

Part 1 Politics and Strategy of
"Lightning War"

Nineteen-hundred-and-thirty-nine carries the dubious distinction of being the year that World War II started.[1] More accurately perhaps, it was the year that all the post–World War I diplomatic efforts to heal a sick world finally and completely failed. To many observers this came as no surprise and the terrible expectation of another world war was confirmed.

During the weeks and months preceding the German attack upon Poland the quarrels of a generation focused on a single issue: Would the German Chancellor Adolf Hitler allow the search for a diplomatic solution to the problems of the Free City of Danzig and the Polish Corridor to continue or would he force a war? It is against this background that the Prime Minister of Great Britain, Neville Chamberlain, spoke to members of the House of Commons in March of 1939 (1) and assured them that his nation would defend Polish independence against all aggressions. Despite this clear warning (France too had joined in the Polish guarantee) Hitler's decision for war had been made, however, and by June the secret plan for the invasion of Poland, "Case White" (2) was fully authorized. Meanwhile, the diplomatic wrangling continued apace.

While Chamberlain struggled to clarify some of the issues during that summer of 1939 by discussion (3), the course was already determined as Hitler outlined his reasons for war (4) to his military commanders. Appeals for peace from world leaders continued to be made, however, in last minute desperate attempts to stave off the conflict. One such appeal (5) was made by the American President, Franklin Roosevelt, during the last week of peace but was virtually lost in the wake of the astounding news that Hitler's Germany had concluded a long-term non-aggression pact (6) with Stalin's Russia.

Several days later, early on the morning of September 1, German armed forces moved into Poland and Hitler issued his first wartime proclamation (7). France and Britain immediately responded with an almost identical

15

warning (8) that demanded Germany's withdrawal under threat of war. When the German Fuehrer ignored the warning the two World War I allies declared war, on September 3 (9).

In the meantime the military position of Poland had moved to the brink of total disaster. After a misunderstanding that briefly delayed Russian action (10) Soviet forces finally moved into eastern Poland (11). Within days (September 17 to 28) Nazi Germany and Communist Russia had agreed on the division of Poland (12) and declared their mutual desire to see the end of the current conflict (13). The first month of World War II had closed with a stunning German victory and the world had witnessed the first example of "Lightning War" (*Blitzkrieg*).

As early as May 1939, Hitler had revealed to his closest military advisors his determination to regain the area ceded to Poland as a result of the Versailles Treaty. By August 1939, the capabilities of the German war machine to realize that goal were beyond question, providing no large power came to Poland's assistance. As noted, both Great Britain and France declared war against Germany (9); however, the fact that they were neither able nor willing to undertake an offensive to rescue Poland sealed the fate of that nation. In addition, virtually secure in the knowledge that there was no immediate danger from the west, Germany was able to draw needed forces—especially mobile armor—for the Polish campaign. In fewer than four weeks (September 1 to 27) German forces numbering some 1,700,000 had completely overwhelmed the 600,000-man Polish army. Germany gained an additional territory—including the Free City of Danzig—of 72,866 square miles and a population of over 22,000,000.

1. Chamberlain Announces Polish Guarantee, March 31, 1939[2]

The right hon. Gentleman the Leader of the Opposition asked me this morning whether I could make a statement as to the European situation. As I said this morning, His Majesty's Government have no official confirmation of the rumours of any projected attack on Poland and they must not, therefore, be taken as accepting them as true.

I am glad to take this opportunity of stating again the general policy of His Majesty's Government. They have constantly advocated the adjustment, by way of free negotiation between the parties concerned, of any differences that may arise between them. They consider that this is the natural and proper course where differences exist. In their opinion there should be no question incapable of solution by peaceful means, and they would see no justification for the substitution of force or threats of force for the method of negotiation.

As the House is aware, certain consultations are now proceeding with other Governments. In order to make perfectly clear the position of His Majesty's Government in the meantime before those consultations are concluded, I now have to inform the House that during that period, in the event of any action which clearly threatened Polish independence, and which the

Polish Government accordingly considered it vital to resist with their national forces, His Majesty's Government would feel themselves bound at once to lend the Polish Government all support in their power. They have given the Polish Government an assurance to this effect.

I may add that the French Government have authorised me to make it plain that they stand in the same position in this matter as do His Majesty's Government.

2. Details of "Case White," June 14, 1939[3] (Excerpts)

1. The commander-in-chief of the army has ordered the working out of a *plan of deployment against Poland* which takes in account the demands of the political leadership for the opening of war by surprise and for quick success.
2. The order of deployment by the High Command, "Fall Weiss" authorizes the Third Army Group (in Fall Weiss 8th Army Headquarters) to give necessary directions and orders to all commands subordinated to it for "Fall Weiss." . . .
4. The orders of deployment "Fall Weiss" will be put into operation on 20 August 1939; all preparations have to be concluded by this date.
. . . .
6. Tenth Corps Command (Gen KdX) and XIII Corps and 1o. Div. can perform the necessary reconnaissance in Silesia while observing the appropriate precautionary measures (civilian clothes, motor vehicle, with civilian license number).
7. The whole correspondence on "Fall Weiss" has to be conducted under the classification Top Secret. This is to be disregarded only if the content of a document, in the judgment of the chief of the responsible command is harmless in every way—even in connection with the other documents.
8. For the middle of July a conference is planned where details on the execution will be discussed. Time and place will be ordered later on. Special requests are to be communicated to Third Army Group before 10 July.
9. I declare it the duty of the Commanding Generals, the divisional commanders and the commandants to limit as much as possible the number of persons who will be informed, and to limit the extent of the information, and ask that all suitable measures be taken to prevent persons not concerned from getting information.

Commander-in-chief of Army Group 3
Signed F. Blaskowitz

Aims of Operation "Fall Weiss"

14 June 1939

1. a. The operation, in order to forestall an orderly Polish mobilization and concentration, is to be opened by surprise with forces which are for the most part armored and motorized, placed on alert in the neighborhood of the border. The initial superiority over the Polish frontier-guards and

surprise that can be expected with certainty are to be maintained by quickly bringing up other parts of the army as well to counteract the marching up of the Polish Army.

Accordingly all units have to keep the initiative against the foe by quick acting and ruthless attacks.

b. If the development of the Political situation should show that a surprise at the beginning of the war is out of question, because of well advanced defense preparations on the part of the Polish Army, the Commander-in-Chief of the army will order the opening of the hostilities only after the assembling of sufficient additional forces. The basis of all preparations will be to surprise the enemy.

Case b—is to be prepared in theory by the High Command only so that necessary changes can be quickly carried out.

3. The British Position on Danzig, July 10, 1939[4]

The Prime Minister: I have previously stated that His Majesty's Government are maintaining close contact with the Polish and French Governments on the question of Danzig. I have nothing at present to add to the information, which has already been given to the House about the local situation. But I may, perhaps, usefully review the elements of this question as they appear to His Majesty's Government.

Racially Danzig is, almost wholly, a German city; but the prosperity of its inhabitants depends to a very large extent upon Polish trade. The Vistula is Poland's only waterway to the Baltic, and the port at its mouth is, therefore, of vital strategic and economic importance to her. Another Power established in Danzig could, if it so desired, block Poland's access to the sea and so exert an economic and military stranglehold upon her. Those who were responsible for framing the present statute of the Free City were fully conscious of these facts, and did their best to make provision accordingly. Moreover, there is no question of any oppression of the German population in Danzig. On the contrary, the administration of the Free City is in German hands, and the only restrictions imposed upon it are not of a kind to curtail the liberties of its citizens. The present settlement, though it may be capable of improvement, cannot in itself be regarded as basically unjust or illogical. The maintenance of the *status quo* had in fact been guaranteed by the German Chancellor himself up to 1944 by the ten-year Treaty which he had concluded with Marshal Pilsudski.

Up till last March Germany seems to have felt that, while the position of Danzig might ultimately require revision, the question was neither urgent nor likely to lead to a serious dispute. But in March, when the German Government put forward an offer in the form of certain desiderata accompanied by the Press campaign, the Polish Government realised that they might presently be faced with a unilateral solution, which they would have to resist with all their forces. They had before them the events which had taken place in Austria, Czecho-Slovakia and the Memelland. Accordingly, they refused to accept the German point of view, and themselves made suggestions for a possible solution of the problems in which Germany was interested. Certain defensive measures were taken by Poland on 23rd March and the reply was sent to Berlin on 26th March. I ask the House to note carefully these dates. It has been freely stated in Germany that it was His Majesty's Government's guarantee which encouraged the Polish Government to take the action which I have described. But it will be observed that our guarantee was not given until 31st March. By 26th March no mention of it, even, had been made to the Polish Government.

Recent occurrences in Danzig have inevitably given rise to fears that it is intended to settle her future status by unilateral action, organised by surreptitious methods, thus presenting Poland and other Powers with a *fait accompli*. In such circumstances any action taken by Poland to restore the situation would, it is suggested, be represented as an act of aggression on her part, and if her action were supported by other Powers they would be accused of aiding and abetting her in the use of force.

If the sequence of events should, in fact, be such as is contemplated on this hypothesis, hon. Members will realise, from what I have said earlier, that the issue could not be considered as a purely local matter involving the rights and liberties of the Danzigers, which incidentally are in no way threatened, but would at once raise graver issues affecting Polish national existence and independence. We have guaranteed to give our assistance to Poland in the case of a clear threat to her independence, which she considers it vital to resist with her national forces, and we are firmly resolved to carry out this undertaking.

I have said that while the present settlement is neither basically unjust nor illogical, it may be capable of improvement. It may be that in a clearer atmosphere possible improvements could be discussed. Indeed, Colonel Beck has himself said in his speech on 5th May that if the Government of the Reich is guided by two conditions, namely, peaceful intentions and peaceful methods of procedure, all conversations are possible. In his speech before the Reichstag on 28th April the German Chancellor said that if the Polish Government wished to come to fresh contractual arrangements governing its relations with Germany he could but welcome such an idea. He added that any such future arrangements would have to be based on an absolutely clear obligation equally binding on both parties.

His Majesty's Government realise that recent developments in the Free City have disturbed confidence and rendered it difficult at present to find an atmosphere in which reasonable counsels can prevail. In face of this situation, the Polish Government have remained calm, and His Majesty's Government hope that the Free City, with her ancient traditions, may again prove, as she has done before in her history, that different nationalities can work together when their real interests coincide. Meanwhile, I trust that all concerned will declare and show their determination not to allow any incidents in connection with Danzig to assume such a character as might constitute a menace to the peace of Europe.

4. FUEHRER SPEECH TO COMMANDERS IN CHIEF, AUGUST 22, 1939[5] (EXCERPT)

I have called you together to give you a picture of the political situation, in order that you may have some insight into the individual factors on which I have based my decision to act and in order to strengthen your confidence.

After this we shall discuss military details.

It was clear to me that a conflict with Poland had to come sooner or later. I had already made this decision in the spring, but I thought that I would first turn against the West in a few years, and only after that against the East. But the sequence of these things cannot be fixed. Nor should one close one's eyes to threatening situations. I wanted first of all to establish a tolerable relationship with Poland in order to fight first against the West. But this plan, which appealed to me, could not be executed, as fundamental points had changed. It became clear to me that, in the event of a conflict with the West, Poland would attack us. Poland is striving for access to the sea. The further development appeared after the occupation of the Memel Territory and it became clear to me that in certain circumstances a conflict with Poland might come at an inopportune moment. I give as reasons for this conclusion:

1. First of all two personal factors:

My own personality and that of Mussolini.

Essentially all depends on me, on my existence, because of my political talents. Furthermore, the fact that probably no one will ever again have the confidence of the whole German people as I have. There will probably never again in the future be a man with more authority than I have. My existence is therefore a factor of great value. But I can be eliminated at any time by a criminal or a lunatic.

The second personal factor is the Duce. His existence is also decisive. If anything happens to him, Italy's loyalty to the alliance will no longer be certain. The Italian Court is fundamentally opposed to the Duce. Above all, the Court regards the expansion of the empire as an encumbrance. The Duce is the man with the strongest nerves in Italy.

The third personal factor in our favour is Franco. We can ask only for benevolent neutrality from Spain. But this depends on Franco's personality. He guarantees a certain uniformity and stability in the present system in Spain. We must accept the fact that Spain does not as yet have a Fascist party with our internal unity.

The other side presents a negative picture as far as authoritative persons are concerned. There is no outstanding personality in England and France.

It is easy for us to make decisions. We have nothing to lose; we have everything to gain. Because of our restrictions our economic situation is such that we can only hold out for a few more years. Göring can confirm this. We have no other choice, we must act. Our opponents will be risking a great deal and can gain only a little. Britain's stake in a war is inconceivably great. Our enemies have leaders who are below the average. No personalities. No masters, no men of action.

Besides the personal factors, the political situation is favourable for us: In the Mediterranean, rivalry between Italy, France and England; in the Far East, tension between Japan and England; in the Middle East, tension which causes alarm in the Mohammedan world.

The English Empire did not emerge stronger from the last war. Nothing was achieved from the maritime point of view. Strife between England and Ireland. The Union of South Africa has become more independent. Concessions have had to be made to India. England is in the utmost peril. Unhealthy industrialization. A British statesman can only view the future with concern.

France's position has also deteriorated, above all in the Mediterranean.

Further factors in our favour are these:

Since Albania, there has been a balance of power in the Balkans. Yugoslavia is infected with the fatal germ of decay because of her internal situation.

Rumania has not grown stronger. She is open to attack and vulnerable. She is threatened by Hungary and Bulgaria. Since Kemal's death, Turkey has been ruled by petty minds, unsteady, weak men.

All these favourable circumstances will no longer prevail in two or three years' time. No one knows how much longer I shall live. Therefore, better a conflict now.

The creation of Greater Germany was a great achievement politically, but militarily it was doubtful, since it was achieved by bluff on the part of the political leaders. It is necessary to test the military [machine]. If at all possible, not in a general reckoning, but by the accomplishment of individual tasks.

The relationship with Poland has become unbearable. My Polish policy hitherto was contrary to the views of the people. My proposals to Poland (Danzig and the Corridor) were frustrated by England's intervention. Poland changed her tone towards us. A permanent state of tension is intolerable. The power of initiative cannot be allowed to pass to others. The present moment is more favourable than in two or three years' time. An attempt on my life or Mussolini's could change the situation to our disadvantage. One cannot for ever face one another with rifles cocked. One compromise solution suggested to us was that we should change our convictions and make kind gestures. They talked to us again in the language of Versailles. There was a danger of losing prestige. Now the probability is still great that the West will not intervene. We must take the risk with ruthless determination. The politician must take a risk just as much as the general. We are faced with the harsh alternatives of striking or of certain annihilation sooner or later.

Reference to previous hazardous undertakings.

I should have been stoned if I had not been proved right. The most dangerous step was the entry into the neutral zone. Only a week before, I got a warning through France. I have always taken a great risk in the conviction that it would succeed.

Now it is also a great risk. Iron nerves, iron resolution.

The following special reasons fortify me in my view. England and France have undertaken obligations which neither is in a position to fulfil. There is no real rearmament in England, but only propaganda. A great deal of harm was done by many Germans, who were not in agreement with me, saying and writing to English people after the solution of the Czech question: The Führer succeeded because you lost your nerve, because you capitulated too soon. This explains the present propaganda war. The English speak of a war of nerves. One factor in this war of nerves is to boost the increase of armaments. But what are the real facts about British rearmament? The naval construction programme for 1938 has not yet been completed. Only the reserve fleet has been mobilized. Purchase of trawlers. No substantial strengthening of the Navy before 1941 or 1942.

Little has been done on land. England will be able to send at most three divisions to the Continent. A little has been done for the Air Force, but it is only a beginning. Anti-aircraft defence is in its initial stages. At the moment England has only 150 anti-aircraft guns. The new anti-aircraft gun has been ordered. It will take a long time before sufficient numbers have been produced. There is a shortage of predictors. England is still vulnerable from the air. This can change in two or three years. At the moment the English Air Force has only 130,000 men, France 72,000, Poland 15,000. England does not want the conflict to break out for two or three years.

The following is typical of England. Poland wanted a loan from England for her rearmament. England, however, only granted credits in order to make sure that Poland buys in England, although England cannot make deliveries. This suggests that England does not really want to support Poland. She is not risking eight million pounds in Poland, although she poured five hundred millions into China. England's position in the world is very precarious. She will not take any risks.

France is short of men (decline in the birth rate). Little has been done for rearmament. The artillery is obsolete. France did not want to embark on this adventure. The West has only two possibilities for fighting against us:

1. Blockade: It will not be effective because of our autarky and because we have sources of supply in Eastern Europe.

2. Attack in the West from the Maginot line: I consider this impossible.

Another possibility would be the violation of Dutch, Belgian and Swiss neutrality. I have no doubt that all these States, as well as Scandinavia, will defend their neutrality with all available means. England and France will not violate the neutrality of these countries. Thus in actual fact England cannot help Poland. There still remains an attack on Italy. Military intervention is out of the question. No one is counting on a long war. If Herr von

Brauchitsch had told me that I would need four years to conquer Poland I would have replied: "Then it cannot be done." It is nonsense to say that England wants to wage a long war.

We will hold our position in the West until we have conquered Poland. We must bear in mind our great production capacity. It is much greater than in 1914–1918.

The enemy had another hope, that Russia would become our enemy after the conquest of Poland. The enemy did not reckon with my great strength of purpose. Our enemies are small fry. I saw them in Munich.

I was convinced that Stalin would never accept the English offer. Russia has no interest in preserving Poland, and Stalin knows that it would mean the end of his régime, no matter whether his soldiers emerged from a war victorious or vanquished. Litvinov's replacement was decisive. I brought about the change towards Russia gradually. In connection with the commercial treaty we got into political conversations. Proposal for a non-aggression pact. Then came a comprehensive proposal from Russia. Four days ago I took a special step, which led to Russia replying yesterday that she is prepared to sign. Personal contact with Stalin is established. The day after tomorrow von Ribbentrop will conclude the treaty. Now Poland is in the position in which I wanted her.

We need not be afraid of a blockade. The East will supply us with grain, cattle, coal, lead and zinc. It is a mighty aim, which demands great efforts. I am only afraid that at the last moment some swine or other will yet submit to me a plan for mediation.

The political objective goes further. A start has been made on the destruction of England's hegemony. The way will be open for the soldiers after I have made the political preparations.

5. ROOSEVELT APPEALS TO ITALIAN KING VICTOR EMMANUEL II FOR PEACE, AUGUST 23, 1939[6]

Again a crisis in world affairs makes clear the responsibility of heads of nations for the fate of their own people and indeed of humanity itself. It is because of traditional accord between Italy and the United States and the ties of consanguinity between millions of our citizens that I feel that I can address Your Majesty in behalf of the maintenance of world peace.

It is my belief and that of the American people that Your Majesty and Your Majesty's Government can greatly influence the averting of an outbreak of war. Any general war would cause to suffer all nations whether belligerent or neutral, whether victors or vanquished, and would clearly bring devastation to the peoples and perhaps to the governments of some nations most directly concerned.

The friends of the Italian people and among them the American people could only regard with grief the destruction of great achievements which

European nations and the Italian nation in particular have attained during the past generation.

We in America having welded a homogeneous nation out of many nationalities, often find it difficult to visualize the animosities which so often have created crises among nations of Europe which are smaller than ours in population and in territory, but we accept the fact that these nations have an absolute right to maintain their national independence if they so desire. If that be sound doctrine then it must apply to the weaker nations as well as to the stronger.

Acceptance of this means peace, because fear of aggression ends. The alternative, which means of necessity efforts by the strong to dominate the weak, will lead not only to war, but to long future years of oppression on the part of victors and to rebellion on the part of the vanquished. So history teaches us.

On April 14th last I suggested in essence an understanding that no armed forces should attack or invade the territory of any other independent nation, and that this being assured, discussions be undertaken to seek progressive relief from the burden of armaments and to open avenues of international trade including sources of raw materials necessary to the peaceful economic life of each nation.

I said that in these discussions the United States would gladly take part. And such peaceful conversations would make it wholly possible for governments other than the United States to enter into peaceful discussions of political or territorial problems in which they were directly concerned.

Were it possible for Your Majesty's Government to formulate proposals for a pacific solution of the present crisis along these lines you are assured of the earnest sympathy of the United States.

The Government of Italy and the United States can today advance those ideals of Christianity which of late seem so often to have been obscured.

The unheard voices of countless millions of human beings ask that they shall not be vainly sacrificed again. Franklin D. Roosevelt.

6. RUSSO-GERMAN NON-AGGRESSION TREATY WITH SECRET PROTOCOL, AUGUST 23, 1939[7]

The Government of the German Reich and the Government of the Union of Soviet Socialist Republics, desirous of strengthening the cause of peace between Germany and the U. S. S. R., and proceeding from the fundamental provisions of the Treaty of Neutrality, which was concluded between Germany and the U. S. S. R. in April 1926, have reached the following agreement:

ARTICLE I

The two Contracting Parties undertake to refrain from any act of violence, any aggressive action and any attack on each other either severally or jointly with other Powers.

Article II

Should one of the Contracting Parties become the object of belligerent action by a third Power, the other Contracting Party shall in no manner lend its support to this third Power.

Article III

The Governments of the two Contracting Parties will in future maintain continual contact with one another for the purpose of consultation in order to exchange information on problems affecting their common interests.

Article IV

Neither of the two Contracting Parties will join any grouping of Powers whatsoever which is aimed directly or indirectly at the other Party.

Article V

Should disputes or conflicts arise between the Contracting Parties over questions of one kind or another, both Parties will settle these disputes or conflicts exclusively by means of a friendly exchange of views or if necessary by the appointment of arbitration commissions.

Article VI

The present Treaty shall be concluded for a period of ten years with the proviso that, in so far as one of the Contracting Parties does not denounce it one year before the expiry of this period, the validity of this Treaty shall be deemed to be automatically prolonged for another five years.

Article VII

The present treaty shall be ratified within the shortest possible time. The instruments of ratification will be exchanged in Berlin. The treaty shall enter into force immediately upon signature.

Done in duplicate in the German and Russian languages.

Moscow, August 23, 1939.

For the Government of the
German Reich:
v. Ribbentrop

With full power of the
Government of the U. S. S. R.:
V. Molotov

Secret Additional Protocol

On the occasion of the signature of the Non-Aggression Treaty between the German Reich and the Union of Soviet Socialist Republics, the undersigned plenipotentiaries of the two Parties discussed in strictly confidential conversations the question of the delimitation of their respective spheres of interest in Eastern Europe. These conversations led to the following result:

1. In the event of a territorial and political transformation in the territories belonging to the Baltic States (Finland, Estonia, Latvia, Lithuania), the northern frontier of Lithuania shall represent the frontier of the spheres of interest both of Germany and the U. S. S. R. In this connection the interest of Lithuania in the Vilna territory is recognized by both Parties.

2. In the event of a territorial and political transformation of the territories belonging to the Polish State, the spheres of interest of both Germany and the U. S. S. R. shall be bounded approximately by the line of the rivers Narev, Vistula, and San.

The question whether the interests of both Parties make the maintenance of an independent Polish State appear desirable and how the frontiers of this State should be drawn can be definitely determined only in the course of further political developments.

In any case both Governments will resolve this question by means of a friendly understanding.

3. With regard to South-Eastern Europe, the Soviet side emphasizes its interest in Bessarabia. The German side declares complete political *désinsement* in these territories.

4. This protocol will be treated by both parties as strictly secret.

Moscow, August 23, 1939.

For the Government of
the German Reich:
v. Ribbentrop

With full power of the
Government of the U. S. S. R.:
V. Molotov

7. FUEHRER PROCLAMATION TO ARMED FORCES, SEPTEMBER 1, 1939[8]

To the Armed Forces—

The Polish Government unwilling to establish good neighbourly relations as aimed at by me wants to force the issue by way of arms.

The Germans in Poland are being persecuted with bloody terror and driven from their homes. Several acts of frontier violation which cannot be tolerated by a great power show that Poland is no longer prepared to respect the Reich's frontiers. To put an end to these mad acts I can see no other way but from now onwards to meet force with force.

The German Armed Forces will with firm determination take up the struggle for the honour and the vital rights of the German people.

I expect every soldier to be conscious of the high tradition of the eternal German soldierly qualities and to do his duty to the last.

Remember always and in any circumstances that you are the representatives of National Socialist Greater Germany.

Long live our people and Reich!

Berlin, 1st September 1939.

(signed) ADOLF HITLER

8. FRENCH WARNING TO GERMANY (TRANSMITTED BY FRENCH AMBASSADOR COULONDRE TO GERMAN FOREIGN MINISTER RIBBENTROP), SEPTEMBER 1, 1939[9]

Your Excellency,

According to instructions from the French Minister for Foreign Affairs, I have the honour to make the following communication:

Early this morning the German Chancellor issued a proclamation to the German army which indicated clearly that he was about to attack Poland.

Information which has reached the French Government and His Majesty's Government in the United Kingdom indicates that German troops have crossed the Polish frontier and that attacks upon Polish towns are proceeding.

In these circumstances it appears to the Governments of France and the United Kingdom that by their action the German Government have created conditions (viz. an aggressive act of force against Poland threatening the independence of that country) which call for the implementation by the Governments of France and the United Kingdom of their undertaking to Poland to come to her assistance.

I have accordingly to inform Your Excellency that unless the German Government are prepared to give the French Government satisfactory assurances that the German Government have suspended all aggressive action against Poland and are prepared promptly to withdraw their forces from Polish territory, the French Government will without hesitation fulfil their obligations to Poland.

I avail myself of this opportunity to renew to Your Excellency the assurance of my highest consideration.

Coulondre

9. Prime Minister Chamberlain's Radio Broadcast, September 3, 1939[10]

I am speaking to you from the Cabinet Room at 10, Downing Street.

This morning the British Ambassador in Berlin handed the German Government a final Note stating that, unless we heard from them by 11 o'clock that they were prepared at once to withdraw their troops from Poland, a state of war would exist between us.

I have to tell you now that no such undertaking has been received, and that consequently this country is at war with Germany.

You can imagine what a bitter blow it is to me that all my long struggle to win peace has failed. Yet I cannot believe that there is anything more or anything different that I could have done and that would have been more successful.

When I have finished speaking certain detailed announcements will be made on behalf of the Government. Give these your closest attention. The Government have made plans under which it will be possible to carry on the work of the nation in the days of stress and strain that may be ahead. But these plans need your help.

You may be taking your part in the fighting services or as a volunteer in one of the branches of Civil Defence. If so you will report for duty in accordance with the instructions you have received. You may be engaged in work essential to the prosecution of war for the maintenance of the life of the people—in factories, in transport, in public utility concerns, or in the supply of other necessaries of life. If so, it is of vital importance that you should carry on with your jobs.

Now may God bless you all. May He defend the right. It is the evil things that we shall be fighting against—brute force, bad faith, injustice, oppression and persecution—and against them I am certain that the right will prevail.

Up to the very last it would have been quite possible to have arranged a peaceful and honourable settlement between Germany and Poland, but Hitler would not have it. He had evidently made up his mind to attack Poland whatever happened, and although he now says he put forward reasonable proposals which were rejected by the Poles, that is not a true statement.

The proposals were never shown to the Poles, nor to us, and, though they were announced in a German broadcast on Thursday night, Hitler did not wait to hear comments on them, but ordered his troops to cross the Polish frontier. His action shows convincingly that there is no chance of expecting that this man will ever give up his practice of using force to gain his will. He can only be stopped by force.

10. TELEGRAM FROM GERMAN AMBASSADOR TO SOVIET UNION TO FOREIGN MINISTRY, SEPTEMBER 10, 1939[11]

MOST URGENT   [Moscow,] September 10, 1939—9:40 p.m.
TOP SECRET
No. 317 of September 10

With reference to my telegram No. 310 of September 9 and to telephone conversation of today with the Reich Foreign Minister.

In today's conference at 4 p.m., Molotov modified his statement of yesterday by saying that the Soviet Government was taken completely by surprise by the unexpectedly rapid German military successes. In accordance with our first communication, the Red Army had counted on several weeks, which had now shrunk to a few days. The Soviet military authorities were therefore in a difficult situation, since, in view of conditions here, they required possibly 2 to 3 weeks more for their preparations. Over 3 million men were already mobilized.

I explained emphatically to Molotov how crucial speedy action of the Red Army was at this juncture.

Molotov repeated that everything possible was being done to expedite matters. I got the impression that Molotov promised more yesterday than the Red Army can live up to.

Then Molotov came to the political side of the matter and stated that the Soviet Government had intended to take the occasion of the further advance of German troops to declare that Poland was falling apart and that it was necessary for the Soviet Union, in consequence, to come to the aid of the Ukrainians and the White Russians "threatened" by Germany. This argument was to make the intervention of the Soviet Union plausible to the masses and at the same time avoid giving the Soviet Union the appearance of an aggressor.

This course was blocked for the Soviet Government by a DNB report yesterday to the effect that, in accordance with a statement by Colonel General Brauchitsch, military action was no longer necessary on the German eastern border. The report created the impression that a German-Polish armistice was imminent. If, however, Germany concluded an armistice, the Soviet Union could not start a "new war."

I stated that I was unacquainted with this report, which was not in accordance with the facts. I would make inquiries at once.

Schulenburg

11. AMERICAN AMBASSADOR TO SOVIET UNION DESCRIBES SOVIET INTERVENTION IN POLAND, SEPTEMBER 17, 1939[12]

The Ambassador in the Soviet Union [Steinhardt] to the
Secretary of State

Moscow, September 17, 1939—7 a.m.
[Received September 17—2:15 a.m.]

550. I am reliably but unofficially informed that under the guise of "restoring order and protecting" the Ukrainians and White Russian minorities Soviet troops entered Eastern Poland along entire frontier operating from Polotsk in White Russia to Kanenets-Podolsk in the Ukraine this morning at dawn.

Please repeat to War Department
Repeated to Riga.

Steinhardt

The Ambassador in the Soviet Union [Steinhardt] to the
Secretary of State

Moscow, September 17, 1939—9 a.m.
[Received 11:42 a.m.]

551. My 550, September 17, 7 p.m. [a.m.]. I received at 8:45 Moscow time this morning the following note signed by Molotov enclosing a copy of a note dated today addressed to the Polish Ambassador here:

Mr. Ambassador: In transmitting to you the enclosed note dated September 17, 1939 of the Government of the Union of Soviet Socialist Republics addressed to the Polish Ambassador in Moscow, I have the honor under instructions from my Government to declare to you that the Union of Soviet Socialist Republics will pursue a policy of neutrality in the relations between the Union of Soviet Socialist Republics and the United States of America.

Accept it, et cetera, Peoples Commissar for Foreign Affairs, signed Molotov.

The following is a full translation of the copy of the note to the Polish Ambassador.

"Mr. Ambassador: The Polish-German [War] has revealed the internal instability of the Polish State. During 10 days of military operations Poland has lost all its industrial regions and cultural centers. Warsaw as the capital of Poland no longer exists. The Polish Government has scattered and gives no signs of life. This means that the Polish State and its Government factually have ceased to exist. By this fact in itself treaties concluded between the Union of Soviet Socialist Republics and Poland have lost their validity. Left to shift for itself and left without leadership Poland has become a convenient field for all kinds of eventualities and unforeseen contingencies which may constitute a threat to the Union of Soviet Socialist Republics. Therefore having been heretofore neutral a [*the?*] Soviet Government can no longer adopt a neutral attitude to these facts. The Soviet Government can also not be indifferent to the fact that the consanguine Ukrainians and White Russians living on the territory of Poland who have been left to the whim of fate should be left defenseless. In view of this situation the Soviet Government has issued instructions to the High Command Red Army to give the order to its forces to cross the Polish frontier and take under their protection the life and property of the population of Western Ukraine and Western White Russia.

At the same time the Soviet Government intends to take all measures in order to extricate the Polish people from the ill-fated war into which they have been led by their unwise leaders and to give them the possibility of living a peaceful life.

Accept, et cetera."

Steinhardt

12. German-Soviet Boundary and Friendship Treaty, September 28, 1939[13]

The Government of the German Reich and the Government of the USSR consider it as exclusively their task, after the disintegration of the former Polish state, to re-establish peace and order in these territories and to assure to the peoples living there a peaceful life in keeping with their national character. To this end, they have agreed upon the following:

ARTICLE I

The Government of the German Reich and the Government of the USSR determine as the boundary of their respective national interests in the territory of the former Polish state the line marked on the attached map, which shall be described in more detail in a supplementary protocol.

ARTICLE II

Both parties recognize the boundary of the respective national interests established in article I as definitive and shall reject any interference of third powers in this settlement.

ARTICLE III

The necessary reorganization of public administration will be effected in the areas west of the line specified in article I by the Government of the German Reich, in the areas east of this line by the Government of the USSR.

ARTICLE IV

The Government of the German Reich and the Government of the USSR regard this settlement as a firm foundation for a progressive development of the friendly relations between their peoples.

ARTICLE V

This treaty shall be ratified and the ratification shall be exchanged in Berlin as soon as possible. The treaty becomes effective upon signature.

Done in duplicate, in the German and Russian languages.

For the Government of the German Reich:	By authority of the Government of the USSR:
v. Ribbentrop	W. Molotov

13. JOINT GERMAN-SOVIET DECLARATION, SEPTEMBER 28, 1939[14]

Declaration of September 28, 1939, by the Government of the German Reich and the Government of the USSR

Moscow, September 28, 1939.

After the Government of the German Reich and the Government of the USSR have, by means of the treaty signed today, definitively settled the problems arising from the disintegration of the Polish state and have thereby created a firm foundation for a lasting peace in Eastern Europe, they mutually express their conviction that it would serve the true interest of all peoples to put an end to the state of war existing at present between Germany on the one side and England and France on the other. Both

Governments will therefore direct their common efforts, jointly with other friendly powers if occasion arises, toward attaining this goal as soon as possible.

Should, however, the efforts of the two Governments remain fruitless, this would demonstrate the fact that England and France are responsible for the continuation of the war, whereupon, in case of the continuation of the war, the Governments of Germany and of the USSR shall engage in mutual consultations with regard to necessary measures.

For the Government	By authority of the
of the German Reich:	Government of the USSR:
v. Ribbentrop	W. Molotov

Part 2. The "Phony War" and the Soviet Union
Fights Finland

Even before the Polish campaign ended Hitler had decided that an attack against the neutral Low Countries would force Great Britain and France into a decisive battle, and while it is clear that his war aim was the military defeat of the western Allies, his ultimate goal was the domination of Europe (18). Ignoring the advice of his military, Hitler ordered the preparations (14) for a western offensive codenamed "Case Yellow," but the weeks and months following Poland's defeat were characterized by general inaction on all sides and the news media began referring to the war as a "phony" one.

Most of the fighting during the closing months of 1939 occurred at sea. Although Hitler had concentrated Germany's war preparations on land conquests, the importance of the Atlantic was not to be ignored and soon German U-boats were taking heavy tolls on British shipping. Two German pocket battleships, the *Graf Spee* and *Deutschland,* provided much of the surface action. The ships were already in the Atlantic at war's outbreak and succeeded in gaining much of the attention of the Royal Navy as well as causing growing concern in the United States.

The United States was already well aware of the necessity to develop additional defenses and it was to this end that the initiative was taken to convene a Western Hemispheric conference in Panama in late September of 1939. One of the resolutions adopted (15), and perhaps the most important, was a defense measure suggested by the United States to create a zone around the Americas free of Europe's war. This was soon followed by the passage of the Neutrality Act of 1939 (16), wherein the United States attempted to carefully state a national position with rules for behavior that would prevent any foreign entanglement.

In October Hitler disclosed that the future of Poland would be bleak indeed if his plans succeeded (17). Later, in a wide-ranging speech to his commanders in November (18) the German leader set forth his distorted images of modern history and discussed Germany's need for more living space (*Lebensraum*).

This strange interlude that had become known as the Phony War was suddenly shattered by a Soviet attack upon Finland. Since the defeat of Poland the Soviet Union had applied pressures to that small nation in an attempt to secure a pact that allowed Soviet military bases to be established there. On November 29 Soviet Foreign Minister V. M. Molotov delivered a radio speech (19) denouncing Finnish intransigence and declared all relations with that nation to be broken. The next day the Soviet invasion of Finland began.

This "Winter War" provided some momentary distraction and a few surprises as well. What had looked like a Russian walkover developed instead into a fiercely fought war of over three months duration. While the western Allies explored various ways of exploiting the situation to their advantage the Finns reached the end of their endurance. Finally, on March 12, 1940, Finland and the Soviet Union concluded a peace agreement (20) that ceded valuable territories to the Communists.

A number of statesmen had succumbed to the notion that there was really not going to be another world war because the first winter was almost over and (despite the Winter War) the power balance of 1939 appeared intact. This proved to be a serious and gross miscalculation of Hitler's intentions. In a top secret directive (21) dated March 1, 1940, he ordered that plans be made ready to invade Denmark and Norway.

Early on the morning of April 9 these plans, codenamed "Case Weser Exercise," were put into force (22) and the respective governments were notified of Germany's intent to "protect" them from becoming a battlefield in the war. It was now quite clear to everyone that the Phony War—if there had ever been one—was now over.

"Case Yellow" (14) was now executed and on May 10 the Germans drove into the Low Countries. Supremely confident of quick victory, Hitler had already issued a directive for the occupying procedures (23). Within a few days time Holland, Belgium, and Luxembourg capitulated before the powerful German advance, and massive British and French forces were trapped on the beaches at the French port of Dunkirk.

While these events were unfolding before a startled world, the British continued—together with Norwegian forces—to battle the Germans for the remnants of Norway. The news of Germany's invasion of the Low Countries plunged the British civil government into crisis and Chamberlain faced a loss of power. Winston Churchill, already reaching for the reins, became the choice to form a new government on May 10. Three days later Churchill delivered what is perhaps his most oft-quoted speech (24) and promised to lead the British people to victory over Hitlerism.

14. Hitler Directive for the Preparation for the Invasion of the Low Countries, and High Command Order, Berlin, October 9, 1939[1]

Directive No. 6
For the Conduct of the War

1. If it should become apparent in the near future that England, and under England's leadership also France are not willing to make an end to the war, I am determined to act actively and aggressively without much delay.

2. If we wait much longer, not only will Belgian and perhaps also Dutch neutrality be lost in favor of the Western Powers, but the military strength of our enemies will grow on an increasing scale, the neutral's confidence in a final German victory will dwindle, and Italy will not be encouraged to join us as a military ally.

3. Therefore I give the following orders for the further military operations.

   a. Preparations are to be made for an attacking operation on the northern wing of the western front, through the areas of Luxembourg, Belgium, and Holland. This attack must be carried out with as much strength and at as early a date as possible.

   b. The purpose of this attacking operation will be, to defeat as strong contingent of the French operational army, as possible, as well as the allies fighting by its side, and at the same time to gain as large an area as possible in Holland, Belgium, and Northern France as a base for conducting a promising air and naval war against England and as a broad area on the immediate front of the vital Ruhr area.

   c. The timing of the attack depends on the readiness of tanks and motorized units for use—this must be speeded up by every possible effort—also on the weather conditions then prevailing and the weather prospects ahead.

4. The air force is to prevent the Anglo-French Air Force from attacking our own army, and, if necessary, to give direct support to the army's advance. In this connection, it will also be essential to prevent the Anglo-French Air Force as well as English landing troops from gaining any hold in Belgium and Holland. [Marginal note in handwriting] It will also be up to the air force to cut the supply lines of those English troops which have already landed. The employment of U-boats in the Channel will soon cease because of heavy losses.

5. The direction of naval warfare must concentrate everything on being able to give direct and indirect support to the operations of the army while this assault lasts.

6. Apart from these preparations for starting the attack in the West according to plan, army and air force must be ready at any time and with increasing strength, in order to be able to meet an Anglo-French invasion of

Belgium as far inside Belgian territory as possible, and to occupy as much of Holland as possible in the direction of the west coast. [Marginal note in handwriting] This kind of procedure would be more desirable in every respect.

7. The camouflage used for these preparations must be that they are merely precautionary measures in view of the threatening concentration of French and English forces on the Franco-Luxembourg and Franco-Belgian borders.

8. I request the commanders in chief to give me, as soon as possible, detailed reports of their intentions on the basis of this directive and from now on, to keep me informed, via the OKW, of the state of the preparations.

[Signed] Adolf Hitler

15. The Declaration of Panama, October 3, 1939[2] (Excerpt)

The Governments of the American Republics meeting at Panamá, have solemnly ratified their neutral status in the conflict which is disrupting the peace of Europe, but the present war may lead to unexpected results which may affect the fundamental interests of America and there can be no justification for the interests of the belligerents to prevail over the rights of neutrals causing disturbances and suffering to nations which by their neutrality in the conflict and their distance from the scene of events, should not be burdened with its fatal and painful consequences.

During the World War of 1914–1918 the Governments of Argentina, Brazil, Chile, Colombia, Ecuador and Peru advanced, or supported, individual proposals providing in principles a declaration by the American Republics that the belligerent nations must refrain from committing hostile acts within a reasonable distance from their shores.

The nature of the present conflagration, in spite of its already lamentable proportions, would not justify any obstruction to inter-American communications which, engendered by important interests, call for adequate protection. This fact requires the demarcation of a zone of security including all the normal maritime routes of communication and trade between the countries of America.

To this end it is essential as a measure of necessity to adopt immediately provisions based on the above-mentioned precedents for the safeguarding of such interests, in order to avoid a repetition of the damages and sufferings sustained by the American nations and by their citizens in the war of 1914–1918.

There is no doubt that the Governments of the American Republics must foresee those dangers and as a measure of self-protection insist that the waters to a reasonable distance from their coasts shall remain free from the commission of hostile acts or from the undertaking of belligerent activities by nations engaged in a war in which the said governments are not involved.

For these reasons the Governments of the American Republics Resolve and Hereby Declare:

1. As a measure of continental self-protection, the American Republics, so long as they maintain their neutrality, are as of inherent right entitled to have those waters adjacent to the American continent, which they regard as of primary concern and direct utility in their relations, free from the commission of any hostile act by any non-American belligerent nation, whether such hostile act be attempted or made from land, sea or air.

. . . .

2. The Governments of the American Republics agree that they will endeavor, through joint representation to such belligerents as may now or in the future be engaged in hostilities, to secure the compliance by them with the provisions of this Declaration, without prejudice to the exercise of the individual rights of each State inherent in their sovereignty.

3. The Governments of the American Republics further declare that whenever they consider it necessary they will consult together to determine upon the measures which they may individually or collectively undertake in order to secure the observance of the provisions of this Declaration.

4. The American Republics, during the existence of a state of war in which they themselves are not involved, may undertake, whenever they may determine that the need therefor exists, to patrol, either individually or collectively, as may be agreed upon by common consent, and in so far as the means and resources of each may permit, the waters adjacent to their coasts within the area above defined. (Approved, October 3, 1939.)

16. United States Neutrality Act of November 3, 1939[3] (Excerpt)

Joint Resolution

To preserve the neutrality and the peace of the United States and to secure the safety of its citizens and their interests.

Whereas the United States, desiring to preserve its neutrality in wars between foreign states and desiring also to avoid involvement therein, voluntarily imposes upon its nationals by domestic legislation the restrictions set out in this joint resolution; and

Whereas by so doing the United States waives none of its own rights or privileges, or those of any of its nationals, under international law, and expressly reserves all the rights and privileges to which it and its nationals are entitled under the law of nations; and

Whereas the United States hereby expressly reserves the right to repeal, change or modify this joint resolution or any other domestic legislation in the interests of the peace, security or welfare of the United States and its people: Therefore be it

Resolved by the Senate and House of Representatives of the United States of America in Congress assembled,

PROCLAMATION OF A STATE OF WAR BETWEEN
FOREIGN STATES

Section 1. (a) That whenever the President, or the Congress by concurrent resolution, shall find that there exists a state of war between foreign states, and that it is necessary to promote the security or preserve the peace of the United States or to protect the lives of citizens of the United States, the President shall issue a proclamation naming the states involved; and he shall, from time to time, by proclamation, name other states as and when they may become involved in the war.

(b) Whenever the state of war which shall have caused the President to issue any proclamation under the authority of this section shall have ceased to exist with respect to any state named in such proclamation, he shall revoke such proclamation with respect to such state.

COMMERCE WITH STATES ENGAGED IN ARMED CONFLICT

Sec. 2. (a) Whenever the President shall have issued a proclamation under the authority of section 1 (a) it shall thereafter be unlawful for any American vessel to carry any passengers or any articles or materials to any state named in such proclamation.

(b) Whoever shall violate any of the provisions of subsection (a) of this section or of any regulations issued thereunder shall, upon conviction thereof, be fined not more than $50,000 or imprisoned for not more than five years, or both. Should the violation be by a corporation, organization, or association, each officer or director thereof participating in the violation shall be liable to the penalty herein prescribed.

(c) Whenever the President shall have issued a proclamation under the authority of section 1 (a) it shall thereafter be unlawful to export or transport, or attempt to export or transport, or cause to be exported or transported, from the United States to any state named in such proclamation, any articles or materials (except copyrighted articles or materials) until all right, title, and interest therein shall have been transferred to some foreign government, agency, institution, association, partnership, corporation, or national. Issuance of a bill of lading under which title to the articles or materials to be exported or transported passes to a foreign purchaser unconditionally upon the delivery of such articles or materials to a carrier, shall constitute a transfer of all right, title, and interest therein within the meaning of this subsection. The shipper of such articles or materials shall be required to file with the collector of the port from or through which they are to be exported a declaration under oath that he has complied with the requirements of this subsection with respect to transfer of right, title, and interest in such articles or materials, and that he will comply with such rules and regulations as shall be promulgated from time to time. Any such declaration so filed shall be a conclusive estoppel against any claim of any citizen of the United States of right, title, or interest in such articles or materials, if such citizen had knowledge of the filing of such declaration; and the exportation or transportation of any articles or materials without filing the declaration required by this subsection shall be a conclusive estoppel against any claim of any citizen of the United States of right, title, or interest in such articles or materials, if such citizen had knowledge of such violation. No loss incurred by any such citizen (1) in connection with the sale or transfer of right, title, and interest in any such articles or materials or (2) in connection with the exportation or transportation of any such copyrighted articles or materials, shall be made the basis of any claim put forward by the Government of the United States.

(d) Insurance written by underwriters on articles or materials included in shipments which are subject to restrictions under the provisions of this joint resolution, and on vessels carrying such shipments shall not be deemed an American interest therein, and no insurance policy issued on such articles or materials, or vessels, and no loss incurred thereunder or by the owners of such vessels, shall be made the basis of any claim put forward by the Government of the United States.

(e) Whenever any proclamation issued under the authority of section 1 (a) shall have been revoked with respect to any state the provisions of this section shall thereupon cease to apply with respect to such state, except as to offenses committed prior to such revocation.

(f) The provisions of subsection (a) of this section shall not apply to transportation by American vessels on or over lakes, rivers, and inland waters bordering on the United States, or to transportation by aircraft on or over lands bordering on the United States; and the provisions of subsection (c) of this section shall not apply (1) to such transportation of any articles or materials other than articles listed in a proclamation referred to in or issued under the authority of section 12 (i), or (2) to any other transportation on or over lands bordering on the United States of any articles or materials other than articles listed in a proclamation referred to in or issued under the authority of section 12 (i); and the provisions of subsections (a) and (c) of this section shall not apply to the transportation referred to in this subsection and subsections (g) and (h) of any articles or materials listed in a proclamation referred to in or issued under the authority of section 12 (i) if the articles or materials so listed are to be used exclusively by American vessels, aircraft, or other vehicles in connection with their operation and maintenance.

(g) The provisions of subsections (a) and (c) of this section shall not apply to transportation by American vessels (other than aircraft) of mail, passengers, or any articles or materials except articles or materials listed in a proclamation referred to in or issued under the authority of section 12 (i) (1) to any port in the Western Hemisphere south of thirty-five degrees north latitude, (2) to any port in the Western Hemisphere north of thirty-five degrees north latitude and west of sixty-six degrees west longitude, (3) to any port on the Pacific or Indian Oceans, including the China Sea, the Tasman Sea, the Bay of Bengal, and the Arabian Sea, and any other dependent waters of either of such oceans, seas, or bays, or (4) to any port on the Atlantic Ocean or its dependent waters south of thirty degrees north latitude. The exceptions contained in this subsection shall not apply to any such port which is included within a combat area as defined in section 3 which applies to such vessels.

(h) The provisions of subsections (a) and (c) of this section shall not apply to transportation by aircraft to mail, passengers, or any articles or materials except articles or materials listed in a proclamation referred to in or issued under the authority of section 12 (i) (1) to any port in the Western Hemisphere, or (2) to any port on the Pacific or Indian Oceans, including the China Sea, the Tasman Sea, the Bay of Bengal, and the Arabian Sea, and any other dependent waters of either of such oceans, seas, or bays. The exceptions contained in this subsection shall not apply to any such port which is included within a combat area as defined in section 3 which applies to such aircraft.

(i) Every American vessel to which the provisions of subsections (g) and (h) apply, and every neutral vessel to which the provisions of subsection (l) apply, shall, before departing from a port or from the jurisdiction of the United States, file with the collector of customs of the port of departure, or if there is no such collector at such port then with the nearest collector of customs, a sworn statement (1) containing a complete list of all the articles and materials carried as cargo by such vessel, and the names and addresses of the consignees of all such articles and materials, and (2) stating the ports at which such articles and materials are to be unloaded and the ports of call of such vessel. All transportation referred to in subsections (f), (g), (h), and (l) of this section shall be subject to such restrictions, rules, and regulations as the President shall prescribe; but no loss incurred in connection with any transportation excepted under the provisions of subsections (g), (h), and (l) of this section shall be made the basis of any claim put forward by the Government of the United States.

(j) Whenever all proclamations issued under the authority of section 1 (a) shall have been revoked, the provisions of subsections (f), (g), (h), (i), and (l) of this section shall expire.

(k) The provisions of this section shall not apply to the current voyage of any American vessel which has cleared for a foreign port and has departed from a port or from the jurisdiction of the United States in advance of (1) the date of enactment of this joint resolution, or (2) any proclamation issued after such date under the authority of section 1 (a) of this joint resolution; but any such vessel shall proceed at its own risk after either of such dates, and no loss incurred in connection with any such vessel or its cargo after either of such dates shall be made the basis of any claim put forward by the Government of the United States.

(l) The provisions of subsection (c) of this section shall not apply to the transportation by a neutral vessel to any port referred to in subsection (g) of this section of any articles or materials (except articles or materials listed in a proclamation referred to in or issued under the authority of section 12 (i) so long as such port is not included within a combat area as defined in section 3 which applies to American vessels.

17. HITLER DISCUSSES POLAND'S FUTURE, OCTOBER 17, 1939[4]

"1) The Armed Forces will welcome it if they can dispose of administrative questions in Poland. On principle, there cannot be two administrations. . . .

. . . .

"3) It is not the task of the administration to make Poland into a model province or a model state of the German order or to put her economically or financially on a sound basis. "The Polish intelligentsia must be prevented from forming a ruling class. The standard of living in the country is to remain low; we want only to draw labor forces from there. Poles are also to be used for the administration of the country. However, the forming of national political groups may not be allowed.

"4) The administration has to work on its own responsibility and must not be dependent on Berlin. We do not want to do there what we do in the Reich. The responsibility does not rest with the Berlin Ministries since there is no German administration unit concerned.

"The accomplishment of this task will involve a hard racial struggle which will not allow any legal restrictions. The methods will be incompatible with the principles otherwise adhered to by us.

"The Governor General is to give the Polish nation only bare living conditions and is to maintain the basis for military security. . . .

"6) . . . Any tendencies towards the consolidation of conditions in Poland are to be suppressed. The 'Polish muddle' must be allowed to develop. The Government of the territory must make it possible for us to purify the Reich territory from Jews and Poles too. Collaboration with new Reich provinces (Posen and West Prussia) only for resettlements (compare Himmler mission).

"Purpose: Shrewdness and severity must be the maxims in this racial struggle in order to spare us from going to battle on account of this country again."

18. FUEHRER CONFERENCE, NOVEMBER 23, 1939[5]

Nov. 23, 1939, 1200 hours. Conference with the Fuehrer, to which all Supreme Commanders are ordered. The Fuehrer gives the following speech:

The purpose of this conference is to give you an idea of the world of my thoughts, which governs me in the face of future events, and to tell you my decisions. The building up of our armed forces was only possible in connection with the ideological [weltanschaulich] education of the German people by the Party. When I started my political task in 1919, my strong belief in final success was based on a thorough observation of the events of the day and the study of the reasons for their occurrence. Therefore, I never lost my belief in the midst of set-backs which were not spared me during my period of struggle. Providence has had the last word and brought me success. On top of that, I had a clear recognition of the probable course of historical events, and the firm will to make brutal decisions. The first decision was in 1919 when I after long internal conflict became a politician and took up the struggle against my enemies. That was the hardest of all decisions. I had, however, the firm belief that I would arrive at my goal. First of all, I desired a new system of selection. I wanted to educate a minority which would take over the leadership. After 15 years, I arrived at my goal, after strenuous struggles and many set-backs. When I came to power in 1933, a period of the most difficult struggle lay behind me. Everything existing before that had collapsed. I had to reorganize everything beginning with the mass of the people and extending it to the armed forces. First reorganization of the interior, abolishment of appearances of decay and defeatist ideas, education to heroism. While reorganizing the interior, I undertook the second task: to release Germany from its international ties. Two particular characteristics are to be pointed out: secession from the League of Nations and denunciation of the disarmament conference. It was a hard decision. The number of prophets who predicted that it would lead to the occupation of the Rhineland was large, the number of believers was very small. I was supported by the nation, which stood firmly behind me, when I carried out my intentions. After that the order for rearmament. Here again there were numerous prophets who predicted misfortunes, and only a few believers. In 1935 the introduction of compulsory armed service. After that militarization of the Rhineland, again a process believed to be impossible at that time. The number of people who put trust in me, was very small. Then the beginning of the fortification of the whole country especially in the west.

One year later, Austria came, this step also was considered doubtful. It brought about a considerable reinforcement of the Reich. The next step was Bohemia, Moravia and Poland. This step also was not possible to accomplish in one campaign. First of all, the western fortification had to be finished. It was not possible to reach the goal in one effort. It was clear to me from the first moment that I could not be satisfied with the Sudeten-German territory. That was only a partial solution. The decision to march into Bohemia was made. Then followed the erection of the Protectorate and with that the basis for the action against Poland was laid, but I wasn't quite clear at that time whether I should start first against the east and then in the west or vice-versa. Moltke often made the same calculations in his time. Under pressure the decision came to fight with Poland first. One might accuse me of wanting to fight and fight again. In struggle I see the fate of all beings. Nobody can avoid a struggle if he does not want to lose out. The increasing number of people requires a larger living space [Lebensraum]. My goal was to create a logical relation between the number of people and the space for them to live in. The struggle must start here. No people can get away from the solution of this task or else it must yield and gradually die out. That is taught by history. First migration of peoples to the southwest, then adaptation of the number of people to the small space by emigration. In the last years, adaptation of the people to insufficient space, by reducing the number of births. This would lead to the death and weakening of the blood of the people. If a people chooses that course all their weaknesses are mobilized. One yields to the force of the outside and uses this force against one's self by killing of the child. This means the greatest cowardice, decimation of the number, and loss of value. I decided a different way: adaptation of the living space to the number of people. One acknowledgement is important. The state has a meaning only if it supports the maintenance of its population potential. In our case 82 millions of people were concerned. That means the greatest responsibility. He who does not want to assume this responsibility is not worthy of belonging to the mass of the people. That gave me the strength to fight. It is one eternal problem to bring the number of Germans to a proper relationship to the available space. Security of the needed space. No calculated cleverness is of any help, solution only with the sword. A people unable to produce the strength to fight must withdraw. Struggles are different than those of 100 years ago. Today we can speak of a racial fight. Today we fight for oilfields, rubber, treasures of the earth, etc. After the peace of Westphalia Germany disintegrated. Disintegration, impotence of the German Reich was determined by decree. This German impotence was removed by the creation of the Reich when Prussia realized her task. Then the opposition between France and England began. Since 1870 England has been against us. Bismarck and Moltke were certain that there would have to be one more action. The danger at that time was of a two-front war. Moltke was at times in favor of a preventive war. To take advantage of the slow progress of the Russian mobilization. German armed might was not fully employed. Insufficient sternness of the leading personalities. The basic thought of Moltke was the offensive. He never thought of the defense. Many opportunities were missed after Moltke's death. The solution was only possible by attacking a country at a favorable moment. Political and military leadership always declared that it was not yet ready. In 1914 there came the war on several fronts. It did not bring the solution of these problems. Today the second act of this drama is being written. For the first time in 67 years it must be made clear that we do not have a two-front war to wage. That which has been desired since 1870 and considered as impossible of achievement has come to pass. For the first time in history we have to fight on only one front, the other front is at present free. But no one can know how long that will remain so. I have doubted for a long time whether I should strike in the east and then in the west. Basically I did not organize the armed forces in order not to strike. The decision to strike was always in me. Earlier or later I wanted to solve the problem. Under pressure it was decided that the east was to be attacked first. If the Polish war was won so quickly, it was due to the superiority of our armed forces. The most glorious appearance in history. Unexpectedly small expenditures of men and material. Now the eastern front is held by only a few divisions. It is a situation which we viewed previously as unachievable.

Now the situation is as follows: The opponent in the west lies behind his fortifications. There is no possibility of coming to grips with him. The decisive question is: how long can we endure this situation? Russia is at present not dangerous. It is weakened by many incidents today. Moreover, we have a pact with Russia. Pacts, however, are only held as long as they serve the purpose. Russia will hold herself to it only so long as Russia considers it to be to her benefit. Even Bismarck thought so. Let one think of the pact to assure our back. Now Russia has far-reaching goals, above all the strengthening of her position in the Baltic. We can oppose Russia only when we are free in the West. Further Russia is striving to increase her influence on the Balkans and is striving toward the Persian Gulf. That is also the goal of our foreign policy. Russia will do that which she considers to benefit her. At the present moment it has retired from internationalism. In case she renounces this, she will proceed to Pan-Slavism. It is difficult to see into the future. It is a fact that at the present time the Russian army is of little worth. For the next one or two years the present situation will remain.

Much depends on Italy, above all on Mussolini, whose death could alter everything. Italy has a great goal for the consolidation of her empire. Those who carry this idea are fascism and the Duce, personally. The court is opposed to that. As long as the Duce lives, then it can be calculated that Italy will seize every opportunity to reach her imperialistic goal. However, it is too much to ask of Italy, that it should join in the battle before Germany has seized the offensive in the west: Just so Russia did not attack until we had marched into Poland. Otherwise Italy will think that France has only to deal with Italy, since Germany is sitting behind its West Wall. Italy will not attack until Germany has taken the offensive against France. Just as the death of Stalin, so the death of the Duce can bring danger to us. Just how easily the death of a statesman can come I myself have experienced recently. The time must be used to the full, otherwise one will suddenly find himself faced with a new situation. As long as Italy maintains this position then no danger from Jugoslavia is to be feared. Just so is the neutrality of Rumania achieved by the position of Russia. Scandinavia is hostile to us because of Marxistic influences, but is neutral now. America is still not dangerous to us because of its neutrality laws. The strengthening of our opponents by America is still not important. The position of Japan is still uncertain, it is not yet certain whether she will join against England.

Everything is determined by the fact that the moment is favorable now: in 6 months it might not be so anymore.

As the last factor I must name my own person in all modesty: irreplaceable. Neither a military nor a civil person could replace me. Assassination attempts may be repeated. I am convinced of the powers of my intellect and of decision. Wars are always ended only by the destruction of the opponent. Everyone who believes differently is irresponsible. Time is working for our adversary. Now there is a relationship of forces which can never be more propitious, but can only deteriorate for us. The enemy will not make peace when the relationship of forces is unfavorable for us. No compromise. Sternness against ourselves. I shall strike and not capitulate. The fate of the Reich depends only on me. I shall deal accordingly. Today we have a superiority such as we have never had before. After 1914 our opponents disarmed themselves of their own accord. England disregarded the construction of her fleet. The fleet is no longer sufficiently large to safeguard the shipping lanes. Only two modern new constructions: Rodney and Nelson. New construction activity only in the cruisers of the Washington class, which were, however, an unsatisfactory type. The new measures can become effective only in 1941. In the Abyssinian war England did not have enough strength to occupy the Tana Sea. At Malta, Gibraltar and London little anti-aircraft protection. Since 1937 a renewal of rearmament. At present however, only a small number of divisions, which must form the nucleus of new divisions. Material for the army being gathered together from all over the world. Not before next summer is a positive action to be expected. The British army has only a symbolic meaning. Rearmament in the air is proceeding. The first phase will end in the spring of 1940. Anti-aircraft has only guns from the last war. A German flyer is safe from English anti-aircraft fire at 6000 meters altitude. The navy will not be fully rearmed before one to two years [1–2 Jahren]. I have the greatest experience in rearmament and I know the difficulties which must be overcome therein.

After 1914 France reduced the length of service. After 1914 decrease of military might. Only in some special branches are we inferior. Only the French Navy was modernized. In the time after the war the French army deteriorated. There were no changes until Germany rearmed and announced her demands.

In summary:
1. The number of active organizations in Germany is greatest.
2. Superiority of the Luftwaffe.
3. Anti-aircraft beyond all competition.
4. Tank corps.
5. Large number of anti-tank guns, five times as many as 1914 machine guns.
6. German artillery has great superiority because of the 10.5 gun.
7. French superiority in howitzers and mortars does not exist.

Numerical superiority, but also the value of the individual soldier is greater than for the others. I am most deeply pained when I hear the opinion that the German army is not individually as valuable as it should be. The infantry in Poland did not accomplish what one should have expected from it. Lax discipline. I believe that the soldiers must be judged in their relative value in comparison with the opponent. There is no doubt that our armed forces are the best. Every German infantryman is better than the French. Not the exhilaration of patriotism but tough determination. I am told that the troops will only advance if the officers lead the way. In 1914 that was also the case. I am told that we were better trained then. In reality we were only better trained on the drill field, but not for the war. I must pay the present leadership the compliment that it is better than it was in 1914. Mention of the collapse while storming Liege. There was nothing like this in the campaign in Poland.

Five million Germans have been called to the colors. Of what importance if a few of them collapse. Daring in the army, navy and Luftwaffe. I can not bear it when one says the army is not in good shape. Everything lies in the hands of the military leader. I can do anything with the German soldier if he is well led. We have succeeded with our small navy in clearing the North Sea of the British. Recognition of the small navy, especially the High Command of the Navy.

We have a Luftwaffe which has succeeded in safeguarding the entire living space of the Germans.

The land army achieved outstanding things in Poland. Even in the West it was not shown that the German soldier is inferior to the French.

Revolution from within is impossible. We are superior to the enemy numerically in the West. Behind the Army stands the strongest armament industry of the world.

I am disturbed by the stronger and stronger appearance of the English. The English are a tough enemy. Above all on defence. There is no doubt that England will be very much represented in France at the latest in six to eight months.

We have an Achilles heel: The Ruhr. The progress of the war depends on the possession of the Ruhr. If England and France push through Belgium and Holland into the Ruhr, we shall be in the greatest danger. That could lead to the paralyzing of the German power of resistance. Every hope of compromise is childish: Victory or defeat! The question is not the fate of a national-socialistic Germany, but who is to dominate Europe in the future. The question is worthy of the greatest efforts. Certainly England and France will assume the offensive against Germany when they are armed. England and France have means of pressure to bring Belgium and Holland to request English and French help. In Belgium and Holland the sympathies are all for France and England. Mention of the incident at Venlo:[6] The man who was shot was not an Englishman, but a Dutch General Staff officer. This was kept silent in the press. The Dutch government asked that the body of the Dutch officer be given up. This is one of their greatest stupidities. The Dutch press does not even mention the incident anymore. At a given time I shall use that to motivate my action. If the French army marches into Belgium in order to attack us, it will be too late for us. We must anticipate them. One more thing. U-boats, mines, and Luftwaffe (also for mines) can strike England effectively, if we have a better starting point. Now a flight to England demands so much fuel that sufficient bomb loads cannot be carried. The invention of a new type mine is of greatest importance for the Navy. Aircraft will be the chief mine layers now. We shall sow the English coast with mines which cannot be cleared. This mine warfare with the Luftwaffe demands a different starting point. England cannot live without its imports. We can feed ourselves. The permanent sowing of mines on the English coasts will bring England to her knees. However, this can only occur if we have occupied Belgium and Holland. It is a difficult decision for me. None has ever achieved what I have achieved. My life is of no importance in all this. I have led the German people to a great height, even if the world does hate us now. I am setting this work on a gamble. I have to choose between victory or destruction. I choose victory. Greatest historical choice, to be compared with the decision of Frederick the Great before the first Silesian war. Prussia owes its rise to the heroism of one man. Even there the closest advisers were disposed to capitulation. Everything depended on Frederick the Great. Even the decisions of Bismarck in 1866 and 1870 were no less great. My decision is unchangeable. I shall attack France and England at the most favorable and quickest moment. Breach of the neutrality of Belgium and Holland is meaningless. No one will question that when we have won. We shall not bring about the breach of neutrality as idiotically as it was in 1914. If we do not break the neutrality, then England and France will. Without attack the war is not to be ended victoriously. I consider it as possible to end the war only by means of an attack. The question as to whether the attack will be successful no one can answer. Everything depends upon the favorable instant. The military conditions are favorable. A prerequisite however, is that the leadership must give an example of fanatical unity from above. There would not be any failures if the leaders always had the courage a rifleman must have.

Individual acknowledgments: The enemy must be beaten only by attack. Chances are different today than during the offensive of 1918. Numerically we can use more than 100 divisions. With respect to men, reserves can be supplied. The material situation is good. Moreover that which is not ready today must be ready tomorrow. The whole thing means the end of the World War, not just of a single action. It concerns not just a single question but the existence or non-existence of the nation.

I ask you to pass on the spirit of determination to the lower echelons.

1. The decision is irrevocable.
2. The only prospect for success, if the whole armed forces are determined.

The spirit of the great men of our history must hearten us all. Fate demands from us no more than from the great men of German history. As long as I live I shall think only of the victory of my people. I shall shrink from nothing and shall destroy everyone who is opposed to me. I have decided to live my life so that I can stand unshamed if I have to die. I want to destroy the enemy. Behind me stands the German people, whose morale can only grow worse. Only he who struggles with destiny can have a good intuition. In the last years I have experienced many examples of intuition. Even in the present development I see the prophecy.

If we come through this struggle victoriously—and we shall come through victoriously—our time will enter into the history of our people. I shall stand or fall in this struggle. I shall never survive the defeat of my people. No capitulation to the outside forces, no revolution from the interior forces.

19. MOLOTOV RADIO ADDRESS OF NOVEMBER 29, 1939[7]

Men and women, citizens of the Soviet Union, the hostile policy pursued by the present Finnish Government towards our country obliges us to take immediate steps to ensure the external security of the State. As you know, during these last two months, the Soviet Government has patiently carried on negotiations with the Finnish Government on proposals which, in the present alarming international situation, it regarded as an indispensable minimum to ensure the safety of the country, and particularly that of Leningrad. During those negotiations, the Finnish Government has adopted an uncompromising and hostile attitude towards our country. Instead of amicably seeking a basis of agreement, those who at present govern Finland, out of deference to the foreign imperialists who stir up hatred against the Soviet Union, have followed a different path. Despite all our concessions, the negotiations have led to no result. Now we see the consequences. During the last few days, on the frontier between the USSR and Finland, the Finnish military clique has begun to indulge in revolting provocations, not stopping short of artillery fire upon our troops near Leningrad, which has caused serious casualties among the Red troops.

The attempts made by our Government to prevent the renewal of these provocations by means of practical proposals addressed to the Finnish Government have not merely met with no support but have again been countered by the hostile policy of the governing circles in Finland. As you have learnt from the Soviet Government's note of yesterday, they have replied to our proposals by a hostile refusal, by an insolent denial of the facts, by an attitude of mockery towards the casualties we have suffered, and by an unconcealed desire to continue to hold Leningrad under the direct threat of their troops. All this has definitely shown that the present Finnish Government, embarrassed by its anti-Soviet connections with the imperialists, is unwilling to maintain normal relations with the USSR. It continues to adopt a hostile position towards our country and will take no heed of the stipulations of the Treaty of Non-aggression concluded between the two countries, being anxious to keep our glorious Leningrad under a military menace. From such a Government and from its insensate military clique nothing is now to be expected but fresh insolent provocations.

For this reason, the Soviet Government was compelled yesterday to declare that it now considered itself released from the engagements which it had undertaken under the Treaty of Non-aggression concluded between the USSR and Finland and which had been irresponsibly violated by the Finnish

Government. In view of the fresh attacks made by Finnish troops against Soviet troops on the Soviet-Finnish frontier, the Government now finds itself compelled to take new decisions. The Government can no longer tolerate the situation created, for which the Finnish Government is entirely responsible. The Soviet Government has come to the conclusion that it could no longer maintain normal relations with the Finnish Government, and for this reason has found it necessary to recall immediately its political and economic representatives from Finland. Simultaneously, the Government gave the order to the Supreme Command of the Red Army and Navy to be prepared for all eventualities and to take immediate steps to cope with any new attacks on the part of the Finnish military clique.

The foreign Press hostile to us declares that our action is aimed at seizing and annexing to the USSR Finnish territory. This is a malicious slander. The Soviet Government never did, and does not now, cherish any such intentions. Nay, more, had Finland herself pursued a friendly policy towards the USSR, the Soviet Government, which has always desired to maintain friendly relations with Finland, would willingly have taken the initiative in making territorial concessions. On that condition, the Soviet Government would have been prepared to discuss favourably even such questions as that of the reunion of the Karelians inhabiting the chief districts of present-day Soviet Karelia with their Finnish kinsmen in a single independent Finnish State. For that, however, it is essential that the Finnish Government should adopt towards the USSR, not a hostile, but a friendly attitude which would correspond to the vital interests of both States. There are some who say that the steps we have taken are directed against the independence of Finland or constitute interference in her internal and external affairs. That is also a malicious slander. We look on Finland, whatever regime prevails there, as an independent sovereign State in the whole of its foreign and domestic policy. It is our steadfast wish that the Finnish people should settle their own internal and external questions as they think fit. The people of the USSR did everything that could be done at the time to create an independent Finland. Our peoples are equally ready in the future to help the Finnish people achieve their free and independent development.

Nor does the USSR intend to infringe in any way the interests of other States in Finland. Questions concerning the relations between Finland and other States are the affair of Finland alone, and the USSR does not consider itself entitled to interfere in the matter. We are solely concerned to ensure the safety of the USSR, and in particular of Leningrad, with its population of three and a half million inhabitants. In the present atmosphere of white heat generated by the war, we cannot allow the solution of this vital and urgent problem to depend on the ill-will of the present rulers in Finland. This problem will have to be solved by the efforts of the USSR itself in friendly collaboration with the Finnish people. We are sure that a favourable solution of this problem of the safety of Leningrad will be the foundation for a solid friendship between the USSR and Finland.

20. Soviet-Finnish Peace Treaty, March 12, 1940[8] (Excerpt)

Article 1

Hostilities between Finland and the U. S. S. R. shall cease immediately in accordance with procedure laid down in the protocol appended to this treaty.

Article 2

The national frontier between the Republic of Finland and the U. S. S. R. shall run along a new line in such fashion that there shall be included in the territory of the U. S. S. R. the entire Karelian Isthmus with the city of Viipuri and Viipuri Bay with its islands, the western and northern shores of Lake Ladoga with the cities of Kexholm and Sortavala and the town of Suojärvi, a number of islands in the Gulf of Finland, the area east of Märkäjärvi with the town of Kuolajärvi, and part of the Rybachi and Sredni peninsulas, all in accordance with the map appended to this treaty.

A more detailed determination and establishment of the frontier line shall be carried out by a mixed commission made up of representatives of the contracting powers, which commission shall be named within ten days from the date of the signing of this treaty.

Article 3

Both contracting parties undertake each to refrain from any attack upon the other and to make no alliance and to participate in no coalition directed against either of the contracting parties.

Article 4

The Republic of Finland agrees to lease to the Soviet Union for thirty years, against an annual rental of eight million Finnish marks to be paid by the Soviet Union, Hanko Cape and the waters surrounding it in a radius of five miles to the south and east and three miles to the north and west, and also the several islands falling within that area, in accordance with the map appended to this treaty, for the establishment of a naval base capable of defending the mouth of the Gulf of Finland against attack; in addition to which, for the purpose of protecting the naval base, the Soviet Union is granted the right of maintaining there at its own expense the necessary number of armed land and air forces.

Within ten days from the date this treaty enters into effect, the government of Finland shall withdraw all its military forces from Hanko Cape, which together with its adjoining islands shall be transferred to the jurisdiction of the U. S. S. R. in accordance with this article of the treaty.

ARTICLE 5

The U. S. S. R. undertakes to withdraw its troops from the Petsamo area which the Soviet state voluntarily ceded to Finland under the peace treaty of 1920.

Finland undertakes, as provided in the peace treaty of 1920, to refrain from maintaining in the waters running along its coast of the Arctic Ocean warships and other armed ships, excluding armed ships of less than one hundred tons displacement, which Finland shall be entitled to maintain without restriction, and also at most fifteen warships or other armed ships, the displacement of none of which shall exceed four hundred tons.

Finland undertakes, as was provided in the same treaty, not to maintain in the said waters any submarines or armed aircraft.

Finland similarly undertakes, as was provided in the same treaty, not to establish on that coast military ports, naval bases, or naval repair shops of greater capacity than is necessary for the above-mentioned ships and their armament.

. . . .

ARTICLE 8

Upon the coming into force of this treaty economic relations between the contracting parties shall be restored, and with this end in view the contracting parties shall enter into negotiations for the conclusion of a trade agreement.

ARTICLE 9

This treaty of peace shall enter into effect immediately upon being signed, and shall be subject to subsequent ratification.

The exchange of instruments of ratification shall take place within ten days in the city of Moscow.

This treaty has been prepared in two original instruments, in the Finnish and Swedish languages and in Russian, at Moscow this twelfth day of March, 1940.

Risto Ryti   V. Molotov
J. K. Paasikivi   A. Zhdanov
R. Walden   A. Vasilevski
Väinö Voionmaa

21. HITLER DIRECTIVE FOR "CASE WESER EXERCISE," MARCH 1, 1940[9]

1. The development of the situation in Scandinavia requires the making of all preparations for the occupation of Denmark and Norway by a part of

the German Armed Forces ("Case Weser Exercise"). This operation should prevent British encroachment on Scandinavia and the Baltic, further it should guarantee our ore base in Sweden and give our navy and air force a wider start line against Britain. The part which the navy and the air force will have to play, within the limits of their capabilities, is to protect the operation against the interference of British naval and air striking forces.

In view of our military and political power in comparison with that of the Scandinavian states, the force to be employed in the "Case Weser Exercise" will be kept as small as possible. The numerical weakness will be balanced by daring actions and surprise execution. On principle we will do our utmost to make the operation appear as a *peaceful* occupation, the object of which is the military protection of the neutrality of the Scandinavian States. Corresponding demands will be transmitted to the governments at the beginning of the occupation. If necessary, demonstrations by the navy and the air force will provide the necessary emphasis. If, in spite of this, resistance should be met with, all military means will be used to crush it.

2. I put in charge of the preparations and the conduct of the operation against Denmark and Norway the Commanding General of the XXI Army Corps, Lt. General of the Infantry v. Falkenhorst (commander of "Group XXI").

In questions of the conduct of operations, the above named is directly under my orders. The staff is to be completed from all the three branches of the armed forces.

The force which will be selected for the purpose of "Case Weser Exercise," will be under separate command. They will not be allocated to other operational theatres.

The part of the air force detailed for the purpose of "Weser Exercise" will be tactically under the orders of Group XXI. After the completion of their task they revert to the command of the High Command of the Air Force.

The employment of the forces which are under direct naval and air force command will take place in agreement with the commander of Group XXI.

The administration and supply of the forces posted to Group XXI will be ensured by the branches of the armed forces themselves according to the demands of the commander.

3. The crossing of the Danish border and the landings in Norway must take place *simultaneously*. I emphasize that the operations must be prepared as quickly as possible. In case the enemy seizes the initiative against Norway, we must be able to apply immediately our own counter measures.

It is most important that the Scandinavian States as well as the western opponents should be *taken by surprise* by our measures. All preparations, particularly those of transport and of readiness, drafting and embarkation of the troops, must be made with this factor in mind.

In case the preparations for embarkation can no longer be kept secret, the leaders and the troops will be deceived with fictitious objectives. The troops may be acquainted with the actual objectives only after putting to sea.

4. *Occupation of Denmark* ("Weser Exercise South").

*   *   *

Added to this, having secured the most important places, the group will break through as quickly as possible from Fuenen [Fyn] to Skagen and to the east coast. In Seeland [Sjaelland] bases will be captured early on. These will serve as starting points for later occupation.

The navy will provide forces for the securing of the connection Nyborg-Korsoer and for swift capture of the "Little Belt" bridge as well as for landing of troops, should the necessity arise. She will also prepare the defense of the coast.

The air force will provide squadrons of which the primary object will be demonstrations and dropping of leaflets. Full use of the existing Danish ground defenses and air defense must be ensured.

5. *Occupation of Norway* ("Weser Exercise North"). *The task of the Group* XXI—capture by surprise of the most important places on the coast by sea and airborne operations.

The navy will take over the preparation and carrying out of the transport by sea of the landing troops as well as the transport of the forces which will have to be brought to Oslo in a later stage of the operation. She will escort supplies and reserves on the way over the sea.

Preparations must be made for speedy completion of coastal defense in Norway.

The air force, after the occupation has been completed, will ensure air defense and will make use of Norwegian bases for air warfare against Britain.

6. Group XXI will make regular reports to the High Command of the Armed Forces concerning the state of preparations and will submit a chronological summary of the progress of preparations. The shortest necessary space of time between the issue of the order for "Weser Exercise," and its execution must be reported.

Intended battle headquarters will be reported.

Code names: Weser Day—day of the operation. Weser Hour—hour of the operation.

[Signed] Adolf Hitler

22. Germany Occupies Denmark and Norway, April 9, 1940[10]

The Chief of the High Command of the Wehrmacht to the Deputy of the Führer and the Higher Reich Authorities

Berlin, April 9, 1940.

Subject: Occupation of Denmark and Norway by the German Wehrmacht.

1) In consequence of the threatened danger of an occupation of Norwegian ports and coastal areas by Anglo-French forces, German troops, on the orders of the Führer and Supreme Commander of the Wehrmacht, crossed

the Danish frontier in the early hours of the morning of April 9 and also landed in Norwegian ports.

At the same time the necessary diplomatic steps were taken with the Danish and Norwegian Governments by political plenipotentiaries appointed by the Führer.

2) The Wehrmacht has orders to render a landing by Allied troops impossible by occupying important bases in Norway, and to establish a safe connection with south Norway by the simultaneous occupation of Denmark. The units of the Wehrmacht detailed for this purpose are under the command of General of Infantry von Falkenhorst, whose official designation is: "Commander, Group XXI."

The troops detailed for the occupation of Denmark are under Corps Command XXXI, commanded by General of the Air Force Kaupisch, subordinate to Commander, Group XXI.

3) The political measures to be taken with the Danish and Norwegian Governments and the extent of German control over the administration and economy of both countries are based on the principle of peaceful occupation, serving to safeguard the neutrality of the northern states. The aim of the political measures is to restrain the Danish and Norwegian Governments from any armed resistance, to induce them to tolerate the German occupation, and to prepare them for loyal cooperation with the German military and civil authorities.

The Governments and administrations of the countries shall continue to function unhindered wherever they are prepared to do so loyally.

The military measures with respect to the authorities and population of both countries take account of this objective.

4) The mission of the Wehrmacht is exclusively military. In political, administrative, and economic matters the occupying troops will only act directly on their own account and intervene or take action in so far as this is absolutely necessary for the execution of their military duties, pending settlement by the civilian authorities.

Measures already introduced by the Wehrmacht, and requests which are still to be submitted in connection with the carrying out of the mission of the Wehrmacht, are set out in the annexes so far as they concern the various high Reich authorities.

5) Denmark and Norway are to the fullest extent *operational areas* as defined militarily. In accord with the character of the occupation, however, the competence to exercise executive power will not be vested in the military authorities in this operational area.

The mission of the Commander, Group XXI, is the military protection and defense of the occupied countries. To this end he exercises supreme military authority and is entitled to take all measures necessary for the fulfillment of his military mission. For Denmark these powers have been vested in the Commander, Corps Command XXXI.

6) In nonmilitary matters representation of the German Reich with the Danish and Norwegian Governments will be effected by the Ministers, or by

plenipotentiaries appointed by the Foreign Ministry. It will be their duty to communicate the German political and military demands to the Danish and Norwegian Governments and to supervise the efforts of the Governments of both countries toward fulfilling the German demands and honoring the assurances given by them.

The foreign policy of the Governments of Denmark and Norway will be regulated according to their conduct.

7) The economic life of the occupied countries should continue to run as smoothly as possible. Intervention is to be resorted to only where necessary for the supply and security of the occupying troops and for ensuring the population's food supply. Representatives of the High Command of the Wehrmacht (Military Economy and Armaments Office) are detailed to the plenipotentiaries of the Foreign Ministry with the object of safeguarding German interests in the armament industry.

Both countries will continue as separate customs and currency areas. The fixed rate of exchange between German and Danish and Norwegian currencies, which will obtain until further notice is:

1 Danish crown = 0.50 RM
1 Norwegian crown = 0.60 RM

The occupation forces have orders to pay exclusively in occupation currency [*Reichskreditkassenscheine*] in the occupied countries. Severe restrictions on purchases are imposed on the occupation forces, and the import of goods into the Reich has been prohibited.

8) The German-Danish frontier will be closed to nonmilitary traffic with effect from the commencement of the occupation. There will be a similar ban on nonmilitary traffic from German ports to Denmark and Norway.

The issue to nonmilitary persons of entry permits to Denmark and Norway is reserved to the High Command of the Wehrmacht in cases involving military jurisdiction, and to the Foreign Ministry in cases involving civilian jurisdiction.

Applications for entry permits in cases involving military jurisdiction are to be addressed to the High Command of the Wehrmacht (Amt Ausland/ Abwehr-Passstelle).

The frontier will be opened as soon as possible for normal business traffic with Denmark and Norway.

9) Telephone and postal traffic from Denmark and Norway overseas with foreign countries will be stopped; that with the Baltic States limited to certain routes and supervised at the request of the officer commanding the occupation forces.

Other telephone and postal traffic from Denmark and Norway to neutral countries will be directed via Germany, and at the same time supervised.

10) The higher Reich authorities are requested, until further notice, to make any communication which may be necessary with the Commander, Group XXI, via the High Command of the Wehrmacht.

The Chief of the High Command
of the Wehrmacht
Keitel

23. FUEHRER DIRECTIVE OF MAY 9, 1940[11]

Subject: Administration of the occupied territories of France, Luxembourg, Belgium, and Holland.

1) The authority conferred on the Commander in Chief of the Army to exercise executive power in the theater of operations, extends also to the widening of the operations resulting from the advance of the German troops beyond the Reich frontier in the west.

2) The Commander in Chief of the Army will set up a military administration for the territories of France, Luxembourg, Belgium, and Holland which are to be occupied. The implementation of the military administration will be delegated to military departments designed for this purpose. The executive bodies will be appointed by the Army.

3) The military administration will be so conducted as to avoid giving the impression that it is intended to annex the occupied territories. The provisions of The Hague Convention on Land Warfare will be observed. The population will be protected and economic life maintained.

4) Hostile acts by the population (guerilla warfare, sabotage, passive resistance, stopping of work as a political demonstration) will be suppressed with the utmost severity.

5) The frontier between the German Reich and the occupied territories of France, Luxembourg, Belgium, and Holland will be closed to nonmilitary passenger and goods traffic as soon as the German troops begin to march in. Exemption from this frontier closure will be subject to the decision of the Commander in Chief of the Army and the departments authorized by him. These are to be restricted to a minimum at first.

The frontier closure will also apply to leading personages and representatives of the highest Reich authorities and departments of the Party. Ordinarily applications for entry permits by these departments will be transmitted through the High Command of the Wehrmacht.

Adolf Hitler

24. WINSTON CHURCHILL'S SPEECH OF MAY 13, 1940[12]

I beg to move,
    That this House welcomes the formation of a Government
    representing the united and inflexible resolve of the nation to
    prosecute the war with Germany to a victorious conclusion.
On Friday evening last I received His Majesty's Commission to form a new Administration. It was the evident wish and will of Parliament and the nation that this should be conceived on the broadest possible basis and that it should include all parties, both those who supported the late Government and also the parties of the Opposition. I have completed the most important part of this task. A War Cabinet has been formed of five Members, representing, with the Opposition Liberals, the unity of the nation. The three party Leaders have agreed to serve, either in the War Cabinet or in high executive

office. The three Fighting Services have been filled. It was necessary that this should be done in one single day, on account of the extreme urgency and rigour of events. A number of other positions, key positions, were filled yesterday, and I am submitting a further list to His Majesty to-night. I hope to complete the appointment of the principal Ministers during to-morrow. The appointment of the other Ministers usually takes a little longer, but I trust that, when Parliament meets again, this part of my task will be completed, and that the administration will be complete in all respects.

I considered it in the public interest to suggest that the House should be summoned to meet to-day. Mr. Speaker agreed, and took the necessary steps, in accordance with the powers conferred upon him by the Resolution of the House. At the end of the proceedings to-day, the Adjournment of the House will be proposed until Tuesday, 21st May, with, of course, provision for earlier meeting, if need be. The business to be considered during that week will be notified to Members at the earliest opportunity. I now invite the House, by the Motion which stands in my name, to record its approval of the steps taken and to declare its confidence in the new Government.

To form an Administration of this scale and complexity is a serious undertaking in itself, but it must be remembered that we are in the preliminary stage of one of the greatest battles in history, that we are in action at many other points in Norway and in Holland, that we have to be prepared in the Mediterranean, that the air battle is continuous and that many preparations, such as have been indicated by my hon. Friend below the Gangway, have to be made here at home. In this crisis I hope I may be pardoned if I do not address the House at any length to-day. I hope that any of my friends and colleagues, or former colleagues, who are affected by the political reconstruction, will make allowance, all allowance, for any lack of ceremony with which it has been necessary to act. I would say to the House, as I said to those who have joined this Government: "I have nothing to offer but blood, toil, tears and sweat."

We have before us an ordeal of the most grievous kind. We have before us many, many long months of struggle and of suffering. You ask, what is our policy? I can say: It is to wage war, by sea, land and air, with all our might and with all the strength that God can give us; to wage war against a monstrous tyranny, never surpassed in the dark, lamentable catalogue of human crime. That is our policy. You ask, what is our aim? I can answer in one word: It is victory, victory at all costs, victory in spite of all terror, victory, however long and hard the road may be; for without victory, there is no survival. Let that be realised; no survival for the British Empire, no survival for all that the British Empire has stood for, no survival for the urge and impulse of the ages, that mankind will move forward towards its goal. But I take up my task with buoyancy and hope. I feel sure that our cause will not be suffered to fail among men. At this time I feel entitled to claim the aid of all, and I say, "Come then, let us go forward together with our united strength."

Part 3. The Fall of France and Great Britain on the Defensive

When Winston Churchill accepted the leadership of British government (24) it was already evident that the crisis he confronted was enormous. In nine short months Hitler had conquered Poland, Denmark, Norway, and the Low Countries, and now France was rapidly weakening. The ease and speed with which Germany had accomplished these victories were astonishing. Faced with the disaster that was unfolding at Dunkirk, the new British Prime Minister found himself helpless to halt the advance of German forces.

The gravity of the situation for America was underscored by a futile peace mission (25) and a speech by the President to Congress (26) that detailed the deteriorating French position. Roosevelt warned of America's own vulnerability, and while he made no public appeal to support the British it was apparent that the United States was moving farther and farther from neutral ground.

Italy meanwhile, eager to partake in the great current events of history and establish a successful Mediterranean empire, declared war on an already defeated France. The world was told the decision in a grandiose speech (27) delivered by Benito Mussolini on June 10, 1940. His action was immediately praised by Hitler (28) as a worthy undertaking compatible with the existing bond of friendship between the two dictatorships. Despite a degree of military coordination with Hitler, Mussolini fully intended to conduct his 'own war'; however, British presence in Malta and North Africa proved too much for Italy's war capacity and German aid soon became essential.

The critical days that followed Mussolini's war declaration witnessed the crumbling of the Third Republic. France's great defense system was rooted in a fixed network of fortifications called the Maginot Line, and as it failed to prove impregnable a stunned and confused people quickly fell prey to a paralyzing defeatism. Beset by disorganization, fear, and chaos France faced an enemy that scorned a defensive credo and moved with all speed around the Maginot Line toward the French interior. The French government, led by the elderly Marshal Henri Pétain, frantically sought to negotiate an armistice that would leave some semblance of autonomy. As the awareness spread that the once proud and great French nation was preparing to surrender, the shock was incalculable. Unable to resist a congratulatory telegram to Hitler, the former German Kaiser, Wilhelm II, broke a self-imposed public silence and dispatched an emotional message (29).

In a final and desperate attempt to hold some of the French government from total collapse Churchill proposed an act of union between the two nations, but Pétain's decision to secure an armistice was final. In an act designed to dramatize the circumstances of the German victory over France the Armistice Treaty (30) was signed in the same railroad car and in the same location as the Armistice of 1918. Hitler had achieved the pinnacle of his astounding career; with amazing swiftness his military machine had won not only a war victory but a much-desired political goal. The Fuehrer had again demonstrated his talent for understanding the time and the situation as opportune and had struck.

While Mussolini occupied Corsica, Savoy, and portions of Provence, German troops moved into the entire coastal region in the west and north of France. The unoccupied area, with strict German liaison, contained the remnants of the French government headquartered in the town of Vichy.

In the process of negotiating an armistice a large question mark of the utmost concern to Great Britain was the ultimate disposition of the powerful French fleet. To Pétain's administration it represented a major bargaining force in their favor, for the Germans fully intended that the French navy would be rendered harmless. For Great Britain, of course, the possibility of gaining the fleet as additional seapower in their own struggle against Hitler was of the greatest significance. It was not to be, however, for as noted in Article 8 of the German-French Armistice Treaty (30) the fleet was neutralized.

The matter did not rest there though because Prime Minister Churchill was determined to try and seize and/or destroy the French fleet. On the afternoon of July 4 Churchill told a fascinated House of Commons that efforts had been undertaken to secure the fleet just as he had ordered (31). This tragic episode between two old allies was to become the source of lasting bitterness that continued long after war's end.

Britain succeeded in sinking and disabling a large part of the French fleet (at Oran), but the loss of that nation from the war was a terrible blow. The failure of the highly vaunted Maginot Line and the French armies to stop—or even seriously delay—Hitler's forces resulted in a military defeat of the greatest magnitude. The many reasons for France's collapse were too puzzling and complex to analyze at the time, but an easily understood and indisputable fact was that Germany had gained a clear and decisive victory in the west just as she had in the east.

Hitler now turned his full attention to England and although he had already ordered invasion preparations (32), in a speech to the Reichstag (33), he reflected the long-standing desire to see peace between the two nations—on Germany's terms and without Churchill's leadership. A few days later, on July 21, and again at the end of the month, Hitler spoke of the "hopeless" (34) position of Great Britain and speculated on the entrance of the Soviet Union into the war against Germany. Short of an armistice with Germany Hitler felt England's chances to be slim unless the United States and Russia entered the war on her side (35). There was not much chance of this happening in Hitler's estimation, as Japan would soon occupy America's attention and Germany had plans for the Soviet Union.

Thus, in that fading summer of 1940 it appeared as if Great Britain's fate was already sealed and she would soon be added to Germany's growing list of nations vanquished. By all odds Britain's future looked just as Hitler had described it; standing alone and with no help in sight it seemed certain that a German invasion was imminent, but the "Battle of Britain" was only beginning.

In that year from 1940 to 1941 the position of the United States began to shift from one of official neutrality to one of open support of the British cause. The swing in that direction was strongly opposed by many powerful groups in America who did not agree that Hitler's expansion in Europe threatened the United States. Despite all opposition the Roosevelt administration moved perceptibly closer to an alliance with Great Britain.

On September 2 it was announced that the United States had recently concluded an agreement (36) with Great Britain to provide fifty overage destroyers to that nation in return for a long-term lease on bases in Newfoundland and the Caribbean. For the United States this constituted a very definite and unequivocal step, for with the "destroyers-for-bases" deal any lingering doubt about the direction of American policy was swept away.

25. Conversation Between Chancellor Hitler and American Under Secretary of State Sumner Welles, Berlin, March 2, 1940[1] (Exerpts)

After a word of thanks for the reception by the Führer, Sumner Welles began with a statement already made at yesterday's conversation with the Foreign Minister regarding the nature of his mission. He explained that the President of the United States had instructed him to go to Italy, Germany, France, and England in order to report to him on the present situation in Europe, and he emphasized, as in yesterday's conversation with the Foreign Minister, that he was not authorized to make any proposals or enter into any commitments in the name of the United States. As in yesterday's conversation, he added that he would consider the statements made to him in the course of his conversations with foreign statesmen as strictly confidential and would use them only for the information of President Roosevelt.

President Roosevelt had given him this mission in order to ascertain whether there were any possibilities at all at the present moment for the establishment of a secure and lasting peace in Europe. President Roosevelt was not interested in any temporary, insecure condition of peace. He was of the opinion that a war of annihilation would bring with it a tremendous destruction of life and of everything that our civilization had taught us to prize, and he was aware that such a war of annihilation would affect every country. The United States also, as the largest neutral country, would feel the effects of such a war on her social, economic, financial, and commercial life.

President Roosevelt had in public statements already declared the readiness of the United States, for its part, after the establishment of a secure and lasting peace, to collaborate fully in the limitation and reduction of armaments and the attainment of a sound economic life.

For all these reasons Sumner Welles had asked for an audience with the Führer and would be grateful if the latter would inform him of his views.

The Führer replied that the first statement he had to make related to the fact that it was not Germany which had declared war on England and France, but that the reverse was the case; that it was not Germany which had war aims that were directed against England and France, but that here, too, the reverse was true. The crux of the matter, therefore, was whether England and France would abandon their war aims or not. The enemy's war aims were known to Germany and were such that they could not be discussed at all. Germany did not now believe that England and France would depart from these war aims, and was therefore of the opinion that the conflict would have to be fought to a finish.

. . . .

For the rest, it should be observed that the economic and disarmament problems which President Roosevelt wished to settle after peace was established had existed for decades. During this long period the other countries had not only not been able to solve any economic or disarmament problem, but had even opposed the sensible proposals that had been made by the Führer for settlements in the disarmament and economic fields.

Only this morning news had come from America that a new boycott had been launched against Germany. Hence it followed that the present atmosphere was not conducive to economic collaboration. In this connection the Führer recalled the boycott movement that started in America when he came to power in a completely democratic way as a result of the German plebiscite and tried, in view of the 7 million unemployed and the collapse of economic life, to expand German trade. Although at that time the German-American trade balance was in America's favor (American sales to Germany of 700 to 900 millions as against German sales of 300 millions to the United States), a boycott movement was at once started against Germany in the United States, and no attempt whatever was made to check it. As it progressed, Germany naturally found herself compelled also to restrict her imports from the United States (namely, to the extent of two-thirds, as compared with a one-third reduction of German sales to America). This reduction could surely not be blamed on the Führer, for Germany's interest had, quite to the contrary, been directed at an extension. In economic matters one should not allow oneself to be swayed by ideological considerations. Germany had carried on trade with the democratic countries just as with Russia, without troubling about the regimes of the trade partners; other countries, however, had allowed themselves to be governed by ideological considerations and had often not wanted to trade with Germany simply because of the difference of the regime and the economic structure. It had often been forgotten in such cases that Germany with its 140 persons to the square kilometer naturally had to have a different economic structure from the United States, in which there were only 13 or 14 persons to the square kilometer. This comparison alone showed that Germany had to produce about 10 times as much per square kilometer as the United States in order to feed herself, etc. And it would have been possible to expand trade but ideological impediments had made this impossible.

. . . .

Sumner Welles replied that his Government had fully recognized the efforts of the Führer to obtain a limitation and reduction of armaments. He was also of the opinion that it must be regarded as a real tragedy for Europe and for the world that the offers the Führer had made in these fields had not been generously examined and put into effect.

Sumner Welles said he was not informed about the boycott against Germany which had broken out in America, according to the latest reports to reach Berlin; he observed that the American Government had at no time promoted or encouraged any sort of boycott movement, since it was one of its fundamental beliefs that no greater harm could be done than by employing economic or financial means for political purposes. The Government of the United States had, therefore, perhaps as the only government in the world, up until very recently sought to lower trade barriers and to remove the artificial obstructions to a free exchange of goods; and it was aware of the fact that nothing was more conducive to a stable condition of peace than a rise in purchasing power and the standard of living and a decrease in unemployment through expansion of world trade.

Sumner Welles stated that he was deeply impressed with the Führer's words and would regret it deeply if he had to feel after this conversation that there was no longer any hope of avoiding the war of annihilation. The American Government took the stand that there was still time to avert this disaster and that certain statesmen could still banish the horrors that threatened the world if a war of annihilation were unleashed. Although the communications that he was receiving from the statesmen had to be treated in confidence, he wanted to say this much about the views of the Duce, that the latter, too, was of the opinion that there was still time to settle the difficulties by peaceful means.

The Führer replied that he had stated at the beginning that this question had nothing to do with Germany, since it was not we who had declared war. If it had been left to Germany absolute peace would now prevail, and if England and France had accepted the Führer's proposal they would probably now for some time have been sitting down together to settle by negotiation the problems still to be solved. Often governments could not act as they wished. Public opinion which was moulded by other elements intervened and often came to dominate the governments.

In principle it was necessary to distinguish three elements:
1. Historical memories, which must not be underestimated;
2. Political interests, which in part were related to security questions and the like;
3. Economic interests.

On the first point the Führer remarked that it was impossible permanently to deny to a great nation the position in the world which was its due by virtue of tradition and history. This applied particularly to Italy and Germany. As much as 500 years before the arrival of the first Europeans in America, half a millennium before Columbus, a great German empire had existed which even then had included all the territories which the Führer had now re-incorporated into the Reich. Perhaps these historical facts receded into the background temporarily for a few hundred years during a period in which these nations slumbered, but, as was plainly shown in the case of Italy and Germany, when the nations regained their strength they immediately reappeared on the surface and asserted themselves.

Second, with regard to the political element the Führer stated that it was an absurdity in the era of nationalism to want to prevent the unification of one people into a great empire. If England or America were split up into different parts, these parts would also strive undeniably to reunite. The same had been evident in the case of Germany and Italy. If now a political coalition had grown accustomed to ignoring such natural tendencies, as in the case of Italy and Germany, it would naturally be awkward if at a certain time these forces became so strong that they could no longer be overlooked. The idea, however, of wanting to prevent the political unification of the German nation, ultimately by war, was simply absurd.

As far as the economic side was concerned, it was simply foolish to want to exclude from raw material sources a people that had to live with 140 persons to the square kilometer. Germany had won her colonies not by conquest and force but by purchase, exchange, and treaty. These colonies had been taken from her without a solution being offered for vital problems connected with this step. Thus a bloc of 80 million people had been plunged into the greatest subsistence difficulties, and a nation that had been deprived in this way of the bases for its existence could not be expected to be grateful for it in the bargain. It was only natural that as soon as this people was restored to strength it would strive to regain the bases of its existence. Germany also failed to understand the "peace-time blockade," which consisted in the fact that certain countries simply reserved to themselves great areas of the world, as had been done in the Ottawa Agreement.

It must be stated, moreover, that world trade was not the only remedy for economic ills. As an example the Führer cited German-American relations. America was producing a surplus of foods, raw materials, and industrial products. Germany was suffering from a shortage of foods and raw materials, but had a surplus of industrial products. America would surely be glad to place at Germany's disposal the available quantities out of her surplus production of food and raw materials, but could not accept industrial exports Germany thought to give in return because she had a surplus industrial production of her own. Thus it was impossible in this way to supply the Central European Lebensraum with all its needs; therefore this Lebensraum must create within itself the bases for its raw materials and food supplies. If this were not done, the greatest economic difficulties would arise. Either the Central European area would be forced to resort to underbidding and dumping or a dangerous state of tension would develop.

The Führer then pointed out that he had proposed to England and France that they proceed to joint collaboration in the economic field after the return of the German colonies. These proposals had been rejected, however. He was not waging war for its own sake; on the contrary, the war meant for him a loss of time if one considered that he had been given the gigantic task of organizing the Central European Lebensraum of the German people and making it viable. The German people were 100 percent behind him in this endeavor.

In summary, the Führer pointed out that if the economic, political, and historical realities which he had just discussed were disregarded, no really lasting and sound condition of peace could be achieved. Respect for these three elements was the condition for a lasting peace. For the rest, Germany did not desire to penetrate the Lebensraum of other great nations, but only to retain what actually belonged to her. She had effected the unification of all the German people as the most natural requirement of the present. She wanted to secure for herself the economic and spatial foundations necessary for her existence. The immense British world empire with its large, unused tracts of land surely had no use for the German colonies. The military argument, too, was not convincing, since Germany was the only power which had not used her colonies for military purposes. If these views were not respected, the Führer said in conclusion, there was no other solution than a life-and-death struggle which Germany, however, was facing with complete confidence.

Sumner Welles stated that he personally fully recognized the work of reconstruction performed by the Führer in the 7 years of his government. He had also recognized very well the significance of the historical and political exigencies of which the Führer had spoken to him. The American Government was of the opinion that there could be no greater guarantee of a lasting and sound peace than a unified, contented, and prosperous German nation.

. . . .

Sumner Welles then pointed out that in economic and disarmament questions the German and the American Governments were of the same opinion on many points, and in this connection asked the Führer whether he agreed with the American Government that after the establishment of a lasting and sound peace which gave the German people every security, in accordance with the principles just described by the Führer, the disarmament and economic problems could be solved simultaneously.

The Führer replied that he was personally of the opinion that the armaments burden had to be reduced because it would otherwise lead to the ruin of all nations. It represented not only the greatest impediment to social reconstruction, but also millions of workers were employed for nonproductive purposes who could better be occupied in other fields for increasing the well-being of the people. There were two possibilities for limiting armaments:

1. By international agreements on the basis of which all the nations would disarm simultaneously according to a definite plan by tedious and involved procedures.

2. By the union of a number of peoples that were ready to disarm, who would pool their defense interests and despite their own disarmament would still remain strong enough collectively to prevail against other nations not willing to disarm; the latter, as a result of the great burden of their armaments, would finally have to collapse. He had made such proposals to England and France, but without success.

Sumner Welles replied that the Government of the United States considered the armaments question one of the most serious problems, just as did the Führer, and agreed with him that it now resulted in diverting the people to work aimed at destruction instead of employing them productively. If rearmament continued, the various countries would be faced with ruin, as the Führer had very correctly observed.

He could not at the moment express himself on the technical procedure for disarmament.

The Führer repeated that the decisive thing was that it was not a matter of the German war aims but the war aims of the others who were seeking the annihilation of Germany. He could assure Mr. Sumner Welles that Germany would never be annihilated. He had been a soldier on the western front for 4 years, and was of the opinion that Germany would not have been defeated then either if there had been another regime at the helm. It was not a question of whether Germany would be annihilated; Germany would know how to defend herself from annihilation, and in the very worst case everyone would be annihilated. Today Germany was in a totally different situation from the last war and he, the Führer, had made all preparations, and made them thoroughly, in order to be able to break the will to annihilation of the others. The German war aim—"peace"—stood opposed to the war aim of the others—"annihilation". The German people, who had learned from the terrible experience of 1918, stood behind him to a man. Anybody who wanted to establish peace had to induce Germany's opponents to abandon their war aims of annihilation. Germany was of the view that America even with the best will in the world—which was recognized by the Germans without question—would find it difficult to attain this goal.

Sumner Welles thanked the Führer for the open and candid way in which he had made his statements. He was deeply impressed with what he had heard and would report it to President Roosevelt as accurately as possible. Responding to a remark by the Führer, Sumner Welles said that the American Government hoped that not only would it be possible to prevent everyone from being destroyed, as the Führer had expressed it, but that not even one of the countries now engaged in the conflict would be destroyed. He took cognizance, moreover, of the fact that the Führer had declared peace to be the German war aim. He would not forget this.

Submitted herewith to the Foreign Minister.

SCHMIDT
Minister

26. PRESIDENT ROOSEVELT'S MESSAGE TO CONGRESS, MAY 16, 1940[2]

The PRESIDENT. Mr. Vice President, Mr. Speaker, Members of the Senate and House of Representatives, these are ominous days—days whose swift and shocking developments force every neutral nation to look at its defenses in the light of new factors. The brutal force of modern offensive war has been loosed in all its horror. New powers of destruction, incredibly swift and deadly, have been developed; and those who wield them are ruthless and daring. No old defense is so strong that it requires no further strengthening and no attack is so unlikely or impossible that it may be ignored.

Let us examine, without self-deception, the dangers which confront us. Let us measure our strength and our defense without self-delusion.

The clear fact is that the American people must recast their thinking about national protection.

Motorized armies can now sweep through enemy territories at the rate of 200 miles a day. Parachute troops are dropped from airplanes in large numbers behind enemy lines. Troops are landed from planes in open fields, on wide highways, and at local civil airports.

We have seen the treacherous use of the "fifth column" by which persons supposed to be peaceful visitors were actually a part of an enemy unit of occupation. Lightning attacks, capable of destroying airplane factories and munition works hundreds of miles behind the lines, are part of the new technique of modern war.

The element of surprise which has ever been an important tactic in warfare had become the more dangerous because of the amazing speed with which modern equipment can reach and attack the enemy's country.

Our own vital interests are widespread. More than ever the protection of the whole American Hemisphere against invasion or control or domination by non-American nations has the united support of the 21 American Republics, including the United States. More than ever this protection calls for ready-at-hand weapons capable of great mobility because of the potential speed of modern attack.

The Atlantic and Pacific Oceans were reasonably adequate defensive barriers when fleets under sail could move at an average speed of 5 miles an hour. Even then by a sudden foray it was possible for an opponent actually to burn our National Capitol. Later the oceans still gave strength to our defense when fleets and convoys propelled by steam could sail the oceans at 15 or 20 miles an hour.

But the new element—air navigation—steps up the speed of possible attack to 200 to 300, miles an hour.

Furthermore, it brings the new possibilities of the use of nearer bases from which an attack or attacks on the American Continents could be made. From the fiords of Greenland it is 4 hours by air to Newfoundland; 5 hours to Nova Scotia, New Brunswick, and Quebec; and only 6 hours to New England.

The Azores are only 2,000 miles from parts of our eastern seaboard, and if Bermuda fell into hostile hands it is a matter of less than 3 hours for modern bombers to reach our shores.

From a base in the outer West Indies the coast of Florida could be reached in 200 minutes.

The islands off the West Coast of Africa are only 1,500 miles from Brazil. Modern planes starting from the Cape Verde Islands can be over Brazil in 7 hours.

And Para, Brazil, is but 4 flying hours to Caracas, Venezuela; and Venezuela but 2½ hours to Cuba and the Canal Zone; and Cuba and the Canal Zone are 2¼ hours to Tampico, Mexico; and Tampico is 2¼ hours to St. Louis, Kansas City, and Omaha.

On the other side of the continent, Alaska, with a white population of only 30,000 people, is within 4 or 5 hours of flying distance to Vancouver, Seattle, Tacoma, and Portland. The islands of the southern Pacific are not too far removed from the west coast of South America to prevent them from becoming bases of enormous strategic advantage to attacking forces.

Surely the developments of the past few weeks have made it clear to all of our citizens that the possibility of attack on vital American zones ought to make it essential that we have the physical, the ready, ability to meet those attacks and to prevent them from reaching their objectives.

This means military implements—not on paper—which are ready and available to meet any lightning offensive against our American interest. It means also that facilities for production must be ready to turn out munitions and equipment at top speed.

We have had the lesson before us over and over again—nations that were not ready and were unable to get ready found themselves overrun by the enemy. So-called impregnable fortifications no longer exist. A defense which allows an enemy to consolidate his approach without hindrance will lose. A defense which makes no effective effort to destroy the lines of supplies and communications of the enemy will lose.

An effective defense, by its very nature, requires the equipment to attack an aggressor on his route before he can establish strong bases within the territory of American vital interests.

Loose talking and thinking on the part of some may give the false impression that our own Army and Navy are not first rate, or that money has been wasted on them.

Nothing could be further from the truth.

In recent years the defensive power of our Army, Navy, and Marine Corps has been very greatly improved.

The Navy is stronger today than at any time in the Nation's history. Today also a large program of new construction is well under way. Ship for ship, ours are equal to or better than the vessels of any foreign power.

The Army likewise is at its greatest peacetime strength. Its equipment in quality and quantity has been greatly increased and improved.

The National Guard and the Reserve strength of the two services are better equipped and better prepared than during any other peacetime period.

On the other side of the picture we must visualize the outstanding fact that since the 1st day of September 1939 every week that has passed has brought new lessons learned from actual combat on land and sea.

I cite examples. Where naval ships have operated without adequate protection by defending aircraft, their vulnerability to air attack has increased. All nations are hard at work studying the need of additional antiaircraft protection.

Several months ago the use of a new type of magnetic mine made many unthinking people believe that all surface ships were doomed. Within a few weeks a successful defensive device against these mines was placed in operation; and it is a fact that the sinkings of merchant ships by torpedo, by mine, or by airplane are definitely much lower than during the similar period of 1915.

Combat conditions have changed even more rapidly in the air. With the amazing progress in the design of planes and engines, the airplane of a year ago is out of date now. It is too slow, it is improperly protected, it is too weak in gunpower.

In types of planes we are not behind the other nations of the world. Many of the planes of the belligerent powers are at this moment not of the latest models. But one belligerent power not only has many more planes than all their opponents combined, but also appears to have a weekly production capacity at the moment that is far greater than that of their opponents.

From the point of view of our own defense, therefore, great additional production capacity is our principal air requisite.

For the permanent record, I ask the Congress not to take any action which would in any way hamper or delay the delivery of American-made planes to foreign nations which have ordered them, or seek to purchase more planes. That, from the point of view of our own national defense, would be extremely short-sighted.

During the past year American production capacity for war planes, including engines, has risen from approximately 6,000 planes a year to more than double that number, due in greater part to the placing of foreign orders.

Our immediate problem is to superimpose on this production capacity a

greatly increased additional production capacity. I should like to see this
Nation geared up to the ability to turn out at least 50,000 planes a year.
Furthermore, I believe that this Nation should plan at this time a program
that would provide us with 50,000 military and naval planes.

The ground forces of the Army require the immediate speeding up of last
winter's program to procure equipment of all kinds, including motor transport and artillery, including antiaircraft guns and full ammunition supplies.
It had been planned to spread these requirements over the next 3 or 4 years.
We should fill them at once.

At this time I am asking the immediate appropriation by the Congress of a
large sum of money for four primary purposes:

First, to procure the essential equipment of all kinds for a larger and
thoroughly rounded-out Army;

Second, to replace or modernize all old Army and Navy equipment with
the latest type of equipment;

Third, to increase production facilities for everything needed for the
Army and Navy for national defense. We require the ability to turn out
quickly infinitely greater supplies;

Fourth, to speed up to a 24-hour basis all existing Army and Navy
contracts, and all new contracts to be awarded.

I ask for an immediate appropriation of $896,000,000, and may I say I
hope there will be speed in giving the appropriation. [Applause.] That sum I
would divide approximately as follows:

    1. For the Army $546,000,000
    2. For the Navy and Marine Corps 250,000,000
    3. To the President to provide for emergencies
       affecting the national security
       and defense 100,000,000

In addition to the above sum, I ask for authorizations for the Army, Navy,
and Marine Corps to make contract obligations in the further sum of
$186,000,000.

And to the President an additional authorization to make contract obligations for $100,000,000.

The total of authorizations is, therefore, $286,000,000.

It is my belief that a large part of the requested appropriation of
$100,000,000, and the requested authorization of $100,000,000 to the President will be used principally for the increase of production of airplanes,
antiaircraft guns, and the training of additional personnel for these
weapons. This would be in addition to the direct estimates for these purposes in the other items requested.

The proposed details of the appropriations and authorizations asked for
will be given to the committees of the Congress.

These estimates do not, of course, duplicate any item now in the pending
war and navy appropriation bills for the year 1941. Nor do they include
supplemental or deficiency estimates which may become necessary by reason
of pending legislation or shortage of funds under existing programs.

There are some who say that democracy cannot cope with the new techniques of government developed in recent years by a few countries—by a few countries which deny the freedoms which we maintain are essential to our democratic way of life. This I reject.

I know that our trained officers and men know more about fighting and the weapons and equipment needed for fighting than any of us laymen; and I have confidence in them.

I know that to cope with present dangers we must be strong in heart and hand; strong in our faith—strong in faith in our way of living.

I, too, pray for peace—that the ways of aggression and force may be banished from the earth—but I am determined to face the fact realistically that this Nation requires a toughness of moral and physical fiber. Those qualities, I am convinced, the American people hold to a high degree.

Our task is plain. The road we must take is clearly indicated. Our defenses must be invulnerable, our security absolute. But our defense as it was yesterday, or even as it is today, does not provide security against potential developments and dangers of the future.

Defense cannot be static. Defense must grow and change from day to day. Defense must be dynamic and flexible, an expression of the vital forces of the Nation and of its resolute will to meet whatever challenge the future may hold. For these reasons, I need hardly assure you that after the adjournment of this session of the Congress I will not hesitate to call the Congress into special session if at any time the situation of the national defense requires it. The Congress and the Chief Executive constitute a team where the defense of the land is concerned.

Our ideal, our objective, is still peace—peace at home and peace abroad. Nevertheless, we stand ready not only to spend millions for defense but to give our service and even our lives for the maintenance of our American liberties.

Our security is not a matter of weapons alone. The arm that wields them must be strong, the eye that guides them clear, the will that directs them indomitable.

These are the characteristics of a free people, a people devoted to the institutions they themselves have built, a people willing to defend a way of life that is precious to them all, a people who put their faith in God. [Prolonged applause.]

27. MUSSOLINI'S STATEMENT OF JUNE 10, 1940[3]

Fighters of land, sea and air, Blackshirts of the revolution and of the legions, men and women of Italy, of the empire and of the Kingdom of Albania, listen!

The hour destined by fate is sounding for us. The hour of irrevocable decision has come. A declaration of war already has been handed to the Ambassadors of Great Britain and France.

We take the field against the plutocratic and reactionary democracies who always have blocked the march and frequently plotted against the existence of the Italian people.

Several decades of recent history may be summarized in these words: Phrases, promises, threats of blackmail, and finally, crowning that ignoble edifice, the League of Nations of fifty-two nations.

Our conscience is absolutely clear.

With you, the entire world is witness that the Italy of fascism has done everything humanly possible to avoid the tempest that envelops Europe, but all in vain.

It would have sufficed to revise treaties to adapt them to changing requirements vital to nations and not consider them untouchable for eternity.

It would have sufficed not to begin the stupid policy of guarantees, which proved particularly deadly for those who accepted them.

It would have sufficed not to reject the proposal the Fuehrer made last October 6 after the campaign in Poland ended.

Now all that belongs to the past.

If today we have decided to take the risks and sacrifices of war, it is because the honor, interests and future firmly impose it since a great people is truly such if it considers its obligations sacred and does not avoid the supreme trials that determine the course of history.

We are taking up arms, after having solved the problem of our continental frontiers, to solve our maritime frontiers. We want to break the territorial and military chains that confine us in our sea because a country of 45,000,000 souls is not truly free if it has not free access to the ocean.

This gigantic conflict is only a phase of the logical development of our revolution. It is the conflict of poor, numerous peoples who labor against starvers who ferociously cling to a monopoly of all riches and all gold on earth.

It is a conflict of fruitful, useful peoples against peoples who are in a decline. It is a conflict between two ages, two ideas.

Now the die is cast and our will has burned our ships behind us.

I solemnly declare that Italy does not intend to drag other peoples bordering on her by sea or land into the conflict. Switzerland, Yugoslavia, Greece, Turkey, and Egypt, take note of these words of mine. It depends on them and only on them if these words are rigorously confirmed or not.

Italians, in a memorable mass meeting in Berlin, I said that according to the rules of Fascist morals when one has a friend one marches with him to the end. This we have done and will continue to do with Germany, her people and her victorious armed forces.

On this eve of an event of import for centuries, we turn our thoughts to His Majesty, the King and Emperor, who always has understood the thought of the country.

Lastly, we salute the new Fuehrer, the chief of great allied Germany.

Proletarian, Fascist Italy has arisen for the third time, strong, proud, compact as never before.

There is only one order. It is categorical and obligatory for every one. It already wings over and enflames hearts from the Alps to the Indian Ocean: Conquer!

And we will conquer in order, finally, to give a new world of peace with justice to Italy, to Europe and to the universe.

Italian people, rush to arms and show your tenacity, your courage, your valor.

28. HITLER TO MUSSOLINI, TELEGRAM, JUNE 10, 1940[4]

The Führer's Headquarters.
June 10, 1940—9:40 p.m.

Duce: The historic decision which you announced today has moved me most profoundly. The whole German people is thinking of you and your country at this moment. The German Wehrmacht is glad to be able to stand at the side of its Italian comrades in battle.

Last September the rulers of Britain and France declared war on the German Reich without any reason. They turned down every offer of a peaceful settlement. Your proposal for mediation, Duce, was also received at the time with a brusque "No." While we have always been very closely linked together ideologically by our two revolutions and politically by treaties, the increasing disregard shown by the rulers in London and Paris for Italy's vital national rights has now finally brought us together in the great struggle for the freedom and future of our peoples.

Duce of Fascist Italy, accept the assurance of the indestructible community of arms between the German and the Italian peoples.

I myself send you as always in loyal comradeship my sincerest greetings.

Yours,   Adolf Hitler

29. FORMER EMPEROR WILHELM II TO ADOLF HITLER, TELEGRAM, JUNE 17, 1940[5]

Doorn, June 17, 1940.

Under the deeply moving impression of the capitulation of France I congratulate you and the whole German Wehrmacht on the mighty victory granted by God, in the words of the Emperor Wilhelm the Great in 1870: "What a turn of events brought about by divine dispensation."

In all German hearts there echoes the Leuthen chorale sung by the victors of Leuthen, the soldiers of the Great King: "Now thank we all our God!"

Wilhelm I. R.

30. German-French Armistice Treaty, June 22, 1940 (German Copy)[6]

The following Armistice Treaty [*Waffenstillstandsvertrag*] has been agreed upon by Colonel General Keitel, Chief of the High Command of the Wehrmacht, appointed by the Führer of the German Reich and Supreme Commander of the German Wehrmacht, on the one hand, and the Plenipotentiaries of the French Government who are vested with full powers, General of the Army Huntziger, chairman of the delegation, M. Noël, Ambassador of France, Vice Admiral Le Luc, General Parisot, Corps Commander, and General of the Air Force Bergeret, on the other:

1. The French Government will order the cessation of hostilities against the German Reich in France, in French possessions, colonies, protectorates, and mandated territories, and at sea. It will order French units, already encircled by German troops, to lay down their arms immediately.

2. In order to safeguard the interests of the German Reich, French territory north and west of the line marked on the attached map will be occupied by German troops. In so far as the parts to be occupied are not yet under the control of German troops, this occupation will be carried out immediately after the conclusion of this Treaty.

3. In the occupied parts of France the German Reich will exercise all the rights of the occupying power. The French Government undertakes to support by every means orders issued in the exercise of those rights and to carry them out with the assistance of the French administration. The French Government will therefore immediately instruct all French authorities and offices of the occupied territory to comply with the orders of the German military commanders and to collaborate with them correctly.

It is the intention of the German Government to reduce to the extent absolutely necessary the occupation of the western coast after the cessation of hostilities with England.

The French Government is free to choose its seat of government in the unoccupied territory, or, if it so desires, to transfer it to Paris. In the latter case, the German Government promises the French Government and its central authorities every necessary facility to enable it to administer the occupied and unoccupied territory from Paris.

4. The French armed forces on land, at sea, and in the air are to be demobilized and disarmed within a period still to be fixed. Excepted from this are only those units which are necessary for the maintenance of internal order. Their strength and armament will be determined by Germany or Italy respectively. Units of the French armed forces in the territory to be occupied by Germany will be speedily withdrawn to the territory not to be occupied and are to be discharged. Before leaving, these troops will lay down their arms and equipment at the places where they happen to be at the time of the entry into force of this Treaty. They will be responsible for orderly delivery to the German troops.

5. As a guarantee that the armistice will be observed, demand can be made for the surrender intact of all guns, tanks, antitank weapons, military aircraft, antiaircraft guns, small arms, transport material and ammunition of those units of the French armed forces which were fighting against Germany and which at the time of the entry into force of this agreement happen to be in territory not to be occupied by Germany. The extent of these surrenders will be determined by the German Armistice Commission.

The surrender of military aircraft can be dispensed with, if all military aircraft still in the possession of the French armed forces are disarmed and placed in safe custody under German supervision.

6. The remaining arms, stocks of ammunition, and war material of all kinds in the unoccupied part of France—except those permitted for the equipment of the authorized French units—are to be stored or placed in safe custody under German or Italian supervision. In this connection the German High Command reserves the right to order all measures necessary to prevent the unauthorized use of these stores. Further manufacture of war material in unoccupied territory is to be stopped immediately.

7. In the territory to be occupied all land and coastal fortifications are to be surrendered intact with their arms, ammunition, equipment, stores, and installations of every kind. Plans of these fortifications, as well as plans of those already captured by the German troops, are to be surrendered. Exact details of explosive charges placed in position, mine fields on land, time fuses, gas barrages, etc., are to be supplied to the German High Command. These obstacles are to be removed by French troops at the request of the German authorities.

8. The French war fleet, with the exception of the part permitted to the French Government for the protection of French interests in its colonial empire, is to be assembled in ports to be specified and is to be demobilized and disarmed under German or Italian supervision. The choice of these ports will be determined by the peacetime stations of the ships. The German Government solemnly declares to the French Government that it does not intend to use for its own purposes in the war the French fleet which is in ports under German supervision, with the exception of those units needed for coastal patrol and for mine sweeping. Furthermore they solemnly and expressly declare that they have no intention of raising any claim to the French war fleet at the time of the conclusion of peace. With the exception of that part of the French war fleet, still to be determined, which is to represent French interests in the colonial empire, all war vessels which are outside French territorial waters are to be recalled to France.

9. The French High Command is to supply the German High Command with detailed information about all mines laid by France, as well as all harbor and coastal barriers and installations for defense and protection.

The clearing of mine fields is to be carried out by French forces to the extent required by the German High Command.

10. The French Government undertakes not to engage in any hostile

actions with any part of the armed forces left to it, or in any other way, against the German Reich.

The French Government will also prevent members of the French armed forces from leaving the country and arms and war material of any kind, ships, aircraft, etc., from being moved to England or to any other foreign country.

The French Government will forbid French nationals to fight against the German Reich in the service of states with which Germany is still at war. French nationals who act contrary to this prohibition will be treated by German troops as franc-tireurs [*Freischärler*].

11. French merchant ships of all kinds including coastal and harbor craft in French hands are to be forbidden to put to sea until further notice. The resumption of merchant shipping will be subject to the approval of the German and Italian Governments respectively.

The French Government will recall French merchant ships which are outside French ports or, if this cannot be done, will order them to proceed to neutral ports.

All German merchant ships which have been captured and which are in French ports will be returned intact on demand.

12. All aircraft on French territory will be immediately prohibited from taking off. Any aircraft taking off without German authority will be regarded by the German Luftwaffe as hostile and treated as such.

Airfields and ground installations of the Air Force in unoccupied territory will be under German and/or Italian supervision as the case may be. Demand may be made that they shall be rendered unusable. The French Government is obligated to make available all foreign aircraft which are in unoccupied territory or to prevent them from continuing their flight. They are to be handed over to the German Wehrmacht.

13. The French Government undertakes to ensure that in the territories to be occupied by German troops all installations equipment and stores of the armed forces are surrendered intact to the German troops. It will further ensure that ports, industrial plants, and shipyards are left in their present condition and not damaged or destroyed in any way. The same applies to all means and routes of communication, in particular to railways, highways, and inland waterways, to the whole telecommunication service and to installations for marking channels for navigation and the coastal lighthouse service. It also undertakes to carry out all repairs necessary thereon as required by the German High Command.

The French Government will ensure that there are available in occupied territory the necessary technical personnel, the amount of rolling stock and other means of transport as under normal peacetime conditions.

14. All radio transmitting stations in French territory are forthwith forbidden to transmit. The resumption of transmissions from the unoccupied part of France will be subject to special arrangements.

15. The French Government undertakes to effect the transit of goods

through the unoccupied territory between the German Reich and Italy to the extent required by the German Government.

16. The French Government, in agreement with the competent German authorities, will arrange for the return of the population to the occupied territory.

17. The French Government undertakes to prevent any removal of economic assets [*Werte*] and stocks [*Vorräte*] from the territory to be occupied by German troops into unoccupied territory or abroad. Such assets and stocks as are in the occupied territory may only be disposed of in agreement with the German Government.

In this connection the German Government will take into consideration the vital needs of the population of the unoccupied territories.

18. The costs of maintenance of the German occupation troops on French territory will be borne by the French Government.

19. All German prisoners of war and civilian prisoners in French custody, including detained or convicted persons who have been arrested and sentenced for acts committed in the interests of the German Reich are to be handed over immediately to the German troops.

The French Government is obligated to hand over on demand all Germans in France, in the French possessions, colonies, protectorates, and mandated territories who are named by the German Government.

The French Government undertakes to prevent German prisoners of war or civilian prisoners from being removed from France to French possessions or abroad. Correct lists are to be supplied of prisoners already removed from France as well as of sick and wounded German prisoners of war unfit for travel, with particulars of their whereabouts. The German High Command will take over the care of German sick and wounded prisoners of war.

20. Members of the French armed forces who are prisoners of war in German hands shall remain prisoners of war until the conclusion of peace.

21. The French Government is liable for securing all objects and assets which, according to this Treaty, are to be surrendered intact, or held at German disposal, or the removal of which outside the country is forbidden. The French Government is obligated to make good all destruction, damage, or removal contrary to this Treaty.

22. The execution of the Armistice Treaty will be regulated and supervised by a German Armistice Commission acting under the instructions of the German High Command. Furthermore the Armistice Commission will be called upon to ensure the necessary conformity between the present Treaty and the Italian-French Armistice Treaty. The French Government will send a delegation to the seat of the German Armistice Commission to represent French wishes and to receive the executive orders of the German Armistice Commission.

23. The present Armistice Treaty will come into force as soon as the French Government has also reached an agreement with the Italian Government on the cessation of hostilities. Hostilities will cease six hours after

the Italian Government has notified the Reich Government that this agreement has been reached. The Reich Government will notify the French Government of this time by radio.

24. The Armistice Treaty will remain in force until the conclusion of the peace treaty. It can be denounced by the German Government at any time and with immediate effect, if the French Government does not carry out the obligations assumed by it in this Treaty:

This Armistice Treaty has been signed in the Forest of Compiègne at 6:50 p.m., German summer time, on June 22, 1940.

Huntziger　　　Keitel

31. CHURCHILL SPEAKS ON FRENCH FLEET SITUATION, JULY 4, 1940[7]

3.54 p.m.

The Prime Minister (Mr. Churchill): It is with sincere sorrow that I must now announce to the House the measures which we have felt bound to take in order to prevent the French Fleet from falling into German hands. When two nations are fighting together under long and solemn alliance against a common foe, one of them may be stricken down and overwhelmed, and may be forced to ask its Ally to release it from its obligations. But the least that could be expected was that the French Government, in abandoning the conflict and leaving its whole weight to fall upon Great Britain and the British Empire, would have been careful not to inflict needless injury upon their faithful comrade, in whose final victory the sole chance of French freedom lay, and lies.

As the House will remember, we offered to give full release to the French from their Treaty obligations although these were designed for precisely the case which arose, on one condition, namely, that the French Fleet should be sailed for British harbours before the separate armistice negotiations with the enemy were completed. This was not done, but on the contrary, in spite of every kind of private and personal promise and assurance given by Admiral Darlan to the First Lord and to his Naval colleague the First Sea Lord of the British Admiralty, an armistice was signed which was bound to place the French Fleet as effectively in the power of Germany and its Italian following as that portion of the French Fleet which was placed in our power when many of them, being unable to reach African ports, came into the harbours of Portsmouth and Plymouth about 10 days ago. Thus I must place on record that what might have been a mortal injury was done to us by the Bordeaux Government with full knowledge of the consequences and of our dangers, and after rejecting all our appeals at the moment when they were abandoning the Alliance, and breaking the engagements which fortified it.

There was another example of this callous and perhaps even malevolent treatment which we received, not indeed from the French nation, who have never been and apparently never are to be consulted upon these transactions, but from the Bordeaux Government. This is the instance. There were over 400 German air pilots who were prisoners in France, many of them perhaps most of them, shot down by the Royal Air Force. I obtained from M. Reynaud a personal promise that these pilots should be sent for safe keeping to England and orders were given by him to that effect; but when M. Reynaud fell, these pilots were delivered over to Germany in order, no doubt, to win favour for the Bordeaux Government with their German masters, and to win it without regard to the injury done to us. The German Air Force already feels acutely the shortage of high grade pilots, and it seemed to me particularly odious, if I may use the word, that these 400 skilled men should be handed over with the sure knowledge that they would be used to bomb this country, and thus force our airmen to shoot them down for the second time over. Such wrongful deeds I am sure will not be condoned by history, and I firmly believe that a generation of Frenchmen will arise who will clear their national honour from all countenance of them.

I said last week that we must now look with particular attention to our own salvation. I have never in my experience seen so grim and sombre a question as what we were to do about the French Fleet discussed in a Cabinet. It shows how strong were the reasons for the course which we thought it our duty to take, that every Member of the Cabinet had the same conviction about what should be done and there was not the slightest hesitation or divergence among them, and that the three Service Ministers, as well as men like the Minister of Information and the Secretary of State for the Colonies, particularly noted for their long friendship with France, when they were consulted were equally convinced that no other decision than that which we took was possible. We took that decision, and it was a decision to which, with aching hearts but with clear vision, we unitedly came. Accordingly early yesterday morning, 3rd July, after all preparations had been made, we took the greater part of the French Fleet under our control, or else called upon them, with adequate force, to comply with our requirements. Two battleships, two light cruisers, some submarines, including a very large one, the "Surcouf," eight destroyers and approximately 200 smaller but extremely useful minesweeping and anti-submarine craft, which lay for the most part at Portsmouth and Plymouth, though there were some at Sheerness, were boarded by superior forces, after brief notice had been given wherever possible to their captains.

This operation was successfully carried out without resistance or bloodshed except in one instance. A scuffle arose through a misunderstanding in the submarine "Surcouf," in which one British leading seaman was killed and two British officers and one rating wounded and one French officer killed and one wounded. For the rest, the French sailors in the main cheerfully accepted the end of a period of uncertainty. A considerable number, 800 or 900, have expressed an ardent desire to continue the war, and some have asked for British nationality. This we are ready to grant without prejudice to the other Frenchmen, numbered by thousands, who prefer to fight on with us as Frenchmen. All the rest of those crews will be immediately repatriated to French ports, if the French Government are able to make arrangements for their reception by permission of their German rulers. We are also repatriating all French troops who were in this country, excepting those who, of their own free will, have volunteered to follow General de Gaulle in the French forces of liberation of whom he is chief. Several French submarines have also joined us independently, and we have accepted their services.

Now I turn to the Mediterranean. At Alexandria, where a strong British battle fleet is lying, there are, besides a French battleship, four French cruisers, three of them modern 8-inch gun vessels, and a number of smaller ships. These have been informed that they cannot be permitted to leave harbour and thus fall within the power of the German conquerors of France. Negotiations and discussions, with the details of which I need not trouble the House, have necessarily been taking place, and measures have now been taken to ensure that those ships, which are commanded by a very gallant Admiral, shall be sunk or otherwise made to comply with our wishes. The anguish which this process has, naturally, caused to the British and French naval officers concerned may be readily imagined, when I tell the House that only this morning, in the air raid upon Alexandria by Italian aircraft, some of the French ships fired heavily and effectively with us against the common enemy. We shall, of course, offer the fullest facilities to all French officers and men at Alexandria who wish to continue the war, and will provide for them and maintain them during the conflict. We have also promised to repatriate all the rest, and every care in our power will be taken, if they allow it, for their safety and their comfort. So much for Alexandria.

But the most serious part of the story remains. Two of the finest vessels of the French fleet, the "Dunkerque" and the "Strasbourg," modern battle cruisers much superior to "Scharnhorst" and "Gneisenau"—and built for the purpose of being superior to them—lay with two battleships, several light cruisers and a number of destroyers and submarines and other vessels at Oran and at its adjacent military port of Mers-El-Kebir on the Northern African shore of Morocco. Yesterday morning, a carefully chosen British officer, Captain Holland, lately Naval Attaché in Paris, was sent on in a destroyer and waited upon the French Admiral Gensoul. After being refused an interview, he presented the following document, which I will read to the House. The first two paragraphs of the document deal with the general question of the Armistice, which I have already explained in my own words. The fourth paragraph begins as follows: This is the operative paragraph:

"It is impossible for us, your comrades up to now, to allow your fine ships to fall into the power of the German or Italian enemy. We are determined to fight on to the end, and if we win, as we think we shall, we shall never forget that France was our Ally, that our interests are the same as hers and that our common enemy is Germany. Should we conquer, we solemnly declare that we shall restore the greatness and territory of France. For this purpose, we must make sure that the best ships of the French Navy are not used against us by the common foe. In these circumstances, His Majesty's Government have instructed me"—

That is, the British Admiral—

"to demand that the French Fleet now at Mers-El-Kebir and Oran shall act in accordance with one of the following alternatives:

(a) Sail with us and continue to fight for victory against the Germans and Italians.

(b) Sail with reduced crews under our control to a British port. The reduced crews will be repatriated at the earliest moment.

If either of these courses is adopted by you, we will restore your ships to France at the conclusion of the war or pay full compensation, if they are damaged meanwhile.

(c) Alternatively, if you feel bound to stipulate that your ships should not be used against the Germans or Italians unless these break the Armistice, then sail them with us with reduced crews, to some French port in the West Indies, Martinique, for instance, where they can be demilitarised to our satisfaction or be perhaps entrusted to the United States and remain safe until the end of the war, the crews being repatriated.

If you refuse these fair offers, I must, with profound regret, require you to sink your ships within six hours.

Finally, failing the above, I have the orders of His Majesty's Government to use whatever force may be necessary to prevent your ships from falling into German or Italian hands."

We had hoped that one or other of the alternatives which we presented would have been accepted, without the necessity of using the terrible force of a British battle squadron. Such a squadron arrived before Oran two hours after Captain Holland and his destroyer. This battle squadron was commanded by Vice-Admiral Somerville, an officer who distinguished himself lately in the bringing-off of over 100,000 Frenchmen during the evacuation from Dunkirk. Admiral Somerville was further provided, besides his battle-ships, with a cruiser force and strong flotillas. All day the parleys continued, and we hoped until the afternoon that our terms would be accepted without bloodshed. However, no doubt in obedience to the orders dictated by the Germans from Wiesbaden, where the Franco-German Armistice Commission is in session, Admiral Gensoul refused to comply and announced his intention of fighting. Admiral Somerville was therefore ordered to complete his mission before darkness fell, and at 5.53 p.m. he opened fire upon this powerful French Fleet, which was also protected by its shore batteries. At 6 p.m. he reported that he was heavily engaged. The action lasted for some 10 minutes and was followed by heavy attacks from our naval aircraft, carried in the "Ark Royal." At 7.20 p.m. Admiral Somerville forwarded a further report, which stated that a battle cruiser of the "Strasbourg" class was damaged and ashore; that a battleship of the "Bretagne" class had been sunk, that another of the same class had been heavily damaged, and that two French destroyers and a seaplane carrier, "Commandant Teste," were also sunk or burned.

While this melancholy action was being fought, either the battle cruiser "Strasbourg" or the "Dunkerque," one or the other, managed to slip out of harbour in a gallant effort to reach Toulon or a North African port and place herself under German control, in accordance with the Armistice terms of the Bordeaux Government—though all this her crew and captain may not have realised. She was pursued by aircraft of the Fleet Air Arm and hit by at least one torpedo. She may have been joined by other French vessels from Algiers, which were well placed to do so and to reach Toulon before we could overtake them. She will, at any rate, be out of action for many months to come.

I need hardly say that the French ships were fought, albeit in this unnatural cause, with the characteristic courage of the French Navy, and every allowance must be made for Admiral Gensoul and his officers who felt themselves obliged to obey the orders they received from their Government and could not look behind that Government to see the German dictation. I fear the loss of life among the French and in the harbour must have been heavy, as we were compelled to use a severe measure of force and several immense explosions were heard. None of the British ships taking part in the action was in any way affected in gun-power or mobility by the heavy fire directed upon them. I have not yet received any reports of our casualties, but Admiral Somerville's Fleet is, in all military respects, intact and ready for further action. The Italian Navy, for whose reception we had also made arrangements and which is, of course, considerably stronger numerically than the Fleet we used at Oran, kept prudently out of the way. However, we trust that their turn will come during the operations which we shall pursue to secure the effectual command of the Mediterranean.

A large proportion of the French Fleet has, therefore, passed into our hands or has been put out of action or otherwise withheld from Germany by yesterday's events. The House will not expect me to say anything about other French ships which are at large except that it is our inflexible resolve to do everything that is possible in order to prevent them falling into the German grip.

I leave the judgment of our action, with confidence, to Parliament. I leave it to the nation, and I leave it to the United States. I leave it to the world and to history.

Now I turn to the immediate future. We must, of course, expect to be attacked, or even invaded, if that proves to be possible—it has not been proved yet—in our own island before very long. We are making every preparation in our power to repel the assaults of the enemy, whether they be directed upon Great Britain, or upon Ireland, which all Irishmen, without distinction of creed or party, should realise is in imminent danger. These again are matters upon which we have clear views. These preparations are constantly occupying our toil from morn till night, and far into the night. But, although we have clear views, it would not, I think, be profitable for us to discuss them in public, or even, so far as the Government are concerned, except under very considerable reserve, in a private session. I call upon all subjects of His Majesty, and upon our Allies, and wellwishers—and they are not a few—all over the world, on both sides of the Atlantic, to give us their utmost aid. In the fullest harmony with our Dominions, we are moving through a period of extreme danger and of splendid hope, when every virtue of our race will be tested, and all that we have and are will be freely staked. This is no time for doubt or weakness. It is the supreme hour to which we have been called.

I will venture to read to the House a message which I have caused to be sent to all who are serving in positions of importance under the Crown, and if the House should view it with sympathy, I should be very glad to send a copy of it to every Member for his own use, not that such exhortations are needed. This is the message:

"On what may be the eve of an attempted invasion or battle for our native land, the Prime Minister desires to impress upon all persons holding responsible positions in the Government, in the Fighting Services, or in the Civil Departments, their duty to maintain a spirit of alert and confident energy. While every precaution must be taken that time and means afford, there are no grounds for supposing that more German troops can be landed in this country, either from the air or across the sea, than can be destroyed or captured by the strong forces at present under arms. The Royal Air Force is in excellent order and at the highest strength it has yet attained. The German Navy was never so weak, nor the British Army at home so strong as now. The Prime Minister expects all His Majesty's servants in high places to set an example of steadiness and resolution. They should check and rebuke expressions of loose and ill-digested opinion in their circles, or by their subordinates.

They should not hesitate to report, or if necessary remove, any officers or officials who are found to be consciously exercising a disturbing or depressing influence, and whose talk is calculated to spread alarm and despondency. Thus alone will they be worthy of the fighting men, who, in the air, on the sea, and on land, have already met the enemy without any sense of being outmatched in martial qualities."

In conclusion, I feel that we are entitled to the confidence of the House and that we shall not fail in our duty, however painful. The action we have already taken should be, in itself, sufficient to dispose once and for all of the lies and rumours which have been so industriously spread by German propaganda and Fifth Column activities that we have the slightest intention of entering into negotiations in any form and through any channel with the German and Italian Governments. We shall, on the contrary, prosecute the war with the utmost vigour by all the means that are open to us until the righteous purposes for which we entered upon it have been fulfilled.

32. OPERATION "SEA LION," JULY 16, 1940[8]

FÜHRER'S DIRECTIVE

Chefsache   Führer's Headquarters, July 16, 1940
Top Secret Military
The Führer and Supreme Commander of the Wehrmacht
OKW/WFA/LNo. 33 160/40 g. Kdos.
By officer only

DIRECTIVE NO. 16

on the Preparation of a Landing Operation Against England

Since England, despite her militarily hopeless situation still shows no sign of willingness to come to terms, I have decided to prepare a landing operation against England, and if necessary to carry it out.

The aim of this operation is to eliminate the English homeland as a base for the carrying on the war against Germany, and if it should become necessary to occupy it completely.

To this end I order the following:

1. The *Landing* must be carried out in the form of a surprise crossing on a broad front approximately from Ramsgate to the area west of the Isle of Wight, in which Luftwaffe units will take the role of artillery, and units of the Navy the role of the engineers. Whether it is practical before the general landing to undertake *subordinate actions,* such as the occupation of the Isle of Wight or of County Cornwall, is to be determined from the standpoint of each branch of the Wehrmacht and the result is to be reported to me. I reserve the decision for myself. The preparations for the entire operation must be completed by *mid-August.*

2. To these preparations also belong the creation of those conditions which make a landing in England possible:

a. The English Air Force must be so beaten down in its morale and in fact, that it can no longer display any appreciable aggressive force in opposition to the German crossing.

b. Mine-free channels must be created.

c. By means of a closely concentrated mine-barrier the Straits of Dover must be sealed off on both *flanks* as well as the western entrance to the Channel at the approximate line Alderney-Portland.

d. The area off the coast must be dominated and given artillery protection by strong coastal artillery.

e. It would be desirable shortly before the crossing to tie down the English naval forces in the North Sea as well as in the Mediterranean (by the Italians), in which connection the attempt should now be made to damage the English naval forces which are in the homeland by air and torpedo attacks in strength.

3. *Organization of the command and of the preparations.*

Under my command and in accordance with my general directives the

Commanders in Chief will command the forces to be used from their branches of the Wehrmacht. The operations staffs of the Commander in Chief of the Army, the Commander in Chief of the Navy, and the Commander in Chief of the Luftwaffe must from August 1 on be located within a radius of at most 50 km. from my headquarters (Ziegenberg). Quartering of the restricted operations staffs of the Commanders in Chief of the Army and Navy together at Giessen appears advisable to me.

Hence for the command of the landing armies the Commander in Chief of the Army will have to employ an Army Group headquarters.

The project will bear the code name *Seeloewe*.

In the preparation and carrying out of the undertaking the following duties will fall to the various branches of the Wehrmacht:

a. *Army:* Will draw up first of all the operational plan and the transport plan for all formations to be shipped as the first wave. The antiaircraft artillery to be transported with the first wave will at the same time be attached to the Army (to the individual crossing groups) until such a time as a division of tasks in support and protection of ground troops, protection of the ports of debarkation and protection of the air bases to be occupied can be carried out. The Army furthermore will distribute the means of transport to the individual crossing groups and establish the embarkation and landing points in agreement with the Navy.

b. *Navy:* Will secure the means of transport and will bring them, corresponding to the desires of the Army and according to the requirements of seamanship, into the individual embarkation areas. In so far as possible ships of the defeated enemy states are to be procured. For every ferrying point it will provide the necessary naval staff for advice on matters of seamanship, with escort vessels and security forces. It will protect, along with the air forces employed to guard the movement, the entire crossing of the channel on both flanks. An order will follow on the regulation of the command relationship during the crossing. It is further the task of the Navy to regulate, in a uniform manner, the building up of the coastal artillery, that is, all batteries of the Army as well as of the Navy, which can be used for firing against sea targets, and to organize the fire control of the whole. As great an amount of *very heavy artillery* as possible is to be employed as quickly as possible to secure the crossing and to protect the flanks from enemy operations from the sea. For this purpose, railway artillery (supplemented by all available captured pieces) less the batteries (K5 and K12) provided for firing on targets on the English mainland, is to be brought up and emplaced by using railway turntables.

Independent of this, the heaviest available platform batteries are to be opposite the Straits of Dover, so emplaced under concrete that they can withstand even the heaviest aerial attacks and thereby dominate permanently within their effective range the Straits of Dover in any circumstances.

The technical work is the responsibility of the Todt Organization.

c. *The mission of the Luftwaffe is:* To hinder interference from the enemy air force. To overcome coastal defense which could do damage to the landing places, to break the first resistance of enemy ground troops and to smash reserves which may be coming up. For this mission closest cooperation of individual units of the Luftwaffe with the crossing units of the Army is necessary. Furthermore, to destroy important transportation routes for the bringing up of enemy reserves, and to attack enemy naval forces, which are coming up, while they are still far away from the crossing points. I request proposals on the use of parachute and glider troops. In this regard it is to be determined in conjunction with the Army if it is worth while here to hold parachute and glider troops in readiness as a *reserve* to be quickly committed in case of emergency.

4. The Wehrmacht Chief of Communications will carry out the necessary preparations for communications connections from France to the English mainland. The installation of the remaining 80 km. East Prussian cable is to be provided for in conjunction with the Navy.

5. I request the commanders in chief to submit to me as soon as possible:

a. The intentions of the Navy and Luftwaffe for achieving the necessary conditions for the crossing of the Channel (see figure 2).

b. The construction of the coastal batteries in detail (Navy).

c. A survey of the tonnage to be employed and the methods of getting it ready and fitting it out. Participation of civilian agencies? (Navy).

d. The organization of aerial protection in the assembly areas for troops about to cross and the means of crossing (Luftwaffe).

e. The crossing and operations plan of the Army, composition and equipment of the first crossing wave.

f. Organization and measures of the Navy and the Luftwaffe for carrying out of the crossing itself, security of the crossing, and support of the landing.

g. Proposals for the commitment of parachute and glider troops, as well as for the detailing and command of antiaircraft artillery, after an extensive occupation of territory on English soil has been made (Luftwaffe).

h. Proposal for the location of the operations staffs of the Commanders in Chief of the Army and of the Navy.

i. The position of Army, Navy, and Luftwaffe on the question whether and what subsidiary actions *before* the general landing are considered practical.

k. Proposal of Army and Navy on the over-all command *during* the crossing.

Adolf Hitler

33. HITLER'S REICHSTAG SPEECH OF JULY 19, 1940[9] (EXCERPT)

Only a few days ago Mr. Churchill reiterated his declaration that he wants war. Some six weeks ago he began to wage war in a field where he apparently considers himself particularly strong—namely, air raids on civilian population, although under the pretense that the raids are directed against so-called military objectives.

Since the bombardment of Friborg these objectives are open towns, market places and villages, burning houses, hospitals, schools, kindergartens and whatever else may come their way. Until now I have hardly had any reprisals.

That does not mean this will be or is my only reply. I know that our answer, which will come some day, will bring upon the people unending suffering and misery. Of course, not upon Mr. Churchill, for he no doubt will already be in Canada where the money and the children of those principally interested in the war already have been sent.

For millions of other persons, great suffering will begin. Mr. Churchill, or perhaps others, for once believe me when I predict a great empire will be destroyed, an empire that it was never my intention to destroy or even to harm.

I do realize that this struggle, if it continues, can end only with the complete annihilation of one or the other of the two adversaries. Mr. Churchill may believe this will be Germany. I know that it will be Britain.

In this hour I feel it to be my duty before my own conscience to appeal once more to reason and common sense in Great Britain as much as elsewhere. I consider myself in a position to make this appeal, since I am not the vanquished, begging favors, but the victor speaking in the name of reason. I can see no reason why this war must go on. I am grieved to think of the sacrifices it will claim.

I should like to avert them. As for my own people, I know that millions of German men, young and old alike, are burning with the desire to settle accounts with the enemy who for the second time has declared war upon us for no reason whatever. But I also know that at home there are many women and mothers who, ready as they are to sacrifice all they have in life, yet are bound to it by their heartstrings.

Possibly Mr. Churchill again will brush aside this statement of mine by saying that it is merely born of fear and of doubt in our final victory. In that case I shall have relieved my conscience in regard to the things to come.

34. HALDER DIARY, JULY 22, 1940[10] (EXCERPT)

2.) . . .
Britain's position is hopeless. The war is won by us. A reversal in the prospects of success is impossible.

d. Navy has been asked: With what time can shipping space be made available? In what way can flank be given Arty. cover? What can be done to provide protection against attacks from the sea? Adm. Raeder will make positive statements by middle of the week.

e. Crossing of Channel appears very hazardous to the Fuehrer. On that account, invasion is to be undertaken only if no other means is left to come to terms with Britain.

f. Britain perhaps sees the following possibilities:

1. Create trouble on the Balkans through Russia, to cut us off from our fuel source, and so paralyze our Air Force.

2. To gain the same ends by inciting Russia against us.

3. To bomb our synthetic oil plants.

g. *Romania:* King Carol has opened way for a peaceful settlement. Has sent a letter to the Fuehrer.

h. If Britain persists in waging war, efforts will be made to confront her with a solid political front, embracing Spain, Italy, Russia.

i. *Britain must be reduced by the middle of September,* at the time when we make the invasion. Will be done by air assaults and submarine warfare. Air Force proposes all-out effort against enemy Air Force; smash enemy fighter strength by luring them off the ground and then make them fight up in the air. Army likewise stresses this necessity and wants to have the air offensive combined with intensified submarine warfare.

k. Appraisal of the effect of the peace feeler: Press initially violent in its rejection, later turned on a softer tune.

. . . .

7.) Stalin is flirting with Britain to keep her in the war and tie us down, with a view to gain time and take what he wants, knowing he could not get it once peace breaks out. He has an interest in not letting Germany become too strong, but there are no indications of any Russian aggressiveness against us.

8.) Our attention must be turned to tackling the Russian problem and prepare planning. The Fuehrer has been given the following information:

a. German assembly will take at least 4–6 weeks.

b. Object: To crush Russian Army or slice as much Russian territory as is necessary to bar enemy air raids on Berlin and Silesian industries. It is desirable to penetrate far enough to enable our Air Force to smash Russia's strategic areas.   (Check with Foreign Armies East.)

c. Political aims: Ukrainian State
    Federation of Baltic States
    White Russia-Finland

Baltic States as a permanent thorn in the flesh.

d. Strength required: 80–100 Divs.; Russia has 50–75 good Divs. If we attack Russia this fall pressure of the air war on Britain will be relieved. United States could supply both Britain and Russia.

e. Operations: What operational objective could be attained? What strength have we available? Timing and area of assembly? Gateways of attack:

Baltic States, Finland, Ukraine.

Protect Berlin and Silesian industrial area.—

Protection of Romanian oil field   (Check with Op. Sec.)

v. Etzdorf:

Romania: Talks with Hungarians at Munich were aimed at urging peaceful compromise. Exchange of letters between Fuehrer and King Carol along this line. Full concurrence of Il Duce. Carol's answer is agreeable to solution.

Bulgaria demands return of about 300,000 nationals.

Hungarian "minimum demand": Arad—Brasov!

Italy: Participation of Italian troops in invasion of Britain has been declined. Ciano is apparently out to get hold of some pawns on the Balkans. Fuehrer wants Italy to defer drive against Suez reported to be planned for near future.

Britain-Russia: The two want to get together. The Russians are afraid of compromising themselves in our eyes; they don't want any war. The official announcements of the Stalin-Cripps talks indicate a very gratifying reserve toward Britain on the part of Stalin. Russia rejects Britain's "balance of power" policy and British terms for trade between the two countries. Russia does not want to claim leadership for coordination of Balkan States, as it would not augment her power. Yet Russia's actual mood shows itself on other occasions (talk between Kalinin and Yugoslav Minister). Here a direct appeal is made for struggle against Germany: "Unite in a solid block."

Britain: Official reaction to Fuehrer speech: rejection, America expects rejection.

Information through Hungarian sources: Britain is fighting shy of concluding peace at this moment. Shift of political power in Britain toward Attlee.

Spain and Portugal: There have been rumors of Spanish intentions to conclude a military alliance with Portugal. We are agreeable. Prerequisite would be that Portugal renounce her alliance with Britain.

German policy: Greater Germanic Reich. There are sympathies for this idea in Denmark, and it is also discussed in Sweden. Germanic sectionalism must be transcended!

35. HALDER DIARY, JULY 31, 1940[11] (EXCERPT)

[Hitler:] . . .

d. In the event that invasion does not take place, our action must be directed to eliminate all factors that let England hope for a change in the situation. To all intents and purposes, the war is won. France has stepped out of the set-up protecting British convoys. Italy is pinning down British forces.

Submarine and air warfare may bring about a final decision, but this may be one or two years off.

Britain's hope lies in Russia and the United States. If Russia drops out of the picture America, too, is lost for Britain, because elimination of Russia would tremendously increase *Japan's power* in the Far East.

Russia is the Far Eastern sword of Britain and the United States, pointed at Japan. Here, an evil wind is blowing for Britain. Japan, like Russia, has her program which she wants to carry through before the end of the war.

[Marginal note:]   *Russia is the factor on which*
   The Russian victory film on the   *Britain is relying the most.*
   Russo-Finnish War!   *Something must have happened*
                                           in London!

The British were completely down; now they have perked up again. Intercepted telephone conversations. Russia is painfully shaken by the swift development of the Western European situation.

All that Russia has to do is to hint that she does not care to have a strong Germany, and the British will take hope, like one about to go under, that the situation will undergo a radical change within six or eight months.

With Russia smashed, Britain's last hope would be shattered. Germany then will be master of Europe and the Balkans.

Decision: Russia's destruction must therefore be made a part of this struggle. Spring 41.

The sooner Russia is crushed, the better. Attack achieves its purpose only if Russian State can be shattered to its roots with one blow. Holding part of the country alone will not do. Standing still for the following winter would be perilous. So it is better to wait a little longer, but with the resolute determination to eliminate Russia. This is necessary also because of contiguity on the Baltic. It would be awkward to have another major power there. If we start in May 41, we would have five months to finish the job in. Tackling it this year still would have been the best, but unified action would be impossible at this time.

Object is destruction of Russian manpower. Operation will be divided into three actions:

First thrust: Kiev and securing flank protection on Dniepr. Air Force will destroy river crossings. Odessa.

Second thrust: Baltic States and drive on Moscow.

Finally: Link-up of northern and southern prongs.

Successively: Limited drive on Baku oil fields.

It will be seen later to what extent Finland and Turkey should be brought in.

Ultimately: Ukraine, White Russia, Baltic States to us. Finland extended to the White Sea.

   7 Divs. will stay in Norway (must be made self-sufficient).
   Ammunition:
   50 " in France
    3 " in Holland and Belgium.
   ___
   60 Divs.
   120 Divs. for the East
   180 Divs.

The greater the number of Divs. we have at the start, the better.
We have 120 Divs. plus 20 Furlough Divs.

36. U.S. Arrangement with Great Britain for Lease of Bases, September 2, 1940 and Roosevelt's Message to Congress, September 3, 1940[12]

Compiled in the Treaty Division
Naval and Air Bases
Arrangement With Great Britain for the Lease of Naval and Air Bases

The texts of the notes exchanged between the British Ambassador at Washington and the Secretary of State on September 2, 1940, under which the Government of the United States acquired the right to lease naval and air bases in Newfoundland, and in the islands of Bermuda, the Bahamas, Jamaica, St. Lucia, Trinidad, and Antigua, and in British Guiana, together with the texts of the message of the President to the Congress and the opinion of the Attorney General dated August 27, 1940, regarding the authority of the President to consummate this arrangement, are as follows:

The British Ambassador to the Secretary of State
British Embassy,
Washington, D.C.,
September 2, 1940.

Sir:

I have the honour under instructions from His Majesty's Principal Secretary of State for Foreign Affairs to inform you that in view of the friendly and sympathetic interest of His Majesty's Government in the United Kingdom in the national security of the United States and their desire to strengthen the ability of the United States to cooperate effectively with the other nations of the Americas in the defence of the Western Hemisphere, His Majesty's Government will secure the grant to the Government of the United States, freely and without consideration, of the lease for immediate establishment and use of naval and air bases and facilities for entrance thereto and the operation and protection thereof, on the Avalon Peninsula and on the southern coast of Newfoundland, and on the east coast and on the Great Bay of Bermuda.

Furthermore, in view of the above and in view of the desire of the United States to acquire additional air and naval bases in the Caribbean and in British Guiana, and without endeavouring to place a monetary or commercial value upon the many tangible and intangible rights and properties involved, His Majesty's Government will make available to the United States for immediate establishment and use naval and air bases and facilities for entrance thereto and the operation and protection thereof, on the eastern side of the Bahamas, the southern coast of Jamaica, the western coast of St. Lucia, the west coast of Trinidad in the Gulf of Paria, in the island of Antigua and in British Guiana within fifty miles of Georgetown, in exchange for naval and military equipment and material which the United States Government will transfer to His Majesty's Government.

All the bases and facilities referred to in the preceding paragraphs will be leased to the United States for a period of ninety-nine years, free from all rent and charges other than such compensation to be mutually agreed on to be paid by the United States in order to compensate the owners of private property for loss by expropriation or damage arising out of the establishment of the bases and facilities in question.

His Majesty's Government, in the leases to be agreed upon, will grant to the United States for the period of the leases all the rights, power, and authority within the bases leased, and within the limits of the territorial waters and air space adjacent to or in the vicinity of such bases, necessary to provide access to and defence of such bases, and appropriate provisions for their control.

Without prejudice to the above-mentioned rights of the United States authorities and their jurisdiction within the leased areas, the adjustment and reconciliation between the jurisdiction of the authorities of the United States within these areas and the jurisdiction of the authorities of the territories in which these areas are situated, shall be determined by common agreement.

The exact location and bounds of the aforesaid bases, the necessary seaward, coast and antiaircraft defences, the location of sufficient military garrisons, stores and other necessary auxiliary facilities shall be determined by common agreement.

His Majesty's Government are prepared to designate immediately experts to meet with experts of the United States for these purposes. Should these experts be unable to agree in any particular situation, except in the case of Newfoundland and Bermuda, the matter shall be settled by the Secretary of State of the United States and His Majesty's Secretary of State for Foreign Affairs.

I have [etc.]   Lothian

The Honourable Cordell Hull,
      Secretary of State of the United States,
        Washington, D.C.

        . . . .

The Secretary of State to the British Ambassador
Department of State,
Washington, September 2, 1940.

Excellency:

I have received your note of September 2, 1940, of which the text is as follows:

[Here follows text of the note, printed above.]

I am directed by the President to reply to your note as follows:

The Government of the United States appreciates the declarations and the generous action of His Majesty's Government as contained in your communication which are destined to enhance the national security of the

United States and greatly to strengthen its ability to cooperate effectively with the other nations of the Americas in the defense of the Western Hemisphere. It therefore gladly accepts the proposals.

The Government of the United States will immediately designate experts to meet with experts designated by His Majesty's Government to determine upon the exact location of the naval and air bases mentioned in your communication under acknowledgment.

In consideration of the declarations above quoted, the Government of the United States will immediately transfer to His Majesty's Government fifty United States Navy destroyers generally referred to as the twelve hundred-ton type.

Accept [etc.]   Cordell Hull

His Excellency
    The Right Honorable
        The Marquess of Lothian, C.H.,
            British Ambassador.

MESSAGE OF THE PRESIDENT

To The Congress Of The United States:

I transmit herewith for the information of the Congress notes exchanged between the British Ambassador at Washington and the Secretary of State on September 2, 1940, under which this Government has acquired the right to lease naval and air bases in Newfoundland, and in the islands of Bermuda, the Bahamas, Jamaica, St. Lucia, Trinidad, and Antigua, and in British Guiana; also a copy of an opinion of the Attorney General dated August 27, 1940, regarding my authority to consummate this arrangement.

The right to bases in Newfoundland and Bermuda are gifts—generously given and gladly received. The other bases mentioned have been acquired in exchange for fifty of our over-age destroyers.

This is not inconsistent in any sense with our status of peace. Still less it is a threat against any nation. It is an epochal and far-reaching act of preparation for continental defense in the face of grave danger.

Preparation for defense is an inalienable prerogative of a sovereign state. Under present circumstances this exercise of sovereign right is essential to the maintenance of our peace and safety. This is the most important action in the reinforcement of our national defense that has been taken since the Louisiana Purchase. Then as now, considerations of safety from overseas attack were fundamental.

The value to the Western Hemisphere of these outposts of security is beyond calculation. Their need has long been recognized by our country, and especially by those primarily charged with the duty of charting and organizing our own naval and military defense. They are essential to the protection of the Panama Canal, Central America, the Northern portion of South America, The Antilles, Canada, Mexico, and our own Eastern and

Gulf Seaboards. Their consequent importance in hemispheric defense is obvious. For these reasons I have taken advantage of the present opportunity to acquire them.

Franklin D. Roosevelt

The White House,
     September 3, 1940.

Chapter II
Europe's New Order, 1940–1941

Part 4. Germany Moves South and East

After the defeat of France the German planning for the invasion of Great Britain (31) was the next move on Hitler's schedule. The beginning was a concentrated air attack against England by Marshal Hermann Goering's powerful Luftwaffe. The German decision to turn from their primary targets of British airfields to the cities was an error that proved disastrous, for it allowed the Royal Air Force the desperately needed relief to develop defense measures for sheer survival. This was to eventually undermine the execution of Operation "Sea Lion," for the R. A. F., at odds of five and six to one, were engaging up to 1000 German attack planes daily and taking heavy tolls. The cost was high, however, for before the Battle of Britain ended many major cities, including London, were to suffer with over 23,000 civilian dead and great destruction.

The peak of the German attack was reached by December of 1940 and the invasion had not yet been launched, for Hitler seemed convinced that the path to peace with Great Britain was an armistice rather than a military defeat.

In the meantime Hitler revealed the conclusion of a new Three Power Pact, signed September 27 with the governments of Italy and Japan (37). The Axis partnership had arrived at a division of the world compatible with their respective political goals and characterized by the terms "Greater East Asia," and the "new order in Europe."

The idea of an invasion was not forgotten (38, art. 6), but by November it had been definitely relegated to a future "possibility." Instead, Hitler had already decided that the expansion of German domination southward would effectively drive the British out of the Mediterranean (38). This was planned to include attacks against British strongholds, provide support of Italy's faltering drive into Egypt, and occupy most of the Balkan states.

Several days after the issuance of his 18th Directive, on November 12, the German Fuehrer conducted a lengthy conversation in Berlin with Soviet

Foreign Minister V. M. Molotov (39). The talk centered on Hitler's concern over a possible renewal of the Russo-Finnish War (19 and 20) and the spheres of influence either agreed upon or implied by the Non-Aggression Treaty of 1939 (6). The importance to the Soviet Union of a British defeat was emphasized by the German leader, and while the long talk covered several subjects it was clear that the real concern was the changing position of the two powers as a result of the war.

It is extremely important when attempting to understand Hitler's reasons for making war on the Soviet Union (40) to recognize the Fuehrer's growing dissatisfaction with what he obviously regarded as Stalin's evasion of treaty agreements (6) and the steady Communist movement into the Baltic and the eastern Mediterranean. These thoughts were no longer in question by November of 1940, for even during Molotov's visit the plans were going ahead for an attack upon the Soviet Union (38, art. 5). The Hitler Directive (40) outlining the attack, called Operation "Barbarossa," was given in December and called for an execution date of May 1941. There were significant references in the order to virtually all the points that Hitler had discussed with Molotov the previous month (39) and the roles that Finland and Rumania were to play as Germany's allies (40,II).

In the meantime Italy had launched an unprovoked attack against Greece on October 28, 1940, and while this appeared to be part of a broad Axis plan of conquest this was not so; it was an independent action taken by Mussolini. It was evident that the Italians had not prepared themselves for more than token resistance, but the war soon turned into a struggle of serious proportions that threatened to swamp Italy's resources. Greece had a small, ill-equipped force of some 150,000 men with a possible reserve of perhaps 600,000 more. Its air force was equally modest, but as the Italian attacks continued Great Britain began to supply reinforcements, supplies, and air support and the battle started to turn around. The Italian invasion slowed and then began a retreat and before the first month was over the Greek counterattack menaced Italy's Adriatic control. What had started as a triumphal march from Albania was rapidly turning into a full-scale rout.

Although Hitler had already authorized plans for the invasion of Greece, Operation "Marita," the target date was for the spring of 1941. The immediate need as the German planners viewed the situation was to provide aid to the Italian forces that had been pushed back to Albania and those that were fighting the British in North Africa; the invasion of Greece could wait.

Mussolini was already heavily committed against the British in North Africa, having begun a drive to push them out of Egypt in September, and with over 250,000 troops the Italians far outnumbered the British garrisons there. The Italian plan to seize the Suez Canal appeared quite feasible at first, but as their forces advanced into Egypt the campaign began to stall and the British started a counterattack in December that resulted in recapturing most of their lost territory. It was at this exact juncture that Hitler ordered (41) additional German forces—there were token German units already there—to go to Italy's aid in both Africa and Albania.

In a top-level military conference in March 1941, Hitler discussed the recent events in Yugoslavia (42) and related the general situation in the Balkans to Germany's own preparations to invade the Soviet Union. The immediate background to this particular conference was the unfolding of a series of complex political events in Yugoslavia that had resulted in the overthrow of Prince Paul's government by a General Simovic. The General, with the backing of the Serbian Orthodox Church, was determined to remain neutral; however, Hitler had already concluded that the use of Yugoslavian bases was vital to the success of future German operations in Greece and the Aegean.

A factor of the utmost importance is that with the advent of a major campaign into the Balkans the operations against the Soviet Union had to be delayed for several weeks (42), a highly significant point in light of the subsequent weather that was encountered by the German armies in Russia. A few days later, on March 30, Hitler reviewed some of the military facts connected with the plan to attack Russia (43) and reiterated his intent to destroy the Communist state.

On April 3 he gave the directions (44) for the plan of action to be taken by his allies in commencing the war against Yugoslavia and Greece. Reserving the top command for himself, the Fuehrer described the positions to be assumed by Hungary, Bulgaria, Rumania, and Italy. On April 6 the Balkan invasion started and by the end of the month the Germans had secured the entire Peninsula.

The loss of Greece as an ally was serious for the British cause, but the loss of that country as a base to continue operations against Germany and Italy was inestimable. The conquest of Crete by the Germans in May and June ended an extremely successful campaign that had brought access to oil reserves, protection for Axis shipping, and bases in vital locations. In addition, Germany had moved quickly to neutralize Turkey in a treaty of friendship signed June 18 (45). Although Turkey had promised active support for Great Britain and France by terms of the Treaty of Ankara in October of 1939 in the event of war in the Mediterranean, that nation continued to maintain a strict neutrality.

On the eve of the invasion of the Soviet Union the position of Germany on the European Continent was supreme and there appeared to be little effect from the flight of Hitler's trusted friend and Deputy Fuehrer Rudolf Hess to England. Hitler's empire had spread from north to south and far beyond just the occupied countries, but for Adolf Hitler, self-proclaimed saviour of the German people, this was not enough; *Lebensraum* or living space in the east was still an aim and in the process the Soviet Union had to be humbled. Several hours before Operation Barbarossa began Hitler expressed some of his motives in launching an eastern war to the Regent of Hungary (46) and outlined what he considered the many transgressions against Germany made by Stalin.

On the morning of June 22 the German General Franz Halder entered a terse statement in his diary (47) noting the beginning of the invasion and the obvious surprise it was for the Russians. Anxious to be of service to such a winning side and desirous of crushing the Soviet Union the Rumanian Premier and General Ion Antonescu issued an enthusiastic war declaration and order of the day (48). Exhorting his people to take up the cause as a holy war, the General informed his people that their hour of history was at hand.

Another kind of joy was expressed that day and it came from the Prime Minister of England. In a radio broadcast the evening of the twenty-second, Winston Churchill welcomed the Russians as partners in the crusade against National Socialism (49).

Although Churchill's war cry was echoed by Stalin (50) the phenomenal success of the Nazi war machine had conditioned the world into believing that it could not be stopped and it would only be a matter of time—and short at that (51)—before the Soviet Union became just another conquered territory. Almost as expected the German gains in Russia were very impressive; attacking on a broad front of some 2,000 miles a massive German force of about 3,000,000 troops, divided into Northern, Central, and Southern Army Groups, broke through Russian defenses in a matter of hours. Advancing at a rate of 25 to 50 miles a day, the invading armies appeared assured of victory before winter. In describing his first successes to Mussolini, Hitler stated that the Soviet Union would fall by October (52) and then only Great Britain remained to defeat.

37. Tripartite Pact: Germany, Italy and Japan, September 27, 1940[1]

Three Powers Pact Between Germany, Italy and Japan

The Governments of Germany, Italy and Japan, considering it as the condition precedent of any lasting peace that all nations of the world be given each its own proper place, have decided to stand by and co-operate with one another in regard to their efforts in Greater East Asia and the regions of Europe respectively wherein it is their prime purpose to establish and maintain a new order of things calculated to promote mutual prosperity and welfare of the peoples concerned.

Furthermore it is the desire of the three Governments to extend cooperation to such nations in other spheres of the world as may be inclined to put forth endeavours along lines similar to their own, in order that their ultimate aspirations for world peace may thus be realized. Accordingly the Governments of Germany, Italy and Japan have agreed as follows:

Article 1

Japan recognizes and respects the leadership of Germany and Italy in the establishment of a new order in Europe.

ARTICLE 2

Germany and Italy recognize and respect the leadership of Japan in the establishment of a new order in Greater East Asia.

ARTICLE 3

Germany, Italy and Japan agree to co-operate in their efforts on the aforesaid lines. They further undertake to assist one another with all political, economic and military means when one of the three Contracting Parties is attacked by a power at present not involved in the European War or in the Sino-Japanese Conflict.

ARTICLE 4

With a view to implementing the present Pact, Joint Technical Commissions the members of which are to be appointed by the respective Governments of Germany, Italy and Japan will meet without delay.

ARTICLE 5

Germany, Italy and Japan affirm that the aforesaid terms do not in any way affect the political status which exists at present as between each of the three Contracting Parties and Soviet Russia.

ARTICLE 6

The present Pact shall come into effect immediately upon signature and shall remain in force for ten years from the date of its coming into force.

At proper time before the expiration of the said term the High Contracting Parties shall, at the request of any one of them, enter into negotiations for its renewal.

In faith whereof, the Undersigned, duly authorized by their respective Governments, have signed this Pact and have affixed hereto their Seals.

Done in triplicate at Berlin, the 27th day of September 1940—in the XVIIIth year of the Fascist Era—, corresponding to the 27th day of the 9th month of the 15th year of Syowa.

> Joachim v. Ribbentrop
> Ciano
> Kurusu

38. HITLER DIRECTIVE NO. 18, NOVEMBER 12, 1940[2]

The measures of the High Commands which are being prepared for the conduct of the war in the near future are to be in accordance with the following guiding principles:

1. *Relations with France*

The aim of my policy toward France is to cooperate with this country in the most effective way for the future prosecution of the war against England. For the time being France will have the role of a "nonbelligerent power" which will have to tolerate German military measures on her territory, in the African colonies especially, and to give support, as far as possible, even by using her own means of defense. The most pressing task of the French is the defensive and offensive protection of their African possessions (West and Equatorial Africa) against England and the de Gaulle movement. From this task the participation of France in the war against England can develop in full force.

Except for the current work of the Armistice Commission, the discussions with France which tie in with my meeting with Marshal Pétain will initially be conducted exclusively by the Foreign Ministry in cooperation with the High Command of the Wehrmacht.

More detailed directives will follow after the conclusion of these discussions.

2. *Spain and Portugal*

Political measures to induce the prompt entry of Spain into the war have been initiated. The aim of *German* intervention in the Iberian Peninsula (code name *Felix*) will be to drive the English out of the Western Mediterranean.

For this purpose:

a) Gibraltar should be taken and the Straits closed;

b) The English should be prevented from gaining a foothold at another point of the Iberian Peninsula or of the Atlantic islands.

For the preparation and execution of the undertaking the following is intended:

Section I:

a) Reconnaissance parties (officers in civilian clothes) will conclude the requisite preparations for the operation against Gibraltar and for the taking over of airfields. As regards camouflage and cooperation with the Spaniards they are bound by the security measures of the Chief of the Foreign Intelligence Department.

b) Special units of the Foreign Intelligence Department in disguised cooperation with the Spaniards are to take over the protection of the Gibraltar area against English attempts to extend the outpost area or prematurely to discover and disturb the preparations.

c) The units designated for the action will assemble in readiness far back of the Franco-Spanish border and without premature explanation being given to the troops. A preliminary alert for beginning the operation will be issued 3 weeks before the troops cross the Franco-Spanish border (but only after conclusion of the preparations regarding the Atlantic islands).

In view of the limited capacity of the Spanish railroads the Army will mainly designate motorized units for the operation so that the railways remain available for supply.

Section II:

a) Directed by observation near Algeciras, Luftwaffe units at a favorable moment will conduct an aerial attack from French soil against the units of the English fleet lying in the harbor of Gibraltar and after the attack they will land on Spanish airports.

b) Shortly thereafter the units designated for commitment in Spain will cross the Franco-Spanish border by land or by air.

Section III:

a) The attack for the seizure of Gibraltar is to be by German troops.

b) Troops are to be assembled to march into Portugal in case the English should gain a foothold there. The units designated for this will march into Spain immediately after the forces designated for Gibraltar.

Section IV:

Support of the Spaniards in closing the Strait after seizure of the Rock, if necessary, from the Spanish-Moroccan side as well.

The following will apply regarding the *strength* of the units to be committed for Operation *Felix*:

Army:

The units designated for Gibraltar must be strong enough to take the Rock even without Spanish help.

Along with this a smaller group must be available to support the Spaniards in the unlikely event of an English attempt at a landing on another part of the coast.

For the possible march into Portugal mobile units are mainly to be designated.

Luftwaffe:

For the aerial attack on the harbor of Gibraltar forces are to be designated which will guarantee abundant success.

For the subsequent operations against naval objectives and for support of the attack on the Rock mainly dive bomber units are to be transferred to Spain.

Sufficient antiaircraft artillery is to be allocated to the army units including its use against ground targets.

Navy:

U-boats are to be provided for combating the English Gibraltar squadron, and particularly in its evacuation of the harbor which is to be expected after the aerial attack.

For support of the Spaniards in closing the Strait the transfer in *individual* coastal batteries is to be prepared in cooperation with the Army.

Italian participation is not envisaged.

The *Atlantic islands* (particularly the Canaries and the Cape Verde Islands) will, as a result of the Gibraltar operation, gain increased importance for the English conduct of the war at sea as well as for our own naval operations. The Commanders in Chief of the Navy and of the Luftwaffe are to study how the

Spanish defense of the Canaries can be supported and how the Cape Verde Islands can be occupied.

I likewise request examination of the question of occupation of Madeira and of the Azores as well as of the question of the advantages and disadvantages which would ensue for the naval and for the aerial conduct of the war. The results of this examination are to be presented to me as soon as possible.

3. *Italian Offensive against Egypt*

If at all, the commitment of German forces comes into consideration only when the Italians have reached Mersa Matrûh. Even then the commitment initially of German air forces is envisaged only if the Italians make available the requisite air bases.

The preparations of the branches of the armed forces for commitment in this or in any other North African theater of war are to be continued within the following framework:

Army:

Holding in readiness of an armored division (composition as previously provided for) for commitment in North Africa.

Navy:

Fitting out of such German ships lying in Italian ports as are suitable as transports for the transfer of the strongest possible units either to Libya or to Northwest Africa.

Luftwaffe:

Preparation for offensive operations against Alexandria and the Suez Canal in order to close the latter against use by the English High Command.

4. *Balkans*

The Commander in Chief of the Army will make preparations in order, in case of necessity, to occupy the *Greek mainland* north of the Aegean Sea, entering from Bulgaria, and thereby make possible the commitment of German air force units against targets in the Eastern Mediterranean, especially against those English air bases which threaten the Rumanian oil area.

In order to be equal to all possible missions and to hold Turkey in check, the commitment of an army group of an approximate strength of 10 divisions is to be the basis for the planning and the calculations for strategic concentration. It will not be possible to count on the railway leading through Yugoslavia for the strategic concentration of these forces. In order to shorten the time needed for the concentration, a prompt reinforcement of the German Army mission in Rumania is to be prepared on a scale which is to be proposed to me.

The Commander in Chief of the Luftwaffe will, in harmony with the intended Army operations, prepare for the employment of German Luftwaffe units in the southeast Balkans and for establishment of an aircraft warning service on the southern border of Bulgaria.

The German Luftwaffe mission in Rumania will be reinforced to an extent to be proposed to me.

The wishes of the *Bulgarians* for equipping their Army (deliveries of weapons and munitions) are to be given favorable treatment.

5. *Russia*

Political discussions have been initiated with the aim of clarifying Russia's attitude for the coming period. Regardless of what results these discussions will have, all preparations for the East which already have been orally ordered, are to be continued.

Directives on this will follow as soon as the outline of the Army's plan of operations is submitted to, and approved by me.

6. *Landing in England*

Because, with changes in the over-all situation, the possibility or necessity may arise to return in the spring of 1941 to Operation *Seelöwe,* the three branches of the armed forces must earnestly try in every way to improve the groundwork for such an operation.

7. *Reports of the Commanders in Chief*

Will be expected by me regarding the measures envisaged in this directive. I shall then issue orders regarding the methods of execution and the synchronization of the individual actions.

In order to guard secrecy, special measures are to be taken for restricting the numbers of the working staffs. This applies particularly for the operation in Spain and for the plans regarding the Atlantic islands.

Adolf Hitler

39. HITLER-MOLOTOV CONVERSATION, NOVEMBER 13, 1940[3] (EXCERPTS) MEMORANDUM BY AN OFFICIAL OF THE FOREIGN MINISTER'S SECRETARIAT

Füh. 33   Berlin, November 15, 1940.

Record of the Conversation Between the Führer and the Chairman of the Council of People's Commissars, Molotov, in the Presence of the Reich Foreign Minister and the Deputy People's Commissar for Foreign Affairs, Dekanozov, as Well as of Counselor of Embassy Hilger and M. Pavlov, Who Acted as Interpreters, in Berlin on November 13, 1940

. . . .

[Hitler mentioned that] The real situation was as follows: In accordance with the German-Russian agreements, Germany recognized that, politically, Finland was of primary interest to Russia and was in her zone of influence. However, Germany had to consider the following two points:

1. For the duration of the war she was very greatly interested in the deliveries of nickel and lumber from Finland, and

2. She did not desire any new conflict in the Baltic Sea which would further curtail her freedom of movement in one of the few merchant shipping regions which still remained to her. It was completely incorrect to assert that Finland was occupied by German troops. To be sure, troops were being transported to Kirkenes via Finland, of which fact Russia had been

officially informed by Germany. Because of the length of the route, the trains had to stop two or three times in Finnish territory. However, as soon as the transit of the troop contingents to be transported had been completed, no additional troops would be sent through Finland. He (the Führer) pointed out that both Germany and Russia would naturally be interested in not allowing the Baltic Sea to become a combat zone again. Since the Russo-Finnish War, the possibilities for military operations had shifted, because England had available long-range bombers and long-range destroyers. The English thereby had a chance to get a foothold on Finnish airports.

In addition, there was a purely psychological factor which was extremely onerous. The Finns had defended themselves bravely, and they had gained the sympathies of the world—particularly of Scandinavia. In Germany too, during the Russo-Finnish War, the people were somewhat annoyed at the position which, as a result of the agreements with Russia, Germany had to take and actually did take. Germany did not wish any new Finnish war because of the aforementioned considerations. However, the legitimate claims of Russia were not affected by that. Germany had proved this again and again by her attitude on various issues, among others, the issue of the fortification of the Åland Islands. For the duration of the war, however, her economic interests in Finland were just as important as in Rumania. Germany expected consideration of these interests all the more, since she herself had also shown understanding of the Russian wishes in the issues of Lithuania and Bucovina at the time. At any rate, she had no political interest of any kind in Finland, and she fully accepted the fact that that country belonged to the Russian zone of influence.

In his reply Molotov pointed out that the agreement of 1939 had referred to a certain stage of the development which had been concluded by the end of the Polish war, while the second stage was brought to an end by the defeat of France, and that they were really in the third stage now. He recalled that by the original agreement, with its Secret Protocol, the common German-Russian boundary had been fixed and issues concerning the adjacent Baltic countries and Rumania, Finland, and Poland had been settled. For the rest, he agreed with the remarks of the Führer on the revisions made. However, if he drew up a balance sheet of the situation that resulted after the defeat of France, he would have to state that the German-Russian agreement had not been without influence upon the great German victories.

. . . .

The Führer replied that if German-Russian collaboration was to show positive results in the future, the Soviet Government would have to understand that Germany was engaged in a life and death struggle, which, at all events, she wanted to conclude successfully. For that, a number of prerequisites depending upon economic and military factors were required, which Germany wanted to secure for herself by all means. If the Soviet Union were in a similar position, Germany on her part would, and would have to, demonstrate a similar understanding for Russian needs. The conditions which Germany wanted to assure did not conflict with the agreements with Russia. The German wish to avoid a war with unforeseeable consequences in the Baltic Sea did not mean any violation of the German-Russian agreements according to which Finland belonged in the Russian sphere of influence. The guarantee given upon the wish and request of the Rumanian Government was no violation of the agreements concerning Bessarabia. The Soviet Union had to realize that in the framework of any broader collaboration of the two countries advantages of quite different scope were to be reached than the insignificant revisions which were now being discussed. Much greater successes could then be achieved, provided that Russia did not now seek successes in territories in which Germany was interested for the duration of the war. The future successes would be the greater, the more Germany and Russia succeeded in fighting back to back against the outside world, and would become the smaller, the more the two countries faced each other breast to breast. In the first case there was no power on earth which could oppose the two countries.

In his reply Molotov voiced his agreement with the last conclusions of the Führer. In this connection he stressed the viewpoint of the Soviet leaders, and of Stalin in particular, that it would be possible and expedient to strengthen and activate the relations between the two countries. However, in order to give those relations a permanent basis, issues would also have to be clarified which were a secondary importance, but which spoiled the atmosphere of German-Russian relations. Finland belonged among these issues. If Russia and Germany had a good understanding, this issue could be solved without war, but there must be neither German troops in Finland nor political demonstrations in that country against the Soviet Russian Government.

The Führer replied that the second point could not be a matter for debate, since Germany had nothing whatsoever to do with these things. Incidentally, demonstrations could easily be staged, and it was very difficult to find out afterward who had been the real instigator. However, regarding the German troops, he could give the assurance that, if a general settlement were made, no German troops would appear in Finland any longer.

. . . .

Molotov replied that he could not understand the German fear that a war might break out in the Baltic. Last year, when the international situation was worse for Germany than now, Germany had not raised this issue. Quite apart from the fact that Germany had occupied Denmark, Norway, Holland, and Belgium, she had completely defeated France and even believed that she had already conquered England. He (Molotov) did not see where in these circumstances the danger of war in the Baltic should come from. He would have to request that Germany take the same stand as last year. If she did that unconditionally, there would certainly be no complications in connection with the Finnish issue. However, if she made reservations, a new situation would arise which would then have to be discussed.

In reply to the statements of Molotov regarding the absence of military danger in the Finnish question, the Führer stressed that he too had some understanding of military matters, and he considered it entirely possible that the United States would get a foothold in those regions in case of participation by Sweden in a possible war. He (the Führer) wanted to end the European war, and he could only repeat that in view of the uncertain attitude of Sweden a new war in the Baltic would mean a strain on German-Russian relations with unforeseeable consequences. Would Russia declare war on the United States, in case the latter should intervene in connection with the Finnish conflict?

When Molotov replied that this question was not of present interest, the Führer replied that it would be too late for a decision when it became so. When Molotov then declared that he did not see any indication of the outbreak of war in the Baltic, the Führer replied that in that case everything would be in order anyway and the whole discussion was really of a purely theoretical nature.

Summarizing, the Reich Foreign Minister pointed out that:

(1) The Führer had declared that Finland remained in the sphere of influence of Russia and that Germany would not maintain any troops there;

(2) Germany had nothing to do with demonstrations of Finland against Russia, but was exerting her influence in the opposite direction;

(3) The collaboration of the two countries was the decisive problem of long-range importance, which in the past had already resulted in great advantages for Russia, but which in the future would show advantages compared with which the matters that had just been discussed would appear entirely insignificant. There was actually no reason at all for making an issue of the Finnish question. Perhaps it was a misunderstanding only. Strategically, all of Russia's wishes had been satisfied by her peace treaty with Finland. Demonstrations in a conquered country were not at all unnatural, and if perhaps the transit of German troops had caused certain reactions in the Finnish population they would disappear with the end of those troop transits. Hence, if one considered matters realistically, there were no differences between Germany and Russia.

The Führer pointed out that both sides agreed in principle that Finland belonged to the Russian sphere of influence. Instead, therefore, of continuing a purely theoretical discussion, they should rather turn to more important problems.

After the conquest of England the British Empire would be apportioned as a gigantic world-wide estate in bankruptcy of 40 million square kilometers. In this bankrupt estate there would be for Russia access to the ice-free and really open ocean. Thus far, a minority of 45 million Englishmen had ruled 600 million inhabitants of the British Empire. He was about to crush this minority. Even the United States was actually doing nothing but picking out of this bankrupt estate a few items particularly suitable to the United

States. Germany, of course, would like to avoid any conflict which would divert her from her struggle against the heart of the Empire, the British Isles. For that reason, he (the Führer) did not like Italy's war against Greece, as it diverted forces to the periphery instead of concentrating them against England at one point. The same would occur during a Baltic War. The conflict with England would be fought to the last ditch, and he had no doubt that the defeat of the British Isles would lead to the dissolution of the Empire. It was a chimera to believe that the Empire could possibly be ruled and held together from Canada. In those circumstances there arose worldwide perspectives. During the next few weeks they would have to be settled in joint diplomatic negotiations with Russia, and Russia's participation in the solution of these problems would have to be arranged. All the countries which could possibly be interested in the bankrupt estate would have to stop all controversies among themselves and concern themselves exclusively with apportioning the British Empire. This applied to Germany, France, Italy, Russia, and Japan.

40. Operation "Barbarossa," December 18, 1940[4]

Führer's Directive

Chefsache   Führer's Headquarters, December 18, 1940.
Top Secret Military
The Führer and Supreme Commander of the Wehrmacht
OKW/WFSt/Abt.L (I) No. 33 408/40 g.K.Chefs
By officer only

Directive No. 21: Operation Barbarossa

The German Wehrmacht must be prepared to *crush Soviet Russia in a quick campaign* (Operation *Barbarossa*) even before the conclusion of the war against England.

For this purpose the *Army* will have to employ all available units, with the reservation that the occupied territories must be secured against surprises.

For the *Luftwaffe* it will be a matter of releasing such strong forces for the eastern campaign in support of the Army that a quick completion of the ground operations can be counted on and that damage to eastern German territory by enemy air attacks will be as slight as possible. This concentration of the main effort in the East is limited by the requirement that the entire combat and armament area dominated by us must remain adequately protected against enemy air attacks and that the offensive operations against England, particularly her supply lines, must not be permitted to break down.

The main effort of the *Navy* will remain unequivocally directed against England even during an eastern campaign.

I shall order the *concentration* against Soviet Russia possibly 8 weeks before the intended beginning of operations.

Preparations requiring more time to get under way are to be started now—if this has not yet been done—and are to be completed by May 15, 1941.

It is of decisive importance, however, that the intention to attack does not become discernible.

The preparations of the High Commands are to be made on the following basis:

I. *General Purpose:*

The mass of the Russian *Army* in western Russia is to be destroyed in daring operations, by driving forward deep armored wedges, and the retreat of units capable of combat into the vastness of Russian territory is to be prevented.

In quick pursuit a line is then to be reached from which the Russian Air Force will no longer be able to attack the territory of the German Reich. The ultimate objective of the operation is to establish a cover against Asiatic Russia from the general line Volga-Archangel. Then, in case of necessity, the last industrial area left to Russia in the Urals can be eliminated by the Luftwaffe.

In the course of these operations the Russian *Baltic Sea Fleet* will quickly lose its bases and thus will no longer be able to fight.

Effective intervention by the Russian *Air Force* is to be prevented by powerful blows at the very beginning of the operation.

II. *Probable Allies and their Tasks:*

1. On the wings of our operation the active participation of *Rumania* and *Finland* in the war against Soviet Russia is to be expected.

The High Command will in due time arrange and determine in what form the armed forces of the two countries will be placed under German command at the time of their intervention.

2. It will be the task of *Rumania* to support with selected forces the attack of the German southern wing, at least in its beginnings; to pin the enemy down where German forces are not committed; and otherwise to render auxiliary service in the rear area.

3. *Finland* will cover the concentration of the German *North Group* (parts of the XXI Group) withdrawn from Norway and will operate jointly with it. Besides, Finland will be assigned the task of eliminating Hangö.

4. It may be expected that *Swedish* railroads and highways will be available for the concentration of the German North Group, from the start of operations at the latest.

III. *Direction of Operations:*

A. *Army* (hereby approving the plans presented to me):

In the zone of operations divided by the Pripet Marshes into a southern and northern sector, the main effort will be made *north* of this area. Two Army Groups will be provided here.

The southern group of these two Army Groups—the center of the entire front—will be given the task of annihilating the forces of the enemy in White Russia by advancing from the region around and north of Warsaw with especially strong armored and motorized units. The possibility of switching strong mobile units to the north must thereby be created in order, in cooperation with the Northern Army Group operating from East Prussia in the general direction of Leningrad, to annihilate the enemy forces fighting in the Baltic area. Only after having accomplished this most important task, which must be followed by the occupation of Leningrad and Kronstadt, are the offensive operations aimed at the occupation of the important traffic and armament center of Moscow to be pursued.

Only a surprisingly fast collapse of Russian resistance could justify aiming at both objectives simultaneously.

The most important assignment of the XXI Group, even during the eastern operations, will still be the protection of Norway. The additional forces available are to be employed in the norther (mountain corps), first to protect the Petsamo region and its ore mines as well as the Arctic Highway, and then to advance jointly with Finnish forces against the Murmansk railroad and stop the supply of the Murmansk region by land.

Whether such an operation with *rather strong* German forces (two or three divisions) can be conducted from the area of and south of Rovaniemi depends upon Sweden's willingness to make the railroads available for such a concentration.

The main body of the Finnish Army will be assigned the task, in coordination with the advance of the German northern wing, of pinning down as strong Russian forces as possible by attacking west of or on both sides of Lake Ladoga, and of seizing Hangö.

By converging operations with strong wings, the Army Group committed *south* of the Pripet Marshes is to aim at the complete destruction west of the Dnieper of the Russian forces standing in the Ukraine. The *main effort* for this is to be made from the area of Lublin in the general direction of Kiev, while the forces in Rumania, crossing the lower Prut, form a widely separated enveloping arm. The Rumanian Army will have the task of pinning down the Russian forces in between.

Once the battles south and north of the Pripet Marshes have been fought, we should aim to achieve as part of the pursuit operation: *in the south,* the prompt seizure of the economically important Donets Basin; *in the north,* rapid arrival at Moscow.

The capture of this city means a decisive success politically and economically and, beyond that, the elimination of the most important railway center.

B. *Luftwaffe:*

Its task will be to paralyze and to eliminate as far as possible the intervention of the Russian Air Force and also to support the Army at its main points of effort, particularly those of Army Group Center and, on the main wing, of Army Group South. The Russian railroads, depending on their importance for the operations, will be cut or, as the case may be, their most important near-by installations (river crossings!) seized by the bold employment of parachute and airborne troops.

In order to concentrate all forces against the enemy Air Force and to give direct support to the Army the armament industry will not be attacked during the main operations. Only after the completion of the mobile operations may such attacks be considered—primarily against the Ural region.

C. *Navy:*

The Navy's role against Soviet Russia is, while safeguarding our own coast, to prevent an escape of enemy naval units from the Baltic Sea. As the Russian Baltic Sea fleet, once we have reached Leningrad, will be deprived of its last base and will then be in a hopeless situation, any larger naval operations are to be avoided before that time.

After the elimination of the Russian fleet it will be a question of protecting all the traffic in the Baltic Sea, including the supply by sea of the northern wing of the Army (mine clearance!).

IV. All orders to be issued by the Commanders in Chief on the basis of this directive must clearly indicate that they are *precautionary measures* for the possibility that Russia should change her present attitude toward us. The number of officers to be assigned to the preparatory work at an early date is to be kept as small as possible; additional personnel should be briefed as late as possible and only to the extent required for the activity of each individual. Otherwise, through the discovery of our preparations—the date of their execution has not even been fixed—there is danger that most serious political and military disadvantages may arise.

V. I expect reports from the Commanders in Chief concerning their further plans based on this directive.

The contemplated preparations of all branches of the armed forces, including their progress, are to be reported to me through the High Command of the Wehrmacht.

Adolf Hitler

41. HITLER DIRECTIVE NO. 22, JANUARY 11, 1941[5]

Support by German forces in the campaign in the
Mediterranean Area

The situation in the Mediterranean area, in which England has committed superior forces against our allies, demands German assistance on strategic, political, and psychological grounds.

Tripolitania must be held, the danger of a collapse of the Albanian front must be averted. Over and above this, the Army Group Cavallero should be capable of starting the attack from Albania in connection with the later operations of the 12th Army.

I. Therefore, I order the following:

1. Blocking unit is to be organized by the Commander in Chief of the Army, which will enable us to render valuable service to our allies in the

defense of Tripolitania especially against British armored divisions. The basis of its composition will be ordered separately.

The preparations are to be scheduled in such a manner, that this unit may be transferred to Tripolis [and] attached to the currently running transports of an Italian armored division and a motorized division (about 20 February).

2. The X Air Corps will keep Sicily as an operational base. Its most important mission will be the combating of British Naval Forces and British sea communications between the western and eastern Mediterranean.

In addition, with the aid of auxiliary landing fields in Tripolitania, the main essentials for the direct support of Army Group Graziani are to be obtained by attacks on British ports of disembarkation and supply bases on the coast of western Egypt and Circenaica.

The Italian Government has been asked to declare a prohibited area between Sicily and the North African coast in order to make the task of the X Air Corps easier and to avoid incidents with neutral ships.

3. German units with the strength of approximately one corps including the 1st Mountain Division and armored forces are to be provided and prepared for the crossing to Albania. Transportation of the 1st Mountain Division is to begin as soon as Italy's agreement is received by the High Command of the Armed Forces. In the meantime, investigations are to be made and the position is to be clarified with the Italian High Command in Albania, as to whether and what further forces can be advantageously employed in Albania in an attack with an operative objective, and how it can be continuously supplied at the same time as the Italian divisions.

The task for the German units will be—

a. First to serve as a reserve in Albania in case new crises should arise there.

b. To facilitate the future transition to the attack of the Italian Army Group with the objective—

To break through the Greek defensive front in a vital sector for a far reaching operation, to open the Narrows west of Salonika from the rear, thereby supporting the frontal attack of the Army "List."

4. The High Command of the Armed Forces with the Italian General Staff will determine the general directions for the chain of command of the German troops to be committed in North Africa and Albania, and for the limitations which are to be made concerning the deployment of these troops.

5. German transports suitable and available in the Mediterranean which are not being used on the convoy run to Tripoli, are to be earmarked for the transfer of the Albanian forces. For troop transports, the Transport Group Ju 52 located in Foggia is to be utilized.

Attempts must be made to complete the transfer of the German forces to Albania before the transport of the blockading unit to Libya begins . . . and use of the bulk of German shipping will be needed for that purpose.

[Signed] A. Hitler
[Initials] J [Jodl] 10/1
K [Keitel] 20/1

42. FUEHRER CONFERENCE ON YUGOSLAVIA, BERLIN, MARCH 27, 1941[6]

The Führer describes Yugoslavia's situation after the coup d'état. States that Yugoslavia was an uncertain factor with respect to the coming *Marita* action and even more in regard to the *Barbarossa* Operation later on. Serbs and Slovenes have never been pro-German. The Governments never sit securely in the saddle because of the nationality problem and the officers' camarilla, which is always inclined toward a coup d'état. In recent times, the country had only one strong man, namely Stojadinović, and Prince Regent Paul, to his own disadvantage, had him overthrown.

The moment for realizing the actual situation in the country and its attitude toward us is favorable to us both for political as well as for military reasons. If the overthrow of the Government were to have taken place during the *Barbarossa* action, the consequences for us would have been much more serious.

The Führer is determined, without waiting for possible loyalty declarations of the new Government, to make all preparations in order to smash Yugoslavia militarily and as a state. No inquiries regarding foreign policy will be made or ultimatums presented. Assurances of the Yugoslav Government which cannot be trusted anyhow in the future will be taken note of. The attack will begin as soon as the means and troops suitable for it are ready.

It is important that action be taken as fast as possible. We will try to get the neighboring states to participate in a suitable way. Actual military support against Yugoslavia is to be asked of Italy, Hungary, and in certain respects of Bulgaria too. Rumania's principal task is to provide cover against Russia. The Hungarian and Bulgarian Ministers have already been notified. Within the course of the day, a message will be addressed to the Duce.

Politically, it is especially important that the blow against Yugoslavia be carried out with inexorable severity and that the military destruction be carried out in a lightning-like operation. In this way, Turkey would presumably be sufficiently deterred and the subsequent campaign against Greece would be influenced in a favorable way. It is to be expected that the Croats will take our side when we attack. They will be assured of political treatment (autonomy later on) in accordance with this. The war against Yugoslavia presumably will be very popular in Italy, Hungary, and Bulgaria, as these states are to be promised territorial acquisitions; the Adriatic coast for Italy, the Banat for Hungary, and Macedonia for Bulgaria.

This plan presupposes that we speed up the schedule of all preparations and employ such strong forces that the Yugoslav collapse will take place within the shortest time.

In this connection, the beginning of Operation Barbarossa will have to be postponed up to 4 weeks.

The military operations are to be conducted in the following way:

1) Beginning of Operation *Marita* as early as possible with the limited objective of capturing Greek Thrace and the basin of Salonika and to win the

high ground of Edessa; for that purpose, a lunge across Yugoslav territory.

2) Thrust from the region south of Sofia in the direction of Skoplje in order to relieve the flank of the Italian front in Albania.

3) Thrust with stronger forces from the area around Sofia in the direction of Niš, then of Belgrade, in cooperation with

4) stronger German forces penetrating from the area around Graz and Klagenfurt in a southeastern direction with the aim of destroying the Yugoslav Army.

Regarding 2) and 3), the forces of the cover group placed in readiness against Turkey, supernumerary units of the southern front and the Army reserves are to be employed also. The cover against the east must be provided on the one hand by Bulgarian forces, reinforced by an armored division which is to be pulled out of Rumania and on the other hand by Rumanian forces which are to be left with one armored division only.

Regarding 4), forces may be taken from the concentration echelon for *Barbarossa* (in this connection, speed is most important). The forces must be sufficiently strong.

The principal task assigned to the Italians is to cease offensive operations against Greece for the time being, to maintain adequate cover toward the Yugoslav frontier and to operate with the Army of the Po from the direction of Istria for the protection of the German right flank.

5) The principal task of the Luftwaffe is to start as early as possible with the destruction of the Yugoslav Air Force ground organization and to destroy the capital, Belgrade, in attacks by waves; and along with this to support the advance of the Army.

For this purpose, it is possible to make use of the Hungarian ground organization.

Commander in Chief of the Army:

The operational plan of the Führer coincides with the ideas which he himself had been thinking about. The date of April 1 can be maintained for the beginning of *Marita* depending on the weather. Start for the rest of the assault groups possible between April 3 and 10, depending on the concentration.

To the question whether the southern assault groups, if they should advance fast will have freedom of action in the further conduct of Operation *Marita,* the Führer gives a reply which is affirmative in principle; he demands, however, that the operations not be allowed to get out of hand but that they be led with a firm hand.

The Commander in Chief of the Army will submit plans before 3:00 a.m.

The Commander in Chief of the Luftwaffe reports that aerial attacks from Bulgaria by the VIII Air Corps could start immediately but that the Luftwaffe would need 2-3 days' time for a larger concentration of air forces. It is intended to bring up rather strong units of fighters and dive bombers into the area of Vienna, Graz, and Hungary. If necessary, to bring up units of the X Air Corps to jump-off bases in southern Italy.

Care will be taken to reinforce the antiaircraft defenses of Vienna, Carinthia, and Styria.

The Führer orders the immediate start of all preparations. He expects the plans of the branches of the Wehrmacht in the course of the evening of March 27. General von Rintelen has orders to fetch the message and oral instructions from the Führer during the night of March 27.

Ch[ristian]

43. HALDER DIARY ENTRY, BERLIN, MARCH 30, 1941[7]

30 March 1941, 1100 hrs. General meeting at Fuehrer's office. Address lasting almost 2½ hours. Situation since 30 June. Mistake of British not to take advantage of chances for peace. Account of subsequent events. Italy's conduct of the war and policies sharply criticized. Advantages for England resulting from Italy's reverses. England puts her hope in the United States and Russia. Detailed review of United States capabilities. Maximum output not before end of four years; problem of shipping. Russia's role and possibilities. Reasons for necessity to clear up the Russian situation. Only the final and drastic solution of all territorial problems will enable us to accomplish our tasks in the air and on the oceans within two years, with the manpower and material resources at our disposal. Our goals in Russia—Crush armed forces, break up state,—

Oberquartiermeister IV—Comments on Russian tanks—respectable; 4.7 cm gun (antitank) a good medium weapon; bulk of antitank guns obsolete.

Numerically, Russian tanks superior to that of any other nation, but they have only a small number of new giant types with long 10 cm guns. (Mammoth models, 42–45 tons.) Air force very large in number, but mostly outmoded; only small number of modern types.

Problems of Russia's vastness—Enormous expanse requires concentration on critical points. Massed planes and tanks must be brought to bear on strategic areas. Our air force cannot cover this entire huge area at one time; at the start of the campaign it will be able to dominate only parts of the enormous front. Hence its operations must be closely coordinated with ground operations. The Russians will cave in under the massive impact of tanks and airplanes.

No illusions about our allies! *Finns* will fight bravely, but they are numerically weak and have not yet recovered from their recent defeat. *Rumanians* are no good at all. Perhaps they could be used as a security force behind very strong natural obstacles (rivers), in quiet sectors. Antonescu has enlarged his army instead of reducing and improving it. The fortunes of large German units must not be tied to the uncertain staying power of the Rumanian forces.

Mines!

Questions regarding Pripet Marshes—flank protection, defenses, mines.

Problems arising if Russians should make strategic withdrawal—not likely, since they are based on both Baltic and the Ukraine. If the Russians want to pull out, they must do so at an early stage; otherwise they cannot get away in good order.

With goals in east achieved we shall need no more than 50–60 divisions (armored). One portion of the ground forces will be discharged into armament production for air force and navy, another portion will be required for other missions, e.g., Spain.

Colonial tasks!

Clash of two ideologies. Crushing denunciation of bolshevism, identified with asocial criminality. Communism is an enormous danger for our future. We must forget the concept of comradeship between soldiers. A Communist is no comrade before nor after the battle. This is a war of extermination. If we fail to grasp this, and though we are sure to beat the enemy, we shall again have to fight the Communist foe 30 years from now. We do not wage war to preserve the enemy.

Future political map of Russia—Northern Russia goes to Finland. Protectorates—Baltic States, Ukraine, White Russia.

War against Russia—Extermination of the Bolshevist commissars and of the Communist intelligentsia. The new states must be Socialist, but without intellectual classes of their own. Growth of a new intellectual class must be prevented. A primitive Socialist intelligentsia is all that is needed. We must fight against the poison of disintegration. This is no job for military courts. The individual troop commander must know the issues at stake. They must be leaders in the fight. The troops must fight back with the methods with which they are attacked. Commissars and GPU men are criminals and must be dealt with as such. This need not mean that the troops get out of hand. Rather the commander must give orders which express the common feelings of his troops.

Embody in CinC Army order—

This fighting will be very different from the fighting in the West. In the East, harshness today means leniency in the future. Commanders must make the sacrifice of overcoming their personal scruples.

Noon—All invited to lunch.

44. Fuehrer's Directive No. 26, April 3, 1941[8]

Chefsache   Führer's Headquarters, April 3, 1941.
Top Secret Military
The Führer and Supreme Commander of the Wehrmacht
OKW/WFSt/Abt. L No. 44395/41 g. K. Chefs.
By officer only

Directive No. 26

Cooperation with our allies in the Balkans

1) The military tasks intended for the *southeastern European states* in the campaign against Yugoslavia result from the political objectives:

Hungary, to whom the Banat will fall, will mainly have to occupy that area, but has declared herself in addition ready to cooperate in the destruction of the enemy.

Bulgaria should get back Macedonia and is therefore principally to be interested in an attack in this direction, but without particular pressure being exerted from the German side. Furthermore the Bulgarians, supported by a German armored unit, will provide the rear cover against Turkey. For that purpose Bulgaria will also employ the three divisions stationed on the Greek border.

Rumania, in her own as well as in the German interest will have to limit her mission to protecting the frontier against Yugoslavia and against Russia. Through the chief of the Wehrmacht mission we should seek to achieve an increase in Rumania's defensive preparedness against Russia. . . . At the very least two-way communications across the Rumanian-Hungarian boundary must proceed between Hungarian and German liaison headquarters without hindrance.

2) The following guiding principles will apply for the *military cooperation* and the organization of command in the coming operation:

I reserve to myself the unified command of this campaign, in so far as the operational objectives of the Italian and Hungarian forces within the framework of the whole operation are concerned. It must be carried on in a way that takes into account the sensibilities of our allies and leaves to the Chiefs of State of Italy and Hungary the possibility of appearing to their peoples and armed forces as sovereign military leaders.

I shall therefore pass on the military demands for the coordination of operations, which are to be transmitted to me by the Commander in Chief of the Army and the Commander in Chief of the Luftwaffe as proposals and wishes, in the form of personal letters to the Duce and Regent Horthy.

The same procedure is to be followed by the Commander in Chief of the Twelfth Army toward the Bulgarian governmental and military authorities.

If single Bulgarian divisions participate in the operations against Yugoslavia, they must be subordinate to the German commanding officers of the given areas.

3) In Hungary a headquarters named "The German General with the High Command of the Hungarian Armed Forces" shall be set up, to whose staff a liaison staff of the Luftwaffe shall also be attached.

This headquarters will serve both [as] my liaison with the Regent, as well as the liaison of the Wehrmacht branches with the Hungarian High Command.

All details of the cooperation with the Italian and Hungarian forces are to be settled by the Wehrmacht branches and by liaison staffs to be exchanged between adjoining armies and air fleets.

4) The *air defense forces* of Rumania and Bulgaria remain integrated in the German air defense of these countries, in so far as they are not employed in the areas of their own armies. Hungary will defend her territory herself,

provided that German units operating there, and the buildings essential to them, are protected by the German Wehrmacht.

5) Apart from the new arrangement regarding the unified command, the agreements with Hungary remain in effect. The Second Italian Army will gain freedom of movement only after the attack of the German Second Army and the motorized group of the XLVI Army Corps begin to take effect. To this end it may become necessary that at first it be made more in a southern than southeastern direction. Limiting the Italian Air Force to protection of the flank and the rear of the front in Albania, to attacks on the Mostar airfield and coastal airports, and to cooperation along the front of the Second Italian Army as soon as it advances to the attack, will be arranged by the OKW.

6) I shall later regulate the *tasks in the occupation* devolving upon the various countries after the campaign. In the manner of the cooperation with the allies even during the operations the brotherhood in arms for the achievement of a common political goal must be stressed in every possible way.

Adolf Hitler

45. German-Turkish Treaty Signed at Ankara, June 18, 1941[9]

The German Reich and the Turkish Republic, desiring to place their relations on a basis of mutual trust and sincere friendship, have agreed, without prejudice to existing obligations of the two countries, to conclude a treaty. For that purpose the following Plenipotentiaries have been appointed:

By the German Reich Chancellor:
   Herr Franz von Papen, Ambassador Extraordinary and Plenipotentiary of the German Reich,
By the President of the Turkish Republic:
   His Excellency M. Sükrü Saracoglu, Deputy from Izmir, Minister of Foreign Affairs,
who, having communicated to each other their full powers, found to be in good and due form, have agreed as follows:

ARTICLE 1

The German Reich and the Turkish Republic undertake mutually to respect the integrity and inviolability of their territories, and not to take measures of any sort aimed directly or indirectly against the other contracting party.

ARTICLE 2

The German Reich and the Turkish Republic undertake in the future to consult with one another in a friendly spirit on all questions affecting their common interests in order to reach an understanding regarding the treatment of such questions.

ARTICLE 3

This Treaty shall enter into force on the day of its signing and shall remain in force from that date for a period of 10 years; the Contracting Parties will consult with one another at the appropriate time about an extension of the Treaty.

The Treaty shall be ratified and the instruments of ratification shall be exchanged as soon as possible in Berlin.

Done in duplicate in the German and Turkish languages, the two texts being equally authentic.

Ankara, June 18, 1941.

Franz v. Papen   S. Saracoglu

46. ADOLF HITLER TO REGENT OF HUNGARY, JUNE 21, 1941[10]

Your Highness: After the German Government had attempted in 1939, through clarification of the mutual spheres of interest, to bring about a relaxation of tension with Soviet Russia, and, if possible, even a friendly cooperation with her, it became nevertheless evident shortly afterward that no essential change in the attitude and tendencies of that Government toward other countries had taken place. On the contrary: Already the occupation of the Baltic countries was undertaken with the insulting justification that they had to be taken under Soviet Russia's protection against a threat from without. And this happened although it was known to the Russian Government that Germany had rejected the earnest plea of Lithuania to send German troops to that country. The Russian attack upon Finland was also a hard blow to the sensibilities of the German people. The attempt of the Soviet Union to penetrate into the Balkans would have led to a dangerous threat not only to German vital interests but to those of the whole of Europe.

On the occasion of the visit to Berlin of Molotov, who had been invited in order that an attempt might again be made to bring about a clarification, the latter addressed a number of questions, or rather, demands to me to which it was impossible for me to assent. They dealt with problems ranging all the way from Finland to the Dardanelles. After the failure of these conversations not only did estrangement set in very quickly between our two countries, but, above all, the military threat to the German eastern frontiers grew increasingly stronger.

About 160 Soviet Russian divisions were concentrated in this area. Despite my confidence in the efficiency of the German transportation system, I was likewise forced in these circumstances slowly to order and carry out strong measures of defense. In the past few weeks the tension became unbearable.

It was obviously the goal of the Russian Government and of its measures to tie down such large German forces in the east that our ability to carry on operations in other theaters of war would be obstructed or at least crippled. Thus time was passing and it was then up to England, or to England and Russia, to decide on the moment when they could seize the initiative from us.

All other measures or statements of the Kremlin were merely phrases to conceal this purpose. Since in recent weeks and especially in the last few days border incidents continued to increase and finally led to bigger and bigger conflicts, I do not believe that I can assume responsibility any longer for continuing to watch idly this slow but sure strangulation of the Reich.

Since this morning extensive defense measures have been taking place along a front that extends practically from the Arctic Ocean to the Black Sea. I am conscious of the gravity of the task but I also believe that I am at the same time acting in the spirit of the whole of European civilization and culture in trying to repel and push back this un-European influence.

How well-founded our view and our decision indeed are, Your Highness will see from those documents that I have now decided to release for publication.

As far as the attitude of Hungary is concerned, Your Highness, I am convinced that in her national consciousness she will appreciate my attitude. I should like at this point to thank Your Highness for the understanding measures of the Hungarian armed forces, which by the mere fact of having strengthened their frontier defenses will prevent Russian flank attacks and tie down Russian forces.

Whatever the immediate consequences of this event may be, the remote ones will surely result in a pacification of Europe and, above all, in the possibility of concentrating all the military forces of the German Reich for the ultimate annihilation of the opponent, who refuses peace only out of sheer lust for war.

Please accept, Your Highness, at this hour my especially cordial and comradely greetings!

Yours,

47. Halder Diary Entry, June 22, 1941[11]

22 June 1941, morning reports show that all armies (except 11th) have started off according to plan. *Tactical surprise appears to have been achieved along the entire line.* The bridges across the Bug and the other rivers of the wet frontier were undefended and are intact in our hands. That the enemy was taken by surprise is evidenced by the fact that events caught the troops in their quarters, that planes stood on the airfields covered up, and that forward elements when seeing themselves unexpectedly attacked, called up the rear for instructions what to do. Other effects of the surprise will result from the general forward rush of the mobile troops. The navy also reports

surprise of the enemy in their sector. He reacted only passively to our actions in the last few days, and now is massed in ports, apparently in fear of mines.

48. ANTONESCU'S ORDER OF THE DAY, JUNE 22, 1941[12] (EXCERPT)

"Free your oppressed brothers from the Red yoke of bolshevism." "Bring old Bessarabia and the woods of Bukovina, your fields and meadows, back into the Fatherland.

"Soldiers, you will fight shoulder to shoulder and heart to heart with the strongest military force on earth.

"You will fight for the soil of Moldavia and for justice in the world. Be worthy of the honor which history, the army of the great Reich and its extraordinary leader Adolf Hitler have given you. Fight to avenge injustice. Our People, our King and your General demand this of you."

49. CHURCHILL'S RADIO ADDRESS OF JUNE 22, 1941[13]

I have taken occasion to speak to you to-night because we have reached one of the climacterics of the war. The first of these intense turning-points was a year ago when France fell prostrate under the German hammer, and when we had to face the storm alone. The second was when the Royal Air Force beat the Hun raiders out of the daylight air, and thus warded off the Nazi invasion of our island while we were still ill-armed and ill-prepared. The third turning-point was when the President and Congress of the United States passed the Lease-and-Lend enactment, devoting nearly 2,000 millions sterling of the wealth of the New World to help us to defend our liberties and their own. Those were the three climacterics. The fourth is now upon us.

At four o'clock this morning Hitler attacked and invaded Russia. All his usual formalities of perfidy were observed with scrupulous technique. A non-aggression treaty had been solemnly signed and was in force between the two countries. No complaint had been made by Germany of its non-fulfilment. Under its cloak of false confidence, the German armies drew up in immense strength along a line which stretches from the White Sea to the Black Sea; and their air fleets and armoured divisions slowly and methodically took their stations. Then, suddenly without declaration of war, without even an ultimatum, German bombs rained down from the air upon the Russian cities, the German troops violated the frontiers; and an hour later the German Ambassador, who till the night before was lavishing his assurances of friendship, almost of alliance, upon the Russians, called upon the Russian Foreign Minister to tell him that a state of war existed between Germany and Russia.

Thus was repeated on a far larger scale the same kind of outrage against every form of signed compact and international faith which we have witnessed in Norway, Denmark, Holland and Belgium, and which Hitler's accomplice and jackal Mussolini so faithfully imitated in the case of Greece.

All this was no surprise to me. In fact I gave clear and precise warnings to Stalin of what was coming. I gave him warning as I have given warning to others before. I can only hope that this warning did not fall unheeded. All we know at present is that the Russian people are defending their native soil and that their leaders have called upon them to resist to the utmost.

Hitler is a monster of wickedness, insatiable in his lust for blood and plunder. Not content with having all Europe under his heel, or else terrorized into various forms of abject submission, he must now carry his work of butchery and desolation among the vast multitudes of Russia and of Asia. The terrible military machine, which we and the rest of the civilized world so foolishly, so supinely, so insensately allowed the Nazi gangsters to build up year by year from almost nothing, cannot stand idle lest it rust or fall to pieces. It must be in continual motion, grinding up human lives and trampling down the homes and the rights of hundreds of millions of men. Moreover it must be fed, not only with flesh but with oil.

So now this bloodthirsty guttersnipe must launch his mechanized armies upon new fields of slaughter, pillage and devastation. Poor as are the Russian peasants, workmen and soldiers, he must steal from them their daily bread; he must devour their harvests; he must rob them of the oil which drives their ploughs; and thus produce a famine without example in human history. And even the carnage and ruin which his victory, should he gain it—he has not gained it yet—will bring upon the Russian people, will itself be only a stepping-stone to the attempt to plunge the four or five hundred millions who live in India, into that bottomless pit of human degradation over which the diabolic emblem of the Swastika flaunts itself. It is not too much to say here this summer evening that the lives and happiness of a thousand million additional people are now menaced with brutal Nazi violence. That is enough to make us hold our breath. But presently I shall show you something else that lies behind, and something that touches very nearly the life of Britain and of the United States.

The Nazi régime is indistinguishable from the worst features of Communism. It is devoid of all theme and principle except appetite and racial domination. It excels all forms of human wickedness in the efficiency of its cruelty and ferocious aggression. No one has been a more consistent opponent of Communism than I have for the last twenty-five years. I will unsay no word that I have spoken about it. But all this fades away before the spectacle which is now unfolding. The past with its crimes, its follies and its tragedies, flashes away. I see the Russian soldiers standing on the threshold of their native land, guarding the fields which their fathers have tilled from time immemorial. I see them guarding their homes where mothers and wives pray—ah yes, for there are times when all pray—for the safety of their loved ones, the return of the breadwinner, of their champion, of their protector. I see the ten thousand villages of Russia, where the means of existence was wrung so hardly from the soil, but where there are still primordial human joys, where maidens laugh and children play. I see advancing upon all this in hideous onslaught the Nazi war machine, with its clanking, heel-clicking, dandified Prussian officers, its crafty expert agents fresh from the cowing and tying-down of a dozen countries. I see also the dull, drilled, docile, brutish masses of the Hun soldiery plodding on like a swarm of crawling locusts. I see the German bombers and fighters in the sky, still smarting from many a British whipping, delighted to find what they believe is an easier and a safer prey.

Behind all this glare, behind all this storm, I see that small group of villainous men who plan, organize and launch this cataract of horrors upon mankind. And then my mind goes back across the years to the days when the Russian armies were our allies against the same deadly foe; when they fought with so much valour and constancy, and helped to gain a victory for all to share in which, alas, they were—through no fault of ours—utterly cut off. I have lived through all this, and you will pardon me if I express my feelings and the stir of old memories.

But now I have to declare the decision of His Majesty's Government—and I feel sure it is a decision in which the great Dominions will, in due course, concur—for we must speak out now at once, without a day's delay. I have to make the declaration, but can you doubt what our policy will be? We have but one aim and one single, irrevocable purpose. We are resolved to destroy Hitler and every vestige of the Nazi régime. From this nothing will turn us—nothing. We will never parley, we will never negotiate with Hitler or any of his gang. We shall fight him by land, we shall fight him by sea, we shall fight him in the air, until with God's help we have rid the earth of his shadow and liberated its peoples from his yoke. Any man or state who fights on against Nazidom will have our aid. Any man or state who marches with Hitler is our foe. This applies not only to organized states but to all representatives of that vile race of quislings who make themselves the tools and agents of the Nazi régime against their fellow-countrymen and the lands of their birth. They—these quislings—like the Nazi leaders themselves, if not disposed of by their fellow-countrymen, which would save trouble, will be delivered by us on the morrow of victory to the justice of the Allied tribunals. That is our policy and that is our declaration. It follows, therefore, that we shall give whatever help we can to Russia and the Russian people. We shall appeal to all our friends and allies in every part of the world to take the same course and pursue it, as we shall, faithfully and steadfastly to the end.

We have offered the Government of Soviet Russia any technical or economic assistance which is in our power, and which is likely to be of service to them. We shall bomb Germany by day as well as by night in ever-increasing measures, casting upon them month by month a heavier discharge of bombs, and making the German people taste and gulp each month a sharper dose of the miseries they have showered upon mankind. It is noteworthy that only yesterday the Royal Air Force, fighting inland over French territory, cut down with very small loss of themselves 28 of the Hun fighting machines in the air above the French soil they have invaded, defiled and profess to hold. But this is only a beginning. From now forward the main expansion of our Air Force proceeds with gathering speed. In another six months the weight of the help we are receiving from the United States in war materials of all kinds, and especially in heavy bombers, will begin to tell.

This is no class war, but a war in which the whole British Empire and Commonwealth of Nations is engaged without distinction of race, creed or party. It is not for me to speak of the action of the United States, but this I will say: if Hitler imagines that his attack on Soviet Russia will cause the slightest division of aims or slackening of effort in the great Democracies who are resolved upon his doom, he is woefully mistaken. On the contrary, we shall be fortified and encouraged in our efforts to rescue mankind from his tyranny. We shall be strengthened and not weakened in determination and in resources.

This is no time to moralize on the follies of countries and governments which have allowed themselves to be struck down one by one, when by united action they could have saved themselves and saved the world from this catastrophe. But when I spoke a few minutes ago of Hitler's blood-lust and the hateful appetites which have impelled or lured him on his Russian adventure, I said there was one deeper motive behind his outrage. He wishes to destroy the Russian power because he hopes that if he succeeds in this, he will be able to bring back the main strength of his army and air force from the East and hurl it upon this Island, which he knows he must conquer or suffer the penalty of his crimes. His invasion of Russia is no more than a prelude to an attempted invasion of the British Isles. He hopes, no doubt, that all this may be accomplished before the winter comes, and that he can overwhelm Great Britain before the fleet and air power of the United States may intervene. He hopes that he may once again repeat, upon a greater scale than ever before, that process of destroying his enemies one by one, by which he has so long thrived and prospered, and that then the scene will be clear for the final act, without which all his conquests would be in vain—namely, the subjugation of the Western Hemisphere to his will and to his system.

The Russian danger is therefore our danger, and the danger of the United States, just as the cause of any Russian fighting for his hearth and home is the cause of free men and free peoples in every quarter of the globe. Let us learn the lessons already taught by such cruel experience. Let us redouble our exertions, and strike with united strength while life and power remain.

50. Stalin's Radio Address of July 3, 1941[14] (Excerpts)

The fact of the matter is that the troops of Germany, as a country at war, were already fully mobilized, and the 170 divisions hurled by Germany against the USSR and brought up to the Soviet frontiers were in a state of complete readiness, only awaiting the signal to move into action, whereas the

Soviet troops had still to effect mobilization and to move up to the frontiers.

It is of no little importance in this connexion that fascist Germany suddenly and treacherously violated the non-aggression pact it concluded in 1939 with the USSR, disregarding the fact that it would be regarded as the aggressor by the whole world. Naturally, our peace-loving country, unwilling to take the initiative in breaking the pact, could not have resorted to perfidy. It may be asked: how could the Soviet Government have consented to conclude a non-aggression pact with such treacherous monsters as Hitler and Ribbentrop? Was this not a mistake on the part of the Soviet Government? Of course not! A non-aggression pact is a pact of peace between two States. It was such a pact that Germany proposed to us in 1939. Could the Soviet Government have declined such a proposal? I think that not a single peace-loving State could decline a peace treaty with a neighbouring Power, even though the latter was headed by such monsters and cannibals as Hitler and Ribbentrop. But that, of course, only on one indispensable condition, namely, that the peace treaty did not encroach either directly or indirectly on the territorial integrity, independence, and honour of the peace-loving State. As you know, the non-aggression pact between Germany and the USSR was precisely such a pact.

What did we gain by concluding the non-aggression pact with Germany? We secured our country peace for a year and a half and the opportunity of preparing its forces to repulse fascist Germany should it risk an attack on our country despite the pact. This was a definite advantage for us and a disadvantage for fascist Germany. What has fascist Germany gained and what has it lost by treacherously tearing up the pact and attacking the USSR? It has gained certain advantageous positions for its troops for a short period, but has lost politically by exposing itself in the eyes of the entire world as a bloodthirsty aggressor. There can be no doubt that this short-lived military gain for Germany is only an episode, while the tremendous political gain of the USSR is a serious and lasting factor that is bound to form the basis for the development of decisive military successes of the Red Army in the war with fascist Germany. . . .

This war with fascist Germany cannot be considered an ordinary war. It is not only a war between two armies; it is also a great war of the entire Soviet people against the German fascist forces. The aim of this national war in defence of our fatherland against the fascist oppressors is not only elimination of the danger hanging over our country, but also to aid all European peoples groaning under the yoke of German fascism. In this war of liberation we shall not be alone. In this great war we shall have loyal allies in the peoples of Europe and America, including the German people who are enslaved by the Hitlerite despots. Our war for the freedom of our fatherland will merge with the struggle of the peoples of Europe and America for their independence, for democratic liberties. It will be a united front of peoples standing for freedom and against enslavement and threats of enslavement by Hitler's fascist armies.

In this connexion, the historic speech of the British Prime Minister, Mr. Churchill, regarding aid to the Soviet Union, and the declaration of the United States Government of its readiness to render aid to our country, which can only evoke a feeling of gratitude in the hearts of the peoples of the Soviet Union, are wholly understandable and significant.

51. HALDER DIARY, JULY 3, 1941[15]

12th Day. . . . It is thus probably no overstatement to say that the Russian Campaign has been won in the space of two weeks. Of course, this does not yet mean that it is closed. The sheer geographical vastness of the country and the stubbornness of the resistance, which is carried on with all means, will claim our efforts for many more weeks to come.
Future plans:

. . . .

b) As soon as the battle in the East changes from an effort to annihilate the enemy armed forces to one of paralyzing the enemy economy, our next tasks in the war against Britain will come to the foreground and require preparation:

Preparations must be made for the offensive against the land route between the Nile and Euphrates, both from Cyrenaica and through Anatolia, and perhaps also for an offensive from the Caucasus against Iran. The former theater, which will always remain dependent of the quantities of supplies we can bring across the sea, and so is subject to incalculable vicissitudes, will assume a secondary role and for the most part will be left to Italian forces. We will have to assign to it only two German Armored Divisions (Fifth light and Fifteenth), which will be brought up to full strength and reinforced by small additional complements. As an initial move for the operations through Anatolia against Syria, possibly supported by a secondary thrust from the Caucasus, we shall have to initiate concentration of the necessary forces in Bulgaria, which at the same time may serve as a means of political pressure to compel Turkey to grant transit for our forces.

52. HITLER-MUSSOLINI CONVERSATION, AUGUST 25, 1941[16] (EXCERPT)

In his first conversation with the Duce immediately after the latter's arrival at Headquarters, the Führer gave the Duce a general outline of the situation, together with a detailed account of the military developments.

The Führer began by acknowledging to the Duce that it had been a wise decision to liquidate Greece along with Yugoslavia before launching the Russian campaign. Greece and Yugoslavia were in reality two potential and active enemies of the Axis, and eliminating them in time proved a great advantage at the moment when it became necessary to take action against

Soviet Russia in order to eliminate the grave Bolshevik menace and to achieve effective control of Europe.

The Führer then made a special point of acknowledging that for the first time since the beginning of the conflict, the German military intelligence service had failed. It had in fact not reported that Russia had a very well armed and equipped army composed for the most part of men imbued with a veritable fanaticism who, despite their racial heterogeneity, were now fighting with blind fury. The Bolshevik army as a whole could be viewed as made up of two large masses: one, the larger, consisting of peasants who fought with unreasoning obstinacy, and the other made up in the main of industrial workers who strongly believed in the words of Marx and fought with fanaticism. For opposite reasons, both were fighting to the last man; the former out of primitive ignorance, the latter because they were bewitched by the mystique of Communism.

The Führer added that he would not let himself be ensnared by the Soviets into continuing the battle inside cities by street fighting, for which the Russians were exceptionally well prepared. He had no intention of destroying the large cities, but would leave them to fall by themselves after he had won the battle of annihilation against the Soviet military forces emplaced around them. That was his plan of Leningrad, which had an urban area comprising about 4 million inhabitants. It would fall as soon as the total destruction of the Soviet forces ringing the city was accomplished. By avoiding street fighting, which yields no useful results, he would above all be able to save important forces.

The Führer had no doubt whatsoever as to the outcome of the struggle. He thought there was no point at the moment in dwelling on a consideration of what might at some future date become a line of resistance set up by the Soviets; he was inclined to believe that the Red military strength would inevitably collapse not later than October under the incessant blows that were being, and would be, inflicted upon them. A contributing factor, as time went on, would be the conquest, already begun and soon to be completed, of the major Soviet industrial centers and mining regions, for example the Don river basin. Whether this collapse would come soon, within a few months, or next spring, could be considered of secondary importance because already the means of victory were in Germany's hands. Inasmuch as the German losses to date, despite the fierceness of the struggle, had not exceeded the low figure of 68,000 men, and the war booty that had fallen into German hands was so immense, far exceeding the needs of the armed forces of the Reich, the Führer had decided to concentrate the production effort from now on exclusively on the construction of submarines, tanks, and antiaircraft artillery.

Regarding military plans for the future, the Führer told the Duce—in absolute secrecy—that after completion of the Russian campaign he intended to deal England the final blow by invading the island. To that end he was now marshaling the necessary resources by preparing the appropriate naval and land material needed for the landing. In the opinion of the Führer, that would mark the final act of the conflict.

Part 5. An Anti-Hitler Coalition Takes Shape

The Soviet Union did not fall after the first German onslaught as Hitler had predicted (52). This does not mean that the German gains were unimpressive; quite the contrary. By November Hitler's forces occupied the remainder of the former Polish state, the Baltic nations, and the Ukraine. In addition, they had advanced deep into the Crimea and the Donets Basin and threatened the cities of Leningrad and Moscow. Determined to end the struggle before winter set in, the intensity of the German attacks increased, but the Russians managed to muster sufficient strength to prevent the capture of Leningrad. German successes were to continue, but it was becoming apparent that the war was not over yet. By the end of November and early December the German advance reached its limits and Russian counterattacks began. With a potential strength of some 10,000,000 men the Red armies were far from being depleted and they had wisely avoided any major engagements with the Germans; instead they had drawn the enemy farther and farther away from his base of supplies and into a freezing and bitter cold.

In the meantime, Prime Minister Winston Churchill, already immeasurably cheered by Russia's entry into the war (49), was exerting increasing pressures to secure more American support. A lengthy telegram from Churchill to Roosevelt in December 1940 (53) does not require extensive interpretation to reach the conclusion that the P. M. was urging the United States to prepare for war. His "prospects for 1941" left little doubt that British dependence on U. S. military and industrial power placed a major responsibility for the war on America.

Churchill did not find the American President unsympathetic to Britain's plight, for there had already been ample demonstration of strong support. The problem was that Roosevelt was bound by a variety of restraints—not the least of which was the law—and obviously could not issue a declaration of war on Germany even to save Great Britain. He could, however, utilize his immense influence and power to provide all forms of aid to that nation. His broadcast to the American people (54), which was delivered shortly after receipt of Churchill's confidential message, made it very plain where the President's sentiments were. In fact, his speech closely paralleled the points made in Churchill's telegram.

The great effectiveness of Roosevelt's policies manifested itself in the passage of a Congressional act on March 11, 1941 (55). This is generally referred to as the "Lend-Lease Act," and was a potent piece of legislation indeed. It was designed to help defend the United States by providing material aid to its allies and was to cost some $50,000,000,000 before World War II closed. The overwhelming bulk of aid provided under this historic act was in the form of war material and went to Great Britain. The United States was to receive some $7,000,000,000 in reciprocal aid. The Lend-Lease Act was a monumental undertaking and contributed most significantly to Allied victory.

Almost simultaneously to the preparation and passage of Lend-Lease the United States embarked on another cooperative venture with Great Britain that may have had even more far-reaching implications. Beginning in January, British naval and military representatives gathered with their American counterparts in Washington to develop a mutual war plan in the event that the United States entered the conflict. The secret ABC (American, British, and Canadian) meeting lasted two months and explored all major aspects involving possible future U. S. participation. The results (56) were extensive and ranged from defining exact military roles to ultimate strategic objectives. The plan—called ABC–1—may well be viewed as having placed the United States in a position of virtually rendering a war commitment.

Secret planning and clandestine meetings did not constitute a war declaration, and while many Americans may have shared some of Roosevelt's strong pro-British feelings they probably didn't believe war was imminent. The President did not neglect an opportunity to press the theme of urgency, however, and to emphasize to his listeners the desperate needs of Great Britain. In a speech before the White House Correspondents' Association in March 1941 (57), he reviewed current events and repeated his "Four Freedoms" statement as well as calling for a national dedication to defeat Naziism. The President's address hardly fell short of a direct war cry.

In the next several months the United States continued to extend its commitments in a quick succession of actions that included agreements relating to the defense of Greenland and Iceland (58 and 61), the proclamation of an unlimited national emergency (60), and a closer military cooperation with Canada (59). These acts quite clearly constituted an abandonment of American neutrality in both thought and action. The Neutrality Act of 1939 (16) now appeared badly out of balance with the administration's position and a different reality of 1941. The Act still contained the arms embargo provisions (16, sec. 2), and the President requested Congress to repeal those portions not in harmony with present practice. This didn't go as smoothly as it might appear in retrospect, for the current of isolationism was strong in America and the Congressional debate grew intense and prolonged before a joint resolution was forthcoming that contained the relevant repeal measures (62).

The importance of the great struggle Russia was making at the time was not forgotten as America and England drew closer in their alignment. The thought that was uppermost was centered on the means to include the Soviets in the growing Anglo-American scheme. This was a serious problem, for the United States was in no position to initiate anything and the British were in dire need themselves. For the moment England could only promise aid to the Soviet Union and sign a mutual pledge to fight the war to the end (63). This pledge became somewhat controversial before the Axis surrenders were finally achieved.

Although both the Soviet Union and Great Britain gave strong voice support to increased economic and military cooperation, the fact remained that most of the cooperation was economic in nature (64). True, the western Allies provided Russia with war supplies, but this fell far short of a second front and everyone concerned was well aware of that. The dimensions of the second front debate were not confined to problems of western logistics only, but were—in part—rooted in Soviet politics, for even with the German war there appeared to be no alteration in the Communist ideology so offensive to democratic governments. The advocacy of world revolution through such instrumentation as the Communist International was not entirely forgotten despite the presence of a common foe and the invasion of the homeland.

In the first of many summit meetings that were to build a close personal bond between them, Roosevelt and Churchill met during August 1941 and reviewed events since the end of the ABC conversations of January-March (56). The meeting is most notable for the release of a mutually signed document containing powerful war and peace aims and called the "Atlantic Charter" (65). It expanded upon Roosevelt's Four Freedoms (57) and added a set of basic principles that anticipated the formation of the United Nations.

53. Churchill to Roosevelt, December 7, 1940[1] (Excerpts)

My Dear Mr. President: As we reach the end of this year I feel that you expect me to lay before you the prospects for 1941. I do so strongly and confidently because it seems to me that the vast majority of American citizens have recorded their conviction that the safety of the United States as well as the future of our two democracies and the kind of civilisation for which they stand are bound up with the survival and independence of the British Commonwealth of Nations. Only thus can those bastions of sea-power, upon which the control of the Atlantic and the Indian Oceans depends, be preserved in faithful and friendly hands. The control of the Pacific by the United States Navy and of the Atlantic by the British Navy is indispensable to the security of the trade routes of both our countries and the surest means to preventing the war from reaching the shores of the United States.

2. There is another aspect. It takes between three and four years to convert the industries of a modern state to war purposes. Saturation point is

reached when the maximum industrial effort that can be spared from
civilian needs has been applied to war production. Germany certainly
reached this point by the end of 1939. We in the British Empire are now only
about half-way through the second year. The United States, I should suppose, was by no means so far advanced as we. Moreover, I understand that
immense programmes of naval, military and air defence are now on foot in
the United States, to complete which certainly two years are needed. It is our
British duty in the common interest as also for our own survival to hold the
front and grapple with Nazi power until the preparations of the United
States are complete. Victory may come before the two years are out; but we
have no right to count upon it to the extent of relaxing any effort that is
humanly possible. Therefore I submit with very great respect for your good
and friendly consideration that there is a solid identity of interest between
the British Empire and the United States while these conditions last. It is
upon this footing that I venture to address you.

3. The form which this war has taken and seems likely to hold does not
enable us to match the immense armies of Germany in any theatre where
their main power can be brought to bear. We can however by the use of sea
power and air power meet the German armies in the regions where only
comparatively small forces can be brought into action. We must do our best
to prevent German domination of Europe spreading into Africa and into
Southern Asia. We have also to maintain in constant readiness in this Island
armies strong enough to make the problem of an overseas invasion insolu-
ble. For these purposes we are forming as fast as possible, as you are already
aware, between fifty and sixty divisions. Even if the United States was our ally
instead of our friend and indispensable partner we should not ask for a large
American expeditionary army. Shipping, not men, is the limiting factor and
the power to transport munitions and supplies claims priority over the
movement by sea of large numbers of soldiers.

4. The first half of 1940 was a period of disaster for the Allies and for the
Empire. The last five months have witnessed a strong and perhaps unexpected recovery by Great Britain; fighting alone but with invaluable aid in
munitions and in destroyers placed at our disposal by the great Republic of
which you are for the third time chosen Chief.

5. The danger of Great Britain being destroyed by a swift overwhelming
blow has for the time being very greatly receded. In its place there is a long,
gradually maturing danger, less sudden and less spectacular but equally
deadly. This mortal danger is the steady and increasing diminution of sea
tonnage. We can endure the shattering of our dwellings and the slaughter of
our civilian population by indiscriminate air attacks and we hope to parry
these increasingly as our science develops and to repay them upon military
objectives in Germany as our Air Force more nearly approaches the strength
of the enemy. The decision for 1941 lies upon the seas; unless we can
establish our ability to feed this Island, to import munitions of all kinds
which we need, unless we can move our armies to the various theatres where

Hitler and his confederate Mussolini must be met, and maintain them there and do all this with the assurance of being able to carry it on till the spirit of the continental dictators is broken, we may fall by the way and the time needed by the United States to complete her defensive preparations may not be forthcoming. It is therefore in shipping and in the power to transport across the oceans, particularly the Atlantic Ocean, that in 1941 the crunch of the whole war will be found. If on the other hand we are able to move the necessary tonnage to and fro across the salt water indefinitely, it may well be that the application of superior air power to the German homeland and the rising anger of the German and other Nazi-gripped populations will bring the agony of civilization to a merciful and glorious end. But do not let us underrate the task.

. . . .

7. The next six or seven months bring the relative battleship strength in home waters to a smaller margin than is satisfactory. The *Bismark* [sic] and the *Tirpitz* will certainly be in service in January. We have already the *King George V* and hope to have the *Prince of Wales* at the same time. These modern ships are of course far better armoured, especially against air attack, than vessels like the *Rodney* and *Nelson* designed twenty years ago. We have recently had to use the *Rodney* on trans-Atlantic escort and at any time when numbers are so small, a mine or a torpedo may alter decisively the strength of the line of battle. We get relief in June when the *Duke of York* will be ready and will be still better off at the end of 1941 when the *Anson* also will have joined. But these two first class, modern, thirty-five thousand ton, fifteen inch gun German battleships force us to maintain a concentration never previously necessary in this war.

. . . .

9. There is a second field of danger: the Vichy Government may either by joining Hitler's new order in Europe or through some manoeuvre such as forcing us to attack an expedition despatched by sea against free French Colonies, find an excuse for ranging with the Axis Powers the very considerable undamaged naval forces still under its control. If the French Navy were to join the Axis, the control of West Africa would pass immediately into their hands with the gravest consequences to our communication between the northern and southern Atlantic, and also affect Dakar and of course thereafter South America.

10. A third sphere of danger is in the Far East. Here it seems clear that the Japanese are thrusting Southward through Indo China to Saigon and other naval and air bases, thus bringing them within a comparatively short distance of Singapore and the Dutch East Indies. It is reported that the Japanese are preparing five good divisions for possible use as an overseas expeditionary force. We have to-day no forces in the Far East capable of dealing with this situation should it develop.

11. In the face of these dangers, we must try to use the year 1941 to build up such a supply of weapons, particularly aircraft, both by increased output

at home in spite of bombardment, and through oceanborne supplies, as will lay the foundation of victory. In view of the difficulty and magnitude of this task, as outlined by all the facts I have set forth to which many others could be added, I feel entitled, nay bound, to lay before you the various ways in which the United States could give supreme and decisive help to what is, in certain aspects, the common cause.

12. The prime need is to check or limit the loss of tonnage on the Atlantic approaches to our Islands. This may be achieved both by increasing the naval forces which cope with attacks, and by adding to the number of merchant ships on which we depend. For the first purpose there would seem to be the following alternatives:

(1) the reassertion by the United States of the doctrine of the freedom of the seas from illegal and barbarous warfare in accordance with the decisions reached after the late Great War, and as freely accepted and defined by Germany in 1935. From this, the United States ships should be free to trade with countries against which there is not an effective legal blockade.

(2) It would, I suggest, follow that protection should be given to this lawful trading by United States forces i.e. escorting battleships, cruisers, destroyers and air flotillas. Protection would be immediately more effective if you were able to obtain bases in Eire for the duration of the war. I think it is improbable that such protection would provoke a declaration of war by Germany upon the United States though probably sea incidents of a dangerous character would from time to time occur. Hitler has shown himself inclined to avoid the Kaiser's mistake. He does not wish to be drawn into war with the United States until he has gravely undermined the power of Great Britain. His maxim is "one at a time." The policy I have ventured to outline, or something like it, would constitute a decisive act of constructive non-belligerency by the United States, and more than any other measure would make it certain that British resistance could be effectively prolonged for the desired period and victory gained.

(3) Failing the above, the gift, loan or supply of a large number of American vessels of war, above all destroyers already in the Atlantic, is indispensable to the maintenance of the Atlantic route. Further, could not United States naval forces extend their sea control over the American side of the Atlantic, so as to prevent molestation by enemy vessels of the approaches to the new line of naval and air bases which the United States is establishing in British islands in the Western Hemisphere. The strength of the United States naval forces is such that the assistance in the Atlantic that they could afford us, as described above, would not jeopardise control over the Pacific.

(4) We should also then need the good offices of the United States and the whole influence of its Government continually exerted, to procure for Great Britain the necessary facilities upon the southern and western shores of Eire for our flotillas, and still more important, for our aircraft, working westward into the Atlantic. If it were proclaimed an American interest that the resistance of Great Britain should be prolonged and the Atlantic route kept open

for the important armaments now being prepared for Great Britain in North America, the Irish in the United States might be willing to point out to the Government of Eire the dangers which its present policy is creating for the United States itself.

His Majesty's Government would of course take the most effective steps beforehand to protect Ireland if Irish action exposed it to a German attack. It is not possible for us to compel the people of Northern Ireland against their will to leave the United Kingdom and join Southern Ireland. But I do not doubt that if the Government of Eire would show its solidarity with the democracies of the English speaking world at this crisis a Council of Defence of all Ireland could be set up out of which the unity of the island would probably in some form or other emerge after the war.

13. The object of the foregoing measures is to reduce to manageable proportions the present destructive losses at sea. In addition it is indispensable that the merchant tonnage available for supplying Great Britain and for waging of the war by Great Britain with all vigour, should be substantially increased beyond the one and a quarter million tons per annum which is the utmost we can now build. The convoy system, the detours, the zig-zags, the great distances from which we now have to bring our imports, and the congestion of our western harbours, have reduced by about one third the value of our existing tonnage. To ensure final victory, not less than three million tons of additional merchant shipbuilding capacity will be required. Only the United States can supply this need. Looking to the future it would seem that production on a scale comparable with that of the Hog Island scheme of the last war ought to be faced for 1942. In the meanwhile, we ask that in 1941 the United States should make available to us every ton of merchant shipping, surplus to its own requirements, which it possesses or controls and should find some means of putting into our "hands" a large proportion of the merchant shipping now under construction for the National Maritime Board.

. . . .

16. I am arranging to present you with a complete programme of munitions of all kinds which we seek to obtain from you, the greater part of which is of course already agreed. An important economy of time and effort will be produced if the types selected for the United States Services should, whenever possible, conform to those which have proved their merit under actual conditions of war. In this way reserves of guns and ammunition and of aeroplanes become interchangeable and are by that very fact augmented. This is however a sphere so highly technical that I do not enlarge upon it.

17. Last of all I come to the question of finance. The more rapid and abundant the flow of munitions and ships which you are able to send us, the sooner will our dollar credits be exhausted. They are already as you know very heavily drawn upon by payments we have made to date. Indeed as you know orders already placed or under negotiation, including expenditures settled or pending for creating munitions factories in the United States,

many times exceed the total exchange resources remaining at the disposal of Great Britain. The moment approaches when we shall no longer be able to pay cash for shipping and other supplies. While we will do our utmost and shrink from no proper sacrifice to make payments across the exchange, I believe that you will agree that it would be wrong in principle and mutually disadvantageous in effect if, at the height of this struggle, Great Britain were to be divested of all saleable assets so that after victory was won with our blood, civilisation saved and time gained for the United States to be fully armed against all eventualities, we should stand stripped to the bone. Such a course would not be in the moral or economic interests of either of our countries. We here would be unable after the war to purchase the large balance of imports from the United States over and above the volume of our exports which is agreeable to your tariffs and domestic economy. Not only should we in Great Britain suffer cruel privations but widespread unemployment in the United States would follow the curtailment of American exporting power.

18.   Moreover I do not believe the Government and people of the United States would find it in accordance with the principles which guide them, to confine the help which they have so generously promised only to such munitions of war and commodities as could be immediately paid for. You may be assured that we shall prove ourselves ready to suffer and sacrifice to the utmost for the Cause, and that we glory in being its champion. The rest we leave with confidence to you and to your people, being sure that ways and means will be found which future generations on both sides of the Atlantic will approve and admire.

19.   If, as I believe, you are convinced, Mr. President, that the defeat of the Nazi and Fascist tyranny is a matter of high consequence to the people of the United States and to the Western Hemisphere, you will regard this letter not as an appeal for aid, but as a statement of the minimum action necessary to the achievement of our common purpose.

I remain,

Yours very sincerely,   Winston S. Churchill

54. Roosevelt Radio Address, Washington, December 29, 1940[2] (Excerpts)

This is not a fireside chat on war. It is a talk on national security; because the nub of the whole purpose of your President is to keep you now, and your children later, and your grandchildren much later, out of a last-ditch war for the preservation of American independence and all of the things that American independence means to you and to me and to ours.

Tonight, in the presence of a world crisis, my mind goes back eight years ago to a night in the midst of a domestic crisis. It was a time when the wheels of American industry were grinding to a full stop, when the whole banking system of our country had ceased to function.

I well remember that while I sat in my study in the White House, preparing to talk with the people of the United States, I had before my eyes the picture of all those Americans with whom I was talking. I saw the workmen in the mills, the mines, the factories; the girl behind the counter; the small shopkeeper; the farmer doing his spring plowing; the widows and the old men wondering about their life's savings.

I tried to convey to the great mass of American people what the banking crisis meant to them in their daily lives.

Tonight, I want to do the same thing, with the same people, in this new crisis which faces America.

We met the issue of 1933 with courage and realism.

We face this new crisis—this new threat to the security of our Nation—with the same courage and realism.

Never before since Jamestown and Plymouth Rock has our American civilization been in such danger as now.

For, on September 27, 1940, by an agreement signed in Berlin, three powerful nations, two in Europe and one in Asia, joined themselves together in the threat that if the United States interfered with or blocked the expansion program of these three nations—a program aimed at world control—they would unite in ultimate action against the United States.

The Nazi masters of Germany have made it clear that they intend not only to dominate all life and thought in their own country, but also to enslave the whole of Europe, and then to use the resources of Europe to dominate the rest of the world.

Three weeks ago their leader stated, "There are two worlds that stand opposed to each other." Then in defiant reply to his opponents, he said this: "Others are correct when they say: 'With this world we cannot ever reconcile ourselves.' . . . I can beat any other power in the world." So said the leader of the Nazis.

In other words, the Axis not merely admits but proclaims that there can be no ultimate peace between their philosophy of government and our philosophy of government.

In view of the nature of this undeniable threat, it can be asserted, properly and categorically, that the United States has no right or reason to encourage talk of peace until the day shall come when there is a clear intention on the part of the aggressor nations to abandon all thought of dominating or conquering the world.

At this moment, the forces of the states that are leagued against all peoples who live in freedom are being held away from our shores. The Germans and Italians are being blocked on the other side of the Atlantic by the British, and by the Greeks, and by thousands of soldiers and sailors who were able to escape from subjugated countries. The Japanese are being engaged in Asia by the Chinese in another great defense.

In the Pacific is our fleet.

Some of our people like to believe that wars in Europe and in Asia are of no concern to us. But it is a matter of most vital concern to us that European and Asiatic war-makers should not gain control of the oceans which lead to this hemisphere.

One hundred and seventeen years ago the Monroe Doctrine was conceived by our Government as a measure of defense in the face of a threat against this hemisphere by an alliance in continental Europe. Thereafter, we stood on guard in the Atlantic with the British as neighbors. There was no "unwritten agreement."

Yet, there was the feeling, proven correct by history, that we as neighbors could settle any disputes in peaceful fashion. The fact is that during the whole of this time the Western Hemisphere has remained free from aggression from Europe or from Asia.

Does anyone seriously believe that we need to fear attack while a free Britain remains our most powerful naval neighbor in the Atlantic? Does anyone seriously believe, on the other hand, that we could rest easy if the Axis powers were our neighbor there?

If Great Britain goes down, the Axis powers will control the continents of Europe, Asia, Africa, Australasia, and the high seas—and they will be in a position to bring enormous military and naval resources against this hemisphere. It is no exaggeration to say that all of us in the Americas would be living at the point of a gun—a gun loaded with explosive bullets, economic as well as military.

We should enter upon a new and terrible era in which the whole world, our hemisphere included, would be run by threats of brute force. To survive in such a world, we would have to convert ourselves permanently into a militaristic power on the basis of war economy.

Some of us like to believe that even if Great Britain falls, we are still safe, because of the broad expanse of the Atlantic and of the Pacific.

But the width of these oceans is not what it was in the days of clipper ships. At one point between Africa and Brazil the distance is less than from Washington to Denver—five hours for the latest type of bomber. And at the north of the Pacific Ocean, America and Asia almost touch each other.

Even today we have planes which could fly from the British Isles to New England and back without refueling. And the range of the modern bomber is ever being increased.

. . . .

There are those who say that the Axis powers would never have any desire to attack the Western Hemisphere. This is the same dangerous form of wishful thinking which has destroyed the powers of resistance of so many conquered peoples. The plain facts are the Nazis have proclaimed, time and again, that all other races are their inferiors and therefore subject to their orders. And most important of all, the vast resources and wealth of this hemisphere constitute the most tempting loot in all the world.

Let us no longer blind ourselves to the undeniable fact that the evil forces which have crushed and undermined and corrupted so many others are already within our own gates. Your Government knows much about them and every day is ferreting them out.

Their secret emissaries are active in our own and neighboring countries. They seek to stir up suspicion and dissension to cause internal strife. They try to turn capital against labor and vice versa. They try to reawaken long slumbering racial and religious enmities which should have no place in this country. They are active in every group that promotes intolerance. They exploit for their own ends our natural abhorrence of war. These trouble-breeders have but one purpose. It is to divide our people into hostile groups and to destroy our unity and shatter our will to defend ourselves.

There are also American citizens, many of them in high places, who, unwittingly in most cases, are aiding and abetting the work of these agents. I do not charge these American citizens with being foreign agents. But I do charge them with doing exactly the kind of work that the dictators want done in the United States.

These people not only believe that we can save our own skins by shutting our eyes to the fate of other nations. Some of them go much further than that. They say that we can and should become the friends and even the partners of the Axis powers. Some of them even suggest that we should imitate the methods of the dictatorships. Americans never can and never will do that.

. . . .

The American appeasers ignore the warning to be found in the fate of Austria, Czechoslovakia, Poland, Norway, Belgium, the Netherlands, Denmark, and France. They tell you that the Axis powers are going to win anyway; that all this bloodshed in the world could be saved; and that the United States might just as well throw its influence into the scale of a dictated peace, and get the best out of it that we can.

They call it a "negotiated peace." Nonsense! Is it a negotiated peace if a gang of outlaws surrounds your community and on threat of extermination makes you pay tribute to save your own skins?

Such a dictated peace would be no peace at all. It would be only another armistice, leading to the most gigantic armament race and the most devastating trade wars in history. And in these contests the Americas would offer the only real resistance to the Axis powers.

With all their vaunted efficiency and parade of pious purpose in this war, there are still in their background the concentration camp and the servants of God in chains.

The history of recent years proves that shootings and chains and concentration camps are not simply the transient tools but the very altars of modern dictatorships. They may talk of a "new order" in the world, but what they have in mind is but a revival of the oldest and the worst tyranny. In that there is no liberty, no religion, no hope.

The proposed "new order" is the very opposite of a United States of

Europe or a United States of Asia. It is not a government based upon the consent of the governed. It is not a union of ordinary, self-respecting men and women to protect themselves and their freedom and their dignity from oppression. It is an unholy alliance of power and pelf to dominate and enslave the human race.

The British people are conducting an active war against this unholy alliance. Our own future security is greatly dependent on the outcome of that fight. Our ability to "keep out of war" is going to be affected by that outcome.

Thinking in terms of today and tomorrow, I make the direct statement to the American people that there is far less chance of the United States getting into war if we do all we can now to support the nations defending themselves against attack by the Axis than if we acquiesce in their defeat, submit tamely to an Axis victory, and wait our turn to be the object of attack in another war later on.

If we are to be completely honest with ourselves, we must admit there is risk in *any* course we may take. But I deeply believe that the great majority of our people agree that the course that I advocate involves the least risk now and the greatest hope for world peace in the future.

The people of Europe who are defending themselves do not ask us to do their fighting. They ask us for the implements of war, the planes, the tanks, the guns, the freighters, which will enable them to fight for their liberty and our security. Emphatically we must get these weapons to them in sufficient volume and quickly enough, so that we and our children will be saved the agony and suffering of war which others have had to endure.

Let not defeatists tell us that it is too late. It will never be earlier. Tomorrow will be later than today.

Certain facts are self-evident.

In a military sense Great Britain and the British Empire are today the spearhead of resistance to world conquest. They are putting up a fight which will live forever in the story of human gallantry.

There is no demand for sending an American Expeditionary Force outside our own borders. There is no intention by any member of your Government to send such a force. You can, therefore, nail any talk about sending armies to Europe as deliberate untruth.

Our national policy is not directed toward war. Its sole purpose is to keep war away from our country and our people.

Democracy's fight against world conquest is being greatly aided, and must be more greatly aided, by the rearmament of the United States and by sending every ounce and every ton of munitions and supplies that we can possibly spare to help the defenders who are in the front lines. It is no more unneutral for us to do that than it is for Sweden, Russia, and other nations near Germany to send steel and ore and oil and other war materials into Germany every day.

We are planning our own defense with the utmost urgency; and in its vast scale we must integrate the war needs of Britain and the other free nations resisting aggression.

This is not a matter of sentiment or of controversial personal opinion. It is a matter of realistic military policy, based on the advice of our military experts who are in close touch with existing warfare. These military and naval experts and the members of the Congress and the administration have a single-minded purpose—the defense of the United States.

This Nation is making a great effort to produce everything that is necessary in this emergency—and with all possible speed. This great effort requires great sacrifice.

. . . .

As planes and ships and guns and shells are produced, your Government, with its defense experts, can then determine how best to use them to defend this hemisphere. The decision as to how much shall be sent abroad and how much shall remain at home must be made on the basis of our over-all military necessities.

We must be the great arsenal of democracy. For us this is an emergency as serious as war itself. We must apply ourselves to our task with the same resolution, the same sense of urgency, the same spirit of patriotism and sacrifice, as we would show were we at war.

We have furnished the British great material support and we will furnish far more in the future.

There will be "bottlenecks" in our determination to aid Great Britain. No dictator, no combination of dictators, will weaken that determination by threats of how they will construe that determination.

The British have received invaluable military support from the heroic Greek Army and from the forces of all the governments in exile. Their strength is growing. It is the strength of men and women who value their freedom more highly than they value their lives.

I believe that the Axis powers are not going to win this war. I base that belief on the latest and best information.

We have no excuse for defeatism. We have every good reason for hope—hope for peace, hope for the defense of our civilization and for the building of a better civilization in the future.

I have the profound conviction that the American people are now determined to put forth a mightier effort than they have ever yet made to increase our production of all the implements of defense, to meet the threat to our democratic faith.

As President of the United States I call for that national effort. I call for it in the name of this Nation which we love and honor and which we are privileged and proud to serve. I call upon our people with absolute confidence that our common cause will greatly succeed.

55. LEND-LEASE ACT (PUBLIC LAW 11), MARCH 11, 1941[3]

AN ACT

Further to promote the defense of the United States, and for other purposes.

Be it enacted by the Senate and House of Representatives of the United States of America in Congress assembled, That this Act may be cited as "An Act to Promote the Defense of the United States."

Sec. 2. As used in this Act—

(a) The term "defense article" means—

(1) Any weapon, munition, aircraft, vessel, or boat;

(2) Any machinery, facility, tool, material, or supply necessary for the manufacture, production, processing, repair, servicing, or operation of any article described in this subsection;

(3) Any component material or part of or equipment for any article described in this subsection:

(4) Any agricultural, industrial or other commodity or article for defense.

Such term "defense article" includes any article described in this subsection: Manufactured or procured pursuant to section 3, or to which the United States or any foreign government has or hereafter acquires title, possession, or control.

(b) The term "defense information" means any plan, specification, design, prototype, or information pertaining to any defense article.

Sec. 3 (a) Notwithstanding the provisions of any other law, the President may, from time to time, when he deems it in the interest of national defense, authorize the Secretary of War, the Secretary of the Navy, or the head of any other department or agency of the Government—

(1) To manufacture in arsenals, factories, and shipyards under their jurisdiction, or otherwise procure, to the extent to which funds are made available therefor, or contracts are authorized from time to time by the Congress, or both, any defense article for the government of any country whose defense the President deems vital to the defense of the United States.

(2) To sell, transfer title to, exchange, lease, lend, or otherwise dispose of, to any such government any defense article, but no defense article not manufactured or procured under paragraph (1) shall in any way be disposed of under this paragraph, except after consultation with the Chief of Staff of the Army or the Chief of Naval Operations of the Navy, or both. The value of defense articles disposed of in any way under authority of this paragraph, and procured from funds heretofore appropriated, shall not exceed $1,300,000,000. The value of such defense articles shall be determined by the head of the department or agency concerned or such other department, agency or officer as shall be designated in the manner provided in the rules and regulations issued hereunder. Defense articles procured from funds

hereafter appropriated to any department or agency of the Government, other than from funds authorized to be appropriated under this Act, shall not be disposed of in any way under authority of this paragraph except to the extent hereafter authorized by the Congress in the Acts appropriating such funds or otherwise.

(3) To test, inspect, prove, repair, outfit, recondition, or otherwise to place in good working order, to the extent to which funds are made available therefor, or contracts are authorized from time to time by the Congress, or both, any defense article for any such government, or to procure any or all such services by private contract.

(4) To communicate to any such government any defense information, pertaining to any defense article furnished to such government under paragraph (2) of this subsection.

(5) To release for export any defense article disposed of in any way under this subsection to any such government.

(b) The terms and conditions upon which any such foreign government receives any aid authorized under subsection (a) shall be those which the President deems satisfactory, and the benefit to the United States may be payment or repayment in kind or property, or any other direct or indirect benefit which the President deems satisfactory.

(c) After June 30, 1943, or after the passage of a concurrent resolution by the two Houses before June 30, 1943, which declares that the powers conferred by or pursuant to subsection (a) are no longer necessary to promote the defense of the United States, neither the President nor the head of any department or agency shall exercise any of the powers conferred by or pursuant to subsection (a); except that until July 1, 1946, any of such powers may be exercised to the extent necessary to carry out a contract or agreement with such a foreign government made before July 1, 1943, or before the passage of such concurrent resolution, whichever is the earlier.

(d) Nothing in this Act shall be construed to authorize or to permit the authorization of convoying vessels by naval vessels of the United States.

(e) Nothing in this Act shall be construed to authorize or to permit the authorization of the entry of any American vessel into a combat area in violation of section 3 of the Neutrality Act of 1939.

Sec. 4. All contracts or agreements made for the disposition of any defense article or defense information pursuant to section 3 shall contain a clause by which the foreign government undertakes that it will not, without the consent of the President, transfer title to or possession of such defense article or defense information by gift, sale, or otherwise, or permit its use by anyone not an officer, employee, or agent of such foreign government.

Sec. 5. (a) The Secretary of War, the Secretary of the Navy, or the head of any other department or agency of the Government involved shall, when any such defense article or defense information is exported, immediately inform the department or agency designated by the President to administer section 6 of the Act of July 2, 1940 (54 Stat. 714), of the quantities, character, value, terms of disposition, and destination of the article and information so exported.

(b) The President from time to time, but not less frequently than once every ninety days, shall transmit to the Congress a report of operations under this Act except such information as he deems incompatible with the public interest to disclose. Reports provided for under this subsection shall be transmitted to the Secretary of the Senate or the Clerk of the House of Representatives, as the case may be, if the Senate or the House of Representatives, as the case may be, is not in session.

Sec. 6. (a) There is hereby authorized to be appropriated from time to time, out of any money in the Treasury not otherwise appropriated, such amounts as may be necessary to carry out the provisions and accomplish the purposes of this Act.

(b) All money and all property which is converted into money received under section 3 from any government shall, with the approval of the Director of the Budget, revert to the respective appropriation or appropriations out of which funds were expended with respect to the defense article or defense information for which such consideration is received, and shall be available for expenditure for the purpose for which such expended funds were appropriated by law, during the fiscal year in which such funds are received and the ensuing fiscal year; but in no event shall any funds so received be available for expenditure after June 30, 1946.

Sec. 7. The Secretary of War, the Secretary of the Navy, and the head of the department or agency shall in all contracts or agreements for the disposition of any defense article or defense information fully protect the rights of all citizens of the United States who have patent rights in and to any such article or information which is hereby authorized to be disposed of and the payments collected for royalties on such patents shall be paid to the owners and holders of such patents.

Sec. 8. The Secretaries of War and of the Navy are hereby authorized to purchase or otherwise acquire arms, ammunition, and implements of war produced within the jurisdiction of any country to which section 3 is applicable, whenever the President deems such purchase or acquisition to be necessary in the interests of the defense of the United States.

Sec. 9. The President may, from time to time, promulgate such rules and regulations as may be necessary and proper to carry out any of the provisions of this Act; and he may exercise any power or authority conferred on him by this Act through such department, agency, or officer as he shall direct.

Sec. 10. Nothing in this Act shall be construed to change existing law relating to the use of the land and naval forces of the United States, except insofar as such use relates to the manufacture, procurement, and repair of defense articles, the communication of information and other noncombatant purposes enumerated in this Act.

Sec. 11. If any provision of this Act or the application of such provision to any circumstance shall be held invalid, the validity of the remainder of the

Act and the applicability of such provision to other circumstances shall not be affected thereby.

Approved, March 11, 1941.

56. ABC–1 (UNITED STATES-BRITISH STAFF CONVERSATIONS), MARCH 27, 1941[4] (EXCERPTS)

GENERAL

1. Staff Conversations were held in Washington from January 29, 1941 to March 27, 1941, between a United States Staff Committee representing the Chief of Naval Operations and the Chief of Staff of the Army, and a United Kingdom Delegation representing the Chiefs of Staff. Representatives of the Chiefs of Staff of the Dominions of Canada, Australia, and New Zealand were associated with the United Kingdom Delegation throughout the course of these conversations, but were not present at joint meetings.

2. The personnel of the United States Staff Committee and of the United Kingdom Delegation comprise the following:

United States Representatives:	British Representatives:
Major-General S. D. Embick	Rear-Admiral R. M. Bellairs
Brigadier-General Sherman Miles	Rear-Admiral V. H. Danckwerts
Brigadier-General L. T. Gerow	Major-General E. L. Morris
Colonel J. T. McNarney	Air Vice-Marshal J. C. Slessor
Rear-Admiral R. L. Ghormley	Captain A. W. Clarke
Rear-Admiral R. K. Turner	
Captain A. G. Kirk	
Captain DeWitt C. Ramsey	
Lt.-Colonel O. T. Pfeiffer	

Secretariat:
Lt.-Colonel W. P. Scobey
Commander L. R. McDowell
Lt.-Colonel A. T. Cornwall-Jones

3. The purposes of the Staff Conference, as set out in the instructions to the two representative bodies, were as follows:

(a) To determine the best methods by which the armed forces of the United States and British Commonwealth, with its present Allies, could defeat Germany and the Powers allied with her, should the United States be compelled to resort to war.

(b) To coordinate, on broad lines, plans for the employment of the forces of the Associated Powers.

(c) To reach agreements concerning the methods and nature of Military Cooperation between the two nations, including the allocation of the principal areas of responsibility, the major lines of the Military strategy to be pursued by both nations, the strength of the forces which each may be able to commit, and the determination of satisfactory command arrangements, both as to supreme Military control, and as to unity of field command in cases of strategic or tactical joint operations.

4. The Staff Conference, interpreting the foregoing instructions in the light of the respective national positions of the two Powers, has reached agreements, as set forth in this and annexed documents, concerning Military Cooperation between the United States and the British Commonwealth and its present Allies should the United States associate itself with them in war against Germany and her Allies.

. . . .

6. The High Command of the United States and United Kingdom will collaborate continuously in the formulation and execution of strategical policies and plans which shall govern the conduct of the war. They and their respective commanders in the field, as may be appropriate, will similarly collaborate in the planning and execution of such operations as may be undertaken jointly by United States and British forces. This arrangement will apply also to such plans and operations as may be undertaken separately, the extent of collaboration required in each particular plan or operation being agreed mutually when the general policy has been decided.

7. The term "Associated Powers" used herein is to be taken as meaning the United States and British Commonwealth, and, when appropriate, includes the Associates and Allies of either Power.

8. The Staff Conference assumes that when the United States becomes involved in war with Germany, it will at the same time engage in war with Italy. In these circumstances, the possibility of a state of war arising between Japan and an Association of the United States, the British Commonwealth and its Allies, including the Netherlands East Indies, must be taken into account.

9. The Conference assumes that the United States will continue to furnish material aid to the United Kingdom, but, for the use of itself and its other associates, will retain material in such quantities as to provide for security and best to effectuate United States-British joint plans for defeating Germany and her Allies. It is recognized that the amount and nature of the material aid which the United States affords the British Commonwealth will influence the size and character of the Military forces which will be available to the United States for use in the war.

10. The broad strategic objective (object) of the Associated Powers will be the defeat of Germany and her Allies.

11. The principles of United States and British national strategic defense policies of which the Military forces of the Associated Powers must take account are:

(a) *United States.*

The paramount territorial interests of the United States are in the Western Hemisphere. The United States must, in all eventualities, maintain such dispositions as will prevent the extension in the Western Hemisphere of European or Asiatic political or Military power.

(b) *British Commonwealth.*

The security of the United Kingdom must be maintained in all circumstances. Similarly, the United Kingdom, the Dominions, and India must maintain dispositions which, in all eventualities, will provide for the ultimate security of the British Commonwealth of Nations. A cardinal feature of British strategic policy is the retention of a position in the Far East such as will ensure the cohesion and security of the British Commonwealth and the maintenance of its war effort.

(c) *Sea Communications.*

The security of the sea communications of the Associated Powers is essential to the continuance of their war effort.

12. The strategic concept includes the following as the principal offensive policies against the Axis Powers:

(a) Application of economic pressure by naval, land, and air forces and all other means, including the control of commodities at their source by diplomatic and financial measures.

(b) A sustained air offensive against German Military power, supplemented by air offensives against other regions under enemy control which contribute to that power.

(c) The early elimination of Italy as an active partner in the Axis.

(d) The employment of the air, land, and naval forces of the Associated Powers, at every opportunity, in raids and minor offensives against Axis Military strength.

(e) The support of neutrals, and of Allies of the United Kingdom, Associates of the United States, and populations in Axis-occupied territory in resistance to the Axis Powers.

(f) The building up of the necessary forces for an eventual offensive against Germany.

(g) The capture of positions from which to launch the eventual offensive.

13. Plans for the Military operations of the Associated Powers will likewise be governed by the following:

(a) Since Germany is the predominant member of the Axis Powers, the Atlantic and European area is considered to be the decisive theatre. The principal United States Military effort will be exerted in that theatre, and operations of United States forces in other theatres will be conducted in such a manner as to facilitate that effort.

(b) Owing to the threat to the sea communications of the United Kingdom, the principal task of the United States naval forces in the Atlantic will be the protection of shipping of the Associated Powers, the center of gravity of the United States effort being concentrated in the Northwestern Approaches to the United Kingdom. Under this conception, the United States naval effort in the Mediterranean will initially be considered of secondary importance.

(c) It will be of great importance to maintain the present British and

Allied Military position in and near the Mediterranean basins, and to prevent the spread of Axis control in North Africa.

(d) Even if Japan were not initially to enter the war on the side of the Axis Powers, it would still be necessary for the Associated Powers to deploy their forces in a manner to guard against eventual Japanese intervention. If Japan does enter the war, the Military strategy in the Far East will be defensive. The United States does not intend to add to its present Military strength in the Far East but will employ the United States Pacific Fleet offensively in the manner best calculated to weaken Japanese economic power, and to support the defense of the Malay barrier by diverting Japanese strength away from Malaysia. The United States intends so to augment its forces in the Atlantic and Mediterranean areas that the British commonwealth will be in a position to release the necessary forces for the Far East.

(e) The details of the deployment of the forces of the Associated Powers at any one time will be decided with regard to the Military situation in all theatres.

(f) The principal defensive roles of the land forces of the Associated Powers will be to hold the British Isles against invasion; to defend the Western Hemisphere; and to protect outlying Military base areas and islands of strategic importance against land, air, or sea-borne attack.

(g) United States' land forces will support United States' naval and air forces maintaining the security of the Western Hemisphere or operating in the areas bordering on the Atlantic. Subject to the availability of trained and equipped organizations, United States' land forces will, as a general rule, provide ground and anti-aircraft defenses of naval and air bases used primarily by United States' forces.

(h) Subject to the requirements of the security of the United States, the British Isles and their sea communications, the air policy of the Associated Powers will be directed towards achieving, as quickly as possible, superiority of air strength over that of the enemy, particularly in long-range striking forces.

(i) United States Army Air Forces will support the United States land and naval forces maintaining the security of the Western Hemisphere or operating in the areas bordering on the Atlantic. Subject to the availability of trained and equipped organizations, they will undertake the air defense of those general areas in which naval bases used primarily by United States forces are located, and subsequently, of such other areas as may be agreed upon. United States Army air bombardment units will operate offensively in collaboration with the Royal Air Force, primarily against German Military power at its source.

(j) United States forces will, so far as practicable, draw their logistic support (supply and maintenance) from sources outside the British Isles. Subject to this principle, however, the military bases, repair facilities, and supplies of either nation will be at the disposal of the Military forces of the other as required for the successful prosecution of the war.

57. ROOSEVELT ADDRESS, WASHINGTON, MARCH 15, 1941[5] (EXCERPTS)

This dinner of the White House Correspondents' Association is unique. It is the first one at which I have made a speech in all these eight years. It differs from the press conferences that you and I hold twice a week. You cannot ask me any questions; and everything I have to say is word for word *"on the record."*

For eight years you and I have been helping each other. I have been trying to keep you informed of the news of Washington and of the Nation and of the world from the point of view of the Presidency. You, more than you realize it, have been giving me a great deal of information about what the people of this country are thinking.

In our press conferences, as at this dinner tonight, we include reporters representing papers and news agencies of many other lands. To most of them it is a matter of constant amazement that press conferences such as ours can exist in any nation in the world.

That is especially true in those lands where freedoms do not exist—where the purposes of our democracy and the characteristics of our country and of our people have been seriously distorted.

Such misunderstandings are not new. I remember that in the early days of the first World War the German Government received solemn assurances from their representatives in the United States that the people of America were disunited; that they cared more for peace at any price than for the preservation of ideals and freedom; that there would even be riots and revolutions in the United States if this Nation ever asserted its own interests.

Let not dictators of Europe and Asia doubt our unanimity now.

Before the present war broke out on September 1, 1939, I was more worried about the future than many people—most people. The record shows I was not worried enough.

That, however, is water over the dam. Do not let us waste time reviewing the past or fixing or dodging the blame for it. History cannot be rewritten by wishful thinking. We, the American people, are writing new history today.

The big news story of this week is this: The world has been told that we, as a united nation, realize the danger which confronts us—and that to meet that danger our democracy has gone into action.

We know that although Prussian autocracy was bad enough, Naziism is far worse.

Nazi forces are not seeking mere modifications in colonial maps or in minor European boundaries. They openly seek the destruction of all elective systems of government on every continent—including our own; they seek to establish systems of government based on the regimentation of all human beings by a handful of individual rulers who have seized power by force.

These men and their hypnotized followers call this a new order. It is not new. It is not order. For order among nations presupposes something enduring—some system of justice under which individuals, over a long period of time, are willing to live. Humanity will never permanently accept a system imposed by conquest and based on slavery.

. . . .

The decisions of our democracy may be slowly arrived at. But when that decision is made, it is proclaimed not with the voice of any one man but with the voice of 130 millions. It is binding on all of us. And the world is no longer left in doubt.

This decision is the end of any attempts at appeasement in our land; the end of urging us to get along with dictators; the end of compromise with tyranny and the forces of oppression.

The urgency is *now.*

We believe firmly that when our production output is in full swing, the democracies of the world will be able to prove that dictatorships cannot win.

But, now, the time element is of supreme importance. Every plane, every other instrument of war, old and new, which we can spare now, we will send overseas. That is commonsense strategy.

The great task of this day, the deep duty which rests upon us is to move products from the assembly lines of our factories to the battle lines of democracy—Now!

We can have speed and effectiveness if we maintain our existing unity. We do not have and never will have the false unity of a people browbeaten by threats and misled by propaganda. Ours is a unity which is possible only among free men and women who recognize the truth and face reality with intelligence and courage.

Today, at last, ours is not a partial effort. It is a total effort and that is the only way to guarantee ultimate safety.

Beginning a year ago, we started the erection of hundreds of plants and we started the training of millions of men.

Then, at the moment the aid-to-democracies bill was passed we were ready to recommend the seven-billion-dollar appropriation on the basis of capacity production as now planned.

The articles themselves cover the whole range of munitions of war and of the facilities for transporting them.

The aid-to-democracies bill was agreed to by both Houses of the Congress last Tuesday afternoon. I signed it one half hour later. Five minutes later I approved a list of articles for immediate shipment. Many of them are on their way. On Wednesday, I recommended an appropriation for new material to the extent of seven billion dollars; and the Congress is making patriotic speed in making the appropriation available.

Here in Washington, we are thinking in terms of speed, and speed now.

And I hope that that watchword will find its way into every home in the Nation.

We shall have to make sacrifices—every one of us. The final extent of those sacrifices will depend upon the speed with which we act Now!

I must tell you tonight in plain language what this undertaking means to you—to your daily life.

Whether you are in the armed services; whether you are a steel worker or a stevedore; a machinist or a housewife; a farmer or a banker; a storekeeper or a manufacturer—to all of you it will mean sacrifice in behalf of country and your liberties. You will feel the impact of this gigantic effort in your daily lives. You will feel it in a way which will cause many inconveniences.

You will have to be content with lower profits from business because obviously your taxes will be higher.

You will have to work longer at your bench or your plow or your machine.

Let me make it clear that the Nation is calling for the sacrifice of some privileges but not for the sacrifice of fundamental rights. Most of us will do that willingly. That kind of sacrifice is for the common national protection and welfare; for our defense against the most ruthless brutality in history; for the ultimate victory of a way of life now so violently menaced.

A half-hearted effort on our part will lead to failure. This is no part-time job. The concepts of "business as usual" and "normalcy" must be forgotten until the task is finished. This is an all-out effort—nothing short of all-out effort will win.

We are now dedicated, from here on, to a constantly increasing tempo of production—a production greater than we now know or have ever known before—a production that does not stop and should not pause.

And so, tonight, I am appealing to the heart and to the mind of every man and every woman within our borders who loves liberty. I ask you to consider the needs of our Nation at this hour and to put aside all personal differences until our victory is won.

The light of democracy must be kept burning. To the perpetuation of this light, each must do his own share. The single effort of one individual may seem very small. But there are 130 million individuals over here. There are many more millions in Britain and elsewhere bravely shielding the great flame of democracy from the blackout of barbarism. It is not enough for us merely to trim the wick or polish the glass. The time has come when we must provide the fuel in ever-increasing amounts to keep the flame alight.

There will be no divisions of party or section or race or nationality or religion. There is not one among us who does not have a stake in the outcome of the effort in which we are now engaged.

A few weeks ago I spoke of four freedoms—freedom of speech and expression, freedom of every person to worship God in his own way, freedom from want, freedom from fear. They are the ultimate stake. They may not be immediately attainable throughout the world but humanity does move toward those ideals through democratic processes. If we fail—if democracy is superseded by slavery—then those four freedoms or even the mention of them will become forbidden things. Centuries will pass before they can be revived.

. . . .

In this historic crisis, Britain is blessed with a brilliant and great leader in Winston Churchill. But, no one knows better than Mr. Churchill himself, that it is not alone his stirring words and valiant deeds which give the British their superb morale. The essence of that morale is in the masses of plain people who are completely clear in their minds about the one essential fact—that they would rather die as free men than live as slaves.

These plain people—civilians as well as soldiers and sailors and airmen—women and girls as well as men and boys—are fighting in the front line of civilization, and they are holding that line with a fortitude which will forever be the pride and the inspiration of all free men on every continent and on every island of the sea.

The British people . . . need ships. From America, they will get ships.

They need planes. From America, they will get planes.

They need food. From America, they will get food.

They need tanks and guns and ammunition and supplies of all kinds. From America, they will get tanks and guns and ammunition and supplies of all kinds.

China likewise expresses the magnificent will of millions of plain people to resist the dismemberment of their Nation. China, through the Generalissimo, Chiang Kai-shek, asks our help. America has said that China shall have our help.

Our country is going to be what our people have proclaimed it must be—the arsenal of democracy.

Our country is going to play its full part.

And when dictatorships disintegrate—and pray God that will be sooner than any of us now dares to hope—then our country must continue to play its great part in the period of world reconstruction.

We believe that the rallying cry of the dictators, their boasting about a master-race, will prove to be pure stuff and nonsense. There never has been, there isn't now, and there never will be, any race of people fit to serve as masters over their fellow men.

The world has no use for any nation which, because of size or because of military might, asserts the right to goose-step to world power over other races. We believe that any nationality, no matter how small, has the inherent right to its own nationhood.

We believe that the men and women of such nations, no matter what size, can, through the processes of peace, serve themselves and serve the world by protecting the common man's security; improve the standards of healthful living; provide markets for manufacture and for agriculture. Through that kind of peaceful service every nation can increase its happiness, banish the terrors of war, and abandon man's inhumanity to man.

Never, in all our history, have Americans faced a job so well worthwhile. May it be said of us in the days to come that our children and our children's children rise up and call us blessed.

58. AGREEMENT RELATING TO DEFENSE OF GREENLAND, APRIL 10, 1941[6]

The Department of State announced April 10 the signing on April 9, 1941 of an agreement between the Secretary of State, acting on behalf of the Government of the United States of America, and the Danish Minister, Henrik de Kauffmann, acting on behalf of His Majesty the King of Denmark in his capacity as sovereign of Greenland.

The agreement recognizes that as a result of the present European war there is danger that Greenland may be converted into a point of aggression against nations of the American Continent, and accepts the responsibility on behalf of the United States of assisting Greenland in the maintenance of its present status.

The agreement, after explicitly recognizing the Danish sovereignty over Greenland, proceeds to grant to the United States the right to locate and construct airplane landing fields and facilities for the defense of Greenland and for the defense of the American Continent.

The circumstances leading up to the agreement are as follows.

On April 9, 1940 the German Army invaded and occupied Denmark, and that occupation continues. In condemning this invasion President Roosevelt said:

> "Force and military aggression are once more on the march against small nations, in this instance through the invasion of Denmark and Norway. These two nations have won and maintained during a period of many generations the respect and regard not only of the American people, but of all peoples, because of their observance of the highest standards of national and international conduct.
>
> "The Government of the United States has on the occasion of recent invasions strongly expressed its disapprobation of such unlawful exercise of force. It here reiterates, with undiminished emphasis, its point of view as expressed on those occasions. If civilization is to survive, the rights of the smaller nations to independence, to their territorial integrity, and to the unimpeded opportunity for self-government must be respected by their more powerful neighbors."

This invasion at once raised questions as to the status of Greenland, which has been recognized as being within the area of the Monroe Doctrine. The Government of the United States announces its policy of maintenance of the *status quo* in the Western Hemisphere.

On May 3, 1940 the Greenland Councils, meeting at Godhavn, adopted a resolution in the name of the people of Greenland reaffirming their allegiance to King Christian X of Denmark, and expressed the hope that so long as Greenland remained cut off from the mother country, the Government of the United States would continue to keep in mind the exposed position of the Danish flag in Greenland and of the native and Danish population of Greenland. The Government of the United States expressed its willingness to assure that the needs of the population of Greenland would be taken care of.

On JULY 25, 1940, the consultation of American Foreign Ministers at Habana declared that any attempt on the part of a non-American state against the integrity or inviolability of the territory, the sovereignty, or the political independence of an American state should be considered an act of aggression, and that they would cooperate in defense against any such aggression. In a further declaration, known as the Act of Habana, it declared that the status of regions in this continent belonging to European powers was a subject of deep concern to all of the governments of the American republics.

During the summer of 1940 German activity on the eastern coast of Greenland became apparent. Three ships proceeding from Norwegian territory under German occupation arrived off the coast of Greenland, ostensibly for commercial or scientific purposes; and at least one of these ships landed parties nominally for scientific purposes, but actually for meteorological assistance to German belligerent operations in the north Atlantic. These parties were eventually cleared out. In the late fall of 1940, air reconnaissance appeared over East Greenland under circumstances making it plain that there had been continued activity in that region.

On March 27, 1941, a German bomber flew over the eastern coast of Greenland and on the following day another German war plane likewise reconnoitered the same territory. Under these circumstances it appeared that further steps for the defense of Greenland were necessary to bring Greenland within the system of hemispheric defense envisaged by the Act of Habana.

The Government of the United States has no thought in mind save that of assuring the safety of Greenland and the rest of the American Continent, and Greenland's continuance under Danish sovereignty. The agreement recognizes explicitly the full Danish sovereignty over Greenland. At the same time it is recognized that so long as Denmark remains under German occupation the Government in Denmark cannot exercise the Danish sovereign powers over Greenland under the Monroe Doctrine, and the agreement therefore was signed between the Secretary of State and the Danish Minister in Washington, acting as representative of the King of Denmark in his capacity as sovereign of Greenland, and with the concurrence of the Governors of Greenland.

The step is taken in furtherance of the traditional friendliness between Denmark and the United States. The policy of the United States is that of defending for Denmark her sovereignty over Greenland, so that she may have a full exercise of it as soon as the invasion is ended. The agreement accordingly provides that as soon as the war is over and the danger has passed, the two Governments shall promptly consult as to whether the arrangements made by the present agreement shall continue or whether they shall then cease.

59. U.S. Exchange of Defense Articles with Canada, April 20, 1941[7]

At the conclusion of a conference between President Roosevelt and Prime Minister Mackenzie King of Canada on April 20, 1941, the following statement was issued:

"Among other important matters, the President and the Prime Minister discussed measures by which the most prompt and effective utilization might be made of the productive facilities of North America for the purposes both of local and hemisphere defense and of the assistance which in addition to their own programs both Canada and the United States are rendering to Great Britain and the other democracies.

"It was agreed as a general principle that in mobilizing the resources of this continent each country should provide the other with the defense articles which it is best able to produce, and, above all, produce quickly, and that production programs should be coordinated to this end.

"While Canada has expanded its productive capacity manyfold since the beginning of the war, there are still numerous defense articles which it must obtain in the United States, and purchases of this character by Canada will be even greater in the coming year than in the past. On the other hand, there is an existing and potential capacity in Canada for the speedy production of certain kinds of munitions, strategic materials, aluminum, and ships, which are urgently required by the United States for its own purposes.

"While exact estimates cannot yet be made, it is hoped that during the next 12 months Canada can supply the United States with between $200,000,000 and $300,000,000 worth of such defense articles. This sum is a small fraction of the total defense program of the United States, but many of the articles to be provided are of vital importance. In addition, it is of great importance to the economic and financial relations between the two countries that payment by the United States for these supplies will materially assist Canada in meeting part of the cost of Canadian defense purchases in the United States.

"Insofar as Canada's defense purchases in the United States consist of component parts to be used in equipment and munitions which Canada is producing for Great Britain, it was also agreed that Great Britain will obtain these parts under the Lease-Lend Act and forward them to Canada for inclusion in the finished article.

"The technical and financial details will be worked out as soon as possible in accordance with the general principles which have been agreed upon between the President and the Prime Minister."

60. U.S. Proclamation of Unlimited National Emergency, May 27, 1941[8]

Proclaiming That an Unlimited National Emergency Confronts This Country, Which

Requires That Its Military, Naval, Air and Civilian Defenses Be Put on the Basis of Readiness to Repel Any and All Acts or Threats of Aggression Directed Toward Any Part of the Western Hemisphere
BY THE PRESIDENT OF THE UNITED STATES OF AMERICA

A Proclamation

Whereas on September 8, 1939 because of the outbreak of war in Europe a proclamation was issued declaring a limited national emergency and directing measures "for the purpose of strengthening our national defense within the limits of peacetime authorizations,"

Whereas a succession of events makes plain that the objectives of the Axis belligerents in such war are not confined to those avowed at its commencement, but include overthrow throughout the world of existing democratic order, and a worldwide domination of peoples and economies through the destruction of all resistance on land and sea and in the air, and

Whereas indifference on the part of the United States to the increasing menace would be perilous, and common prudence requires that for the security of this nation and of this hemisphere we should pass from peacetime authorizations of military strength to such a basis as will enable us to cope instantly and decisively with any attempt at hostile encirclement of this hemisphere, or the establishment of any base for aggression against it, as well as to repel the threat of predatory incursion by foreign agents into our territory and society,

Now, therefore, I, Franklin D. Roosevelt, President of the United States of America, do proclaim that an unlimited national emergency confronts this country, which requires that its military, naval, air and civilian defenses be put on the basis of readiness to repel any and all acts or threats of aggression directed toward any part of the Western Hemisphere.

I call upon all the loyal citizens engaged in production for defense to give precedence to the needs of the nation to the end that a system of government that makes private enterprise possible may survive.

I call upon all our loyal workmen as well as employers to merge their lesser differences in the larger effort to insure the survival of the only kind of government which recognizes the rights of labor or of capital.

I call upon loyal state and local leaders and officials to cooperate with the civilian defense agencies of the United States to assure our internal security against foreign directed subversion and to put every community in order for maximum productive effort and minimum waste and unnecessary frictions.

I call upon all loyal citizens to place the nation's needs first in mind and in action to the end that we may mobilize and have ready for instant defensive use all of the physical powers, all of the moral strength and all of the material resources of this nation.

In witness whereof I have hereunto set my hand and caused the seal of the United States of America to be affixed.

Done at the City of Washington this twenty-seventh day of May, in the year of [SEAL] our Lord nineteen hundred and forty-one, and of the Independence of the United States of America the one hundred and sixty-fifth.

By the President: Franklin D. Roosevelt
  Cordell Hull
    Secretary of State

61. U.S. DEFENSE OF ICELAND, JULY 7, 1941[9]

The text of a message from the President to the Congress, dated July 7, 1941, transmitting a message received from the Prime Minister of Iceland and the reply of the President of the United States, relating to use of United States forces in Iceland, follows:

To the Congress of the United States:

I am transmitting herewith for the information of the Congress a message I received from the Prime Minister of Iceland on July first and the reply I addressed on the same day to the Prime Minister of Iceland in response to this message.

In accordance with the understanding so reached, forces of the United States Navy have today arrived in Iceland in order to supplement, and eventually to replace, the British forces which have until now been stationed in Iceland in order to insure the adequate defense of that country.

As I stated in my message to the Congress of September third last regarding the acquisition of certain naval and air bases from Great Britain in exchange for certain over-age destroyers, considerations of safety from overseas attack are fundamental.

The United States cannot permit the occupation by Germany of strategic outposts in the Atlantic to be used as air or naval bases for eventual attack against the Western Hemisphere. We have no desire to see any change in the present sovereignty of those regions. Assurance that such outposts in our defense-frontier remain in friendly hands is the very foundation of our national security and of the national security of every one of the independent nations of the New World.

For the same reason substantial forces of the United States have now been sent to the bases acquired last year from Great Britain in Trinidad and in British Guiana in the south in order to forestall any pincers movement undertaken by Germany against the Western Hemisphere. It is essential that Germany should not be able successfully to employ such tactics through sudden seizures of strategic points in the south Atlantic and in the north Atlantic.

The occupation of Iceland by Germany would constitute a serious threat in three dimensions:

The threat against Greenland and the northern portion of the North American Continent, including the Islands which lie off it.

The threat against all shipping in the north Atlantic.

The threat against the steady flow of munitions to Britain—which is a matter of broad policy clearly approved by the Congress.

It is, therefore, imperative that the approaches between the Americas and those strategic outposts, the safety of which this country regards as essential to its national security, and which it must therefore defend, shall remain open and free from all hostile activity or threat thereof.

As Commander-in-Chief I have consequently issued orders to the Navy that all necessary steps be taken to insure the safety of communications in the approaches between Iceland and the United States, as well as on the seas between the United States and all other strategic outposts.

This Government will insure the adequate defense of Iceland with full recognition of the independence of Iceland as a sovereign state.

In my message to the Prime Minister of Iceland I have given the people of Iceland the assurance that the American forces sent there would in no way interfere with the internal and domestic affairs of that country, and that immediately upon the termination of the present international emergency all American forces will be at once withdrawn, leaving the people of Iceland and their Government in full and sovereign control of their own territory.

Franklin D. Roosevelt

The White House,
   July 7, 1941.

62. U.S. Repeal of Arms Embargo, November 17, 1941[10]

Joint Resolution To Repeal Sections 2, 3, and 6 of the Neutrality Act
Of 1939, and for Other Purposes

Resolved by the Senate and House of Representatives of the United States of America in Congress assembled, That section 2 of the Neutrality Act of 1939 (relating to commerce with States engaged in armed conflict), and section 3 of such Act (relating to combat areas), are hereby repealed.

Sec. 2. Section 6 of the Neutrality Act of 1939 (relating to the arming of American vessels) is hereby repealed; and, during the unlimited national emergency proclaimed by the President on May 27, 1941, the President is authorized, through such agency as he may designate, to arm, or to permit or cause to be armed, any American vessel as defined in such Act. The provisions of section 16 of the Criminal Code (relating to bonds from armed vessels on clearing) shall not apply to any such vessel.

Approved, November 17, 1941, 4:30 p.m., E. S. T.

63. Anglo-Soviet Agreement, July 12, 1941[11]

AGREEMENT BETWEEN HIS MAJESTY'S GOVERNMENT IN THE UNITED KINGDOM AND THE GOVERNMENT OF THE UNION OF SOVIET SOCIALIST REPUBLICS PROVIDING FOR JOINT ACTION IN THE WAR AGAINST GERMANY, WITH PROTOCOL. SIGNED AT MOSCOW, JULY 12TH, 1941.

AGREEMENT.

His Majesty's Government in the United Kingdom and the Government of the Union of Soviet Socialist Republics have concluded the present Agreement and declare as follows:

(1) The two Governments mutually undertake to render each other assistance and support of all kinds in the present war against Hitlerite Germany.

(2) They further undertake that during this war they will neither negotiate nor conclude an armistice or treaty of peace except by mutual agreement.

The present Agreement has been concluded in duplicate in the English and Russian languages.

Both texts have equal force.

Moscow, the twelfth of July, nineteen hundred and forty-one.

By authority of His Majesty's Government in the United Kingdom:

(L. S.) R. Stafford Cripps,
His Majesty's Ambassador
Extraordinary and Plenipotentiary
in the Union of Soviet Socialist
Republics.

By authority of the Government of Union of Soviet Socialist Republics:

(L. S.) V. Molotov,
The Deputy President of the Council of
People's Commissars and People's
Commissar for Foreign Affairs of
Union of Soviet Socialist Republics.

64. Anglo-American Assistance to Soviet Union, August 15, 1941[12]

JOINT MESSAGE FROM THE PRESIDENT OF THE UNITED STATES AND THE PRIME MINISTER OF GREAT BRITAIN TO THE PRESIDENT OF THE SOVIET OF PEOPLE'S COMMISSARS OF THE U. S. S. R.

We have taken the opportunity afforded by the consideration of the report of Mr. Harry Hopkins on his return from Moscow to consult together as to how best our two countries can help your country in the splendid defense that you are making against the Nazi attack. We are at the moment cooperating to provide you with the very maximum of supplies that you most urgently need. Already many shiploads have left our shores and more will leave in the immediate future.

We must now turn our minds to the consideration of a more long term policy, since there is still a long and hard path to be traversed before there can be won that complete victory without which our efforts and sacrifices would be wasted.

The war goes on upon many fronts and before it is over there may be further fighting fronts that will be developed. Our resources though immense are limited, and it must become a question as to where and when those resources can best be used to further the greatest extent our common effort. This applies equally to manufactured war supplies and to raw materials.

The needs and demands of your and our armed services can only be determined in the light of the full knowledge of the many factors which must be taken into consideration in the decisions that we make. In order that all of us may be in a position to arrive at speedy decisions as to the apportionment of our joint resources, we suggest that we prepare for a meeting to be held at Moscow, to which we would send high representatives who could discuss these matters directly with you. If this conference appeals to you, we want you to know that pending the decisions of that conference we shall continue to send supplies and material as rapidly as possible.

We realize fully how vitally important to the defeat of Hitlerism is the brave and steadfast resistance of the Soviet Union and we feel therefore that we must not in any circumstances fail to act quickly and immediately in this matter on planning the program for the future allocation of our joint resources.

Franklin D Roosevelt
Winston S Churchill

65. The Atlantic Charter, August 14, 1941[13]

Declaration of Principles, Known as the Atlantic Charter, by the President of the United States and the Prime Minister of the United Kingdom

The President of the United States and the Prime Minister, Mr. Churchill, representing His Majesty's Government in the United Kingdom, have met at sea.

They have been accompanied by officials of their two Governments, including high-ranking officers of their Military, Naval, and Air Services.

The whole problem of the supply of munitions of war, as provided by the Lease-Lend Act, for the armed forces of the United States and for those countries actively engaged in resisting aggression has been further examined.

Lord Beaverbrook, the Minister of Supply of the British Government, has joined in these conferences. He is going to proceed to Washington to discuss further details with appropriate officials of the United States Government. These conferences will also cover the supply problems of the Soviet Union.

The President and the Prime Minister have had several conferences. They have considered the dangers to world civilization arising from the policies of military domination by conquest upon which the Hitlerite government of Germany and other governments associated therewith have embarked, and have made clear the stress which their countries are respectively taking for their safety in the face of these dangers.

They have agreed upon the following joint declaration:

Joint declaration of the President of the United States of America and the Prime Minister, Mr. Churchill, representing His Majesty's Government in the United Kingdom, being met together, deem it right to make known certain common principles in the national policies of their respective countries on which they base their hopes for a better future for the world.

First, their countries seek no aggrandizement, territorial or other;

Second, they desire to see no territorial changes that do not accord with the freely expressed wishes of the peoples concerned;

Third, they respect the right of all peoples to choose the form of government under which they will live; and they wish to see sovereign rights and self-government restored to those who have been forcibly deprived of them;

Fourth, they will endeavor, with due respect for their existing obligations, to further the enjoyment by all States, great or small, victor or vanquished, of access, on equal terms, to the trade and to the raw materials of the world which are needed for their economic prosperity;

Fifth, they desire to bring about the fullest collaboration between all nations in the economic field with the object of securing, for all, improved labor standards, economic advancement, and social security;

Sixth, after the final destruction of the Nazi tyranny, they hope to see established a peace which will afford to all nations the means of dwelling in safety within their own boundaries, and which will afford assurance that all the men in all the lands may live out their lives in freedom from fear and want;

Seventh, such a peace should enable all men to traverse the high seas and oceans without hindrance;

Eighth, they believe that all of the nations of the world, for realistic as well as spiritual reasons, must come to the abandonment of the use of force. Since no future peace can be maintained if land, sea, or air armaments continue to be employed by nations which threaten, or may threaten, aggression outside of their frontiers, they believe, pending the establishment of a wider and permanent system of general security, that the disarmament of such nations is essential. They will likewise aid and encourage all other practicable measures which will lighten for peace-loving peoples the crushing burden of armaments.

Franklin D Roosevelt
Winston S Churchill

Chapter III
From War in Europe to World War, 1941–1942

Part 6. The "Greater East Asia Co-Prosperity Sphere"

The year of 1941 saw the conflagration in Europe become a war of worldwide dimensions. Between 1939 and 1941 German expansion had proceeded to cover most of Europe and was well into Russia. During the same period the United States had moved into the position of virtually waging an undeclared war against the Hitler régime, but the decision to go to war was made for the Americans by Japan's strike at Pearl Harbor in December 1941. The Pacific and the Far East now became theatres of war and World War II had begun.

These events were not entirely unexpected despite the great American shock over Japan's actions. For a number of years the Japanese Empire had been in the process of expansion and followed an undisguised, aggressive foreign policy. Japan had succeeded in establishing puppet states taken from former Chinese territories and carried on a persistent level of warfare against that nation. China, now divided domestically into two antagonistic factions of Nationalists and Communists, was unable to present a united front against Japanese aggression.

The determination of Japan to create and dominate a "Greater East Asia Co-Prosperity Sphere" had been announced in November 1938, and the open pursuit of economic and military control in the Far East was launched. Japan's leaders fully intended to create an economic sphere that would supply the raw materials necessary for complete independence from western nations and any threat of boycott. Japan had moved rapidly from a policy of decrying its lack of sufficient living space to one of encouraging population growth in order to handle its "new responsibilities." In early 1941 the Imperial Cabinet set an immediate goal of 100,000,000 people (66).

The German Chancellor Hitler was pleased by every action of Japan that moved her closer to war's entry and a possible conflict with the Soviet Union. It was, no doubt, in this encouraging mood that the Fuehrer offered to Japan the prospects of greater cooperation in anticipation of that nation's attack upon the United States (67). Interestingly, at this date of March 1941,

Hitler had set the plans in motion for the invasion of Russia (40) but did not wish this revealed to his Far Eastern ally (67, final para.). Of course, Japan and the Soviet Union were already in the negotiation stage for a mutual neutrality pact, and it was soon announced (68). A pledge to respect each other's territory was included.

Japan's plan for an East Asia Co-Prosperity Sphere called for the expulsion of all the western powers from Asia and the Pacific. Some of this had already been accomplished by the war in Europe, for with the defeat of France and Holland their colonial territories were left without adequate protection. The ability of Great Britain to defend holdings in the Far East was also greatly diminished and therefore the single power remaining was the United States. Japan's decision to eliminate American power was based upon a boldly conceived plan to attack the U. S. Pacific Fleet located in Hawaii. The initial planning was directed by Admiral Isoroku Yamamoto who commanded the Japanese Combined Fleet. The "Yamamoto Plan" was put forth in early 1941 and practiced during the spring and summer months (69). The final testing took place in November of 1941.

These events had unfolded amidst a backdrop of political struggle in Japan between the moderates led by Premier Prince Konoye and the militarists headed by General Hideki Tojo. In mid-October the struggle climaxed with Tojo forming a new cabinet (70), and shortly thereafter the reasons for making war against the United States and Great Britain were developed (71); at the same time a schedule was prepared for "hastening the conclusion of war" against their chosen enemies (72).

The diplomatic role that Japan played during the month of November was a complex one indeed. In an extremely interesting document drawn by the Imperial Council in the presence of Emperor Hirohito on November 5 (73), a set of policies was agreed upon for Japan's national conduct for the next critical weeks.

The relations of Japan and the United States had been steadily deteriorating since Japan's invasion of China in 1937. Since Japan did not recognize the conflict officially as a war, preferring to call it the "China Incident," the American President decided to accept that definition at face value and continue to extend aid to China (an official war would have meant strict adherence to a neutrality position). It is difficult to assess the wisdom of Roosevelt's move for it also meant that Japan could continue—and did—to purchase all sorts of materials from the United States. After the war in Europe began the relations between the United States and Japan worsened rapidly and the announcement of Japan's alliance with Germany and Italy in 1940 (37) was a clear warning to America.

The efforts at finding diplomatic solutions continued to occupy the two governments, however, or at least their respective foreign offices. On the surface some progress seemed to appear in the on-going negotiations during the latter months of 1941, and in November the United States proposed a comprehensive settlement to Japan that covered all of their mutual differences in the Pacific (74). However, at virtually the same moment that the U. S. proposal was going forth Roosevelt received a report of Japanese troop movements into French Indo-China and asked for a clarification. Far from denying the report, Japan verified it and placed the blame on Chinese aggressions (75). The following day, December 6, the American President took the extraordinary step of dispatching a message directly to the Japanese Emperor expressing his great concern over the turn of events (76).

Japan's answer on December 7 was a total rejection of Roosevelt's message and a presentation of Japan's own interpretation of current affairs (77). The reply was interesting enough in light of what had been happening, but the timing was nothing short of incredible, for the attack on Pearl Harbor was already under way and had been for over an hour. The response of American Secretary of State Hull was brief and immediate (78).

The early morning air attack by Japan on American Pacific installations in Hawaii was almost over by noon, but the devastation was sufficient to cripple the Pacific Fleet. At the same time there were assaults on the islands of Guam, Midway, and Wake as well as Hong Kong, Thailand, Malaya, and the Philippines.

Approximately three hours after the attacks began, Japan announced a declaration of war against the United States and Great Britain (79). In a brief but striking speech to the American Congress on December 8 President Roosevelt requested a declaration of war against Japan (80). The speech lasted barely six minutes, and with only one dissenting member Congress voted for war. On December 11 Congress approved a similar action against Germany and Italy after both of those nations had declared war on the United States. In a special meeting before the German Reichstag that morning Hitler, in a lengthy recapitulation of events since the start of the war, announced not only the declaration against the United States by Germany but the determination of Italy and Japan to join in a common effort (81).

66. Japan's Population Policy, January 1941[1]

EXTRACT FROM JAPAN TIMES & *ADVERTISER*, January 23, 1941

Fundamental principles of Japan's population policy were decided on at the special Cabinet meeting in the official residence of the Premier Wednesday, Domei reports.

Mr. Naoki HOSHINO, president of the Cabinet Planning Board, made detailed explanations on the policy while the Welfare, Education, and War Ministers expressed their opinions.

With minor changes, in wording, however, the draft of a bill relating to the population policy was unanimously approved by the members of the Cabinet. In this connection a statement was issued by the Board of Information immediately after the meeting.

According to this statement, the Government has been brought to establish a new population policy to increase the population of this country quickly and incessantly, to enhance the quality of the Japanese, and to correct the distribution of the Japanese race so as to secure the leadership of Japan over East Asia.

GOAL at 100,000,000

To this end, the goal for the total population of Japan proper in 1945 has been set at 100,000,000. This is to enable Japan to expand its population without stop, to surpass other countries in the rate of population increase as well as in the quality of race, to secure adequate man power for military and economic purposes, and to keep the supremacy of Japan over other races in East Asia.

The Government will make payments to newlyweds, cut the marriageable age by three years. The goal is five children per couple.

Efforts will be made to heighten the birth rate, and lower the death rate, and for the propagation of the view of the world based on family and race instead of the individual.

For heightening the birth rate in this country, marriages will be promoted by special bureaus designated by the Government, expenditures on weddings will be restricted, employment of women over 20 will be restricted as much as possible, and priority in materials will be given to prolific families.

Birth Control Banned

At the same time, various systems will be instituted for the protection of mothers and infants, and birth control through the practice of abortion and use of medicines will be prohibited strictly.

In order to lower the death rate, the Government will make special efforts for the prevention of tuberculosis as well as the protection of infants from death. According to a Government plan, the death rate in Japan will be reduced by 35 per cent in the next 20 years.

As a means of elevating the quality of the nation, the Government will try to redistribute population with stress laid on the reduction of the population of large cities such as Tokyo and Osaka.

Farmers Held Static

At the same time, it will keep the farming population in this country at a certain level as the farming villages are considered to be the best source of soldiers and laborers. It will expand sports facilities for the rearing of stout and healthy youths, and institute a system through which young men can receive special spiritual and physical training for a certain period of time. . . .

67. GERMAN COOPERATION WITH JAPAN, MARCH 5, 1941[2]

Directive No. 24
Regarding Cooperation With Japan

The Führer has ordered the following regarding cooperation with Japan:

1) The *aim* of the cooperation initiated by the Tripartite Pact must be *to bring Japan into active operations in the Far East* as soon as possible. This will tie down strong English forces and the focal point of the interests of the United States of America will be diverted to the Pacific.

In view of the still undeveloped military preparedness of her foes, Japan's prospects of success will be the better, the sooner the intervention occurs. The *Barbarossa* Operation creates especially favorable political and military conditions for this.

2) For the *preparation* of the cooperation it is necessary to strengthen *Japanese military power* by every means.

To that end, the commanders in chief of the branches of the Wehrmacht will extensively and liberally comply with Japanese requests for the communication of German war and battle experience, and for aid in the field of war economy and of a technical nature. Reciprocity is desirable, but must not impede the negotiations. This naturally concerns in the main such Japanese requests as could have application in military operations within a short time.

With respect to special cases, the Führer reserves his decision.

3) The *coordination of plans* of operations on both sides pertains to the High Command of the Navy.

The following principles apply hereto:

a) The quick defeat of England is to be designated as the common aim in the conduct of the war, thereby keeping the U. S. A. out of the war. Otherwise Germany has neither political, nor military, nor economic interests in the Far East which give occasion to reservations respecting Japanese intentions.

b) The great successes which Germany has achieved in the *war against merchant shipping* make it appear peculiarly appropriate that strong Japanese forces be directed to the same purpose. In addition, every possibility of assistance in Germany's war against merchant shipping is to be exploited.

c) The *situation* of the [Tripartite] Pact Powers with respect to *raw materials* requires that Japan take over those territories which it needs to continue the war, especially if the United States intervenes. Rubber deliveries must take place even after Japan's entry into the war, since they are vital to Germany.

d) *The seizure of Singapore,* England's key position in the Far East, would signify a decisive success for the combined warfare of the three Powers.

Moreover, attacks directed against other bases of the English sea power system—against those of American sea power only if America's entry into the war cannot be prevented—are likely to weaken the power system of the enemy and, just as in the case of attack upon his sea communications, to tie down essential forces of all kinds (Australia).

A date for the beginning of operational conversations cannot yet be fixed.

4) In the *military commissions* to be set up under the Tripartite Pact only those subjects should be discussed which concern the *three* Powers in the same fashion. This will primarily include the problems of economic warfare.

Dealing with them in detail is the task of the main commission in concert with the High Command of the Wehrmacht.

5) No hint of the *Barbarossa Operation* must be given to the Japanese.

The Chief of the High Command
of the Wehrmacht
signed in draft: Keitel

68. Soviet-Japanese Pact and Frontier Declaration, April 13, 1941[3]

The Treaty
A Neutrality Pact
Between the Union of Soviet Socialist Republics and Japan

The Presidium of the Supreme Soviet of the U. S. S. R. and His Majesty the Emperor of Japan, guided by a desire to strengthen peaceful and friendly relations between the two countries, decided to conclude a pact on neutrality, for the purpose of which they appointed as their representatives:

For the Presidium of the Supreme Soviet of the U. S. S. R., Vyacheslaff Molotoff, Chairman of the Council of People's Commissars and People's Commissar for Foreign Affairs.

For His Majesty the Emperor of Japan, Yosuke Matsuoka, Minister of Foreign Affairs, Ju San Min, Cavalier of the Order of the Sacred Treasure, First Class; and Yoshitsugu Tatekawa, Ambassador Extraordinary and Plenipotentiary in the U. S. S. R., Lieut. Gen., Ju San Min, Cavalier of the Order of the Rising Sun, First Class, and the Order of the Golden Kite, Fourth Class.

Who, after the exchange of their credentials, which were found in due and proper form, agreed on the following:

Article I

Both contracting parties undertake to maintain peaceful and friendly relations between them and mutually respect the territorial integrity and inviolability of the other contracting party.

Article II

Should one of the contracting parties become the object of hostilities on the part of one or several third Powers the other contracting party will observe neutrality throughout the duration of the conflict.

Article III

The present pact comes into force from the day of its ratification by both contracting parties and remains valid for five years. In case neither of the contracting parties denounces the pact one year before expiration of the term, it will be considered automatically prolonged for the next five years.

Article IV

The present pact is subject to ratification as soon as possible. Instruments of ratification shall be exchanged in Tokyo also as soon as possible.

In confirmation whereof the above-named representatives signed the present pact in two copies, drawn up in the Russian and Japanese languages, and affixed thereto their seals.

Done in Moscow April 13, 1941, which corresponds to the 13th Day of the Fourth Month of the 16th Year of Shown.

Signed by:

Molotoff,
Yosuke Matsuoka
Yoshitsugu Tatekawa.

Frontier Declaration

In conformity with the spirit of the neutrality pact concluded April 13, 1941, between the U. S. S. R. and Japan the Governments of the U. S. S. R. and Japan, in the interests of ensuring peaceful and friendly relations between the two countries, solemnly declare that the U. S. S. R. pledges to respect the territorial integrity and inviolability of Manchukuo, and Japan pledges to respect the territorial integrity and inviolability of the Mongolian People's Republic.

Moscow, April 13, 1941.
Signed on behalf of the Government of Japan by

Yosuke Matsuoka
Yoshitsugu Tatekawa

69. DETAILS OF THE "YAMAMOTO PLAN," APRIL 1941[4]

(Excerpts from International Military Tribunal for the Far East, 1946–1948)
"Q Admiral, [Osami Nagano, Former Chief, Naval General] who was the originator of the plan to attack Pearl Harbor?

"A After being studied by the Combined Fleets the plan was brought forth in the spring of 1941 by Admiral YAMAMOTO. It was a great secret in the Combined Fleets whereby Admiral YAMAMOTO and only one or two other officers knew of it.

"Q When was the plan as prepared by Admiral YAMAMOTO first called to your attention, Admiral?

"A I first found out about this plan officially in October 1941. I heard prior to that that such a plan was being studied.

"Q Admiral, when did you become Chief of the Naval General Staff?

"A In April 1941.

"Q And is it not a fact that this plan of Admiral YAMAMOTO's was called to your attention at that time?

"A No, it was not. I believe it was at that time that YAMAMOTO first thought of the plan.

"Q Now, Admiral, you stated that the first time the plan had been called to your attention officially was in October 1941. When was the plan called to your attention unofficially?

"A About July I heard that they were training or practicing such a plan.

"Q And is it not a fact, Admiral, and again I ask you not to answer me too literally but to answer my questions from your knowledge even though you were not personally present and from your knowledge as Naval Chief of Staff as to what was going on in connection with Naval activities in the light of the fact that you were Chief of Staff and as such had general knowledge of Naval activities, is it not a fact that the Japanese Navy started practicing to place into execution the YAMAMOTO plan to attack Pearl Harbor in the spring of 1941?

"A The plan came into being in the spring but it was not practiced until summer.

"Q And what do you mean by summer?

"A I am not sure but I believe it was about the beginning of July. The Combined Fleets went into Kagoshima and there they practiced coming in low over the mountains and dive bombing.

"Q And is it not a fact also, Admiral, that in addition to those maneuvers, that the fleet also practiced with a specially designed torpedo for use in shallow water such as was known to be the situation in Pearl Harbor?

"A The torpedo was completed during those maneuvers. The Combined Fleets spent a lot of time trying out this torpedo and experimenting with it."

. . . .

"Q Now, Admiral, I believe yesterday or the day before you mentioned, or you stated that the Japanese Navy started practicing on the Pearl Harbor plan some time in the summer of 1941. That was correct, was it not?

"A Yes, I believe the Fleet started training in the summer as you say.

"Q Do you remember just about what month in the summer of 1941, Admiral?

"A I don't remember too clearly but I am sure it was some time in the summer.

"Q Would you say it was possibly some time in July, 1941?

"A Yes.

"Q As I have the details here, the experiments and training were held at Sukamo, Saiki, Kagoshima and Konoye. Is that correct?

"A Sukamo is a very suitable place for training and the Navy has consistently used it for such, but I believe the training of dive bombing and coming in low over the mountains which was utilized in the attack on Pearl Harbor was practiced at Kagoshima."

70. INTERROGATION OF HIDEKI TOJO ON EVENTS OF OCTOBER 1941[5] (EXCERPT)

"Q Did you feel, at the time the KONOYE Cabinet fell on or about 17 October 1941, that war should be declared against the United States and the other three nations?

"A At that time I felt, as War Minister, that the opportune time for fighting was in danger of being lost and the Imperial Conference had set the middle ten days of October as the limit for waiting for a favorable diplomatic break.

"Q Was it not because of the fact that you, as War Minister, favored war with the United States that the KONOYE Cabinet fell on or about 17 October 1941?

"A Theoretically, yes. KONOYE thought that a diplomatic solution was still possible if Japan would withdraw troops from China, but the Army felt that there would be no guarantee that the unlawful acts of the Chinese, which had caused the Incident, would not be resumed if the troops were withdrawn before their purpose had been achieved, and the Army could not bear to so withdraw the troops."

71. JAPAN'S REASONS FOR WAR AGAINST THE UNITED STATES AND GREAT BRITAIN, NOVEMBER 11, 1941[6] (NOTES FROM IMPERIAL CONFERENCE

Principal reasons alleged for the commencement
of hostilities against the U.S.A. and Britain.

(Draft)

11 November SHOWA 16 (1941)
Draft adopted at the Liaison Conference

1. That it is the unshakable national policy of our Empire to establish permanent peace by creating a new order in Greater East Asia, and to voluntarily contribute to world peace.

2. That the China Affair aims, in accordance with this national policy, to do away with all causes which disturb the stability of Greater East Asia, and to realize the results of co-prosperity of all peoples, building upon peace on the basis of the New Order, and that Japan must do all in her power to bring it to a successful issue.

3. That the United States and Britain have been trying for a long time in the Far East to obstruct the measures and actions of the Japanese Empire. Above all, with the outbreak of the China Affair, they have openly increased their measures of assistance of the Chungking Régime and stealthily gave rein to their inordinate ambition to dominate the Far East at the expense of China. In addition, they have persuaded other powers to strengthen the encirclement of Japan, and also adopted such measures as the direct disruption of economic relations with our Empire, and reinforced military preparations. Thus they have threatened the security of our Empire by daring to conduct virtual war operations against us.

4. That our Empire, exhausting every possible means and putting up with the unbearable, has proposed to the United States the peaceful settlement of the situation and has already conducted negotiations with the United States for the past 8 months. However, there is a fundamental opposition between the assertions of Japan and the United States in regard to the establishment of a lasting peace in the Far East. We can hardly realize our national policy and can by no means bring about the stability of Greater East Asia if we once accede to the assertions of the United States.

Under such circumstances, all the efforts exerted by us during the past four years in order to successfully prosecute the China Affair would come to naught. This our Empire cannot tolerate from the standpoint of her existence and prestige.

5. That in the attitudes of the United States and Britain we can read nothing but a hasty move to satisfy their own inordinate ambitions, and see

no trace of a sincere desire on their part for world peace, and to rescue mankind [from] unfortunate disasters.

Greater East Asia is now on the brink of a crisis, and the existence of our Empire is in jeopardy.

Such being the situation, we are compelled to rise up to take up arms on the side of our allies to smash all the obstacles in our way.

72. JAPAN'S PLAN FOR A QUICK CONCLUSION TO THE WAR, NOVEMBER 12, 1941[7]

GENERAL OUTLINE FOR HASTENING THE CONCLUSION OF WAR AGAINST THE UNITED STATES, GREAT BRITAIN, NETHERLANDS, AND THE CHUNGKING REGIME.

FOREIGN MINISTRY
Dated: Nov 12 1941

1. A 'No-Separate-Peace Agreement' shall be concluded with both Germany and Italy.

2. Through mutual consent with Germany, we shall mediate for peace between Germany and the Soviet Union and restore our trans-continental communication with Germany. On the other hand, while adjusting our relation with the Soviet Union, we shall take measures to promote her advancement into the direction of India and Persia.

3. We shall completely cut off the supply route to the Chungking Regime, and bring all the concessions in China under Japan's power. On the other hand, we shall induce and utilize the Chinese merchants residing in the South Sea to strengthen our oppression upon the Chungking Regime, thereby contributing to the settlement of the Incident.

4. The independence of the Philippine Islands shall be recognized and proclaimed to the world at the earliest possible occasion after the occupation of the Islands.

5. Independence shall be allowed to part of the Dutch East Indies while other necessary areas shall be maintained by Japan.

6. We shall give independence to Burma and thus incite and promote India's independent movement.

7. We shall support Thailand's movement against England for the recovery of lost territories, (French Indo-China shall maintain her status-quo).

8. Regarding our administrative policy in the occupied areas, we shall not oppress the lives of the people; and shall adopt, as far as possible a non-interference policy towards their internal affairs, thereby shall earn the hearts of the people.

9. When the time becomes suitable, we shall declare our intentions to guarantee an equal supply of tin and rubber in the South Seas to the United States and Great Britain.

(Remarks)

(1) Judging from the fact proved in World War I, the policy to utilize

Americans of German descent for the purpose to break up the public opinion in the United States may at least be considered, but it will prove impracticable and fruitless. (2) We cannot expect much from activities in Central and South America.

73. JAPAN'S POLICIES FOR NOVEMBER 1941[8]

Measures to be taken towards Foreign Countries relative to the Outline for the execution of National Policies, which was decided at the Council in the presence of the Emperor held on November 5.

Liaison Conference Division
November 13, 1941.
Policy Towards Germany and Italy.

When the present negotiations with the United States of America break down and a war with her becomes unavoidable (presumed to be after November 25th), the Japanese Government shall notify Germany (and Italy), without delay, of our intention to start war against the United States of America and Britain as soon as our war preparations are ready, and shall open necessary negotiations with them in connection with the following matters, telling them that these are a part of our war preparations:

1. Participation of Germany (and Italy) in the war against the United States of America.

2. No separate peace.

Remarks:

If we are requested by Germany to join in the war against the Soviet Union, we shall reply that we will not enter it for the time being. It cannot be helped if, as a result of it, Germany's participation in the war against the United States of America is delayed thereby.

Policy towards Britain

Prompt measures shall be taken directly or through the medium of the United States of America to make Britain accept, and positively cooperate with us in the matters included in the understandings reached in the negotiations between Japan and the United States of America.

In order to conceal our intentions, no other special diplomatic measures shall be taken.

Policy towards the Dutch East Indies

In order to help conceal and disguise our intentions, we shall open as soon as possible a series of diplomatic negotiations [with the Dutch East Indies], in the form of continuation of previous negotiations, with the chief object of obtaining commodities needed by our country.

Policy towards the Soviet Union

Diplomatic negotiations [with the Soviet Union] shall be continued in conformity with Item I of the Outline of Diplomatic Negotiations with the Soviet Union, which was decided at the Liaison Conference of Imperial Headquarters and the Government held on August 4th, 1941.

Policy towards Thailand

1. Just before commencing the advance into [Thailand], the following demands shall be made and their immediate compliance obtained:

Our troops shall advance [into Thailand], as prearranged, even if our demands are rejected by Thailand. However, efforts shall be made to localize as much as possible military collision between Japan and Thailand.

(a) Right of passage of Japanese troops through her territory and the grant of various facilities incidental thereto.

(b) Immediate enforcement of measures to avoid possible collisions between the troops of Japan and Thailand, owing to the passage of Japanese troops.

(c) Conclusion of a joint defence agreement, if Thailand desires it.

Note: No special change in our attitude towards Thailand shall be made before the commencement of the negotiations. In particular, great care shall be taken to conceal our plan of opening war.

2. After the penetration of our troops, we shall immediately open negotiations with the Government of Thailand for concrete arrangements on the following matters:

(a) Matters concerning the passage and stationing of Japanese troops.

(b) Provision, construction and enlargement of military establishments.

(c) Provision of necessary traffic and communication facilities as well as factory facilities.

(d) Matters concerning billeting and sustenance for the Japanese troops passing through or stationed in Thailand.

(e) Loans to defray necessary military expenditure.

Remarks: In the negotiations on Items 1 and 2, we shall definitely promise to respect her sovereignty and territorial integrity in conformity with the Outline of Policies towards French Indo-China and Thailand, which was decided at the Liaison Conference of Imperial Headquarters and the Government held on February 1st, 1941.

Moreover, depending on the attitude of Thailand, we shall try to turn the negotiations to our advantage by suggesting that we will in future consider the cession of a part of Burma or Malay to Thailand.

Policy towards China

The following measures shall be taken, bearing in mind the necessity of preserving our all-round fighting power to cope with a protracted world war by avoiding military attrition in China as far as possible and also bearing in mind the probable decrease of our military strength in the future:

1. To drive out the military forces of the United States of America and Britain in China.

2. To place under our actual control enemy concessions in China (including the Legation Quarter in Peking) and important enemy interests (such as the maritime customs and mines), but care shall be taken to lighten as far as possible our burden in respect to man-power and materials.

Note: Though the International Settlements and the Legation Quarter in

Peking shall be brought under our actual control after driving out the enemy's military forces, these areas shall not be completely taken over since they also include interests of countries friendly to us.

3. The above mentioned plans shall be carried out only after the declaration of war against the United States of America and Britain, lest our intentions be revealed.

4. Our right of belligerency against the Chungking Regime shall not be obtained by a declaration or other formalities, but the actual effect of belligerency will be obtained by a declaration of war against the United States of America and Britain.

5. Among the enemy interests in China, even those interests connected with the National Government shall, if necessary, be brought under our control for the time being, and adjustment made separately.

6. The activities of influential Chinese in the occupied area shall be encouraged and fostered as far as possible, so as to win the people's mind to Sino-Japanese cooperation and thereby gradually establish localized peace in the areas where this is possible.

7. In our economic relations with China, we shall lay special stress upon the acquisition of goods. For this purpose reasonable adjustments shall be made in the various existing restrictions.

74. UNITED STATES NOTE TO JAPAN, NOVEMBER 26, 1941[9]

"Oral

"*Strictly confidential*

"November 26, 1941.

"The representatives of the Government of the United States and of the Government of Japan have been carrying on during the past several months informal and exploratory conversations for the purpose of arriving at a settlement if possible of questions relating to the entire Pacific area based upon the principles of peace, law and order and fair dealing among nations. These principles include the principle of inviolability of territorial integrity and sovereignty of each and all nations; the principle of non-interference in the internal affairs of other countries; the principle of equality, including equality of commercial opportunity and treatment; and the principle of reliance upon international cooperation and conciliation for the prevention and pacific settlement of controversies and for improvements of international conditions by peaceful methods and processes.

"It is believed that in our discussions some progress has been made in reference to the general principles which constitute the basis of a peaceful settlement covering the entire Pacific area. Recently the Japanese Ambassador has stated that the Japanese Government is desirous of continuing the conversations directed toward a comprehensive and peaceful settlement in the Pacific area; that it would be helpful toward creating an atmosphere favorable to the successful outcome of the conversations if a temporary *modus vivendi* could be agreed upon to be in effect while the conversations looking to a peaceful settlement in the Pacific were continuing. On November 20 the Japanese Ambassador communicated to the Secretary of State proposals in regard to temporary measures to be taken respectively by the Government of Japan and the Government of the United States, which measures are understood to have been designed to accomplish the purposes above indicated.

"The Government of the United States most earnestly desires to contribute to the promotion and maintenance of peace and stability in the Pacific area, and to afford every opportunity for the continuance of discussions with the Japanese Government directed toward working out a broad-gauge program of peace throughout the Pacific area. The proposals which were presented by the Japanese Ambassador on November 20 contain some features which, in the opinion of this Government, conflict with the fundamental principles which form a part of the general settlement under consideration and to which each Government has declared that it is committed. The Government of the United States believes that the adoption of such proposals would not be likely to contribute to the ultimate objectives of ensuring peace under law, order and justice in the Pacific area, and it suggests that further effort be made to resolve our divergences of views in regard to the practical application of the fundamental principles already mentioned.

"With this object in view the Government of the United States offers for the consideration of the Japanese Government a plan of a broad but simple settlement covering the entire Pacific area as one practical exemplification of a program which this Government envisages as something to be worked out during our further conversations.

"The plan therein suggested represents an effort to bridge the gap between our draft of June 21, 1941 and the Japanese draft of September 25 by making a new approach to the essential problems underlying a comprehensive Pacific settlement. This plan contains provisions dealing with the practical application of the fundamental principles which we have agreed in our conversations constitute the only sound basis for worthwhile international relations. We hope that in this way progress toward reaching a meeting of minds between our two Governments may be expedited."

"*Strictly confidential, tentative*
        and without commitment

                                              "November 26, 1941.
"Outline of Proposed Basis for Agreement Between the United States and Japan
"Section I

               "*Draft Mutual Declaration of Policy*
"The Government of the United States and the Government of Japan both being solicitous for the peace of the Pacific affirm that their national policies

are directed toward lasting and extensive peace throughout the Pacific area, and they have no territorial designs in that area, that they have no intention of threatening other countries or of using military force aggressively against any neighboring nation, and that, accordingly, in their national policies they will actively support and give practical application to the following fundamental principles upon which their relations with each other and with all other governments are based:

"(1) The principle of inviolability of territorial integrity and sovereignty of each and all nations.

"(2) The principle of non-interference in the internal affairs of other countries.

"(3) The principle of equality, including equality of commercial opportunity and treatment.

"(4) The principle of reliance upon international cooperation and conciliation for the prevention and pacific settlement of controversies and for improvement of international conditions by peaceful methods and processes.

"The Government of Japan and the Government of the United States have agreed that toward eliminating chronic political instability, preventing recurrent economic collapse, and providing a basis for peace, they will actively support and practically apply the following principles in their economic relations with each other and with other nations and peoples:

"(1) The principle of non-discrimination in international commercial relations.

"(2) The principle of international economic cooperation and abolition of extreme nationalism as expressed in excessive trade restrictions.

"(3) The principle of non-discriminatory access by all nations to raw material supplies.

"(4) The principle of full protection of the interests of consuming countries and populations as regards the operation of international commodity agreements.

"(5) The principle of establishment of such institutions and arrangements of international finance as may lend aid to the essential enterprises and the continuous development of all countries and may permit payments through processes of trade consonant with the welfare of all countries.

"Section II

"*Steps To Be Taken by the Government of the United States and by the Government of Japan*

"The Government of the United States and the Government of Japan propose to take steps as follows:

"1. The Government of the United States and the Government of Japan will endeavor to conclude a multilateral non-aggression pact among the British Empire, China, Japan, the Netherlands, the Soviet Union, Thailand and the United States.

"2. Both Governments will endeavor to conclude among the American, British, Chinese, Japanese, the Netherland and Thai Governments an agreement whereunder each of the Governments would pledge itself to respect the territorial integrity of French Indochina and, in the event that there should develop a threat to the territorial integrity of Indochina, to enter into immediate consultation with a view to taking such measures as may be deemed necessary and advisable to meet the threat in question. Such agreement would provide also that each of the Governments party to the agreement would not seek or accept preferential treatment in its trade or economic relations with Indochina and would use its influence to obtain for each of the signatories equality of treatment in trade and commerce with French Indochina.

"3. The Government of Japan will withdraw all military, naval, air and police forces from China and from Indochina.

"4. The Government of the United States and the Government of Japan will not support—militarily, politically, economically—any government or regime in China other than the National Government of the Republic of China with capital temporarily at Chungking.

"5. Both Governments will give up all extraterritorial rights in China, including rights and interests in and with regard to international settlements and concessions, and rights under the Boxer Protocol of 1901.

"Both Governments will endeavor to obtain the agreement of the British and other governments to give up extraterritorial rights in China, including rights in international settlements and in concessions and under the Boxer Protocol of 1901.

"6. The Government of the United States and the Government of Japan will enter into negotiations for the conclusion between the United States and Japan of a trade agreement, based upon reciprocal most-favored-nation treatment and reduction of trade barriers by both countries, including an undertaking by the United States to bind raw silk on the free list.

"7. The Government of the United States and the Government of Japan will, respectively, remove the freezing restrictions on Japanese funds in the United States and on American funds in Japan.

"8. Both Governments will agree upon a plan for the stabilization of the dollar-yen rate, with the allocation of funds adequate for this purpose, half to be supplied by Japan and half by the United States.

"9. Both Governments will agree that no agreement which either has concluded with any third power or powers shall be interpreted by it in such a way as to conflict with the fundamental purpose of this agreement, the establishment and preservation of peace throughout the Pacific area.

"10. Both Governments will use their influence to cause other governments to adhere to and to give practical application to the basic political and economic principles set forth in this agreement."

75. Japan Explains Troops in French Indochina to Roosevelt, December 5, 1941[10]

"Reference is made to your inquiry about the intention of the Japanese Government with regard to the reported movements of Japanese troops in French Indo-China. Under instructions from Tokyo, I wish to inform you as follows:

"As Chinese troops have recently shown frequent signs of movements along the northern frontier of French Indo-China bordering on China, Japanese troops, with the object of mainly taking precautionary measures, have been reinforced to a certain extent in the northern part of French Indo-China. As a natural sequence of this step, certain movements have been made among the troops stationed in the southern part of the said territory. It seems that an exaggerated report has been made of these movements. It should be added that no measure has been taken on the part of the Japanese Government that may transgress the stipulations of the Protocol of Joint Defense between Japan and France."

76. Roosevelt to Hirohito, December 6, 1941[11]

"Almost a century ago the President of the United States addressed to the Emperor of Japan a message extending an offer of friendship of the people of the United States to the people of Japan. That offer was accepted, and in the long period of unbroken peace and friendship which has followed, our respective nations, through the virtues of their people and the wisdom of their rulers have prospered and have substantially helped humanity.

"Only in situations of extraordinary importance to our two countries need I address to Your Majesty messages on matters of state. I feel I should now so address you because of the deep and far-reaching emergency which appears to be in formation.

"Developments are occurring in the Pacific area which threaten to deprive each of our nations and all humanity of the beneficial influence of the long peace between our two countries. Those developments contain tragic possibilities.

"The people of the United States, believing in peace and in the right of nations to live and let live, have eagerly watched the conversations between our two Governments during these past months. We have hoped for a termination of the present conflict between Japan and China. We have hoped that a peace of the Pacific could be consummated in such a way that nationalities of many diverse people could exist side by side without fear of invasion; that unbearable burdens of armaments could be lifted for them all;

and that all peoples would resume commerce without discrimination against or in favor of any nation.

"I am certain that it will be clear to Your Majesty, as it is to me, that in seeking these great objectives both Japan and the United States should agree to eliminate any form of military threat. This seemed essential to the attainment of the high objectives.

"More than a year ago Your Majesty's Government concluded an agreement with the Vichy Government by which five or six thousand Japanese troops were permitted to enter into Northern French Indo-China for the protection of Japanese troops which were operating against China further north. And this Spring and Summer the Vichy Government permitted further Japanese military forces to enter into Southern French Indo-China for the common defense of French Indo-China. I think I am correct in saying that no attack has been made upon Indo-China, nor that any has been contemplated.

"During the past few weeks it has become clear to the world that Japanese military, naval and air forces have been sent to Southern Indo-China in such large numbers as to create a reasonable doubt on the part of other nations that this continuing concentration in Indo-China is not defensive in its character.

"Because these continuing concentrations in Indo-China have reached such large proportions and because they extend now to the southeast and the southwest corners of that Peninsula, it is only reasonable that the people of the Philippines, of the hundreds of Islands of the East Indies, of Malaya and of Thailand itself are asking themselves whether these forces of Japan are preparing or intending to make attack in one or more of these many directions.

"I am sure that Your Majesty will understand that the fear of all these peoples is a legitimate fear inasmuch as it involves their peace and their national existence. I am sure that Your Majesty will understand why the people of the United States in such large numbers look askance at the establishment of military, naval and air bases manned and equipped so greatly as to constitute armed forces capable of measures of offense.

"It is clear that a continuance of such a situation is unthinkable.

"None of the peoples whom I have spoken of above can sit either indefinitely or permanently on a keg of dynamite.

"There is absolutely no thought on the part of the United States of invading Indo-China if every Japanese soldier or sailor were to be withdrawn therefrom.

"I think that we can obtain the same assurance from the Governments of the East Indies, the Governments of Malaya and the Government of Thailand. I would even undertake to ask for the same assurance on the part of the Government of China. Thus a withdrawal of the Japanese forces from Indo-China would result in the assurance of peace throughout the whole of the South Pacific area.

"I address myself to Your Majesty at this moment in the fervent hope that Your Majesty may, as I am doing, give thought in this definite emergency to ways of dispelling the dark clouds. I am confident that both of us, for the sake of the peoples not only of our own great countries but for the sake of humanity in neighboring territories, have a sacred duty to restore traditional amity and prevent further death and destruction in the world."

77. JAPAN'S ANSWER OF DECEMBER 7, 1941[12]

"Memorandum

"1. The Government of Japan, prompted by a genuine desire to come to an amicable understanding with the Government of the United States in order that the two countries by their joint efforts may secure the peace of the Pacific Area and thereby contribute toward the realization of world peace, has continued negotiations with the utmost sincerity since April last with the Government of the United States regarding the adjustment and advancement of Japanese-American relations and the stabilization of the Pacific Area.

"The Japanese Government has the honor to state frankly its views concerning the claims the American Government has persistently maintained as well as the measures the United States and Great Britain have taken toward Japan during these eight months.

"2. It is the immutable policy of the Japanese Government to insure the stability of East Asia and to promote world peace and thereby to enable all nations to find each its proper place in the world.

"Ever since China Affair broke out owing to the failure on the part of China to comprehend Japan's true intentions, the Japanese Government has striven for the restoration of peace and it has consistently exerted its best efforts to prevent the extension of war-like disturbances. It was also to that end that in September last year Japan concluded the Tripartite Pact with Germany and Italy.

"However, both the United States and Great Britain have resorted to every possible measure to assist the Chungking régime so as to obstruct the establishment of a general peace between Japan and China, interfering with Japan's constructive endeavours toward the stabilization of East Asia. Exerting pressure on the Netherlands East Indies, or menacing French Indo-China, they have attempted to frustrate Japan's aspiration to the ideal of common prosperity in cooperation with these regions. Furthermore, when Japan in accordance with its protocol with France took measures of joint defence of French Indo-China, both American and British Governments, wilfully misinterpreting it as a threat to their own possessions, and inducing the Netherlands Government to follow suit, they enforced the assets freezing order, thus severing economic relations with Japan. While manifesting thus an obviously hostile attitude, these countries have strengthened their military preparations perfecting an encirclement of Japan, and have brought about a situation which endangers the very existence of the Empire.

"Nevertheless, to facilitate a speedy settlement, the Premier of Japan proposed, in August last, to meet the President of the United States for a discussion of important problems between the two countries covering the entire Pacific area. However, the American Government, while accepting in principle the Japanese proposal, insisted that the meeting should take place after an agreement of view had been reached on fundamental and essential questions.

"3. Subsequently, on September 25th the Japanese Government submitted a proposal based on the formula proposed by the American Government, taking fully into consideration past American claims and also incorporating Japanese views. Repeated discussions proved of no avail in producing readily an agreement of view. The present cabinet, therefore, submitted a revised proposal, moderating still further the Japanese claims regarding the principal points of difficulty in the negotiation and endeavoured strenuously to reach a settlement. But the American Government, adhering steadfastly to its original assertions, failed to display in the slightest degree a spirit of conciliation. The negotiation made no progress.

"Therefore, the Japanese Government, with a view to doing its utmost for averting a crisis in Japanese-American relations, submitted on November 20th still another proposal in order to arrive at an equitable solution of the more essential and urgent questions which, simplifying its previous proposal, stipulated the following points:

"(1) The Governments of Japan and the United States undertake not to dispatch armed forces into any of the regions, excepting French Indo-China, in the Southeastern Asia and the Southern Pacific area.

"(2) Both Governments shall cooperate with the view to securing the acquisition in the Netherlands East Indies of those goods and commodities of which the two countries are in need.

"(3) Both Governments mutually undertake to restore commercial relations to those prevailing prior to the freezing of assets.

"The Government of the United States shall supply Japan the required quantity of oil.

"(4) The Government of the United States undertakes not to resort to measures and actions prejudicial to the endeavours for the restoration of general peace between Japan and China.

"(5) The Japanese Government undertakes to withdraw troops now stationed in French Indo-China upon either the restoration of peace between Japan and China or the establishment of an equitable peace in the Pacific Area; and it is prepared to remove the Japanese troops in the southern part of French Indo-China to the northern part upon the conclusion of the present agreement.

"As regards China, the Japanese Government, while expressing its readiness to accept the offer of the President of the United States to act as 'introducer' of peace between Japan and China as was previously suggested, asked for an undertaking on the part of the United States to do nothing prejudicial to the restoration of Sino-Japanese peace when the two parties have commenced direct negotiations.

"The American Government not only rejected the above-mentioned new proposal, but made known its intention to continue its aid to Chiang Kai-shek; and in spite of its suggestion mentioned above, withdrew the offer of the President to act as so-called 'introducer' of peace between Japan and China, pleading that time was not yet ripe for it. Finally on November 26th, in an attitude to impose upon the Japanese Government those principles it has persistently maintained, the American Government made a proposal totally ignoring Japanese claims, which is a source of profound regret to the Japanese Government.

"4. From the beginning of the present negotiation the Japanese Government has always maintained an attitude of fairness and moderation, and did its best to reach a settlement, for which it made all possible concessions often in spite of great difficulties. As for the China question which constitutes an important subject of the negotiation, the Japanese Government showed a most conciliatory attitude. As for the principle of non-discrimination in international commerce, advocated by the American Government, the Japanese Government expressed its desire to see the said principle applied throughout the world, and declared that along with the actual practice of this principle in the world, the Japanese Government would endeavour to apply the same in the Pacific area including China, and made it clear that Japan had no intention of excluding from China economic activities of third powers pursued on an equitable basis. Furthermore, as regards the question of withdrawing troops from French Indo-China, the Japanese Government even volunteered, as mentioned above, to carry out an immediate evacuation of troops from Southern French Indo-China as a measure of easing the situation.

"It is presumed that the spirit of conciliation exhibited to the utmost degree by the Japanese Government in all these matters is fully appreciated by the American Government.

"On the other hand, the American Government, always holding fast to theories in disregard of realities, and refusing to yield an inch on its imprac-tical principles, caused undue delay in the negotiation. It is difficult to understand this attitude of the American Government and the Japanese Government desires to call the attention of the American Government especially to the following points:

"1. The American Government advocates in the name of world peace those principles favorable to it and urges upon the Japanese Government the acceptance thereof. The peace of the world may be brought about only by discovering a mutually acceptable formula through recognition of the reality of the situation and mutual appreciation of one another's position. An attitude such as ignores realities and imposes one's selfish views upon others will scarcely serve the purpose of facilitating the consummation of negotiations.

"Of the various principles put forward by the American Government as a basis of the Japanese-American Agreement, there are some which the Japanese Government is ready to accept in principle, but in view of the world's actual condition it seems only a utopian ideal on the part of the American Government to attempt to force their immediate adoption.

"Again, the proposal to conclude a multilateral non-aggression pact between Japan, United States, Great Britain, China, the Soviet Union, the Netherlands and Thailand, which is patterned after the old concept of collective security, is far removed from the realities of East Asia.

"2. The American proposal contained a stipulation which states—'Both Governments will agree that no agreement, which either has concluded with any third power or powers, shall be interpreted by it in such a way as to conflict with the fundamental purpose of this agreement, the establishment and preservation of peace throughout the Pacific area.' It is presumed that the above provision has been proposed with a view to restrain Japan from fulfilling its obligations under the Tripartite Pact when the United States participates in the war in Europe, and, as such, it cannot be accepted by the Japanese Government.

"The American Government, obsessed with it own views and opinions, may be said to be scheming for the extension of the war. While it seeks, on the one hand, to secure its rear by stabilizing the Pacific Area, it is engaged, on the other hand, in aiding Great Britain and preparing to attack, in the name of self-defense, Germany and Italy, two Powers that are striving to establish a new order in Europe. Such a policy is totally at variance with the many principles upon which the American Government proposes to found the stability of the Pacific Area through peaceful means.

"3. Whereas the American Government, under the principles it rigidly upholds, objects to settle international issues through military pressure, it is exercising in conjunction with Great Britain and other nations pressure by economic power. Recourse to such pressure as a means of dealing with international relations should be condemned as it is at times more inhumane than military pressure.

"4. It is impossible not to reach the conclusion that the American Government desires to maintain and strengthen, in coalition with Great Britain and other Powers, its dominant position it has hitherto occupied not only in China but in other areas of East Asia. It is a fact of history that the countries of East Asia for the past hundred years or more have been compelled to observe the *status quo* under the Anglo-American policy of imperialistic exploitation and to sacrifice themselves to the prosperity of the two nations. The Japanese Government cannot tolerate the perpetuation of such a situation since it directly runs counter to Japan's fundamental policy to enable all nations to enjoy each its proper place in the world.

"The stipulation proposed by the American Government relative to

French Indo-China is a good exemplification of the above-mentioned American policy. Thus the six countries,—Japan, the United States, Great Britain, the Netherlands, China, and Thailand,—excepting France, should undertake among themselves to respect the territorial integrity and sovereignty of French Indo-China and equality of treatment in trade and commerce would be tantamount to placing that territory under the joint guarantee of the Governments of those six countries. Apart from the fact that such a proposal totally ignores the position of France, it is unacceptable to the Japanese Government in that such an arrangement cannot but be considered as an extension to French Indo-China of a system similar to the Nine Power Treaty structure which is the chief factor responsible for the present predicament of East Asia.

"5. All the items demanded of Japan by the American Government regarding China such as wholesale evacuation of troops or unconditional application of the principle of non-discrimination in international commerce ignored the actual conditions of China, and are calculated to destroy Japan's position as the stabilizing factor of East Asia. The attitude of the American Government in demanding Japan not to support militarily, politically or economically any régime other than the régime at Chungking, disregarding thereby the existence of the Nanking Government, shatters the very basis of the present negotiation. This demand of the American Government falling, as it does, in line with its above-mentioned refusal to cease from aiding the Chungking régime, demonstrates clearly the intention of the American Government to obstruct the restoration of normal relations between Japan and China and the return of peace to East Asia.

"5. [Sic] In brief, the American proposal contains certain acceptable items such as those concerning commerce, including the conclusion of a trade agreement, mutual removal of the freezing restrictions, and stabilization of yen and dollar exchange, or the abolition of extra-territorial rights in China. On the other hand, however, the proposal in question ignores Japan's sacrifices in the four years of the China Affair, menaces the Empire's existence itself and disparages its honour and prestige. Therefore, viewed in its entirety, the Japanese Government regrets that it cannot accept the proposal as a basis of negotiation.

"6. The Japanese Government, in its desire for an early conclusion of the negotiation, proposed simultaneously with the conclusion of the Japanese-American negotiation, agreements to be signed with Great Britain and other interested countries. The proposal was accepted by the American Government. However, since the American Government has made the proposal of November 26th as a result of frequent consultation with Great Britain, Australia, the Netherlands and Chungking, and presumably by catering to the wishes of the Chungking régime in the questions of China, it must be concluded that all these countries are at one with the United States in ignoring Japan's position.

"7. Obviously it is the intention of the American Government to conspire with Great Britain and other countries to obstruct Japan's efforts toward the establishment of peace through the creation of a new order in East Asia, and especially to preserve Anglo-American rights and interests by keeping Japan and China at war. This intention has been revealed clearly during the course of the present negotiation. Thus, the earnest hope of the Japanese Government to adjust Japanese-American relations and to preserve and promote the peace of the Pacific through cooperation with the American Government has finally been lost.

"The Japanese Government regrets to have to notify hereby the American Government that in view of the attitude of the American Government it cannot but consider that it is impossible to reach an agreement through further negotiations.

"December 7, 1941."

78. Oral Response of American Secretary of State Hull to Japanese Note of December 7, 1941[13]

"I must say that in all my conversations with you [the Japanese Ambassador] during the last nine months I have never uttered one word of untruth. This is borne out absolutely by the record. In all my 50 years of public service I have never seen a document that was more crowded with infamous falsehoods and distortions—infamous falsehoods and distortions on a scale so huge that I never imagined until today that any Government on this planet was capable of uttering them."

79. Japan's Declaration of War on the United States and Great Britain, December 8, 1941[14]

Imperial Rescript.

WE, by grace of heaven, Emperor of Japan, seated on the Throne of the line unbroken for ages eternal, enjoin upon ye, Our loyal and brave subjects:

We hereby declare war on the United States of America and the British Empire. The men and officers of Our Army and Navy shall do their utmost in prosecuting the war, Our public servants of various departments shall perform faithfully and diligently their appointed tasks, and all other subjects of Ours shall pursue their respective duties; the entire nation with a united will shall mobilize their total strength so that nothing will miscarry in the attainment of our war aims.

To insure the stability of East Asia and to contribute to world peace is the far-sighted policy which was formulated by Our Great Illustrious Imperial Grandsire and Our Great Imperial Sire succeeding Him, and which We lay constantly to heart. To cultivate friendship among nations and to enjoy prosperity in common with all nations has always been the guiding principle of Our Empire's foreign policy. It has been truly unavoidable and far from Our wishes that Our Empire has now been brought to cross swords with America and Britain. More than four years have passed since the government of the Chinese Republic, failing to comprehend the true intentions of Our Empire, and recklessly courting trouble, disturbed the peace of East Asia and compelled Our Empire to take up arms. Although there has been re-established the National Government of China, with which Japan has effected neighbourly intercourse and co-operation, the regime which has survived at Chungking, relying upon American and British protection, still continues its fratricidal opposition. Eager for the realization of their inordinate ambition to dominate the Orient, both America and Britain, giving support to the remaining [T. N. Chungking] regime, have, under the false name of peace, aggravated the disturbances in East Asia. Moreover, these two Powers, inducing other countries to follow suit, increased military preparations on all sides of Our Empire to challenge us. They have obstructed by every means our peaceful commerce, and finally resorted to a direct severance of economic relations, menacing gravely the existence of Our Empire.

Patiently have We waited and long have We endured, in the hope that Our Government might retrieve the situation in peace. But our adversaries, showing not the least spirit of conciliation, have unduly delayed a settlement; and in the meantime, they have intensified the economic and military pressure to compel thereby Our Empire to submission. This trend of affairs would, if left unchecked, not only nullify Our Empire's efforts of many years for the sake of the stabilization of East Asia, but also endanger the very existence of Our nation. The situation being such as it is, Our Empire for its existence and self-defence has no other recourse but to appeal to arms and to crush every obstacle in its path.

The hallowed spirits of Our Imperial Ancestors guarding Us from above, We rely upon the loyalty and courage of Our subjects in Our confident expectation that the task bequeathed by Our Forefathers will be carried forward, and that the sources of evil will be speedily eradicated and an enduring peace immutably established in East Asia, preserving thereby the glory of Our Empire.

The 8th day of the 12th month of the 16th year of Showa.

HIROHITO

80. Roosevelt Asks for Declaration of War on Japan, December 8, 1941[15]

[Released to the press by the White House December 8]
To The Congress of the United States:

Yesterday, December 7, 1941—a date which will live in infamy—the

United States of America was suddenly and deliberately attacked by naval and air forces of the Empire of Japan.

The United States was at peace with that Nation and, at the solicitation of Japan, was still in conversation with its Government and its Emperor looking toward the maintenance of peace in the Pacific. Indeed, one hour after Japanese air squadrons had commenced bombing in Oahu, the Japanese Ambassador to the United States and his colleague delivered to the Secretary of State a formal reply to a recent American message. While this reply stated that it seemed useless to continue the existing diplomatic negotiations, it contained no threat or hint of war or armed attack.

It will be recorded that the distance of Hawaii from Japan makes it obvious that the attack was deliberately planned many days or even weeks ago. During the intervening time the Japanese Government has deliberately sought to deceive the United States by false statements and expressions of hope for continued peace.

The attack yesterday on the Hawaiian Islands has caused severe damage to American naval and military forces. Very many American lives have been lost. In addition American ships have been reported torpedoed on the high seas between San Francisco and Honolulu.

Yesterday the Japanese Government also launched an attack against Malaya.

Last night Japanese forces attacked Hong Kong.

Last night Japanese forces attacked Guam.

Last night Japanese forces attacked the Philippine Islands.

Last night the Japanese attacked Wake Island.

This morning the Japanese attacked Midway Island.

Japan has, therefore, undertaken a surprise offensive extending throughout the Pacific area. The facts of yesterday speak for themselves. The people of the United States have already formed their opinions and well understand the implications to the very life and safety of our Nation.

As Commander-in-Chief of the Army and Navy I have directed that all measures be taken for our defense.

Always will we remember the character of the onslaught against us.

No matter how long it may take us to overcome this premeditated invasion, the American people in their righteous might will win through to absolute victory.

I believe I interpret the will of the Congress and of the people when I assert that we will not only defend ourselves to the uttermost but will make very certain that this form of treachery shall never endanger us again.

Hostilities exist. There is no blinking at the fact that our people, our territory, and our interests are in grave danger.

With confidence in our armed forces—with the unbounded determination of our people—we will gain the inevitable triumph—so help us God.

I ask that the Congress declare that since the unprovoked and dastardly attack by Japan on Sunday, December seventh, a state of war has existed between the United States and the Japanese Empire.

Franklin D Roosevelt

The White House,
  December 8, 1941.

81. HITLER'S REICHSTAG SPEECH, DECEMBER 11, 1941[16] (EXCERPTS)

In their unshakable determination not to lay down arms until the common war against the United States of America and Britain has been brought to a successful conclusion, the German Government, the Italian Government, and the Japanese Government have agreed upon the following provisions:

Article 1. Germany, Italy and Japan jointly and with every means at their disposal shall proceed with the war forced upon them by the United States of America and Britain until victory is achieved.

Article 2. Germany, Italy and Japan undertake not to conclude an armistice or peace with the United States of America or Britain except in complete mutual agreement.

Article 3. After victory has been achieved Germany, Italy and Japan will continue in closest co-operation with a view to establishing a new and just order along the lines of the Tripartite Agreement concluded by them on Sept. 27, 1940.

Article 4. The present agreement will come into force with its signature, and will remain valid as long as the Tripartite Pact of Sept. 27, 1940. The high contracting parties will in good time before the expiry of this term of validity enter into consultation with each other as to the future development of their co-operation, as provided under Article 8 of the present agreement.

. . . .

Just as we were pitiless in our struggle for power, we shall be equally pitiless in our struggle to maintain the nation. At a moment when thousands of our best men are dying, no German can expect to live if he attempts to denigrate the sacrifices made at the front. No matter what camouflage he uses to disturb the German front, to undermine our people's resistance, to weaken the authority of the regime, to sabotage the achievements of the internal front—he will perish. I am now head of the strongest military force in the world, of the strongest air force and the most gallant navy. Behind me is the National Socialist party, with which I grew great and which grew great with me and by me. I thank the President, I thank God, for the opportunity given to me and to the German nation for our generation, too, to write a page in the book of honour of German history.

Part 7. The First Phase of Global War

The initial reaction to Japan's attack upon the United States and Great Britain varied from surprise and anger to considerable satisfaction and outright joy, depending, of course, on the source queried. In the Allied camp it meant that Roosevelt's administration no longer had any restricting influences and a total war effort could be undertaken. This new force was more than evident in the message that the American President delivered to Congress on January 6, 1942 (82).

Despite the grim situation confronting the western Allies, and especially America, it was generally understood that the initial step was to develop a mutual war plan. The first wartime conference between Roosevelt and Churchill met in Washington beginning in the final week of December (83). The British leader and his staff of civilian and military advisers remained in the American capital until almost mid-January, and this first Washington Conference, codenamed "Arcadia," was the beginning of numerous meetings that adopted a format of strong personal diplomacy.

Actually the basic strategy was already in existence with the ABC–1 Conversations that had taken place in February-March of 1941 (56). In a far-reaching series of agreements, the United States and British Chiefs of Staff (soon to be called the Combined Chiefs) not only reaffirmed the earlier decisions recognizing Germany and the European war as the "decisive theatre," but developed a blueprint for the Grand Strategy (84). Later, in a brief but interesting meeting on January 4, Roosevelt and Churchill with their respective military advisers dealt with several specific subjects (85), among them the plans for an invasion of North Africa.

Amidst the important Washington talks—both formal and informal—a background was being established for an even broader form of collaboration by many more nations. The common basis that provided the initiative for action was the opposition to aggression, and some foundation stones had already been laid with the Lend-Lease Act (55) and the Atlantic Charter (65). There now emerged a declaration by nations worldwide that pledged their people and their resources to the defeat of the Axis powers (86), and the first United Nations Declaration was born.

It is important to remember that the uniting of nations against a common enemy did not necessarily insure general harmony nor erase old enmities. This proved particularly true in the wartime relations between Great Britain and the Soviet Union. There was little history of mutual interests or friendship since 1917, and although the world situation altered dramatically with Hitler's attack on Russia in June 1941, it did not wipe out the many years of Anglo-Soviet hostility and suspicion. A view of some of these concerns is afforded by a memorandum from the British Foreign Secretary

Anthony Eden (87) written several days before Pearl Harbor. It is noteworthy for its revelation of basic problems that continued to remain problems despite the stresses of war. Eden visited Moscow shortly thereafter and spent two weeks conferring with Stalin, and although the Soviet leader asked for British recognition on a number of frontier questions at war's end, the Foreign Secretary refused any commitment (88). He did, however, succeed in gaining Soviet agreement to the U. N. Declaration (86).

The Axis partnership was not entirely free of strain although at the outset they had the great advantage of having taken and maintaining the offensive while the Allies could only plan to do so at some future date. The best that the United States and Great Britain could hope to do in the Far East and the Pacific area was to avoid general defeat and keep some of their forces intact. Japan had, meanwhile, captured Hong Kong, the Malay Peninsula, Singapore, the Dutch East Indies, Guam and Wake Islands, and in May 1942, the Philippines. Additional Japanese landings were made in Burma, Ceylon, New Britain, the Solomons, New Guinea, and the Aleutian Islands. The United States reeled under these attacks and the staggering losses that resulted, and the government could do little but regroup its forces and attempt to gain badly needed time (a brief but bright moment had been provided by an American air raid on Tokyo by carrier-based planes led by Colonel Doolittle on April 18, 1942).

The advantages enjoyed by the Axis powers during early 1942 included a record of extensive victories already achieved, and now the possibility of closely coordinating their war efforts with combined strategies and resources. Almost immediately Hitler pointed out to the Japanese Ambassador the value of his intent to push Germany's submarine warfare right up to America's Atlantic sea ports, and encouraged his new war ally to adopt a code of ruthlessness (89).

The kind of cooperation that Hitler really sought, however, was a Japanese commitment to war against the Soviet Union. This was not an illogical expectation in light of their past associations (67) and mutual dislike of Communism, but Japan did have a neutrality treaty with Russia (68), and the plans the Empire developed in November did not include a war on their neighbor (73). The advantage to both Japan and the Soviet Union in maintaining neutrality toward each other was obvious and Japan recognized that the Soviets were not likely to make the first move (90). The possible development of a stalemate between Germany and Russia, with Japan playing the role of mediator by forcing a peace upon the Russians under threat of war, appeared to be a much stronger likelihood in Japanese thinking at this stage of the war (91).

Japan's primary concern was and remained western oriented, not eastern. After the initiation of war in December, Japan followed a "Basic Plan for the Greater East Asia War," and by early 1942 had already established itself in an area designated as "a perimeter for the defense of the Southern Resources Area and the Japanese Mainland" (92). This vast region, extending over the Dutch East Indies and into the Central Pacific, provided a self-sufficiency in war resources for the entire Empire. There appeared to be little doubt in the minds of Japan's military leaders that they could hold onto what they had seized and protect their chosen perimeter (93).

The most important American stronghold in Japan's new perimeter during those critical days was the Philippine Islands. With a strength that barely exceeded 30,000 regulars (including some 12,000 Philippine Scouts) and a newly formed citizens army of approximately 100,000 men, it was clearly only a matter of time before that area too fell under Japanese rule. The small mixed Philippine force under the command of General Douglas MacArthur retreated to the Bataan Peninsula and several islands in Manila Bay, including Corregidor. Before the surrender, however, MacArthur was ordered to a new command post in Australia, and General Jonathan Wainwright was left in command. In what has become a minor war epic, Wainwright presided over the final surrender of the Philippines and by May 6, 1942, it was all over (94). From Australia General MacArthur radioed President Roosevelt his analysis of Japan's next move (95) and the news was not encouraging for America.

82. Roosevelt's Message to Congress, January 6, 1942[1] (Excerpts)

Exactly 1 year ago today I said to this Congress:

When the dictators are ready to make war upon us, they will not wait for an act of war on our part * * *. They—not we—will choose the time and the place and the method of their attack.

We now know their choice of the time: a peaceful Sunday morning—December 7th, 1941.

We know their choice of the place: an American outpost in the Pacific.

We know their choice of the method: the method of Hitler himself.

Japan's scheme of conquest goes back half a century. . . .

But the dreams of empire of the Japanese and Fascist leaders were modest in comparison with the gargantuan aspirations of Hitler and his Nazis. Even before they came to power, in 1933, their plans for conquest had been drawn. Those plans provided for ultimate domination, not of any one section of the world but of the whole earth and all the oceans on it.

With Hitler's formation of the Berlin-Rome-Tokyo alliance, all these plans of conquest became a single plan. Under this, in addition to her own schemes of conquest, Japan's role was to cut off our supply of weapons of war to Britain, Russia, and China—weapons which increasingly were speeding the day of Hitler's doom. The act of Japan at Pearl Harbor was intended to stun us—to terrify us to such an extent that we would divert our industrial and military strength to the Pacific area, or even to our own continental defense.

The plan failed in its purpose. We have not been stunned. We have not been terrified or confused. This reassembling of the Seventy-seventh Congress is proof of that; for the mood of quiet, grim resolution which here prevails bodes ill for those who conspired and collaborated to murder world peace.

That mood is stronger than any mere desire for revenge. It expresses the will of the American people to make very certain that the world will never so suffer again.

. . . .

For the first time since the Japanese and the Fascists and the Nazis started along their bloodstained course of conquest they now face the fact that superior forces are assembling against them. Gone forever are the days when the aggressors could attack and destroy their victims one by one, without unity of resistance. We of the united nations will so dispose our forces that we can strike at the common enemy wherever the greatest damage can be done.

The militarists in Berlin and Tokyo started this war. But the massed, angered forces of common humanity will finish it.

Destruction of the material and spiritual centers of civilization—this has been and still is the purpose of Hitler and his Italian and Japanese chessmen. They would wreck the power of the British Commonwealth and Russia and China and the Netherlands, and then combine all their forces to achieve their ultimate goal—the conquest of the United States.

They know that victory for us means victory for freedom.

They know that victory for us means victory for the institution of democracy—the ideal of the family—the simple principles of common decency and humanity.

They know that victory for us means victory for religion.

And they could not tolerate that. The world is too small to provide adequate "living room" for both Hitler and God.

In proof of that, the Nazis have now announced their plan for enforcing their new German pagan religion throughout the world—the plan by which the Holy Bible and the cross of mercy would be displaced by Mein Kampf and the swastika and the naked sword.

Our own objectives are clear: The objective of smashing the militarism imposed by war lords upon their enslaved peoples; the objective of liberating the subjugated nations; the objective of establishing and securing freedom of speech, freedom of religion, freedom from want, and freedom from fear everywhere in the world.

We shall not stop short of these objectives; nor shall we be satisfied merely to gain them and call it a day. I know that I speak for the American people—and I have good reason to believe I speak also for all the other peoples who fight with us—when I say that this time we are determined not only to win the war, but also to maintain the security of the peace which will follow.

But modern methods of warfare make it a task, not only of shooting and fighting, but an even more urgent one of working and producing.

Victory requires the actual weapons of war and the means of transporting them to a dozen points of combat.

It will not be sufficient for us and the other united nations to produce a slightly superior supply of munitions to that of Germany, Japan, Italy, and the stolen industries in the countries which they have overrun.

The superiority of the united nations in munitions and ships must be overwhelming—so overwhelming that the Axis nations can never hope to catch up with it. In order to attain this overwhelming superiority the United States must build planes and tanks and guns and ships to the utmost limit of our national capacity. We have the ability and capacity to produce arms not only for our own forces but also for the armies, navies, and air forces fighting on our side.

And our overwhelming superiority of armament must be adequate to put weapons of war at the proper time into the hands of those men in the conquered nations, who stand ready to seize the first opportunity to revolt against their German and Japanese oppressors, and against the traitors in their own ranks, known by the already infamous name of "Quislings." As we get guns to the patriots in those lands, they too will fire shots heard around the world.

This production of ours in the United States must be raised far above its present levels, even though it will mean the dislocation of the lives and occupations of millions of our own people. We must raise our sights all along the production line. Let no man say it cannot be done. It must be done—and we have undertaken to do it.

I have just sent a letter of directive to the appropriate departments and agencies of our Government, ordering that immediate steps be taken:

1. To increase our production rate of airplanes so rapidly that in this year, 1942, we shall produce 60,000 planes, 10,000 more than the goal set a year and a half ago. This includes 45,000 combat planes—bombers, dive-bombers, pursuit planes. The rate of increase will be continued, so that next year, 1943, we shall produce 125,000 airplanes, including 100,000 combat planes.

2. To increase our production rate of tanks so rapidly that in this year, 1942, we shall produce 45,000 tanks; and to continue that increase so that next year, 1943, we shall produce 75,000 tanks.

3. To increase our production rate of antiaircraft guns so rapidly that in this year, 1942, we shall produce 20,000 of them; and to continue that increase so that next year, 1943, we shall produce 35,000 antiaircraft guns.

4. To increase our production rate of merchant ships so rapidly that in this year, 1942, we shall build 8,000,000 deadweight tons as compared with a 1941 production of 1,100,000. We shall continue that increase so that next year, 1943, we shall build 10,000,000 tons.

These figures and similar figures for a multitude of other implements of war will give the Japanese and Nazis a little idea of just what they accomplished in the attack on Pearl Harbor.

. . . .

Only this all-out scale of production will hasten the ultimate all-out victory. Speed will count. Lost ground can always be regained—lost time never. Speed will save lives; speed will save this Nation which is in peril; speed will save our freedom and civilization—and slowness has never been an American characteristic.

As the United States goes into its full stride, we must always be on guard against misconceptions which will arise naturally or which will be planted among us by our enemies.

We must guard against complacency. We must not underrate the enemy. He is powerful and cunning—and cruel and ruthless. He will stop at nothing which gives him a chance to kill and to destroy. He has trained his people to believe that their highest perfection is achieved by waging war. For many years he has prepared for this very conflict—planning, plotting, training, arming, fighting. We have already tasted defeat. We may suffer further setbacks. We must face the fact of a hard war, a long war, a bloody war, a costly war.

We must, on the other hand, guard against defeatism. That has been one of the chief weapons of Hitler's propaganda machine—used time and again with deadly results. It will not be used successfully on the American people.

We must guard against divisions among ourselves and among all the other united nations. We must be particularly vigilant against racial discrimination in any of its ugly forms. Hitler will try again to breed mistrust and suspicion between one individual and another, one group and another, one race and another, one government and another. He will try to use the same technique of falsehood and rumor-mongering with which he divided France from Britain. He is trying to do this with us even now. But he will find a unity of will and purpose against him, which will persevere until the destruction of all his black designs upon the freedom and safety of the people of the world.

We cannot urge this war in a defensive spirit. As our power and our resources are fully mobilized, we shall carry the attack against the enemy—we shall hit him and hit him again wherever and whenever we can reach him.

We must keep him far from our shores, for we intend to bring this battle to him on his own home grounds.

American armed forces must be used at any place in all the world where it seems advisable to engage the forces of the enemy. In some cases these operations will be defensive, in order to protect key positions. In other cases, these operations will be offensive, in order to strike at the common enemy, with a view to his complete encirclement and eventual total defeat.

American armed forces will operate at many points in the Far East.

American armed forces will be on all the oceans helping to guard the essential communications which are vital to the united nations.

American land and air and sea forces will take stations in the British Isles, which constitute an essential fortress in this world struggle.

American armed forces will help to protect this hemisphere and also bases outside this hemisphere which could be used for an attack on the Americans.

If any of our enemies, from Europe or from Asia, attempt long-range raids by "suicide" squadrons of bombing planes, they will do so only in the hope of terrorizing our people and disrupting our morale. Our people are not afraid of that. We know that we may have to pay a heavy price for freedom. We will pay this price with a will. Whatever the price, it is a thousand times worth it. No matter what our enemies in their desperation may attempt to do to us, we will say, as the people of London have said, "We can take it." And what's more, we can give it back—and we will give it back—with compound interest.

When our enemies challenged our country to stand up and fight they challenged each and every one of us. And each and every one of us has accepted the challenge—for himself and for the Nation.

There were only some four hundred United States marines who in the heroic and historic defense of Wake Island inflicted such great losses on the enemy. Some of those men were killed in action, and others are now prisoners of war. When the survivors of that great fight are liberated and restored to their homes they will learn that a hundred and thirty million of their fellow citizens have been inspired to render their own full share of service and sacrifice.

Our men on the fighting fronts have already proved that Americans today are just as rugged and just as tough as any of the heroes whose exploits we celebrate on the Fourth of July.

Many people ask, "When will this war end?" There is only one answer to that. It will end just as soon as we make it end, by our combined efforts, our combined strength, our combined determination to fight through and work through until the end—the end of militarism in Germany and Italy and Japan. Most certainly we shall not settle for less.

83. White House Press Release, December 22, 1941[2] (First Washington Conference)

There is, of course, one primary objective in the conversations to be held during the next few days between the President and the British Prime Minister and the respective staffs of the two countries. That purpose is the defeat of Hitlerism throughout the world.

It should be remembered that many other nations are engaged today in this common task. Therefore, the present conferences in Washington should be regarded as preliminary to further conferences which will officially include Russia, China, the Netherlands and the Dominions. It is expected that there will thus be evolved an over-all unity in the conduct of the war. Other nations will be asked to participate to the best of their ability in the over-all objective.

It is probable that no further announcements will be made until the end of the present conferences, but it may be assumed that the other interested nations will be kept in close touch with this preliminary planning.

84. Memorandum by the United States and British Chiefs of Staff, December 31, 1941[3] (First Washington Conference)

American-British Grand Strategy

Note: The circulation of this paper should be restricted to the United States and British Chiefs of Staff and their immediate subordinates.

I. Grand Strategy

1. At the A-B Staff conversations in February, 1941, it was agreed that Germany was the predominant member of the Axis Powers, and consequently the Atlantic and European area was considered to be the decisive theatre.

2. Much has happened since February last, but notwithstanding the entry of Japan into the War, our view remains that Germany is still the prime enemy and her defeat is the key to victory. Once Germany is defeated, the collapse of Italy and the defeat of Japan must follow.

3. In our considered opinion, therefore, it should be a cardinal principle of A-B strategy that only the minimum of force necessary for the safeguarding of vital interests in other theatres should be diverted from operations against Germany.

II. Essential Features of our Strategy

The essential features of the above grand strategy are as follows.
Each will be examined in greater detail later in this paper.

a. The realization of the victory programme of armaments, which first and foremost requires the security of the main areas of war industry.

b. The maintenance of essential communications.

c. Closing and tightening the ring around Germany.

d. Wearing down and undermining German resistance by air bombardment, blockade, subversive activities and propaganda.

e. The continuous development of offensive action against Germany.

f. Maintaining only such positions in the Eastern theatre as will safeguard vital interests (see paragraph 18) and denying to Japan access to raw materials vital to her continuous war effort while we are concentrating on the defeat of Germany.

III. Steps to be Taken in 1942 to Put into Effect the Above General Policy

The Security of Areas of War Production

5. In so far as these are likely to be attacked, the main areas of war industry are situated in:—

a. The United Kingdom.

b. Continental United States, particularly the West Coast.

c. Russia.

6. The United Kingdom.—To safeguard the United Kingdom it will be

necessary to maintain at all times the minimum forces required to defeat invasion.

7. The United States.—The main centers of production on or near the West Coast of United States must be protected from Japanese sea-borne attack. This will be facilitated by holding Hawaii and Alaska. We consider that a Japanese invasion of the United States on a large scale is highly improbable, whether Hawaii or Alaska is held or not.

8. The probable scale of attack and the general nature of the forces required for the defense of the United States are matters for the United States Chiefs of Staff to assess.

9. Russia.—It will be essential to afford the Russians assistance to enable them to maintain their hold on Leningrad, Moscow, and the oilfields of the Caucasus, and to continue their war effort.

Maintenance of Communications

10. The main sea routes which must be secured are:—

a. From the United States to the United Kingdom.

b. From the United States and the United Kingdom to North Russia.

c. The various routes from the United Kingdom and the United States to Freetown, South America, and the Cape.

d. The routes in the Indian Ocean to the Red Sea and Persian Gulf, to India and Burma, to the East Indies, and to Australasia.

e. The route through the Panama Canal, and the United States coastal traffic.

f. The Pacific routes from the United States and the Panama Canal to Alaska, Hawaii, Australia, and the Far East.

In addition to the above routes, we shall do everything possible to open up and secure the Mediterranean route.

11. The main air routes which must be secured are:—

a. From the United States to South America, Ascension, Freetown, Takoradi, and Cairo.

b. From the United Kingdom to Gibraltar, Malta and Cairo.

c. From Cairo to Karachi, Calcutta, China, Malaya, Philippines, Australasia.

d. From the United States to Australia via Hawaii, Christmas Island, Canton, Palmyra, Samoa, Fiji, New Caledonia.

e. The routes from Australia to the Philippines and Malaya via the Netherlands East Indies.

f. From the United States to the United Kingdom via Newfoundland, Canada, Greenland, and Iceland.

g. From the United States to the United Kingdom via the Azores.

h. From the United States to Vladivostok, via Alaska.

12. The security of these routes involves:—

a. Well-balanced A-B naval and air dispositions.

b. Holding and capturing essential sea and air bases.

Closing and Tightening the Ring Around Germany

13. This ring may be defined as a line running roughly as follows:
Archangel—Black Sea—Anatolia—The Northern Seaboard of the Mediterranean—The Western Seaboard of Europe.

This main object will be to strengthen this ring, and close the gaps in it, by sustaining the Russian front, by arming and supporting Turkey, by increasing our strength in the Middle East, and by gaining possession of the whole North African coast.

14. If this ring can be closed, the blockade of Germany and Italy will be complete, and German eruptions, e.g. towards the Persian Gulf, or to the Atlantic seaboard of Africa, will be prevented. Furthermore, the seizing of the North African coast may open the Mediterranean to convoys, thus enormously shortening the route to the Middle East and saving considerable tonnage now employed in the long haul around the Cape.

The Undermining and Wearing Down of the German Resistance

15. In 1942 the main methods of wearing down Germany's resistance will be:

    a. Ever-increasing air bombardment by British and American Forces.
    b. Assistance to Russia's offensive by all available means.
    c. The blockade.
    d. The maintenance of the spirit of revolt in the occupied countries, and the organization of subversive movements.

Development of Land Offensives on the Continent

16. It does not seem likely that in 1942 any large scale land offensive against Germany except on the Russian front will be possible. We must, however, be ready to take advantage of any opening that may result from the wearing down process referred to in paragraph 15 to conduct limited land offensives.

17. In 1943 the way may be clear for a return to the Continent, across the Mediterranean, from Turkey into the Balkans, or by landings in Western Europe. Such operations will be the prelude to the final assault on Germany itself, and the scope of the victory program should be such as to provide means by which they can be carried out.

The Safeguarding of Vital Interests in the Eastern Theatre

18. The security of Australia, New Zealand, and India must be maintained, and the Chinese war effort supported. Secondly, points of vantage from which an offensive against Japan can eventually be developed must be secured. Our immediate object must therefore be to hold:—

    a. Hawaii and Alaska.
    b. Singapore, the East Indies Barrier, and the Philippines.
    c. Rangoon and the route to China.
    d. The Maritime Provinces of Siberia.

The minimum forces required to hold the above will have to be a matter of mutual discussion.

85. ROOSEVELT-CHURCHILL MEETING, JANUARY 4, 1942[4] (FIRST WASH-
INGTON CONFERENCE)

Present

United States	United Kingdom
President Roosevelt	Prime Minister Churchill
Secretary Stimson	Admiral Pound
Secretary Knox	Field Marshal Dill
Mr. Hopkins	Air Chief Marshal Portal
General Marshall	Brigadier Hollis
Admiral Stark	
Admiral King	
Lieutenant General Arnold	
Rear Admiral Turner	
Brigadier General Gerow	
Captain McCrea	
Commander Libby	
Major Sexton	

United States Minutes

Secret

Subject: General Plans.

The President stated that there were one or two matters on which he desired clarification because certain Army-Navy action depended on political considerations.

The first matter was that it was problematical what would happen to the French, both in France and in West and North Africa, and that plans must be prepared for any situation which might arise.

The second consideration was the situation in Brazil—that at the present time we can do no more than guess, but that it was of great importance that we keep our lines of communication with Europe open.

Third, that we must be prepared to take Army-Navy action if no additional developments occur in either of these areas and the situation appears to be working in our direction. We must work on the basis that the Ireland and Iceland expeditions are in shape to proceed without delay in such a manner that these operations could be halted if other considerations intervened. We cannot, at this time, make a decision with reference to Africa and Brazil, but we must be ready to take proper action if both of these situations blow up in our face, and also we must be ready if nothing happens in either of these places; that the Secretary of War is correct when he says that we can take no chances on the possibility of our first major expedition being a failure; that if the risk looks great, we must think twice before we go ahead.

Subject: Relief of Troops in Northern Ireland.

The Secretary of War stated that the expedition to Northern Ireland has been agreed upon, and the sailing date has been set. The question is, are the British ready for us?

Field Marshal Dill stated that he would see that all arrangements were made to receive the American troops.

The Secretary of War stated that he wanted to be certain that when the American troops arrive in Ireland they will not have to "roost on the rocks."

Mr. Churchill stated that the British would take full responsibility for accommodating the American troops when they arrive; that the three divisions which were being relieved could be moved to England; that he felt it was of tremendous importance to begin this movement at once.

The President asked how many American planes were being sent to Northern Ireland.

General Arnold replied, "Two pursuit groups, about 160 planes."

The President asked if the British were going to withdraw their planes from Northern Ireland.

Air Marshal Portal replied that at present they have none in Northern Ireland; however, that the presence of American planes in Ireland would be of great assistance to the British because it would obviate the necessity of the British dispatching planes to that area in case Ireland were invaded, and that accommodations would be provided for the air units also.

Subject: Gymnast Plan.

It was agreed that the British plans for the occupation of Northwestern Africa would be known as Gymnast; British plans with American participation would be known as Super-Gymnast.

The Secretary of War stated that the Army representatives had just completed a meeting with the Navy, and that in his opinion, the situation depended on political considerations—(1) an invitation; (2) would the Spanish be able to delay a German invasion of the Iberian Peninsula in sufficient time to permit the occupation to be completed?

The President observed that we should discount any idea that the Spanish would offer opposition to the Germans.

The Secretary of War then stated that the crucial matter in the occupation depended as to whether the American-British forces could establish a canopy of air protection until the landing could be completed; that this meant the employment of considerable carrier forces, and that the matter was still under discussion; that he was troubled by the possibility that the Germans could quickly establish themselves in the Iberian Peninsula and employ a dangerous force against this operation; that the Germans are already on the ground; that they have a considerable knowledge of the situation in Africa and that what we need is a fifth column in the North African area; that our chances of success in this plan will fade as time goes on.

The President observed that, on the supposition that the Germans would move in immediately, it would take them as long to complete the occupation as it would us; that they would have the same problem as we have; that in this event he did not think that we could stand idly by and permit them to become established.

With reference to the time required to complete Super-Gymnast, Mr. Churchill observed that it had not required the Japs four months to get ashore in Luzon.

Admiral Turner stated that Casablanca was the only suitable port and it was small; that it will take each convoy two weeks to unload; that there are other small ports along the coast, but we could only furnish air protection for one of these.

Mr. Churchill observed that if we could complete the movement in one month, the opposition (from the Germans) would undoubtedly be small, but that if it takes four months we would probably be blasted out.

The Secretary of War stated that only one port is thoroughly available; that in other possible landing places, the force would have to land from an open roadstead, and he admitted that he could not understand why it would still take four months even if the British are not landing there but at Algiers.

The President asked if any investigation of the possibilities at Rio [de] Oro had been made.

Admiral Turner replied that the communications were very bad there and it would involve a movement over a desert road of 700 or 800 miles.

Mr. Churchill observed that if carriers are going to be involved in this movement, the time factor for unloading would have to be reduced because the Germans could assemble a strong U-boat concentration, and that the loss of carriers could not be afforded at this time.

The Secretary of War observed that, under the plans, the carriers would be moving out without delay; that there were two possibilities being studied—one to carry assembled Army planes on the carriers, and the other to use Navy planes.

Admiral Turner stated that carriers could not remain in the Casablanca area more than ten days; that two plans were possible—one to carry Army planes and have them fly off the carrier and immediately establish themselves in landing fields adjacent to Casablanca. This plan would not appear as feasible as the possibility of having Navy planes furnish the initial air canopy while fields were being established. These Navy planes could then return to the carriers, a matter which would be impossible for Army planes. Then after the fields were established the Army planes could be flown to them and landed. (Note: The point of this is that Army pursuit planes cannot land on the decks of a carrier.)

The Secretary of War stated that from our experience in the Philippines it was of vital importance to have several dispersed fields, and that the basic necessity was to establish this canopy of air protection immediately following the beginning of the operation.

Mr. Churchill observed that the first wave should be accommodated in two or three days, and that even if the Germans hear about the movement, it would take them some time, at least ten days, to move supplies and get ready for an attack from Spain.

The Secretary of War asked how many ships could unload at Casablanca at once.

Admiral Turner replied that not more than ten or twelve could unload at once; that the first convoy would have twenty-two or twenty-three ships; that it would take two weeks for each convoy to unload; that the Americans had thought it could be done in ten days but the British believed two weeks.

The President asked that if the Commander was ordered to unload in one week instead of two, could he do it?

Admiral Turner replied that two weeks was the best estimate that they could make.

The Secretary of the Navy quoted General Arnold as saying that German fighters could not operate at Casablanca from bases in Spain; that Colonel Donovan's organization was attempting to get detailed information concerning the Casablanca area.

The President observed that he and Mr. Churchill and the two staffs appeared to know very little about the region, and that a matter of outstanding consideration was the possibility that the Germans might move into the area first.

The Secretary of War observed that he couldn't understand the lack of military intelligence concerning this area.

Admiral Turner stated that the Joint Planning Committee had a mass of information available, but there were still certain factors which could be obtained only by detailed inspection of the ground.

The Secretary of War stated that essential points should be boiled down to the matter as to whether it would be possible to get and keep air control, and whether it would be possible to land and disperse in fields around Casablanca.

The President asked concerning the sea conditions in the area.

Admiral Turner stated there was a large surf with a heavy roll at this time of the year.

Admiral King proposed a solution of using three carriers—one to carry Navy fighters, the other Army fighters, and the third, heavy Army bombers. While the Navy fighters were furnishing the canopy, the Army heavy bombers would carry supplies such as gasoline, bombs, etc., and land them on the fields at which it was desired to base the Army fighters. This would avoid the delay necessary to move the supplies to these fields. He thought that this could be done in three weeks and then the carriers could move out.

The President observed that the two-weeks period to completely unload one convoy seemed awfully slow for people who were in a hurry.

Mr. Churchill suggested that the landing be practiced at some place which would be similar to actual anticipated conditions, and the determination made as to how long it would actually take. While this was being done, the general plans for the operation would go forward.

General Marshall pointed out that an operation similar to this is being undertaken at the present time.

The President asked, in the amphibious exercises which had been held lately, how long had been taken to unload.

Admiral King replied that it had taken 48 hours to unload 12,000 men, but that this had not included heavy equipment.

The President then stated that the matter of the invitation is in the lap of the gods, but that we must be ready to have the transports sail within one week after the time it was received (if it is received).

Marshal Dill observed that if we did this, it would hold up other transportation which was needed for other purposes.

Admiral King stated that we could hold the ships in readiness.

General Marshall pointed out that present plans contemplate the sailing of the Ireland relief expedition on January 15; and if this convoy had already sailed, and it was desired to initiate Super-Gymnast, it would require three or four weeks to get it back, that meanwhile, effort would be made to figure out every possible way in which this expedition could be put across; that everyone agreed as to the strategic importance of the expedition; that we would push for information and explore all possibilities.

Mr. Churchill stated that he attached tremendous importance to the January 15 movement; that it was of great importance to the morale of the British to have American troops move into Ireland at this time. He suggested that planners push ahead with their plans for Super-Gymnast but make no diversion of shipping on the Ireland relief; that we should take no real ships from real jobs; and that we could talk about the matter again in a few days.

Admiral Pound observed that if the Ireland relief (Magnet) is undertaken, there would not be sufficient ships immediately available for Super-Gymnast.

Mr. Churchill inquired as to the possibility of using some of the fast, large ships for Magnet to move unescorted.

Admiral Pound agreed that the risks of using an unescorted fast ship are not too heavy, but that the price is frightful if the ship would be sunk.

Admiral King observed that he believed that a fast ship moving unescorted had a better chance of reaching its destination than slow-moving convoys.

The Secretary of War made the following summary: Assuming that the Magnet force now goes ahead as planned, we should try to get, in addition, twenty-two or twenty-three ships for the first convoy of Super-Gymnast so that if it becomes feasible to put Super-Gymnast into operation, the Magnet force will not interfere; that the first expedition on Super-Gymnast would consist of certain marines and Air Corps units but would not contain armored forces; that even if the British would make a landing at Algiers, some armoured forces should be provided for the first convoy in Super-Gymnast.

Admiral Turner thought that we could get enough ships (exclusive of Magnet) for the first U.S. convoy on Super-Gymnast; however, we could not dispatch the second convoy on Super-Gymnast until the Magnet ships get back.

Mr. Churchill said that under no circumstances should we delay Magnet going ahead.

Admiral Pound observed that the *Queen Mary* would be ready in a week, and that the *Queen Elizabeth*, the *Aquitania* and *Normandie* would also be available.

Admiral King suggested that we might send a token force (Magnet) on the *Queen Mary* and leave the other ships to rest on events.

Admiral Turner stated that we are all set for 21,000 men (Magnet) to sail on the fifteenth of January.

General Marshall stated that we will have troops ready to go as fast as the ships are ready to carry them.

The President stated that we might transport 6,000 men on the *Queen Mary* for Magnet and use the rest of the available space for cargo; that the matter should be given further study; and that we should get more information regarding Northwest Africa.

Mr. Churchill then asked "Then you rule that the *Queen Mary* can be used for this transportation?"

The President nodded apparent agreement.

Admiral Pound asked if an additional use could be made of American ships which had been turned over to the British for convoy from the Middle East to the Far East.

Admiral King stated that he would be willing to permit the British to make any emergency use of these ships that was desirable.

Admiral Stark stated that he would talk to Admiral Pound concerning the matter.

At 6:30 P.M. the Conference adjourned.

86. United Nations Declaration, January 1, 1942[5]

A Joint Declaration by the United States, the United Kingdom, the Union of Soviet Socialist Republics, China, Australia, Belgium, Canada, Costa Rica, Cuba, Czechoslovakia, Dominican Republic, El Salvador, Greece, Guatemala, Haiti, Honduras, India, Luxembourg, Netherlands, New Zealand, Nicaragua, Norway, Panama, Poland, South Africa, Yugoslavia
The Governments signatory hereto,

Having subscribed to a common program of purposes and principles embodied in the Joint Declaration of the President of the United States of America and the Prime Minister of the United Kingdom of Great Britain and Northern Ireland dated August 14, 1941, known as the Atlantic Charter.

Being convinced that complete victory over their enemies is essential to defend life, liberty, independence and religious freedom, and to preserve

human rights and justice in their own lands as well as in other lands, and that they are now engaged in a common struggle against savage and brutal forces seeking to subjugate the world,
DECLARE:

(1) Each Government pledges itself to employ its full resources, military or economic, against those members of the Tripartite Pact and its adherents with which such government is at war.

(2) Each Government pledges itself to cooperate with the Government signatory hereto and not to make a separate armistice or peace with the enemies.

The foregoing declaration may be adhered to by other nations which are, or which may be, rendering material assistance and contributions in the struggle for victory over Hitlerism.

Done at Washington

January First, 1942

87. BRITISH FOREIGN SECRETARY EDEN'S MEMORANDUM, DECEMBER 4, 1941[6]

The United States Government will no doubt be aware that in conversation with Mr. Harriman and Lord Beaverbrook during the Moscow conference, Stalin mentioned peace objectives, the payment by Germany of war damage, and the possible extension of the Anglo-Russian agreement of July 12 to a treaty of alliance not only for the period of the war but for the post-war period as well. There was no serious discussion of these points at the time. But on the 11th November, in response to a suggestion that His Majesty's Government should send two senior generals to discuss military matters at Moscow, the Prime Minister received a message from Stalin [in] which he expressed the desire that clarity should be established in the relations between the two Governments and the view that it was necessary for this purpose that an understanding should be reached not only on military matters but on war aims and on plans for the post-war organization of peace. The terms of the message were such as to leave no doubt that Stalin was in a mood of suspicion and even resentment to a degree that might adversely affect the cooperation of the two Governments in the prosecution of the war, and His Majesty's Government decided that every effort must be made to dissipate these feelings.

2. Fortunately, a few days later, a verbal message was received from Stalin through the Soviet Ambassador, evidently designed to soften the asperities of the former message, and we seized this opportunity of informing Stalin that our intention was to see the war through to the end in alliance with Russia and that when the war was won we expected that Soviet Russia, the British Commonwealth and the United States of America would meet at the council table of the victors as the three principal partners and agencies by

which Nazis would have been destroyed. We added that the fact that Russia is a Communist state and Britain and the United States are not and don't intend to be was not an obstacle to our making a good plan for our mutual safety and rightful interests. Stalin was also informed that I should be ready to meet him in the early future at Moscow or elsewhere to discuss both military questions and the field of war aims and post-war aims.

3. Stalin has heartily welcomed this proposal and it is intended that I should proceed in the very near future.

4. I intend, of course, to make it clear from the outset that the association of the United States Government in the matter of war aims and postwar aims is of essential importance, that our obligations to them and to our allies have to be taken into account and that the United States Government must be kept fully informed.

5. On the other hand, the Soviet Ambassador indicated some time ago that his Government felt that they might have been consulted beforehand regarding the issue of the Atlantic Charter (although, of course, M. Maisky announced at the Inter-Allied Conference on September 24 his Government's agreement with its fundamental principles) and our accumulated information leads us to suppose that certain suspicions of our intention exist in Stalin's mind which it is essential, if possible, to eradicate. These appear to be:

(a) That we aim at excluding Russia from the peace and postwar settlement.

(b) That we shall not be prepared to take what the Soviet Government may regard as sufficiently drastic measures at the peace settlement to render Germany innocuous.

6. Our main aim in the conversations will be:

(a) As far as possible to allay the suspicions and resentment referred to in the immediately preceding paragraph.

(b) For the rest to give Stalin as much satisfaction as possible without entering into commitments.

(c) To secure his agreement to certain points to which Soviet assent is important, viz.,

I. Reaffirmation both of the Atlantic Charter, and of certain passages of Stalin's speech of November 6, undertaking not to interfere in the internal affairs of other nations;

II. The principle of the disarmament of Germany;

III. The encouragement of confederations of the weaker European States.

7. His Majesty's Government realize, of course, that Soviet participation in international postwar commodity schemes and studies of postwar reconstruction such as those which it is proposed that the two should undertake will require the consent of other participating governments. His Majesty's Government are aware that this may give rise to some controversy.

But as the Soviet Government have shown a disposition to make the readiness of His Majesty's Government to discuss with them postwar problems a test of confidence, we feel it indispensable to give the Soviet Government an indication of our own attitude in this matter.

8. His Majesty's Government have so far reached no decision as to the extent to which the enemy powers should be required to compensate their victims for the spoliation inflicted upon them. The Soviet Government on the other hand have shown some inclination to expect indemnification in certain respects. In the forthcoming talk His Majesty's Government hope to dissuade the Soviet Government from definitely committing themselves at this stage to such a policy.

88. Eden Summary of Moscow Talks, December 1941[7]

Begin summary.

At my first conversation with M. Stalin, M. Stalin set out in some detail what he considered should be the postwar territorial frontiers in Europe; and in particular his ideas regarding the treatment of Germany. He proposed the restoration of Austria as an independent state, the detachment of the Rhineland from Prussia as an independent state or protectorate, and possibly the constitution of an independent state of Bavaria. He also proposed that East Prussia should be transferred to Poland and the Sudetenland returned to Czechoslovakia. He suggested that Yugoslavia should be restored and even receive certain additional territories from Italy, that Albania should be reconstituted as an independent state, and that Turkey should receive the Dodecanese, with possibly readjustments in favour of Greece as regards islands in the Aegean important to Greece. Turkey might also receive certain districts in Bulgaria, and possibly also in Northern Syria.

In general the occupied countries, including Czechoslovakia and Greece, should be restored to their prewar frontiers, and Mr. Stalin was prepared to support any special arrangements for securing bases, et cetera, for the United Kingdom in Western European countries, e.g., France, Belgium, the Netherlands, Norway and Denmark. As regards the special interests of the Soviet Union, Stalin desired the restoration of the position in 1941, prior to the German attack, in respect of the Baltic States, Finland and Bessarabia. The 'Curzon Line' should form the basis for the future Soviet-Polish frontier, and Rumania should give special facilities for bases, et cetera, to the Soviet Union, receiving compensation from territory now occupied by Hungary.

In the course of this first conversation, Stalin generally agreed with the principle of restitution in kind by Germany to the occupied countries, more particularly in regard to machine tools, et cetera, and ruled out money reparations as undesirable. He showed interest in a postwar military alliance between the 'democratic countries,' and stated that the Soviet Union had no objection to certain countries of Europe entering into a federal relationship, if they so desired.

In the second conversation, M. Stalin pressed for the immediate recognition by His Majesty's Government of the future frontiers of the USSR, more particularly in regard to the inclusion within the USSR of the Baltic States and the restoration of the 1941 Finnish-Soviet frontier. He made the conclusion of any Anglo-Soviet agreement dependent on agreement on this point. I, for my part, explained to M. Stalin that in view of our prior undertakings to the United States Government it was quite impossible for His Majesty's Government to commit themselves at this stage to any postwar frontiers in Europe, although I undertook to consult His Majesty's Government in the United Kingdom, the United States Government, and His Majesty's Governments in the Dominions on my return.

At the fourth meeting, on the 20th December M. Stalin agreed to my proposal that I should consult His Majesty's Government in the United Kingdom, the Dominion Governments and the United States Government on my return to the United Kingdom. He suggested that meanwhile the signature of any Anglo-Soviet agreements should be postponed with a view to 'signing a proper treaty, or two treaties,' after I had been able to consult the 'Governments concerned (. . .) within the next 2 or 3 weeks.' M. Stalin said that he was sure that, whether the treaties were signed or not, Anglo-Soviet relations would improve with the progress of the war, which 'compelled many countries to discard their prejudices and preconceived views.' He did not think that 'failure to sign the treaties now (i.e. during my Moscow visit) should be regarded in too tragic a light. If the treaties were signed in London in 2 or 3 weeks time it would come to much the same thing. Our relations would meanwhile be based on the July agreement, and they would become closer.' At this meeting M. Stalin communicated the text of the draft communiqué which was eventually issued at midnight of the 28/29th December.

After this meeting M. Stalin was my host at a banquet attended by most of the leading political and military figures in the USSR, which lasted until 5 a.m. and was marked by the greatest cordiality.

As regards the Far East, M. Stalin did not consider that he was yet strong enough to continue the campaign against Germany and also to provoke hostilities with Japan. He said that he hoped by next spring to have restored his Far Eastern army to the strength which it had before he had been obliged to draw upon it for reinforcements in the West. He did not undertake to declare war on Japan next spring, but only to reconsider the matter then, although he would prefer that hostilities should be opened by the Japanese, as he seemed to expect might be the case.

M. Stalin expressed himself as satisfied with the course of developments in Persia, and agreed that it was in our joint interest that Turkey should remain outside the war as a buffer against further German penetration eastwards. He even advocated territorial offers to Turkey with a view to strengthening the determination of the Turkish Government to continue their present policy.

End summary.

89. Hitler Conversation with Japanese Ambassador Oshima, January 3, 1942[8] (Excerpts)

The Führer, using a map, explains to the Japanese Ambassador the present position of marine warfare in the Atlantic, emphasizing that what he considers his most important task is to get the U-boat warfare going in full swing. The U-boats are being re-organized. Firstly, he had recalled all U-boats operating in the Atlantic. As mentioned before, they would now be posted outside United States ports. Later, they would be off Freetown and the larger boats even as far down as Capetown.

. . . .

After having given further explanations on the map, the Führer pointed out that, however many ships the United States built, one of their main problems would be the lack of personnel. For that reason even merchant ships would be sunk without warning with the intention of killing as many of the crew as possible. Once it gets around that most of the seamen are lost in the sinkings, the Americans would soon have difficulties in enlisting new people. The training of sea-going personnel takes a very long time. We are fighting for our existence and our attitude cannot be ruled by any humane feelings. For this reason he must give the order that in case foreign seamen could not be taken prisoner, which is in most cases not possible on the sea, U-boats were to surface after torpedoing and shoot up the lifeboats.

Ambassador Oshima heartily agreed with the Führer's comments, and said that the Japanese, too, are forced to follow these methods.

90. Yamamoto Secret Operation Order No. 1, November 1, 1941[9] (Excerpt)

Policy toward the Soviet Union. The strength of Soviet forces on the Soviet-Manchukuoan border is formidable. The Union of Socialistic Soviet Republics is maintaining a vigilant alert awaiting developments. However, if the Empire does not attack the Soviet Union, it is believed that the Soviet Union will not commence hostilities.

91. Japanese Institute of Total War, "The Construction of East Asia," February 1942[10] (Excerpt)

When the war situation is unfavorable to Germany, it shall be the general rule that no efforts will be made to bring about peace between Germany and the Soviet Union. However, we must be prepared to exert great pressure on the Soviet Union in case of unavoidable necessity, and to expect a peace which may not be necessarily satisfactory.

. . . .

If there should arise good prospect that peace between Germany and the

U. S. S. R. would cause Soviet alienation from America and Britain and reduce the threat against Japan, we shall mediate for peace between Germany and the Soviet Union by bringing, if necessary, pressure to bear at a period when the war situation is favorable to Germany.

To force peace on the Soviet Union by hinting at a declaration of war against her if she should refuse to suspend hostilities.

92. Japan's "Basic Plan for the Greater East Asia War," December 1941[11] (Excerpt)

I. The seizure of the Southern Areas which are rich in resources; the attack on the United States Fleet in Hawaii, and the seizure of strategic areas and positions for the establishment of a perimeter for the defense of the Southern Resources Area and the Japanese Mainland. The area to be seized was that within the line which joins the Kuriles, Marshalls (including Wake), Bismarcks, Timor, Java, Sumatra, Malaya and Burma.

II. Consolidation and strengthening of the defensive perimeter.

III. The interception and destruction of any attacking strength which might threaten the defensive perimeter or the vital areas within the perimeter. Concurrently with intercept operations the activation of plans to destroy the United States will to fight.

By the successful accomplishment of the three phases of this plan the Japanese hoped to attain the goal of this war, making Japan self-sufficient.

93. American Interrogation of Japanese General Ija Kawabe, Tokyo, November 26, 1945[12] (Excerpts)

Q. Just after the start of the war, in early 1942, were you familiar with the overall plan of the defense perimeter that it was the intention of JAPAN to hold?

A. I will have to first of all say that at that time I was not on the General Staff so it has to be just hearsay, my personal opinion and what I heard as rumors. But I think that the extent of the Japanese line was to have been what it was in about March 1942; in other words, SUMATRA, JAVA, and BORNEO.

Q. What was the then current opinion in your circles as to the ability of JAPAN to hold that line?

A. I felt, or my associates felt, that if we stopped at this line which I just mentioned, we were confident that we could hold it. The feeling in the Bureau of Aeronautics was that if we had stopped at that line and then made subsequent strategical moves and political moves, we could have held the extent which was held in March 1942.

Q. What was the current opinion as to the greatest danger to that line, the greatest threat?

A. As far as the extent of thinking of the Bureau of Aeronautics went, we felt that some time, eventually, there would be a counter-attack from the U. S. Forces. But from what direction that would come, the Bureau of Aeronautics people hadn't given it consideration. . . .

A. As I said before, the original plan was to maintain the line mentioned before. But then, at that time, it was found that the U. S. Forces were weaker than had been originally expected, so the Japanese forces fanned out to PORT MORESBY, BISMARK [*sic*], etc.

94. MESSAGES FROM AMERICAN GENERAL WAINWRIGHT, PHILIPPINES, APRIL AND MAY 1942[13] (EXCERPTS)

April 9:

Shortly after flag of truce passed through the front line this morning, hostilities ceased for the most part in Bataan. At about 10 o'clock this morning General King was sent for, to confer with the Japanese commander. He has not returned, as of 7 o'clock p.m., nor has result of conference been disclosed. Since the fall of Bataan the hostile air force has renewed its attack on Corregidor. This island was heavily bombed this afternoon but has suffered no damage of military consequence.

May 5:

As I write this we are subjected to terrific air and artillery bombardment and it is unreasonable to expect that we can hold out for long. We have done our best, both here and on Bataan, and although beaten we are still unashamed.

95. GENERAL MACARTHUR'S RADIO MESSAGE TO ROOSEVELT, MAY 8, 1942[14]

The fall of Corregidor and the collapse of resistance in the Philippines, with the defeat in Burma, brings about a new situation in this theater. At least two enemy divisions and all the air force in the Philippines will be released for other missions. Japanese troops in Malaya and the Netherlands East Indies are susceptible of being regrouped for an offensive effort elsewhere since large garrisons will not be required because of the complacency of the native population. The Japanese Navy is as yet unchallenged and is disposed for further offensive effort. A preliminary move is now under way probably initially against New Guinea and the line of communications between the United States and Australia. The series of events releases an enormously dangerous enemy potential in the Western Pacific. That the situation will remain static is most improbable. I am of the opinion that the Japanese will not undertake large operations against India at this time. That area is undoubtedly within the scope of their military ambitions but it would be strategically advisable for them to defer it until a later date. On the other hand, the enemy advance toward the south has been supported by the establishment of a series of bases while his left is covered from the Mandated Islands. He is thus prepared to continue in that direction. Moreover, operations in these waters will permit the regrouping of his naval and air forces to meet a threat from the East. Such is not the case in a movement towards India. He must thrust into the Indian Ocean without adequate supporting bases, relinquishing the possibility of concentrating his naval strength in either ocean. The military requirements for a decisive Indian campaign are so heavy that it cannot be undertaken under those conditions. On the other hand, a continuation of his southern movement at this time will give added safety for his eventual move to the west. In view of this situation I deem it of the utmost importance to provide adequate security for Australia and the Pacific Area, thus maintaining a constant frontal defense and a flank threat against further movement to the southward. This should be followed at the earliest possible moment by offensive action or at least by a sufficiently dangerous initial threat of offensive action to affect the enemy plans and dispositions. . . .

The first step in the execution of this conception is the strengthening of the position in this area. At this time there are present all the elements to produce another disaster. If serious enemy pressure were applied against Australia prior to the development of adequate and balanced land, sea, and air forces, the situation would be extremely precarious. The extent of territory to be defended is so vast and the communication facilities are so poor that the enemy, moving freely by water, has a preponderant advantage. . . . In view of the enemy potentialities I consider it essential for the security of this country that it be reinforced as follows . . . two aircraft carriers in order to provide a balanced sea force and a reasonable coverage of the adjacent sea areas; an increase from 500 to 1000 front line planes in U. S. Air Forces with an adequate flow of replacement personnel and material to maintain Table of Organization strength; one U. S. Army Corps of three first-class divisions capable of executing a tactical offensive movement. Such a force will give reasonable assurance of a successful defense of Australia and will provide an adequate base for counter offensive action. I cannot too strongly represent that the defensive force here must be built up before hostile direct pressure is applied for it would then be too late. We must anticipate the future or we will find ourselves once more completely outnumbered. . . .

Chapter IV

The War Turns, 1942–1943

Part 8. The High Tide of Axis Aggression

As World War II assumed truly global proportions in 1941–42, the changes were not just in the military dimensions characteristic of the conflict since 1939. In some parts of the Allied camp the struggle against Axis-ruled Europe and a Japanese-dominated Asia now merged into one fight. This approach was most strongly favored by the Americans; however, some reservations remained with the other two Allies, Great Britain and the Soviet Union. The reservations came because of a greater priority to not only defeat Hitler first but also to concentrate maximum effort on securing a political outcome most favorable to each of the respective powers. Quite clearly there was a conflict here that continued to deepen as victory over the Hitler forces neared.

In the first full year of global war it is doubtful if either Great Britain or the U.S.S.R. could have really provided the United States with much more support than they did, for their own resources were already stretched to the breaking point. To Americans being driven out of the Pacific and fearing even more devastating Japanese attacks, the question of giving top priority to the European war was a matter for debate, however, for many obviously did not share the Russo-British aim as fully as their Allies did.

In evaluating the Pacific situation during the first half of 1942, the American Air Force General Arnold presented a war report that succinctly described the powerful gains that had been made so quickly by the Japanese Empire (96). The rapidity and ease of their conquests was both frightening and astonishing and gave full encouragement to continue with the Basic Plan for the Greater East Asia War (92). This consisted of extending the original defense perimeters into the Aleutian Islands, the mid-Pacific, and south to Australia. The wisdom of this decision was not questioned by the Japanese military, but a number of senior naval officers were highly skeptical (97).

In implementing their war plans the Japanese prepared to sever all Allied communications with Australia in a series of operations that included an

211

attack on Port Moresby and the seizure of Midway Island (Points 1, 2 and 4, Doc. 97). The attempted invasion of the New Guinea harbor of Port Moresby was intercepted by American naval forces, and in the subsequent Battle of the Coral Sea in May a standoff resulted. This did not deter Japanese plans for the Midway attack, however, and during the first three days of June a bloody battle for the Island took place. In their first significant defeat, Japan was beaten back with a loss of several major warships, some 300 aircraft, and almost 5,000 men. American losses were less than half these figures and United States' planners regarded the battle for Midway as the first severe blow against Japanese military might (98).

During early 1942 the United States, Great Britain, and Canada established a Pacific War Council and with representatives from Australia, China, the Netherlands, New Zealand, and the Philippines a first meeting was held in April. Thereafter, conferences were held almost on a weekly basis with the American President as chairman. At the twelfth meeting, on June 25, 1942, the situations in the Pacific, Asia, and India were discussed (99), and important planning to seize the initiative was drafted.

Meanwhile, Great Britain and the Soviet Union had completed an alliance in May in London (100) that formally replaced the Moscow pledges of July 12, 1941(63). The new treaty enlarged upon the earlier Anglo-Soviet Agreement, and significantly it contained important political and economic references to the post-war period. The agreement did not, however, touch upon the highly important question of a second front by the western Allies in Europe nor did it reflect any of the growing Soviet anxiety in this regard.

The complexities that surrounded the whole subject of a second European front were creating concerns of major proportion for the Allies. The problems ranged from military planning to political decisions. The Americans tended to view the planning and execution of a cross-Channel invasion as purely military in scope and to be undertaken as soon as possible. Of course, Soviet leadership held much the same approach and wanted a new European front in 1942. The British view was that of caution based on longer experience with the Germans and a fear that if an invasion was mounted too soon it would fail, for the Allies were simply not strong enough in 1942.

The outlines of the controversy surrounding when and how a second front would be opened were revealed in a Churchill message to Roosevelt when the Prime Minister, after posing a number of basic questions, concluded that "Gymnast," the proposed invasion of North Africa, was the more prudent course for 1942 (101). The two replies from the American General Marshall, one stating the case for going ahead on a European invasion, Operation "Bolero" (102), and the other advising against any American involvement in the Middle East (103), expressed much of the American sentiment.

These matters were still undecided in July, when the American Chiefs of Staff traveled to London to confer with their British counterparts. Before the meeting took place, however, the British had already concluded that Gymnast was the only plan that contained a reasonable chance for success that year, and prepared themselves to reject American pressures for a French landing. The British position is clearly reflected in the notes of General Alan Brooke, Chief of the Imperial General Staff, for the London meetings of July 20 through 24 (104). The British arguments won the decision to go forward with Gymnast preparations, now renamed "Torch," by Winston Churchill, and by August 21 a working draft was completed (105).

The British Prime Minister assumed the onerous burden of visiting Stalin in Moscow during August to personally convey the news of the delay in second front operations for 1942. The exchange between the two leaders (106) reveals a great bitterness and disappointment on Stalin's part and a certain stubbornness to entirely accept the rejection of a second front. The Soviet charge that it represented a promise broken was denied by Churchill and he presented the Allied arguments for Torch, insisting that it constituted a second front. A French landing was projected for 1943.

Operation Torch called for an invasion of West and North Africa by an Anglo-American force commanded by General Dwight Eisenhower while the British Eighth Army, led by General Bernard Montgomery, pushed westward from Egypt. Montgomery's operation was to begin first, and he methodically outlined his plan while assessing the enemy's strength in a pre-battle address to his officers (107). The attack was aimed at the forces under German General Erwin Rommel at El Alamein on October 23. Rommel, in Germany recovering from an illness, returned to Africa to assume command, but it was already too late. Despite a counterattack and bolstered by a message from Hitler expressing fullest confidence in victory (108), Rommel was forced by Montgomery into a westward retreat.

While Churchill informed Stalin of the planned operations in Africa (109), Hitler addressed the Party leadership in Munich and informed them that, despite recent reversals, "if a blow does not knock a man down it only makes him stronger" (110). Soon thereafter, however, Churchill told the world of the successes of Allied operations against Rommel and especially Britain's role at El Alamein (111). Significantly, he also noted Britain's intent to hold to her pre-war territories. In a world broadcast on November 29 Churchill fulfilled his promise to tell the public the details of the invasion of North Africa and stressed the important progress made by the Allied powers (112). The Prime Minister did not hold out false hopes, however, and warned his listeners of the grim struggle ahead, while assuring them of growing Allied strength and confidence.

96. First War Report of General Arnold[1] (Excerpt)

(January 4, 1944)

Given time, Japan's first rapid series of conquests could be converted to form part of an enviably self-sufficient economic unit. A matchless combination of resources—nickel, tin, manganese, bauxite, rubber, oil—were seized in Malaya and the Netherlands East Indies. These are the raw materials of empire. No traditional mode of naval or land warfare could possibly have broken the defensive ring that Japan counted on for consolidation. In point of fact, the ring is still largely intact.

Japan had the drop on us. Her great offensive had secured a powerful interlocking system of air bases stretching from Formosa to Burma, Malaya, the Dutch East Indies, and on through New Guinea to the Solomons and Marshalls. This network of airfields made it possible for her to concentrate even short range fighter planes at any point—quickly—for either offensive or defensive purposes. Japan—and Germany—realized at the outset that no operation, whether sea or ground, could be successfully conducted without an air umbrella.

In the first phase of the Pacific war it was all we could do to isolate Japan's Aleutian salient, to protect our pipeline to Australia and to dam the flow of Japanese might into Australia itself. True, General Ralph Royce raided the Philippines in specially equipped B-25's, and a few days later (April 18, 1942) General Doolittle and his men took off from the carrier Hornet on our first sweep over the Japanese mainland. But these were little more than gallant episodes in a holding war at a time when we could do no more than to hold.

Offense is the essence of air power. This principle of modern war was amply demonstrated in the Coral Sea and Midway actions of May and June respectively. In both engagements, Army Air Force bombers, operating with Navy aircraft and surface ships, helped dramatically to confirm the long standing conviction of this country's air leaders—air power, properly deployed and employed, can stop a sea-borne force. In the Coral Sea nineteen enemy ships were sunk or damaged. At Midway, American forces sank at least 10 vessels, including 4 aircraft carriers and 2 heavy cruisers. They damaged a number of other ships and destroyed an estimated 275 airplanes.

97. Japan's Basic Plan is Extended, 1942[2] (Excerpt)

Upon the successful completion of the first phase, and influenced by the unexpected ease with which their initial operations were carried out, the activation of the second phase was delayed and plans were formulated for further expansion.

These expansion plans were for the purpose of extending Japanese control of the Pacific and provided for the following:

> (1) The capture of Port Moresby in order to strengthen the defenses of New Guinea and the Bismarcks.
> (2) The capture of Midway in order to strengthen the defenses of the Central Pacific and to force a decisive engagement with the United States Fleet.
> (3) The invasion of the Western Aleutians in order to reinforce the defenses of the Northern Area.
> (4) The seizure of New Caledonia, Fiji and Samoa in order to cut lines of

communication between the United States and Australia. This latter step was contingent on the successful completion of the others and was scheduled to be activated subsequent to the capture of Midway.

Upon completion of these expansion operations, the consolidation of position was to be completed as follows:

    (1) The Northern Area, June 1942.
    (2) The Solomons and Eastern New Guinea Area, November 1942.
    (3) The Southern Areas, January 1943.
    (4) General consolidation of all occupied areas, March 1943.

SUPPORTING PLANS

In support of the basic plan, plans were formulated for the conduct of the following operations:

(1) *Raids on advanced Allied bases.* —These operations were for the purpose of preventing the strengthening of Allied positions as operational bases.

    (a) Air raids on Port Darwin. This was carried out on 19 February 1942.

    (b) Air raid on Ceylon. Raids by carrier forces were carried out on 5 and 13 April 1942.

    (c) Air raids on Hawaii. These were to be conducted by seaplanes refueling from submarines at French Frigate Shoals and if possible by land based planes operating from Midway subsequent to its capture.

    (d) Raids on Diégo-Suarez and Sydney by midget submarines. These were carried out on 31 May 1942.

Every effort was made and every opportunity seized to reduce Allied air and surface strength by raiding tactics.

(2) *Operations Against Allied Lines of Communication.* —The Japanese expected to accomplish much through the use of German submarine blockade tactics, and plans were made to employ such tactics in the Pacific and Indian Oceans. Carrier and land based aircraft were to be employed when ever possible against lines of communication. They also planned to operate auxiliary cruisers in the Southern Pacific and East Indian Oceans at the outbreak of the war.

(3) *Operations for the Protection of Japanese Lines of Communication.* —Until about the end of 1942 shipping losses were comparatively light and no comprehensive plans for the protection of shipping were in effect. With the sudden rise in shipping losses the following countermeasures were taken to protect their lines of communications;

    (a) Convoy operations were organized and a system of shipping control established.

    (b) Surface escort units were organized and additional escort vessels provided.

    (c) Antisubmarine patrols were activated and search and reconnaissance operations increased. A refuge policy for shipping was established.

    (d) Small type vessels were employed for transportation in advanced areas.

    (e) Development of improved antisubmarine weapons and the training of personnel in antisubmarine warfare were undertaken.

(4) *Air Defense Operations in the Home Islands.* —Although this was an Army responsibility, the Japanese Navy acted in an assisting capacity. Air defense plans provided for the following:

(a) Employment of concentration in the use of intercept fighters.

(b) Installation of antiaircraft batteries in the vicinity of metropolitan and industrial areas.

(c) Installation of radar at strategic points.

(d) Stationing of patrol vessels to the east and south of the Home Islands.

(e) Improvement of fighter performance; research toward development of improved types.

(f) Measures for the dispersal and removal to underground installations of industrial activities, and the evacuation of industrial areas.

(g) Strengthening of air defense organizations.

98. INTERROGATION OF JAPANESE NAVAL MINISTER ADMIRAL YONAI[3] (EXCERPT)

(November 17, 1945)

Q. Admiral, we would like to have your opinion, and discuss it as you will, on what do you consider the turning point of the war, the occasion or the situation where there were definite indications of the doubtful successful conclusion of the war?

A. To be very frank, I think that the turning point was the start. I felt from the very beginning that there was no chance of success, but of course this is not an answer to your question. Once the war had started, I would pick either MIDWAY or our retreat from GUADALCANAL as the turning point, after which I was certain there was no chance for success. Later on, of course, it was the loss of SAIPAN followed by LEYTE, and I felt that that was the end.

Q. Why do you pick MIDWAY and why do you pick the retreat from GUADALCANAL?

A. I pick MIDWAY principally from the naval standpoint because of the heavy fleet losses suffered there.

99. TWELFTH MEETING OF THE PACIFIC WAR COUNCIL, WASHINGTON, JUNE 25, 1942[4] (EXCERPTS)

The President stated that, on behalf of the regular members of the Pacific War Council, he wished to extend cordial greetings to the Prime Minister of Great Britain (Mr. Churchill), the Prime Minister of Canada (Mr. King), and the Foreign Minister of the Netherlands (Dr. van Kleffens), remarking as he did so that the Council would be pleased to receive the observations and comments of these distinguished visitors.

In general, the President remarked that there was "no particular news." It now appears that the Japanese carrier strength has been reduced from twelve to seven. Three or four of the original twelve were no doubt converted merchant types, and not having been built as carriers they no doubt lacked certain desirable features, but nevertheless up until now they have been able to carry on pretty successfully in their appointed roles. The attrition that has gone on against the Japanese carrier strength has been very gratifying. In addition, with the loss of each of the aircraft carriers concerned there must have been a correspondingly heavy loss of embarked aircraft.

With reference to the Aleutian situation, the President stated that he was "somewhat disturbed." Continual fog, rain and wind make aircraft operations against the enemy in this area very difficult. So far as can now be determined, the enemy forces in this area are "small, even somewhat infinitesimal as regards ships and men." Looking at the Pacific problem as a whole and without attempting to evaluate the relative importance of the south and central Pacific, it would appear nevertheless that the north Pacific is definitely in third place insofar as priority of attention on our part is concerned. With the remark that Canada appeared to be "somewhat excited," the President asked the Prime Minister of Canada (Mr. King) for his comments. To this, the Prime Minister of Canada (Mr. King) replied, "We are not much excited; we feel that we are in good company."

The President then requested that the Prime Minister of Great Britain present his views on the general situation. The Prime Minister of Great Britain (Mr. Churchill) replied substantially as follows: "I have, of course, been concerned about Libya. We think that with reinforcements which are now enroute to that theatre, the situation will be gotten in hand. I wish to here state with what inexpressible relief we learned of the results of the fighting in the Pacific, both in the Coral Sea and Midway areas. The change in the list of Japanese ships as a result of those two engagements is, to say the least, refreshing. I can now disclose that in the latter part of March and in early April we were much alarmed for the safety of Bengal and Ceylon. Very different is that position now. Into India we have put three divisions, with more on the way. There are more British troops in India now than have ever been there before. The Eastern Fleet will be built up to full strength by August. This will not alone improve our position in the Far East, but we will be in a position to do something of positive help to China, and I wish to say here and now that we will extend ourselves to the utmost to aid our Oriental ally. It is our very definite hope that we will be able to take the offensive in the Bay of Bengal area not later than November 1942. What has happened in Libya will not set back this date. The Japanese are making their first important and decided move to wipe out Chinese resistance. Everything points to early action on the part of the Japanese against Siberia. With a war on his western front, Mr. Stalin no doubt views the possible attack on Siberia by the Japanese without enthusiasm. The United Nations can rest assured that

Britain will spare no means or methods to bring the aggressor nations to their early and ultimate downfall."

At this point the President remarked that the Japanese are in such a position that heavy withdrawals of troops from the southwest cannot be made since there is much resistance by guerrillas going on in the East Indies and the Philippine Islands. To this, both the Foreign Minister of the Netherlands (Dr. van Kleffens) and the President of the Philippine Commonwealth (Mr. Quezon) added vigorous agreement. The President further remarked that the Japanese were encountering much resistance in Timor on the part of the Portuguese and that the Australian troops and New Guinea natives in the Australian Mandates were helping "harass the invader." The President further stated that authority had been given General MacArthur to purchase at a good price all rubber which could be smuggled into Australia; this will unquestionably help to keep alive the resistance against the Japanese.

The President of the Philippine Commonwealth (Mr. Quezon) remarked that he had recently received information that Colonel Roxas, the one whom the President had designated as his successor in case he were killed or fell into the hands of the enemy, was still fighting bravely against the Japanese in central Mindanao.

At this point the Prime Minister of Great Britain (Mr. Churchill) stated that he would "like to remark in conclusion" that he thought it wise for the Council to adopt an offensive policy embodying (1) Operations against the enemy to the northward from Australia; (2) Counterstrokes against the enemy from India; (3) Maintenance of guerrillas wherever they were located.

The President remarked that he felt it most essential that the guerrillas be assisted in every possible way. "Every Japanese killed by the Guerrillas hastens the end of the war." Plans for the offensive to the north from Australia are now in a most confidential and advanced state of completion. Cooperation from British seaborne forces in Trincomalee, the Prime Minister informs me, can confidently be counted upon.

The Australian Minister (Sir Owen Dixon) suggested that early consideration be given to opening up a channel through Torres Strait. To this remark the President replied that the matter was being "attended to."

The Prime Minister of Great Britain (Mr. Churchill) told the Council that he had a very gratifying conversation with Rear Admiral Sherman, lately in command of the U.S.S. Lexington, and that Rear Admiral Sherman had particularly impressed him with the capabilities of dive bombers and torpedo planes.

The Chinese Minister for Foreign Affairs (Mr. Soong) remarked that he had just received a despatch from his government in which it was stated that aircraft were being used for transportation purposes in the Indian area in an injudicious manner, in that this type of transportation was being employed where other and slower transportation would do. The President directed that Captain McCrea take up this matter with the Joint Chiefs of Staff.

The President then informed the Council that information had been received that the Germans, Italians, and Japanese were planning a commercial air route between their countries via Rangoon and the Middle East. Consideration was also being given to flying a northern route across Siberia and Russia, but that route was looked upon with little favor because of the usually adverse weather conditions. The President remarked that everything possible should be done "to make their venture a failure. . . ."

The Prime Minister of Great Britain (Mr. Churchill) at this point read a letter which he had received from General Smuts recommending that every effort be made to recover Rangoon and the Burma route. The import of General Smuts' letter was that it was most important to support China and that the quickest and best way to do so would be to reestablish the Burma route as a supply line to the heart of China. In conclusion, the Prime Minister of Great Britain (Mr. Churchill) remarked that General Smuts' proposal had his entire approval and hearty endorsement. "I have great confidence in General Smuts' judgment."

The President remarked that the immediate goal of the allied nations was to construct "more and more planes and arms per month." In that manner we shall bring the full force of our resources to bear at the earliest possible moment, on the aggressor nations.

100. ANGLO-SOVIET ALLIANCE, MAY 26, 1942[5] (EXCERPT)

Part I.
Article I.
In virtue of the alliance established between the United Kingdom and the Union of Soviet Socialist Republics the High Contracting Parties mutually undertake to afford one another military and other assistance and support of all kinds in the war against Germany and all those States which are associated with her in acts of aggression in Europe.
Article II.
The High Contracting Parties undertake not to enter into any negotiations with the Hitlerite Government or any other Government in Germany that does not clearly renounce all aggressive intentions, and not to negotiate or conclude except by mutual consent any armistice or peace treaty with Germany or any other State associated with her in acts of aggression in Europe.
Part II.
Article III.
(1) The High Contracting Parties declare their desire to unite with other like-minded States in adopting proposals for common action to preserve peace and resist aggression in the post-war period.

(2) Pending the adoption of such proposals, they will after the termination of hostilities take all the measures in their power to render impossible a

repetition of aggression and violation of the peace by Germany or any of the States associated with her in acts of aggression in Europe.

Article IV.

Should one of the High Contracting Parties during the post-war period become involved in hostilities with Germany or any of the States mentioned in Article III (2) in consequence of an attack by that State against that Party, the other High Contracting Party will at once give to the Contracting Party so involved in hostilities all the military and other support and assistance in his power.

This article shall remain in force until the High Contracting Parties, by mutual agreement, shall recognise that it is superseded by the adoption of the proposals contemplated in Article III (I). In default of the adoption of such proposals, it shall remain in force for a period of twenty years and thereafter until terminated by either High Contracting Party, as provided in Article VIII.

Article V.

The High Contracting Parties, having regard to the interests of the security of each of them, agree to work together in close and friendly collaboration after the re-establishment of peace for the organisation of security and economic prosperity in Europe. They will take into account the interests of the United Nations in these objects, and they will act in accordance with the two principles of not seeking territorial aggrandisement for themselves and of non-interference in the internal affairs of other States.

Article VI.

The High Contracting Parties agree to render one another all possible economic assistance after the war.

Article VII.

Each High Contracting Party undertakes not to conclude any alliance and not to take part in any coalition directed against the other High Contracting Party.

Article VIII.

The present Treaty is subject to ratification in the shortest possible time and the instruments of ratification shall be exchanged in Moscow as soon as possible.

It comes into force immediately on the exchange of the instruments of ratification and shall thereupon replace the Agreement between the Government of the Union of Soviet Socialist Republics and His Majesty's Government in the United Kingdom, signed at Moscow on the 12th July, 1941.

Part I of the present Treaty shall remain in force until the re-establishment of peace between the High Contracting Parties and Germany and the Powers associated with her in acts of aggression in Europe.

Part II of the present Treaty shall remain in force for a period of twenty years. Thereafter, unless twelve months' notice has been given by either Party to terminate the Treaty at the end of the said period of twenty years, it shall continue in force until twelve months after either High Contracting Party shall have given notice to the other in writing of his intention to terminate it.

It witness whereof the above-named Plenipotentiaries have signed the present Treaty and have affixed thereto their seals.

Done in duplicate in London on the 26th day of May, 1942, in the English and Russian languages, both texts being equally authentic.

Anthony Eden.   V. Molotov.

101. CHURCHILL TO ROOSEVELT, JUNE 20, 1942[6]

Mr. President:

1. The continued heavy sinkings at sea constitute our greatest and most immediate danger. What further measures can be taken now to reduce sinkings other than those in actual operations which must be faced? When will this convoy start in the Caribbean and Gulf of Mexico? Is there needless traffic which could be reduced? Should we build more escort vessels at the expense of merchant tonnage, and if so to what extent?

2. We are bound to persevere in the preparation for BOLERO if possible in 1942 but certainly in 1943. The whole of this business is now going on. Arrangements are being made for a landing of six or eight Divisions on the coast of Northern France early in September. However the British Government would not favour an operation that was certain to lead to disaster for this would not help the Russians whatever their plight, would compromise and expose to Nazi vengeance the French population involved and would gravely delay the main operation in 1943. We hold strongly to the view that there should be no substantial landing in France this year unless we are going to stay.

3. No responsible British military authority has so far been able to make a plan for September 1942 which had any chance of success unless the Germans become utterly demoralized, of which there is no likelihood. Have the American Staffs a plan? If so, what is it? What forces would be employed? At what points would they strike? What landing-craft and shipping are available? Who is the officer prepared to command the enterprise? What British forces and assistance are required? If a plan can be found which offers a reasonable prospect of success His Majesty's Government will cordially welcome it and will share to the full with their American comrades the risks and sacrifices. This remains our settled and agreed policy.

4. But in case no plan can be made in which any responsible authority has good confidence, and consequently no engagement on a substantial scale in France is possible in September 1942, what else are we going to do? Can we afford to stand idle in the Atlantic theatre during the whole of 1942? Ought we not to be preparing within the general structure of BOLERO some other

operation by which we may gain positions of advantage and also directly or indirectly to take some of the weight off Russia? It is in this setting and on this background that the operation GYMNAST should be studied.

102. MARSHALL TO ROOSEVELT, JUNE 23, 1942[7]

Memorandum For The President:

The following are my comments on the Prime Minister's memorandum to the President, . . . ; the paragraphing corresponds to that of the Prime Minister's memorandum:

PARAGRAPH 1—SHIPPING

The Prime Minister's questions in this paragraph touch on matters which are primarily Naval. The Army Air Corps is developing anti-submarine measures with a special group of planes and scientists at Langley Field which give great promise.

The importance of a ship-building program properly proportioned as to escort and merchant tonnage is under active study by the Combined Chiefs of Staff.

PARAGRAPH 2—BOLERO

Any military operation against odds may lead to disaster. In case of a threatened Russian collapse immediate and drastic measures will be indicated for the United Nations. An operation supported by the entire British Air Force based in the UK and by a large increment from the U. S. Army Air Force has better chance of success than any other. A landing on the coast of France this year should aim at permanent occupation.

PARAGRAPH 3—SCHEME FOR BOLERO, 1942

a. *Plan*

The United States, through General Marshall, presented in London outlines of plans for a cross-channel operation in the fall of 1942 to be undertaken (a) should Russian collapse appear imminent, or (b) should a perceptible German weakening be detected. The former would admittedly be the most difficult, but its execution is predicated on a desperate situation. Detailed operational plans for these operations have not been developed here as it was agreed, and is logical, that this should be done in England.

While the difficulties involved in an operation against the mainland of Europe in 1942 are formidable, it is not believed that they are insurmountable. The Germans, by clever utilization of every conceivable method, overcame what were commonly accepted as insurmountable obstacles in virtually all of their great thrusts, March 21, 1918, Norway, Flanders in 1940, Crete, etc. All possible methods to overcome the recognised obstacles involved have not yet been fully exploited. The potential power of the immense Air Force concentrated in the UK, alone introduces many possibilities for new departures. The use of bombers for transport, smoke, protective barriers, feints, etc. is yet to be exploited.

b. *Forces to be employed*

The United States now has 50,000 soldiers in UK including one Infantry and one Armored Division and a Parachute battalion. The First Infantry Division is now assembling in the Northeast preparatory to embarking for England. The schedule calls for transporting to UK before the end of August the First Division above referred to, two more parachute battalions, 20,000 Air Force personnel, and over 40,000 other troops. By the end of August there will be five heavy bombardment air groups, five fighter groups, and two transport groups in England. Should conditions require, at least one more division could be sent in August.

c. *Landing Sites*

The operation involves a Channel crossing, probably in the Pas de Calais area, but the Cherbourg peninsula, the Channel Islands, and the Brest peninsula are to be considered, if only for diversion effect.

d. *Landing Craft and Shipping*

It is estimated that for the fall operation there will be available in the UK the following landing craft from US and UK production:

    199 tank lighters and tank landing craft of varied sizes
    583 personnel carriers
    311 vehicle and AA-carrying craft
     30 support craft of different sizes.

The total carrying capacity of the above amounts to over 20,000 men, 1,000 tanks and 300 light vehicles, and is sufficient to transport at least a reinforced division. These are all special types of craft, yet the possibilities of improvising landing craft have not been exhausted. The transport of troops and supplies by air are also to be considered.

The number of vehicles assigned to divisions for the assault is being reduced and only the lightest types are to be employed. It may thus become possible to transport the combat elements of two divisions by water, with more by air.

e. *Commander*

I think the comment on this should be, the U. S. is prepared to furnish a commander, or will accept a qualified British commander. But unity of command is regarded as imperative.

f. *British Assistance Required*

Minimum requirements are indicated in subpar. b above. Additional ground forces may be necessary. All available British airborne troops will be needed as well as the assistance of the entire RAF in England.

PARAGRAPH 4—INTERIM PLANS

There is no reason why we should "stand idle in the Atlantic Theater during the whole of 1942." Even before the BOLERO operation is begun, an aggressive, continuous air offensive should be maintained. Such an offensive, followed by the cross-channel operation, would be the best means of taking some of the weight off Russia. As a minimum it would, in our opinion, bring on a major air battle over Western Europe. This air battle in itself would probably be the greatest single aid we could give to Russia.

The operation GYMNAST has been studied and re-studied. It is a poor substitute for BOLERO. It would require the diversion of means essential to BOLERO, thereby emasculating our main blow to which we should contribute our utmost resources. An outstanding disadvantage is the fact that the operation, even though successful, may not result in withdrawing planes, tanks, or men from the Russian Front.

G. C. Marshall
Chief of Staff

103. MARSHALL TO ROOSEVELT, JUNE 23, 1942[8]

MEMORANDUM FOR THE PRESIDENT:
Subject: American forces in the Middle East.

The matter of locating large American ground forces in the Middle East was discussed Sunday night. The desirability of the United States taking over control of operations in that area was mentioned. It is my opinion, and that of the Operations staff, that we should not undertake such a project.

The controlling reasons are logistical, serious confusion of command (further complicated by strong racial and religious prejudices), and the indecisive nature of the operation.

The leakage or wastage of strength logistically in operating in such distant theaters is tremendous. We are necessarily involved in the Southwest Pacific at 8,000 miles, the central Pacific at 3,000 miles, Alaska at 2,000, the Caribbean at 1,000, Greenland and Iceland at 3,000; we have the drain of the Ferry Service across Africa into the Middle East, and the lease-loan shipments to India for China. Now, if we undertake to support large forces in the Middle East, it is our opinion that we have denied the probability of assembling American forces of decisive power in any theater in this war.

The importance of the Middle East and a protected supply through the Mediterranean are evident. The influence on Italy of a North African frontier in the hands of the United Nations would be great, but it would be only an influence with the hope of gaining a foothold on the southern but indecisive fringe of the European continent. We would still be a long distance from Germany, with extremely difficult natural intervening obstacles.

You are familiar with my view that the decisive theater is Western Europe. That is the only place where the concerted effort of our own and the British forces can be brought to bear on the Germans. A large venture in the Middle East would make a decisive American contribution to the campaign in

Western Europe out of the question. Therefore, I am opposed to such a project.

GCM
Chief of Staff

104. Notes from General Alan Brooke's Diary, July 1942[9] (Excerpts)

"July 20th ... At 12:30 we went round to 10 Downing Street to meet the American Chiefs of Staff with the P. M. We had originally intended to meet them at 10 a. m. 'off the record' for a private talk, but the P. M. very suspicious and had informed me at Chequers that Marshall was trying to assume powers of Commander-in-Chief of American troops, which was the President's prerogative.

"After lunch at 3 p. m. we met Marshall and King and had long arguments with them. Found both of them still hankering after an attack across the Channel this year to take the pressure off the Russians. They failed to realise that such action could only lead to the loss of some six divisions without achieving any results. The next argument was that we should take advantage of German preoccupation in Russia to establish a bridgehead for 1943 operations. Had to convince them that there was no hope of such a bridgehead surviving the winter. Next discussed alternative operation in North Africa, which they are not much in favour of, preferring the Pacific.

"Rushed back to War Office to see Secretary of State, Vice Chief of Imperial General Staff, Deputy Chief of Imperial General Staff, Director of Military Operations, Director of Military Intelligence, and Military Secretary. After dinner put in two hours' hard work and was then sent for to 10 Downing Street. There I found Hopkins, Harriman and Beaverbrook with the P. M. He kept me up, alone with him, after the others had left, giving him till 1 a. m. results of my talks with Marshall and King.

"July 21st. A short C. O. S. which started at 10 a. m. leading up to a meeting at 11 a. m. with American C. O. S. Disappointing start. Found ourselves much where we had started yesterday morning, except that Marshall admitted that he saw no opportunity of staging an offensive in Europe to assist Russians by September. He missed the point that after September the Russians might be past requiring assistance and that the weather, at any rate at that season, was such as to make cross-Channel operations practically impossible. We went on arguing for two hours, during which King remained with a face like a Sphinx, and with only one idea, to transfer operations to the Pacific. Finally we parted at 1 p. m. and I felt we had made little headway. We are to meet again at 11 a. m. to-morrow. ...

"... At 11 p. m. I had to go back to 10 Downing Street. Both Eden and Hopkins were there, and I was not allowed to join them for fear that Marshall and King should hear of it and feel that I had been briefed by

Hopkins against them according to President's wishes. P. M. therefore came up to Cabinet Room to see me and to find out results of our morning meeting. Got home by 12:30 a. m.

"July 22nd ... At 11 a. m. met American Chiefs of Staff again. They handed in a written memorandum adhering to an attack on Cherbourg salient as the preliminary move to a general attack in 1943. The memorandum drew attention to the advantages, but failed to recognise the main disadvantage that there was no hope of our still being in Cherbourg by next spring. I put all the disadvantages to them. They did not return to the attack, but stated that they would now have to put the matter up to the President and wished to see the P. M. first. I therefore fixed up for a 3 p. m. meeting with the P. M. and went round to explain to him how matters stood, and to discuss with him the most profitable line of action. ...

"At 3 p. m. we all went to Downing Street and remained there till 4 p.m. P. M. informed American chiefs that he was in agreement with the opinion of his Chiefs of Staff, and would put the whole matter before the War Cabinet at 5:30 p. m.

"At the Cabinet meeting I had to open the ball by putting results of all our meetings before the Cabinet, and then marshalling the case against the Cherbourg attack in 1942. I had no trouble in convincing the Cabinet who were unanimously against it. American Chiefs are therefore now wiring to America and we are waiting for next phase of our meeting. I hope they will not be as exhausting as the last seven hours of discussion.

"This evening Chiefs of Staff gave dinner to Americans at Claridge's. On the whole, went well.

"July 23rd. My birthday—59! I don't feel like it. A difficult C. O. S. at which we discussed the necessary measures to guard against German attacks through Persia on Abadan oilfields should Russian resistance break. ...

"Whilst lunching received message that P. M. wanted Chiefs of Staff to meet him at 10 Downing Street at 3 p. m. Arrived there to be told latest developments in our negotiations with Americans. Roosevelt had wired back accepting fact that Western Front in 1942 was off. Also that he was in favour of attack in North Africa and was influencing his Chiefs in that direction. They were supposed to be working out various aspects with their staff and will probably meet us to-morrow. Winston anxious that I should not put Marshall off Africa by referring to Middle East dangers in 1943. Told him I must put whole strategical picture in front of Americans. Foresee difficulties ahead of me.

. . . .

"July 24th. During our C. O. S. meeting we received a note from Marshall saying that American Chiefs of Staff would be ready to see us at 12 noon. I was a bit nervous as to what they might have been brewing up since our last meeting. ... However, they produced a paper containing almost everything that we had asked them to agree to at the start. We sat with them till 1:30 p. m. and only made minor alterations to their draft. We then parted till 3 p. m.

When we met again to examine the redraft, we settled that the British
C. O. S. should present the paper to the P. M. and to the Cabinet for their
approval before final signature by them and Americans as a 'Combined
Chiefs of Staff Document.' They all agreed to giving up immediate attack on
Continent, and to prepare plans for attack on North Africa to be carried out
if re-entry into Europe was impossible next year. In order to obtain this we
were prepared to accept an American armoured division in Persia and to
stand certain cuts in proposed air allotments. At 4:30 p. m. we met P. M. and I
put Memorandum to him. He was delighted with it and passed it at once. At 5
p.m. Cabinet meeting . . . to discuss Stalin's reply to stopping Northern
Convoy and intimation that Western Front was not possible. It was an
unpleasant reply.

"Then P. M. got me to put our Memorandum to the Cabinet. From the
start things went wrong. . . . I perspired heavily in my attempts to pull things
straight and was engaged in heated arguments. . . . In the end I triumphed
and had the Memorandum passed without a word altered. Any change
would have been fatal. The Americans had gone a long way to meet us, and I
should have hated to have to ask them for more.

"A very trying week, but it is satisfactory to feel that we have got just what
we wanted out of U. S. Chiefs. Just been told that I am for Chequers
tomorrow night.

105. OPERATION "TORCH," AUGUST 21, 1942[10]

HEADQUARTERS
EUROPEAN THEATER OF OPERATIONS
UNITED STATES ARMY
NORFOLK GROUP
OUTLINE PLAN
OPERATION "TORCH"

21 August 1942.

1. This outline plan was prepared jointly by a British-American group of
planners, under the direction of the Commanding General, European Theater of Operations, United States Army. It is designed to initiate and give
direction to more detailed planning.

2. *IMMEDIATE OBJECT:* A Combined land, sea, and air assault against
the Mediterranean Coast of ALGERIA, with a view to the earliest possible
occupation of TUNISIA, and the establishment in FRENCH MOROCCO of
a striking force which can insure control of the STRAITS of GIBRALTAR,
by moving rapidly, if necessary, into SPANISH MOROCCO.

3. *DATE OF ASSAULT:* (Tentative—see covering letter)
15th October, 1942, D. I (equivalent to U. S. "D" Day).

Practically every consideration of strategy and policy dictates that this
operation be initiated at the earliest possible date, the earlier the better. With

this in mind, every aspect of the problem has been investigated, with a view to launching the attack on October 15.

4. *ASSAULT PHASE:* Simultaneous Assaults at ORAN, ALGIERS, and BONE.

(a) *ORAN*—Two pre-dawn landings, each by a Force of approximately one Regimental Combat Team (British equivalent, one Brigade Group), one in the vicinity of GULF of ARZEU (20 miles EAST of ORAN) and one at the BAY DES ANDALOUSES.

Aggregate Assault Force: Four Regimental Combat Teams, of which three are Assault Loaded, and one composite light armored force, Assault Loaded.

Objective: To secure the Port of ORAN and the nearby airdromes of LA SENIA and TAFAROUI.

Proposed Composition Assault Forces: One amphibiously trained U. S. infantry division, plus one Regimental Combat Team and one composite light armored force of about one Regiment, together with auxiliary troops and including part of the ground echelons required for the U. S. TORCH Air Force. Three Infantry Regiments and the armored Regiment to be Combat Loaded.

(b) *ALGIERS*—Three pre-dawn landings, each by one Regimental Combat Team, one near SIDI FERRUCH (15 miles WEST of ALGIERS), one near CASTIGLIONE (20 miles S. W. of ALGIERS) and one near AIN TAYA (11 miles EAST of ALGIERS).

Aggregate Assault Force: Four Regimental Combat Teams, of which three are Assault Loaded.

Objective: To secure the Port of ALGIERS and the airdromes at MAISON BLANCHE and HUSSEIN DEY.

Proposed Composition Assault Forces: One British Division, with one U. S. Regimental Combat Team, attached (from 34th U. S. Division) under command of C. G. 78th Division (British). A senior American representative of the Allied C. in C. will accompany this force, to treat with any French authorities who may be willing to collaborate.

(c) *BONE*—A pre-dawn landing in the vicinity of CAPE DE GARDE, NORTH of the city, by approximately one Regimental Combat Team.

Aggregate Assault Force: One U. S. "Ranger" battalion with the remainder of the force British. The balance of the force will arrive in a second convoy on D. 2.

Objective: To secure the Port of BONE and the airdrome near DOZZERVILLE (6½ miles SOUTH of BONE).

5. *BUILD-UP PHASE:* On the assumption that ORAN and ALGIERS will have been captured by the end of D. 3, the movement of supporting and follow-up troops into these Ports and BONE should be timed for D. 4.

(a) *ALGIERS and EASTWARD:* To consolidate our position, and to build up a force which can prevent an enemy landing in TUNISIA or Westward, a total of six divisions (2 armored and 4 infantry) will be required, including the landing forces.

The striking force in TUNISIA will be built up by land, sea and possibly air movement eastward from ALGIERS and BONE, with advance elements starting as quickly as possible.

(b) *ORAN and WESTWARD:* To consolidate our position in ORAN and FRENCH MOROCCO, and to build up striking forces which could occupy SPANISH MOROCCO if required, a total of seven divisions (2 armored and 5 Infantry) will be required, including the landing forces.

The second convoy will land air forces and an armored division to strike West, open up communications through MOROCCO and seize CASA-BLANCA from the rear. Should French resistance cease while this convoy is in transit, it might however be diverted into CASABLANCA. Thereafter, the build-up would continue through both Parts.

The ultimate dispositions envisaged are:

One Division to garrison each of CASABLANCA and ORAN areas.

One Division to keep open communications between CASA-BLANCA and ORAN.

One Division to form a striking force on the South-East border of SPANISH MOROCCO.

Three Divisions to form a striking force on the South-West border of SPANISH MOROCCO.

(c) *Time Factors:* After Assault units have been brought up to normal scale of transport and equipment, the probable rate of build-up will be:

Through ALGIERS .... 1½ Div. per month.
BONE .... ⅔ Div. per month.
ORAN .... 1 Div. per month.
CASABLANCA .... 1 Div. per month.

Providing escorts are available to bring in two convoys per month. This rate of flow must be maintained until at least the thirteen divisions contemplated are in the theater.

6. *ALLOCATION OF TASKS:*

(a) *AMERICAN:* The Assault at ORAN, the occupation of the ORAN area and of FRENCH MOROCCO, the establishment and maintenance of communications between ORAN and CASABLANCA and the build-up of a striking force opposite SPANISH MOROCCO.

(b) *BRITISH:* The assaults at ALGIERS and BONE, the occupation of ALGERIA (except the ORAN area) and TUNISIA. As, however, it has been deemed expedient for political reasons that all Assaults should be led by U. S. troops, one U. S. Combat Team allotted to the British Force for ALGIERS and the U. S. Ranger battalion, allotted to the British Force for BONE, will land first.

7. *ULTIMATE TROOP BASIS:* As a matter of policy, it is necessary to bear in mind the British man-power situation and its relation to troop availability. In addition to this factor there is the vital necessity for economy in the use of shipping.

Since a strong force must be maintained in GREAT BRITAIN for the defense of that island, as well as to furnish troops for other theaters, it is apparent that, after a certain point has been reached, each British division sent to the new NORTH AFRICAN front must be replaced by an equivalent American Unit.

The urgent need for utilizing, in the earlier stages of the operation, those troops which are most available, requires that some British divisions be employed. However, American forces should be used as far as practicable in the build-up phase. Of the estimated 13 Divisions required for the entire operation it is considered that approximately 9 should be American and 4 British with a corresponding proportion of service units.

8. *AVIATION:* Aviation will provide air cover and support for the initial Assault, protection of bases and communications, and support for the subsequent land operations.

Assaults at ORAN and ALGIERS will be supported by carrier-based aviation until airdromes for land-based aviation have been secured.

As soon as airdromes ashore can be secured and stocked, aircraft will be flown to them.

Fighters for the relief of the carrier-based fighters will be flown in from GIBRALTAR.

Bombers will be flown from the UNITED KINGDOM after the bases have been secured.

A reserve of long-range U. S. fighters will be established in the UNITED KINGDOM as emergency relief of the carrier-fighters, in the event that GIBRALTAR is rendered untenable.

For the ultimate build-up of a striking force, bomber aircraft will be flown direct from the UNITED KINGDOM and from the UNITED STATES via the UNITED KINGDOM or WEST AFRICA.

The requirements for air support are so critical to the success of the operation that the provision of the necessary air forces must be given the highest priority.

Details of the Air Plan are contained in the Air Annex.

9. *NAVAL:* The mission of the Naval forces will be:
   (a) To safeguard the overseas movements.
   (b) To support and land the military forces at their respective objectives.
   (c) To maintain the sea lines of communications.
To accomplish the above it will be necessary to provide forces for the following tasks:
   (1) Fleet covering forces against surface attacks in the ATLANTIC.

(2) Anti-submarine protection to each group of Assault shipping and to each subsequent convoy.

(3) Close Naval support for the landings, to include bombardment, A. A. protection and minesweeping.

(4) Air cover to the assaults (except that at BONE) and to Naval surface forces and shipping, until shore-based aircraft are established on captured airdromes.

(5) A covering force in the Mediterranean to guard against Axis and Vichy French Forces.

(6) Naval base staffs for the operation of captured ports and maintenance of underwater defenses and local patrols.

(7) Naval reconnaissance, in conjunction with Air Forces when necessary.

(8) A Naval force, based on MEDITERRANEAN Ports, for offensive action during the build-up phase and during the forward movement into TUNISIA. "TORCH" is conceived as essentially an amphibious operation, in which the eastward advance along the MEDITERRANEAN will be possible only through the employment of effective Naval craft for the protection of ports, convoys, landing craft and beaches, as well as counteraction to prevent interference with land movements along the coast by hostile Naval forces.

106. STALIN-CHURCHILL EXCHANGE, AUGUST 13 AND 14, 1942[11]

J. V. Stalin to W. Churchill
MEMORANDUM

As a result of the exchange of views in Moscow on August 12 I have established that Mr. Churchill, the British Prime Minister, considers it impossible to open a second front in Europe in 1942.

It will be recalled that the decision to open a second front in Europe in 1942 was reached at the time of Molotov's visit to London, and found expression in the agreed Anglo-Soviet Communique released on June 12 last.

It will be recalled further that the opening of a second front in Europe was designed to divert German forces from the Eastern Front to the West, to set up in the West a major centre of resistance to the German fascist forces and thereby ease the position of the Soviet troops on the Soviet-German front in 1942.

Needless to say, the Soviet High Command, in planning its summer and autumn operations, counted on a second front being opened in Europe in 1942.

It will be readily understood that the British Government's refusal to open a second front in Europe in 1942 delivers a moral blow to Soviet public opinion, which had hoped that the second front would be opened, complicates the position of the Red Army at the front and injures the plans of the Soviet High Command.

I say nothing of the fact that the difficulties in which the Red Army is involved through the refusal to open a second front in 1942 are bound to impair the military position of Britain and the other Allies.

I and my colleagues believe that the year 1942 offers the most favourable conditions for a second front in Europe, seeing that nearly all the German forces—and their crack troops too—are tied down on the Eastern Front, while only negligible forces, and the poorest, too, are left in Europe. It is hard to say whether 1943 will offer as favourable conditions for opening a second front as 1942. For this reason we think that it is possible and necessary to open a second front in Europe in 1942. Unfortunately I did not succeed in convincing the British Prime Minister of this, while Mr. Harriman, the U. S. President's representative at the Moscow talks, fully supported the Prime Minister.

J. STALIN

August 13, 1942

W. CHURCHILL TO J. V. STALIN

AIDE-MEMOIRE

In reply to Premier Stalin's Aide-Mémoire of August 13th the Prime Minister of Great Britain states:

1. The best second front in 1942, and the only large-scale operation possible from the Atlantic, is "Torch." If this can be effected in October it will give more aid to Russia than any other plan. It also prepares the way for 1943 and has the four advantages mentioned by Premier Stalin in the conversation of August 12th. The British and United States Governments have made up their minds about this and all preparations are proceeding with the utmost speed.

2. Compared with "Torch," the attack with 6 or 8 Anglo-American Divisions on the Cherbourg Peninsula and the Channel Islands would be a hazardous and futile operation. The Germans have enough troops in the West to block us in this narrow peninsula with fortified lines, and would concentrate all their air forces in the West upon it. In the opinion of all the British Naval, Military and Air authorities the operation could only end in disaster. Even if the lodgment were made, it would not bring a single division back from Russia. It would also be far more a running sore for us than for the enemy, and would use up wastefully and wantonly the key men and the landing craft required for real action in 1943. This is our settled view. The Chief of the Imperial General Staff will go into details with the Russian Commanders to any extent that may be desired.

3. No promise has been broken by Great Britain or the United States. I point to paragraph 5 of my Aide-Mémoire given to Mr. Molotov on the 10th June, 1942, which distinctly says: "We can, therefore, give no promise." This Aide-Mémoire followed upon lengthy conversations, in which the very small chance of such a plan being adopted was made abundantly clear. Several of these conversations are on record.

4. However, all the talk about an Anglo-American invasion of France this year has misled the enemy, and has held large air forces and considerable military forces on the French Channel coast. It would be injurious to all

common interests, especially Russian interests, if any public controversy arose in which it would be necessary for the British Government to unfold to the nation the crushing argument which they conceive themselves to possess against "Sledgehammer."[12] Widespread discouragement would be caused to the Russian armies who have been buoyed up on this subject, and the enemy would be free to withdraw further forces from the West. The wisest course is to use "Sledgehammer" as a blind for "Torch," and proclaim "Torch," when it begins, as the second front. This is what we ourselves mean to do.

5. We cannot admit that the conversations with Mr. Molotov about the second front, safeguarded as they were by reservations both oral and written, formed any ground for altering the strategic plans of the Russian High Command.

6. We reaffirm our resolve to aid our Russian allies by every practicable means.

W. CH.

August 14th, 1942

107. Notes for General Montgomery's Address to Officers, October 22, 1942[13]

Address to Officers—"Lightfoot"   19/20 Oct. 1942

1. Back history since August. The mandate; my plans to carry it out, the creation of 10 corps. Leadership-equipment-training.
2. Interference by Rommell [*sic*] on 31 Aug.
3. The basic framework of the Army plan for Lightfoot as issued on 14 Sep. To destroy enemy armour.
4. Situation in early October. Untrained Army. Gradually realized that I must recast the plan so as to be within the capability of the troops. The new plan; the "crumbling" operations. A reversal of accepted methods.
5. *Key points in the Army plan.* Three phases.
   30 corps break-in.
   10 corps break through. } Fighting for position and the
   13 corps break in.   tactical advantage.
   The dog-fight, and "crumbling" operations.
   The final "break" of the enemy.
6. *The enemy.*
   His sickness; low strengths, small stocks of petrol, ammunition, food.
   Morale is good, except possibly Italians.
7. *Ourselves.*
   Immense superiority in guns, tanks, men.
   Can fight a prolonged battle, and will do so.
   25 pdr 832
    6 pdr 753   1200 tanks (470 heavy)
    2 pdr 500
   Morale on the top lines.

8. *General conduct of the battle.*
   Methodical progress; destroy enemy part by part, slowly and surely.
   Shoot tanks and shoot Germans.
   He cannot last a long battle; we can.
   We must therefore keep at it hard; no unit commander must relax the pressure; Organize ahead for a "dog fight" a week. Whole affair about 10 days, (12).
   Don't expect spectacular results too soon.
   Operate from firm bases.
   Quick re-organization on objectives.   If we do all this,
   Keep balanced.   victory is certain.
   Maintain offensive eagerness.
   Keep up the pressure.
12. Morale—measures to get it. Addresses.
   Every soldier in the Army a fighting soldier.
   No non-fighting man. All trained to kill Germans.
   My message to the troops.
11. The issues at stake.
10. The troops to remember what to say if they are captured.
   Rank, name, and number.

108. Hitler Message to Rommel, November 3, 1942[14]

I and the German people are watching the heroic defensive battle being fought in Egypt. We have loyal confidence in your powers of leadership as well as in the courage of the German and Italian troops under your command. In the situation in which you now find yourself, there can be no other consideration than to hold fast, never retreat, hurl every gun and every man into the fray. During the next few days there will be important air reinforcements transferred to the Commander in Chief South. The *Duce* and the *Commando Supremo* will also strain every muscle to see to it that you are supplied with the means to continue the battle. The enemy has numerical superiority, but he, too, will come to the end of his resources. It would not be the first time in history that the stronger will has prevailed against the stronger battalions of the enemy. You can show your troops no other way than that which leads to victory or death.

109. Churchill Message to Stalin, November 5, 1942[15]

I promised to tell you when our army in Egypt had gained a decisive victory over Rommel. General Alexander now reports that enemy's front is broken and that he is retreating westwards in considerable disorder. Apart from the troops in the main battle, there are six Italian and two German divisions in the desert to the South of our advance along the coast. These have very little mechanical transport or supplies, and it is possible that a very heavy toll will be taken in the next few days. Besides this, Rommel's only line of retreat is along the coastal road which is now crammed with troops and transport and under continuous attack of our greatly superior Air Force.

2. *Most Secret.* For yourself alone. "Torch" is imminent on a very great scale. I believe political difficulties about which you expressed concern have been satisfactorily solved. The military movement is proceeding with precision.

3. I am most anxious to proceed with the placing of twenty British and American Squadrons on your southern flank as early as possible. President Roosevelt is in full accord and there is no danger now of a disaster in Egypt. Before anything can be done, however, it is necessary that detailed arrangements should be made about landing grounds, etc., between your officers and ourselves. Kindly let me know as soon as possible how you would like this consultation to be arranged. The Squadrons it is proposed to send were stated in my telegram of October 9th, in accordance with which we have been making such preparations as were possible pending arrangements with you.

4. Let me further express to you, Premier Stalin, and to M. Molotov, our congratulations on the ever glorious defence of Stalingrad and on the decisive defeat of Hitler's second campaign against Russia. I should be glad to know from you how you stand in the Caucasus.

5. All good wishes for your anniversary.

110. HITLER'S MUNICH SPEECH, NOVEMBER 8, 1942[16] (EXCERPTS)

Destiny will give the victory to him who most deserves it. We could have had victory in 1918, but the German people did not deserve it. There will be no repetition of 1918. Why are we fighting so far from home to-day? To keep the war from our home country and spare it the fate which has befallen only a few German towns.

The enemy is making a great mistake if he thinks he can repeat the history of the last war. Mr. Eden, this snobbish dandy, says the English have experience in governing. It would be truer to say experience in robbing and plundering. If they govern as efficiently as they boast, why don't they leave India? No, they cannot govern. They can only subjugate peoples and push them into misery. If now this super-scoundrel Roosevelt comes and says Germany must be rescued by American methods I reply: "You cannot help your own people. You plunged them into war because you saw no other way out."

. . . .

We know what would be in store for us if the other side won. Because of that, there can be no sort of compromise, and no more peace offers will come from us. The last one was in 1940. Since then there has been nothing else but the word ' ·ht.' I said before that if the World Jewry thinks it can wipe us out it will find that it will be the World Jewry which will be extinguished. A great many Jews who laughed then are not laughing now, and those who are laughing now will not be laughing soon.

Our enemies make out their smallest successes to be of world-shaking importance. Then the tables are turned and they are down again. Stalin thought we would attack in the central sector, but our aims were directed against one particular town. It was this special town that I wanted. Please do not believe I wanted it because it is called after Stalin. I wanted it because of its importance as a junction. We stopped the traffic of 30,000,000 tons of fuel and 9,000,000 tons of petrol. That is why we took Stalingrad. That is why we have got it now except for some very small parts. If anybody asks why we do not take immediately the remaining strong-points held by the enemy, I reply, 'Because they are not worth a second Verdun.' I can assure you that there are no more vessels steaming up the Volga. That is what really matters.

People ask, 'Why are we taking so long over Stalingrad?' We are taking so long because we do not want mass murder. Enough blood is flowing as it is. If the enemy wanted to attack, I for one would not wish to stop him, for defence is always cheaper. He could bleed to death. The enemy accuses us of mistakes. Was it a mistake to occupy the Ukraine, to seize the iron ore, the oil, the wheatfields?

In North Africa the enemy has moved forward and back, but what matters in this war is the final result, and that you can leave to us. We cannot score new successes every week. That is impossible. It is also unnecessary. What is necessary is that we should hold what we have. On that you can depend.

. . . .

If a blow does not knock a man down it only makes him stronger. Wherever the fronts may be, Germany will always hit back and go over to the attack. When to-day Roosevelt launches an attack against North Africa under the pretext of protecting it against Germany and Italy we need not waste words about the lies of this old scoundrel. The decisive last word will certainly not be spoken by Herr Roosevelt. You may be sure of that. We shall prepare all counter-blows, as always, thoroughly, and they will come, as always, in due time. When the British first landed in Boulogne, six months later their dreams had come to an end. It came differently from what they thought, and it will come differently again.

111. CHURCHILL'S MANSION HOUSE SPEECH, NOVEMBER 10, 1942[17] (EXCERPT)

We have not so far in this war taken as many German prisoners as they have taken British, but these German prisoners will no doubt come in in droves at the end just as they did last time. I have never promised anything but blood, tears, toil, and sweat. Now, however, we have a new experience. We have victory. The bright gleam has caught the helmets of our soldiers, and warmed and cheered all our hearts.

The late M. Venizelos observed that in all her wars England—he should have said Britain, of course—always wins one battle—the last. It would seem to have begun rather earlier this time. General Alexander, with his brilliant comrade and lieutenant, General Montgomery, has gained a glorious and decisive victory in what I think should be called the Battle of Egypt. Rommel's army has been defeated. It has been routed. It has been very largely destroyed as a fighting force.

This battle was not fought for the sake of gaining positions or so many square miles of desert territory. General Alexander and General Montgomery fought it with one single idea. They meant to destroy the armed force of the enemy, and to destroy it at the place where the disaster would be most far-reaching and irrecoverable.

All the various elements in our line of battle played their parts—Indian troops, Fighting French, the Greeks, the representatives of Czechoslovakia and the others who took part. The Americans rendered powerful and invaluable service in the air. But as it happened—as the course of the battle turned—it has been fought throughout almost entirely by men of British blood from home and from the Dominions on the one hand, and by Germans on the other. The Italians were left to perish in the waterless desert or surrender as they are doing.

The fight between the British and the Germans was intense and fierce in the extreme. It was a deadly grapple. The Germans have been outmatched and outfought with the very kind of weapons with which they had beaten down so many small peoples, and also large unprepared peoples. They have been beaten by the very technical apparatus on which they counted to gain them the domination of the world. Especially is this true of the air and of the tanks and of the artillery, which has come back into its own on the battlefield. The Germans have received back again that measure of fire and steel which they have so often meted out to others.

Now this is not the end. It is not even the beginning of the end. But it is, perhaps, the end of the beginning. Henceforth Hitler's Nazis will meet equally well armed, and perhaps better armed troops. Henceforth they will have to face in many theatres of war that superiority in the air which they have so often used without mercy against others, of which they boasted all around the world, and which they intended to use as an instrument for convincing all other peoples that all resistance to them was hopeless. When I read of the coastal road crammed with fleeing German vehicles under the blasting attacks of the Royal Air Force, I could not but remember those roads of France and Flanders, crowded, not with fighting men, but with helpless refugees—women and children—fleeing with their pitiful barrows and household goods, upon whom such merciless havoc was wreaked. I have, I trust, a humane disposition, but I must say I could not help feeling that what was happening, however grievous, was only justice grimly reclaiming her rights.

It will be my duty in the near future to give to Parliament a full and particular account of these operations. All I will say of them at present is that the victory which has already been gained gives good prospect of becoming decisive and final so far as the defence of Egypt is concerned.

Let me, however, make this clear, in case there should be any mistake about it in any quarter. We mean to hold our own. I have not become the King's First Minister in order to preside over the liquidation of the British Empire. For that task, if ever it were prescribed, someone else would have to be found, and, under democracy, I suppose the nation would have to be consulted. I am proud to be a member of that vast commonwealth and society of nations and communities gathered in and around the ancient British monarchy, without which the good cause might well have perished from the face of the earth. Here we are, and here we stand, a veritable rock of salvation in this drifting world.

112. Public Radio Broadcast By Churchill, London, November 29, 1942[18] (Excerpts)

Since we rang the bells for Alamein, the good cause has prospered. The Eighth Army has advanced nearly four hundred miles, driving before them in rout and ruin the powerful forces, or the remnants of the powerful forces, which Rommel boasted and Hitler and Mussolini believed would conquer Egypt. Another serious battle may be impending at the entrance to Tripolitania. I make it a rule not to prophesy about battles before they are fought. Everyone must try to realise the immense distances over which the North African war ranges, and the enormous labours and self-denial of the troops who press forward relentlessly, twenty, thirty, forty and sometimes fifty miles in a single day. I will say no more than that we may have the greatest confidence in Generals Alexander and Montgomery, and in our soldiers and airmen who have at last begun to come into their own.

At the other side of Africa, a thousand miles or more to the westward, the tremendous joint undertaking of the United States and Britain which was fraught with so many hazards has also been crowned with astonishing success. To transport these large armies of several hundred thousand men, with all their intricate elaborate modern apparatus, secretly across the seas and oceans, and to strike to the hour, and almost to the minute, simultaneously at a dozen points, in spite of all the U-boats and all the chances of weather, was a feat of organisation which will long be studied with respect. It was rendered possible only by one sovereign fact—namely the perfect comradeship and understanding prevailing between the British and American staffs and troops. This majestic enterprise is under the direction and responsibility of the President of the United States, and our First British Army is serving under the orders of the American Commander-in-Chief, General Eisenhower, in whose military skill and burning energy we put our faith, and whose orders to attack we shall punctually and unflinchingly obey. Behind all lies the power of the Royal Navy, to which is joined a powerful

American Fleet; the whole under the command of Admiral Cunningham, and all subordinated to the Allied Commander-in-Chief.

. . . .

I have been speaking about Africa, about the 2,000 miles of coastline fronting the underside of subjugated Europe. From all this we intend, and I will go so far as to say we expect, to expel the enemy before long. But Africa is no halting-place: it is not a seat but a springboard. We shall use Africa only to come to closer grips. Anyone can see the importance to us of re-opening the Mediterranean to military traffic and saving the long voyage round the Cape. Perhaps by this short cut and the economy of shipping resulting from it, we may strike as heavy a blow at the U-boats as has happened in the whole war; but there is another advantage to be gained by the mastery of the North African shore: we open the air battle upon a new front. In order to shorten the struggle, it is our duty to engage the enemy in the air continuously on the largest scale and at the highest intensity. To bring relief to the tortured world, there must be the maximum possible air fighting. Already, the German Air Force is a wasting asset; their new construction is not keeping pace with their losses; their front line is weakening both in numbers and, on the whole, in quality. The British, American and Russian Air Forces, already together far larger, are growing steadily and rapidly; the British and United States expansion in 1943 will be, to put it mildly, well worth watching: all we need is more frequent opportunities of contact. The new air front, from which the Americans and also the Royal Air Force are deploying along the Mediterranean shore, ought to give us these extra opportunities abundantly in 1943. Thirdly, our operations in French North Africa should enable us to bring the weight of the war home to the Italian Fascist state, in a manner not hitherto dreamed of by its guilty leaders, or still less by the unfortunate Italian people Mussolini has led, exploited and disgraced. Already the centres of war industry in Northern Italy are being subjected to harder treatment than any of our cities experienced in the winter of 1940. But if the enemy should in due course be blasted from the Tunisian tip, which is our aim, the whole of the South of Italy—all the naval bases, all the munition establishments and other military objectives wherever situated—will be brought under prolonged, scientific, and shattering air attack.

It is for the Italian people, forty millions of them, to say whether they want this terrible thing to happen to their country or not. One man, and one man alone, has brought them to this pass. There was no need for them to go to war; no one was going to attack them. We tried our best to induce them to remain neutral, to enjoy peace and prosperity and exceptional profits in a world of storm. But Mussolini could not resist the temptation of stabbing prostrate France, and what he thought was helpless Britain, in the back. Mad dreams of imperial glory, the lust of conquest and booty, the arrogance of long-unbridled tyranny, led him to his fatal, shameful act. In vain I warned him: he would not hearken. On deaf ears and a stony heart fell the wise, far-seeing appeals of the American President. The hyena in his nature broke all bounds of decency and even commonsense. To-day his Empire is gone. We have over a hundred Italian generals and nearly three hundred thousand of his soldiers in our hands as prisoners of war. Agony grips the fair land of Italy. This is only the beginning, and what have the Italians to show for it? A brief promenade by German permission along the Riviera; a flying visit to Corsica; a bloody struggle with the heroic patriots of Yugoslavia; a deed of undying shame in Greece; the ruins of Genoa, Turin, Milan; and this is only a foretaste. One man and the régime he has created have brought these measureless calamities upon the hard-working, gifted, and once happy Italian people, with whom, until the days of Mussolini, the English-speaking world had so many sympathies and never a quarrel. How long must this endure?

We may certainly be glad about what has lately happened in Africa, and we may look forward with sober confidence to the moment when we can say: one continent relieved. But these successes in Africa, swift and decisive as they have been, must not divert our attention from the prodigious blows which Russia is striking on the Eastern Front. All the world wonders at the giant strength which Russia has been able to conserve and to apply. The invincible defence of Stalingrad is matched by the commanding military leadership of Stalin. When I was leaving the Kremlin in the middle of August, I said to Premier Stalin: "When we have decisively defeated Rommel in Egypt, I will send you a telegram." And he replied: "When we make our counteroffensive here" (and he drew the arrow on the map), "I will send you one." Both messages have duly arrived, and both have been thankfully received.

. . . .

I know of nothing that has happened yet which justifies the hope that the war will not be long, or that bitter and bloody years do not lie ahead. Certainly the most painful experiences would lie before us if we allowed ourselves to relax our exertions, to weaken the discipline, unity and order of our array, if we fell to quarrelling about what we should do with our victory before that victory had been won. We must not build on hopes or fears, but only on the continued faithful discharge of our duty, wherein alone will be found safety and peace of mind. Remember that Hitler with his armies and his secret police holds nearly all Europe in his grip. Remember that he has millions of slaves to toil for him, a vast mass of munitions, many mighty arsenals, many fertile fields. Remember that Göring has brazenly declared that whoever starves in Europe, it will not be the Germans. Remember that these villains know their lives are at stake. Remember how small a portion of the German Army we British have yet been able to engage and to destroy. Remember that the U-boat warfare is not diminishing but growing, and that it may well be worse before it is better. Then, facing the facts, the ugly facts as well as the encouraging facts, undaunted, then we shall learn to use victory as a spur to further efforts, and make good fortune the means of gaining more.

This much only will I say about the future, and I say it with an acute consciousness of the fallibility of my own judgment. It may well be that the war in Europe will come to an end before the war in Asia. The Atlantic may be calm, while in the Pacific the hurricane rises to its full pitch. If events should take such a course, we should at once bring all our forces to the other side of the world, to the aid of the United States, to the aid of China, and above all to the aid of our kith and kin in Australia and New Zealand, in their valiant struggle against the aggressions of Japan. While we were thus engaged in the Far East, we should be sitting with the United States and with our ally Russia and those of the United Nations concerned, shaping the international instruments and national settlements which must be devised if the free life of Europe is ever to rise again, and if the fearful quarrels which have rent European civilisation are to be prevented from once more disturbing the progress of the world. It seems to me that should the war end thus, in two successive stages, there will be a far higher sense of comradeship around the council table than existed among the victors at Versailles. Then the danger had passed away. The common bond between the Allies had snapped. There was no sense of corporate responsibility such as exists when victorious nations who are masters of one vast scene are, most of them, still waging war side by side in another. I should hope, therefore, that we shall be able to make better solutions—more far-reaching, more lasting solutions— of the problems of Europe at the end of this war than was possible a quarter of a century ago. It is not much use pursuing these speculations farther at this time. For no one can possibly know what the state of Europe or of the world will be, when the Nazi and Fascist tyrannies have been finally broken. The dawn of 1943 will soon loom red before us, and we must brace ourselves to cope with the trials and problems of what must be a stern and terrible year. We do so with the assurance of ever-growing strength, and we do so as a nation with a strong will, a bold heart and a good conscience.

Part 9. The Year for Global Strategy

By the beginning of 1943 the Allies, though far from victory, had begun to assume a much more confident posture. Axis expansion had been halted and the broad outlines of an overall war strategy were being implemented in successive steps. During January of that year Allied leaders gathered in Morocco at Casablanca for a conference; Stalin, engaged by military operations at home, did not attend.

In preparation for conference discussion, a British Chiefs of Staff paper (113) outlined American-British strategy and noted in the opening paragraph that the "days of plugging holes are over. We must now agree on a plan that will lead to victory, quickly and decisively." Generally acknowledging the growing resources of the United States, the question was posed as to how these vast resources were to be employed for maximum efficiency. Germany still remained the nation with greatest potential and the force that had to be destroyed first. Several subjects were of prime importance for discussion, such as a cross-Channel invasion of France, the bomber offensive against Germany, and the possibility of eliminating Italy from the war in the near future.

A discussion by the Combined Chiefs of Staff at Casablanca centered upon the Pacific situation shortly after the conference opened (114). The disappointment—even bitterness—of some Americans engaged in the Pacific war at the lesser priority given to Japan's defeat was clearly evident in the discussions. Despite the basic decisions outlined by the Casablanca meeting that were of major importance in reaffirming the course of the conflict, the conference is perhaps best known for President Roosevelt's "unconditional surrender" announcement.

By all accounts the phrase "unconditional surrender" came from Roosevelt at a luncheon meeting with Churchill on January 23. The following day the American President held a press conference and revealed a number of aspects of the Casablanca meeting, including the unconditional surrender statement (115). The exact value of announcing the unconditional surrender position at Casablanca is difficult to assess. Clearly it represented a logical stance for the western powers to assume in view of their World War I experiences with Germany. However, there were other considerations and perhaps the most important at the moment for both Roosevelt and Churchill was an inability to fix a date for the opening of a second front. Thus, a promise to pursue enemy defeat to the bitter end without compromise had to suffice for Stalin—at least for the moment.

Shortly after the unconditional surrender statement, the two western leaders informed Stalin of the results of the Casablanca meeting and stressed their positive plans to launch Mediterranean operations in the near future, including the invasion of Sicily (Operation "Husky"). In later communications with the Communist leader the possibility of a second front in late summer was broached, and an exchange of messages during February and March revealed the great anxieties surrounding that extremely difficult problem (116, 117 and 118).

By the time of the third Washington Conference (May 11–27, 1943) the planning for the Sicilian invasion was well advanced and Operation Husky was scheduled to begin in July. The Conference dealt with further operations planned against Italy, the air war over Europe, and increased efforts in the Pacific theatre (119). The continued operations against Japan envisioned an "overwhelming air offensive" and ultimately an invasion of the home islands. Japan's plans remained rooted in protective measures, for their earlier established defense perimeter (92); however, this had to be modified as the Allied offensive increased in strength. The Japanese response was a series of operational plans, beginning with the "Z" and "Y" Plans about May 1943, that generally called for greater strengthening of already existing defenses.

An interesting development in Allied relations occurred at this time that was to eliminate a long-standing irritant for many western statesmen. On May 15 it was announced in Moscow that the Communist International (Comintern) was dissolving, and later Stalin granted an interview explaining the Soviet reasoning behind such a move (120). Despite this improvement, there is no indication that it changed the immediate course of Allied talks. The long-planned Allied invasion of France had been discussed by Roosevelt and Churchill at Washington during May, and it was evident even before the meeting that there would be no attempt before 1944. It does not appear from the exchange of correspondence among the "Big Three," however, that Stalin had abandoned hope that there was still a chance for a second front in 1943 until so informed in June (121). Churchill's reply (122) to Stalin elicited an interesting message in return that showed his deep disappointment (123). Stalin's words that the western leaders were showing a "disregard of vital Soviet interests" illustrated the growing differences that were beginning to manifest themselves among Allies.

113. ALLIED STRATEGY FOR 1943[1] (EXCERPTS)

American-British Strategy January 3, 1943

1. Our combined resources have increased to the point where we have been able to wrest the initiative from Germany and Italy, and to pin down the Japanese in the Southwest Pacific. The days of plugging holes are over. We must now agree on a plan that will lead to victory, quickly and decisively.

2. The main factors bearing on the war are:

(a) The fighting power of Germany is on the wane and her oil situation is at the moment critical. What she needs above all, is a period for recuperation.

(b) All that stands between Germany and the opportunity for recuperation with an abundant oil supply, is Russia. The Russian war effort is also the greatest single drain on the power and hope of Germany and must be sustained and assisted at all costs.

(c) The Japanese war effort is incapable of much expansion provided communications with Germany are kept severed.

(d) The offensive power of the United States is growing. The main problem is to decide how her armed forces can best be deployed against the enemy.

(e) The war potential of the British Empire is not capable of much more overall expansion. The bulk of the British armed forces are already directed against Germany. As long as Germany is in the field, a considerable proportion of these forces must continue to be located in the United Kingdom and Home Waters.

(f) Shipping is vital—not only to maintain the British war effort but to deploy the forces of the United Nations against the enemy.

(g) Submarine warfare is now the only means whereby Germany could cripple our offensive action.

3. The resources of the United Nations are insufficient to defeat Germany and Japan simultaneously. We must therefore either concentrate on defeating Germany while holding Japan, or vice versa. The arguments may be summarized as follows:

(a) If Germany were allowed breathing space to recuperate, she might well become unbeatable. Provided we maintain limited pressure on Japan, she can never become unbeatable.

(b) By concentrating on Germany we uphold Russia. By concentrating on Japan we should cause little, if any, relief to the Russians. Moreover, for a given amount of shipping more United States forces can be deployed against Germany than against Japan.

(c) In order to defeat Japan, we should need to concentrate against her so large a naval force that the security of the United Kingdom and of Atlantic Sea communications would be seriously jeopardized.

(d) If we do not bring sufficient pressure to bear on Japan there is a risk of China dropping out of the fight. We must therefore continue to give China such support as will ensure that she will not give up the struggle.

(e) Important though China is as an ally against Japan, Russia is far more important as an ally against Germany. Moreover, after the defeat of Germany, Russia might be a decisive factor in the war against Japan, whereas China could never help us in the war against Germany.

4. It is clear from the above that we should persist in the strategic policy adopted at the first Washington Conference, namely, that we should bend all our efforts to the early and decisive defeat of Germany, diverting only the minimum force necessary to hold Japan.

Holding Japan

5. The operations in the Southwest Pacific during the last few months have forced the Japanese to make this area their principal theater of operations. These have directly relieved the threat to Australasia, India and the Indian Ocean, and have indirectly assisted Russia by staving off a Japanese attack on the Maritime provinces. The best way of holding Japan is to continue limited offensive operations on a scale sufficient to contain the bulk of the Japanese forces in the Pacific. It is necessary to define the broad action required to implement this strategy.

6. The only way of bringing material help to China is to open the Burma Road. The reconquest of Burma should therefore be undertaken as soon as resources permit.

Defeat of Germany

7. The occupation of Germany will ultimately be necessary. For the present, however, Northwest Europe may be likened to a powerful fortress which can be assaulted only after adequate preparation. To make a fruitless assault before the time is ripe would be disastrous for ourselves, of no assistance to Russia and devastating to the morale of occupied Europe. We

cannot yet bring to bear sufficient forces to overcome the German garrison of France and the low countries, which can rapidly concentrate against us in superior strength and behind powerful coast defenses.

. . . .

Invasion of the Continent

9. If we go for the maximum "Bolero" with the intention of assaulting the Continent in 1943 we must be ready to strike by September. Thereafter weather conditions will progressively deteriorate. The strongest Anglo-American force which we could assemble in the United Kingdom by that date for an attack upon Northern France would be some 13 British and 9 United States divisions with perhaps a further 3 United States divisions collecting in the United Kingdom. 6 divisions are probably the maximum which could be organized as assault forces.

. . . .

ANNEX I
THE BOMBER OFFENSIVE

1. The aim of the bomber offensive is the progressive destruction and dislocation of the enemy's war industrial and economic system, and the undermining of his morale to a point where his capacity for armed resistance is fatally weakened.

2. In estimating the prospective results of the air offensive it is important not to be misled by the limited results attained in the past 2 ½ years. Bombing methods and technique have been passing through a phase of rapid development, new navigational aids and other ancillary equipment which should bring about a great advance in bombing accuracy are being introduced, the training of air crews has been improved, and better tactical methods, showing great promise, have been devised.

3. As a result, the British Bomber Force will attain far higher standards of efficiency and accuracy in night bombing in the future than have been possible in the past. We have gained a lead over the German defenses, and we do not believe that they will be able to develop countermeasures sufficient to offset our advantage.

4. In spite of the progress made during recent months by the United States Bomber Command in the bombing of targets in occupied territory, it is still an open question whether regular penetration of the defenses of Germany by daylight will be practicable without prohibitive losses. While every effort should continue to be made to achieve success by day, it is important to arrange that, if the daylight bombing of Germany proves impracticable, it will be possible to convert the United States Bomber Command from a primarily day to a primarily night force with the least possible delay and loss of efficiency.

5. The result attained with a given bombing effort does not vary directly with the scale of that effort, but tends to become progressively more fruitful as the effort increases. Moreover experience shows that, as the bombing

effort mounts above a certain level the defenses become saturated and the aircraft casualty rate is reduced.

6. While the enemy's attention is focussed on Russia, the Allies have the initiative in strategic bombing which is the chief method by which they can at present inflict direct damage on Germany and Germans. We must therefore exploit it to the full.

7. British heavy bombers are in steadily increasing production. In parallel, the build-up of United States heavy bombers in the United Kingdom will increase our combined strengths at little cost to shipping space, once the transfer of American ground personnel has been completed.

8. It is not claimed that the bomber offensive will at once shatter the enemy's morale. It is claimed that it already has an appreciable and will have an increasing effect on the enemy's distributive system and industrial potential—an effect which the German high command and German people will fear more and more.

9. We recommend that we should aim at operating a force of 3,000 British and United States heavy and medium bombers from the United Kingdom by the end of 1943. Without drawing on reserve stocks, this increase in the Allied bomber force in the United Kingdom will only involve an increase in petrol import requirements of about 350,000 tons in 1943—a very small proportion of total requirements.

ANNEX II
PLAN OF ACTION IN THE MEDITERRANEAN

1. Communications prevent our maintaining large forces in Southern Russia. It would be unwise to operate against Southern France except in conjunction with an offensive across the Channel, and difficult to operate in the Balkans unless either Italy goes out of the war or Turkey comes into it. To exploit our African successes, therefore, our plan of action will be:

(a) To bring about the collapse of Italy.
(b) To bring Turkey into the war.
(c) To seize any chance offered by (a) or (b) to operate in the Balkans.

ELIMINATION OF ITALY
Amphibious Operations

2. Once North Africa is cleared, it will be necessary to seize one or other of the island bases—Sicily, Sardinia or Corsica—in order to increase the pressure on Italy. Since we cannot capture Corsica until we have Sardinia, the initial choice will lie between Sicily and Sardinia.

3. Plans for both these operations are already being prepared and should be pressed forward as a matter of urgency. We do not, however, feel able at this stage to express a definite opinion as to which of the two alternatives should be chosen.

. . . .

ACTION IN THE BALKANS AFTER THE COLLAPSE OF ITALY

18. In the event of an Italian collapse, our further action in the Mediter-

ranean will be influenced by Germany's concentration and distribution of her forces and by the attitude of Turkey. Action in the Balkans might result in the following benefits:

(a) We should obtain bases for air attack on Romanian oilfields and refineries, and for fanning the already glowing embers of revolt in the Balkans.

(b) We should (i) be able to interrupt the Danube supply route to Germany, (ii) create a threat to the German southern lines of communication to South Russia, (iii) cut Axis sea communications between the Mediterranean and the Black Sea.

(c) The raw materials of the Balkans (particularly oil, chrome and copper) are vitally important to the Axis. The loss of chrome and copper, together with the cutting of Axis sea communications in the Aegean, on which the Axis supply of chrome from Turkey largely depends, would deprive Germany of almost all her sources of these indispensable products.

Plan of Action

19. Our plan of action for developing our effort against the Balkans might be

(a) Intensification of subversive activity in the Balkans, and supply of arms and equipment to the Patriot forces in Greece, Yugoslavia and Albania, and

(b) When the time is ripe, the despatch of Allied land and air forces to act as a rallying point for offensive action of insurgent forces in this area.

ANNEX III
CROSS-CHANNEL OPERATIONS

1. We intend to return to the Continent the moment the time is ripe.

2. Subject to the prior claims of the Mediterranean, and of the bomber offensive, therefore, our policy should be to assemble the maximum British and United States forces in the United Kingdom for invasion of the Continent in the event of a sudden crack in German military power.

3. For example, it is possible that continued pressure on the Russian Front, the bombing offensive from the United Kingdom and offensives in the Mediterranean might combine seriously to weaken Germany and to bring Italy to surrender during the summer. It might then be justifiable to forego further offensives in the Mediterranean and to concentrate rapidly for a Cross-Channel operation....

114. Pacific Situation, January 14, 1943[2] (Excerpts)

(Casablanca Meeting)
Combined Chiefs of Staff Minutes

Secret

COMBINED STRATEGY

Sir Allen [*sic*] Brooke said that he would like to hear the views of the United States Chiefs of Staff regarding the situation in the Pacific.

Admiral King stated that of the nine fronts on which the United Nations are now engaged, four are in the Pacific. These include the Alaska-Aleutian area, the Hawaiian-Midway area, the South and Southwest Pacific areas, and the Burma-China area.

. . . .

Admiral King said that had we been set at the time of Midway, we could have made great progress in an attack on the Solomon Islands. The operation was in preparation in July and took place on August 7th but we did not have sufficient force even at that time to exploit our success beyond the occupation of Tulagi and Guadalcanal. The Japanese reaction there was more violent and sustained than had been anticipated. Another reason why we could not proceed further with the Solomon operations was that Operation Torch had been decided upon and much of our available means had to be diverted to it.

. . . .

Admiral King stated that he felt the Philippines should be our objective rather than the Netherlands East Indies. The Philippines could be captured by a flank action whereas the capture of the Netherlands East Indies must of necessity be the result of a frontal attack. The most likely intermediate objective, once Rabaul is captured, is Truk and thence to the Marianas.

Prior to the war, every class at the Naval War College was required to play the game of the Pacific Islands involving the recapture of the Philippines. There are three ways in which the Philippines may be taken: first, the direct route which would constitute a frontal attack; second, the southern route which is outflanked by the enemy along much of its course; and third, the northern route through the Aleutians to the northern tip of the Island of Luzon. The northern route would include establishing a base in the northwestern Marshall Islands and then proceeding to Truk and the Marianas. The Marianas are the key of the situation because of their location on the Japanese line of communications. Any line of action decided upon requires considerable force, especially air strength. All of the necessary operations are amphibious.

. . . .

Admiral King stated that the Japanese are now replenishing Japan with raw materials and also fortifying an inner defense ring along the line of the Netherlands East Indies and the Philippines. For these reasons, he believed that it was necessary for the United Nations to prevent the Japanese having time to consolidate their gains. He compared this situation with the present desire of the United Nations to avoid giving Germany a respite during the winter months.

. . . .

General Marsahll stated that the peace of mind of the United States Chiefs of Staff was greater now than it had been a year ago. The Japanese are now on the defensive and must be careful of a surprise move from us. However, he pointed out that we must still worry about the locations of the Japanese aircraft carriers because they constitute a constant threat against our line of communications and for raiding purposes against our west coast.

We must not allow the Japanese any pause. They fight with no idea of surrendering and they will continue to be aggressive until attrition has defeated them. To accomplish this, we must maintain the initiative and force them to meet us. . . .

115. The "Unconditional Surrender" Statement, January 24, 1943[3] (Excerpts)

(Casablanca Meeting)
Transcript of Press Conference

THE PRESIDENT: This meeting goes back to the successful landing operations last November, which as you all know were initiated as far back as a year ago, and put into definite shape shortly after the Prime Minister's visit to Washington in June.

After the operations of last November, it became perfectly clear, with the successes, that the time had come for another review of the situation, and a planning for the next steps, especially steps to be taken in 1943. That is why we came here, and our respective staffs came with us, to discuss the practical steps to be taken by the United Nations for prosecution of the war. We have been here about a week.

. . . .

I think it can be said that the studies during the past week or ten days are unprecedented in history. Both the Prime Minister and I think back to the days of the first World War when conferences between the French and British and ourselves very rarely lasted more than a few hours or a couple of days. The Chiefs of Staffs have been in intimate touch; they have lived in the same hotel. Each man has become a definite personal friend of his opposite number on the other side.

Furthermore, these conferences have discussed, I think for the first time in history, the whole global picture. It isn't just one front, just one ocean, or one continent—it is literally the whole world; and that is why the Prime Minister and I feel that the conference is unique in the fact that it has this global aspect.

. . . .

Another point. I think we have all had it in our hearts and heads before, but I don't think that it has ever been put down on paper by the Prime Minister and myself, and that is the determination that peace can come to the world only by the total elimination of German and Japanese war power.

Some of you Britishers know the old story—we had a General called U. S. Grant. His name was Ulysses Simpson Grant, but in my, and the Prime Minister's, early days he was called "Unconditional Surrender" Grant. The elimination of German, Japanese and Italian war power means the unconditional surrender by Germany, Italy and Japan. That means a reasonable assurance of future world peace. It does not mean the destruction of the population of Germany, Italy, or Japan, but it does mean the destruction of the philosophies in those countries which are based on conquest and the subjugation of other people.

(this meeting is called the "unconditional surrender" meeting)

While we have not had a meeting of all of the United Nations, I think that there is no question—in fact we both have great confidence that the same purposes and objectives are in the minds of all of the other United Nations—Russia, China, and all the others.

And so the actual meeting—the main work of the Committee—has been ended, except for a certain amount of resultant paper work—has come to a successful conclusion. I call it a meeting of the minds in regard to all military operations, and, thereafter, that the war is going to proceed against the Axis Powers according to schedule, with every indication that 1943 is going to be an even better year for the United Nations than 1942.

THE PRIME MINISTER: I agree with everything that the President has said, and I think it was a very happy decision to bring you gentlemen here to Casablanca to this agreeable spot, Anfa Camp, which has been the center— the scene—of much the most important and successful war conference which I have ever attended or witnessed. Nothing like it has occurred in my experience, which is a long while—the continuous work, hours and hours every day from morning until often after midnight, carried on by the Staffs of both sides, by all the principal officers of the two nations who are engaged in the direction of the war.

116. Stalin-Churchill Message, February 16, 1943[4]

MOST SECRET AND PERSONAL MESSAGE
FROM PREMIER STALIN
TO THE PRIME MINISTER, MR. CHURCHILL

On February 12 I received your message on the forthcoming Anglo-American military operations.

Thanks for the additional information on the Casablanca decisions. On the other hand, I cannot but state certain considerations with reference to your message, which you tell me is a common reply conveying also the President's opinion.

It appears from your message that the date—February—which you had fixed earlier for completing the operations in Tunisia is now set back to April. There is no need to demonstrate at length the undesirability of this delay in operations against the Germans and Italians. It is now, when the Soviet troops are still keeping up their broad offensive, that action by the

Anglo-American troops in North Africa is imperative. Simultaneous pressure on Hitler from our front and from yours in Tunisia would be of great positive significance for our common cause and would create most serious difficulties for Hitler and Mussolini. It would also expedite the operations you are planning in Sicily and the Eastern Mediterranean.

As to the opening of a second front in Europe, in particular in France, it is planned, judging by your communication, for August or September. As I see it, however, the situation calls for shortening these time limits to the utmost and for the opening of a second front in the West at a date much earlier than the one mentioned. So that the enemy should not be given a chance to recover, it is very important, to my mind, that the blow from the West, instead of being put off till the second half of the year, be delivered in spring or early summer.

According to reliable information at our disposal, since the end of December, when for some reason the Anglo-American operations in Tunisia were suspended, the Germans have moved 27 divisions, including five armoured divisions, to the Soviet-German front from France, the Low Countries and Germany. In other words, instead of the Soviet Union being aided by diverting German forces from the Soviet-German front, what we get is relief for Hitler, who, because of the let-up in Anglo-American operations in Tunisia, was able to move additional troops against the Russians.

The foregoing indicates that the sooner we make joint use of the Hitler camp's difficulties at the front, the more grounds we shall have for anticipating early defeat for Hitler. Unless we take account of this and profit by the present moment to further our common interests, it may well be that, having gained a respite and rallied their forces, the Germans might recover. It is clear to you and us that such an undesirable miscalculation should not be made.

2. I have deemed it necessary to send this reply to Mr. Roosevelt as well.

3. Thank you for your cordial congratulations on the liberation of Rostov. This morning our troops have taken Kharkov.

February 16, 1943

117. CHURCHILL-STALIN MESSAGE, MARCH 11, 1943[5]

PERSONAL AND MOST SECRET MESSAGE
FROM THE PRIME MINISTER, MR. WINSTON CHURCHILL,
TO MARSHAL STALIN

Mr. Roosevelt has sent me a copy of his reply to your message of February 16th. I am well enough to reply myself.

2. Our first task is to clear the Axis out of North Africa by an operation, the code name of which is in my immediately following message. We hope

that this will be accomplished towards the end of April, by which time about a quarter of a million Axis troops will be engaged by us.

3. Meanwhile all preparations are being pressed forward to carry out the operation "Husky," which is the new code word . . . in June, a month earlier than we had planned at Casablanca.

4. Plans are also being investigated for operations in the Eastern Mediterranean such as:

(a) Capture of Crete and/or Dodecanese, and

(b) A landing in Greece.

The timing of these operations is largely governed by the result of "Husky" and the availability of the necessary assemblage of shipping and landing craft. The assistance of Turkey and the use of Turkish air fields would, of course, be of immense value. At the right time I shall make a request of them.

5. The Anglo-American attempt to get Tunis and Bizerta at a run was abandoned in December because of the strength of the enemy, the impending rainy season, the already sodden character of the ground and the fact that communications stretched 500 miles from Algiers and 160 from Bone through bad roads and a week's travelling over single-track French railways. It was only possible to get supplies up to the Army by sea on a small scale owing to the strength of the enemy air and submarine attack. Thus it was not possible to accumulate petrol or other supplies in forward areas. Indeed it was only just possible to nourish the troops already there. The same was true of the air, and improvised air fields became quagmires. When we stopped attacking there were about 40,000 Germans in Tunisia apart from Italians and from Rommel who was still in Tripoli. The German force in North Tunisia is now more than double that figure, and they are rushing over every man they can in transport aircraft and destroyers. Some sharp local reverses were suffered towards the end of last month, but the position has now been restored. We hope that the delays caused by this set-back will be repaired by the earlier advance of Montgomery's army which should have six divisions (200,000 men) operating from Tripoli with sufficient supplies against the Mareth position before the end of March. Already on the 6th March Montgomery's army repulsed Rommel's forestalling attack with heavy losses. The British and American armies in the northern sector of Tunisia will act in combination with Montgomery's battle.

6. I thought that you would like to know these details of the story, although it is on a small scale compared with the tremendous operations over which you are presiding.

7. The British Staffs estimate that about half the number of the divisions which were sent to the Soviet-German front from France and the Low Countries since last November have already been replaced mainly by divisions from Russia and Germany, and partly by new divisions formed in France. They estimate that at the present time there are thirty German divisions in France and the Low Countries.

8. I am anxious that you should know, for your own most secret information, exactly what our military resources are for an attack upon Europe across the Mediterranean or the Channel. By far the larger part of the British Army is in North Africa, in the Middle East and in India and there is no physical possibility of moving it by sea back to the British Isles. By the end of April we shall have five British divisions or about 200,000 men in Northern Tunisia in addition to General Montgomery's army of some six divisions and we are bringing two specially trained British divisions from Iran, sending one from this country to reinforce them for "Husky," a total of fourteen. We have four mobile British divisions, the two Polish divisions, one Free French division and one Greek division in the Middle East. There is the equivalent of four static divisions in Gibraltar, Malta and Cyprus. Apart from the garrisons and frontier troops, there are ten or twelve divisions formed and forming in India for reconquering Burma after the monsoon and reopening contact with China (see my immediately following message for the code word of this operation). Thus we have under British command, spread over a distance of some 6,300 miles from Gibraltar to Calcutta, thirty-eight divisions including strong armoured and a powerful proportion of air forces. For all these forces active and definite tasks are assigned for 1943.

9. The gross strength of a British division, including Corps, army, and lines of communication troops, may be estimated at about 40,000 men. There remain in the United Kingdom about nineteen formed divisions, four home defence divisions and four drafting divisions, of which sixteen are being prepared for a cross-Channel operation in August. You must remember that our total population is 46,000,000 and that the first charge upon it is the Royal Navy and Mercantile Marine, without which we could not live. Thereafter comes our very large Air Force, about 1,200,000 strong, and the needs of munitions, agriculture and air raid defence. Thus the entire manhood and womanhood of the country is, and has been, for some time, fully absorbed.

10. The United States had an idea in July last to send twenty-seven divisions, each of a gross strength of between 40,000 and 50,000 men, to the United Kingdom for the invasion of France. Since then they have sent seven divisions to the operation "Torch" and three more are to go. In this country there is now only one American division and no more are expected for two months at least. They hope to have four divisions available by August in addition to a strong air force. This is no disparagement of the American effort. The reason why these performances have fallen so far short of the expectations of last year is not that the troops do not exist, but that the shipping at our disposal and the means of escorting it do not exist. There is in fact no prospect whatever of bringing anything more than I have mentioned into the United Kingdom in the period concerned.

11. The bomber offensive from the United Kingdom has been going steadily forward. During February over 10,000 tons of bombs were dropped

on Germany and on German-occupied territory, and 4,000 tons have fallen
on Germany since the beginning of March. Our Air Staff estimates that out
of a German first line strength of 4,500 combat aircraft about 1,780 are now
on the Russian front, the remainder being held opposite us in Germany and
on the Western and Mediterranean fronts. Besides this, there is the Italian
Air Force with a first line strength of 1,385 aircraft, the great bulk of which is
opposed to us.

12. With regard to the attack across the Channel it is the earnest wish of
the President and myself that our troops should be in the general battle in
Europe which you are fighting with such astounding prowess. But in order
to sustain the operations in North Africa, the Pacific, and India, and to carry
supplies to Russia the import programme into the United Kingdom has been
cut to the bone and we have eaten and are eating into reserves. However, in
case the enemy should weaken sufficiently we are preparing to strike earlier
than August and plans are kept alive from week to week. If he does not
weaken, a premature attack with inferior and insufficient forces would
merely lead to a bloody repulse, Nazi vengeance on the local population if
they rose, and a great triumph for the enemy. The actual situation can only
be judged nearer the time and in making, for your own personal information, this declaration of our intentions there I must not be understood to
limit our freedom of decision.

March 11th, 1943

118. Stalin-Churchill Message, March 15, 1943[6]

PERSONAL AND SECRET MESSAGE
FROM PREMIER J. V. STALIN
TO THE PRIME MINSTER, MR. W. CHURCHILL

I have received your reply to my message of February 16. It appears from
your communication that Anglo-American operations in North Africa are
not being hastened, but are, in fact, being postponed till the end of April.
Moreover, even this date is given in rather vague terms. In other words, at
the height of fighting against the Hitler troops, in February and March, the
Anglo-American offensive in North Africa, far from having been stepped
up, has been called off, and the date fixed by yourself has been set back.
Meanwhile Germany has succeeded in moving from the West 36 divisions,
including six armoured ones, to be used against Soviet troops. The difficulties that this has created for the Soviet Army and the extent to which it has
eased the German position on the Soviet-German front will be readily
appreciated.

For all its importance "Husky" can by no means replace a second front in

France, but I fully welcome, of course, your intention to expedite the operation.

I still regard the opening of a second front in France as the important thing. You will recall that you thought it possible to open a second front as early as 1942 or this spring at the latest. The grounds for doing so were weighty enough. Hence it should be obvious why I stressed in my previous message the need for striking in the West not later than this spring or early summer.

The Soviet troops fought strenuously all winter and are continuing to do so, while Hitler is taking important measures to rehabilitate and reinforce his Army for the spring and summer operations against the U.S.S.R.; it is therefore particularly essential for us that the blow from the West be no longer delayed, that it be delivered this spring or in early summer.

I have studied the arguments you set out in paragraphs 8, 9 and 10 as indicative of the difficulties of Anglo-American operations in Europe. I grant the difficulties. Nevertheless, I think I must give a most emphatic warning, in the interest of our common cause, of the grave danger with which further delay in opening a second front in France is fraught. For this reason the vagueness of your statements about the contemplated Anglo-American offensive across the Channel causes apprehension which I cannot conceal from you.

March 15, 1943

119. Allied Combined Chiefs' Plan For Japan's Defeat, May 14, 1943[7]

Strategic Plan For The Defeat Of Japan

1. A brief discussion of a strategic plan for the defeat of Japan is contained in Enclosure "A."

2. The plan is based on the following overall strategic concept for the prosecution of the war.

a. In cooperation with Russia and other Allies to force an unconditional surrender of the Axis in Europe.

b. Simultaneously, in cooperation with other Pacific Powers concerned, to maintain and extend unremitting pressure against Japan with the purpose of continually reducing her Military power and attaining positions from which her ultimate unconditional surrender can be forced.

c. Upon the defeat of the Axis in Europe, in cooperation with other Pacific Powers and, if possible, with Russia, to direct the full resources of the United States and Great Britain to force the unconditional surrender of Japan. If, however, conditions develop which indicate that the war as a whole can be brought more quickly to a successful conclusion by the earlier mounting of a major offensive against Japan, the strategical concept set forth herein may be reversed.

3. In view of the long period covered and the inevitable changes in conditions that cannot be foreseen, it is not practicable to divide the plan into definitely coordinated phases. With this reservation in regard to timing and coordination, the plan is expressed as follows:

Phase I
    a. *Continue and Augment Existing Undertakings in and From China.*
       Chinese Forces assisted by U. S. Forces.
    b. *Recapture Burma.*
       British Forces assisted by U. S. and Chinese Forces.
    c. *Open a Line of Communications to the Celebes Sea.*
       United States Forces.

Phase II
    a. *Operations To Open the Strait of Malacca and To Compel Wide Dispersion of Enemy Forces.*
       British Forces
    b. *Recapture the Philippines.*
       United States Forces.
    c. *Prepare To Capture Hong Kong.*
       Chinese Forces.

Phase III
    a. *Continue Operations To Open the Strait of Malacca and To Compel Wide Dispersion of Enemy Forces.*
       British Forces.
    b. *Secure Control of the Northern Part of the South China Sea, and Assist in the Capture of Hong Kong.*
       United States Forces.
    c. *Capture Hong Kong.*
       Chinese Forces.

Phase IV
    Establish Air Bases in Japanese Occupied China From Which To Launch an Overwhelming Bombing Offensive Against Japan.
    Chinese Forces, assisted by British and U. S. Forces.

Phase V
    Conduct an Overwhelming Air Offensive Against Japan.
    U. S. Forces, assisted by British and Chinese Forces.

Phase VI
    Invade Japan.
    U. S. Forces, assisted by British and Chinese Forces.

Enclosure "A"
STRATEGIC PLAN FOR THE DEFEAT OF JAPAN
    4. *Objective of the Plan*
       The United Nations war objective is the unconditional surrender of the

Axis Powers. The accomplishment of this objective may require the invasion of Japan.

5. *Most Probable Japanese Courses of Action*

Japan's most probable courses of actions are to direct her major effort toward securing and exploiting the territory she controls, and eliminating China from the war.

6. *The Invasion of Japan*

Since the invasion of Japan is a vast undertaking, it should not be attempted until Japanese power and will to resist have been so reduced that favorable conditions for invasion obtain. Under these conditions the invasion of Japan is considered feasible.

It is probable that the reduction of Japan's power and will to resist may only be accomplished by a sustained, systematic, and large-scale air offensive against Japan itself.

7. *An Overwhelming Air Offensive Against Japan*

An air offensive on the required scale can only be conducted from bases in China.

8. *Recapture Burma*

The attainment of bases in China for the air offensive against Japan is dependent on the continuation of China in the war, and on the establishment of adequate supply routes, not only to maintain China, but also to maintain United Nations forces which are to operate in and from China. The recapture of Burma is a prerequisite to the attainment of adequate bases in China. The capacity of the Burma Road supplemented by the air route from India is inadequate to support the air and ground forces required to implement an air offensive on the required scale. The seizure of a port in China to augment the supply routes through Burma is essential.

9. *The Seizure of a Port in China*

Hong Kong is the most suitable port which may be seized initially. Its seizure requires an offensive from the interior of China by forces supported through Burma, and, probably by supplementary amphibious operations. Control of the South China Sea by the United Nations will be necessary to prevent Japan from successfully opposing these measures.

10. *A Line of Communications to Hong Kong*

The most feasible sea route from the United States to Hong Kong is through the Celebes and Sulu Seas; that from the United Kingdom is through the Strait of Malacca. The establishment of these routes will require the neutralization of Japanese bases in the northern East Indies, the Philippines, Formosa, and on the Asiatic mainland south of Hong Kong. Control of these areas will prevent Japan from supporting her forces in the Netherlands East Indies and will deny her the economic advantages she receives from that area. Operations to open a line of communications to Hong Kong and to control the South China Sea are considered feasible.

11. *A Line of Communications From Hawaii to the Celebes Sea*

This line of communications to the Celebes Sea will be established by advancing in the Central and Southwest Pacific areas with a view to shortening the sea route, providing for its security, and denying to the enemy bases and means by which he may interfere with the line of communications.

12. *A Line of Communications Through the Strait of Malacca*

Although the supply of forces in China will come mainly from the United States, operations to open the Strait of Malacca, after the reconquest of Burma, are a vital part of the plan. The enemy must be continuously compelled to disperse his forces throughout the Pacific and Asiatic areas thus exposing them to attrition on an additional front in Southeastern Asia. This area is one of British strategic responsibility, and is a suitable and feasible undertaking for British Commonwealth Forces.

13. *Control of the Seas*

Since control of the seas in the western Pacific by the United Nations may force the unconditional surrender of Japan before invasion and even before Japan is subjected to an intensive air offensive, every means to gain this control will be undertaken by the United States. The establishment of the line of communications to the Celebes Sea will be used as the vehicle to gain this end. The selection of intermediate objectives which will compel the enemy to expose his naval forces will be the greatest single factor in determining the enemy positions to be seized.

Attrition of enemy shipping, air, and naval resources will be a continuing objective. Raids on Japanese lines of communication, and carrier-based air raids on Japanese positions extending to Japan itself, will be implemented as our naval strength increases.

120. Stalin Interview to Reuter's on Comintern, May 28, 1943[8]

"The dissolution of the Communist International is proper and timely because it facilitates the organisation of the common onslaught of all freedom-loving nations against the common enemy—Hitlerism. The dissolution of the Communist International is proper because:

(a) It exposes the lie of the Hitlerites to the effect that 'Moscow' allegedly intends to intervene in the life of other nations and to "Bolshevise" them. An end is now being put to this lie.

(b) It exposes the calumny of the adversaries of Communism within the Labour movement to the effect that Communist Parties in various countries are allegedly acting not in the interests of their people but on orders from outside. An end is now being put to this calumny too.

(c) It facilitates the work of patriots of all countries for uniting the progressive forces of their respective countries, regardless of party or religious faith, into a single camp of national liberation—for unfolding the struggle against Fascism.

(d) It facilitates the work of patriots of all countries for uniting all freedom-loving peoples into a single international camp for the fight against the menace of world domination by Hitlerism, thus clearing the way to the future organisation of a companionship of nations based upon their equality.

I think that all these circumstances taken together will result in a further strengthening of the United Front of the Allies and other united nations in their fight for victory over Hitlerite tyranny. I feel that the dissolution of the Communist International is perfectly timely—because it is exactly now, when the Fascist beast is exerting its last strength, that it is necessary to organise the common onslaught of freedom-loving countries to finish off this beast and to deliver the people from Fascist oppression."

121. STALIN-ROOSEVELT MESSAGE, JUNE 11, 1943[9]

PERSONAL AND SECRET MESSAGE
FROM PREMIER J. V. STALIN
TO THE PRESIDENT, MR. ROOSEVELT

Your message informing me of certain decisions on strategic matters adopted by you and Mr. Churchill reached me on June 4. Thank you for the information.

It appears from your communication that the decisions run counter to those reached by you and Mr. Churchill earlier this year concerning the date for a second front in Western Europe.

You will doubtless recall that the joint message of January 26, sent by you and Mr. Churchill, announced the decision adopted at the time to divert considerable German ground and air forces from the Russian front and bring Germany to her knees in 1943.

Then on February 12 Mr. Churchill communicated on his own behalf and yours the specified time of the Anglo-American operation in Tunisia and the Mediterranean, as well as on the west coast of Europe. The communication said that Great Britain and the United States were vigorously preparing to cross the Channel in August 1943 and that if the operation were hindered by weather or other causes, then it would be prepared with an eye to being carried out in greater force in September 1943.

Now, in May 1943, you and Mr. Churchill have decided to postpone the Anglo-American invasion of Western Europe until the spring of 1944. In other words, the opening of the second front in Western Europe, previously postponed from 1942 till 1943, is now being put off again, this time till the spring of 1944.

Your decision creates exceptional difficulties for the Soviet Union, which straining all its resources, for the past two years, has been engaged against the main forces of Germany and her satellites, and leaves the Soviet Army, which is fighting not only for its country, but also for its Allies, to do the job alone, almost single-handed, against an enemy that is still very strong and formidable.

Need I speak of the disheartening negative impression that this fresh postponement of the second front and the withholding from our Army, which has sacrificed so much, of the anticipated substantial support by the Anglo-American armies, will produce in the Soviet Union—both among the people and in the Army?

As for the Soviet Government, it cannot align itself with this decision, which, moreover, was adopted without its participation and without any attempt at a joint discussion of this highly important matter and which may gravely affect the subsequent course of the war.

122. CHURCHILL-STALIN MESSAGE, JUNE 19, 1943[10] (EXCERPT)

PERSONAL AND MOST SECRET MESSAGE
FROM THE PRIME MINISTER, MR. WINSTON CHURCHILL,
TO MARSHAL J. V. STALIN

I have received a copy of your telegram of about the 11th June to the President. I quite understand your disappointment but I am sure we are doing not only the right thing but the only thing that is physically possible in the circumstances. It would be no help to Russia if we threw away a hundred thousand men in a disastrous cross-Channel attack such as would, in my opinion, certainly occur if we tried under present conditions and with forces too weak to exploit any success that might be gained at very heavy cost. In my view and that of all my expert military advisers we should, even if we got ashore, be driven off as the Germans have forces already in France superior to any we could put there this year, and can reinforce far more quickly across the main lateral railways of Europe than we could do over the beaches or through any of the destroyed Channel ports we might seize. I cannot see how a great British defeat and slaughter would aid the Soviet armies. It might, however, cause the utmost ill-feeling here if it were thought it had been incurred against the advice of our military experts and under pressure from you. You will remember that I have always made it clear in my telegram sent to you that I would never authorise any cross-Channel attack which I believed would lead to only useless massacre.

123. STALIN-CHURCHILL MESSAGE, JUNE 24, 1943[11]

PERSONAL AND SECRET MESSAGE
FROM PREMIER J. V. STALIN
TO THE PRIME MINISTER, MR. W. CHURCHILL

Your message of June 19 received.

I fully realise the difficulty of organising an Anglo-American invasion of Western Europe, in particular, of transferring troops across the Channel. The difficulty could also be discerned in your communications.

From your messages of last year and this I gained the conviction that you and the President were fully aware of the difficulties of organising such an operation and were preparing the invasion accordingly, with due regard to the difficulties and the necessary exertion of forces and means. Even last year you told me that a large-scale invasion of Europe by Anglo-American troops would be effected in 1943. In the Aide-Memoire handed to V. M. Molotov on June 10, 1942, you wrote:

> "Finally, and most important of all, we are concentrating our maximum effort on the organisation and preparation of a large-scale invasion of the Continent of Europe by British and American forces in 1943. We are setting no limit to the scope and objectives of this campaign, which will be carried out in the first instance by over a million men, British and American, with air forces of appropriate strength."

Early this year you twice informed me, on your own behalf and on behalf of the President, of decisions concerning an Anglo-American invasion of Western Europe intended to "divert strong German land and air forces from the Russian front." You had set yourself the task of bringing Germany to her knees as early as 1943, and named September as the latest date for the invasion.

In your message of January 26 you wrote:

> "We have been in conference with our military advisers and have decided on the operations which are to be undertaken by the American and British forces in the first nine months of 1943. We wish to inform you of our intentions at once. We believe that these operations, together with your powerful offensive, may well bring Germany to her knees in 1943."

In your next message, which I received on February 12, you wrote, specifying the date of the invasion of Western Europe decided on by you and the President:

> "We are also pushing preparations to the limit of our resources for a cross-Channel operation in August, in which British and United States units would participate. Here again, shipping and assault-landing craft will be the limiting factors. If the operation is delayed by the weather or other reasons, it will be prepared with stronger forces for September."

Last February, when you wrote to me about those plans and the date for invading Western Europe, the difficulties of that operation were greater than they are now. Since then the Germans have suffered more than one defeat: they were pushed back by our troops in the South, where they suffered appreciable loss, they were beaten in North Africa and expelled by the Anglo-American troops; in submarine warfare, too, the Germans found themselves in a bigger predicament than ever, while Anglo-American superiority increased substantially; it is also known that the Americans and British have won air superiority in Europe and that their navies and mercantile marines have grown in power.

It follows that the conditions for opening a second front in Western

Europe during 1943, far from deteriorating, have, indeed, greatly improved.

That being so, the Soviet Government could not have imagined that the British and U. S. Governments would revise the decision to invade Western Europe, which they had adopted early this year. In fact, the Soviet Government was fully entitled to expect that the Anglo-American decision would be carried out, that appropriate preparations were under way and that the second front in Western Europe would at last be opened in 1943.

That is why, when you now write that "it would be no help to Russia if we threw away a hundred thousand men in a disastrous cross-Channel attack," all I can do is remind you of the following:

First, your own Aide-Memoire of June 1942 in which you declared that preparations were under way for an invasion, not by a hundred thousand, but by an Anglo-American force exceeding one million men at the very start of the operation.

Second, your February message, which mentioned extensive measures preparatory to the invasion of Western Europe in August or September 1943, which, apparently, envisaged an operation, not by a hundred thousand men, but by an adequate force.

So when you now declare: "I cannot see how a great British defeat and slaughter would aid the Soviet armies," is it not clear that a statement of this kind in relation to the Soviet Union is utterly groundless and directly contradicts your previous and responsible decisions, listed above, about extensive and vigorous measures by the British and Americans to organise the invasion this year, measures on which the complete success of the operation should hinge?

I shall not enlarge on the fact that this responsible decision revoking your previous decisions on the invasion of Western Europe, was reached by you and the President without Soviet participation and without inviting its representatives to the Washington conference, although you cannot but be aware that the Soviet Union's role in the war against Germany and its interest in the problems of the second front are great enough.

There is no need to say that the Soviet Government cannot become reconciled to this disregard of vital Soviet interests in the war against the common enemy.

You say that you "quite understand" my disappointment. I must tell you that the point here is not just the disappointment of the Soviet Government, but the preservation of its confidence in its Allies, a confidence which is being subjected to severe stress. One should not forget that it is a question of saving millions of lives in the occupied areas of Western Europe and Russia and of reducing the enormous sacrifices of the Soviet armies, compared with which the sacrifices of the Anglo-American armies are insignificant.

June 24, 1943

Chapter V
The Beginning of Major Allied Offensives:
1943–1944

Part 10. Planning the Assault on "Festung Europa"

By mid-1943 a major concern of the western Allies was the preparation of a cross-Channel invasion for 1944. Recent history suggests that that concern, as noted in Part 9, was complex and became even more complicated before the invasion was finally launched. The earlier plans, beginning with "Sledgehammer" in 1942, were tentative and generally modest in scale relative to that stage of the war. Many factors influenced the Allied attempts to arrive at a course of action mutually acceptable, but the noticeable lack of trained manpower and landing craft was singularly important. The Anglo-American differences on a second front operation were equally important and the inability to resolve these barriers resulted in the passage of valuable months, and the decision reached by simple default eventually favored the proponents of a Mediterranean campaign. Operation Bolero (the buildup of American forces in Great Britain) was possibly a logical outcome of compromise in planning the French invasion, but it is probably more accurate to regard the resulting interval as wasted time.

The conference at Casablanca contributed little to the second front controversy beyond airing the already familiar arguments between the two western Allies. The creation of a Combined Planning Staff and the subsequent appointment of British General Frederick Morgan to coordinate and plan for an invasion in northern France was, however, a positive step. Morgan, with the impressive title of Chief of Staff to the Supreme Allied Commander ("COSSAC"), was charged with an almost impossible task: planning an operation not fully accepted in principle by British leadership while simultaneously trying to gather a nucleus from which to build an invasion force.

By the time of the third Washington Conference, in May, the plans for Operation Husky (see 117 and 118) were under way, and in terms of available resources that operation assumed priority. During the intervening period from May to August the first Quebec Conference met, and Morgan continued to direct preparation of a plan for a full-scale attack against the Continent in 1944. The operation was codenamed "Overlord" (originally "Roundup") and by July (124) Morgan had completed the major outlines for preliminary consideration. There were, however, still issues to face that stirred heated discussions at the Quebec meeting (August 17–27).

The problems that surfaced revealed the complexities surrounding the Allied disagreements, and introduced other growing concerns. At a Combined Chiefs meeting on August 20, an interesting exchange between Generals Alan Brooke and Marshall revealed increasing Allied anxieties over future Russian plans (125). The range of options appeared for the moment to favor the Soviets, since the eventuality of either a German peace offer in the east or an internal collapse were strong prospects. The western Allies had not finished discussions on a second front, and any invasion force gathered to meet an emergency (also one of Morgan's responsibilities and codenamed "Rankin") might arrive on the Continent "too late," i.e., the Soviet armies would already be there and they would get credit for liberating Europe from the Nazis. A military evaluation of the Russian front confirmed the growing power of the Soviet armies and marked "a new phase in the war in the east" (126).

The work at Allied conferences increasingly reflected the superior offensive position being achieved. This became evident at Quebec in the "Conclusions Report" presented by the Combined Chiefs of Staff (127). The sections on Operation Overlord (Points 11 and 12) that fixed a target date of May 1944 and provided the Operation the highest priority are noteworthy, and Morgan's duties to continue to provide for an "Emergency Return to the Continent" were extended.

During the May meeting in Canada the Allied leaders were notified that Generals Eisenhower and Alexander had completed the occupation of Sicily and had captured over 130,000 Italian and German soldiers and some 1,000 aircraft in the process. The stage was thus set for an attack against the Italian mainland. Meanwhile, Mussolini lost the support of his Fascist followers and the king, and he was arrested on July 25. Mussolini's successor, Marshal Pietro Badoglio, showed every willingness to surrender to the Allies and secret talks were begun despite the goal of unconditional surrender (115), which applied to Italy as fully as it did to Germany and Japan.

On September 1 General Eisenhower briefed the Combined Chiefs of Staff about the Italian situation (128), and shortly thereafter presented Badoglio the armistice conditions (129). On September 8 Eisenhower released the news that Italy had accepted the terms. Italy soon began to participate on the Allied side, but the German forces in Italy remained formidable until the war ended.

The foreign secretaries of Great Britain, the United States, and the Soviet Union met in Moscow in October 1943 and conducted a series of important negotiations. The Moscow Conference of Foreign Secretaries issued several significant documents, among them a declaration on general security that pledged support for a "general international organisation, based on the principle of the sovereign equality of all peace-loving states" (130). The Axis leadership was warned that they would be held legally responsible for their actions (Part 15, 187), and they were later tried in Nuremberg and Tokyo.

The Germans entered their fifth year of war against a background of increasing Allied confidence and power. An analysis of the German situation was included in a lengthy report presented to the Reich and Gau leaders by the Chief of the German General Staff in November 1943 (131). The report interestingly noted the "repeated and prolonged setbacks for the year," and although the report praised the strong will of the German forces to resist, its general tone was pessimistic.

During late November and the first part of December the Allied meetings were continued in Cairo and Teheran. The Cairo meeting of Roosevelt, Churchill, and China's Chiang Kai-shek (attending for the first time) concentrated on military operations planned against Japan (see Part 11 fol.). At Teheran Joseph Stalin replaced Chiang, and the major topic was the continuation of the European struggle. The date for Overlord was finally fixed (132) at Teheran, and the three leaders pledged additional support for the government of Iran (133), which had played a significant geographic role in the transport of Allied goods to the Soviet Union.

124. DIGEST OF OPERATION "OVERLORD," LONDON, JULY 27, 1943[1]
(C. O. S. S. A. C.)

The object of Operation "Overlord" is to mount and carry out an operation with forces and equipment established in the United Kingdom, and with target date the 1st of May, 1944, to secure a lodgement on the Continent from which further offensive operations can be developed. The lodgement area must contain sufficient port facilities to maintain a force of some twenty-six to thirty divisions, and enable that force to be augmented by follow-up shipments from the United States or elsewhere of additional divisions and supporting units of the rate of three to five divisions per month.

SELECTION OF A LODGEMENT AREA

2. In order to provide sufficient port facilities to maintain these large forces, it will be necessary to select a lodgement area which includes a group of major ports. We must plan on the assumption that ports, on capture, will be seriously damaged and probably blocked. It will take some time to restore normal facilities. We shall thus be forced to rely on maintenance over beaches for an extended period.

3. A study of the beaches on the Belgian and Channel coasts shows that the beaches with the highest capacity for passing vehicles and stores inland are those in the Pas de Calais, and the Caen-Cotentin area. Of these, the Caen beaches are the most favourable, as they are, unlike the others, sheltered from the prevailing winds. Naval and air considerations point to the area between the Pas de Calais and the Cotentin as the most suitable for the initial landing, air factors of optimum air support and rapid provision of airfields indicating the Pas de Calais as the best choice, with Caen as an acceptable alternative.

4. Thus, taking beach capacity and air and naval considerations together, it appears that either the Pas de Calais area or the Caen-Cotentin area is the most suitable for the initial main landing.

5. As the area for the initial landing, the Pas de Calais has many obvious advantages such that good air support and quick turn round for our shipping can be achieved. On the other hand, it is a focal point of the enemy fighters disposed for defence, and maximum enemy air activity can be brought to bear over this area with the minimum movement of his air forces. Moreover, the Pas de Calais is the most strongly defended area on the whole French coast. The defences would require very heavy and sustained bombardment from sea and air: penetration would be slow, and the result of the bombardment of beach exits would severely limit the rate of build-up. Further, this area does not offer good opportunities for expansion. It would be necessary to develop the bridgehead to include either the Belgian ports as far as Antwerp or the Channel ports Westwards to include Havre and Rouen. But both an advance to Antwerp across the numerous water obstacles, and a long flank march of some 120 miles to the Seine ports must be considered unsound operations of war unless the German forces are in a state not far short of final collapse.

6. In the Caen-Cotentin area it would be possible to make our initial landing either partly on the Cotentin Peninsula and partly on the Caen beaches, wholly in the Cotentin or wholly on the Caen beaches. An attack with part of our forces in the Cotentin and part on the Caen beaches is, however, considered to be unsound. It would entail dividing our limited forces by the low-lying marshy ground and intricate river system at the neck of the Cotentin Peninsula; thus exposing them to defeat in detail.

7. An attack against the Cotentin Peninsula, on the other hand, has a reasonable chance of success, and would ensure the early capture of the port of Cherbourg. Unfortunately, very few airfields exist in the Cotentin, and that area is not suitable for rapid airfield development. Furthermore, the narrow neck of the Peninsula would give the Germans an easy task in preventing us from breaking out and expanding our initial bridgehead. Moreover, during the period of our consolidation in the Cotentin the Germans would have time to reinforce their coastal troops in the Caen area, rendering a subsequent amphibious assault in that area much more difficult.

8. There remains the attack on the Caen beaches. The Caen sector is

weakly held; the defences are relatively light and the beaches are of high capacity and sheltered from the prevailing winds. Inland the terrain is suitable for airfield development and for the consolidation of the initial bridgehead; and much of it is unfavourable for counterattacks by Panzer divisions. Maximum enemy air opposition can only be brought to bear at the expense of the enemy air defence screen covering the approaches to Germany; and the limited number of enemy airfields within range of the Caen area facilitates local neutralisation of the German fighter force. The sector suffers from the disadvantage that considerable effort will be required to provide adequate air support to our assault forces and some time must elapse before the capture of a major port.

After a landing in the Caen sector it would be necessary to seize either the Seine group of ports or the Brittany group of ports. To seize the Seine ports would entail forcing a crossing of the Seine, which is likely to require greater forces than we can build up through the Caen beaches and the port of Cherbourg. It should, however, be possible to seize the Brittany ports between Cherbourg and Nantes and on them build up sufficient forces for our final advance Eastwards.

Provided that the necessary air situation can first be achieved, the chances of a successful attack and of rapid subsequent development are so much greater in this sector than in any other that it is considered that the advantages far outweigh the disadvantages.

THE LODGEMENT AREA SELECTED

9. In the light of these factors, it is considered that our initial landing on the Continent should be effected in Caen area, with a view to the eventual seizure of a lodgement area comprising the Cherbourg-Brittany group of ports (from Cherbourg to Nantes).

OPENING PHASE UP TO THE CAPTURE OF CHERBOURG

10. The opening phase in the seizing of this lodgement area would be the effecting of a landing in the Caen sector with a view to the early capture and development of airfield sites in the Caen area, and of the port of Cherbourg.

11. The main limiting factors affecting such an operation are the possibility of attaining the necessary air situation; the number of offensive divisions which the enemy can make available for counter attack in the Caen area; the availability of landing ships and craft and of transport aircraft; and the capacity of the beaches and ports in the sector.

12. Although the strength of the G. A. F. [German Air Force] available in 1944 on the Western front cannot be forecast at this stage, we can confidently expect that we shall have a vast numerical superiority in bomber forces. The first-line strength of the German fighter force is, however, showing a steady increase and although it is unlikely to equal the size of the force at our

disposal, there is no doubt that our fighters will have a very large commitment entailing dispersal and operations at maximum intensity. Our fighters
will also be operating under serious tactical disadvantages in the early stages,
which will largely offset their numerical superiority. Before the assault takes
place, therefore, it will be necessary to reduce the effectiveness of the G.A.F.,
particularly that part which can be brought to bear against the Caen area.

13. The necessary air situation to ensure a reasonable chance of success
will therefore require that the maximum number of German fighter forces
are contained in the Low Countries and North-West Germany, that the
effectiveness of the fighter defence in the Caen area is reduced and that air
reinforcements are prevented from arriving in the early stages from the
Mediterranean. Above all, it will be necessary to reduce the over-all strength
of the German fighter force between now and the date of the operation by
destruction of the sources of supply, by the infliction of casualties by bringing
on air battles, and, immediately prior to the assault, by the disorganisation of
G. A. F. installations and control system in the Caen area.

14. As it is impossible to forecast with any accuracy the number and
location of German formations in reserve in 1944, while, on the other hand,
the forces available to us have been laid down, an attempt has been made in
this paper to determine the wisest employment of our own forces and then to
determine the maximum number of German formations which they can
reasonably overcome. Apart from the air situation, which is an over-riding
factor, the practicability of this plan will depend principally on the number,
effectiveness and availability of German divisions present in France and the
Low Countries in relation to our own capabilities. This consideration is
discussed below (paragraph 35).

15. A maximum of thirty and a minimum of twenty-six equivalent divisions are likely to be available in the United Kingdom for cross-Channel
operations on the 1st May 1944. Further build-up can be at the rate of three
to five divisions per month.

16. Landing ships and craft have been provided to lift the equivalent of
three assault divisions and two follow-up divisions, without "overheads," and
it has been assumed that the equivalent of an additional two divisions can be
afloat in ships.

17. Airborne forces amounting to two airborne divisions and some five or
six parachute regiments will be available, but, largely owing to shortage of
transport aircraft, it is only possible to lift the equivalent of two-thirds of one
airborne division simultaneously, on the basis of present forecasts.

18. Even if additional landing ships and craft could be made available, the
beaches in the Caen area would preclude the landing of forces greater than
the equivalent of the three assault and two follow-up divisions, for which
craft have already been provided. Nevertheless, an all-round increase of at
least 10 per cent in landing ships and craft is highly desirable in order to
provide a greater margin for contingencies within the framework of the
existing plan. Furthermore, sufficient lift for a further assault division could
most usefully be employed in an additional landing on other beaches.

19. There is no port of any capacity within the sector although there are a number of small ports of limited value. Maintenance will, therefore, of necessity be largely over the beaches until it is possible to capture and open up the port of Cherbourg. In view of the possibilities of interruption by bad weather it will be essential to provide early some form of improvised sheltered waters.

20. Assuming optimum weather conditions, it should be possible to build up the force over the beaches to a total by D plus 6 of the equivalent of some eleven divisions and five tank brigades and thereafter to land one division a day until about D plus 24.

PROPOSED PLAN

Preliminary Phase.

21. During the preliminary phase, which must start forthwith, all possible means including air and sea action, propaganda, political and economic pressure, and sabotage, must be integrated into a combined offensive aimed at softening the German resistance. In particular, air action should be directed towards the reduction of the German air forces on the Western front, the progressive destruction of the German economic system and the undermining of German morale.

22. In order to contain the maximum German forces away from the Caen area diversionary operations should be staged against other areas such as the Pas de Calais and the Mediterranean Coast of France.

Preparatory Phase.

23. During this phase air action will be intensified against the G. A. F., particularly in North-West France, with a view to reducing the effectiveness of the G. A. F. in that area, and will be extended to include attacks against communications more directly associated with movement of German reserves which might affect the Caen area. Three naval assault forces will be assembled with the naval escorts and loaded at ports along the South Coast of England. Two naval assault forces carrying the follow-up forces will also be assembled and loaded, one in the Thames Estuary and one on the West Coast.

The Assault.

24. After a very short air bombardment of the beach defences three assault divisions will be landed simultaneously on the Caen beaches, followed up on D day by the equivalent of two tank brigades (United States regiments) and a brigade group (United States regimental combat team). At the same time, airborne forces will be used to seize the town of Caen; and subsidiary operations by commandos and possibly by airborne forces will be undertaken to neutralise certain coast defences and seize certain important river crossings. The object of the assault forces will be to seize the general line of Grandcamp-Bayeux-Caen.

Follow-up and Build-up Phase.

25. Subsequent action will take the form of a strong thrust Southwards

and South-Westwards with a view to destroying enemy forces, acquiring sites for airfields, and gaining depth for a turning movement into the Cotentin Peninsula directed on Cherbourg. When sufficient depth has been gained a force will advance into the Cotentin and seize Cherbourg. At the same time a thrust will be made to deepen the bridgehead South-Eastwards in order to cover the construction and operation of additional airfields in the area South-East of Caen.

26. It is considered that, within fourteen days of the initial assault, Cherbourg should be captured and the bridgehead extended to include the general line Trouville-Alencon-Mont St. Michel. By this date, moreover, it should have been possible to land some eighteen divisions and to have in operation about fourteen airfields from which twenty-eight to thirty-three fighter-type squadrons should be operating.

FURTHER DEVELOPMENTS AFTER CAPTURE OF CHERBOURG

27. After the capture of Cherbourg the Supreme Allied Commander will have to decide whether to initiate operations to seize the Seine ports or whether he must content himself with first occupying the Brittany ports. In this decision he will have to be guided largely by the situation of the enemy forces. If the German resistance is sufficiently weak, an immediate advance could be made to seize Havre and Rouen. On the other hand, the more probable situation is that the Germans will have retired with the bulk of their forces to hold Paris and the line of the Seine, where they can best be covered by their air forces from North-East France and where they may possibly be reinforced by formations from Russia. Elsewhere they may move a few divisions from Southern France to hold the crossings of the Loire and will leave the existing defensive divisions in Brittany.

It will therefore most probably be necessary for us to seize the Brittany ports first, in order to build up sufficient forces with which we can eventually force the passage of the Seine.

28. Under these circumstances, the most suitable plan would appear to be to secure first the left flank and to gain sufficient airfields for subsequent operations. This would be done by extending the bridgehead to the line of the River Eure from Dreux to Rouen and thence along the line of the Seine to the sea, seizing at the same time Chartres, Orléans and Tours.

29. Under cover of these operations a force would be employed in capturing the Brittany ports; the first step being a thrust Southwards to seize Nantes and St. Nazaire, followed by subsidiary operations to capture Brest and the various small ports of the Brittany Peninsula.

. . . .

COMMAND AND CONTROL

31. In carrying out Operation "Overlord" administrative control would be greatly simplified if the principle were adopted that the United States

forces were normally on the right of the line and the British and Canadian forces on the left.

MAJOR CONDITIONS AFFECTING SUCCESS OF THE OPERATION

32. It will be seen that the plan for the initial landing is based on two main principles—concentration of force and tactical surprise. Concentration of the assault forces is considered essential if we are to ensure adequate air support and if our limited assault forces are to avoid defeat in detail. An attempt has been made to obtain tactical surprise by landing in a lightly defended area—presumably lightly defended as, due to its distance from a major port, the Germans consider a landing there unlikely to be successful. This action, of course, presupposes that we can offset the absence of a port in the initial stages by the provision of improvised sheltered waters. It is believed that this can be accomplished.

33. The operation calls for a much higher standard of performance on the part of the naval assault forces than any previous operation. This will depend upon their being formed in sufficient time to permit of adequate training.

34. Above all, it is essential that there should be an over-all reduction in the German fighter force between now and the time of the surface assault. From now onwards every practical method of achieving this end must be employed. This condition, above all others, will dictate the date by which the amphibious assault can be launched.

35. The next condition is that the number of German offensive divisions in reserve must not exceed a certain figure on the target date if the operation is to have a reasonable chance of success. The German reserves in France and the Low Countries as a whole, excluding divisions holding the coast, G. A. F. divisions and training divisions, should not exceed on the day of the assault twelve full-strength first-quality divisions. In addition, the Germans should not be able to transfer more than fifteen first-quality divisions from Russia during the first two months. Moreover, on the target date the divisions in reserve should be so located that the number of first-quality divisions which the Germans could deploy in the Caen area to support the divisions holding the coast should not exceed three divisions on D day, five divisions by D plus 2, or nine divisions by D plus 8.

During the preliminary period, therefore, every effort must be made to dissipate and divert German formations, lower their fighting efficiency and disrupt communications.

36. Finally, there is the question of maintenance. Maintenance will have to be carried out over beaches for a period of some three months for a number of formations, varying from a maximum of eighteen divisions in the first month to twelve divisions in the second month, rapidly diminishing to nil in the third month. Unless adequate measures are taken to provide sheltered waters by artificial means, the operation will be at the mercy of the

weather. Moreover, special facilities and equipment will be required to prevent undue damage to craft during this extended period. Immediate action for the provision of the necessary requirements is essential.

37. Given these conditions—a reduced G. A. F., a limitation in the number or effectiveness of German offensive formations in France, and adequate arrangements to provide improvised sheltered waters—it is considered that Operation "Overlord" has a reasonable prospect of success. To ensure these conditions being attained by the 1st May, 1944, action must start *now* and every possible effort made by all means in our power to soften German resistance and to speed up our own preparations.

125. 113TH MEETING OF COMBINED CHIEFS OF STAFF, AUGUST 20, 1943[2] (EXCERPT)

9. *MILITARY CONSIDERATIONS IN RELATION TO RUSSIA*

SIR ALAN BROOKE outlined the present position in Russia. In general, the Russians were in a stronger position than ever before. He believed that they had reserves available for further offensives in the Autumn. Hungary was understood to be seeking to negotiate a separate peace and neither Rumania nor Finland were desirous of remaining in the war. The Germans would, he thought, be forced to hold all their existing divisions on the Russian front or even to reinforce them. This would facilitate our operations in Italy and OVERLORD. He did not believe that there was any chance of the Germans achieving a negotiated peace with the Russians who had too much to wipe off the slate.

GENERAL MARSHALL referred to the forming of a "Free Germany" movement within Russia. From reports he had received, it appeared that Russia was turning an increasingly hostile eye on the capitalistic world, of whom they were becoming increasingly contemptuous. Their recent "Second Front" announcement, no longer borne of despair, was indicative of this attitude. He would be interested to know the British Chiefs of Staff's views on the possible results of the situation in Russia with regard to the deployment of Allied forces—for example, in the event of an overwhelming Russian success, would the Germans be likely to facilitate our entry into the country to repel the Russians?

SIR ALAN BROOKE said that he had in the past often considered the danger of the Russians seizing the opportunity of the war to further their ideals of international communism. They might try to profit by the chaos and misery existing at the end of the hostilities. . . .

There would, however, SIR ALAN BROOKE considered, be Russian demands for a part of Poland, at least part of the Baltic States, and possibly concessions in the Balkans. If she obtained these territories, she would be anxious to assist us in maintaining the peace of Europe.

126. ALLIED REPORT ON RUSSIAN FRONT, AUGUST 1943[3] (EXCERPT)

The Russian Front. Since early spring two-thirds of Germany's ground strength (203 divisions) has been on the Russian front, with very heavy offensive concentrations near Orel and Belgorod. It is believed that the Germans planned an early operation to pinch off the Kursk salient at least, but that it was suspended on account of the sudden collapse in Tunisia. On 5 July, the Germans launched a violent attack northward and eastward from Belgorod, which failed, apparently with severe losses. A complementary attack southward from Orel made no headway. The Russians seized the initiative and launched a heavy converging attack on Orel, where the German position now appears to be precarious. This situation, if not preliminary to more extensive operations (as was the Russian Kharkov offensive in the spring of 1942), marks a new phase in the war in the east, with the Russians conducting a mid-summer offensive and the Germans professing to welcome a positional battle of attrition.

On the whole front, Russian ground strength is to the German as three to two. The superiority of German communications, staff work, and fighting skill may yet compensate for this disparity. Russian staff planning, however, has improved since 1941–42.

Germany has, on the Russian front, some 2,000 aircraft, of which 1,170 are bombers of all types. Available information indicates that the U. S. S. R. air strength is numerically superior in the ratio of approximately two to one. But due to a large proportion of obsolescent aircraft and to a low rate of serviceability its overall effectiveness has until recently been low. As a result, the Germans have been able to prevent the U. S. S. R. from establishing effective air superiority in any large sector. This advantage is rapidly being lost as the proportion of first-line aircraft is increased and combat efficiency improved.

127. REPORTS OF CONCLUSIONS REACHED BY COMBINED CHIEFS OF STAFF, QUEBEC, AUGUST 24, 1943[4] (EXCERPTS)

I. OVER-ALL OBJECTIVE

2. In conjunction with Russia and other Allies to bring about at the earliest possible date, the unconditional surrender of the Axis powers.

II. OVER-ALL STRATEGIC CONCEPT FOR THE PROSECUTION OF THE WAR

3. In cooperation with Russia and other Allies to bring about at the earliest possible date, the unconditional surrender of the Axis in Europe.

4. Simultaneously, in cooperation with other Pacific Powers concerned to maintain and extend unremitting pressure against Japan with the purpose of continually reducing her Military power and attaining positions from which her ultimate surrender can be forced. The effect of any such exten-

sion on the over-all objective to be given consideration by the Combined Chiefs of Staff before action is taken.

5. Upon the defeat of the Axis in Europe, in cooperation with other Pacific Powers and, if possible, with Russia, to direct the full resources of the United States and Great Britain to bring about at the earliest possible date the unconditional surrender of Japan.

. . . .

8. The U-Boat War

a. *Progress Report*

We have had encouraging reports from the Chiefs of the two Naval Staffs regarding the U-boat war. We have approved recommendations made by the Allied Submarine Board which should result in further strengthening our anti-U-boat operations. The Board has been directed to continue and expand its studies in search of further improvements.

. . . .

9. The Defeat of the Axis in Europe

We have approved the following operations in 1943–44 for the defeat of the Axis Powers in Europe.

10. The Bomber Offensive

The progressive destruction and dislocation of the Germany military, industrial and economic system, the disruption of vital elements of lines of communication, and the material reduction of German air combat strength by the successful prosecution of the Combined Bomber Offensive from all convenient bases is a prerequisite to Overlord (barring an independent and complete Russian victory before Overlord can be mounted). This operation must therefore continue to have highest strategic priority.

. . . .

12. We have approved the outline plan of General Morgan for Operation Overlord and have authorized him to proceed with the detailed planning and with full preparations.

. . . .

19. Emergency Return to the Continent

We have examined the plans that have been prepared by General Morgan's staff for an emergency operation to enter the Continent. We have taken note of these plans and have directed that they be kept under continuous review with particular reference to the premises regarding the attainment of air superiority and the number of troops necessary for the success of these operations.

128. Eisenhower Report on Italy, September 1, 1943[5] (Excerpt)

(a) Italy is in fact an occupied country and its government has no freedom of independent action. The most that could be expected from any governmental decision would be the influence (on) certain portions of the

Italian armed forces to act in our favor and possibly to inspire something in the order of a general strike.

(b) The German occupation of Italy has become so strong as to change materially the estimates on which AVALANCHE [Allied Amphibious Attack on the Port of Salerno] was originally planned. While apparently the German strength south of Rome has not been greatly increased since the retirement of German forces out of HUSKY, yet, subject to limitations of transportation, the large German reserves concentrated in the north of Italy could be used aggressively at any moment that the German Commander believed such action desirable. Our own air action can do something to delay movements of such reserves, but it is not strong enough to impose the almost complete paralysis of communications that was achieved in Sicily.

(c) At this moment, the Italians are far more frightened by the German strength and reprisals within the country than they are of our threat of invasion or even of our bombing operations. They are particularly concerned about the Rome area, and it appears certain that they will make no attempt whatsoever to agree to an Armistice unless assured of some help in the Rome area to stiffen up the resistance which the Italian formations in that region might make against German occupation of the city. We believe that the employment of an Airborne Division for this purpose, under the conditions we have laid down to determine good faith on the part of the Italians, would be a good gamble, because the success of AVALANCHE may very likely turn upon obtaining a degree of Italian help that will materially delay movement of German forces.

(d) Consequently, under my instructions to support any Italian units that would actually fight the Germans, I have determined to employ an Airborne Division in the Rome area if we can be sufficiently assured of the good faith of the Italians.

(e) Our rate of build up in AVALANCHE has been previously reported and, as you know, is painfully slow. However, the decisions of the Combined Chiefs of Staff at QUADRANT clearly visualized the vigorous prosecution of my mission of knocking Italy out of the War. Since this can be done only by seizing a substantial port, I have no thought of abandoning plans for AVALANCHE. But I do consider it absolutely necessary to get every possible atom of support I can from the Italian formations.

(f) Nothing that I am doing now or will do in the future implies any promises to any particular government or heads of government with respect to their status after occupation by Allied Forces.

(g) We attempt to keep the Combined Chiefs of Staff fully informed of every development in these tangled negotiations. The only reason that more frequent reports have not been submitted is because of the lack of decisiveness in the representations of General C and General Z and consequent lack of progress in negotiation. They are merely frightened individuals that are trying to get out of a bad mess in the best possible way and their attitude is, I believe, indicative of that of the whole country.

My own belief is that the Italians will probably allow this situation to drift and will not seek a formal armistice. They are too badly demoralized to face up to consequences and are not sufficiently assured of the safety of Rome.

129. Italian Military Armistice, Fairfield Camp, Sicily, September 3, 1943[6]

The following conditions of an Armistice are presented by

GENERAL DWIGHT D. EISENHOWER

Commander-in-Chief of the Allied Forces,

acting by authority of the Governments of the United States and Great Britain and in the interest of the United Nations, and are accepted by

MARSHAL PIETRO BADOGLIO

Head of the Italian Government

1. Immediate cessation of all hostile activity by the Italian armed forces.

2. Italy will use its best endeavors to deny, to the Germans, facilities that might be used against the United Nations.

3. All prisoners or internees of the United Nations to be immediately turned over to the Allied Commander in Chief, and none of these may now or at any time be evacuated to Germany.

4. Immediate transfer of the Italian Fleet and Italian aircraft to such points as may be designated by the Allied Commander in Chief, with details of disarmament to be prescribed by him.

5. Italian merchant shipping may be requisitioned by the Allied Commander in Chief to meet the needs of his military-naval program.

6. Immediate surrender of Corsica and of all Italian territory, both islands and mainland, to the Allies, for such use as operational bases and other purposes as the Allies may see fit.

7. Immediate guarantee of the free use by the Allies of all airfields and naval ports in Italian territory, regardless of the rate of evacuation of the Italian territory by the German forces. These ports and fields to be protected by Italian armed forces until this function is taken over by the Allies.

8. Immediate withdrawal to Italy of Italian armed forces from all participation in the current war from whatever areas in which they may be now engaged.

9. Guarantee by the Italian Government that if necessary it will employ all its available armed forces to insure prompt and exact compliance with all the provisions of this armistice.

10. The Commander in Chief of the Allied Forces reserves to himself the right to take any measure which in his opinion may be necessary for the protection of the interests of the Allied Forces for the prosecution of the war, and the Italian Government binds itself to take such administrative or other action as the Commander in Chief may require, and in particular the Commander in Chief will establish Allied Military Government over such parts of Italian territory as he may deem necessary in the military interests of the Allied Nations.

11. The Commander in Chief of the Allied Forces will have a full right to impose measures of disarmament, demobilization, and demilitarization.

12. Other conditions of a political, economic and financial nature with which Italy will be bound to comply will be transmitted at a later date.

The conditions of the present Armistice will not be made public without prior approval of the Allied Commander in Chief. The English will be considered the official text.

Marshal Pietro Badoglio,   Dwight D. Eisenhower,
   Head of Italian Government.   General, U. S. Army,
                                                Commander in Chief,
                                                          Allied Forces.

130. Moscow Declaration on General Security, October 30, 1943[7]

THE GOVERNMENTS of the United States of America, the United Kingdom, the Soviet Union and China:

united in their determination, in accordance with the Declaration by the United Nations of January 1, 1942, and subsequent declarations, to continue hostilities against those Axis powers with which they respectively are at war until such powers have laid down their arms on the basis of unconditional surrender;

conscious of their responsibility to secure the liberation of themselves and the peoples allied with them from the menace of aggression; recognizing the necessity of ensuring a rapid and orderly transition from war to peace and of establishing and maintaining international peace and security with the least diversion of the world's human and economic resources for armaments; jointly declare:

1. That their united action, pledged for the prosecution of the war against their respective enemies, will be continued for the organization and maintenance of peace and security.

2. That those of them at war with a common enemy will act together in all matters relating to the surrender and disarmament of that enemy.

3. That they will take all measures deemed by them to be necessary to provide against any violation of the terms imposed upon the enemy.

4. That they recognize the necessity of establishing at the earliest practicable date a general international organization, based on the principle of the sovereign equality of all peace-loving states, and open to membership by all such states, large and small, for the maintenance of international peace and security.

5. That for the purpose of maintaining international peace and security pending the re-establishment of law and order and the inauguration of a system of general security, they will consult with one another and as occasion requires with other members of the United Nations with a view to joint action on behalf of the community of nations.

6. That after the termination of hostilities they will not employ their military forces within the territories of other states except for the purposes envisaged in this declaration and after joint consultation.

7. That they will confer and co-operate with one another and with other members of the United Nations to bring about a practicable general agreement with respect to the regulation of armaments in the post-war period.

131. Germany's Strategic Position in the Beginning of the 5th Year of the War, Munich, November 7, 1943[8] (Excerpts)

Lecture by the Chief of the General Staff of the Armed Forces (West) to the Reich and Gau leaders, delivered in Munich on 7 November 1943.
. . . .

Introduction

Reichsleiter Bormann has requested me to give you a review today of the strategic position in the beginning of the 5th year of war.

I must admit that it was not without hesitation that I undertook this none too easy task. It is not possible to do it justice with a few generalities. It is not necessary to say openly what is. No one—the Fuehrer has ordered—may know more or be told more than he needs for his own immediate task, but I have no doubt at all in my mind, Gentlemen, but that you need a great deal in order to be able to cope with your tasks. It is in your Gaus, after all, and among their inhabitants that all the enemy propaganda, the defeatism, and the malicious rumors concentrate that try to find themselves a plan among our people. Up and down the country the devil of subversion strides. All the cowards are seeking a way out, or—as they call it—a political solution. They say, we must negotiate while there is still something in hand, and all these slogans are made use of to attack the natural sense of the people that in this war there can only be a fight to the end. Capitulation is the end of the Nation, the end of Germany. Against this wave of enemy propaganda and cowardice you need more than force. You need to know the true situation and for this reason I believe that I am justified in giving you a perfectly open and uncolored account of the state of affairs. This is no forbidden disclosure of secrets, but a weapon which may perhaps help you to fortify the morale of the people. For this war will not only be decided by force of arms but by the will to resist of the whole people. Germany was broken in 1918 not at the front but at home. Italy suffered not military defeat but morale defeat. She broke down internally. The result has been not the peace she expected but—through the cowardice of these criminal traitors—a fate a thousand times harder than continuation of the war at our side would have brought to the Italian people. I can rely on you, Gentlemen, that since I give concrete figures and data concerning our own strength, you will treat these details as your secret; all the rest is at your disposal without restriction for application in your activities as leaders of the people.

. . . .

If today, in view of the repeated and prolonged setbacks of the year 1943, the question comes up again and again, whether we had not thoroughly underestimated the strength of the Bolshevik opponent, the answer to this question in regard to the execution of individual part-operations, may certainly be said to be 'Yes.' But as regards the decision to attack as a whole and that of holding on to this decision for as long as possible, there can be no doubts. As in politics so in the conduct of war—the issue is not merely one of arithmetical sums, and one of the most important lessons taught by war is that correct estimation of the opponent is one of the hardest of all tasks, and that even when everything has been correctly summed up, there still remains much that is imponderable and only becomes clear in the course of the battle itself.

One clarification of the situation is however to be perceived in that, as a result of our advance into the dark unknown which is Russia, we have taken the measure not only of the strength in personnel involved but also of a standard of equipment which has forced us in our turn to institute a state of totalitarian warfare and a technical counterblast such as left to ourselves we were hardly likely to have produced. One can only think with a shudder of what would have happened if we had adopted a waiting attitude in the face of this danger and, sooner or later, have been overrun by it.

. . . .

The first two years of war saw Germany and its later allies running a victorious course almost unparalleled in history. The campaigns in Poland, Norway, France, in North Africa, in the Balkans, and the attack on Russia as far as the Donetz, up to the gates of Moscow and up to the Volkhov created a wide forefield for the defense of Europe and as a result of the occupation and making safe of rich areas of raw materials and food, provided the premises for a long war. Superior leadership, better employment of the modern means of war, a superior air arm and the exceptionally high fighting value and morale of our troops faced by opponents inferior on each of these counts have produced these successes. Nevertheless, during this period of the war, in which our superiority on land was undisputed, and our superiority in the air was able to make good, at all events in the coastal district, our hopeless inferiority at sea, in our last grasp at the palm of victory success has eluded us. The landing in England, prepared for down to the smallest detail but with improvised transport resources only, could not be dared while the British Air arm had not been completely beaten. And this we were not able to do, just as we have not been able completely to shatter the Soviet Armed Forces. Later generations will not be able to reproach us with not having dared the utmost and spared no effort to achieve these aims which would have decided the war.

But no one could take it upon himself to allow the German air arm to bleed to death in the Battle of Britain in view of the struggle which still lay before us against Soviet Russia.

In the East however, the natural catastrophe of the winter of 1941 imposed an imperative halt on even the sternest resolution. [Following paragraph struck out:]

Our third objective, that of drawing Spain into the war on our side, and thereby creating the possibility of seizing Gibraltar, was wrecked by the resistance of the Spanish or, better say, Jesuit Foreign Minister, Sorano Sunjer.

It therefore became clear that we could no longer count upon an early end to the war, but that it would be hard and difficult and confront the whole nation with great hardships.

After the first set-backs on the Eastern front and in the North African theater of war in the winter of 1943, the Reich and its Allies once again gathered together all their strength in order to defeat this Eastern opponent finally by a new assault and to deprive the British of their Egyptian base of operations. The great operation against the Caucasus and the Delta of the Nile failed, however, owing to insufficient strength and inadequate supplies. For the first time our Western opponents showed themselves to be superior both on the technical side and numerically in the air over the Mediterranean. The Soviet Russian Command also continued to stabilize the front at Stalingrad and before the Caucasus, and after that in wintertime using newly-formed strong reserves continued to break-through the petrified over-extended fronts on the Volga and along the Don—largely occupied moreover by the troops of our Allies. The 6th Army, consisting of the best German formations, inadequately supplied and exposed to the storms of winter, succumbed to enemy superiority.

Similarly, the Western Powers were able to bring together in Egypt a concentration of land, sea, and air forces which held us up at the very gates of Egypt and after the battle of El Alamein forced us to retreat, and finally, following on the landing of strong Anglo-American armies in French North Africa, to surrender the entire African position. Again some of the best German divisions fell a victim to the stranglehold of a superior enemy air force on our supplies by sea, although not before they had won for us a certain gain in time which was worth every sacrifice.

At the end of the winter fighting of 1942/43 and after the loss of the

African Army the armed forces of Germany and her allies were strained to the utmost. It proved possible to re-form the 5th Armored Army and the 6th Army—but four armies of our allies were lost for good.

The tactical reserves in the East would, it is true be exceptionally well equipped, but their numbers would no longer be increased to such a pitch as to make it possible to envisage any extensive operations. Gone was the great mobility of the Army and, excepting on the Russian theater of war, gone also our superiority in the air. The superior economic strength of our opponents and their greater reservoir of manpower, concentrated to form a point of gravity against Europe, was beginning to tell. The complete failure of Italy in all domains and the absence of any munitions production worthy of the name among our other Allies could not be adequately compensated by the tremendous efforts made by Germany.

Of necessity therefore the initiative was bound to pass over to the opposing side and the Reich, and the European nations fighting at Germany's side, to go over to the defensive.

So when the positions pushed out beyond the European front to the South had been taken by the enemy, in July 1943, the enemy attack started: In the East to regain the territories lost there and in the South against the Fortress Europe proper at its weakest point. In the meantime the air arms of the Anglo-Americans had already begun the grand assault on the production hearths and morale of our people at home.

In the Far East Japan's struggle has developed on much the same lines, with the difference, however, that the Japanese had pushed their advanced positions very much farther away from the Motherland proper and the Anglo-Saxons did not here undertake any attacks on a large scale for the reason that they had directed their point of gravity against Europe.

It was at this stage of the war that the Italian betrayal took place. Its main features will be known to you from what appeared in the press. Actually it was even more dramatic than the newspapers showed. For the Supreme Command it was perhaps one of the hardest problems which it had as yet had to master. That the removal and arrest of the Duce could not end otherwise than by the defection of Italy was completely clear to the Fuehrer from the first, although many politically less well-trained eyes thought to see in it rather an improvement in our position in the Mediterranean and our coop-eration with the Italians. There were many personages at this time who failed to understand the Fuehrer's GHQ in its political and military actions. For these were directed towards overthrowing the new Government and liberating the Duce. Only the smallest possible circle might know of this. On the military side in the meantime everything was to be done to stop enemy penetration of the Southern front as far South as possible, that is, on Sicily.

That the enemy would bring this point of gravity to bear on some point further West in the Mediterranean—of that there was not the slightest doubt; the distribution of his shipping and landing space made this clear. Where however would this point be? On Sardinia, on Corsica, in Apulia, in

Calabria, or—if the thesis of betrayal were true—why not in Rome itself, or near Leghorn or Genoa? If he did not do this, then our job was to hold as much of Italy as possible in order not to let the base of the enemy air forces come near to the Alps. If the enemy is successful in a landing in Northern Italy then all the German formations in Central and Southern Italy would be lost. Moreover no grounds must be given which might serve the Italians as a moral pretext for their betrayal, or by premature hostile action to commit the betrayal ourselves. In the meantime the traitors simply oozed with amiability and assurances of faith, and even got as far as to make some of our officers who came into contact with them daily doubtful of the truth of the betrayal-hypothesis. This was nothing to be wondered at, for to the German officers such depths of infamy were simply incomprehensible.

The situation became more and more difficult. It was perhaps the only time in this war when at times I myself hardly knew what I should suggest to the Fuehrer. The measures to be taken in the event of open betrayal had been decided in every detail. The watchword 'Axis' would set them in motion. In the meantime however all the divisions, which the Fuehrer at once caused to be moved from the West to Upper Italy, were operatively idle there—and that at a time when the East front, subjected to severe assault, was begging for reserves more urgently than ever.

How much meanwhile we had been able to find out through our troops and through the bordering Gau's—keen as sleuth-hounds on the track of Italian machinations—in the matter of manifestly hostile actions and preparations is known to you all. However, somehow or other the Italians explained it all ways, either as a misunderstanding or with excuses.

In this insupportable position the Fuehrer agreed to slash through the Gordian knot by a political and military ultimatum. Then on the morning of the 7 September the enemy landing fleet appeared at Salerno and on the afternoon of 8 September news of the Italian capitulation flew through the ether. Even now however, at the last moment, the freedom of action of the Command was still held up: the Italians refused to admit the authenticity of the wireless message. The password itself therefore would not be given but only the 'stand-by' for the troops, until at last at 19.15 this most monstrous of all betrayals in history was confirmed by the Italian political authorities themselves. What followed was both a drama and a tragedy. Only at a later date will it be possible to gather together and set forth all the grotesque details. The more disillusioned the troops and the German Command, the harder the reaction.

132. MILITARY CONCLUSIONS OF THE TEHERAN CONFERENCE, DECEMBER 1, 1943[9]

The Conference:—

(1) Agreed that the Partisans in Yugoslavia should be supported by supplies and equipment to the greatest possible extent, and also by commando operations:

(2) Agreed that, from the military point of view, it was most desirable that Turkey should come into the war on the side of the Allies before the end of the year:

(3) Took note of Marshal Stalin's statement that if Turkey found herself at war with Germany, and as a result Bulgaria declared war on Turkey or attacked her, the Soviet would immediately be at war with Bulgaria. The Conference further took note that this fact could be explicitly stated in the forthcoming negotiations to bring Turkey into the war:

(4) Took note that Operation Overlord would be launched during May 1944, in conjunction with an operation against Southern France. The latter operation would be undertaken in as great a strength as availability of landing-craft permitted. The Conference further took note of Marshal Stalin's statement that the Soviet forces would launch an offensive at about the same time with the object of preventing the German forces from transferring from the Eastern to the Western Front:

(5) Agreed that the military staffs of the three Powers should henceforward keep in close touch with each other in regard to the impending operations in Europe. In particular it was agreed that a cover plan to mystify and mislead the enemy as regards these operations should be concerted between the staffs concerned.

133. Allied Declaration on Iran, December 1, 1943[10]

The President of the United States, the Premier of the U. S. S. R., and the Prime Minister of the United Kingdom, having consulted with each other and with the Prime Minister of Iran, desire to declare the mutual agreement of their three Governments regarding their relations with Iran.

The Governments of the United States, the U. S. S. R., and the United Kingdom recognize the assistance which Iran has given in the prosecution of the war against the common enemy, particularly by facilitating the transportation of supplies from overseas to the Soviet Union.

The Three Governments realize that the war has caused special economic difficulties for Iran, and they are agreed that they will continue to make available to the Government of Iran such economic assistance as may be possible, having regard to the heavy demands made upon them by their world-wide military operations and to the world-wide shortage of transport, raw materials, and supplies for civilian consumption.

With respect to the post-war period, the Governments of the United States, the U. S. S. R., and the United Kingdom are in accord with the Government of Iran that any economic problems confronting Iran at the close of hostilities should receive full consideration, along with those of other members of the United Nations, by conferences or international agencies held or created to deal with international economic matters.

The Governments of the United States, the U. S. S. R., and the United Kingdom are at one with the Government of Iran in their desire for the maintenance of the independence, sovereignty and territorial integrity of

Iran. They count upon the participation of Iran, together with all other peace-loving nations, in the establishment of international peace, security and prosperity after the war, in accordance with the principles of the Atlantic Charter, to which all four Governments have subscribed.

Part 11. Strategy For Japan's Defeat

Allied operations in the Pacific became offensive following the battle for Midway (98) but on a definitely limited scale. In the New Guinea area, stretching west from the Solomons, a vast region of water and islands became a major battleground. Unlike land warfare, the Pacific battle area contained many "fronts" simultaneously as the American and Japanese forces fought for possession of island strongholds some hundreds—even thousands—of miles apart.

By mid-1943 the Allies began a strong push to drive the Japanese from the Solomon Islands and destroy their base of operations at Rabaul on New Britain. Within this setting the Allied leaders met at Quebec in August (see Part 10) and drafted a "Long-Term Strategy" aimed at Japan's ultimate defeat (134). The participants confidently anticipated that following Germany's defeat "vast resources . . . will become available to the United Nations" to pour into the war against Japan. Their goal was to bolster China's defenses and develop United States air power throughout the Southeast Asia theatre. An insight into some of the problems that confronted the American participants in the South East Asia Command (SEAC) is glimpsed in an interesting note (135) from American General Joseph Stilwell's political adviser (prepared for Roosevelt). The conduct of war demands unity of purpose for would-be partners, and the White House press release of December 1 announced the goals of "the three great Allies" (United States, Great Britain, and China) engaged in punishing Japanese aggression (136).

One of President Roosevelt's major interests was to persuade Stalin to commit Soviet forces to the war against Japan, but since the long promised second front had not materialized he approached the subject circumspectly. He informed Marshal Stalin about the planning of naval operations in the Pacific, and his carefully worded message reflected his full awareness of the Soviet position vis-à-vis Japan; yet it asked for a commitment (137). A few days later the U. S. Chiefs of Staff issued a memorandum at the second Cairo meeting (December 3) which discussed Japan's eventual defeat. The memorandum almost included the assumption that Russia would enter the war (138).

Japan, meanwhile, retreated farther into the western New Guinea area and started preparing a new plan geared to a changed defensive position. The "A" Operations Plan (139), as it was called, was never completed, however, because the American forces moved too quickly. The attack against Palau in March and the capture of Hollandia in April prevented the Japanese from readying the plan. Thus the U. S. attack in the Philippine Sea resulted in disastrous Japanese carrier and air group losses. Consequently the Japanese discarded the "A" Plan in favor of the "Sho" Plan in July 1944 (140). The United States now controlled most of the Central Pacific, forcing Japan's new defense range to assume almost north-south proportions stretching from Timor north through the Philippines, Formosa, and the home islands. The summary of Allied progress in the Pacific in September (141) revealed they had indeed made impressive gains.

As the war came closer to the home islands the Japanese military frantically sought to delay the onslaught. The introduction of a special attack unit called the *Kamikaze* was born of desperation, and volunteer pilots undertook suicide missions against American warships. These methods were extraordinary even for wartime and they attracted special notice during the sea battles for the recovery of the Philippines in October. It became obvious that enemy fighter planes were deliberately diving into American ships. These actions created widespread fear and consternation because the western soldier found them inconceivable; however, the creation of a *Kamikaze* corps was compatible with Japanese beliefs on life and death (142).

The American penetration of Japan's defense lines resulted in a severance of the Sixteenth and Nineteenth Armies (estimated 200,000 men) in the Netherlands East Indies and the loss of important war supplies. Two graphic reports by General MacArthur during September recounted the successful landings on the coast of Leyte Island in the Philippines (143) and commented on the effects the war was having upon the Japanese people (144).

134. REPORTS OF CONCLUSIONS REACHED BY COMBINED CHIEFS OF STAFF, QUEBEC, AUGUST 24, 1943[1] (EXCERPTS)

THE WAR AGAINST JAPAN

20. Long-Term Strategy

We have made a preliminary study of long-term strategy for the defeat of Japan and are of the opinion that the following factors require particular emphasis:

a. The dependence of Japan upon air power, naval power, and shipping for maintaining her position in the Pacific and Southeast Asia.

b. The consequent need for applying the maximum attrition to Japan's air force, naval forces and shipping by all possible means in all possible areas.

c. The advantage to be gained and the time to be saved by a more extensive use of the superior air resources at the disposal of the United

Nations, both in the strategic field and in conjunction with operations on land.

21. We consider that great advantage may be obtained, by modern and untried methods, from the vast resources which, with the defeat of Germany, will become available to the United Nations. We have in mind:

a. A project rapidly to expand and extend the striking power of the United Nations air forces in China as well as of the ground troops for their defense by employing the large numbers of load carrying aircraft available to open an "air road" to China.

b. The employment of lightly equipped jungle forces, dependent largely upon air supply lines.

c. The use of special equipment, such as artificial harbors, HAB-BAKUKS, etc., to enable the superior power of the United Nations to be deployed in unexpected and undeveloped areas.

22. From every point of view operations should be framed to force the defeat of Japan as soon as possible after the defeat of Germany. Planning should be on the basis of accomplishing this within 12 months of that event. Decisions as to specific operations which will insure a rapid course of events must await further examination on the lines indicated above.

. . . .

24. We are agreed that the reorientation of forces from the European Theater to the Pacific and Far East should be started as soon as the German situation, in our opinion, so allows.

25. The principle has been accepted that the forces to carry out operations from the East, including the Southwest Pacific, shall be provided by the United States, and for operations from the West by Great Britain, except for special types not available to Great Britain which will be provided by the United States. The employment of Dominion forces will be a matter of discussion between all Governments concerned.

. . . .

27. Operations in the Pacific 1943–44
We approve the proposals of the United States Chiefs of Staff for operations in the Pacific in 1943–44 as follows:
28. Gilberts
The seizure and consolidation of the Gilberts preparatory to a further advance into the Marshalls.
29. Marshalls
The seizure of the Marshall Islands (including Wake and Kusaie) preparatory to a westward advance through the Central Pacific.
30. Ponape
The capture of Ponape preparatory to operations against the Truk area.
31. Carolines (Truk Area)
The seizure of the eastern Carolines as far west as Woleai and the establishment of a fleet base at Truk.
32. Palau Islands
The capture of the Palaus including Yap.

33. Operations Against Guam and the Japanese Marianas
The seizure of Guam and the Japanese Marianas.

34. Paramushiru
Consideration of operations against Paramushiru and the Kuriles.

35. Operations in the New Guinea-Bismarcks-Admiralty Islands Subsequent to Current Operations
The seizure or neutralization of eastern New Guinea as far west as Wewak and including the Admiralty Islands and Bismarck Archipelago. *Rabaul is to be neutralized rather than captured.*

36. Operations in New Guinea Subsequent to the Wewak-Kavieng Operation
An advance along the north coast of New Guinea as far west as Vogelkop, *by step-by-step airborne-water-borne advances.*

37. Operations in India-Burma-China Theater, 1943–44
To carry out operations for the capture of Upper Burma in order to improve the air route and establish overland communications with China. Target date mid-February 1944.

. . . .

39. To continue the preparation of India as a base for the operations eventually contemplated in the Southeast Asia Command.

40. To continue to build up and increase the air routes and air supplies of China, and the development of air facilities, with a view to:

a. Keeping China in the war.
b. Intensifying operations against the Japanese.
c. Maintaining increased U. S. and Chinese Air Forces in China.
d. Equipping Chinese ground forces.

41. We have decided that our main effort should be put into offensive operations with the object of establishing land communications with China and improving and securing the air route. Priorities cannot be rigid and we therefore propose to instruct the Supreme Commander in formulating his proposals to regard this decision as a guide and to bear in mind the importance of the longer term development of the lines of communication.

. . . .

46. Southeast Asia Command
General
The vigorous and effective prosecution of large-scale operations against Japan in Southeast Asia, and the rapid development of the air route through Burma to China, necessitate the reorganization of the High Command in the Indian Theater. It has, therefore, been decided that the Command in India should be divided from the operational Command in Southeast Asia as described below:

47. Command in Asia
The administration of India as a base for the forces in Southeast Asia will remain under the control of the Commander in Chief, India. . . .

. . . .

General Stilwell will be Deputy Supreme Allied Commander of the Southeast Asia Theater and in that capacity will command the Chinese troops operating into Burma and all U. S. air and ground forces committed to the Southeast Asia Theater.

. . . .

55. General Stilwell will continue to have the same direct responsibility to Generalissimo Chiang Kai-shek as heretofore. His dual function under the Supreme Allied Commander and under the Generalissimo is recognized.

135. Memorandum By General Stilwell's Political Adviser (Davies), Cairo, November 1943[2]

THE CHINA AND SOUTH EAST ASIA THEATERS: SOME POLITICAL CONSIDERATIONS

The mission of the South East Asia Command is to defeat the enemy in and presumably occupy former British and Dutch colonies and Thailand. French Indochina may later be included.

In so far as we participate in SEAC operations, we become involved in the politically explosive colonial problems of the British, Dutch and possibly French. In so doing, we compromise ourselves not only with the colonial peoples of Asia but also the free peoples of Asia, including the Chinese. Domestically, our Government lays itself open to public criticism—"why should American boys die to recreate the colonial empires of the British and their Dutch and French satellites?" Finally, more Anglo-American misunderstanding and friction is likely to arise out of our participation in SEAC than out of any other theater.

By concentrating our Asiatic effort on operations in and from China we keep to the minimum our involvement in colonial imperialism. We engage in a cause which is popular with Asiatics and the American public. We avoid the mutual mistrust and recrimination over the colonial question, potentially so inimical to harmonious Anglo-American relations.

General Stilwell has submitted a plan for increased American effort in the China theater. It envisages, among other things, the recapture of Canton, Hong Kong and Shanghai and a possible attack on Formosa. He proposes to use American and Chinese forces to accomplish this. The Chinese welcome this plan. It gives them something to fight for. They have slight interest in entering Burma, Thailand and French Indochina for only the territorial benefit of the British and the French. But their own territory and Formosa (which they claim) provide a real incentive.

The Chinese Army is great in size. But it is relatively untrained and generally corrupt. However much of the Generalissimo and his Army may in principle wish to assume the offensive, they cannot effectively do so excepting under firm American guidance. American leadership can concretely be exercised only as General Stilwell is given bargaining power, for the Chinese are sharp, practical traders. All aid and concessions to China must therefore be made in consultation with and through General Stilwell.

It is not proposed that with a concentration of effort on the China theater we should forthwith turn our backs on SEAC. In cooperation with SEAC we need to retake North Burma immediately and so reopen a land route to China. But after the recapture of North Burma there comes a parting of the ways.

The British will wish to throw their main weight southward for the repossession of colonial empire. Our main interest in Asia will lie to the East from whence we can strike directly and in coordination with other American offensives at the center of Japan's new Empire.

136. WHITE HOUSE PRESS RELEASE, DECEMBER 1, 1943[3]

PRESS COMMUNIQUÉ

President Roosevelt, Generalissimo Chiang Kai-Shek and Prime Minister Churchill, together with their respective military and diplomatic advisers, have completed a conference in North Africa. The following general statement was issued:

"The several military missions have agreed upon future military operations against Japan. The three great Allies expressed their resolve to bring unrelenting pressure against their brutal enemies by sea, land and air. This pressure is already rising.

"The three great Allies are fighting this war to restrain and punish the aggression of Japan. They covet no gain for themselves and have no thought of territorial expansion. It is their purpose that Japan shall be stripped of all the islands in the Pacific which she has seized or occupied since the beginning of the first World War in 1914, and that all the territories Japan has stolen from the Chinese, such as Manchuria, Formosa, and the Pescadores, shall be restored to the Republic of China. Japan will also be expelled from all other territories which she has taken by violence and greed. The aforesaid three great powers, mindful of the enslavement of the people of Korea, are determined that in due course Korea shall become free and independent.

"With these objects in view the three Allies, in harmony with those of the United Nations at war with Japan, will continue to persevere in the serious and prolonged operations necessary to procure the unconditional surrender of Japan."

137. ROOSEVELT TO STALIN, NOVEMBER 29, 1943[4]

ADVANCE PLANNING FOR NAVAL OPERATIONS IN NORTHWESTERN PACIFIC

I would like to arrange with you at this time for the exchange of information and for such preliminary planning as may be appropriate under the present conditions for eventual operations against Japan when Germany has been eliminated from the war. The more of this preliminary planning that can be done, without undue jeopardy to the situation, the sooner the war as a whole can be brought to a conclusion.

Specifically, I have in mind the following items:

a. We would be glad to receive combat intelligence information concerning Japan.

b. Considering that the ports for your Far Eastern submarine and destroyer force might be threatened seriously by land or air attack, do you feel it desirable that the United States should expand base facilities sufficiently to provide for these forces in U. S. bases?

c. What direct or indirect assistance would you be able to give in the event of a U. S. attack against the northern Kuriles?

d. Could you indicate what ports, if any, our forces could use, and could you furnish data on these ports in regard to their naval use as well as port capacities for dispatch of cargo?

These questions can be discussed as you may find appropriate with our Military Mission in Moscow, similar to the procedure suggested for plans regarding air operations.

138. Memorandum By the U. S. Chiefs of Staff, Cairo, December 3, 1943[5] (Excerpts)

C. C. S. 397 (Revised)

SPECIFIC OPERATIONS FOR THE DEFEAT OF JAPAN, 1944

1. We are agreed that every effort should be exerted to bring the U. S. S. R. into the war against Japan at the earliest practicable date, and that plans should be prepared in that event.

2. We are agreed that plans should be prepared for operations in the event that Germany is defeated earlier than the fall of 1944.

. . . .

4. *General.* In addition to the specific objectives hereinafter indicated, supporting operations should be conducted. Both the specific and supporting operations will be designed to destroy the Japanese Fleet at an early date; to secure maximum attrition of enemy air forces; to intensify air, submarine, and mining operations against enemy shipping and lines of communication; to establish air and sea blockade of the main Japanese islands; to continue efforts to keep China in the war; and to enable us to launch land and carrier-based air operations against Japan.

5. *North Pacific.* Plans for the North Pacific involve the augmentation of base facilities and defensive installations in the Aleutians in preparation for entry into the Kuriles and Soviet territory in the event of Russian collaboration. Naval surface and submarine action, including raids on the Japanese fishing fleet will be carried out. Preparations will be made for executing very long range strategic bombing against the Kuriles and northern Japan.

6. *Central, South and Southwest Pacific.* The advance along the New

Guinea-N. E. I.-Philippine axis will proceed concurrently with operations for the capture of the Mandated Islands. A strategic bombing force will be established in Guam, Tinian, and Saipan for strategic bombing of Japan proper. Air bombardment of targets in the N. E. I.-Philippine Area and the aerial neutralization of Rabaul will be intensified.

7. *China.* Our efforts in the China area should have as their objective the intensification of land and air operations in and from China and the buildup of the U. S. A. A. F. and the Chinese army and air forces. It shall include also the establishing, without materially affecting other approved operations, of a very long range strategic bombing force at Calcutta, with advanced bases at Chengtu to attack vital targets in the Japanese "inner zone."

8. *Southeast Asia.* In the Southeast Asia Area operations should be carried out for the capture of Upper Burma in order to improve the air route and establish overland communications with China. . . .

9. As more carriers become available, the operations set forth should be supplemented, between scheduled operational dates as practicable, with massed carrier task force strikes against selected vital targets.

10. The completion of these operations will place the United Nations in positions from which to use most advantageously the great air, ground, and naval resources which will be at our disposal after Germany is defeated.

139. JAPAN'S "A" OPERATIONS PLAN, MAY 1944[6]

The objective of this plan was to concentrate all available forces for a decisive action against United States attacking forces.

The tasks to be performed were as follows:

(a) Consolidation of decisive battle forces was to be expedited. The enemy fleet's main force was to be contacted and destroyed sometime subsequent to the latter part of May, in the general area between the Central Pacific and the Philippines, or in the area south of the Timor-Java-Sumatra line. Unless otherwise directed, participation in any decisive action prior to the time when the forces could be thoroughly organized was to be avoided. Insofar as possible, the seas close to the bases where the Mobile Fleet was based were to be selected as the scene for the decisive battle.

(b) In the event that the enemy's attack materialized prior to the time of completion of the organization of the Mobile Fleet, decisive action employing naval surface forces was to be avoided and land-based air and local defense forces would be employed in intercepting and destroying the attacking force. In this eventuality every effort was to be made to avoid excessive losses of shore-based air, except where such losses would have a favorable effect on the ensuing decisive action.

(c) At the opportune moment when preparations for the decisive action had been completed, the entire force was to be thrown against the enemy's main strength in an effort to contact and destroy it.

(d) In preparation for the decisive action, priority was to be given to preparations for air operations by construction of air bases and by stock piling of fuel and ammunition. The Army and Navy were to cooperate in these preparations, and share all air bases jointly.

The disposition of forces prescribed by this plan was:

(a) Naval Surface Forces: The forces of the First Mobile Fleet, consisting of Battleship Divisions 1 and 3, Carrier Divisions 1, 2, and 3, Cruiser Divisions 4, 5, and 7, and Destroyer Squadrons 2 and 10, were to stand by in the Central and Southern Philippines.

(b) Naval Air Forces: The First Air Fleet, consisting of Air Flotillas 61 and 62, was to be deployed in the Central Pacific (Marianas-Western Carolines), Philippines, and the area north of Australia.

140. JAPAN'S "SHO" OPERATIONS PLAN, JULY 1944[7]

The operational policy of this plan was:

(a) By means of an all-out coordinated effort of land, sea, and air forces, to fight a decisive action in defense of the Home Islands, Nansei Shoto, Formosa, and Philippine areas. Only under favorable conditions would a decisive action be fought in defense of the Nanpo Shoto.

In accordance with the estimate of the probable areas of action, and in order to facilitate preparations and to establish command relationships the following four plans were drawn up:

Sho Number 1—Philippine Area.

Sho Number 2—Formosa-Nansei Shoto-Southern Kyushu Areas.

Sho Number 3—Kyushu-Shikoku-Honshu Areas.

Sho Number 4—Hokkaido Area.

As the Sho Number 1 and Number 2 were considered most likely to be activated, priority was given to strengthening the defenses in these areas. After a brisk discussion between the Army and Navy, it was agreed that an all-out land defense would be made only if the action were to occur in the Northern Philippines. If the action were to occur in the central or southern part, only air and surface forces would seek decisive action.

The tasks to be performed were:

(a) Destruction of enemy forces at the point of attack, by air, sea, and land forces concentrating on carriers and transports. The primary target for the Naval air forces was to be the United States Carrier Task Force; for Army air forces, the convoys.

(b) Disposition of air strength in depth, and conservation of this strength until just before the attempt to land.

(c) All-out air attacks and surface torpedo attacks when the enemy fleet and convoys approached sufficiently close to the objective.

(d) Maintenance of a counter landing force in readiness; a counter landing if a favorable opportunity occurs.

The initial disposition of forces prescribed by this plan:

(a) Naval Surface Forces

(1) Inland Sea area: The 3rd Fleet, consisting of Carrier Divisions 1, 3, and 4, and Destroyer Squadrons 10 and 11; the 6th Fleet consisting of Submarine Squadrons 7, 8, and 11, plus Battleship Division 2 of the 2d Fleet.

(2) Ominato area: The 5th Fleet consisting of Cruiser Division 21 and Destroyer Squadron 1.

(3) Philippines area: Southwest Area Fleet consisting of Cruiser Division 16 plus some destroyers.

(4) Singapore area: The 2d Fleet consisting of Battleship Divisions 1 and 3, Cruiser Divisions 4, 5, and 7, and Destroyer Squadron 2, plus one half of Destroyer Squadron 10.

(b) Army and Navy Air Forces

(1) Northeast and Home Islands areas: Army, the 1st, 10th, 11th, and 12th Air Divisions plus Training Command Aircraft; Navy, the 3d and 12th Air Fleets plus Air Groups of the 3d Fleet.

(2) Nansei Shoto-Formosa areas: The Army 8th Air Division and the Navy 2d Air Fleet (this air fleet was later sent to the Philippines).

(3) Philippines-Area north of Australia: The Army 4th Air Army and the Navy 1st Air Fleet.

141. U. S. Progress Report on Pacific Operations, September 12, 1944[8]

TOP SECRET   [Quebec]
C. C. S. 676
GENERAL PROGRESS REPORT ON RECENT OPERATIONS IN THE PACIFIC

The enclosure, compiled from reports of the area commanders in the Pacific, is presented for the information of the Combined Chiefs of Staff.

Enclosure

TOP SECRET
PROGRESS OF PACIFIC AND SOUTHWEST PACIFIC OPERATIONS
15 November 1943–15 September 1944

North Pacific

1. Operations in the North Pacific have been limited to periodic air raids and surface ship bombardment of Paramushiru and Shimushu and other islands in the northern Kuriles. Concurrently the establishment of bases to support future operations in the North Pacific is being carried to completion.

Central Pacific

2. In furtherance of the approved strategic concept of the war against Japan, the amphibious forces of the Pacific Ocean Areas, supported tactically and strategically by combatant units of the U. S. Pacific Fleet, have

successively occupied principal objectives in the Gilbert, Marshall and Marianas Islands.

3. The Gilbert Islands operations were initiated on 17 November 1943, and resulted in the occupation of Tarawa, Makin, and Apamama. Tarawa was well defended. In particular the beach defenses were extensive and difficult to overcome.

4. The Marshall Islands operations were initiated the 31st of January and resulted in the occupation of Kwajalein and Majuro Atolls. This was followed by the occupation in mid-February of Eniwetok.

5. Operations for the seizure of Saipan were initiated on the 15th of June. This was followed by the occupation of Tinian and Guam in late July.

6. The next operation scheduled in this area is the occupation of the Palaus. The target date is 15 September 1944.

7. From bases established in the Marshalls and Gilberts continuous air raids have been conducted against isolated Japanese held islands. Particular attention has been given to neutralization of Truk. These operations have been coordinated with similar operations conducted from bases in the Southwest Pacific.

8. During the operations for the occupation of the Marianas strong units of the Japanese Fleet were engaged by air action from our carriers in the Philippine Seas. Severe damage was inflicted on the Japanese in this engagement.

9. The submarine campaign in the Western Pacific has been prosecuted with vigor and the results attained have been most gratifying. Heavy toll has been taken of Japanese shipping as well as of escorting forces.

10. The occupation of the Marianas has presented the opportunity for development of bases for VLR [very long range] bombers for operations against Japan Proper. Preparations for conducting these operations are underway with all speed.

South Pacific

11. Operations in the South Pacific have been principally harassing operations against the isolated Japanese garrisons by air forces. The Royal New Zealand Air Force participated in combat missions with U. S. Army and Navy air units from bases in the South Pacific. The South Pacific area is being progressively "rolled-up." Bases developed in that area are currently being used for rehabilitation of troops for further operations in the Western Pacific. The naval base at Espíritu Santo has proved very useful in repairing battle damage. Repairs have been successfully accomplished on all classes of ships.

12. On 15 February, the 3rd New Zealand Division (less one brigade) seized Green Island.

Southwest Pacific

13. A U. S. task force landed in the Arawe area of New Britain on 15 December 1943 and terminated organized enemy resistance on 16 January 1944.

14. One U. S. marine division, supported by Allied air and naval forces,

landed in the Gloucester area on 26 December 1943 and succeeded in capturing the airfields by 30 December. Japanese killed were 3,686 as against our losses of 326. As a result of the Arawe and Cape Gloucester operations, western New Britain was secured by the middle of March.

15. Preceded by heavy naval and air bombardment, a successful, unopposed landing was made near Saidor on 2 January 1944. The airstrip was captured and ready for landing of transport aircraft by 7 January. Commencing 16 January, the remainder of the U. S. division employed reinforced the original landing. In expanding the beachhead, only weak resistance was encountered.

16. One U. S. cavalry division, supported by naval and air force units, made initial landings in the Admiralty Islands on 29 February 1944. The landing was made in Hayne Harbor, Los Negros Island, against little resistance and Momote airdrome was seized on D-day. Several enemy counterattacks were repulsed resulting in large Japanese casualties and by 23 March enemy forces on Los Negros were completely surrounded. Adjacent islands in the group were reduced and occupied and by the middle of April complete control of the Admiralty Islands had been obtained.

17. Two independent task forces, under the command of the Sixth Army, made simultaneous landings at Aitape and Hollandia on 22 April 1944. Landings were preceded by heavy naval bombardment and air strafing attacks.

    a. The Hollandia Task Force made landings in the Humboldt Bay and Tanahmerah Bay areas respectively and formed a pincers movement in attacking the three airstrips. Only slight enemy resistance was encountered and by 1 May control of the area had been definitely established.

    b. The Aitape Task Force established landings against practically no opposition and the airdrome was reported operational by 25 April.

    c. The element of surprise played an important part in the success of both operations resulting in an estimated 54,000 troops to the eastward being cut off.

18. A U. S. task force, supported by air and naval forces, made unopposed landings on Wakde Island and near Arara on 17 May 1944. All enemy resistance on Wakde was overcome by 18 May. The Arara perimeter was extended between the Tementoe River and the Tor River on 17 May with increasing enemy resistance west of the Tor River. Strong enemy attacks failed to penetrate the perimeter and were repulsed. The task force perimeter was extended and by 3 July included the Maffin airdrome. Casualties suffered by the Japanese are 3,650 killed and 70 prisoners. Active patrolling is continuing.

19. On 27 May 1944 one U. S. infantry division, with the support of air and naval forces, made landings in the Biak Island areas and encountered little opposition initially. Enemy strength developed on 5 June and the Mokmer airstrip was crossed on 7 June under artillery, mortar and machine gun fire. Artillery fire prevented work on the Mokmer airdrome until 11 June and the enemy launched several unsuccessful counterattacks in an

effort to regain the field. Boroke, Sorido and Mokmer dromes were entirely cleared of enemy artillery and small arms fire by 22 June. General patrolling and mopping up operations continue.

20. One U. S. regimental combat team, closely supported by air and naval forces, landed unopposed near the Kamiri drome on Noemfoor Island on 2 July 1944. On 3 July and 4 July three U. S. parachute battalions were dropped on the Kamiri strip, assisting the infantry. By 6 July enemy resistance had been overcome and the Kamiri, Koransoren and Namber dromes were firmly held.

21. A U. S. infantry task force made an unopposed landing near Cape Opmarai in the Cape Sansapor area on 30 July 1944. No opposition other than patrol skirmishes has been encountered and active patrolling continues. Japanese dead for the period 30 July to 10 August numbered 92.

22. Air operations conducted in the Southwest Pacific Area have been especially effective in neutralizing Japanese forces and enabling the Allies to conduct further offensive actions aimed at gaining complete control. In all advances, their mission in each case called for securing airfields and other bases from which to conduct further operations. Air supremacy has been achieved to such an extent that only in isolated instances are the Japanese offering any determined air resistance.

23. Australian land force activity in the Southwest Pacific Area consisted primarily of participation in the Finschhafen and Kaiapit-Dumpu operations and the occupation of the Madang-Sepik River coast line. The 9th Australian Division captured Finschhafen on 2 October 1943 and drove the remaining Jap troops to Satelberg. Satelberg fell on 29 November. Elements of the 9th Australian Division, utilizing armor to great advantage, then advanced up Huon Peninsula coast line to contact U. S. Saidor Task Force at Yaut River, southeast of Saidor, to complete occupation of Huon Peninsula on 10 February.

Simultaneously, the 7th Australian Division was deployed into the Ramu Valley to reinforce independent Australian units and to stop the threatened Jap drive overland through the Ramu-Markham Valley from Madang. The 11th Australian Division relieved the 7th Australian Division 8 January and continued the Australian advance to a final juncture with U. S. troops near Yalua on 13 April. Subsequently, U. S. troops were withdrawn and the Australian units continued pressure on the Jap forces which withdrew up the New Guinea coast toward Wewak. By 6 June Australian troops had reached Hansa Bay and are now in contact along the Sepik River.

During this period, the RAAF carried on continued attacks from the Darwin area. Australian fighter units attached to U. S. task forces were used in each of the landings along the New Guinea coast as the initial occupation forces with their light P-40's.

They operated in the advance airdromes before the airdromes were suitable for the operation of U. S. units equipped with heavier aircraft.

The Netherlands East Indies Air Forces operating in the Southwest Pacific Area consist of the 18th Medium Bomber Squadron and the 120th Fighter

Squadron. Elements of these forces participated in daily bombing and strafing strikes against enemy shipping and installations in the Aroe-Tanimbar-Kai and Timor areas.

24. Future operations in this area will advance our forces into the southern and central Philippines via Morotai, Talaud, Sarangani and the Leyte-Samar area, with a target date of 20 December for Leyte-Samar.

142. KAMIKAZE CORPS, INTERROGATION OF INOGUCHI, OCTOBER 15, 1945[9] (EXCERPTS)

(U. S. Interrogation of Japanese Officers)

TOKYO   15 October 1945

Interrogation of: Captain INOGUCHI, Rikibei, IJN, Chief of Staff of First Air Fleet throughout the PHILIPPINE Campaign.

. . . .

TRANSCRIPT

Q. What was your position in the Philippines in 1944-1945?

A. Operations and Plans, Staff of First Air Fleet.

Q. Was the First Air Fleet combined with the Second Air Fleet during the time of our attacks there?

A. At the beginning they were separate. 22 October they combined with the Second Air Fleet. They had a single staff but remained under separate operation. Kamikaze was begun by the First Air Fleet.

Q. Were the plans of the First Air Fleet and surface forces combined in the SHO Operations?

A. They were.

Q. Who made the plans for coordination?

A. The Imperial Headquarters (Daihonei). Admiral TOYODA was the Senior Navy Member of the Imperial Headquarters.

Q. Does the plan cover the complete SHO Operation?

A. The entire study of the SHO Operation is not in the plan. It is divided into three phases (3 plans), but the whole plan was directed at the same objective.

Q. I am not so much interested in the Kamikaze, but in the air cover for Admiral KURITA's fleet. Is this covered in the plan?

A. Yes, it is covered in the plan. Due to bad weather they never received cover and the Air Fleet was not able to get into the air. There was a very bad cloud bank between LUZON and BATANGAS. U. S. planes of your Task Force were able to escape through this cloud bank.

Q. Where were your planes on LUZON?

A. NICHOLS Field—and we had an insufficient number of aircraft in the command to complete the mission.

I would like to read you the history of Kamikaze which I have prepared and perhaps you will find the answer to your questions in it.

Admiral ONISHI ordered the organization of the Kamikaze on 19 October 1944. They were ready to go on 20 October, but no opportunity presented itself. On 25 October the first Kamikaze attack was made, having a great morale-raising effect. Although the attacks were ordered by the Commander in Chief (1st Air Fleet), in fact it was originated by the feeling of all combatants in the PHILIPPINE Area. All were beginning to think that there was no way but suicide to save the situation; there were many volunteers.

For example, on 15 October, Admiral ARIMA, Commander of the 26th Air Squadron, himself dove into an aircraft carrier. Admiral ARIMA lit the fuse of the ardent wishes of his men in order to bring their wishes into reality. At this time we in the PHILIPPINES thought about the approach of the crisis, owing to the odds. So we felt as follows: we must give our lives to the Emperor and Country, this is our inborn feeling. I am afraid you cannot understand it well, or you may call it desperate or foolish. We Japanese base our lives on obedience to Emperor and Country. On the other hand, we wish for the best place in death, according to Bushido. Kamikaze originates from these feelings.

It was the incarnation of these feelings. We believe in absolute obedience to the supreme authority who is unselfish, and whose concern is the welfare and peace of mankind. By this means we can accomplish peace. In view of this—from this standpoint, the Kamikaze deserved the consideration of the whole world.

The center of Kamikaze is morale. To achieve Kamikaze, the ordinary technique of the pilot is sufficient, no special training methds are necessary. Certain points about special attack are given. But to pilots who have had short training and least flight experience we give the essence of Kamikaze attack in the shortest period possible. Later on we gave them training in Kamikaze night attack.

As soon as our reconnaissance flight consisting of several planes ascertained the location of the enemy, then the Kamikaze units would start. Our Kamikaze units tried to make their operations secret so they did not start to attack until preparation was completed and the location of the enemy fleet ascertained. Each unit consisted of five planes; one unit after another would take off in the usual method. The method of attack changed in accordance with the attacks of the Task Force.

Later the method of attack was changed. Small number of planes were deployed to many bases. The other method was to deploy a large number of planes at only a few bases. This method has the advantage of providing many supporting planes. It was useful when defense of your carriers was very effective. This method was also used when we were going to attack the enemy at the landing point.

It is to be regretted that the number of bombers we had were insufficient and cruising radius of planes inadequate.

Q. Were any of the men refused permission to make Kamikaze attacks because they were considered valuable for other missions?

A. Anybody who felt that he wanted to, could do so, and he was pledged to carry out his feelings for the Emperor. The only trouble with the U. S. way of looking at it is if you start out on a mission with the idea of coming back you won't proceed to carry out the mission with 100% efficiency. The main point of failure was the short cruising radius of the planes. When we dispersed a small number of Kamikaze planes to a large number of bases it confused the enemy but lacked cover. When a large number of planes were based at a small number of bases it gave more opportunity for cover but lessened their opportunity to attack objects from many angles.

Q. Were you cognizant of overall air and fleet plans of the PHILIPPINE Campaign?

A. Only with air operations plans of my base.

Q. Were those plans made up by your staff or made up by GHQ?

A. From GHQ. The details and execution of over-all plans were left up to us.

Q. Was the use of Kamikaze envisaged by GHQ?

A. No, they were purely and simply a policy of that base.

Q. First Air Fleet started Kamikaze?

A. Yes.

Q. But the Domei News Agency announced that they were training Kamikaze pilots in August 1944?

A. There is absolutely no basis for such a statement and possibly what they meant was that the Japanese war was going badly and that the nation would use suicide as a policy, not that the Kamikaze was a definite plan.

Q. Were Army and Navy pilots in the first Kamikaze attack?

A. Navy only. Members of the 201st Air Group. This sort of thing has to come up from the bottom and you can't order such a thing. At no time were Kamikaze tactics ordered.

Q. Do you know whether the carrier force under Admiral OZAWA took part in this campaign?

A. A Task Force under his command participated in the attack.

Q. Was it intended that the pilots from the carriers should carry out Kamikaze attacks?

A. There was no plan as to whether carrier-based pilots would take part in the action and it depended on the unit in the area and the responsibility for carrying out the Operations Plan. In the PHILIPPINE Campaign it was the First Air Fleet's responsibility. Because of lack of personnel and planes they felt that it was their responsibility to evolve some tactics that would cope with the situation. Later on when the Second Air Fleet came into the picture in the PHILIPPINE action they, too, had some Kamikaze flyers. But the main point is that initially the Kamikaze concept was a method of coping with local situations and not the result of an overall policy handed down from GHQ.

Q. Did any of the carrier pilots join your forces on shore or take part in the operations?

A. The carrier-based planes were actively engaged between the period 24th and 25th, after which they joined our land-based forces.

Q. Did any of them carry out Kamikaze attacks from carriers or from your base?

A. Generally it was from a land base that the Kamikaze attacks started.

Q. When was the Baka (Oka) bomb invented?

A. Approximately August 1944. The name was given to the bomb by a Navy petty officer.

Q. Did it come from GERMANY originally?

A. Maybe; my opinion is absolutely no. It has no connection with the German plan.

Q. Doesn't the fact that construction of Oka was begun in August 1944 indicate a general plan for the use of Kamikaze attacks?

A. The Oka did not precede the Kamikaze plan.

Q. How do you reconcile the two dates, August for Oka and October for Kamikaze?

A. While there may have been overall conceptions of the Kamikaze idea outside the PHILIPPINES, there was no connection. The Kamikaze spirit is uniformly Japanese. They may have very well been thinking about it at Imperial Headquarters but the first were put into practice in the PHILIPPINES. I do not know of any Kamikaze ideas in the Imperial Headquarters.

Q. Did they have Special Attack Units training in Japan?

A. There was no connection; that is, in the plans and policies. The Special Attack is a submarine attack. The common thing with all these attacks is the Kamikaze idea.

Q. In carrying out Kamikaze attacks in the PHILIPPINES was any special method of approach used to avoid radar detection?

A. The main method was to have planes, of course, drop window etc., in order to distract, while the other planes made the main attack.

Q. But as to the altitude of approach, was there any specific instructions?

A. Altitude policy was to fly as high as possible, about 18,000 feet (6000 meters). We tried various altitudes. Came in at 18,000 feet and as soon as they realized that the radar had picked them up they would go down to as low as 80 or 90 meters. After they became accustomed to your defense tactics they found that the easiest altitude was about 3000 meters.

Q. What was the best type for dive attack?

A. Tactics changed with the type of planes. A fighter would come in at 3000 or 4000 meters and then when sighting the enemy would go down to 500 meters and perform a 45° dive.

Q. Did they prefer to attack from astern, ahead, or on the beam?

A. Preferred to aim at the forward elevator from astern. We found that diving from astern and aiming for forward elevators reduced the efficiency of the target's evasive action.

Q. Did they have priority on targets, were they specifically instructed as to what targets to attack, and who issued those instructions?

A. It depended; on certain days, aircraft carriers; on other days, destroyers, etc. It was usually embodied in the Operations Plan handed down by the Commander of the Air Fleet.

Q. Why was it that Kamikaze pilots, when attacked by our fighters, did not attempt evasive tactics?

A. In such cases, if they were quite far off from their main objective, they would take evasive tactics. Sometimes it was too late.

. . . .

Q. What percentage of hits were obtained in relation to the number of Kamikaze planes employed in the PHILIPPINE Campaign and at OKINAWA?

A. Approximately one-sixth of all Kamikaze planes used in the PHILIP-PINES hit their target. My estimate of the OKINAWA figure was approx-imately one-ninth.

Q. To defend the homeland what percentage of Kamikaze planes were expected to hit targets?

A. I think that it would have depended a lot on the point at which you would have landed. We probably would have used inexperienced pilots and the figure would be probably only one-ninth or one-tenth successful. An-other factor in the low score was that we had no defense against fighters.

Q. Were they going to make Kamikaze attacks at night or day, and what type of planes?

A. The plan was to use them primarily at twilight or on bright moonlight nights. SHIRAGIKU, ZERO fighters and WILLOW.

Q. Did you plan to use pathfinder planes equipped with radar during KETSU Operations (Defense of Japan)?

A. There were two few radar equipped planes to plan any considerable use of them in the KETSU Operation. Certain reconnaissance planes were equipped with radar such as FRANCES and MYRT. In my opinion, if it came to KETSU Operations, there would be no need for pathfinder planes for Kamikaze.

Q. Was it planned to use Kamikaze planes after the landings on the beaches?

A. The plan was to wait until the very last moment, until the American forces were dispersed as little as possible and thus inflict a greater amount of damage.

. . . .

Q. How many flying hours did the Navy Kamikaze pilots have in (a) the PHILIPPINE Campaign (b) the OKINAWA Campaign?

A. Most of the men in the PHILIPPINE Campaign had about 300 hrs., but in the OKINAWA Campaign we had Kamikaze pilots with as little as 100 hours.

Q. Were Kamikaze pilots during the PHILIPPINE Campaign limited to those having 300 hours or less in order to conserve the more experienced flying personnel?

A. Every one of the pilots hoped to get into the Kamikaze Corps but several
   of them, with the most flight time, were prevented by order of the
   Commanding Officer from doing so as he wanted them for torpedo
   bombing.
Q. Why did he limit it to torpedo bombing attack?
A. We felt that torpedo bombing took a greater amount of accuracy.
Q. In the middle of September our carrier force attacked in the PHILIP-
   PINES. Do you know the total loss from those attacks?
A. We lost 200 planes in one attack in one day. About 60 fighters in one day.
   The total loss in September from the carrier strikes was about 1000.

143. MacArthur Report on Leyte Landing, September 1944[10]

In a major amphibious operation we have seized the eastern coast of Leyte
Island in the Philippines, 600 miles north of Morotai and 2,500 miles from
Milne Bay from whence our offensive started nearly 16 months ago. This
point of entry in the Visayas is midway between Luzon and Mindanao and at
one stroke splits in two the Japanese forces in the Philippines. The enemy's
anticipation of attack in Mindanao caused him to be caught unawares in
Leyte and beachheads in the Tacloban area were secured with small casualties. The landing was preceded by heavy naval and air bombardments which
were devastating in effect. Our ground troops are rapidly extending their
positions and supplies and heavy equipment are already flowing ashore in
great volume. The troops comprise elements of the 6th U. S. Army, to which
are attached units from the Central Pacific, with supporting elements.

The naval forces consist of the 7th U. S. Fleet, the Australian Squadron,
and supporting elements of the 3rd U. S. Fleet. Air support was given by
naval carrier forces, the Far East Air Force, and the RAAF.

The enemy's forces of an estimated 225,000 include the 14th Army Group
under command of Field Marshal Count Terauchi, of which seven divisions
have already been identified: 16th, 26th, 30th, 100th, 102nd, 103rd, and
105th.

The strategic result of capturing the Philippines will be decisive. The
enemy's so-called Greater East Asia Co-Prosperity Sphere will be cut in two.
His conquered empire to the south comprising the Dutch East Indies, and
the British possessions of Borneo, Malaya and Burma will be severed from
Japan proper. The great flow of transportation and supply upon which
Japan's vital war industry depends will be cut as will the counter supply of his
forces to the south. A half million men will be cut off without hope of support
and with ultimate destruction at the leisure of the Allies a certainty. In broad
strategical conception the defensive line of the Japanese which extends
along the coast of Asia from the Japan Islands through Formosa, the Philippines, the East Indies, to Singapore and Burma will be pierced in the center
permitting an envelopment to the south and to the north. Either flank will be
vulnerable and can be rolled up at will.

144. MacArthur Comments on the Enemy, September 1944[11]

We now dominate the Moluccas. I rejoice that it has been done with so little loss. Our campaign is entering upon its decisive stage. Japanese ground troops still fight with the greatest tenacity. The military quality of the rank and file remains of the highest. Their officer corps, however, deteriorates as you go up the scale. It is fundamentally based upon a caste and feudal system and does not represent strict professional merit. Therein lies Japan's weakness. Her sons are strong of limb and stout of heart but weak in leadership. Gripped inexorably by a military hierarchy, that hierarchy is now failing the nation. It has had neither the imagination nor the foresighted ability to organize Japanese resources for a total war. Defeat now stares Japan in the face. Its barbaric codes have dominated Japanese character and culture for centuries and have practiced a type of national savagery at strange variance with many basic impulses of the Japanese people. Its successful domination has been based largely on the people's belief in its infallibility. When public opinion realizes that its generals and admirals have failed in the field of actual combat and campaign, the revulsion produced in Japanese thought will be terrific. Therein lies a basis for ultimate hope that the Japanese citizen will cease his almost idolatrous worship of the military and readjust his thoughts along more rational lines. No sophistry can disguise the fact from him that the military had failed him in this his greatest hour of need. That failure may mark the beginning of a new and ultimately happier era for him; his hour of decision is close at hand.

Part 12. The Battle for Hitler's Europe

By late 1943 the premature optimism of the Allies that the war might soon end was replaced by the harsh realization that a bitter struggle for Europe lay ahead. The rumors of a separate peace or a possible German collapse disappeared amidst the grim preparations for invading the Continent in 1944 (124).

A major goal of the Allied planning was to secure air superiority over the Germans before the invasion began, and while this seemed a certainty there were factors that could not be controlled. For example, the direction of German planning and production prior to 1944 had recognized the increasing Allied strength in heavy bombing planes and the Germans began to prepare accordingly. The resulting concentration on fighter planes and home defense measures eventually presented difficult obstacles for the Allied bomber forces. The most unpredictable factor, of course, was the weather. From mid-October 1943 until late February of 1944 the weather was unfavorable for extensive and continued Allied bomber operations over Germany.

Fortunately for the Allies the weather cleared briefly during February to permit massive air strikes. The American Eighth Air Force carried out a series of attacks that equaled the previous year's entire effort (almost 4,000 bombing missions and over 10,000 tons of explosives dropped within a five day period). The weather break had been short but the results were significant, and the air strikes represented the beginning of the end for the Luftwaffe. The German air force had already become a defensive instrument and the Allied attacks during February clearly indicated that German air defenses were too weak. As their war production dropped the Germans sought desperate measures to prevent a further weakening of industrial output, but they were too late—a decisive stage of the war had been reached (145).

The situation was becoming abundantly evident in the news from the European war theatre and Allied optimism was strongly reflected in official pronouncements. Marshal Stalin reviewed German retreats since Stalingrad in his May Day speech and declared the war already lost (146). The Soviet leader urged Hitler's "underlings," Rumania, Hungary, Finland, and Bulgaria, to abandon Germany and avoid total disaster (see 154, 155, 156, and 157). Within weeks the Allies captured Rome and invaded France to establish the long-awaited second front.

On June 4 Allied forces entered the Italian capital amidst a holiday atmosphere and found the city bruised but largely intact (147). That morning a special announcement from Hitler's headquarters to the Vatican officially recognized Rome as an open city, and a later message the same day explained the Fuehrer's decision (148). On June 5, Winston Churchill telegraphed the Rome details to Stalin and provided him last minute news on the pending invasion of France (149). Ironically, the news of the Allied landings the next day was first broadcast by the German News Agency (150) with a brief message. An appeal by French Marshal Pétain to his countrymen requested "rigorous discipline" be exercised to maintain calm (151). The British Prime Minister provided a far more graphic description of the invasion; he spoke of the grand scale of the Allied undertaking to the House of Commons (152).

The German resistance proved strong but the success of the Normandy landings was quickly apparent and the pessimistic report forwarded to Hitler on July 15 by Rommel provided the German dictator a dismal picture indeed (153). It was evident to all but the most fanatic that Germany would soon be invaded, and before the end of July a desperate group of German officers and civilians made an abortive move to kill Hitler (see Part 15).

In the weeks following, the Allies landed more than a million men and they advanced rapidly in a series of fortuitous breakouts. By August the Germans had lost almost two field armies and were retreating steadily eastward beyond the Seine. Meanwhile, the long-planned invasion of southern France began when the American Seventh Army attacked German forces southwest of Cannes (Operation "Dragoon"). The Allies, however, soon encountered logistical problems on the western front, and although they penetrated the German defenses at certain points they were unable to complete the breakthroughs necessary to end the war. Bad weather and rough terrain compounded the problem and Eisenhower accordingly decided to advance into Germany on a broad front. Much to the disappointment of his individual commanders (e.g., Patton and Montgomery) Eisenhower held to his decision.

During September-October 1944, Stalin's May Day words (146) proved prophetic and Germany's allies, one after the other, sought armistices with the Allied powers. Beginning with Finland's decision to accept the Soviet terms in early September (154), the defections proceeded quickly, and Rumania (155), Bulgaria (156), and finally Hungary (157) had sought peace by January 1945.

The United States launched a major drive to reach the Rhine in November but it was stalled by adverse weather and strong German defenses. Before the year was out Hitler directed a powerful counterattack in the Ardennes region (Battle of the Bulge) and terrible casualties were exacted on both sides. Although the Allies didn't reach the Rhine as planned, Germany's reserves were exhausted and the battle for Hitler's Europe entered its final phase as 1944 closed.

145. STATEMENTS ON ALLIED AIR ATTACK ON MAY 12, 1944 BY AMERICAN GENERAL ARNOLD[1] AND GERMAN ARMAMENTS MINISTER SPEER[2]

[Arnold]

The Luftwaffe could not prevent us from attacking any portion of the Reich. We were ready to begin a major offensive against the heart of Germany's entire military machine. Our targets were the oil refineries and synthetic plants which pumped the lifeblood of a mechanized army.

On 12 May, AAF heavy bombers escorted by fighters attacked synthetic oil-production facilities at Brux, Merseburg, Bohlan, Zeitz, and Lutzkendorf.

[Speer]

On May 8, 1944, I returned to Berlin to resume my work. I shall never forget the date May 12, four days later. On that day the technological war was decided. Until then we had managed to produce approximately as many weapons as the armed forces needed, in spite of their considerable losses. But with the attack of nine hundred and thirty-five daylight bombers of the American Eighth Air Force upon several fuel plants in central and eastern Germany, a new era in the air war began. It meant the end of German armaments production.

146. STALIN'S ORDER OF THE DAY, MAY 1, 1944[3]

Since the defeat of the Germans at Stalingrad the Red Army has been conducting a practically incessant offensive and has advanced from the Volga to the Sereth, from the Caucasus to the Carpathians. In the winter campaign of 1943–44 the Red Army won the historic battle for the Dnieper and the W. Ukraine, crushed the powerful German defences at Leningrad and in the Crimea, and overwhelmed the German defences on the Bug, Dniester, Pruth, and Seveth. Nearly the entire Ukraine, Moldavia, the Crimea, the Leningrad and Kalinin regions, and a considerable part of White Russia have been cleared of the invaders; the metallurgical industries of the South, the ore of Krivoi Rog, Kerch, and Nikopol, and the fertile lands between the Dnieper and Pruth restored to the Motherland; and tens of millions of Soviet people liberated from Fascist slavery. The Red Army has emerged on our State frontiers with Rumania and Czechoslovakia and is now battling on Rumanian territory. A considerable contribution to these successes has been made by our great Allies, the United States and Great Britain, who hold a front in Italy against the Germans, divert a considerable part of the German troops from us, supply us with valuable raw materials and armaments, and subject military objectives in Germany to systematic bombing, thus undermining the enemy's military might. Under the blows of the Red Army the Fascist bloc is falling to pieces. Fear and confusion reign among Hitler's Rumanian, Hungarian, Finnish, and Bulgarian Allies. These underlings cannot now fail to see that Germany has lost the war. Rumania, Hungary, Finland, and Bulgaria have only one possibility of escaping disaster—to break with the Germans and withdraw from the war. The sooner the peoples of these countries realise to what an impasse the Hitlerites have brought them, the sooner they will withdraw all support from their German enslavers, the less will be the sacrifice and destruction caused to those countries by the war, and the more they can count on understanding from the democratic countries.

The Red Army has liberated more than three-quarters of occupied Soviet land from the German yoke. The object now is to clear the whole of our land from the invaders and re-establish the Soviet State frontiers along the entire line from the Black Sea to the Barents Sea. But our tasks cannot be confined to the expulsion of the enemy from the Motherland. The German troops now resemble a wounded beast compelled to crawl back to its lair— Germany—in order to heal its wounds. But a wounded beast which has retired to its lair does not cease to be a dangerous beast. To rid our country and the countries allied with us from the danger of enslavement, the wounded German beast must be pursued and finished off in its lair. And while pursuing the enemy we must deliver from German bondage our brother Poles and Czechoslovaks and the peoples of Western Europe allied with us who are under the heel of Hitlerite Germany. This task is more difficult than the expulsion of German troops from the Soviet Union. It can be accomplished only on the condition of joint efforts by the Soviet Union, Great Britain, and the United States, by joint blows from the east dealt by our troops and from the west by our Allies. Only this combined blow can completely crush Hitlerite Germany.

147. ALLIED ARMIES ENTER ROME, JUNE 4, 1944[4] (NEWS RELEASE)

The world-famous historic monuments, churches, palaces, and buildings of Rome were found intact, and Allied troops penetrating into the heart of the city found the Lateran Square, the Colosseum, the Forum, the Corso (Rome's main thoroughfare), etc., in perfect order. The Fifth Army was accompanied by many officials of AMG who, some months earlier, had drafted elaborate plans for the administration and safeguarding of Rome and the feeding of her citizens (whose numbers had been swollen to 2,000,000 by some 500,000 refugees from the battle areas and bombed cities). It was officially announced that Maj.-Gen. Harry H. Johnston, U. S. Army, had been appointed Military Governor of Rome, with Brig.-Gen. Edgar E. Hume, U. S. Army, as head of AMG in Rome (he formerly occupied a similar position in Naples), and that very great quantities of food had been accumulated to feed the population (which had been very short of food during the German and Fascist occupation, the bread ration being only 100 grammes a day and fantastic "black market" prices prevailing), that soup kitchens would be set up if needed, and that there would be milk for mothers and infants and special supplies for hospitals. In the evening of June 5 Brig.-Gen. Hume announced that, after inspection by AMG, Rome had been found in general in excellent condition; that such damage as had occurred (mainly to houses in outer suburbs which had been the scene of fighting) could be rapidly repaired; and that no major demolitions had been found. There was some damage to the water supply (owing to pumping machinery being out of order and not to destruction of aqueducts), while the electricity and telephonic systems were only partly functioning (due mainly to the effects of earlier Allied bombings), but, unlike Naples, the sewers and gasworks were untouched; within 24 hours, however, the electricity supply had been partially restored and running water was available in many districts, and it was announced that an electric cable was being laid across the recent battlefields from Naples which would very shortly restore entirely the city's electricity supply. As at Naples, many AMG legal, welfare, health, labour, and education officers entered Rome with the troops, and it was announced that arrangements had been made for 3,000 Carabinieri specially recruited in Naples and the South to take over police duties in 10 districts of Rome under Allied police officers.

148. SPECIAL REPORT ISSUED BY HITLER'S HEADQUARTERS, JUNE 4, 1944[5]

"As the front line in Italy was gradually approaching nearer to the city of Rome there was the danger that Rome, one of the oldest cultural centres of the world, would be directly involved in the present fighting. Hitler has ordered the withdrawal of the German troops to the N. W. of Rome in order to prevent its destruction. The struggle in Italy will be continued with unshakable determination with the aim of breaking the enemy attacks and forging final victory for Germany and her Allies. The necessary measures for an eventual German victory are being taken in close collaboration with Fascist Italy and the other Allied Powers. The year of the invasion will bring Germany's enemies an annihilating defeat at the most decisive moment."

149. CHURCHILL TO STALIN, JUNE 5, 1944[6]

You will have been pleased to learn of the Allied entry into Rome. What we have always regarded as more important is the cutting off of as many enemy divisions as possible. General Alexander is now ordering strong armoured forces northward on Terni, which should largely complete the cutting off of all the divisions which were sent by Hitler to fight south of Rome. Although the amphibious landing at Anzio and Nettuno did not immediately fructify, as I had hoped when it was planned, it was a correct strategical move and brought its reward in the end. First it drew ten divisions from the following places:

1 from France, 1 from the Rhineland,
4 from Yugoslavia and Istria,
1 from Denmark, and 3 from North Italy.

Secondly, it brought on a defensive battle in which, though we lost about 25,000 men, the Germans were repulsed and much of the fighting strength of their divisions was broken with a loss of about 30,000 men. Finally the Anzio landing has made possible the kind of movement for which it was originally planned, only on a far larger scale. General Alexander is concentrating every effort now on the entrapping of the divisions south of Rome. Several have retreated into the mountains leaving a great deal of their heavy weapons behind, but we hope for a very good round-up of prisoners and material. As soon as this is over we shall decide how best to use our armies in Italy to support the main adventure. British, Americans, Free French and Poles have all broken or beaten in frontal attack the German troops opposite them and there are various important options which will soon have to be considered.

2. I have just returned from two days at General Eisenhower's Headquarters watching troops embark. The difficulties of getting proper weather conditions are very great, especially as we have to consider the fullest

employment of the vast naval and ground forces in relation to the tides, waves, fog and cloud. With great regret General Eisenhower was forced to postpone for one night, but the weather forecast has undergone a most favourable change and tonight we go. We are using 5,000 ships and have available 11,000 fully mounted aircraft.

150. German News Agency Release, June 6, 1944 (By Capt. Sertorius, Military Correspondent)[7]

"They are coming! With this shout of satisfaction and relief the German soldier welcomed the enemy during the first World War, when after weeks of artillery preparation he showed himself on the battlefield. The German soldiers have always wished the invasion to come so that they could show their moral supremacy in a fight not marked by material inferiority, such as was the case in Africa and Italy. All our hopes and expectations are thus expressed in the words—'They are coming.' It is good that they should come."

151. Pétain's Paris Radio Broadcast, June 6, 1944[8]

"Frenchmen! The British and American armies have landed on our soil. France is thus becoming a battlefield. Officials, civil servants, railwaymen, workers, stay at your posts to keep the essential services of the nation going and carry out the duties assigned to you. Frenchmen, do not pile up misfortune by acts which will bring about terrible reprisals. It would be the French people who would have to bear the consequences. Do not listen to defeatists; they will lead us to disaster. France can only save herself by observing the most rigorous discipline. Therefore obey the orders of the Government. Everyone must remain in his place. The trend of the battle may lead the German Army to take special measures in the battle areas. Accept this necessity. This is my urgent advice in the interest of your safety. I implore you, Frenchmen, to think above all of the mortal danger to which our country would be exposed if this solemn warning were not heeded."

152. Churchill's Announcement to House of Commons, June 6, 1944[9]

I have also to announce to the House that during the night and the early hours of this morning the first of the series of landings in force upon the European continent has taken place. In this case the liberating assault fell upon the coast of France. An immense armada of upwards of 4000 ships, together with several thousand smaller craft, crossed the Channel. Massed airborne landings have been successfully effected behind the enemy lines, and landings on the beaches are proceeding at various points at the present time. The fire of the shore batteries has been largely quelled. The obstacles that were constructed in the sea have not proved so difficult as was apprehended. The Anglo-American Allies are sustained by about 11,000 first-line aircraft, which can be drawn upon as may be needed for the purposes of the battle. I cannot of course commit myself to any particular details. Reports are coming in in rapid succession. So far the commanders who are engaged report that everything is proceeding according to plan. And what a plan! This vast operation is undoubtedly the most complicated and difficult that has ever taken place. It involves tides, winds, waves, visibility, both from the air and the sea standpoint, and the combined employment of land, air, and sea forces in the highest degree of intimacy and in contact with conditions which could not and cannot be fully foreseen.

There are already hopes that actual tactical surprise has been attained, and we hope to furnish the enemy with a succession of surprises during the course of the fighting. The battle that has now begun will grow constantly in scale and in intensity for many weeks to come, and I shall not attempt to speculate upon its course. This I may say however. Complete unity prevails throughout the Allied Armies. There is a brotherhood in arms between us and our friends of the United States. There is complete confidence in the Supreme Commander, General Eisenhower, and his lieutenants, and also in the commander of the Expeditionary Force, General Montgomery. The ardour and spirit of the troops, as I saw myself, embarking in these last few days was splendid to witness. Nothing that equipment, science, or forethought could do has been neglected, and the whole process of opening this great new front will be pursued with the utmost resolution both by the commanders and by the United States and British Governments whom they serve.

153. ROMMEL TO HITLER, JULY 15, 1944[10]

C.-in-C. Army Group B   H. Q. 15 July

The situation on the Normandy front is growing worse every day and is now approaching a grave crisis.

Due to the severity of the fighting, the enemy's enormous use of material—above all, artillery and tanks—and the effect of his unrestricted command of the air over the battle area, our casualties are so high that the fighting power of our divisions is rapidly diminishing. Replacements from home are few in number and, with the difficult transport situation, take weeks to get to the front. As against 97,000 casualties (including 2,360 officers)—i.e. an average of 2,500 to 3,000 a day—replacements to date number 10,000, of whom about 6,000 have actually arrived at the front.

Material losses are also huge and have so far been replaced on a very small scale; in tanks, for example, only 17 replacements have arrived to date as compared with 225 losses.

The newly arrived infantry divisions are raw and, with their small establishment of artillery, anti-tank guns and close-combat anti-tank weapons, are in no state to make a lengthy stand against major enemy attacks coming after hours of drum-fire and heavy bombing. The fighting has shown that with this use of material by the enemy, even the bravest army will be smashed piece by piece, losing men, arms and territory in the process.

Due to the destruction of the railway system and the threat of the enemy air force to roads and tracks up to 90 miles behind the front, supply conditions are so bad that only the barest essentials can be brought to the front. It is consequently now necessary to exercise the greatest economy in all fields, and especially in artillery and mortar ammunition. These conditions are unlikely to improve, as enemy action is steadily reducing the transport capacity available. Moreover, this activity in the air is likely to become even more effective as the numerous air-strips in the bridgehead are taken into use.

No new forces of any consequence can be brought up to the Normandy front except by weakening Fifteenth Army's front on the Channel, or the Mediterranean front in southern France. Yet Seventh Army's front, taken over all, urgently requires two fresh divisions, as the troops in Normandy are exhausted.

On the enemy's side, fresh forces and great quantities of war material are flowing into his front every day. His supplies are undisturbed by our air force. Enemy pressure is growing steadily stronger.

In these circumstances we must expect that in the foreseeable future the enemy will succeed in breaking through our thin front, above all, Seventh Army's, and thrusting deep into France. Apart from the Panzer Group's sector reserves, which are at present tied down by the fighting on their own front and—due to the enemy's command of the air—can only move by night, we dispose of no mobile reserve for defence against such a breakthrough. Action by our air force will, as in the past, have little effect.

The troops are everywhere fighting heroically, but the unequal struggle is approaching its end. It is urgently necessary for the proper conclusion to be drawn from this situation. As C.-in-C. of the Army Group I feel myself in duty bound to speak plainly on this point.

(Signed)   ROMMEL

154. Broadcast of Finnish Premier M. Hackzell, September 2, 1944[11] (Excerpts)

"The Finnish Diet met this evening in secret session to deal with the question of restoring peaceful relations between Finland and the U. S. S. R. Throughout the early part of the year the Finnish Government in vain

sought a solution, but, through the latest military and political developments, the question has become more urgent. Changes have taken place
in Finland's military situation which may be regarded as unexpectedly unfavourable and which necessitate a reassessment of the position.

. . . .

The worsening of the military position in the last few months has affected
not only us. Our co-belligerents have suffered a similar fate. As a consequence of several landings Germany is about to lose occupied France and
holds only the northern part of Italy. In the Balkans she has lost her most
noteworthy ally and another has proclaimed its neutrality. The Soviet Union
has for the most part reached its former frontiers and even crossed them at
some points. It is becoming more and more obvious that Germany, to
overcome her present difficult situation, must limit the field of her military
operations and try to use the means at her disposal to defend the homeland.

Everyone who has closely followed the development of the atmosphere in
official German circles has observed that many well-informed circles no
longer hope for victory but are striving for a political decision. This change
in Germany has caused Finnish-German relations to enter upon a new
phase. The Finnish-German brotherhood in arms was founded upon the
realistic advantage Germany has derived from co-operation with Finland
ever since it became apparent that armed conflict between Germany and the
Soviet Union was unavoidable. Finland was important to Germany when it
was a case of establishing and maintaining mastery in the Baltic and the
Arctic regions.

. . . .

Surveying the developments from this point of view, it is apparent that the
political interests which have caused Germany to support our struggle for 3
years are vanishing. We are approaching a phase of developments when
Germany can no longer help us to the same extent, making us rely more and
more upon our own resources, which should not be over-estimated. During
the whole period of collaboration, which began in 1941, relations between
Finland and Germany have been based solely on mutual military interests
without any political agreement.

. . . .

After thorough preliminary preparations the Government handed to the
Soviet Envoy in Stockholm (Mme. Kollontai) on Aug. 25 a written request
asking if the Soviet Government was prepared to receive a delegation appointed by the Finnish Government to negotiate an armistice or peace or
both. On Aug. 29 the Soviet Envoy handed to Finland's Envoy in Stockholm
the reply to this request, with the comment that the Soviet Union and Great
Britain together had agreed to this reply, which also had been communicated
to the U.S. Government for approval. The United States has had no comment to make on the reply.

It was demanded that the Finnish Government should make an official
announcement of having broken off relations with Germany and demand
from Germany the withdrawal within 2 weeks of her troops from Finnish

territory, this day to be calculated from the day on which the Finnish Government agreed to the preliminary conditions, but in any case the German troops must be withdrawn by September 15 at the latest. Provided that the Finnish Government conformed with these preliminary conditions, and only then, would the Soviet Union be prepared to receive a Finnish Government delegation in Moscow. The Soviet reply thus deviated in one respect to our advantage from the reply which we received to our inquiry in June—namely, that on our fulfilling the preliminary conditions we shall be in a position to open negotiations without having laid down our arms. In addition the terms have been communicated to us in the name of Great Britain and have been approved by the U. S. Government. After having considered the armistice terms the Finnish Government came to the conclusion that despite the stipulated preliminary conditions it should open negotiations with the object of obtaining an armistice or peace with the Soviet Union. To approve this request appears also to be in accordance with Germany's own interests because of the fact that Germany if she acts in this way will be remembered with gratitude by our people as a country with whom we have been brothers-in-arms and who really wished us well.

Fellow-citizens, this is briefly the position. We have taken the first step to restore peaceful relations with our great neighbour in the East.

155. ALLIED ARMISTICE WITH RUMANIA, SEPTEMBER 12, 1944[12] (EXCERPT)

The Government and High Command of Rumania, recognizing the fact of the defeat of Rumania in the war against the Union of Soviet Socialist Republics, the United States of America, and the United Kingdom, and the other United Nations, accept the armistice terms presented by the Governments of the above-mentioned three Allied Powers, acting in the interests of all the United Nations.

On the basis of the foregoing the representative of the Allied (Soviet) High Command, Marshal of the Soviet Union, R. Ya. Malinovski, duly authorized thereto by the Governments of the United States of America, the Soviet Union, and the United Kingdom, acting in the interests of all the United Nations, on the one hand, and the representatives of the Government and High Command of Rumania, Minister of State and Minister of Justice L. Patrascanu, Deputy Minister of Internal Affairs, Adjutant of His Majesty the King of Rumania, General D. Damaceanu, Prince Stirbey, and Mr. G. Popp, on the other hand, holding proper full-powers, have signed the following conditions:

1. As from August 24, 1944, at 4 a. m., Rumania has entirely discontinued military operations against the Union of Soviet Socialist Republics in all theatres of war, has withdrawn from the war against the United Nations, has broken off relations with Germany and her satellites, has entered the war and will wage war on the side of the Allied Powers against Germany and

Hungary for the purpose of restoring Rumanian independence and sovereignty, for which purpose she provides not less than 12 infantry divisions with Corps Troops.

156. ALLIED ARMISTICE WITH BULGARIA, OCTOBER 28, 1944[13] (EXCERPT)

The Government of Bulgaria accepts the armistice terms presented by the Governments of the United States of America, the Union of Soviet Socialist Republics and the United Kingdom, acting on behalf of all the United Nations at war with Bulgaria.

Accordingly, the representative of the Supreme Allied Commander in the Mediterranean, Lieutenant-General Sir James Gammell, and the representative of the Soviet High Command, Marshal of the Soviet Union F. I. Tolbukhin, duly authorized thereto by the Governments of the United States of America, the Union of Soviet Socialist Republics and the United Kingdom, acting on behalf of all the United Nations at war with Bulgaria, on the one hand, and representatives of the Government of Bulgaria, Mr. P. Stainov, Minister of Foreign Affairs, Mr. D. Terpeshev, Minister without Portfolio, Mr. N. Petkov, Minister without Portfolio, and Mr. P. Stoyanov, Minister of Finance, furnished with due powers, on the other hand, have signed the following terms:

1. (a) Bulgaria, having ceased hostilities with the U. S. S. R. on September 9, and severed relations with Germany on September 6 and with Hungary on September 26, has ceased hostilities against all the other United Nations.

(b) The Government of Bulgaria undertakes to disarm the German armed forces in Bulgaria and to hand them over as prisoners of war. The Government of Bulgaria also undertakes to intern nationals of Germany and her satellites.

(c) The Government of Bulgaria undertakes to maintain and make available such land, sea and air forces as may be specified for service under the general direction of the Allied (Soviet) High Command. Such forces must not be used on Allied territory except with the prior consent of the Allied Government concerned.

(d) On the conclusion of hostilities against Germany, the Bulgarian armed forces must be demobilized and put on a peace footing under the supervision of the Allied Control Commission.

157. ALLIED ARMISTICE WITH HUNGARY, JANUARY 20, 1945[14] (EXCERPT)

The Provisional National Government of Hungary, recognizing the fact of the defeat of Hungary in the war against the Soviet Union, the United Kingdom, the United States of America, and other United Nations, accepts the armistice terms presented by the Governments of the above-mentioned three powers, acting on behalf of all the United Nations which are in a state of war with Hungary.

On the basis of the foregoing the representative of the Allied (Soviet) High Command, Marshal of the Soviet Union K. E. Voroshilov, duly authorized thereto by the Governments of the Soviet Union, the United Kingdom, and the United States of America, acting on behalf of all the United Nations which are at war with Hungary, on the one hand, and the representatives of the Provisional National Government of Hungary, Minister of Foreign Affairs, Mister Gyöngyösi Janos, Minister of Defense Colonel General Vörös Janos and State Secretary of the Cabinet of Ministers Mister Balogh Istvan, on the other, holding proper full powers, have signed the following conditions:

1. (a) Hungary has withdrawn from the war against the Union of Soviet Socialist Republics and other United Nations, including Czechoslovakia, has severed all relations with Germany and has declared war on Germany.

(b) The Government of Hungary undertakes to disarm German armed forces in Hungary and to hand them over as prisoners of war. The Government of Hungary also undertakes to intern nationals of Germany.

(c) The Government of Hungary undertakes to maintain and make available such land, sea and air forces as may be specified for service under the general direction of the Allied (Soviet) High Command. In this connection Hungary will provide not less than eight infantry divisions with corps troops. These forces must not be used on allied territory except with the prior consent of the allied government concerned.

(d) On the conclusion of hostilities against Germany, the Hungarian armed forces must be demobilized and put on a peace footing under the supervision of the Allied Control Commission.

Chapter VI
The End of the War

Part 13. The Defeat of Nazi Germany

It was apparent to all who followed the relentless progress of the Allies toward victory in 1944 that an end to the war in Europe was very near. In the west the successful invasion of Normandy was history and Allied forces were poised for the final drive into Germany. In the east Soviet power was equally successful and German defenses were crumbling before the onslaught. A strong address by Stalin to the Central Committee of the Communist Party on the twenty-seventh anniversary of the Russian Revolution in November 1944 dramatically detailed the course of the war with the Germans that year (158).

As 1945 opened, the tasks that still confronted the Allies were the defeat of Japan and preparations for the ensuing peace settlements. The job of finishing the war against Japan weighed more heavily upon the United States than on Great Britain, and Stalin had not committed the Soviet Union to the conflict. The Soviet position represented a problem in persuasion for Franklin Roosevelt which was successfully surmounted at Yalta in February (159). The possible admission of France as a partner in the post-war administration of Germany, the discussion of a government for Poland, and the planning of a final peace conference imposed lesser, but still important, concerns on the Allied leaders.

The problems that faced the Allies in 1945 resulted because they were winning the war and the conference that met at Yalta during February was intended to resolve most of them (see Part 17). Ironically, the Yalta (Crimean) Conference, called in a spirit of almost unlimited optimism by three world powers on the threshold of the greatest military victory in the history of mankind, is remembered as the most controversial of the wartime conferences.

The period following Yalta was strange and critical. It was strange because the spirit of confidence evident as the conference began seemed to evaporate as soon as it was over. The situation grew critical because of the growing differences among the Allies over the meaning and interpretation of their respective behavior toward Germany as the war closed. The Soviets openly evinced the suspicion that the two western Allies were deliberately stalling to allow continued fighting on the eastern front, and they implied that General Marshall had purposely supplied false intelligence to that end (160). In addition, Stalin expressed the belief that Roosevelt and Churchill were attempting to circumvent the unconditional surrender pledge of Casablanca by negotiating with the Germans in Italy to effect a surrender there without adequate Soviet participation (161).

As the war ground to its inevitable conclusion, Germany became the final battleground. During March and April Allied forces advanced from both east and west upon an ever-shrinking German army. On April 12 Roosevelt died and Harry Truman became the new member of the Big Three. Before that fateful month ended Benito Mussolini and Adolf Hitler also died. The Duce and his mistress, Clara Petacci, were caught by Italian partisans while attempting to escape to Switzerland and were executed on April 28. Hitler chose to remain in Berlin, and as the city capitulated to the Soviet forces, he ended his life amidst the total collapse of the German nation on April 30.

Before Hitler committed suicide he witnessed the destruction of his empire and the attempts of several Nazi leaders to surrender Germany to the Allies. On April 29, in the Berlin Chancellory Bunker, Hilter prepared his will (162) and a political testament (163) as his last words for posterity. The day after Hitler's death his chosen successor, Admiral Karl Doenitz, personally broadcast the news from Hamburg and issued his orders for the day (164). The wording of Doenitz' message clearly indicated that the Fuehrer had "fallen" in battle, presumably fighting against Russian soldiers somewhere in Berlin.

As the last hours of the war approached, confusion began to build in Allied capitals in anticipation of the news that the war in Europe was over. By prior agreement the Allies proposed to make a simultaneous announcement at a specified time. But as the hour neared, the situation became more complicated, and this is reflected in the U. S. State Department memorandum (165) of May 7 and Stalin's message to Truman of the same date (166). The dilemma was partially resolved by the military surrenders at Rheims on May 7 and in Berlin on May 8 (167). At the end of the war against Hitler, President Truman declared a day of prayer (168). Several months later General George Marshall outlined the reasons for the German defeat, as described by captured members of the High Command, in his "Biennial Report to the Secretary of War" (169).

158. STALIN SPEECH ON 27TH ANNIVERSARY OF RUSSIAN REVOLUTION, NOVEMBER 1944[1] (EXCERPTS)

"The decisive success of the Red Army this year and the expulsion of the Germans from Soviet territory were predetermined by the succession of shattering blows which our troops dealt the German forces beginning as far back as last January and following throughout the year. The first blow was

struck in January at Leningrad and Novgorod, which broke up the permanent German defences, flung the enemy back to the Baltic, and resulted in
the liberation of the Leningrad Region. The second was struck in February
and March on the River Bug, when the Red Army flung the Germans
beyond the Dniester and freed the Ukraine W(est) of the Dnieper. The third
was struck in April and May in the Crimea, when the Germans were flung
into the Black Sea and the Crimea and Odessa delivered. The fourth was
struck in June in Karelia, when the Red Army routed the Finnish forces,
liberated Viborg and Petrozavodsk, and flung the Finns back into the interior of Finland, liberating the greater part of the Karelo-Finnish Soviet
Republic. The fifth was struck in June and July when the Red Army utterly
routed the German forces at Vitebsk, Bobruisk, and Mogilev, culminating in
the encirclement of 30 German divisions at Minsk; as a result of this blow our
forces: (a) liberated the whole White Russian Soviet Republic; (b) gained the
Vistula and liberated a considerable part of Poland, our Ally; (c) gained the
Niemen and liberated the greater part of the Lithuanian Soviet Republic;
and (d) forced the Niemen and approached the frontiers of Germany. The
sixth was struck in July and August in the West Ukraine, when the Red Army
routed the German force at Lvov, flung them beyond the San and Vistula,
liberated the Western Ukraine, forced the Vistula, and set up a strong
bridgehead W(est) of Sandomir. The seventh was struck in August in the
Kishinev and Jassy area, when our troops utterly routed the German and
Rumanian forces. As a result of this blow: (a) the Moldavian Soviet Republic
was liberated; (b) Germany's Rumanian ally was put out of action and
declared war on Germany and Hungary; (c) Germany's Bulgarian ally was
put out of action and likewise declared war on Germany; (d) the road was
opened for our troops to Hungary, Germany's last ally in Europe; and (e) the
opportunity arose to reach out a helping hand to Yugoslavia. The eighth
blow was struck in September and October in the Baltic, when the Red Army
routed the German forces at Tallinn and Riga. As a result of this: (a) The
Estonian Soviet Republic was liberated; (b) the greater part of the Latvian
Soviet Republic was liberated; (c) Germany's Finnish ally was put out of
action and declared war on Germany; (d) over 30 German divisions found
themselves cut off from Prussia and gripped in pincers between Tukums and
Libau where they are now being hammered to a finish by our troops. In
October the ninth blow was launched by our troops between the Tisza and
the Danube in Hungary; its purpose is to put Hungary out of the war and
turn her against Germany. As a result of this blow, which has not yet been
consummated, our forces: (a) rendered direct assistance to Yugoslavia in
driving out the Germans and liberating Belgrade; (b) obtained the opportunity of crossing the Carpathians and stretching out a helping hand to
Czechoslovakia, part of whose territory has already been freed. Lastly, at the
end of October, a blow was dealt in N(orth) Finland, when the German
troops were thrown out of the Petsamo area and our troops, pursuing the
Germans, entered the territory of Norway.

    Such are the principal operations carried out by the Red Army during the past year, which have led to the expulsion of the German forces from our country. As a result of these operations 120 divisions of the Germans and their Allies have been routed and put out of action. Instead of the 257 divisions that faced our front last year, of which 207 were German, we now have against our front a total of only 204 German and Hungarian divisions, German divisions numbering 180. It must be admitted that in this war Hitlerite Germany with her Fascist army has proved a more powerful, crafty, and experienced adversary than Germany and her army were in any war of the past. In this war the Germans succeeded in exploiting the productive forces of nearly the whole of Europe and the considerable armies of their vassal states. If, in spite of these favourable conditions for the prosecution of the war, Germany nevertheless finds herself on the brink of imminent destruction, the explanation is that her chief adversary, the Soviet Union, has surpassed her in strength.

This year the Red Army has not been operating against the German forces single-handed, as was the case in previous years, but together with the forces of our Allies. The Teheran Conference was not held for nothing. Its decision on a joint blow at Germany from west, east, and south began to be carried out with astounding precision. Simultaneously with the summer operations of the Red Army on the Soviet-German front, the Allied forces launched the invasion of France and organised powerful offensive operations which compelled Germany to wage war on two fronts. The troops and navies of our Allies accomplished a mass landing operation on the coast of France unparalleled in history for scope and organisation, and overcame the German fortifications with consummate skill. Thus Germany found herself gripped in a vice between two fronts. The enemy failed to withstand the joint blows of the Red Army and the Allied forces. The enemy's resistance was broken, and his troops in a short time were thrown out of Central Italy, France, Belgium, and the Soviet Union and flung back to the German frontier.

There can be no doubt that without the opening of the Second Front in Europe, which contains as many as 75 German divisions, our troops would not have been able to break the resistance of the German forces and throw them out of the Soviet Union in such a short time. But it is equally indubitable that without the powerful offensive operations of the Red Army in the summer of this year, which held as many as 200 German divisions, our Allies could not have coped so quickly with the German forces and thrown them out of Central Italy, France, and Belgium. The task is to keep Germany gripped in this vice between the two fronts. That is the key to victory.

If the Red Army was able successfully to fulfil its duty to its country and drive the Germans from the Soviet land it was because of the unreserved support it received in the rear from our whole country. 'Everything for the Front!' has been the watchword this year in the selfless work of all Soviet people—workers, peasants, intellectuals—as well as in the directing activities of our Government and Party bodies. With the war in its fourth year our factories are producing several times as many tanks, planes, guns, mortars, and ammunition as in its opening phase. In the rehabilitation of agriculture the most difficult period lies behind us. With the fertile lands of the Don and Kuban restored to our country, after the liberation of the Ukraine, our agriculture is recovering rapidly from its grave losses. The Soviet railways have stood a strain that the transport of other countries would hardly be able to bear. All this indicates that the economic foundation of the Soviet State has proved to possess infinitely greater vitality than the economy of the enemy States....To-day the Red Army has more tanks, guns, and planes than the German Army. As for quality, our war material is far superior to that of the enemy. Just as the Red Army in its long and arduous single-handed struggle won military victory over the Fascist forces, so the working people of the Soviet rear won an economic victory over the enemy in their long fight against Hitlerite Germany and her associates. The Soviet people have denied themselves many necessities, have consciously accepted serious material privations, in order to give more for the front. Our people has justly won for itself the fame of a heroic nation....

159. Yalta Agreement Regarding Soviet Entry into the War Against Japan, February 11, 1945[2]

The leaders of the three Great Powers—the Soviet Union, the United States of America and Great Britain—have agreed that in two or three months after Germany has surrendered and the war in Europe has terminated the Soviet Union shall enter into the war against Japan on the side of the Allies on the condition that:

1. The status quo in Outer-Mongolia (The Mongolian People's Republic) shall be preserved;

2. The former rights of Russia violated by the treacherous attack of Japan in 1904 shall be restored, viz:

(a) the southern part of Sakhalin as well as all the islands adjacent to it shall be returned to the Soviet Union,

(b) the commercial port of Dairen shall be internationalized, the preeminent interests of the Soviet Union in this port being safe-guarded and the lease of Port Arthur as a naval base of the USSR restored,

(c) the Chinese-Eastern Railroad and the South-Manchurian Railroad which provides an outlet to Dairen shall be jointly operated by the establishment of a joint Soviet-Chinese Company it being understood that the preeminent interests of the Soviet Union shall be safe-guarded and that China shall retain full sovereignty in Manchuria;

3. The Kuril islands shall be handed over to the Soviet Union.

It is understood, that the agreement concerning Outer-Mongolia and the ports and railroads referred to above will require concurrence of Generalissimo Chiang Kai-Shek. The President will take measures in order to obtain this concurrence on advice from Marshal Stalin.

The Heads of the three Great Powers have agreed that these claims of the Soviet Union shall be unquestionably fulfilled after Japan has been defeated.

For its part the Soviet Union expresses its readiness to conclude with the National Government of China a pact of friendship and alliance between the USSR and China in order to render assistance to China with its armed forces for the purpose of liberating China from the Japanese yoke.

J. Stalin

Franklin D. Roosevelt

Winston S. Churchill

160. Red Army General Antonov to American General Deane, March 30, 1945[3]

Copy. Secret

To Major-General John R. Deane,

Head of the Military Mission

of the U. S. A. in the U. S. S. R.

Dear General Deane,

Please convey to General Marshall the following:

On February 20 I received a message from General Marshall through General Deane, saying that the Germans were forming two groups for a counter-offensive on the Eastern Front: one in Pomerania to strike in the direction of Thorn and the other in the Vienna-Moravská Ostrava area to advance in the direction of Lódź. The southern group was to include the 6th S. S. Panzer Army. On February 12 I received similar information from Colonel Brinkman, head of the Army Section of the British Military Mission.

I am very much obliged and grateful to General Marshall for the information designed to further our common aims, which he so kindly made available to us.

At the same time it is my duty to inform General Marshall that the military operations on the Eastern Front in March did not bear out the information furnished by him. For the battles showed that the main group of German troops, which included the 6th S. S. Panzer Army, had been concentrated, not in Pomerania or in the Moravská Ostrava area, but in the Lake Balaton area, whence the Germans launched their offensive in an attempt to break through to the Danube and force it south of Budapest.

Thus, the information supplied by General Marshall was at variance with the actual course of events on the Eastern Front in March.

It may well be that certain sources of this information wanted to bluff both Anglo-American and Soviet Headquarters and divert the attention of the Soviet High Command from the area where the Germans were mounting their main offensive operation on the Eastern Front.

Despite the foregoing, I would ask General Marshall, if possible, to keep me posted with information about the enemy.

I consider it my duty to convey this information to General Marshall solely for the purpose of enabling him to draw the proper conclusions in relation to the source of the information.

Please convey to General Marshall my respect and gratitude.

Truly yours,
Army General Antonov
Chief of Staff of the Red Army

March 30, 1945

161. Stalin to Roosevelt, April 7, 1945[4] (Excerpt)

Personal and Secret From Premier J. V. Stalin
To The President, Mr. F. Roosevelt

I have received your message of April 5.

In my message of April 3 the point was not about integrity or trustworthiness. I have never doubted your integrity or trustworthiness, just as I have never questioned the integrity or trustworthiness of Mr. Churchill. My point is that in the course of our correspondence a difference of views has arisen over what an Ally may permit himself with regard to another and what he may not. We Russians believe that, in view of the present situation on the fronts, a situation in which the enemy is faced with inevitable surrender, whenever the representatives of one of the Allies meet the Germans to discuss surrender terms, the representatives of the other Ally should be enabled to take part in the meeting. That is absolutely necessary, at least when the other Ally seeks participation in the meeting. The Americans and British, however, have a different opinion—they hold that the Russian point of view is wrong. For that reason they have denied the Russians the right to be present at the meeting with the Germans in Switzerland. I have already written to you, and I see no harm in repeating that, given a similar situation, the Russians would never have denied the Americans and British the right to attend such a meeting. I still consider the Russian point of view to be the only correct one, because it precludes mutual suspicions and gives the enemy no chance to sow distrust between us.

2. It is hard to agree that the absence of German resistance on the Western Front is due solely to the fact that they have been beaten. The Germans have 147 divisions on the Eastern Front. They could safely withdraw from 15 to 20 divisions from the Eastern Front to aid their forces on the Western Front. Yet they have not done so, nor are they doing so. They are fighting desperately against the Russians for Zemlenice, an obscure station in Czechoslovakia, which they need just as much as a dead man needs a poultice, but they surrender without any resistance such important towns in the heart of Germany as Osnabrück, Mannheim and Kassel. You will admit that this behaviour on the part of the Germans is more than strange and unaccountable.

3. As regards those who supply my information, I can assure you that they

are honest and unassuming people who carry out their duties conscientiously and who have no intention of affronting anybody. They have been tested in action on numerous occasions. Judge for yourself. In February General Marshall made available to the General Staff of the Soviet troops a number of important reports in which he, citing data in his possession, warned the Russians that in March the Germans were planning two serious counter-blows on the Eastern Front, one from Pomerania towards Thorn, the other from the Moravská Ostrava area towards Łódź. It turned out, however, that the main German blow had been prepared, and delivered, not in the areas mentioned above, but in an entirely different area, namely, in the Lake Balaton area, south-west of Budapest. The Germans, as we now know, had concentrated 35 divisions in the area, 11 of them armoured. This, with its great concentration of armour, was one of the heaviest blows of the war. Marshal Tolbukhin succeeded first in warding off disaster and then in smashing the Germans, and was able to do so also because my informants had disclosed—true with some delay—the plan for the main German blow and immediately apprised Marshal Tolbukhin. Thus I had yet another opportunity to satisfy myself as to the reliability and soundness of my sources of information.

162. Hitler's Private Will and Testament, April 29, 1945[5]

As I did not consider that I could take responsibility, during the years of struggle, of contracting a marriage, I have now decided, before the closing of my earthly career, to take as my wife that girl who, after many years of faithful friendship, entered, of her own free will, the practically besieged town in order to share her destiny with me. At her own desire she goes as my wife with me into death. It will compensate us for what we both lost through my work in the service of my people.

What I possess belongs—in so far as it has any value—to the Party. Should this no longer exist, to the State; should the State also be destroyed, no further decision of mine is necessary.

My pictures, in the collections which I have bought in the course of years, have never been collected for private purposes, but only for the extension of a gallery in my home town of Linz on Donau.

It is my most sincere wish that this bequest may be duly executed.

I nominate as my Executor my most faithful Party comrade,

Martin Bormann.

He is given full legal authority to make all decisions. He is permitted to take out everything that has a sentimental value or is necessary for the maintenance of a modest simple life, for my brothers and sisters, also above all for the mother of my wife and my faithful co-workers who are well known to him, principally my old Secretaries Frau Winter etc. who have for many years aided me by their work.

I myself and my wife—in order to escape the disgrace of deposition or capitulation—choose death. It is our wish to be burnt immediately on the spot where I have carried out the greatest part of my daily work in the course of a twelve years' service to my people.

Given in Berlin, 29th April 1945, 4:00 A.M.

[Signed] A. Hitler

[Witnesses]

Dr. Joseph Goebbels
Martin Bormann
Colonel Nicholas von Below

163. HITLER's POLITICAL TESTAMENT, APRIL 29, 1945[6] (EXCERPT)

First Part of the Political Testament

More than thirty years have now passed since I in 1914 made my modest contribution as a volunteer in the first world war that was forced upon the Reich.

In these three decades I have been actuated solely by love and loyalty to my people in all my thoughts, acts, and life. They gave me the strength to make the most difficult decisions which have ever confronted mortal man. I have spent my time, my working strength, and my health in these three decades.

In is untrue that I or anyone else in Germany wanted the war in 1939. It was desired and instigated exclusively by those international statesmen who were either of Jewish descent or worked for Jewish interests. I have made too many offers for the control and limitation of armaments, which posterity will not for all time be able to disregard for the responsibility for the outbreak of this war to be laid on me. I have further never wished that after the first fatal world war a second against England, or even against America, should break out. Centuries will pass away, but out of the ruins of our towns and monuments the hatred against those finally responsible whom we have to thank for everything, International Jewry and its helpers, will grow.

Three days before the outbreak of the German-Polish war I again proposed to the British ambassador in Berlin a solution to the German-Polish problem—similar to that in the case of the Saar district, under international control. This offer also cannot be denied. It was only rejected because the leading circles in English politics wanted the war, partly on account of the business hoped for and partly under influence of propaganda organized by International Jewry.

I have also made it quite plain that, if the nations of Europe are again to be regarded as mere shares to be bought and sold by these international conspirators in money and finance, then that race, Jewry, which is the real criminal of this murderous struggle, will be saddled with the responsibility. I further left no one in doubt that this time not only would millions of children of Europe's Aryan people die of hunger, not only would millions of grown men suffer death, and not only hundreds of thousands of women and children be burnt and bombed to death in the towns, without the real criminal having to atone for this guilt, even if by more humane means.

After six years of war, which in spite of all setbacks, will go down one day in history as the most glorious and valiant demonstration of a nation's life purpose, I cannot forsake the city which is the capital of this Reich. As the forces are too small to make any further stand against the enemy attack at this place and our resistance is gradually being weakened by men who are as deluded as they are lacking in initiative, I should like by remaining in this town, to share my fate with those, the millions of others, who have also taken upon themselves to do so. Moreover I do not wish to fall into the hands of an enemy who requires a new spectacle organized by the Jews for the amusement of their hysterical masses.

I have decided therefore to remain in Berlin and there of my own free will to choose death at the moment when I believe the position of the Führer and Chancellor itself can no longer be held.

I die with a happy heart, aware of the immeasurable deeds and achievements of our soldiers at the front, our women at home, the achievements of our farmers and workers and the work, unique in history, of our youth who bear my name.

That from the bottom of my heart I express my thanks to you all, is just as self-evident as my wish that you should, because of that, on no account give up the struggle, but rather continue it against the enemies of the Fatherland, no matter where, true to the creed of a great Clausewitz. From the sacrifice of our soldiers and from my own unity with them unto death, will in any case spring up in the history of Germany, the seed of a radiant renaissance of the National Socialist movement and thus of the realization of a true community of nations.

Many of the most courageous men and women have decided to unite their lives with mine until the very last. I have begged and finally ordered them not to do this, but to take part in the further battle of the Nation. I beg the heads of the Armies, the Navy and the Air Force to strengthen by all possible means the spirit of resistance of our soldiers in the National Socialist sense, with special reference to the fact that also I myself, as founder and creator of this movement, have preferred death to cowardly abdication or even capitulation.

May it, at some future time, become part of the code of honor of the German officer—as is already the case in our Navy—that the surrender of a district or of a town is impossible, and that above all the leaders here must march ahead as shining examples, faithfully fulfilling their duty unto death.

Second Part of the Political Testament

Before my death I expel the former Reichsmarschall Hermann Göring from the party and deprive him of all rights which he may enjoy by virtue of the decree of June 29th, 1941; and also by virtue of my statement in the

Reichstag on September 1st, 1939, I appoint in his place Grossadmiral Dönitz, President of the Reich and Supreme Commander of the Armed Forces.

Before my death I expel the former Reichsführer-SS and Minister of the Interior Heinrich Himmler, from the party and from all offices of State. In his stead I appoint Gauleiter Karl Hanke as Reichsführer-SS and Chief of the German Police, and Gauleiter Paul Giesler as Reich Minister of the Interior.

. . . .

Although a number of men, such as Martin Bormann, Dr. Goebbels etc., together with their wives, have joined me of their own free will and did not wish to leave the capital of the Reich under any circumstances, but were willing to perish with me here, I must nevertheless ask them to obey my request, and in this case set the interests of the nation above their own feelings. By their work and loyalty as comrades they will be just as close to me after death, as I hope that my spirit will linger among them and always go with them. Let them be hard, but never unjust, above all let them never allow fear to influence their actions, and set the honour of the nation above everything in the world. Finally, let them be conscious of the fact that our task, that of continuing the building of a National Socialist State, represents the work of the coming centuries, which places every single person under an obligation always to serve the common interest and to subordinate his own advantage to this end. I demand of all Germans, all National Socialists, men, women and all the men of the Armed Forces, that they be faithful and obedient unto death to the new government and its President.

Above all I charge the leaders of the nation and those under them to scrupulous observance of the laws of race and to merciless opposition to the universal poisoner of all peoples, international Jewry.

Given in Berlin, this 29th day of April 1945.   4:00 a. m.
                                                     Adolf Hitler.

Witnessed by
Dr. Josef Fuhr.   Wilhelm Buergdorf.
Martin Bormann.   Hans Krebs.

164. Doenitz's Order of the Day, May 1, 1945[7] (Excerpts)

German Armed Forces, my comrades.

The *Fuehrer* has fallen. Faithful to his great ideal to save the nations of Europe from Bolshevism, he has given his life and has met a hero's death. In him one of the greatest heroes of German history has appeared. With proud respect and grief we lower our standards.

The *Fuehrer* has designated me to be the head of the State and Supreme Commander. . . . I am resolved to continue the struggle against the Bolsheviks. . . . Against the British and Americans I am bound to continue to fight as far and as long as they impede me in the struggle against Bolshevism. . . .

German soldiers! Do your duty! The existence of our people is at stake.

165. U. S. State Department Memorandum, May 7, 1945[8]

Memorandum of Telephone Conversation, by the Acting Secretary of State [Grew] [Washington,] May 7, 1945—1:45 p. m.

Admiral Leahy telephoned me and said that the situation on the announcement of V-E Day was terribly confused and he wanted me to know the background of the latest information. He stated that we have an agreement with Stalin and Churchill to make the announcement at 9 o'clock tomorrow morning but Churchill today raised the devil because he said he had to make the announcement right away and wanted to make it at noon today. Admiral Leahy said the President declined to do it then and said that he had arranged with Stalin and Churchill to announce it at 9 o'clock and he could not violate his agreement without the assent of Stalin. Admiral Leahy said they had been trying to get in touch with Stalin but so far have had nothing from him except the vague thought that he doesn't know the terms and can't make an announcement as yet. Admiral Leahy said he had heard later through BBC that Churchill was going to make the announcement at 3 o'clock. He said that he also had heard that de Gaulle is going to announce it at 2 o'clock. He stated that nobody has any control over de Gaulle and that this action was typical of him. I agreed with Admiral Leahy and remarked that de Gaulle was acting just like a naughty boy. Admiral Leahy said he spoke to the President about 20 minutes ago and thought it was definite for 9 o'clock tomorrow morning. He said that the only way the thing would be stopped would be for Stalin to ask us not to announce it yet. Admiral Leahy also said that he had been in touch with Eisenhower who said he had made no announcement and has kept it as secret as it could be kept. He said he would not make any announcement until it was released here. I said I understood it had leaked through AP. Admiral Leahy said the Germans are talking freely in plain language about it so everyone knows it. I said at any rate the only people who would be displeased about the whole thing would be the newspapermen.

166. Stalin to Truman, Moscow, May 7, 1945[9]

I am in receipt of your message of May 7, about announcing Germany's surrender. The Supreme Command of the Red Army is not sure that the order of the German High Command on unconditional surrender will be executed by the German armies on the Eastern Front. We fear, therefore, that if the Government of the U. S. S. R. announces today the surrender of Germany we may find ourselves in an awkward position and mislead the Soviet public. It should be borne in mind that the German resistance on the Eastern Front is not slackening but, judging by the intercepted radio messages, a considerable grouping of German troops have explicitly declared their intention to continue the resistance and to disobey Dönitz's surrender order.

For this reason the Command of the Soviet troops would like to wait until the German surrender takes effect and to postpone the Government's announcement of the surrender till May 9, 7 p. m. Moscow time.

167. ACT OF MILITARY SURRENDER, BERLIN, GERMANY, MAY 8, 1945[10]

1. We the undersigned, acting by authority of the German High Command, hereby surrender unconditionally to the Supreme Commander, Allied Expeditionary Force and simultaneously to the Supreme High Command of the Red Army all forces on land, at sea, and in the air who are at this date under German control.

2. The German High Command will at once issue orders to all German military, naval and air authorities and to all forces under German control to cease active operations at 2301 hours Central European time on 8th May 1945, to remain in the positions occupied at that time and to disarm completely, handing over their weapons and equipment to the local allied commanders or officers designated by Representatives of the Allied Supreme Commands. No ship, vessel, or aircraft is to be scuttled, or any damage done to their hull, machinery or equipment, and also to machines of all kinds, armament, apparatus, and all the technical means of prosecution of war in general.

3. The German High Command will at once issue to the appropriate commanders, and ensure the carrying out of any further orders issued by the Supreme Commander, Allied Expeditionary Force and by the Supreme High Command of the Red Army.

4. This act of military surrender is without prejudice to, and will be superseded by any general instrument of surrender imposed by, or on behalf of the United Nations and applicable to GERMANY and the German armed forces as a whole.

5. In the event of the German High Command or any of the forces under their control failing to act in accordance with this Act of Surrender, the Supreme Commander, Allied Expeditionary Force and the Supreme High Command of the Red Army will take such punitive or other action as they deem appropriate.

6. This Act is drawn up in English, Russian and German languages. The English and Russian are the only authentic texts.

Signed at Berlin on the 8. day of May, 1945
Friedeburg   Keitel   Stumpf
On behalf of the German High Command
In The Presence of:

On behalf of the   On behalf of the
Supreme Commander   Supreme High Command
Allied Expeditionary Force   of the Red Army
A. W. Tedder   G. Zhukov
At the signing also were present as witnesses:
F. de Lattre-Tassigny   Carl Spaatz
General Commanding in Chief   General, Commanding United
First French Army   States Strategic Air Forces

168. Truman Proclamation, May 8, 1945[11] (Excerpt)

The Allied armies, through sacrifice and devotion and with God's help, have wrung from Germany a final and unconditional surrender. The western world has been freed of the evil forces which for five years and longer have imprisoned the bodies and broken the lives of millions upon millions of free-born men. They have violated their churches, destroyed their homes, corrupted their children, and murdered their loved ones. Our Armies of Liberation have restored freedom to these suffering peoples, whose spirit and will the oppressors could never enslave.

Much remains to be done. The victory won in the West must now be won in the East. The whole world must be cleansed of the evil from which half the world has been freed. United, the peace-loving nations have demonstrated in the West that their arms are stronger by far than the might of dictators or the tyranny of military cliques that once called us soft and weak. The power of our peoples to defend themselves against all enemies will be proved in the Pacific war as it has been proved in Europe.

For the triumph of spirit and of arms which we have won, and for its promise to peoples everywhere who join us in the love of freedom, it is fitting that we, as a nation, give thanks to Almighty God, who has strengthened us and given us the victory.

NOW, THEREFORE, I, HARRY S TRUMAN, President of the United States of America, do hereby appoint Sunday, May 13, 1945, to be a day of prayer.

I call upon the people of the United States, whatever their faith, to unite in offering joyful thanks to God for the victory we have won and to pray that He will support us to the end of our present struggle and guide us into the way of peace.

I also call upon my countrymen to dedicate this day of prayer to the memory of those who have given their lives to make possible our victory.

169. GENERAL MARSHALL'S "BIENNIAL REPORT TO THE SECRETARY OF WAR," SEPTEMBER 1945[12] (EXCERPTS)

The steps in the German defeat, as described by captured members of the High Command, were:

1. *Failure to invade England.* Hitler's first military setback occurred when, after the collapse of France, England did not capitulate. According to Colonel General Jodl, Chief of the Operations Staff of the German High Command, the campaign in France had been undertaken because it was estimated that with the fall of France, England would not continue to fight. The unexpectedly swift victory over France and Great Britain's continuation of the war found the General Staff unprepared for an invasion of England. Although the armistice with France was concluded on 22 June 1940, no orders to prepare for the invasion of Britain were issued prior to 2 July. Field Marshal Kesselring stated that he urged the invasion since it generally was believed in Germany that England was in a critical condition. Field Marshal Keitel, Chief of Staff of German Armed Forces, however, stated that the risk was thought to be the existence of the British fleet. He said the army was ready but the air force was limited by weather, the navy very dubious. Meanwhile, in the air blitz over England the German Air Force had suffered irreparable losses from which its bombardment arm never recovered.

2. *The Campaign of 1941 in the Soviet Union.* In the autumn of 1941 after the battle of Vysma, the Germans stood exhausted but apparently victorious before Moscow. According to Jodl, the General Staff of the armed forces considered that one last energetic push would be sufficient to finish the Soviets. The German High Command had neither envisioned nor planned for a winter campaign. A sudden change in the weather brought disaster. The Red Army defense, a terrific snowstorm, and extremely unseasonable cold in the Christmas week of 1941 precipitated the strategic defeat of the German armed forces. Impatient of all restraint, Hitler publicly announced that he had more faith in his own intuition than in the judgment of his military advisers. He relieved the Commander in Chief of the Army, General von Brauschitsch. It was the turning point of the war.

3. *Stalingrad.* Even after the reverse before Moscow in 1941, Germany might have avoided defeat had it not been for the campaign in 1942 which culminated in the disaster at Stalingrad. Disregarding the military lessons of history, Hitler, instead of attacking the Soviet armies massed in the north, personally planned and directed a campaign of which the immediate objectives were to deprive the Soviet Union of her vital industries and raw materials by cutting the Volga at Stalingrad and seizing the Caucasian oil fields. Beyond these concrete objectives was evidently the Napoleonic dream of a conquest of the Middle East and India by a gigantic double envelopment with one pincer descending from the Caucasus through Tiflis and the other from North Africa across Egypt, Palestine, and the Arabian desert. The campaign collapsed before Stalingrad with the magnificent Russian defense

of that city and in the northern foothills of the Caucasus, where a breakdown of German transport to the front left the German armor stalled for 3 weeks for lack of fuel in the critical summer months of 1942. Field Marshal Keitel in reviewing this campaign remarks that Germany failed completely to estimate properly the reserve of Russian industrial and productive power east of the Urals. The statement of both Keitel and Jodl is that neither was in favor of the Stalingrad campaign, but that the recommendations of the High Command were overruled by Adolf Hitler.

4. *Invasion of North Africa.* Allied landings in North Africa came as a surprise to the German High Command. Field Marshal Kesselring, who, at the time, was commanding all German forces in the Mediterranean except Rommel's desert task force, states that his headquarters did expect a landing and had requested reinforcement by a division. However, Kesselring's fears were not heeded by Hitler and Goering. Allied security and deception measures for the landing operations were found to have been highly effective. Only when the Allied fleets and convoys were streaming through the Straits of Gibraltar did the Germans realize that something very special was under way, and even then false conclusions were drawn: either that the Allies intended to land in rear of Rommel in the Middle East, or that these were British reinforcements en route to the Far East, or supplies for starving Malta. Since no advance preparations had been made by the Germans to repel such an Allied invasion of North Africa, all subsequent efforts to counter the Allies suffered from hasty improvisation. Defense continued, however, because, as Field Marshal Keitel now states, since evacuation was impossible, the Germans had only the choice of resisting or surrendering.

5. *The Invasion of France.* All German headquarters expected the Allied invasion of France. According to Colonel General Jodl, both the general direction and the strength of the initial assault in Normandy were correctly estimated; but Field Marshal Keitel states that the Germans were not sure exactly where the Allies would strike and considered Brittany as more probable because of the three major U-boat bases located in that region. Both agree that the belief of the German High Command that a second assault would be launched, probably by an army under General Patton, held large German forces in the Pas-de-Calais area. Both Keitel and Jodl believed that the invasion could be repulsed or at worst contained, and both named the Allied air arm as the decisive factor in the German failure.

Prior to the invasion, important divergencies of opinion developed between Field Marshal von Rundstedt, Commander in Chief West, and Rommel, commander of the threatened army group. Rundstedt desired to hold his armored forces in a group around Paris and in Eastern France; Rommel to push them forward to positions in readiness close to the coast. The Rommel view prevailed. Von Rundstedt was subsequently relieved by Colonel General von Kluge.

Soon after the Allied capture of Cherbourg, dissension again broke out in the High Command. Von Kluge and Rommel wished to evacuate all South-western France, blocking or destroying its usable ports. They believed that a continuation of the fight in Normandy could only end with the destruction of their Western armies and that they should withdraw before disintegration began. Von Kluge recommended defense on the general line: lower Seine-Paris-Fontainebleau-Massif Central. Hitler refused to accept this recommendation, relieved Kluge from command, and reappointed Von Rundstedt as Commander in Chief West. Under direct instructions, Rundstedt continued the battle of Normandy to its final denouement. Hitler himself ordered the Avranches-Mortain counterattack and was much surprised when it completely failed. Keitel expresses further surprise at the audacious exploitation of the American break-through at Avranches during this counterattack, and particularly of the thrust toward Brest.

6. *The Ardennes Counterattack*. The German offensive in December 1944 was Hitler's personal conception. According to Jodl, the objective of the attack was Antwerp. It was hoped that overcast weather would neutralize Allied air superiority, and that an exceptionally rapid initial break-through could be achieved. Other German officers believe that this operation was reckless in the extreme, in that it irreparably damaged the comparatively fresh armored divisions of the Sixth Panzer Army, the principal element of Germany's strategic reserve, at a moment when every available reserve was needed to repulse the expected Soviet attack in the east.

7. *The Crossing of the Rhine*. Even after the failure of the German counteroffensive in the Ardennes, the Germans believed that the Rhine line could be held. The loss of the Remagen bridge, however, exploded this hope. The entire Rhine defensive line had to be weakened in the attempt to contain the bridgehead, and the disorderly German retreat in the Saar and Palatinate rendered easy the subsequent drive eastward of the Allied armies toward Hamburg, Leipzig, and Munich.

Part 14. Allied Victory in the Far East

In early 1944, long before the invasion of the Philippines began, the American military planners expected to bypass those islands and carry the war to Japan with B-29s based in China. However, a major Japanese offensive in China, launched in the spring of 1944, proved too much for Chiang's forces and the United States was forced to abandon the plan to use Chinese bases. The problem was complicated by the mutual dislike of Chiang and his American military adviser, General Stilwell. General Stilwell was convinced that Chiang spent more effort on routing the Chinese Communists than the Japanese. The Americans subsequently decided to invade the Philippines and use Luzon and the Mariana Islands as strategic bombing bases. The B-29 was capable of nonstop flights of 1400 miles, making all of Japan vulnerable to massive air raids by late 1944.

By the middle of January 1945, it became evident that Japan desperately needed a new strategic defense plan. Despite the situation that demanded new planning, it was difficult to proceed because a controversy developed over the air defense of the home islands. The Japanese army favored locating the major defense effort over the East China Sea even at the expense of drawing away home defense resources. The Navy favored delaying any commitment to larger-scale air operations and judged the Army's plan premature at best. The increased American air power in striking range of Japan proper, however, made it clear that delay was impossible. The Imperial General Headquarters then used the Army plan as the basis of a draft of a general policy presented to the Emperor called "Outline of Army and Navy Operations" (170). The Emperor approved the policy on January 20 and it became the basis of home defense planning for the rest of the war.

The United States had achieved air superiority over Japan and could launch raids at will. American air superiority was reflected in planned operations for Japan's defeat (171), but it was apparent that the destruction of cities and killing of thousands of people alone might not eliminate Japan's will or capacity to wage war. The situation, however, required frequent reevaluations of Japan's position because of the American air superiority but also because the war in Europe was ending and the Soviets could be expected to move forces to the Far East. Japan's Imperial General Headquarters Army Section prepared a detailed directive (172) in March based upon the January 20 policy (164), ordering their commands to prepare for an invasion of the home islands.

Meanwhile, President Truman announced the defeat of Germany and called upon Japan to surrender unconditionally (173), but there was little optimism that the Japanese would heed his message. The bloody battles for Iwo Jima and Okinawa had resulted in heavy American losses and Japanese resistance was unyielding. The Americans were increasingly convinced that Japan would never surrender without a sweeping invasion of the home islands. At this juncture the role of nuclear weapon research became increasingly important. The United States, aided by scientists from several nations, had developed an atomic bomb, and the time for the first test was at hand.

The general assumption of most of the officials and scientists engaged in the Manhattan Project was that the weapon would be employed against the enemy if it could be produced in time. Some scientists, however, had misgivings, and in "A Report to the Secretary of War" in June 1945 (174), they outlined the thoughts and reservations that would haunt the post-war world. The Report was apparently ignored because a group of British and American officials agreed, in July, that the bomb should be used against Japan (175). It is interesting to note the footnote urging extreme caution about sharing the details of the bomb with the Soviets at the pending Potsdam Conference.

There was considerable uncertainty as to how the bomb would perform, so it was decided to test it in New Mexico. One of the leading scientists on the project, E. O. Lawrence, vividly described the awesome power of the new and terrible weapon (176). When the momentous test occurred President Truman was attending the Potsdam Conference, and he informed Churchill and Stalin that the test was successful. The decision to use the bomb against Japan was President Truman's sole responsibility and despite the generally positive agreement his decision evoked, Truman made another appeal for Japanese surrender. Together with Great Britain and China, the United States issued a proclamation from Potsdam that warned Japan of the consequences of delay (177).

The Potsdam Declaration presented a surrender formula to Japan, and it was also intended to reassure the Japanese people that the terms were just; but it was rejected by Japan's leaders even before the Potsdam meeting ended. The first atomic bomb was then dropped on Hiroshima on August 6. President Truman released a dramatic account of the bombing in a prearranged statement (178), and on the next day the Soviet Union attacked Japanese strongholds in Mongolia, Manchuria, and North Korea.

The Soviet attacks began against Japan's Kwantung Army before dawn and quickly advanced on all fronts. Japan did not get the full text of Russia's declaration of war until it was intercepted from a Tass radio message on August 9, the day on which a second bomb was dropped, on Nagasaki (179). Japan's Premier Suzuki and the Imperial War Guidance Council then agreed to accept the surrender terms outlined in the Potsdam Declaration (see 177), but stipulated certain conditions (180). Those conditions were refused by the Allies, and the Emperor, broadcasting to the Japanese people for the first time on August 15, told them of the sad state of their nation (181). Almost simultaneously the Soviet Union and China concluded an alliance treaty pledging mutual war support against Japan (182). The war was officially over on September 2, 1945 (183).

170. Japan's "Outline of Army and Navy Operations," January 20, 1945[1]

1. General Policy

a. The final decisive battle of the war will be waged in Japan Proper.

b. The armed forces of the Empire will prepare for this battle by immediately establishing a strong strategic position in depth within the confines of a national defense sphere delineated by the Bonin Islands, Formosa, the coastal sector of east China, and southern Korea.

c. The United States will now be considered Japan's principal enemy.

Operational planning of all headquarters will be directed toward interception and destruction of American forces, all other theaters and adversaries assuming secondary importance.

2. Preparation and Conduct of Operations

a. Resistance will continue in the Philippines so as to delay as long as possible the enemy's approach to the Homeland defense perimeter.

b. Key strongpoints to be developed within the perimeter defense zone include Iwo Jima, Formosa, Okinawa, the Shanghai district, and the south Korean coast. The main defensive effort will be made in the Ryukyus area. Preparations in the perimeter defense zone will be completed during February and March 1945.

c. When the enemy penetrates the defense zone, a campaign of attrition will be initiated to reduce his preponderance in ships, aircraft, and men, to obstruct the establishment and use of advance bases, to undermine enemy morale, and thereby to seriously delay the final assault on Japan. The air forces will make a maximum effort over the perimeter defense zone. Enemy troops that succeed in getting ashore at points on the Homeland defense perimeter will be dealt with by those ground forces on the spot without reinforcement from other theaters.

d. Emphasis in ground preparations will be laid on Kyushu and Kanto. Strong air defenses will be established along key lines of communication, such as the Shimonoseki and Korea Straits, and at important ports and communications centers such as Tokyo, Nagoya, Osaka-Kobe, and the Moji-Kokura-Yawata area.

e. During the delaying operations in the forward area, preparation for the decisive battle will be completed in Japan Proper by the early fall of 1945.

f. In general, Japanese air strength will be conserved until an enemy landing is actually underway on or within the defense sphere. The Allied invasion fleet will then be destroyed on the water, principally by sea and air special-attack units.

171. U. S. Chiefs of Staff Memorandum, "Operations for Defeat of Japan," January 22, 1945[2]

1. The agreed over-all objective in the war against Japan has been expressed as follows (C. C. S. 417/9):

To force the unconditional surrender of Japan by:

(1) Lowering Japanese ability and will to resist by establishing sea and air blockades, conducting intensive air bombardment, and destroying Japanese air and naval strength.

(2) Invading and seizing objectives in the industrial heart of Japan.

2. The United States Chiefs of Staff have adopted the following as a basis for planning in the war against Japan:

The concept of operations for the main effort in the Pacific is (C. C. S. 417/10):

a. Following the Okinawa operation to seize additional positions to intensify the blockade and air bombardment of Japan in order to create a situation favorable to:

b. An assault on Kyushu for the purpose of further reducing Japanese capabilities by containing and destroying major enemy forces and further intensifying the blockade and air bombardment in order to establish a tactical condition favorable to:

c. The decisive invasion of the industrial heart of Japan through the Tokyo Plain.

3. The following sequence and timing of operations have been directed by the United States Chiefs of Staff and plans prepared by theater commanders:—

Objectives	Target Date
Continuation of operations in the Philippines (Luzon, Mindoro, Leyte)	—
Iwo Jima	19 February 1945
Okinawa and extension therefrom in the Ryukus	1 April–August 1945

4. Until a firm date can be established when redeployment from Europe can begin, planning will be continued for an operation to seize a position in the Chusan-Ningpo area and for invasion of Kyushu-Honshu in the winter of 1945–1946.

5. Examination is being conducted of the necessity for and cost of operations to maintain and defend a sea route to the Sea of Okhotsk when the entry of Russia into the war against Japan becomes imminent. Examination so far has shown that the possibility of seizing a position in the Kuriles for that purpose during the favorable weather period of 1945 is remote due to lack of sufficient resources. The possibility of maintaining and defending such a sea route from bases in Kamchatka alone is being further examined.

6. The United States Chiefs of Staff have also directed examination and preparation of a plan of campaign against Japan in the event that prolongation of the European war requires postponement of the invasion of Japan until well into 1946.

172. JAPANESE HOMELAND DEFENSE PLAN, APRIL 8, 1945[3] (EXCERPTS)

1. The forthcoming decisive operation in the Homeland and adjacent areas will be referred to as the KETSU-GO Operation. Designations of the component operations will be as follows:

KETSU No. 1 Hokkaido, Karafuto, and the Kurile Islands

No. 2 Northern Honshu
No. 3 Kanto District
No. 4 Nagoya-Shizuoka area
No. 5 Western Honshu and Shikoku
No. 6 Kyushu
No. 7 Korea

2. Operational Policy

a. The Imperial Army will hasten preparations to meet and crush the attack of U. S. forces in the above key areas. Emphasis will be on the Kanto area (Ketsu No. 3) and Kyushu (Ketsu No. 6).

b. Preparations for operations prescribed in this plan will fall into the following general phases:

First   April through July
Second   August through September
Third   from 1 October

Emergency preparations in Kyushu will be completed by early June. Dispositions will continue to be strengthened during the second phase, and all tactical plans completed. Final deployment of field units and perfection of the field positions will be completed in the early part of the third phase.

c. Air Operations

(1) A close watch will be maintained over all enemy fleet movements, particularly transport convoys. Air search over the approaches to the Homeland will be continuous and aggressive.

(2) Enemy amphibious task forces attempting to invade the Homeland will be destroyed on the water.

(3) The primary target of the air offensive will be transports.

(4) All air operations will be curtailed rigorously until the enemy convoy approaches. Fighting strength will be preserved until the moment for the decisive effort.

(5) Air support for ground forces will be restricted to liaison missions and tactical reconnaissance in extreme emergencies.

(6) Long-range, surprise air raids against such enemy bases as Iwo Jima and Okinawa will be carried out.

d. Ground Operations

(1) The ground forces will win the final decision by overwhelming and annihilating the enemy landing force in the coastal area before the beachhead is secure.

(2) Speedy maneuver of the largest possible force against the enemy landing sector is the key to success in such operations. As many local reserves as possible must be maneuvered into the expected landing sector as soon as it becomes known that the enemy intends to land. After the enemy has landed, additional ground troops from other parts of the Homeland will be deployed to the area in accordance with the plan prescribed in Para. 3 below.

(3) In the event of simultaneous invasions of more than one area, the main Japanese counteroffensive will be directed at the main enemy landing. Delaying actions will be fought in other localities. This principle will apply both tactically and strategically.

(4) If the location of the enemy's main landing is undetermined, the main Japanese force will be committed in the area which presents the most favorable terrain for offensive operations. Delaying actions will be conducted in other localities. This principle will apply both tactically and strategically.

(5) Large-scale and thorough construction of fortifications will be carried out with emphasis on those field positions designed to provide jumping-off, rallying, and support points for local offensives.

(6) Special security precautions will be taken at vital installations to forestall enemy airborne penetrations.

. . . .

g. Guerrilla Resistance and Internal Security

(1) We will strive to realize our operational objectives through exploitation of the traditional spirit of "Every citizen a soldier."

(2) Guerrilla resistance will aim at the obstruction of enemy activities and the attrition of enemy strength through guerrilla warfare, espionage, deception, raids on rear areas, and demolition of enemy installations. Such resistance will be carried out as part of the overall operation to assist line units, to meet enemy airborne operations and small secondary amphibious landings, and to cut off and harass enemy elements which penetrate into the interior.

(3) Internal security will aim at protecting military activities, vital communications, transport, power sources, and secret areas. If necessary, internal security will quell public disorder arising as a result of air raids, bombardment, invasion, propaganda, and natural disaster.

(4) Forces for guerrilla resistance and internal security will be drawn from the entire body of the citizenry as the situation may dictate. Guard units and civilian defense organizations will provide manpower, organized around small elements of the field forces as a guiding nucleus. Such units will be under the command of the various district army commands.

3. Redeployment Plan

a. In event of an enemy invasion of Kyushu, the following steps will be taken:

(1) Four line combat divisions will be dispatched to Sixteenth Area Army from forces available to Thirteenth and Fifteenth Area Armies in central and western Honshu and Shikoku.

(2) Preparations will be made for the advance of a second increment. Three or four additional divisions will be dispatched from the

Eleventh Area Army in northern Honshu and from Twelfth Area Army in the Kanto district to the Osaka-Kobe area, where they will be held in readiness for further advance to Kyushu.

b. In event of an enemy landing in the Kanto district, without a prior landing in other areas, the following steps will be taken:

(1) Three line combat divisions from Eleventh Area Army in northern Honshu, three from Fifteenth Area Army in the Osaka-Kobe area, and two from Sixteenth Area Army in Kyushu will be immediately sent to Twelfth Area Army and held in readiness in Nagano Prefecture as a mass counterattack force.

(2) If the situation permits, two line combat divisions will be speedily dispatched by Thirteenth Area Army from the Nagoya area to Twelfth Area Army in the Kanto district.

(3) Preparations will be made for the advance of a second increment. Two line combat divisions will be sent by Fifth Area Army in Hokkaido to Eleventh Area Army in northern Honshu, and five divisions from Sixteenth Area Army on Kyushu to Fifteenth Area Army in the Osaka-Kobe district, all these divisions to be held in readiness for further advance to the Kanto district.

173. TRUMAN CALLS FOR JAPANESE SURRENDER, MAY 8, 1945[4]

NAZI GERMANY has been defeated.

The Japanese people have felt the weight of our land, air and naval attacks. So long as their leaders and the armed forces continue the war the striking power and intensity of our blows will steadily increase and will bring utter destruction to Japan's industrial war production, to its shipping, and to everything that supports its military activity.

The longer the war lasts, the greater will be the suffering and hardships which the people of Japan will undergo—all in vain. Our blows will not cease until the Japanese military and naval forces lay down their arms in *unconditional surrender*.

Just what does the unconditional surrender of the armed forces mean for the Japanese people?

It means the end of the war.

It means the termination of the influence of the military leaders who have brought Japan to the present brink of disaster.

It means provision for the return of soldiers and sailors to their families, their farms, their jobs.

It means not prolonging the present agony and suffering of the Japanese in the vain hope of victory.

Unconditional surrender does not mean the extermination or enslavement of the Japanese people.

174. "A Report to the [U. S.] Secretary of War," June 1945[5] (Excerpts)

(Presented By Some Atomic Scientists)

The only reason to treat nuclear power differently from all the other developments in the field of physics is the possibility of its use as a means of political pressure in peace and sudden destruction in war. All present plans for the organization of research, scientific and industrial development, and publication in the field of nucleonics are conditioned by the political and military climate in which one expects those plans to be carried out. Therefore, in making suggestions for the postwar organization of nucleonics, a discussion of political problems cannot be avoided. The scientists on this Project do not presume to speak authoritatively on problems of national and international policy. However, we found ourselves, by the force of events, during the last five years, in the position of a small group of citizens cognizant of a grave danger for the safety of this country as well as for the future of all the other nations, of which the rest of mankind is unaware. We therefore feel it our duty to urge that the political problems, arising from the mastering of nuclear power, be recognized in all their gravity, and that appropriate steps be taken for their study and the preparation of necessary decisions. We hope that the creation of the Committee by the Secretary of War to deal with all aspects of nucleonics, indicates that these implications have been recognized by the government. We believe that our acquaintance with the scientific elements of the situation and prolonged preoccupation with its world-wide political implications, impose on us the obligation to offer to the Committee some suggestions as to the possible solution of these grave problems.

. . . .

The development of nuclear power not only constitutes an important addition to the technological and military power of the United States, but also creates grave political and economic problems for the future of this country.

Nuclear bombs cannot possibly remain a "secret weapon" at the exclusive disposal of this country for more than a few years. The scientific facts on which their construction is based are well known to scientists of other countries. Unless an effective international control of nuclear explosives is instituted, a race for nuclear armaments is certain to ensue following the first revelation of our possession of nuclear weapons to the world. Within ten years other countries may have nuclear bombs, each of which, weighing less than a ton, could destroy an urban area of more than ten square miles. In the war to which such an armaments race is likely to lead, the United States, with its agglomeration of population and industry in comparatively few metropolitan districts, will be at a disadvantage compared to nations whose population and industry are scattered over large areas.

We believe that these considerations make the use of nuclear bombs for an early unannounced attack against Japan inadvisable. If the United States were to be the first to release this new means of indiscriminate destruction upon mankind, she would sacrifice public support throughout the world, precipitate the race for armaments, and prejudice the possibility of reaching an international agreement on the future control of such weapons.

Much more favorable conditions for the eventual achievement of such an agreement could be created if nuclear bombs were first revealed to the world by a demonstration in an appropriately selected uninhabited area.

In case chances for the establishment of an effective international control of nuclear weapons should have to be considered slight at the present time, then not only the use of these weapons against Japan, but even their early demonstration, may be contrary to the interests of this country. A postponement of such a demonstration will have in this case the advantage of delaying the beginning of the nuclear armaments race as long as possible.

If the government should decide in favor of an early demonstration of nuclear weapons, it will then have the possibility of taking into account the public opinion of this country and of the other nations before deciding whether these weapons should be used against Japan. In this way, other nations may assume a share of responsibility for such a fateful decision.

175. USE OF ATOMIC WEAPONS IN WAR AGAINST JAPAN, JULY 4, 1945[6]

Minutes of a Meeting of the Combined Policy Committee
[Extracts]

TOP SECRET
MINUTES OF COMBINED POLICY COMMITTEE MEETING HELD
    AT THE PENTAGON ON JULY 4TH, 1945—9:30 A. M.
Present:
    Members: The Secretary of War, Chairman
              Field Marshal Sir Henry Maitland Wilson
              The Hon. C. D. Howe
              Dr. Vannevar Bush
    By Invitation: The Right Hon. The Earl of Halifax
              Sir James Chadwick
              Major General L. R. Groves
              Mr. George Harrison
    Joint Secretaries: Mr. Harvey H. Bundy
              Mr. Roger Makins
              . . . .

3. USE OF WEAPON AGAINST THIRD PARTIES

Field Marshal Wilson stated that the British Government concurred in the use of the T. A. [Tube Alloy-Bomb Codename] weapon against Japan. He added that the Prime Minister might wish to discuss this matter with the President at the forthcoming meeting in Berlin.

The Committee:—Took note that the Governments of the United Kingdom and the United States had agreed that T. A. weapons should be used by
the United States against Japan, the agreement of the British Government
having been communicated by Field Marshal Sir Henry Maitland Wilson.

4. DISCLOSURE OF INFORMATION BY THE TWO GOVERNMENTS ON THE USE OF THE WEAPON

. . . .

The Chairman said he was thinking of an earlier period, viz., the forthcoming meeting with Stalin. His own opinion had been very much influenced by the probable use within a few weeks after the meeting. If nothing
was said at this meeting about the T. A. weapon, its subsequent early use
might have a serious effect on the relations of frankness between the three
great Allies. He had therefore advised the President to watch the atmosphere at the meeting. If mutual frankness on other questions was found to
be real and satisfactory, then the President might say that work was being
done on the development of atomic fission for war purposes; that good
progress had been made; and that an attempt to use a weapon would be
made shortly, though it was not certain that it would succeed. If it did
succeed, it would be necessary for a discussion to be held on the best method
of handling the development in the interests of world peace and not for
destruction. If Stalin pressed for immediate disclosure the President might
say that he was not prepared to take the matter further at the present
time. . . .

. . . .

Harvey H. Bundy
Roger Makins
Joint Secretaries

176. "THOUGHTS BY E. O. LAWRENCE," JULY 16, 1945[7]

TOP SECRET [Near Alamogordo Air Base?], July 16, 1945.
Thoughts By E. O. Lawrence

Our group assembled at a point 27 miles from the bomb site about two in
the morning. We were on a plain extending all the way to the bomb and
although I did not notice carefully the mountains seemed to be some miles
away. We could see in the distance lights defining the position of the bomb
and at about four a. m. our radio picked up conversations between the B-29s
and the ground organization.

We soon learned that zero hour was 5:30 a. m. which was just break of
dawn. Naturally our tenseness grew as zero hour approached. We were
warned of the probable brilliance of the explosion—so bright it would blind
one looking directly at it for sometime and there was even danger of sun-
burn!

I decided the best place to view the flame would be through the window of the car I was sitting in, which would take out ultraviolet, but at the last minute decided to get out of the car (evidence indeed I was excited!) and just as I put my foot on the ground I was enveloped with a warm brilliant yellow white light—from darkness to brilliant sunshine in an instant and as I remember I momentarily was stunned by the surprise. It took me a second thought to tell myself, "this is indeed it!!" and then through my dark sun glasses there was a gigantic ball of fire rising rapidly from the earth—at first as brilliant as the sun, growing less brilliant as it grew boiling and swirling into the heavens. Ten or fifteen thousand feet above the ground it was orange in color and I judge a mile in diameter. At higher levels it became purple and this purple afterglow persisted for what seemed a long time (possibly it was only for a minute or two) at an elevation of 20–25,000 feet. This purple glow was due to the enormous radioactivity of the gases. (The light is in large part due to nitrogen of the air and in the laboratory we occasionally produce it in miniature with the cyclotron.)

In the earlier stages of rise of the flame the clouds above were illuminated and as the flame rose it was a grand spectacle also to see the great clouds immediately above melt away before our eyes.

The final phase was the column of hot gases, smoke and dust funneling from the earth into the heavens to 40,000 feet. The column was to me surprisingly narrow until high elevations were reached when it foamed out considerably. The great funnel was visible a long time. We could still make it out as we drove away a half hour later.

But to retrace, a little over two minutes after the beginning of the flash the shock wave hit us. It was a sharp loud crack and then for about a minute thereafter there were resounding echoes from the surrounding mountains. The pressure of the shock wave was not great enough to be disturbing but the noise was very loud and sharp, indeed. The noise of the shock wave was a sharp crack like that of a giant firecracker set off a few yards away—or perhaps like the report of 37 mm artillery at a distance of about one hundred yards.

A number of observers near me were looking right at the explosion through welder's goggles (or the same dark glass) and they told me the light through these glasses was so bright as to blind them for an instant.

As I was not actively concerned with the problems of Y, I had on occasions asked my colleagues there what the event would be like and their predicted picture of the event was borne out completely. I am amazed that the whole business went off so exactly as their calculations had predicted.

The grand, indeed almost cataclysmic proportion of the explosion produced a kind of solemnity in everyone(')s behavior immediately afterwards. There was restrained applause, but more a hushed murmuring bordering on reverence in manner as the event was commented upon(.) Dr. Charles Thomas (Monsanto) spoke to me of this being the greatest single event in the history of mankind, etc. etc.

As far as all of us are concerned although we knew the fundamentals were sound and that the explosion could be produced, we share a feeling that we have this day crossed a great milestone in human progress.

Ernest O. Lawrence

177. POTSDAM PROCLAMATION, JULY 26, 1945[8]

PROCLAMATION BY THE HEADS OF GOVERNMENTS, UNITED STATES, CHINA AND THE UNITED KINGDOM

(1) We, the President of the United States, the President of the National Government of the Republic of China and the Prime Minister of Great Britain, representing the hundreds of millions of our countrymen, have conferred and agree that Japan shall be given an opportunity to end this war.

(2) The prodigious land, sea and air forces of the United States, the British Empire and of China, many times reinforced by their armies and air fleets from the west are poised to strike the final blows upon Japan. This military power is sustained and inspired by the determination of all the Allied nations to prosecute the war against Japan until she ceases to resist.

(3) The result of the futile and senseless German resistance to the might of the aroused free peoples of the world stands forth in awful clarity as an example to the people of Japan. The might that now converges on Japan is immeasurably greater than that which, when applied to the resisting Nazis, necessarily laid waste to the lands, the industry and the method of life of the whole German people. The full application of our military power, backed by our resolve, will mean the inevitable and complete destruction of the Japanese armed forces and just as inevitably the utter devastation of the Japanese homeland.

(4) The time has come for Japan to decide whether she will continue to be controlled by those self-willed milita(r)istic advisers whose unintelligent calculations have brought the Empire of Japan to the threshold of annihilation, or whether she will follow the path of reason.

(5) Following are our terms. We will not deviate from them. There are no alternatives. We shall brook no delay.

(6) There must be eliminated for all time the authority and influence of those who have deceived and misled the people of Japan into embarking on world conquest, for we insist that a new order of peace, security and justice will be impossible until irresponsible militarism is driven from the world.

(7) Until such a new order is established and until there is convincing proof that Japan's war-making power is destroyed, points in Japanese territory to be designated by the Allies shall be occupied to secure the achievement of the basic objectives we are here setting forth.

(8) The terms of the Cairo Declaration shall be carried out and Japanese sovereignty shall be limited to the islands of Honshu, Hokkaido, Kyushu, Shikoku and such minor islands as we determine.

(9) The Japanese military forces, after being completely disarmed, shall

be permitted to return to their homes with the opportunity to lead peaceful and productive lives.

(10) We do not intend that the Japanese shall be enslaved as a race or destroyed as (a) nation, but stern justice shall be meted out to all war criminals, including those who have visited cruelties upon our prisoners. The Japanese government shall remove all obstacles to the revival and strength(en)ing of democratic tendencies among the Japanese people. Freedom of speech, of religion, and of thought, as well as respect for the fundamental human rights shall be established.

(11) Japan shall be permitted to maintain such industries as will sustain her economy and permit the exaction of just reparations in kind, but not those industries which would enable her to re-arm for war. To this end, access to, as distinguished from control of raw materials shall be permitted. Eventual Japanese participation in world trade relations shall be permitted.

(12) The occupying forces of the Allies shall be withdrawn from Japan as soon as these objectives have been accomplished and there has been established in accordance with the freely expressed will of the Japanese people a peacefully inclined and responsible government.

(13) We call upon the Government of Japan to proclaim now the unconditional surrender of all the Japanese armed forces, and to provide proper and adequate assurances of their good faith in such action. The alternative for Japan is prompt and utter destruction.

Potsdam July 26, 1945

> Harry S Truman
> Winston Churchill
> by H. S. T.
> President of China
> by wire

178. Truman Announces Use of A-Bomb At Hiroshima, August 6, 1945[9]

Sixteen hours ago an American airplane dropped one bomb on Hiroshima, an important Japanese Army base. That bomb had more power than 20,000 tons of T. N. T. It had more than two thousand times the blast power of the British "Grand Slam" which is the largest bomb ever yet used in the history of warfare.

The Japanese began the war from the air at Pearl Harbor. They have been repaid many fold. And the end is not yet. With this bomb we have now added a new and revolutionary increase in destruction to supplement the growing power of our armed forces. In their present form these bombs are now in production and even more powerful forms are in development.

It is an atomic bomb. It is a harnessing of the basic power of the universe. The force from which the sun draws its power has been loosed against those who brought war to the Far East.

Before 1939, it was the accepted belief of scientists that it was theoretically possible to release atomic energy. But no one knew any practical method of doing it. By 1942, however, we knew that the Germans were working feverishly to find a way to add atomic energy to the other engines of war with which they hoped to enslave the world. But they failed. We may be grateful to Providence that the Germans got the V-1's and V-2's late and in limited quantities and even more grateful that they did not get the atomic bomb at all.

The battle of the laboratories held fateful risks for us as well as the battles of the air, land and sea, and we have now won the battle of the laboratories as we have won the other battles.

Beginning in 1940, before Pearl Harbor, scientific knowledge useful in war was pooled between the United States and Great Britain, and many priceless helps to our victories have come from that arrangement. Under that general policy the research on the atomic bomb was begun. With American and British scientists working together we entered the race of discovery against the Germans.

The United States had available the large number of scientists of distinction in the many needed areas of knowledge. It had the tremendous industrial and financial resources necessary for the project and they could be devoted to it without undue impairment of other vital war work. In the United States the laboratory work and the production plants, on which a substantial start had already been made, would be out of reach of enemy bombing, while at that time Britain was exposed to constant air attack and was still threatened with the possibility of invasion. For these reasons Prime Minister Churchill and President Roosevelt agreed that it was wise to carry on the project here. We now have two great plants and many lesser works devoted to the production of atomic power. Employment during peak construction numbered 125,000 and over 65,000 individuals are even now engaged in operating the plants. Many have worked there for two and a half years. Few know what they have been producing. They see great quantities of material going in and they see nothing coming out of these plants, for the physical size of the explosive charge is exceedingly small. We have spent two billion dollars on the greatest scientific gamble in history—and won.

But the greatest marvel is not the size of the enterprise, its secrecy, nor its cost, but the achievement of scientific brains in putting together infinitely complex pieces of knowledge held by many men in different fields of science into a workable plan. And hardly less marvelous has been the capacity of industry to design, and of labor to operate, the machines and methods to do things never done before so that the brain child of many minds came forth in physical shape and performed as it was supposed to do. Both science and industry worked under the direction of the United States Army, which achieved a unique success in managing so diverse a problem in the advancement of knowledge in an amazingly short time. It is doubtful if such another combination could be got together in the world. What has been done is the greatest achievement of organized science in history. It was done under high pressure and without failure.

We are now prepared to obliterate more rapidly and completely every productive enterprise the Japanese have above ground in any city. We shall destroy their docks, their factories, and their communications. Let there be no mistake; we shall completely destroy Japan's power to make war.

It was to spare the Japanese people from utter destruction that the ultimatum of July 26 was issued at Potsdam. Their leaders promptly rejected that ultimatum. If they do not now accept our terms they may expect a rain of ruin from the air, the like of which has never been seen on this earth. Behind this air attack will follow sea and land forces in such numbers and power as they have not yet seen and with the fighting skill of which they are already well aware.

The Secretary of War, who has kept in personal touch with all phases of the project, will immediately make public a statement giving further details.

His statement will give facts concerning the sites at Oak Ridge near Knoxville, Tennessee, and at Richland near Pasco, Washington, and an installation near Santa Fe, New Mexico. Although the workers at the sites have been making materials to be used in producing the greatest destructive force in history they have not themselves been in danger beyond that of many other occupations, for the utmost care has been taken of their safety.

The fact that we can release atomic energy ushers in a new era in man's understanding of nature's forces. Atomic energy may in the future supplement the power that now comes from coal, oil, and falling water, but at present it cannot be produced on a basis to compete with them commercially. Before that comes there must be a long period of intensive research.

It has never been the habit of the scientists of this country or the policy of this Government to withhold from the world scientific knowledge. Normally, therefore, everything about the work with atomic energy would be made public.

But under present circumstances it is not intended to divulge the technical processes of production or all the military applications, pending further examination of possible methods of protecting us and the rest of the world from the danger of sudden destruction.

I shall recommend that the Congress of the United States consider promptly the establishment of an appropriate commission to control the production and use of atomic power within the United States. I shall give further consideration and make further recommendations to the Congress as to how atomic power can become a powerful and forceful influence towards the maintenance of world peace.

179. SOVIET DECLARATION OF WAR AGAINST JAPAN, AUGUST 9, 1945[10]

With the defeat and capitulation of Hitlerite Germany, Japan remains the only great Axis power continuing the war.

With the rejection by the Japanese Government of the 26 July demand of the United States, Great Britain and China, for the unconditional surrender of the Japanese armed forces, the proposal of the Japanese Government to the Soviet Union with regard to mediation in the Far East loses its basis. In view of Japan's refusal to surrender, the Allied nations have submitted to the Soviet Government a proposal that it join the war against Japanese aggression, in order to hasten the end of the conflict, reduce the number of victims, and contribute to the early restoration of universal peace.

The Soviet Government, fulfilling its obligations to its Allies, has accepted this proposal by the Allied nations and has joined in their declaration of July 26. The Soviet Government considers that a policy such as it has adopted is the only means of expediting the return of peace, freeing the several peoples from further sacrifices and suffering and helping the Japanese nation avoid the dangers and destruction suffered by Germany after her refusal to surrender unconditionally.

For the foregoing reasons, the Soviet Government declares that as of tomorrow, 9 August, a state of war will exist between the Soviet Union and Japan.

180. KIDO DIARY ENTRY, AUGUST 9, 1945[11]

"At 1:30 p. m. Premier SUZUKI called at my office and reported that the Supreme War Guidance Council has decided to accept the Potsdam Declaration on the following conditions: (1) Preservation of the Imperial Dynasty, (2) Independent evacuation of troops, (3) Handling in our own country of persons responsible for the war, and (4) No guarantee occupation."

181. BROADCAST BY JAPAN'S EMPEROR, AUGUST 15, 1945[12]

After pondering deeply the general trend of the world situation and the actual state of Our Empire, We have decided to effect a settlement of the present crisis by resort to an extraordinary measure. To Our good and loyal subjects, we hereby convey Our will.

We have commanded Our Government to communicate to the Governments of the United States, Great Britain, China and the Soviet Union that Our Empire accepts the terms of their Joint Declaration.

To strive for the common prosperity and happiness of all nations as well as the security and well-being of Our subjects is the solemn obligation handed down to Us by Our Imperial Ancestors, and We keep it close to heart. Indeed, We declared war on America and Britain out of Our sincere desire to ensure Japan's self-preservation and the stabilization of East Asia. It was not Our intention either to infringe upon the sovereignty of other nations or to seek territorial aggrandizement.

The hostilities have now continued for nearly four years. Despite the gallant fighting of the Officers and Men of Our Army and Navy, the diligence and assiduity of Our servants of State, and the devoted service of Our hundred million subjects—despite the best efforts of all—the war has not necessarily developed in Our favor, and the general world situation also is not to Japan's advantage. Furthermore, the enemy has begun to employ a new and cruel bomb which kills and maims the innocent and the power of which to wreak destruction is truly incalculable.

Should We continue to fight, the ultimate result would be not only the obliteration of the race but the extinction of human civilization. Then, how should We be able to save the millions of Our subjects and make atonement to the hallowed spirits of Our Imperial Ancestors? That is why We have commanded the Imperial Government to comply with the terms of the Joint Declaration of the Powers.

To those nations which, as Our allies, have steadfastly cooperated with the Empire for the emancipation of East Asia, We cannot but express Our deep regret. Also, the thought of Our subjects who have fallen on the field of battle or met untimely death while performing their appointed tasks, and the thought of their bereaved families, rends Our heart, and We feel profound solicitude for the wounded and for all war-sufferers who have lost their homes and livelihood.

The suffering and hardship which Our nation yet must undergo will certainly be great. We are keenly aware of the innermost feelings of all ye, Our subjects. However, it is according to the dictates of time and fate that We have resolved, by enduring the unendurable and bearing the unbearable, to pave the way for a grand peace for all generations to come.

Since it has been possible to preserve the structure of the Imperial State, We shall always be with ye, Our good and loyal subjects, placing Our trust in your sincerity and integrity. Beware most strictly of any outburst of emotion which may engender needless complications, and refrain from fraternal contention and strife which may create confusion, lead ye astray and cause ye to lose the confidence of the world. Let the nation continue as one family from generation to generation with unwavering faith in the imperishability of Our divine land and ever mindful of its heavy burden of responsibility and the long road ahead. Turn your full strength to the task of building a new future. Cultivate the ways of rectitude, foster nobility of spirit, and work with resolution so that ye may enhance the innate glory of the Imperial State and keep pace with the progress of the world. We charge ye, Our loyal subjects, to carry out faithfully Our will.

182. Chinese-Soviet Alliance Treaty, August 14, 1945[13]

Art. 1: Both countries undertake jointly with the other United Nations to wage war against Japan until final victory and to render each other all necessary military and other help in this war.

Art. 2: They undertake not to enter into separate negotiations with Japan and not to conclude an armistice without mutual consent with the present Japanese Government or any other Government or authority established in Japan which will not clearly renounce all aggressive intentions.

Art. 3: They undertake after the end of the war against Japan to take jointly all measures in their power to prevent a repetition of aggression and violation of the peace by Japan. If one country becomes the victim of aggression the other will immediately render all military and other aid and support at her disposal, the article to remain in force until such time as, at the request of both countries, responsibility for the prevention of further aggression by Japan is placed in the hands of the United Nations Organisation.

Art. 4: They undertake not to conclude an alliance of any kind or to take part in any coalition directed against the other country.

Art. 5: Both countries, taking into account the protection and economic development of each country, agree to work together in friendly co-operation after the advent of peace and to act on the principle of mutual respect of each other's sovereign and territorial rights and not to interfere in the internal affairs of the other contracting party.

Art. 6: They agree to give each other all possible economic help in the post-war period to speed up their reconstruction and to bring about the well-being of the world.

Art. 7: This agreement respects the rights and obligations of the high contracting Powers and all member Powers of the United Nations.

Art. 8: The agreement is to come into force immediately after ratification and to remain valid for 30 years and, if neither country gives notice of termination, for an indefinite period thereafter, subject to each country being able to give one year's notice of termination.

183. Japan's Surrender, September 2, 1945[14]

INSTRUMENT OF SURRENDER

We, acting by command of and in behalf of the Emperor of Japan, the Japanese Government and the Japanese Imperial General Headquarters, hereby accept the provisions set forth in the declaration issued by the heads of the Governments of the United States, China and Great Britain on 26 July 1945, at Potsdam, and subsequently adhered to by the Union of Soviet Socialist Republics, which four powers are hereafter referred to as the Allied Powers.

We hereby proclaim the unconditional surrender to the Allied Powers of the Japanese Imperial General Headquarters and of all Japanese armed forces and all armed forces under Japanese control wherever situated.

We hereby command all Japanese forces wherever situated and the Japanese people to cease hostilities forthwith, to preserve and save from damage all ships, aircraft, and military and civil property and to comply with all requirements which may be imposed by the Supreme Commander for the Allied Powers or by agencies of the Japanese Government at his direction.

We hereby command the Japanese Imperial Headquarters to issue at once orders to the Commanders of all Japanese forces and all forces under Japanese control wherever situated to surrender unconditionally themselves and all forces under their control.

We hereby command all civil, military and naval officials to obey and enforce all proclamations, orders and directives deemed by the Supreme Commander for the Allied Powers to be proper to effectuate this surrender and issued by him or under his authority and we direct all such officials to remain at their posts and to continue to perform their non-combatant duties unless specifically relieved by him or under his authority.

We hereby undertake for the Emperor, the Japanese Government and their successors to carry out the provisions of the Potsdam Declaration in good faith, and to issue whatever orders and take whatever action may be required by the Supreme Commander for the Allied Powers or by any other designated representative of the Allied Powers for the purpose of giving effect to that Declaration.

We hereby command the Japanese Imperial Government and the Japanese Imperial General Headquarters at once to liberate all allied prisoners of war and civilian internees now under Japanese control and to provide for their protection, care, maintenance and immediate transportation to places as directed.

The authority of the Emperor and the Japanese Government to rule the state shall be subject to the Supreme Commander for the Allied Powers who will take such steps as he deems proper to effectuate these terms of surrender.

Chapter VII
Victory Without Peace

Part 15. Occupied Europe, Resistance and Liberation

The geographical area dominated by Germany in 1941–42 was enormous. Hitler's power extended from the Atlantic to the Caucasus and from Scandinavia to the Mediterranean. At the beginning, Germany's victories were military not political achievements. Later, however, the Nazis promised that every defeated nation was to have a place in Hitler's "new order."

In some conquered areas the relationship to German rule was long and stormy, while in others the situation varied in accordance with the treatment they received from the Germans. That treatment, in turn, rested upon Nazi dogma. The nations west and north of Germany were "acceptable" racially, and their populations would fit into the higher echelons of the new order.

The territories of Eastern Europe with large Slavic populations were a different matter. There the Nazi racial views applied to Poland early in the war made it clear that the people were to have "only bare living conditions" (17). After the invasion of Russia in June 1941, Germany ruled over additional millions of eastern peoples and a huge territory. The excitement shared by Hitler and his top aides in contemplating the new conquests was revealed in a secret Fuehrer conference in Berlin on July 16, 1941 (184).

The German administration of western occupied states was different, however—following the German attack on Russia there was increased resistance against German authority in the west. The resistance was manifested in underground organizations and sabotage directed toward the German occupiers. It was evident that Europe's Communist parties had joined the resistance. In December 1941 Hitler issued a decree (185) demanding that stringent measures be taken against any and all resisters. The decree was signed by General Keitel, and in later correspondence dealing with its implementation reference was made to removing offenders under cover of "night and fog," thus the order took that title. The Night and Fog Decree was soon directed at the Jewish populations of German-occupied states and became the administrative vehicle for their mass deportation to Germany.

German control extended over more and more territory, and the problems of German administration increased correspondingly; the most notable involved the large Jewish population. The doctrine of Aryan supremacy extolled by the National Socialists allowed no place in the new order for the Jewish people. The Nazi racist doctrine was apparent before the war, but as nation after nation came under German control the number of Jews subject to Hitler dramatically increased and the "problem" became a major concern to the Nazi planners.

Reinhard Heydrich, Himmler's SS deputy, abandoned all pretense at arranging a humane settlement when he was directed by Hermann Goering to develop a plan that would solve the Jewish problem once and for all. A conference was called at Wannsee near Berlin on January 20, 1942, and there Heydrich's plan (the Wannsee Protocol) was presented as the "Final Solution of the Jewish Question" (186). Despite the great secrecy that surrounded Nazi operations to suppress and kill subjected peoples, the Allies were aware that terrible crimes were being committed and at the Moscow Conference of Foreign Secretaries in 1943 (see Part 10) Roosevelt, Churchill, and Stalin warned Germany's leaders that they would be held accountable for their deeds when the war ended (187).

By 1943 resistance to German domination reached nearly uncontrollable proportions in some areas. The degree of resistance was related to the proximity of fighting fronts in most instances, and as the combat theatres inched closer to Germany more people joined the battle. For example, in Greece a unified underground force was formed by mid-1943 and the National Guerilla Bands was born (188).

Prime Minister Churchill, in a lengthy speech to the House of Commons in early 1941, provided the world an insightful account of the resistance efforts of the occupied peoples, those newly liberated and, in the case of Italy, former allies of Germany (189). Ironically, Churchill carefully noted that Poland, without a unified underground, would not be fully effective against the Germans until and unless a cooperative arrangement was concluded with Soviet forces already in the Polish area. A few months later, in August, the Polish underground army openly revolted against the German forces in Warsaw and waited in vain for the Soviet army to come to their aid. The politics of war proved more powerful than the challenge of a common enemy.

Opposition to Hitler's regime came not only from the conquered peoples but from Germans themselves (190). German prisoners of war in Russia were a source of early opposition, and the nucleus of a propaganda unit that proved useful to the Allied cause was found amidst the thousands of Germans captured at Stalingrad. The opposition was encouraged and nurtured by the Soviets, and some German officers and men, many of high rank and reputation at home, formed a "National Committee of Free Germany" and addressed their manifesto to all Germans, armed and unarmed, in July 1943.

The appeal of the Free Germany movement represented a legitimate dimension of German opposition to Hitler but it was primarily a propaganda weapon ultimately under Soviet control. The German opposition was incapable of attempting an overthrow of the Hitler government, so it was of limited value to both Germany and the Allies. This stark fact was well understood by the people within Germany who began plotting against Hitler in 1941. The difficulty of securing a unity of goals, while preparing a physical assault and reconciling changing personnel, civilian and military, in wartime proved insurmountable until 1944, when a plan emerged that appeared realizable. A fascinating report of German efforts to open negotiations with the Allies was compiled by the U. S. Office of Strategic Services (OSS) in May 1944 (191).

The attempt against Hitler's life on July 20, 1944, unfortunately failed, and the Nazi leader escaped, shaken but generally unharmed (192). The Fuehrer himself broadcast the details of the event the next day (193).

The news of the abortive assassination and the reaction to Hitler's "version" of what was behind the attempt and exactly what transpired varied, but essentially the mood was negative. After all, the course of the war was already decided and Hitler's death would not alter the outcome. The German struggle might have been shortened, but the Allies had come too far to compromise, and the consensus was to pursue the goal of Germany's total surrender. Victory was close and Europe was being liberated from German control at an exhilarating pace (194). The news of an attack on Hitler's life could not compete with the euphoria of freedom close at hand (195).

184. Fuehrer Conference, July 16, 1941[1] (Excerpts)

A conference attended by Reichsleiter Rosenberg, Reich Minister Lammers, Field Marshal Keitel, the Reichsmarschall, and me was held today by order of the Führer at 3:00 p. m. in his quarters. The conference began at 3:00 p. m. and, including a break for coffee, lasted until about 8:00 p. m.

By way of introduction the Führer emphasized that he wished first of all to make some basic statements. Various measures were now necessary; this was confirmed, among other events, by an assertion made in an impudent Vichy newspaper that the war against the Soviet Union was Europe's war and that therefore, it had to be conducted for Europe as a whole. Apparently the Vichy paper meant to say by these hints that it ought not to be the Germans alone who benefited from this war, but that all European states ought to benefit from it.

It was essential that we not proclaim our aims before the whole world; also this was not necessary, but the chief thing was that we ourselves know what we wanted. In no case should our own way be made more difficult by superfluous declarations. Such declarations were superfluous because we could do everything wherever we had the power, and what was beyond our power we would not be able to do anyway.

What we told the world about the motives for our measures ought to be conditioned, therefore, by tactical reasons. We ought to proceed here in exactly the same way as we did in the cases of Norway, Denmark, Holland, and Belgium. In these cases too we said nothing about our aims, and if we were clever we would continue in the same way.

We shall then emphasize again that we were forced to occupy, administer, and secure a certain area; it was in the interest of the inhabitants that we provide order, food, traffic, etc., hence our measures. It should not be recognizable that thereby a final settlement is being initiated! We can nevertheless take all necessary measures—shooting, resettling, etc.—and we shall take them.

But we do not want to make any people into enemies prematurely and unnecessarily. Therefore we shall act as though we wanted to exercise a mandate only. It must be clear to us, however, that we shall never withdraw from these areas.

Accordingly we should act:

1. To do nothing which might obstruct the final settlement, but to prepare for it only in secret;

2. To emphasize that we are liberators.

In particular:

The Crimea has to be evacuated by all foreigners and to be settled by Germans only.

. . . .

In principle we have now to face the task of cutting up the giant cake according to our needs, in order to be able: first, to dominate it; second, to administer it; and third, to exploit it.

The Russians have now given an order for partisan warfare behind our front. This partisan war again has some advantages for us; it enables us to exterminate everyone who opposes us.

Principles:

Never again must it be possible to create a military power west of the Urals, even if we have to wage war for a hundred years in order to attain this goal. All successors of the Führer must know: Security for the Reich exists only if there are no foreign military forces west of the Urals; it is Germany who undertakes the protection of this area against all possible dangers. Our iron principle must be and must remain:

We must never permit anybody but the Germans to carry arms!

This is especially important; even when it seems easier at first to enlist the armed support of foreign, subjugated nations, it is wrong to do so. This will prove some day to be to our disadvantage absolutely and unavoidably. Only the German may carry arms, not the Slav, not the Czech, not the Cossack, nor the Ukrainian!

. . . .

Even if we divide up certain areas at once, we shall always proceed in the role of protectors of the Right and of the population. The terms which are necessary at this time should be selected in accordance with this principle: We shall not speak of new Reich territory, but of the task which became necessary because of the war.

In particular:

In the Baltic territory the country up to the Düna will now have to be administered in agreement with Field Marshal Keitel.

Reichsleiter Rosenberg emphasizes that in his opinion a different treatment of the population is desirable in every Commissariat. In the Ukraine we should start with attention to cultural matters; there we ought to awaken the historical consciousness of the Ukrainians, establish a university at Kiev, and the like.

The Reichsmarschall on the other hand states that we have to think first of securing our food supply; everything else can come later.

(Incidental question: Is there still anything like an educated stratum in the Ukraine, or do upper class Ukrainians exist only as emigrants outside present day Russia?)

Rosenberg continues, also in the Ukraine certain efforts toward independence should be encouraged.

The Reichsmarschall asks the Führer to indicate what areas had been promised to other states.

The Führer replies, Antonescu desired Bessarabia and Odessa with a strip (of land) leading west-northwest from Odessa.

Upon objections made by the Reichsmarschall and Rosenberg, the Führer replies that the new frontiers desired by Antonescu contained little outside the old Rumanian frontiers.

The Führer stresses furthermore that nothing definite had been promised to the Hungarians, Turks, and Slovaks.

The Führer then submits for consideration whether the former Austrian part of Galicia ought to be added immediately to the General Government; upon objections being voiced the Führer decides that this part shall not be added to the General Government but shall only be placed at the same time under Reich Minister Frank (Lwów).

The Reichsmarschall considers it right to assign East Prussia several parts of the Baltic region, e.g., the Forest of Bialystok.

The Führer emphasizes that the entire Baltic area must become Reich territory.

Likewise the Crimea, including a considerable hinterland (the area north of the Crimea) must become Reich territory; the hinterland must be as large as possible.

Rosenberg had misgivings about this because of the Ukrainians living there.

(Incidentally: It appeared several times that Rosenberg has a soft spot for the Ukrainians; thus he wishes to enlarge the former Ukraine to a considerable extent.)

The Führer emphasizes further that the Volga colony too will have to become Reich territory, also the district around Baku; the latter will have to become a German concession (military colony).

. . . .

Rosenberg then states he had received a letter from Ribbentrop who desired the participation of the Foreign Ministry; but he asked the Führer to state that the internal organization of the newly acquired areas was no concern of the Foreign Ministry. The Führer absolutely shares this view. For the time being it will suffice for the Foreign Ministry to appoint a liaison officer to Reichsleiter Rosenberg.

. . . .

Reichsleiter Rosenberg then broached the question of providing for the security of the administration.

The Führer tells the Reichsmarschall and the Field Marshal that he had always urged that the police regiments be provided with armored cars; this has proved to be most necessary for police operations within the newly-occupied eastern territories, because a police regiment equipped with the appropriate number of armored cars of course could perform much service. Otherwise though, the Führer pointed out the security protection was very thin. However, the Reichsmarschall was going to transfer all his training fields to the new territories, and if necessary even Junker 52's could drop bombs in case of riots. Naturally this giant area would have to be pacified as quickly as possible; the best solution was to shoot anybody who looked askance.

Field Marshal Keitel emphasizes that the inhabitants themselves ought to be made responsible for their affairs because it was of course impossible to put a sentry in front of every shed or railway station. The inhabitants had to understand that anybody who did not perform his duties properly would be shot, and that they would be held responsible for every offense.

Upon a question of Reichsleiter Rosenberg the Führer replied that newspapers, e.g., for the Ukraine too, would have to be reestablished, in order to obtain means of influencing the inhabitants.

185. HITLER'S "NIGHT AND FOG" DECREE, DECEMBER 7, 1941[2]

Secret

The Fuehrer and Supreme Commander of the Armed Forces
Directives for the Prosecution of Criminal Acts against the
Reich or the Occupying Power in the Occupied Territories
of 7 December 1941

Since the beginning of the Russian campaign, Communist elements and other anti-German circles have increased their assaults against the Reich and the occupation force in the occupied territories. The extent and the danger of these activities necessitate the most severe measures against the malefactors in order to intimidate them. To begin with, the following directives should be observed:

I

In case of criminal acts committed by non-German civilians and which are directed against the Reich or the occupation force, endangering their safety or striking force, the death penalty is indicated in principle.

II

Criminal acts contained in paragraph I, will on principle, be tried in the occupied territories only when it appears probable that death sentences are going to be passed on the offenders, or, at least, the main offenders, and if the trial and the execution of the death sentence can be carried out without delay. In other cases the offenders, or, at least, the main offenders, are to be taken to Germany.

III

Offenders who are being taken to Germany are subject to court martial procedure there only if particular military interests should require this. German and foreign agencies will be told upon inquiries on such offenders that they were arrested and that the state of the proceeding does not allow further information.

IV

The commanders in the occupied territories and the judicial authorities, within their jurisdiction, will be personally held responsible for the execution of this decree.

V

The Chief of the High Command of the Armed Forces will decide in which of the occupied territories this decree shall be applied. He is authorized to furnish explanations, to issue supplements, and implementation directives. The Reich Minister of Justice will issue implementation directives within his jurisdiction.

By Order:
The Chief of the High Command of the Armed Forces
[Signed] Keitel

186. WANNSEE PROTOCOL, JANUARY 20, 1942[3] (EXCERPTS)

At the beginning of the meeting the Chief of Security Police and the SD, SS Lieutenant General Heydrich, reported his entrustment by the Reich Marshal to service as Commissioner for the Preparation of the Final Solution of the European Jewish Problem and pointed out that the officials had been invited to the conference in order to clear up the fundamental problems. The Reich Marshal's request to have a draft submitted to him on the organizational, factual, and material requirements with respect to the Final Solution of the European Jewish Problem, necessitated this previous general consultation by all the central offices directly concerned, in order that there should be coordination in the policy.

The primary responsibility for the administrative handling of the Final Solution of the Jewish Problem will rest centrally with the Reich Leader SS and the Chief of the German Police (Chief of the Security Police and the SD)—regardless of geographic boundaries.

The Chief of the Security Police and the SD thereafter gave a brief review of the battle conducted up to now. The most important aspects are—

a. Forcing the Jews out of the various fields of the community life of the German people.

b. Forcing the Jews out of the living space of the German people.

In execution of these efforts there was undertaken—as the only possible provisional solution—the acceleration of the emigration of the Jews from Reich territory on an intensified and methodical scale.

By decree of the Reich Marshal, a Reich Central Office for Jewish Emigration was set up in January 1939, and the director of this office was entrusted to the Chief of the Security Police and the SD. It had in particular the task—

a. Of taking all steps for the preparation for an intensified emigration of the Jews.

b. Of steering the emigration stream.

c. Of expediting the emigration in individual cases.

The objective of these tasks was to clear the German living space of Jews in a legal way.

The disadvantages which such a forcing of emigration brought with it were clear to all the authorities. But in view of the lack of alternative solutions, they had to be accepted in the beginning.

. . . .

Meanwhile, in view of the dangers of an emigration during the war and in view of the possibilities in the East, the Reich Leader SS and Chief of the German Police had forbidden the emigrating of the Jews.

III. The emigration program has now been replaced by the evacuation of the Jews to the East as a further solution possibility, in accordance with previous authorization by the Fuehrer.

These actions are of course to be regarded only as a temporary substitute; nonetheless, here already, the coming Final Solution of the Jewish Question is of great importance.

In the course of this Final Solution of the European Jewish Problem, approximately 11 million Jews are involved. They are distributed among the individual countries as follows:

	Country	Number
A.	Original Reich Territory [Altreich]	131,800
	Austria	43,700
	Eastern Territories	420,000
	Government General	2,284,000
	Bialystok	400,000

Protectorate Bohemia and Moravia   74,200
Estonia—free of Jews
Latvia   3,500
Lithuania   34,000
Belgium   43,000
Denmark   5,600
France: Occupied territory   165,000
            Unoccupied territory   700,000
Greece   69,600
The Netherlands   160,800
Norway   1,300

B.   Bulgaria   48,000
     England   330,000
     Finland   2,300
     Ireland   4,000
     Italy, including Sardinia   58,000
     Albania   200
     Croatia   40,000
     Portugal   3,000
     Rumania, including Bessarabia   342,000
     Sweden   8,000
     Switzerland   18,000
     Serbia   10,000
     Slovakia   88,000
     Spain   6,000
     Turkey (European part)   55,500
     Hungary   742,800
     U. S. S. R. 5,000,000
          Ukraine 2,994,684
          White Russia, excluding Bialystok   446,484
                    TOTAL   over   11,000,000

In the Jewish population figures given for the various foreign countries
however, only those of Jewish faith are included as the stipulations for
defining Jews along racial lines still are in part lacking there.

....

Under proper direction the Jews should now in the course of the Final
Solution be brought to the East in a suitable way for use as labor. In big labor
gangs, with separation of the sexes, the Jews capable of work are brought to
these areas and employed in road building, in which task undoubtedly a
great part will fall out through natural diminution.

The remnant that finally is able to survive all this—since this is undoubtedly the part with the strongest resistance—must be treated accordingly
since these people, representing a natural selection, are to be regarded as the
germ cell of a new Jewish development. (See the experience of history.)

In the program of the practical execution of the Final Solution, Europe is combed through from the West to the East. The Reich area, including the Protectorate of Bohemia and Moravia, will have to be taken in advance, alone, for reasons of the housing problem and other social and political necessities.

The evacuated Jews are brought first group by group into the so-called transit ghettos, in order to be transported from there farther to the East.

An important prerequisite for the whole execution of the evacuation, so SS Lieutenant General Heydrich explained further, is the exact establishment of the category of persons who are to be included.

It is intended not to evacuate Jews over 65 years of age, but to remove them to a ghetto for the aged—Theresienstadt is under consideration.

Along with these old age classes of the perhaps 280,000 Jews who on 31 October 1941 were in Germany proper and in Austria—perhaps 30 percent are over 65 years old—there will also be taken into the ghettos for the aged the Jews who are serious war wounded cases and Jews with war decorations (Iron Cross, First Class). With this appropriate solution the many petitions for exceptions will be eliminated with one blow.

The beginning of the individual larger evacuation actions will be very much dependent on the military development. With regard to the handling of the Final Solution in the European areas occupied and influenced by us, it was proposed that the competent officials in the Foreign Office should confer with the competent specialists of the Security Police and the SD.

In Slovakia and Croatia the matter is no longer too difficult as the most essential problems in this respect have already been solved there. In Rumania likewise the government has meanwhile appointed a Commissioner for Jewish Affairs. For settling the problem in Hungary it will be necessary in the near future to force upon the Hungarian Government acceptance of an adviser on Jewish problems.

With regard to taking up the preparations for the settling of the problem in Italy, SS Lieutenant General Heydrich thinks a liaison with the Police Chief in these matters is suitable.

In occupied and unoccupied France the taking of the Jews for evacuation can in all probability proceed without great difficulties.

Under State Secretary Luther stated at this point that in a more basic treatment of this problem in a few countries, such as in the northern countries, difficulties would come up, and it is therefore advisable to postpone these countries for the time being. In consideration of the small number of Jews in question there this postponement constitutes no appreciable limitation anyway.

On the other hand, the Foreign Office sees no great difficulties for the south and west of Europe.

SS Major General Hofmann intends to ask to have an official of the Race and Settlement Main Office sent along to Hungary for general orientation, when the affair is started there by the Chief of the Security Police and the SD. It was decided to assign this official of the Race and Settlement Main Office, who is not to be active, temporarily in the official capacity of assistant to the Police Attaché.

IV. In the course of the Final Solution plans, the Nuernberg Laws are in a certain degree to form the basis, and accordingly the complete settlement of the problem is to include also the solution of the mixed marriage and the Mischling problems.

In connection with a letter of the Chief of the Reich Chancellery, the Chief of the Security Police and the SD discussed the following points, for the time being theoretically:

1. Treatment of the first degree Mischlings.—First degree Mischlings [Persons Partly Jewish] are to be treated the same as the Jews as regards the Final Solution of the Jewish Problem. From this treatment exception will be made in the case of—

a. First degree Mischlings married to persons of German blood, from whose marriage there are children (2d degree Mischlings). These second degree Mischlings are to have essentially the same position as Germans.

b. First degree Mischlings for whom the exception approvals for certain groups have been accorded previously by the highest authorities of the Party and the State.

Each individual case must be examined and the possibility is not to be excluded that the decision may be retaken in the Mischling's disfavor.

Conditions for the granting of an exception must always be the fundamental merits of the Mischling concerned himself. (Not merits of the racial German parent or marriage partner.)

The first degree Mischling excepted from the evacuation is to be sterilized in order to prevent any offspring and to settle the Mischling problem once and for all. The sterilization takes place on a voluntary basis. It is, however, the condition for remaining in the Reich. The sterilized Mischling is afterwards to be free from all restrictive stipulations to which he has previously been subject.

2. Treatment of the second degree Mischlings.—The second degree Mischlings are to be treated in principle like persons of German blood with exception of the following cases in which the second degree Mischlings are to have the same position as Jews:

a. Derivation of the second degree Mischling from a bastard marriage (both parents Mischlings).

b. Racially especially unfavorable appearance of the second degree Mischling, so that even in appearance he is considered a Jew.

c. Especially bad police and political appraisal of the second degree Mischling which shows that he feels and conducts himself like a Jew.

But even in these cases exceptions are not to be made if the second degree Mischling is married to a person of German blood.

3. Marriages between full Jews and persons of German blood.
....

4. Marriages between first degree Mischlings and persons of German blood.
....

5. Marriages between first degree Mischlings and first degree Mischlings or Jews.
....

6. Marriages between first degree Mischlings and second degree Mischlings.

187. ALLIED DECLARATION ON GERMAN ATROCITIES, NOVEMBER 1, 1943[4]

THE UNITED KINGDOM, the United States and the Soviet Union have received from many quarters evidence of atrocities, massacres and cold-blooded mass executions which are being perpetrated by the Hitlerite forces in the many countries they have overrun and from which they are now being steadily expelled. The brutalities of Hitlerite domination are no new thing and all the peoples or territories in their grip have suffered from the worst form of government by terror. What is new is that many of these territories are now being redeemed by the advancing armies of the liberating Powers and that in their desperation, the recoiling Hitlerite Huns are redoubling the ruthless cruelties. This is now evidenced with particular clearness by monstrous crimes of the Hitlerites on the territory of the Soviet Union which is being liberated from the Hitlerites, and on French and Italian territory.

Accordingly, the aforesaid three allied Powers, speaking in the interests of the thirty-two [thirty-three] United Nations, hereby solemnly declare and give full warning of their declaration as follows:

At the time of the granting of any armistice to any government which may be set up in Germany, those German officers and men and members of the Nazi party who have been responsible for, or have taken a consenting part in the above atrocities, massacres and executions, will be sent back to the countries in which their abominable deeds were done in order that they may be judged and punished according to the laws of these liberated countries and of the free governments which will be created therein. Lists will be compiled in all possible detail from all these countries having regard especially to the invaded parts of the Soviet Union, to Poland and Czechoslovakia, to Yugoslavia and Greece, including Crete and other islands, to Norway, Denmark, the Netherlands, Belgium, Luxemburg, France and Italy.

Thus, the Germans who take part in wholesale shootings of Italian officers or in the execution of French, Dutch, Belgian or Norwegian hostages or of Cretan peasants, or who have shared in the slaughters inflicted on the people of Poland or in territories of the Soviet Union which are now being swept clear of the enemy, will know that they will be brought back to the scene of their crimes and judged on the spot by the peoples whom they have outraged. Let those who have hitherto not imbrued their hands with innocent blood beware lest they join the ranks of the guilty, for most assuredly the three allied Powers will pursue them to the uttermost ends of the earth and will deliver them to their accusers in order that justice may be done.

The above declaration is without prejudice to the case of the major criminals, whose offences have no particular geographical localisation and who will be punished by the joint decision of the Governments of the Allies.
(Signed):   Roosevelt
                                       Churchill
                                       Stalin

188. Greek 'National Bands' Agreement, July 1943[5]

1. All guerilla bands will be known for military purposes as the National Guerilla Bands of Greece, which title will be the only one used by Middle East. It is, of course, understood that each organisation may use its own names within Greece and its own system of command.

2. Greece shall be divided into military areas appointed as independent territorial districts. In an area where there are bands of only one organisation, all military decisions will be taken by its HQ in accordance with the orders of the Joint GHQ. In an area where there is more than one organisation, the different bands will co-operate fully in all military actions, either under a joint HQ of the area appointed by the co-operating bands, or under a commander appointed by the Joint GHQ after consultation with the respective commanders and the British Liaison Officer of the area concerned. In special circumstances the Joint GHQ may itself appoint a commander to execute an operation ordered by the Middle East.

3. The bands of one area will not enter another area except in cases of emergency, or as a result of mutual agreement of the respective directing authorities, or as a result of an order issued by Joint GHQ in accordance with the military requirements of the Middle East. This clause aims at the insurance of the proper distribution of forces with regard to the local military requirements.

4. All guerillas of one organisation recognise the guerillas of another organisation. Every guerilla is free to voice his opinion on any matter in public, provided he does not denounce or say anything against other guerilla bands, their principles or ideals, or against any member of another organisation.

5. Any organisations or persons are free to raise guerilla bands in any area so long as they accept the conditions of the agreement and come under the orders of the Joint GHQ. All guerillas within the same area have equal rights. Any disputes will be settled by common agreement of HQs of the respective bands or, if necessary, by the Joint GHQ.

6. All guerilla bands in the plains will help guerilla bands and the civil population in the mountains in the supply of food. The Joint GHQ reserves the rights to arrange by mutual agreement between the different organisations the distribution of food supplies in cases of shortages.

7. The bands of different areas will give maximum assistance to each other in cases of military action against the enemy, either when asked by the commander concerned, or of their own accord when the situation demands it. In cases of general action, orders from Joint GHQ should state the extent of help to be given.

8. There must be no barbarism against anyone by any member of any guerilla band. No one must be kept under permanent arrest or be executed without fair trial and complete proof of the facts.

9. Any Greek guerilla who in the past or up to the date of the signing of this agreement has transferred his allegiance to another organisation will be given complete amnesty. All Greeks enlisting as guerillas have been and will be free to join any organisation they wish.

10. All military stores now being sent to Greece should be accepted as a gesture of the United Nations' appreciation of the great and gallant effort being made by their Greek allies to resist and overthrow the Axis. The distribution of stores will be undertaken by Joint GHQ. Any area contravening these conditions will have supplies stopped.

11. For the better direction of the struggle, and for the co-ordination of all military actions, a Joint GHQ will be formed, composed of representatives of all guerilla bands recognised throughout Greece or occupying large areas, as well as a representative of Middle East. Similar Joint HQs may be formed for areas and smaller districts, according to the strength of the different bands. All smaller independent bands may be represented on the Joint GHQ by liaison officers.

12. The role of the British officers attached to Joint HQs shall be that of liaison officers to Middle East. In cases of disputes between co-operating bands affecting the requirements of Middle East, the nearest British Liaison Officer will be immediately informed.

NOTE.—These terms are to be published in the Press, read to all guerillas, and will be broadcast on the Cairo and London radio stations.

189. Churchill Speech to House of Commons, February 22, 1944[6] (Excerpts)

I must now turn from actual military operations to the European political scene which influences all military affairs so vehemently. In this war of so many nations against the Nazi tyranny there has at least been a common principle at work throughout Europe, and among the conquered peoples there is a unity of hatred and desire to revolt against the Germans such as has never been known against any race before. The penalties of national defeat are frightful. After the blinding flash of catastrophe, the stunning blow, the gaping wounds, there comes the onset of the diseases of defeat. The central principle of the nation's life is broken and all healthy normal control vanishes.

There are few societies that can withstand the conditions of subjugation. Indomitable patriots take different paths, quislings and collaborationists of all kinds abound, guerilla leaders, each with their personal followers, quarrel and fight. There are already in Greece and Yugoslavia factions engaged in civil war one with another and animated by hatreds more fierce than those which should be reserved for the common foe. Among all these varied forces the German oppressor develops his intrigues with cynical ruthlessness and merciless cruelty. It is hard enough to understand the politics of one's own country; it is almost impossible to understand those of foreign countries. The sanest and safest course for us to follow is to judge all parties and factions dispassionately by the test of their readiness and ability to fight the Germans, and thus lighten the burden of the Allied troops. It is no time for ideological prejudices for one side or the other, and certainly we have not indulged ourselves in this way at all. Thus in Italy we are working for the present through the Government of the King and Badoglio, in Yugoslavia we give our aid to Marshal Tito, in Greece, in spite of the fact that a British officer was murdered by the guerilla organisation called 'Elas,' we are doing our best to bring about a reconciliation or at least a working agreement between the opposing forces.

I will say a word about each of these unhappy countries; the principle which should govern us and which we are certainly following. We signed the Italian armistice on the basis of unconditional surrender with King Victor Emanuel and Marshal Badoglio, who were, and up to the present are, the legitimate Government of Italy. On their authority the Italian Navy, not without risk and loss, surrendered to us, and practically all Italian troops and airmen who were not dominated by the Germans also obeyed the orders they received from the Crown. Since then these Italian forces have co-operated with us to the best of their ability and nearly 100 Italian ships of war are discharging valuable services in the Mediterranean and the Atlantic. Italian troops have entered the front line in Italy, and although on one occasion they suffered severe casualties they continue to fight alongside our men. Very much larger numbers are engaged in indispensable services to the Allied armies behind the front. Italian airmen are also fighting at our side. The battle in Italy, for reasons which I have explained, will be hard and long. I am not yet convinced that any other Government can be formed at the present time in Italy which would command the same obedience from the Italian armed forces.

. . . .

On the other side of the Adriatic, in the vast mountain regions of Yugoslavia, Albania, and Greece, an area of perhaps 800 miles from north to south and 300 or 400 miles from east to west, the magnificent resistance to the German invaders is in full and violent progress. With the surrender of

Italy, with which I think Great Britain had something to do, having fought the Italians since the summer of 1940, 62 Italian divisions ceased to be a hostile fighting factor. Forty-three were disbanded and enslaved, apparently without any of the safeguards which attach to prisoners of war, by the Germans; 10 were disbanded by the guerrillas in the Balkans; and 9, which were stationed in the south of Italy or in Corsica and Sardinia, came over to the Allies. Confronted with this situation, Hitler decided to reinforce the Balkan Peninsula heavily, and at the present time no fewer than 20 German divisions are engaged in the Balkans. That is to say, there are 25 German divisions in Italy, of which 18 are in the present battle south of Rome, and another 20 are spread over the vast area of the Balkans.

In Yugoslavia, in spite of the most ferocious and murderous cruelties and reprisals perpetrated by the Germans not only against hostages but against the village populations, including women and children, the Partisan forces have the upper hand. The Germans hold the principal towns and try to keep the railways working. They can march their columns of troops hither and thither about the country. They own the ground they stand on but nothing else. All the rest belongs to the valiant Partisans. The German losses have been very heavy, and so far as actual fighting is concerned, greatly exceed the losses of the Partisans, but the killing of hostages and civilians in cold blood adds to the German score, and adds to our score against the Germans.

In Yugoslavia two main forces are engaged in the field. First, there are the guerrilla bands under Gen. Mihailovitch. These were the first to take the field, and represent to a certain extent the forces of old Serbia. For some time after the defeat of the Yugoslav Army, these forces maintained a guerrilla [sic]. We were not able to send them any aid or supplies, except a few droppings from aeroplanes. The Germans retaliated for any guerrilla activities by shooting batches of 400 or 500 people in Belgrade. Gen. Mihailovitch, I much regret to say, drifted gradually into the position where some of his commanders made accommodations with the Italian and German troops, which resulted in their being left alone in certain mountain areas and in return doing very little or nothing against the enemy. However, a new and far more formidable champion appeared on the scene. In the autumn of 1941 Marshal Tito's Partisans began a wild and furious war for existence against the Germans. They wrested weapons from the Germans' hands; they grew in numbers rapidly; no reprisals, however bloody, whether upon hostages or the villages, deterred them. For them, it was death or freedom. Soon they began to inflict heavy injury upon the Germans and became masters of wide regions. Led with great skill, organised on the guerrilla principle, they were at once elusive and deadly. They were here, there, and everywhere. Large-scale offensives have been launched against them by the Germans, but in every case the Partisans, even when surrounded, have escaped, after inflicting great losses and toll upon the enemy.

The Partisan movement soon outstripped in numbers the forces of Gen. Mihailovitch. Not only Croats and Slovenes, but large numbers of Serbians joined with Marshal Tito, and he has at this moment more than 250,000 men with him and large quantities of arms taken from the enemy or from the Italians. These men are organised, without losing their guerrilla qualities, into a considerable number of divisions and corps. The whole movement has taken shape and form without losing the guerrilla quality without which it could not possibly succeed. These forces are, at this moment, holding in check no fewer than 14 out of 20 German divisions in the Balkans. Around and within these heroic forces, a national and unifying movement has developed. The Communist element had the honour of being the beginners, but as the movement increased in strength and numbers, a modifying and unifying process has taken place, and national conceptions have supervened. In Marshal Tito the Partisans have found an outstanding leader, glorious in the fight for freedom.

. . . .

I took occasion to raise personally with Marshal Stalin the question of the future of Poland. I pointed out that it was in fulfilment of our guarantee to Poland that Great Britain declared war upon Nazi Germany, that we had never weakened in our resolve, even during the period when we were all alone, and that the fate of the Polish nation holds a prime place in the thoughts and policy of H.M. Government and the British Parliament. It was with great pleasure that I heard from Marshal Stalin that he, too, was resolved upon the creation and maintenance of a strong, integral, independent Poland as one of the leading powers of Europe. He has several times repeated these declarations in public, and I am convinced that they represent the settled policy of the Soviet Union. I may remind the House that we ourselves have never in the past guaranteed, on behalf of H.M. Government, any particular frontier line to Poland. We did not approve of the Polish occupation of Vilna in 1920. The British view in 1919 stands expressed in the so-called Curzon Line, which attempted to deal, at any rate partially, with the problem. I have always held the opinion that all questions of territorial settlement and readjustment should stand over until the end of the war, and that the victorious Powers should then arrive at formal and final agreement governing the articulation of Europe as a whole. That is still the wish of H. M. Government. However, the advance of the Russian armies into Polish regions in which the Polish underground army is active makes it indispensable that some kind of friendly working agreement should be arrived at to govern the wartime conditions and enable all anti-Hitlerite forces to work together with the greatest advantage against the common foe. During the last few weeks the Foreign Secretary and I have laboured with the Polish Government in London with the object of establishing a working arrangement upon which the fighting forces can act, and upon which, I trust, an increasing structure of good will and comradeship may be built between Russia and Poland.

I have an intense sympathy with the Poles, that heroic race whose national spirit centuries of misfortune cannot quench, but I also have sympathy with the Russian standpoint. Twice in our lifetime Russia has been violently assaulted by Germany. Many millions of Russians have been slain and vast tracts of Russian soil devastated as a result of repeated German aggression. Russia has the right to reassurance against future attacks from the West, and we are going all the way with her to see that she gets it, not only by the might of her arms but by the approval and assent of the United Nations. The liberation of Poland may presently be achieved by the Russian armies, after these armies have suffered millions of casualties in breaking the German military machine. I cannot feel that the Russian demand for reassurance about her western frontiers goes beyond the limits of what is reasonable or just. Marshal Stalin and I also agreed upon the need for Poland to obtain compensation at the expense of Germany both in the north and in the west.

190. MEMORANDUM OF THE BISHOP OF CHICHESTER OF JUNE 1942 ABOUT A TALK WITH PASTOR SCHONFELD AND DIETRICH BONHOEFFER AND EDEN LETTER OF JULY 17, 1942[7]

I

At the end of May two German pastors [SCHONFELD and BONHOEF-FER] came from Berlin to Stockholm to meet the Bishop of Chichester there. They arrived independently of each other and one of them only stayed 48 hours [BONHOEFFER]. The bishop talked with them individually as well as together on four different days. Both men are well-known to the bishop and have worked together with him for many years in connection with the ecumenical movement, the world church council and in various stages of the German ecclesiastical fight. One of them lives in Switzerland but visits Germany continuously. The other lives in Berlin and is one of the leaders of the confessional church; the "Gestapo" has prohibited him from speaking or preaching.

Their intention was:

A. To give information about a strong organized resistance movement within Germany which has worked out plans for the overthrow of the whole HITLER regime (including HIMMLER, GÖRING, GOEBBELS, the ringleaders of the "Gestapo," the "SS" and the "SA") and for the establishment of a new German government, consisting of:

1. Representatives of strongly anti-National Socialist forces in the army and the central state administration.

2. Former trade-union leaders.

3. Representatives of the Protestant and Catholic churches.

They commit themselves to the following policy:

(a) Renunciation of agression [sic]

(b) Immediate abolition of the Nuremberg Laws and cooperation for an international solution of the Jewish problem.

(c) Gradual retreat of the German forces from the occupied and assaulted contries [sic].

(d) Withdrawal of the support of Japan, and instead support of the Allies in order to finish the war in the Far East.

(e) Cooperation with the Allies to rebuild the areas which were destroyed or damaged by war.

B. To ask whether the Allies, under the presupposition that the whole of the HITLER regime has been overthrown, would be ready to negotiate a peace settlement with a new German Government which would provide the following:

1. The establishment of a system of law and social justice in Germany, combined with a far-reaching distribution of responsibilities to the individual states.

2. The creation of economic interdependence among the various nations of Europe, a step which would be justified in itself as well as being the most effective guarantee against militarism.

3. The establishment of a representative federation of free nations or states which would include a free Polish and a free Czech nation.

4. The establishment of a European army for the control of Europe under central leadership in which the German army could participate.

II

CHARACTER OF THE OPPOSITION

The opposition had already been developing or [sic] some time and already existed before the war. Now the war gives it an opportunity that only waits to be seized. The opposition crystallized in the autumn of 1941 and could have seized an opportunity in 1941, when many officers refused to continue to fight in Russia. But nobody took the leadership.

HITLER's last speech, in which he claimed quite openly to stand above all law, showed the full lawlessness of the regime more and more clearly to the German people. The opposition has full trust in the strength of the German army and is willing to continue fighting the war to its bitter end in case the Allies should refuse to negotiate with the new government of a Germany freed from HITLER, after the overthrow of the whole HITLER regime; but it believes, too, that the continuation of the war, on the present or a still greater scale, under these circumstances would sentence still further millions to destruction, especially in the occupied countries. It also believes that a continuation of the fight to a decision would be suicidal in Europe. From that springs the wish first to destroy HITLER and his regime and then to reach a peace settlement under which all nations of Europe would become economically dependent upon each other, by which means they would be allied in some way or other and would be defended against an aggression by possession of adequate European military forces. Although the opposition entertains some doubts in regard to Russia, it nevertheless hopes (based on impressions which some higher Russian officers have made on German officers) for the possibility of reaching an understanding.

III

ORGANIZATION OF THE OPPOSITION

The opposition is based on members of the state administration, the state police, on former trade-union leaders and high officers of the army. It has connections in each ministry, military official in all large cities, commanding officers, and others who are in key positions in close proximity to the generals. It has armed contact men in the broadcasting stations, in the big factories, in the main offices of army supply and gas supply. It is impossible to give the figures of the opposition. The main thing is that everywhere key positions are in the hands of members of the opposition and that key positions are of great importance in Germany.

The following names were supplied, of men who are said to be closed [sic] connected with the resistance movement:

General BECK	chief of the general staff before the Czechoslovakian crisis in 1938, 60 years old
General VON HAMMERSTEIN	chief of the general staff before BECK
GOERDELER	ex-commissioner of prices, mayor of Leipzig. Leader of the civilian front
LEUSCHNER	former president of the United Trade Unions
KAISER	leader of the Catholic Trade Unions

All persons mentioned above are said to be convinced Christians, the most important of them being BECK and GOERDELER.

Certain other persons of a less pronounced Christian character would be available, as for instance SCHACHT. Most of the field marshals are trustworthy, especially VON KLUGE, VON BOCK, KÜCHLER and possibly WITZLEBEN. It was asked whether England would favour a monarchy in Germany, in which case Prince LOUIS FERDINAND would be considered. But it was not said whether he is a member of the opposition or not. After the death in action of the oldest son of the Crown Prince, he had been fetched by HITLER from the United States. He had served in the FORD factory as a worker and is now living on an estate in East Prussia. He is a Christian, shows honest social interest and is known to one of the German pastors. The leaders of the Protestant and Catholic churches are also in close relationship with the resistance movement as a whole, particularly Bishop WURM from Wurttemberg (Protestant) and Bishop PREYSING from Berlin, who is acting as spokesman of the Catholic bishops. (At the same time it should be mentioned that many members of the opposition are not only filled with deep repentance about the crimes which are committed in the name of Germany, but even say: "A Christian does not wish to evade any atonement or any chaos that God's will lays upon him.")

IV

PROCEDURE OF THE OPPOSITION

The opposition knows about the threatened rebellion against HITLER within the Nazi party by HIMMLER and his comrades; but while a successful coup d'état by HIMMLER could be useful to the opposition, a total overthrow of HITLER and HIMMLER and the whole regime is indispensable. The plan of the opposition consists in a cleaning-up operation which would have to be carried through at home and in the occupied countries as simultaneously as possible. After that, a new government would be set up. The opposition is aware of the necessity of an effective police control everywhere in Germany and in the occupied and assaulted countries in order to safeguard the new government; and it appears as if the presence of the Allied army as helper in maintaining order would be necessary and welcome, the more so if it were possible to combine with the Allied army the army of a neutral power for this maintenance of order.

V

QUESTIONS OF THE OPPOSITION DIRECTED TO THE GOVERN-MENTS OF THE ALLIES

Now that the procedure and the plans of the opposition have been presented, the question arises of what support can be given to its leaders in order to start the operation and to cope with all dangers connected with it. For example, questions like the following are posed:

1. Would the Allied governments be willing to negotiate bona fide for a peace as it has been described in paragraph I, B with a new German government which is set up along the guiding principles of paragraph I, A?

(The answer to that could be given privately to a representative of the opposition by way of a neutral country.)

2. Could the Allies now declare publicly to the world and in the clearest words that if HITLER and the whole regime is overthrown they would be willing to talk with a new German government with a view toward reaching a peace settlement of kind as described in paragraph I, B, which renounces every aggression and commits itself to a mode of procedure as described in paragraph I, A?

VI

METHODS OF COMMUNICATION

Agreements were made by which every reaction of influential British authorities of which the Bishop of Chichester should learn can be imparted via neutral channels. The British Ambassador in Stockholm was also fully informed about the contents of the talks. On his advice the Bishop of Chichester let the two Germans [sic] pastors know that of necessity not only the American and Russian and other Allied governments as well would be concerned by this, but that the Foreign Office might be of the opinion that the situation is much too uncertain to justify an exchange of opinion of any kind. If, however, on the other hand it would be thought desirable to receive further enlightenment, a confidential meeting between a German representative of the Foreign Office or any other suitable person could be arranged in Stockholm.

. . . .

EDEN LETTER TO THE BISHOP OF CHICHESTER
Personal and confidential

Foreign Office, S.W. 1
17th July, 1942

My dear Bishop,

When you visited me on 30th June you were kind enough to let me have a memorandum on your talk with two German pastors whom you had met in

Stockholm at the end of May, together with a report on a statement by one of the pastors.

These interesting documents have by now been carefully examined. Without challenging the honest conviction of your informers in the least, I have no doubt that it would be contrary to the interest of our nation to provide them with any answer whatever. I know well that this decision will be somewhat disappointing to you, but in view of the delicate circumstances connected with it I cannot do other than ask you to accept it, something that you will surely understand.

Sincerely yours,

ANTHONY EDEN

191. OVERTURES TO THE U. S. BY GERMAN (MILITARY AND CIVILIAN) OPPOSITION FOR SEPARATE PEACE, 1944[8]

Washington, May 16, 1944.

1. Since early 1944 the OSS representative in Bern has been approached periodically by two emissaries of a German group proposing to attempt an overthrow of the Nazi regime. The group includes Leuschner, socialist leader and former Minister of Interior in Hesse; Oster, a general formerly the righthand man of Canaris, arrested in 1943 by the Gestapo, kept under surveillance after his release, and recently discharged from official functions by Keitel; Goerdler, former Major of Leipzig; and General Beck. The last two men have been described by the OSS representatives as leaders of the group; it is from them that the two emissaries have brought proposals for negotiation.

2. Early in April the emissaries talked with the OSS representative in Bern, conveying the suggestion of a deal between this German opposition group and the Western Allies. The group expressed their willingness and preparation to attempt ousting Hitler and the Nazis. They stated their belief that the time in which successful action could be carried out was rapidly shortening. They said they were the only group able to profit by personal approach to Hitler and other Nazi chiefs, and the only one controlling enough arms and enough influence in the Wehrmacht to accomplish the purpose of Nazi overthrow. The group stated that the German generals now commanding in the West—particularly Rundstedt and Falkenhausen— would be ready to cease resistance and aid Allied landings, once the Nazis had been ousted. They thought that similar arrangements might be worked out for the reception of Allied airborne forces at strategic points in Germany. While ready to attempt a coup, the group did not guarantee success.

3. The condition on which the group expressed willingness to act was that they would deal directly with the Western Allies alone after overthrowing the Nazi regime. As precedent for excluding the USSR from all negotiations they cited the recent example of Finland, which they said dealt solely with Moscow. The group based this condition on the conservative character of their membership and supporters. However, the group declared their will-

ingness to cooperate with any leftist elements except the Communists; in February they had described Leuschner as an acceptable type of head for an interim government, assuming that neither the military nor the Communists would dominate during the transition period. The group feared political and ideological sway over Central Europe by Bolshevism, with a mere exchange of Nazi totalitarianism for a totalitarianism of the radical left accompanied by the submergence of democracy and Christian culture. They stated that if capitulation were to be made primarily to the Soviet Union, it would have to be carried out by another group in Germany.

4. The OSS representative expressed to the emissaries his conviction that the United States and Great Britain would not act regarding Germany without the concert of Russia. In commenting on the opposition group's proposal, he expressed skepticism of their capability since Beck and Goerdler have been so prominently mentioned as potential leaders that the Gestapo must be aware of the situation and is only waiting to crack down until plans have gone farther or because the Gestapo may wish to keep an anchor to westward.

5. In May 1944, approximately one month after the April visit of the emissaries to the OSS representative, they received an oral message by courier from the opposition group. Now mentioned as members were also Halder, Zeitzler, Heusinger (chief of operations for Zeitzler), Olbr[i]cht (chief of the German Army Administration), Falkenhausen, and Rundstedt. The group was reported ready to help Allied units get into Germany if the Allies agreed that the Wehrmacht should continue to hold the Eastern Front. They proposed in detail: (1) three Allied airborne divisions should land in the Berlin region with the assistance of the local Army commanders, (2) major amphibious landings should be undertaken at or near Bremen and Hamburg, (3) landings in France should follow, although Rommel cannot be counted on for cooperation, (4) reliable German units in the area of Munich would isolate Hitler and other high Nazis in Ober Salzburg. The opposition group is reported to feel that Germany has lost the war and that the only chance of avoiding Communism in Germany is to facilitate occupation of as large a section of Europe as possible by American and British forces before collapse on the Eastern Front.

6. The emissaries, who had remained in Switzerland, replied to the courier that discussion of the plan would be unavailing because of the proviso concerning the USSR. Later the group dispatched to them a telegram advising no further action "for the time being." The emissaries think nevertheless that the subject is still open. They have characterized the group's proviso as unrealistic, and regard as the core of the proposal only the plan that American and British forces should become entrenched in Germany before the Russians; they urged that it was entirely a military matter if some of the German generals wish to assist the Allied invasion and try to take over the Nazi regime. The OSS representative reiterated to the emissaries that Great Britain and the United States would adhere to their Russian commitments. In answer to the objection that point (1) of the group's plan (paragraph 5, above, on page 3) might be regarded by the Allies as a trap,

they stated that since they were not military men they could only say that sufficient opportunity for requisite precautions would be presented in the form of direct prior contact with German military authorities. The emissaries said that Zeitzler had been won over by Heusinger and Olbr[i]cht; they added that he was preoccupied in respect of military matters with the Eastern Front, that he would cooperate in any plan to bring about a systematic liquidation of that front in order to escape the blame for a military disaster there—which he greatly fears.

7. One of the opposition group's emissaries acknowledged his lack of confidence in the political courage of the German generals, on the basis of past experience, and said the Allies might do well to ignore their proposition if there were assurance of early victory and a speedy Allied occupation of Germany. The OSS representative at Bern is convinced of the sincerity of this intermediary, as the result of investigation and of experience with him. The representative is of the opinion that there are some German generals who wish to liquidate their responsibility in the war by collaborating in the construction of an Anglo-American bulwark against the pressure of the USSR in Europe, and he is convinced that the two emissaries are in contact with such a group. Doubtful that the group would have the determination to act effectively at the appropriate time and sensitive to the problem of Soviet relations in the effectuation of any plan in which the group might participate, he believes that the group's activities may nevertheless be useful to undermine the morale of the top echelon in the Wehrmacht.

192. GERMAN NEWS RELEASE, JULY 20, 1944[9] (6:20 p. m.)

"An attempt on the life of the Führer was made with high explosives to-day. The following persons of his entourage were severely injured: Lt.-Gen. Schmundt, Col. Brandt, and collaborator Berger. Slighter injuries were suffered by Col.-Gen. Jodl, as well as by Generals Korten, Buhl, Bodenschatz, Heusinger, and Scherff, Lt.-Col. Borgmann, Admirals Voss and von Puttkamer, and Naval Captain Assman. Hitler received slight burns and a concussion, but no injuries. He at once began work again. He then received Mussolini for a long meeting as previously arranged. Shortly after the attempt Marshal Göring came to Hitler."

193. HITLER BROADCAST, JULY 21, 1944[10] (EXCERPT)

"For the third time an attempt on my life has been planned and carried out. If I speak to you to-day it is first in order that you should hear my voice and that you should know that I myself am unhurt and well. Second, in order that you should know about a crime unparalleled in German history. A very small clique of ambitious, irresponsible, mad, and criminally stupid officers have formed a plot to eliminate me and the German Wehrmacht Command. The bomb was placed by Col. Count Stauffenberg. It exploded 2 metres to my right. One of those with me has died. A number of collaborators very dear to me were very severely injured. I myself sustained only some very minor scratches, bruises, and burns. I regard this as a confirmation of the task imposed on me by Providence to continue on the road of my life as I have done hitherto. For I may confess to the nation that since the days when I moved into the Wilhelmstrasse I had only one thought—to dedicate my life ever since I realised that the war could no longer be postponed. I have lived for worry, work, and nothing but worry through days unnumbered and sleepless nights.

Suddenly, at a moment when the German army is engaged in a bitter struggle a small group emerged in Germany, just as in Italy, in the belief that they could repeat the 1918 stab in the back. But this time they have made a bad mistake. The circle of these conspirators is very small, and has nothing in common with the spirit of the German Wehrmacht, and above all none with the German people. It is a miniature group of criminal elements which will be ruthlessly exterminated. I therefore now order that no military authority, no leader of any unit, no private in the field is to obey any orders emanating from these groups of usurpers. I also order that it is everyone's duty to arrest, or, if they resist, to kill at sight anyone issuing or handing on such orders.

I have, therefore, to create order once and for all, nominated Reich-Minister Himmler to be C.-in-C. of the Home Army (Heimatheer). I have summoned Col.-Gen. Guderian to join my General Staff and to replace the Chief of the General Staff (Gen. Zeitzler) who has been taken to hospital. Another proved Eastern Front commander has been called in by me to assist him. There has been no change in any other office in the Reich.

I am convinced that with the emergence of this tiny clique of traitors and destroyers there has at long last been created in our rear that atmosphere which the fighting front needs. For is it possible that out there hundreds of thousands and millions of brave men sacrifice their lives, while at home a small, filthy, ambitious, self-seeking group should seek to sow the seeds of despair? This time we shall get quits with them in the way that National Socialists are accustomed. I am convinced that every decent officer, every gallant soldier, will comprehend this at this hour."

194. General Eisenhower's Broadcast on Morning of June 6, 1944 to People of Western Europe[11]

"I have this message for all of you. Although the initial assault may not have been made in your own country, the hour of your liberation is approaching. All patriots, men and women, young and old, have a part to play in the achievement of final victory. To members of resistance movements I say, 'Follow the instructions you have received.' To patriots who are not members of organised resistance groups I say, 'Continue your passive resistance, but do not needlessly endanger your lives; wait until I give you the signal to rise.'

Citizens of France! I am proud to have again under my command the gallant forces of France. Fighting beside their Allies, they will play a worthy part in the liberation of their homeland. Effective civil administration of France must be provided by Frenchmen. All persons must continue in their present duties unless otherwise instructed."

195. FRENCH PROVISIONAL GOVERNMENT PROCLAMATION, AUGUST 23, 1944[12]

"Aug. 23, 1944. Paris is free! The Provisional Government of the Republic salutes the dead and martyrs of Paris, as well as the soldiers of the Allied and French armies who have fallen in 5 years of battle. It pays homage to the National Council of Resistance; to the Paris Committee of Liberation; to the patriots who directed and inspired the fight against the enemy and his accomplices; to the people of Paris which has won its battle for freedom. Paris—risen to join in the war effort—stands in the vanguard for the ultimate battle for the liberation of the nations. Its fall had been a sign of mourning. Its liberation heralds victory. By their sacrifices and their immeasurable sufferings the people of Paris will have opened the road to new progress and new hopes. Vive Paris! Vive la liberté! Vive la République!"

Part 16. Independence Movements: Middle East, India, China, Indonesia

The impact of World War II upon the areas now referred to as the Third World was immense. Many of the long-range ramifications of that tumultuous impact are still with us and show no immediate signs of abatement. The history of Third World independence developed rapidly because the diverse forces of war hastened change and encouraged action. Europeans knew in 1940 that their world was being dramatically changed by contemporary events but they never anticipated the influence that change would have elsewhere.

During the course of the war the Allied and Axis powers occasionally issued statements referring to their colonial holdings or spheres of influence dominated by them prior to the war. Those statements were generally made within the larger context of their pursuit of victory, and they sought maximum support from allied or occupied subordinates. Many of the subordinate states found themselves on opposite sides, but that made little difference in their surge toward self-determination; the only common denominator in their drive for independence appeared to be their colonial or former colonial status.

Since colonial rule was a historical characteristic of western nation-states, the greater hostility was logically directed toward them rather than toward the Soviet Union. The Communist anti-imperialist philosophy was widely accepted by many independence leaders even before the onset of the war, which provided an unexpected opportunity, a revolutionary opportunity, to force the issue of independence. Japan secured broad support by promoting her own ambitious expansion under the banner of "Asia for the Asians."

The complexity of situations that involved people desirous of independence defies generalization, for no two instances were alike and any attempt to place these struggles in perspective within the vast canvas of World War II is extremely difficult. Actually, few of the new "nationalists" exerted much influence on the course of the war even though some of them successfully exploited the conflict for their own benefit and most eventually achieved independence.

The period 1939 to 1945 was climactic for the proponents of Zionism, a movement born in the 19th century to achieve the return of Jews to Palestine. Zionist leaders, buttressed by British support for a Jewish homeland (Balfour Declaration) and the creation of a Palestine mandate following World War I, were confident they would achieve full and guaranteed independence when World War II closed. However, Pan-Arabism was an equally powerful counterforce to any increase in Jewish settlement, and the conflict between Jew and Arab created a crisis in early 1939, when Great Britain announced a policy favoring restricted Jewish emigration to Palestine for a ten year period (White Paper).[1]

During the war Zionist supporters urged the establishment of an independent Jewish state in Palestine with control over its own immigration policy (Biltmore Program). Soon after the war in Europe the first Zionist conference since 1939 met in London in August 1945, and delegations from many nations—some newly liberated—listened to Zionist leaders articulate their feelings and hopes (196). Before the conference ended the membership achieved consensus on a political declaration condemning the British White Paper and pledging full support for the immediate establishment of a Jewish state from Palestine (197).

The Zionist position strengthened during the war and the Zionist arguments for full independence were sympathetically supported by the major powers. The question of an independent Jewish state was complicated because Great Britain, the traditional western power in the Middle East, was reluctantly withdrawing from that role to meet more pressing responsibilities and the United States and Russia had yet to formulate their Mid-East policies. The situation was further complicated by

Pan-Arab aspirations rooted in Islamic unity and the Arab view that a Jewish state in Palestine was a threat. The war also spurred Arab ambitions and by 1943 leaders from Egypt, Iraq, Syria, and Saudi Arabia had voiced an interest in creating a Pan-Arab organization that would fit into a post-war world and a United Nations structure. In March 1945 representatives of Egypt, Syria, Lebanon, Transjordan, Saudi Arabia, and Iraq signed a "Pact of the Union of Arab States" in Cairo (198).

The Arab Pact refused to accept the Zionist position on Palestine and Jewish immigration. The problem was discussed by President Roosevelt and the King of Saudi Arabia earlier and the American President assured King Ibn Saud that no moves hostile to Arab interests would be made. Roosevelt also pledged United States support—short of force—of full independence for Syria and Lebanon (199).

The latent nationalism unleashed by the war rarely resulted in a smooth transition to independence. The historical origins of Indian nationalism are found long before 1939, and the resulting problems remained long after 1945. The history of India's struggle for independence reveals that World War II simply forced the issue and a quicker transfer of power from British to Indian rule was the result. The internal difficulties that beset India because of the conflict between Hindu and Moslem often prevented the Indian Congress and the Moslem league from working together for independence even in wartime. This did not blunt the nationalist thrust, however, since both sides hammered at continued British control. The comments from a wartime speech in 1943 by Mr. Jinnah, President of the Moslem League, illustrates the Indian attitude toward British colonialism (200). The Hindu-Moslem conflict remained unresolved but the British position toward Mr. Gandhi and the Congress Party is reflected in the views of the Viceroy, Field Marshal Lord Wavell (201). Gandhi, however, despite setbacks and incarceration continued to personify India's struggle for independence (202).

The Far East imposed far different circumstances than India and the Middle Eastern nations, but internal struggles for unity and leadership illustrated that there were common goals that applied more to China than to other states and pre-dated World War II. Yet, the impact of the war cannot be minimized when examining decolonization (see Part 6). The United States and Great Britain announced in 1942 their respective intentions to abandon all extraterritorial rights and other special privileges at war's end (203), and several months later their promises were formalized in a Sino-British treaty (204). The United States offered a similar treaty.

The renunciation of territorial control was easier for the western Allies than the problem of internal Chinese politics. During the war the United States closely supported the government of Nationalist China (Kuomintang) led by Chiang Kai-shek, but before the war was over the Americans were trying to reconcile the Nationalists with the Chinese Communist Party. The disunity significantly distracted the war effort, and the United States unsuccessfully tried to bring the two factions together into a coalition throughout the war years. Mao Tse-tung issued a report in May 1945 "On the Coalition Government" that outlined the conditions for cooperation (205; see also 135).

Soviet Russia planned to recognize the Nationalist government (182), so it was hoped that a coalition might be formed; but Chiang Kai-shek refused and World War II ended with the struggle unresolved. Immediately following the war the Nationalist-Communist rivalry centered on Manchuria, which was occupied by Russian forces. Russia suddenly evacuated the area in April 1946 and Chinese Communist troops moved in. Thereafter Russia supported Mao Tse-tung, and the United States supported the Nationalist government of Chiang Kai-shek. The China struggle thus became an adjunct to the ensuing Cold War.

Quite clearly, the Japanese occupation in China did not produce an internal unity of action. The drive for independence in Indonesia was not smooth either, but there was more unity of purpose. The impact of the war was direct, since Japan occupied the area in 1942 (see Part 7). During 1942 Queen Wilhelmina recognized the Indonesian desire for independence by announcing a plan for a new post-war structure of the Netherlands Empire (206). When the war ended Great Britain accepted responsibility for evacuating the Japanese forces from Indonesia in the face of a declaration of independence from the Provisional Indonesian Republican Government in Java under nationalist leader Dr. Soekarno (Sukarno), issued on August 17, 1945 (207). The independence movements examined here illustrate the accelerated politics of war, and Indonesia like the others continued its drive for self-government into the post-war era, gaining full independence in 1946.

196. SPEECH BY ZIONIST LEADER WEIZMANN, AUGUST 1945[2] (EXCERPTS)

"Our reunion takes place in the shadow of the greatest catastrophe that has befallen our people since the destruction of the Temple. The reality has exceeded our worst fears. The great and powerful European Jewry of 10 years ago is no more. We have instead a broken remnant.

. . . .

We shall never forget that it was England which, at the turning-point in world history produced by the last war, stretched out a friendly hand to the Jewish people. The Balfour Declaration released our pent-up energies and enabled us to attain the strength we now possess in Palestine. But on the eve of the present war—under the stress of the impending conflict, and as part of a futile attempt to ward it off—the British Government went back on the solemn promise and set, in the White Paper of 1939, a course diametrically opposed to that indicated by the Balfour Declaration. It did so unilaterally, in defiance alike of Britain's pledged word, of international obligations, and of the authority of the League of Nations.

Probably the most tragic result of this policy has been the preventable loss of life. Hedged in as it was by the White Paper restriction, Palestine was able to take in during the war some 65,000 Jews, most of whom would have been dead to-day if they had stayed in Europe. But for the impediments placed in our way by the White Paper policy, many tens of thousands more—perhaps hundreds of thousands—might have been saved. When the White Paper was issued we proclaimed our uncompromising opposition and our determination to bring about its reversal. I myself informed the then Prime Minister of our resolution, and he said he understood me perfectly. But when war came I wrote immediately to the Prime Minister pledging our whole-hearted and unreserved co-operation in the war effort. That pledge we have carried through to the full, in Palestine and throughout the world.

The injustice and anachronism of the White Paper policy are even more grossly patent now than they were in 1939. The European tragedy stands out as a fearful vindication of the truth of Zionist teaching. The Jewish people will not achieve 'freedom from fear' save by the re-establishment of its statehood in Palestine. The words of Herzl, that 'the Jewish State is a world need,' have never been more true than they are to-day. A new policy for Palestine, opening the way for a more comprehensive solution of the Jewish problem, is the imperative need of the hour. The cardinal elements of that policy must be the acceptance of the Jewish claim to statehood in the one country in the world which the Jewish people can call its own; the recognition of the Jewish right to free immigration and settlement in Palestine; and the adoption of a practical programme, political and economic, designed to achieve the speediest possible transformation of Palestine into a Jewish State.

The Arabs will remain secure in their possessions, their linguistic, cultural, and religious identity, their enjoyment of complete equality of rights, and in their natural ties with their brethren in neighbouring countries. It is in those countries, incomparably larger and potentially richer than Palestine, with their immense unutilised resources of land and water, that Arab nationalism and statehood will find ample scope to work itself out constructively. The Arabs have a vast empire to inherit, but Jerusalem is to Jewry what Mecca, Medina, Baghdad, Damascus, and Cairo all rolled into one are to the Arabs. Arab countries have tremendous gains to register in terms of political emancipation and potential unity as a result of the last and the present war—gains which I do not begrudge them but which, in simple truth, must be admitted to be utterly incommensurate with their sufferings and sacrifices and with their contributions to the common struggle. Is that struggle to bring to the Arabs the fulfilment of all their hopes and to the Jews nothing? The Jewish people must be given (their) rightful place in the family of nations. Palestine as a Jewish State must be one of the fruits of victory.

Our appeal goes out to all the United Nations, and more especially to the 2 major allies of Britain, the U. S. A. and the U. S. S. R., on whose harmonious

collaboration the hopes of the world are pinned. Delay means the prolongation of agony for the survivors in Europe, crystallisation in Palestine, growing tension, and finally a crisis. Unless there is a clear lead, the position is
bound to deteriorate and chaos may ensue. We are a patient people. So long
as there is a reasonable certainty that relief is at hand we are prepared to wait.
But our people in Europe are going under, while in the Middle East new
facts are being created which are calculated to prejudge the issue. It cannot
be expected that a people should look with equanimity on the agony of their
brothers who have survived so fearful a holocaust, and on the liquidation of
their National Home—whose foundations have been laid with so much
devotion, effort, and sacrifice.

Most urgent of all is the question of immigration. Our proposals have been
submitted to H. M. Government in 2 memoranda, of October 1944 and May
1945. At the same time we asked the Government to place at our disposal
100,000 immigration permits for immediate use, as the first instalment of
the post-war immigration programme, to enable us to satisfy the most
pressing and urgent requirements. The decision on this question should be
given speedily. We ask for the opening of the gates of our country to let our
people in. We appeal to all governments to grant free right of exit to all Jews
wishing to leave and immigrate to Palestine."

197. POLITICAL DECLARATION OF WORLD ZIONIST CONFERENCE, LON-
DON, AUGUST 1945[3]

1. The Conference notes with deep regret and resentment that the White
Paper of 1939 is, even after the termination of the war, still in force. The
White Paper constituted a repudiation of the international pledge undertaken towards the Jewish people; it violated the natural and historic right of
the Jews acknowledged in the Mandate to return to their homeland; it
confined their freedom of settlement within a small fraction of the country;
it condemned the Jews to remain in Palestine, as in all countries of their
dispersion, a permanent minority; it denied to the Jews the right enjoyed by
every nation to be free and independent in its country.

2. But for the White Paper hundreds of thousands who perished in
Europe could have been saved in time by being admitted to Palestine.
Children for whom the Jewish Agency sought in vain to obtain immigration
permits on the outbreak of the war, an application which was refused on
account of the White Paper, were subsequently burned in the death furnaces
of Maidanek and other extermination centres.

3. The White Paper was issued without the approval of the League of
Nations and without consultation with the Government of the United States.
The only organ of the League of Nations to which the White Paper was
referred, the Permanent Mandates Commission, declared it to be incompatible with the provisions of the Mandate. Mr. Winston Churchill stated at the

time that the White Paper contained 'a plain breach of a solemn obligation,' and speaking for the Labour party Mr. Herbert Morrison declared that it would not be automatically binding upon a Labour Government.

4. A concession to Arab terrorism, which raged in Palestine from 1936 onwards with the support of Hitler and Mussolini, the White Paper was designed to gain Arab support in the event of a war with the Axis. But it failed to achieve even that practical objective, as witness the open alliance with Hitler of Rashid Ali of Baghdad, and of the then Mufti of Jerusalem.

5. The Jews of Palestine were the only national entity in the Middle East which mobilised its whole potential for the support of Great Britain and her Allies. The war effort of the Jews in Palestine, military and economic, was unique in the Middle East. The Jewish Brigade took a gallant part in the final defeat of the enemy on the Italian front.

6. Only some 60,000 Jews managed to escape from Europe to Palestine during the war. A hundred times as many—some 6,000,000 men, women, and children—were put to death by the Nazis and their satellites. What happened to our people in Europe did not and could not happen to any people in the world which has a country and a State of its own. The vast majority of the Jewish people throughout the world feel that they have no chance of 'freedom from fear' unless the status of the Jews as individuals and as a nation has been made equal to that of all normal peoples, and the Jewish State of Palestine has been established.

7. The return of Jews to Palestine and their settlement in it has not proceeded and will not proceed at the expense of others. The Arabs and other inhabitants of Palestine will continue to benefit, not less than in the past, from the increasing economic opportunities. In addition to full equality of rights they will enjoy every freedom in organising autonomously their religious, cultural, and social affairs. Jewish immigration and settlement will continue to be based, as hitherto, on the development of resources untapped by others. The Arab States, with their underpopulated and underdeveloped territories, will find in the Jewish State a faithful ally; it will contribute to the best of its ability to the progress of its neighbours.

8. The Conference endorses the declaration of the Jewish Agency for Palestine, communicated at the time to H. M. Government, that the White paper is devoid of any moral and legal validity. Now that the war has ended, the Jews cannot possibly acquiesce in the continuation of the White Paper under any circumstances whatsoever, whether in its present or in any modified form. There can be no solution to the inseparable twin problems of the Jewish people and Palestine except by constituting Palestine, undivided and undiminished, as a Jewish State in accordance with the purpose of the Balfour Declaration.

9. Any delay in the solution of the problem, any attempt at half-measures, any decision which, however favourable, remains on paper and is not faithfully and speedily implemented, would not meet the tragedy of the hour and

might only increase suffering amongst the Jewish people and tension in Palestine.

10. The Conference proclaims its full endorsement of the following requests submitted by the Jewish Agency to H. M. Government on May 22, 1945:

a. That an immediate decision be announced to establish Palestine as a Jewish State.

b. That the Jewish Agency be invested with all necessary authority to bring to Palestine as many Jews as it may be found necessary and possible to settle, and to develop, fully and speedily, all the resources of the country, especially land and power resources.

c. That an international loan and other help be given for the transfer of the first 1,000,000 Jews to Palestine, and for the economic development of the country.

d. That reparations in kind from Germany be granted to the Jewish people for the rebuilding of Palestine, and—as a first instalment—that all German property in Palestine be used for the settlement of Jews from Europe.

e. That international facilities be provided for the exit and transit of all Jews who wish to settle in Palestine.

The Conference begs to address an urgent appeal to H. M. Government to implement these requests without delay. It appeals to the principal Allies of H. M. Government and to all the United Nations to give H. M. Government their full moral and material support in the adoption and implementation of this policy.

198. ARAB LEAGUE PACT, CAIRO, MARCH 22,1945[4]

Art. 1. The League of the Arab States is composed of the independent Arab States which have signed this pact.

Any independent Arab State has the right to become a member of the League. If it desires to do so, it shall submit a request which will be deposited with the permanent Secretariat-General and submitted to the Council at the first meeting held after submission of the request.

Art. 2. The League has as its purpose the strengthening of the relations between the member states; the coordination of their policies in order to achieve cooperation between them and to safeguard their independence and sovereignty; and a general concern with the affairs and interests of the Arab countries. It has also as its purpose the close cooperation of the member states, with due regard to the organization and circumstances of each state, on the following matters:

A. Economic and financial affairs, including commercial relations, customs, currency, and questions of agriculture and industry.

B. Communications: this includes railroads, roads, aviation, navigation, telegraphs, and posts.

C. Cultural affairs.

D. Nationality, passports, visas, execution of judgments, and extradition of criminals.

E. Social affairs.

F. Health problems.

Art. 3. The League shall possess a Council composed of the representatives of the member state of the League; each state shall have a single vote, irrespective of the number of its representatives.

It shall be the task of the Council to achieve the realization of the objectives of the League and to supervise the execution of agreements which the member states have concluded on the questions enumerated in the preceding article, or on any other questions.

It likewise shall be the Council's task to decide upon the means by which the League is to cooperate with the international bodies to be created in the future in order to guarantee security and peace and regulate economic and social relations.

Art. 4. For each of the questions listed in Article 2 there shall be set up a special committee in which the member states of the League shall be represented. These committees shall be charged with the task of laying down the principles and extent of cooperation. Such principles shall be formulated as draft agreements, to be presented to the Council for examination preparatory to their submission to the aforesaid states.

Representatives of the other Arab countries may take part in the work of the aforesaid committees. The Council shall determine the conditions under which these representatives may be permitted to participate and the rules governing such representation.

Art. 5. Any resort to force in order to resolve disputes arising between two or more member states of the League is prohibited. If there shall arise among them a difference which does not concern a state's independence, sovereignty, or territorial integrity, and if the parties to the dispute have recourse to the Council for the settlement of the difference, the decision of the Council shall then be enforceable and obligatory.

In such a case, the states between whom the difference has arisen shall not participate in the deliberations and decisions of the Council.

The Council may lend its good offices for the settlement of all differences which threaten to lead to war between two member states, or a member state and a third state, with a view to bringing about their reconciliation.

Decisions of arbitration and mediation shall be taken by majority vote.

Art. 6. In case of aggression or threat of aggression by one state against a member state, the state which has been attacked or threatened with aggression may demand the immediate convocation of the Council.

The Council shall by unanimous decision determine the measures necessary to repulse the aggression. If the aggressor is a member state, his vote shall not be counted in determining unanimity.

If, as a result of the attack, the government of the state attacked finds itself unable to communicate with the Council, that state's representative in the Council shall have the right to request the convocation of the Council for the purpose indicated in the foregoing paragraph. In the event that this representative is unable to communicate with the Council, any member state of the League shall have the right to request the convocation of the Council.

Art. 7. Unanimous decisions of the Council shall be binding upon all member states of the League; majority decisions shall be binding only upon those states which have accepted them.

In either case the decisions of the Council shall be enforced in each member state according to its respective fundamental laws.

Art. 8. Each member state shall respect the systems of government established in the other member states and regard them as exclusive concerns of those states. Each shall pledge to abstain from any action calculated to change established systems of government.

Art. 9. States of the League which desire to establish closer cooperation and stronger bonds than are provided by this Pact may conclude agreements to that end.

Treaties and agreements already concluded or to be concluded in the future between a member state and another State shall not be binding or restrictive upon other members.

Art. 10. The permanent seat of the League of Arab States is established in Cairo. The Council may, however, assemble at any other place it may designate.

Art. 11. The Council of the League shall convene in ordinary session twice a year, in March and in October. It shall convene in extraordinary session upon the request of two member states of the League whenever the need arises.

Art. 12. The League shall have a permanent Secretariat-General which shall consist of a Secretary-General, Assistant Secretaries, and an appropriate number of officials.

The Council of the League shall appoint the Secretary-General by a majority of two-thirds of the states of the League. The Secretary-General, with the approval of the Council, shall appoint the Assistant Secretaries and the principal officials of the League.

The Council of the League shall establish an administrative regulation for the functions of the Secretariat-General and matters relating to the staff.

The Secretary-General shall have the rank of Ambassador and the Assistant Secretaries that of Ministers Plenipotentiary.

The first Secretary-General of the League is named in an Annex to this Pact.

Art. 13. The Secretary-General shall prepare the draft budget of the

League and shall submit it to the Council for approval before the beginning of each fiscal year.

The Council shall fix the share of the expenses to be borne by each state of the League. This share may be reconsidered if necessary.

Art. 14. The members of the Council of the League as well as the members of the committees and the officials who are to be designated in the administrative regulation shall enjoy diplomatic privileges and immunity when engaged in the exercise of their functions.

The buildings occupied by the organs of the League shall be inviolable.

Art. 15. The first meeting of the Council shall be convened at the invitation of the Head of the Egyptian Government. Thereafter it shall be convened at the invitation of the Secretary-General.

The representatives of the member States of the League shall alternatively assume the Presidency of the Council at each of its ordinary sessions.

Art. 16. Except in cases specifically indicated in this Pact, a majority vote of the Council shall be sufficient to make enforceable decisions on the following matters:

A. Matters relating to personnel.

B. Adoption of the budget of the League.

C. Establishment of the administrative regulations for the Council, the committees, and the Secretariat-General.

D. Decisions to adjourn the sessions.

Art. 17. Each member State of the League shall deposit with the Secretariat-General one copy of every treaty or agreement concluded or to be concluded in the future between itself and another member state of the League or a third state.

Art. 18. If a member state contemplates withdrawal from the League, it shall inform the Council of its intention one year before such withdrawal is to go into effect.

The Council of the League may consider any state which fails to fulfill its obligations under this Pact as having become separated from the League, this to go into effect upon unanimous decision of the States, not counting the state concerned.

Art. 19. This Pact may be amended with the consent of two-thirds of the states belonging to the League, especially in order to make firmer and stronger the ties between the member states, to create an Arab Tribunal of Arbitration, and to regulate the relations of the League with any international bodies to be created in the future to guarantee security and peace.

Final action on an amendment cannot be taken prior to the session following the session in which the motion was initiated.

If a state does not accept such an amendment it may withdraw at such time as the amendment goes into effect, without being bound by the provisions of the preceding article.

Art. 20. This Pact and its Annexes shall be ratified according to the basic laws in force among the High Contracting Parties.

The instruments of ratification shall be deposited with the Secretariat-General of the Council and the Pact shall become operative as regards each ratifying state fifteen days after the Secretariat-General has received the instruments of ratification from four states.

This Pact has been drawn up in Cairo in the Arabic language on this 8th day of Rabi II, thirteen hundred and sixty-four (22 March 1945), in one copy which shall be deposited in the safe keeping of the Secretariat-General.

An identical copy shall be delivered to each state of the League.

(1) *Annex Regarding Palestine.* Since the termination of the last great war the rule of the Ottoman Empire over the Arab countries, among them Palestine, which had become detached from that Empire, has come to an end. She has come to be independent in herself, not subordinate to any other state.

The Treaty of Lausanne proclaimed that her future was to be settled by the parties concerned.

However, even though she was as yet unable to control her own affairs, the Covenant of the League (of Nations) in 1919 made provision for a regime based upon recognition of her independence.

Her international existence and independence in the legal sense cannot, therefore, be questioned, any more than could the independence of the other Arab countries.

Although the outward manifestations of this independence have remained obscured for reasons beyond her control, this should not be allowed to interfere with her participation in the work of the Council of the League.

The States signatory to the Pact of the Arab League are therefore of the opinion that, considering the special circumstances of Palestine, and until that country can effectively exercise its independence, the Council of the League should take charge of the selection of an Arab representative from Palestine to take part in its work.

(2) *Annex Regarding Cooperation With Countries Which Are Not Members of the Council of the League.* Whereas the member states of the League will have to deal in the Council as well as in the committees with matters which will benefit and affect the Arab world at large:

And Whereas the Council has to take into account the aspirations of the Arab countries which are not members of the Council and has to work toward their realization;

Now therefore, it particularly behooves the states signatory to the Pact of the Arab League to enjoin the Council of the League, when considering the admission of those countries to participation in the committees referred to in the Pact, that it should do its utmost to cooperate with them, and furthermore, that it should spare no effort to learn their needs and understand their aspirations and hopes; and that it should work thenceforth for their best interests and the safeguarding of their future with all the political means at its disposal.

(3) *Annex Regarding the Appointment of a Secretary-General of the League.* The states signatory to this Pact have agreed to appoint His Excellency Abd-ul-

Rahman 'Azzam Bey, to be Secretary-General of the League of Arab States.

This appointment is made for two years. The Council of the League shall hereafter determine the new regulations for the Secretariat-General.

199. MEMORANDUM OF CONVERSATION BETWEEN KING OF SAUDI ARABIA AND PRESIDENT ROOSEVELT, FEBRUARY 14, 1945[5] (EXCERPT)

I

The President asked His Majesty for his advice regarding the problem of Jewish refugees driven from their homes in Europe. His Majesty replied that in his opinion the Jews should return to live in the lands from which they were driven. The Jews whose homes were completely destroyed and who have no chance of livelihood in their homelands should be given living space in the Axis countries which oppressed them. The President remarked that Poland might be considered a case in point. The Germans appear to have killed three million Polish Jews, by which count there should be space in Poland for the resettlement of many homeless Jews.

His Majesty then expounded the case of the Arabs and their legitimate rights in their lands and stated that the Arabs and the Jews could never cooperate, neither in Palestine, nor in any other country. His Majesty called attention to the increasing threat to the existence of the Arabs and the crisis which has resulted from continued Jewish immigration and the purchase of land by the Jews. His Majesty further stated that the Arabs would choose to die rather than yield their lands to the Jews.

His Majesty stated that the hope of the Arabs is based upon the word of honor of the Allies and upon the well-known love of justice of the United States, and upon the expectation that the United States will support them.

The President replied that he wished to assure His Majesty that he would do nothing to assist the Jews against the Arabs and would make no move hostile to the Arab people. He reminded His Majesty that it is impossible to prevent speeches and resolutions in Congress or in the press which may be made on any subject. His reassurance concerned his own future policy as Chief Executive of the United States Government.

His Majesty thanked the President for his statement and mentioned the proposal to send an Arab mission to America and England to expound the case of the Arabs and Palestine. The President stated that he thought this was a very good idea because he thought many people in America and England are misinformed. His Majesty said that such a mission to inform the people was useful, but more important to him was what the President had just told him concerning his own policy toward the Arab people.

II

His Majesty stated that the problem of Syria and the Lebanon was of deep concern to him and he asked the President what would be the attitude of the United States Government in the event that France should continue to press intolerable demands upon Syria and the Lebanon. The President replied that the French Government had given him in writing their guarantee of the independence of Syria and the Lebanon and that he could at any time write to the French Government to insist that they honor their word. In the event that the French should twart the independence of Syria and the Lebanon, the United States Government would give to Syria and the Lebanon all possible support short of the use of force.

200. SPEECH BY MR. JINNAH, PRESIDENT OF THE MOSLEM LEAGUE, DECEMBER 24, 1943[6] (EXCERPTS)

"Mr. Churchill has said that he has not taken office to preside over the liquidation of the British Empire. I would say voluntary liquidation is more honourable than a compulsory one . . . and the British Empire will have to be liquidated one day. We are now impressing on British statesmen that the only honest way for Britain is to 'divide and quit.' . . . Lord Wavell, like a soldier-Viceroy, has spoken in plain language. In that respect he has made a great contribution to India's political problems. He is no more embarrassed by his mental bag which he found it necessary to jettison in the Mediterranean before he crossed the Suez Canal. Having put the political issue into cold storage indefinitely Lord Wavell has said that he is concentrating on winning the war. It is really astonishing that he, representing the Crown and speaking with responsibility, thinks that he can win this war while he is totally indifferent to the political situation. . . . With all humility I say to the British Government: you have got to get the whole-hearted and enthusiastic support of some Party in this country if not all.

. . . Lord Wavell's appeal for co-operation is really a flagrant abuse of the word. Without being given any real share or authority in the Government we are asked to do the work of camp followers, menials, and subservients. Can he expect any self-respecting organisation to acceptthat position? The British Government are pursuing a definite policy. They do not want co-operation from any Party. Congress decided to non-co-operate and resorted to mass civil disobedience. We have offered the hand of co-operation for the object of winning the war, provided it is accepted as that of a confident friend with a share and authority in the Government and that a definite promise is given that we shall reap our share in the fruits of victory when we win it. That has been rejected and yet our organisation is being treated like the Congress. They would like to outlaw the Moslem League. We are quite ready for it.

. . . We shall never rest content until we seize the territories that belong to us and rule over them."

201. STATEMENT BY LORD WAVELL, VICEROY OF INDIA, MARCH 28, 1944[7] (EXCERPT FROM LETTER TO MR. GANDHI)

I regret that I must view the present policy of Congress as hindering and not forwarding Indian progress to self-government and development. During a war in which the success of the United Nations against the Axis powers is vital both to India and the world, as you yourself have recognised, the

Working Committee of Congress declined to co-operate, ordered Congress Ministries to resign, and decided to take no part in the administration of the country or in the war effort which India was making to assist the United Nations. At the greatest crisis of all for India, at a time when Japanese invasion was possible, the Congress Party decided to pass a resolution calling on the British to leave India, which could not fail to have the most serious effect on our ability to defend the frontiers of India against the Japanese. I am quite clear that India's problems cannot be solved by an immediate and complete withdrawal of the British.

I do not accuse you or Congress of any wish deliberately to aid the Japanese. But you are too intelligent a man not to have realised that the effect of your resolution must be to hamper the presecution of the war, that you had lost confidence in our ability to defend India, and were prepared to take advantage of our supposed military straits to gain political advantage. I do not see how those responsible for the safety of India could have acted otherwise than they did and could have failed to arrest those who sponsored the resolution.

202. PRESS RELEASE ON MR. GANDHI, JULY 9, 1944[8]

"Mr. Gandhi, after his release, assured more than one friend that he would ask Congress to participate in an interim Government and help the Allies' war effort in India. In public and private he has repudiated the sabotage activities indulged in during his detention. Mr. Gandhi wants only national control over civil affairs and all those things which affect the lives of the people. He made it clear that his own anti-war creed would not stand in the way of a National Government's efforts or of Allied operations in India. As for the future, what Mr. Gandhi wants is nothing more than what the British Government has on recent occasions solemnly assured would belong to India after the war, namely, such independence as all other free nations of the civilised world will enjoy in the new order."

203. EXTRATERRITORIAL RIGHTS ABANDONED BY BRITAIN AND U.S.A., LONDON, OCTOBER 9, 1942 (U. S. DECLARATION ISSUED IN WASHINGTON)[9]

"H. M. Government have declared in public pronouncements on Jan. 14, 1939, July 18, 1940, and June 11, 1941, that they were prepared at the conclusion of hostilities in the Far East to negotiate with the Chinese Government for the abrogation of the extraterritorial rights and privileges hitherto enjoyed by their nationals in China. Similar pronouncements have been made by the U. S. Government, with whom H. M. Government have been in consultation.

In order to emphasise their friendship and solidarity with their Chinese allies, H. M. Government have now decided to proceed further in this matter at once. Accordingly, the Foreign Secretary made a communication to the Chinese Charge d'Affaires in London on Oct. 9, indicating that H. M. Government hoped in the near future to open discussions with the Chinese Government and to present for their consideration a draft treaty for the immediate relinquishment of extraterritorial rights and privileges in China and for the settlement of questions intimately connected therewith.

H. M. Government have recently been engaged in an exchange of views with the U. S. Government on this question. They have been pleased to learn that a similar communication was made by the U. S. Government on the same day to the Chinese Ambassador in Washington, and the fact that the two Governments have found it possible to take similar action in this important matter has occasioned lively satisfaction in London."

204. SINO-BRITISH TREATY, CHUNGKING, JANUARY 11, 1943[10]

(Sino-American Treaty Signed in Washington)

Art. I defines the territories to which the Treaty applies: on the British side, the United Kingdom, India, and the Colonial Empire, and on the Chinese side, all the territories of the Chinese Republic, including those at present occupied by the enemy.

Art. II ends the practice by which British subjects could be tried by British Consular or other courts in China, in the following terms: "All treaties or agreements in force between H. M. the King and H. E. the President of China which authorize his Majesty or his representatives to exercise jurisdiction over nationals or companies of his Majesty in the territory of the Republic of China are hereby abrogated. The nationals and companies of H.M. the King shall be subject in China to the jurisdiction of the Government of the Republic of China, in accordance with the principles of international law and practice."

Art. III relinquishes British rights under the Peking (Boxer) Protocol of 1901, which gave foreign Powers the right *inter alia* to station troops at Peking and elsewhere and placed the diplomatic quarter of Peking under foreign control.

Art. IV relinquishes British rights in the Shanghai and Amoy International Settlements and provides for the rendition to China of the British Concessions at Tientsin and Canton. Britain undertakes to help the Chinese Government in reaching any necessary agreements with other Governments for transferring the administration of such settlements to China. The Chinese Government, on their side, undertake when taking over control of the official assets of the settlements, to assume and discharge all official obligations connected with them and to recognise all legitimate rights therein.

Articles V and VI state that the existing rights and titles to real property in China possessed by British nationals and companies are indefeasible and not to be questioned except upon legal proof of fraudulent acquisition; no such rights and titles may be alienated to nationals of third Powers without the consent of the Chinese Government. The right is also established of both British and Chinese nationals to travel, live and trade throughout the territories of the other party, with each party according the other in its territories national treatment in regard to legal proceedings and taxation. "National treatment means the same treatment as that accorded to the natives of the country concerned."

Art. VII provides for Consular appointments and privileges, including the right of Consuls to visit their nationals under detention.

Art. VIII looks forward to a wider treaty and declares that any outstanding questions will be decided in accordance with the principles of international law.

Art. IX provides for ratification and exchange of instruments at Chungking as soon as possible.

The Treaty was accompanied by an exchange of Notes dealing with the following subjects:

Shipping: Overseas merchant vessels will receive most-favoured-nation treatment and may come to such ports as are or may be opened to such traffic. Each party relinquishes any special rights of coastal trade and inland navigation in the territories of the other.

Naval Vessels: The special rights accorded to British warships in Chinese waters under older treaties are relinquished, and both Governments will in future extend to each other on the visits of their warships mutual courtesy in accordance with ordinary international usage.

British Court Cases: Previous judgments of British courts in China will be considered as *res judicata*. Uncompleted cases can, at the request of the plaintiffs, be remitted to the appropriate Chinese courts, which shall apply the law which the former British court would have applied.

Real Property: May be acquired in future by nationals of both parties in the territory of the other in accordance with British and Chinese laws and regulations.

205. DIGEST OF SPEECH BY MAO TZE-TUNG, MAY 1, 1945[11]

(Presented By Yenan Radio Broadcast)

Yenan, May 1—"On the Coalition Government" was the title of the political report given by Chairman Mao Tze-tung, leader of the Chinese Communist Party to the Seventh Congress of the Chinese Communist Party.

Mao Tze-tung pointed out that the "unification of all parties and groups and non-party representatives to form a provisional democratic coalition government so as to carry out democratic reform to overcome the present crisis, mobilize and unify the national forces of the war of resistance to effectively collaborate with the Allies in fighting and defeating the Japanese aggressor, and to secure the thorough-liberation of the Chinese are the basic demands of the Chinese people at present."

NATIONAL ASSEMBLY

China needs a coalition government, said Mao Tze-tung, not only during the war but also after the war. "After the victory of the war of resistance, the National Assembly based on a broad, democratic foundation should be called to form a regular democratic government of a similar coalition nature, embracing more broadly all parties and groups of non-party representatives. This Government will lead the liberated people of the entire Nation to build up an independent, free, unified, prosperous and strong new country. After China has had a democratic elective system, the Government should be a coalition working on the basis of a commonly recognized new democratic program no matter whether the Communist Party is the majority or minority party in the National Assembly."

IMMEDIATE FORMATION

Mao Tze-tung repeatedly urged the necessity of immediate formation of a coalition government. One party dictatorship, dictatorship of the anti-population [sic] group within the Kuomintang, said Mao Tze-tung, is not only "a fundamental obstacle to the mobilization and unification or the strength of the Chinese people in the war of resistance, it is also the [colossal] embryo of the civil war."

If such dictatorship is not abolished and replaced by a democratic coalition government, then "not only will it be impossible to carry out any democratic reform within the Kuomintang-controlled areas and mobilize all the people and army there effectively to collaborate with the Allies thoroughly to defeat the aggressors, but it will also lead to a calamity as [words missing] war."

SIGNS OF CIVIL WAR

Mao Tze-tung pointed out: "The principal ruling clique within the Kuomintang is still upholding the reactionary policy of dictatorship and civil war. Many signs disclose that they have been, and especially now, are preparing to launch a civil war and are only waiting till certain Allied troops have driven the Japanese from certain parts of China. . . ."

MOCKERY OF DEMOCRACY

Speaking of Kuomintang authorities who talk of "convoking a national assembly to return the reins of the Government to the people" and yet refuse a coalition government, Mao Tze-tung called this "a mockery" of democracy. He exposed the dark designs of the reactionary clique within the Kuomintang as that of "being bent on convoking a so-called 'National Assembly' entirely under its thumb which will [push] an anti-democratic so-called 'constitution,' maintaining dictatorship."

"This will enable it to put up a show of 'returning the reins of government to the people' by putting on a cloak of 'legality' on the illegal so-called 'national' government without popular support, clamped on the Chinese people through appointment by only several dozens of Kuomintang members. There will then be an excuse for issuing punitive orders against anyone who disagrees."

Issuing a serious warning against such an action of the Kuomintang authorities, Mao Tze-tung said "popular heroes stand in danger of pushing themselves into a blind alley." At the same time he also declared that "Whenever the Kuomintang Government abandons its erroneous policy, at present in force, and consents to democratic reform, we are willing to resume negotiations with it. But such negotiations must be based on a general policy of the war of resistance, unity, and democracy. We can never agree with any measure, proposition or other empty talk which departs from this general policy, no matter how well they sound."

In order to promote the setting up of a coalition government, Mao Tze-tung proposed to the liberated areas that "a conference of people's representatives in [all] of liberated China should be called in Yenan as soon as possible to discuss the unification of [action] of all liberated areas, lead the anti-Japanese democratic movement of the people in Kuomintang-controlled areas and the underground movement of the people in the occupied areas, and promote the unity of the entire Nation and formation of a coalition government."

TWO COURSES OPEN

In analyzing the concrete conditions in China's anti-Japanese war, Chairman Mao Tze-tung pointed out that for a long time there has obviously been two courses in China. These are, he said, "the course of the Kuomintang Government which oppresses the people and passively carries on armed resistance, and the course of the Chinese people who have awakened and united to get her to carry out the peoples war."

CONTRAST IN AREAS

In order to explain clearly these two diametrically opposed courses, Mao Tze-tung vividly compared and contrasted the liberated areas and the areas under Kuomintang rule. He said: "The Chinese liberated areas now extend to over 906,000 square kilometers with 95.5 million population. In these vast liberated areas all essential policies of the anti-Japanese national united front have been put into force, and popularly elected governments, through cooperation between [words missing] and the representatives of other parties and groups have been set up or are in the process of being set up. These are really local coalition governments which have mobilized the entire people."

DEMOCRATIC PATTERN

He also said: "Chinese liberated areas have become a democratic pattern for China and the center of gravity for cooperation with our allies to drive out the Japanese aggressors and to liberate the Chinese people. The troops in the liberated areas have expanded to 910,000 and the people's volunteers to over 2,200,000. These troops have become the main force in the war of resistance, and as soon as they receive modern equipment they will become still more invincible and able finally to defeat the Japanese aggressors."

In areas under Kuomintang rule, on the contrary, as a consequence of the anti-popular and anti-democratic policies of Kuomintang authorities, "there were military defeats, loss of huge territories, and economic as well as financial crises. These gave rise to a serious crisis of the people, reduced to the hardest life, people complaining loudly and insistently and people staging revolts. Kuomintang troops have been reduced by more than half their strength."

BATTLEFRONTS

As [to?] the conditions in the battlefronts in Kuomintang-controlled areas and liberated areas, Mao Tze-tung pointed out that since 1939 the Japanese aggressors' bayonet has mainly been pointed at the liberated areas. In 1945, 64 percent of the Japanese forces invading China and 95 percent of the puppet forces in China were opposed by troops in the liberated areas.

In 1944 the Japanese aggressors launched a war for effecting a through continental line and found Kuomintang troops devoid of the power of resistance. It was only at this period that some changes occurred in the proportion of the share in armed resistance by the two above-mentioned battlefronts. However, even at present, troops in liberated areas are still opposing 56 percent of the Japanese troops invading China, while there is absolutely no change in the proportion of the puppet troops they are opposing.

PUPPET TROOPS

Mao Tze-tung pointed out that among the 800,000 puppet troops the majority were entire units that went over to the Japanese under Kuomintang officers or were organized by Kuomintang officers who had gone over. Kuomintang reactionary elements are supporting these puppet troops morally and organizationally in order that they may cooperate with the Japanese aggressors to attack Chinese liberated areas. Besides, these reactionary elements mobilized a large number of troops to blockade and attack the Shensi,

Kansu, and Ninghsia border region and other liberated areas. These troops reached the number of 797,000, and even now they have not been reduced.

Many Chinese and foreigners never heard of such a serious situation in China because of the Kuomintang news censorship policy. Mao said: "Many people only know that there is a Mihailovich in Yugoslavia, but they never knew that there were scores of Mihailovichs in China."

Concerning these two courses, Mao Tze-tung drew the following conclusion: "One is the course of victory, in spite of the fact that it is carried on under such adverse conditions as in the liberated areas, absolutely without outside help. The other is the course of defeat, even though it is carried on under such extremely favorable conditions as in the Kuomintang-controlled areas aided by foreign supplies."

206. Broadcast of Queen Wilhelmina of Holland, December 6, 1942[12]

"Without anticipating the recommendations of the future conference," she said, "I visualize that they will be directed towards a Commonwealth in which the Netherlands, Indonesia, Surinam and Curacao will take part, with complete freedom of conduct for each part regarding its internal affairs, but with a readiness to render mutual assistance. Such a combination of independence and collaboration can give the Kingdom and its parts the strength to carry fully their responsibility, both externally and internally. This would leave no room for discrimination according to race or nationality. Only the ability of the individual citizens and the needs of the various groups of the population will determine the policy of the Government."

207. Sukarno Proclamation, August 17, 1945[13]

We the people of Indonesia hereby declare Indonesia's independence. Matters concerning the transfer of power and other matters will be executed in an orderly manner and in the shortest possible time.

         On behalf of the Indonesian people
         (signed) Soekarno   Hatta

Part 17. Peace Aims and Post-war Planning

The experience of the victors in World War I, who had made little preparation for peace, was a lesson that the Allied leaders of World War II learned well. Great Britain and the United States were determined to construct a basis for post-war planning and peace that would reflect the ideals of freedom, so these two nations agreed in 1941 to work for a "better future for the world" (65). The Atlantic Charter represented a statement of principles essential to future planning, and it was also the product of two democratic governments. A third Allied partner, the U. S. S. R., harbored somewhat different aspirations for the world. Some of the differences of approach in post-war planning between the western Allies and the Soviet Union were fundamental and proved insurmountable later. However, the pressures for wartime cooperation temporarily obscured their differences, and objections from either camp during the war would have only served the Axis cause.

The Soviet Union, together with other nations including the United States and Great Britain, participated in the United Nations Declaration (86) and endorsed, by signature, the earlier Atlantic Charter. The principles embodied in these documents were reiterated throughout the period of wartime collaboration in one form or another (see 100, 129, 130, and 133). The Allied cooperation also appeared to be successful when applied to more specific problems, and by 1944 it was obvious that if the invasion of France was successful the three major powers would soon be jointly administering much of Europe.

In preparing for those responsibilities the European Advisory Commission (EAC) was formed to study and advise on occupation zones, to draft surrender terms, and to ready an administrative structure for post-war Germany and Austria (208). There was little disagreement among the Big Three on questions of demilitarization, political decentralization, and punishment of war criminals. The determination to destroy German war potential by eliminating its industrial zones found early favor as a cooperative goal, and one of the first proposals came from the United States at the second Quebec Conference, in 1944. The "Morgenthau Plan" (209), as it was called, stipulated among other things that Germany's post-war production was to concentrate on agricultural goods.

By November and December of 1944, Allied reports detailed the beginnings of occupation policy in the western Rhine area. Their descriptions of various problems encountered in administering captured German territory provided a glimpse of the future (210).

During several weeks from August to October 1944, delegations from the United States, Great Britain, China, and the Soviet Union met in Washington and developed a series of tentative proposals on the subject of an international organization for maintaining peace after the war. General agreement was reached on a number of basic questions. Shortly thereafter, at the Yalta meeting in February 1945, the United States, Great Britain, and the Soviet Union agreed on a United Nations Conference to deal with the proposed world organization to be held in America in April (211). In addition, a variety of other subjects bearing upon the post-war world were agreed upon. Later, at a press conference, President Roosevelt spoke of additional U. N. responsibilities for the Pacific after Japan's defeat (212; see also 159). In June the Charter of the United Nations was completed and signed by representatives of fifty nations (213). Following the Polish ratification as the fifty-first member nation in October the Charter became effective.

The final Allied conference of the war took place in July and August of 1945 at Potsdam (Berlin) (214). The personnel had changed, since Truman replaced Roosevelt and Clement Attlee replaced Churchill before the conference ended; Stalin was the sole survivor of the wartime trio.

208. STRANG MEMORANDUM ON GERMANY AND AUSTRIA IN THE POST-SURRENDER PERIOD, MAY 31, 1944[1] (ANNEX 1 AND 2)

[Annex 1]
DRAFT GENERAL DIRECTIVE FOR GERMANY IN THE
POST-SURRENDER PERIOD

1. This directive relates to the period after Germany's surrender and will govern your action in relation to general matters not covered by particular directives.

2. You will on all occasions and by all means emphasize and display the Allied character of the occupation of Germany. You will tolerate no action by any German individual or organisation which seeks to undermine the unity of the Allies.

3. You will bear in mind and seek to promote the purposes of the occupation of Germany, which are—

(a) To complete the disarmament of Germany and the destruction of the German war machine.

(b) To convince the German people that they have suffered a total military defeat, in order to break for ever the legend of the invincibility of German arms, and to correct the belief that aggression pays.

(c) To destroy the National Socialist Party and system, and to do everything possible to uproot and discredit National Socialist doctrines.

(d) To ensure that German militarism and National Socialism do not continue to operate underground or in some other guise.

(e) To lay the foundations for the rule of law in Germany, and for eventual peaceful co-operation in international life by Germany.

(f) To encourage individual and collective responsibility in Germans.

4. You should bear in mind that positive action in the sense of (e) and (f) above must be taken by the Germans rather than by the United Nations on

their behalf; but one purpose of the occupation is to make it possible for Germans to take such action. Direct action by the United Nations will, however, be needed under (a), (b), (c) and (d).

5. You will strictly forbid and vigorously suppress any political activity by remnants of the National Socialist Party, or any groups that seek to propagate its doctrines or any similar ones. In particular, you will tolerate no continuance of discrimination against individual Germans on grounds of race or religion. Your attitude towards other political activities in Germany will be governed by the overriding necessity for the maintenance of military security. Subject to such security, you will not forbid political activities, including public demonstrations or meetings. You will be careful not to lend your support or authority to any particular political party or policy in Germany, but you should be aware that the United Nations hope to encourage any movement in Germany towards decentralisation or federalism. Movements of a separatist character will also be looked on with favour by the United Nations, but you should be careful that such movements (though they may be favoured at a later stage) should not at the outset be compromised by being given the appearance of being actively promoted by the Allies.

6. Subject again to the necessity for maintaining military security and a smooth administration, you will, so far as possible, permit freedom of speech and freedom of the press, and you will encourage the formation of free Trades Unions.

7. You will do all you can to foster freedom of religion and the maintenance of respect for the churches in Germany; though you should take steps to ensure that religious activities are not used as a cloak for the spreading of undesirable political ideas or of propaganda directed against any of the United Nations.

8. In general, the attitude to the German population of all forces and agencies under your command or control should be just, but firm and distant. You will strongly discourage fraternisation between Allied forces and the German population. In particular, you will reduce to a minimum all contact between forces under your command and German forces not yet demobilised. In general, contact with German officials should be as little as is necessary in order to ensure the adequate supervision of administration.

9. All Germans appointed to official positions (e.g., in the police of the administration) should understand that they hold office only during good behaviour.

[Annex 2]
DRAFT GENERAL DIRECTIVE FOR AUSTRIA IN THE POST-SURRENDER PERIOD

1. This directive relates to the period after Germany's surrender and will govern your action in relation to general Austrian matters not covered by particular directives.

2. You will on all occasions and by all means emphasise and display the

Allied character of the occupation of Austria. You will tolerate no action by any Austrian individual or organisation which seeks to undermine the unity of the Allies.

3. You will bear in mind and seek to promote the purposes of the occupation of Austria, which are:—

(a) To disarm Austrians embodied in the German services, and to destroy the German war machine in so far as it exists or is based in Austrian territory.

(b) To demonstrate the complete defeat of Germany; to destroy the legend of the invincibility of German arms; and to correct the belief that aggression pays.

(c) To destroy the National Socialist party and system in Austria, and to uproot and discredit National Socialist doctrines.

(d) To make clear to Austria that association with Germany has brought her to disaster, and to fortify her will not to renew that association.

(e) To assist in the process of disentangling the national life of Austria, in every sphere, from Germany.

(f) To assist in the establishment of a free, independent and prosperous Austria, based on the rule of law, ready and able to co-operate in international life.

4. You will observe that the purposes of the occupation of Austria differ from those defined for the case of Germany. This difference will much influence the character of Allied occupation in Austria, which in this case is intended to be exercised in the interests of the country occupied as well as in those of the United Nations. It is probable that proportionately fewer Allied troops will be engaged in the occupation of Austria than in that of Germany; and that the occupation will end sooner than that of Germany. Though it will be of great importance that occupying forces in Germany should be respected by the inhabitants, this will be of even more importance in Austria, and the impression to be aimed at is of a different kind. You should bear in mind that—in a certain sense—Austria already has a six-years' experience of being occupied.

5. You will strictly forbid and vigorously suppress any political activity by remnants of the National Socialist party in Austria, or any groups which seek to propagate its doctrines or any similar ones. In particular you will tolerate no continuance of discrimination against individual Austrians on grounds of race or religion. You will also forbid any political activity or propaganda based on pan-Germanism or seeking to renew in any way the association of Austria with Germany.

6. Your attitude towards other political activities in Austria will be governed by the over-riding necessity for the maintenance of military security; this will, however, leave you more latitude than will be the case in Germany. Subject to this necessity, you will not forbid political activities, including public demonstrations or meetings. But you will be careful, in the absence of further instructions, not to lend your support or authority to any particular party or policy in Austria.

7. Subject again to the necessity for maintaining military security and a smooth administration, you will encourage freedom of speech and freedom of the Press, and the formation of free Trades Unions.

8. You will do all you can to foster freedom of religion and the maintenance of respect for the churches in Austria; but you should take steps to ensure that religious activities are not used as a cloak for the spreading of undesirable political ideas or of propaganda directed against any of the United Nations.

9. In general, the attitude to the Austrian population of all forces and agencies under your command or control should be firm and just, but more friendly than in Germany. You will exercise your discretion in regard to the degree of fraternisation to be permitted between Allied forces and the Austrian population. You will, however, reduce to a minimum all contact between forces under your command and Austrian forces not yet demobilised. Similarly, contact with Austrian officials can be more friendly and forthcoming than will be desirable in Germany.

10. After Germany's surrender, your first concern in Austria will be to ensure the functioning of a central administration. This task will be complicated by the fact that no such administration has existed since 1939, when the seven Reichsgaue into which Austria was divided were made directly dependent on Berlin. It will be necessary to build up a central machine in Vienna to take control of Austrian affairs in many spheres. You should encourage the Austrians themselves to undertake this task, and you should do so as far as possible without prejudicing the question of the political and constitutional future of Austria. In selecting Austrians for posts in this central administration, you should have regard to administrative competence. There is no objection to you using suitable Austrian émigrés for this purpose. Some time is bound to elapse before sufficient representative Austrians of the right type emerge to form a central administration. You should, therefore, yourself be prepared not only to control the Austrian administration in the general interests of the United Nations, but also to supplement its personnel, where necessary, by providing the services of Allied officers and officials.

11. In Austria there is no intermediate administrative unit between the Reichsgaue and the Kreise, and the principal link for civil administration must, therefore, be the former until it is possible to restore the old Austria Länder.

12. Some time must elapse before it becomes possible for an Austrian Government to be formed, though it is to be hoped that this may be done with as brief a delay as possible. You should bear in mind that, even after the surrender of Germany, Austria will remain technically a part of Germany, till she is formally constituted as an independent State. During this time there can in any case be no independent Austrian Government, and Austria will, of course, remain as much subject to control by the United Nations as Germany. In Austria this control will be exercised as far as possible by organisations and staffs separate from those operating in Germany; and you

will use this period for helping to carry out the process referred to in paragraph 3(e) above.

13. For the "disentangling" of Austria from Germany, you will be given fuller instructions at a later stage. But at the earliest moment you will control the passage of persons across the frontier between Austria and Germany in both directions.

14. You should bear in mind that the problem of purging the administration (on which you will have received a particular directive) will not be the same in Austria as in Germany. In Austria it will be necessary to get rid not merely of extreme National Socialists, who will be, if anything, more firmly in control of the administration there than in Germany, but also of the many Reich Germans who hold Austrian posts. The necessity for removing these, in which process you should act in concert with whatever Austrian elements you may have established in the central administration at Vienna, may for some time increase the number of Allied officers you will have to provide to assist that administration.

209. "Morgenthau Plan," September 5, 1944[2]

TOP SECRET   [Washington, September 5, 1944.]
SUGGESTED POST-SURRENDER PROGRAM FOR GERMANY
   1. *Demilitarization of Germany*
   It should be the aim of the Allied Forces to accomplish the complete demilitarization of Germany in the shortest possible period of time after surrender. This means completely disarming the German Army and people (including the removal or destruction of all war material), the total destruction of the whole German armament industry, and the removal or destruction of other key industries which are basic to military strength.
   2. *Partitioning of Germany*
   (a) Poland should get that part of East Prussia which doesn't go to the U. S. S. R. and the southern portion of Silesia. . . .
   (b) France should get the Saar and the adjacent territories bounded by the Rhine and the Moselle Rivers.
   (c) As indicated in part 3 an International Zone should be created containing the Ruhr and the surrounding industrial areas.
   (d) The remaining portion of Germany should be divided into two autonomous, independent states, (1) a South German state comprising Bavaria, Wuerttemberg, Baden and some smaller areas and (2) a North German state comprising a large part of the old state of Prussia, Saxony, Thuringia and several smaller states.
   There shall be a custom union between the new South German state and Austria, which will be restored to her pre-1938 political borders.
   3. *The Ruhr Area*
   (The Ruhr, surrounding industrial areas, as shown on the attached

map, including the Rhineland, the Kiel Canal, and all German territory north of the Kiel Canal.)

Here lies the heart of German industrial power, the caldron of wars. This area should not only be stripped of all presently existing industries but so weakened and controlled that it can not in the foreseeable future become an industrial area. The following steps will accomplish this:

(a) Within a short period, if possible not longer than 6 months after the cessation of hostilities, all industrial plants and equipment not destroyed by military action shall either be completely dismantled and removed from the area or completely destroyed. All equipment shall be removed from the mines and the mines shall be thoroughly wrecked.

It is anticipated that the stripping of this area would be accomplished in three stages:

(i) The military forces immediately upon entry into the area shall destroy all plants and equipment which cannot be removed.

(ii) Removal of plants and equipment by members of the United Nations as restitution and reparation (Paragraph 4).

(iii) All plants and equipment not removed within a stated period of time, say 6 months, will be completely destroyed or reduced to scrap and allocated to the United Nations.

(b) All people within the area should be made to understand that this area will not again be allowed to become an industrial area. Accordingly, all people and their families within the area having special skills or technical training should be encouraged to migrate permanently from the area and should be as widely dispersed as possible.

(c) The area should be made an international zone to be governed by an international security organization to be established by the United Nations. In governing the area the international organization should be guided by policies designed to further the above stated objectives.

4. *Restitution and Reparation*

Reparations, in the form of recurrent payments and deliveries, should not be demanded. Restitution and reparation shall be effected by the transfer of existing German resources and territories, e.g.,

(a) by restitution of property looted by the Germans in territories occupied by them;

(b) by transfer of German territory and German private rights in industrial property situated in such territory to invaded countries and the international organization under the program of partition;

(c) by the removal and distribution among devastated countries of industrial plants and equipment situated within the International Zone and the North and South German states delimited in the section on partition;

(d) by forced German labor outside Germany; and

(e) by confiscation of all German assets of any character whatsoever outside of Germany.

5. *Education and Propaganda*

(a) All schools and universities will be closed until an Allied Commission of Education has formulated an effective reorganization program. It is contemplated that it may require a considerable period of time before any institutions of higher education are reopened. Meanwhile the education of German students in foreign universities will not be prohibited. Elementary schools will be reopened as quickly as appropriate teachers and textbooks are available.

(b) All German radio stations and newspapers, magazines, weeklies, etc. shall be discontinued until adequate controls are established and an appropriate program formulated.

6. *Political Decentralization*

The military administration in Germany in the initial period should be carried out with a view toward the eventual partitioning of Germany into three states. To facilitate partitioning and to assure its permanence the military authorities should be guided by the following principles:

(a) Dismiss all policy-making officials of the Reich government and deal primarily with local governments.

(b) Encourage the reestablishment of state governments in each of the states (Länder) corresponding to 18 states into which Germany is presently divided and in addition make the Prussian provinces separate states.

(c) Upon the partition of Germany, the various state governments should be encouraged to organize a federal government for each of the newly partitioned areas. Such new governments should be in the form of a confederation of states, with emphasis on states' rights and a large degree of local autonomy.

7. *Responsibility of Military for Local German Economy*

The sole purpose of the military in control of the German economy shall be to facilitate military operations and military occupation. The Allied Military Government shall not assume responsibility for such economic problems as price controls, rationing, unemployment, production, reconstruction, distribution, consumption, housing, or transportation, or take any measures designed to maintain or strengthen (the German economy, except those which are essential to military) operations. The responsibility for sustaining the German economy and people rests with the German people with such facilities as may be available under the circumstances.

8. *Controls Over Development of German Economy*

During a period of at least twenty years after surrender adequate controls, including controls over foreign trade and tight restrictions on capital imports, shall be maintained by the United Nations designed to prevent in the newly-established states the establishment or expansion of key industries basic to the German military potential and to control other key industries.

9. *Punishment of War Crimes and Treatment of Special Groups*

There is attached (Appendix B) a program for the punishment of certain war crimes and for the treatment of Nazi organizations and other special groups.

10. *Wearing of Insignia and Uniforms*

(a) No person in German[y] (except members of the United Nations and neutral countries) shall be permitted to wear any military insignia of rank or branch of service, service ribbons or military medals.

(b) No such person shall be permitted to wear, after 6 months from the cessation of hostilities any military uniform or any uniform of any quasi military organizations.

11. *Prohibition on Parades*

No military parades shall be permitted anywhere in German(y) and all military bands shall be disbanded.

12. *Aircraft*

All aircraft (including gliders), whether military or commercial, will be confiscated for later disposition. No German shall be permitted to operate or to help operate such aircraft, including those owned by foreign interests.

13. *United States Responsibility*

(a) The responsibility for the execution of the post-surrender program for Germany set forth in this memorandum is the joint responsibility of the United Nations. The execution of the joint policy agreed upon should therefore eventually be entrusted to the international body which emerges from United Nations discussions.

Consideration of the specific measures to be taken in carrying out the joint program suggests the desirability of separating the task to be performed during the initial period of military occupation from those which will require a much longer period of execution. While the U. S., U. K. and U. S. S. R. will, for practical reasons, play the major role (of course aided by the military forces of other United Nations) in demilitarizing Germany (point 1) the detailed execution of other parts of the program can best be handled by Germany's continental neighbors.

(b) When Germany has been completely demilitarized there would be the following distribution of duties in carrying out the German program:

(i) The U. S. would have military and civilian representation on whatever international commission or commissions may be established for the execution of the whole German program and such representatives should have adequate U. S. staffs.

(ii) The primary responsibility for the policing of Germany and for civil administration in Germany would be assumed by the military forces of Germany's continental neighbors. Specifically these should include Russian, French, Polish, Czech, Greek, Yugoslav, Norwegian, Dutch and Belgian soldiers.

(c) Under this program United States troops could be withdrawn within a relatively short time. Actual withdrawal of United States troops should not precede agreement with the U. S. S. R. and the U. K. on the principles set forth in this memorandum.

14. *Appointment of an American High Commissioner*

An American High Commissioner for Germany should be appointed as soon as possible, so that he can sit in on the development of the American views on this problem.

210. ALLIED REPORTS ON GERMANY, NOVEMBER AND DECEMBER, 1944[3] (EXCERPTS)

REPORT ON GERMANY FOR WEEK ENDING NOVEMBER 25, 1944
CIVIL ADMINISTRATION

Recent reports indicate an increasing difficulty in inducing people to suggest names of possible officials. In all places, however, where Military Government has been established and the initial difficulty of finding the most suitable persons available has been overcome, administration is working quite smoothly.

At VICHT, the Burgermeister, though lacking in previous administrative experience is working satisfactorily. He enjoys the respect of the civilian population (prior to appointment he was a local schoolmaster) and is receiving considerable assistance from the local postmaster. Both these officials are eagerly following the directions of Military Government officers.

From PALENBERG it is reported that a civilian Fuel Administrator has been appointed—his duties consist of the transportation, under police supervision of a limited quantity of coal to a central point where a rationed issue to civilians will be made.

LEGAL

Two interesting cases are reported by First US Army. A Military Government Summary Court at Eilendorf, Germany, convicted Franz Gottfries of disobeying a circulation restriction and sentenced him to serve 45 days in prison and to pay a fine of twenty marks. The fine and the sentence were approved by the reviewing authority. The Intermediate Military Government Court sitting at KORNELIMUNSTER convicted Maria Jensen of concealing records of the NS Frauenschaft and sentenced her to a term of six years imprisonment. The reviewing authority reduced the sentence to two years.

PUBLIC SAFETY

A close scrutiny and control of civilian population and activities is being maintained. It is reported that German nationals are being encountered who are not in possession of identity cards. A few German soldiers, in civilian clothing, have been apprehended and turned over to CIC.

Telephone connections have been re-established in EIGEL SHOVEN for the use of the local air raid warning service.

FINANCE

First US Army reports that financial conditions throughout occupied areas are spotty. Some banks are operating satisfactorily, others not at all. In spite of cash gain by reopened banks, cash holdings are extremely low in relation to deposits, representing only an insignificant fraction thereof. It is too early to draw definite conclusions as to willingness of German bankers, outside of the Reichsbank, to cooperate with Military Government, although those in small banks reopened so far have shown willingness. The flight of managers and personnel from the bigger places indicates unwillingness to cooperate. As to the Reichsbank, evidence provided by AACHEN and STOLBERG indicates we cannot expect any voluntary cooperation. In the field of public finance, some towns have adequate cash or facilities at hand for essential requirements; others are badly off. Resumption of normal conditions generally is a long way off. Circulation restrictions required by military necessity and absence of records and officials will hamper tax collections in many cases. Collections now are unsatisfactory.

. . . .

LABOUR

The 60-hour week seems to be in general operation in Germany and is causing many complaints especially from women, some of whom state that they too are expected to work 60 hours, although the regulation is 56 for women. Some employers are interpreting the demand for total effort as a call to increase hours, without regard to their workers' health or to optimum production. Employers who can succeed in completing their production quota in under 60 hours are expected to release a corresponding number of workers for other firms, and are penalized for "cornering the labour market" if they do not. This in itself is likely to discourage any increase in output per man-hour, as it is to the interest neither of employers or workers.

The strain is even greater in enterprises which have been transferred underground for greater protection against air attacks, so that daylight, has to a great extent to be foregone and the supply of fresh air, despite the highly developed air-conditioning plants, is hardly comparable with that in factories above-ground.

Workers are supplied with warm food, medical attention, extra rations and special holidays. They are given also special stimulants, such as sweets with Vitamin C, which are administered in doses of up to 100 g in the first stages of exhaustion and have increased working capacity by 20 to 25 per cent.

The latest method is to combine these stimulants with alcohol, making a liquor which is said to have proved exceptionally valuable for ensuring peak performance.

A curfew has been imposed for all foreign workers in Germany. Camp leaders have been ordered to see that everyone is in camp by 9 p.m. in winter and 10 p.m. in summer. The purpose of the decree is stated by the Dutch workers paper, VAN HONK, to be guaranteed a night's rest in these nerve-cracking times. Camp leaders, may, however, allow *reliable* men to return after the curfew.

The Labour Office has also issued a warning to employers that they must not engage foreign workers except through official channels. No doubt this warning is partly due to the numbers of foreign workers who have escaped and are trying to work their way across Germany towards the Western Front.

. . . .

REPORT ON GERMANY FOR WEEK ENDING DECEMBER 9, 1944
CIVIL ADMINISTRATION

Reports from the most recently occupied sectors of Germany indicate that destruction to towns and villages is now much more severe than in the early stages of the German battle and that evacuation Eastwards of the civilian population is still being carried out. BETTENDORF and SIERSDORF are reported to be 90% destroyed. LOVERICH and FLOVERICH to have suffered 50% destruction. The town of DUERSBOSLAR was completely evacuated when occupied and almost all the population had disappeared from GEILENKIRCHEN, PUFFENDORF, EDEREN, FREIALDENHA-VEN, MERZENHAUSEN, ALDENHOVEN and GEREONSWEILER.

In Landkreiss MONSCHAU, in an effort to improve control in the distribution of existing supplies of food, fuel and civilian clothing a conference was called by the local Military Government officer and attended by the Landrat of the Kreis together with the acting burgermeisters of ZWEIFALL, ROTT, and ROETGEN.

Acting burgermeister KEISCHGENS of BEND, near SCHEVEN-HUTTE has been removed from office on security grounds and now is being held in a local prisoner of war cage. Gemeinde STEINEBRUCK has a new burgermeister in the person of Johann Marx of Urb.

The burgermeister of SCHERPENSEEL and five secretaries are working without compensation for their services. All records were destroyed or removed by the Nazis upon their departure.

Officials appointed by the Military Government in the Gemeinden of UBACH and PALENBERG have proved reliable, and civil administration in these communities is functioning effectively.

PUBLIC SAFETY

In general no change is reported. Military Government enactments are being posted in the ESCHWEILER area and Military Government officers in this town are assisting in the screening of local inhabitants.

At EILENDORF Nazi Party members are reporting daily in compliance with orders and several former German soldiers found in the town have been handed over to Prisoner of War authorities. Billets have been allotted to a considerable number of troops and the fire department has been reorganized and is ready for service.

From AACHEN reports indicate that considerable progress has been made in reorganising the administration of the local prison.

Civilian circulation is prohibited in SCHERPENSEEL except for shopping, water carrying and harvesting. Emergency passes which permit circulation after curfew are issued only to priests and to doctors.

POLITICAL

The burgermeister of SCHERPENSEEL maintains that, prior to American occupation, there were about fifty Nazi party members out of a total population of 1,274. Of the fifty, only twelve allegedly were genuine Nazis. A certain number of professional party workers had been sent in, but they left with the retreating German forces. This stated disinclination for Nazism is attributed to preponderant Catholic and peasant opinion and influence.

. . . .

AGRICULTURE

Farm Production. In certain occupied German territory farm production has been seriously interfered with by tactical operations. The majority of German farmers have left their farms, being evacuated by the Germans as refugees, or forced to leave their land by Allied tactical commanders. In some areas, cattle are roaming the countryside unattended. Many milk cows are going dry due to the inability of the remaining farmers to milk them: crops in the field are not being dug: leaking roofs and lack of permission to issue gasoline for threshing is causing considerable quantities of grain to rot in the barns. There are some vegetables available, but the lack of transport and inability of civilians to cross Divisional and Corps boundaries, makes it difficult to get much of these into cities.

The area uncovered to date is rather rich in potatoes, cattle, dairy products and root crops for animals. It is not a wheat area although some rye is grown. It is stated that one half of the cattle in the area may have to be slaughtered for lack of fodder and farm help to care for them.

Available Stocks of Food. There were practically no large stocks of food uncovered and those which are available are located in homes, shops and farms. Although the rural areas will be able to feed themselves for sometime, it was felt that imported Civil Affairs food would be needed in the AACHEN region within 30–60 days (depending on the number of persons returning to evacuated cities), to keep people from starving. The area appears to have sufficient meat for some months, potatoes for at least 60 days, vegetables for the present, but there is a shortage of flour and there will be an acute milk shortage within a month or two. In AACHEN, an effort is being made to collect all food stocks from bombed stores, warehouses and homes, so that it may be distributed as a ration later.

. . . .

PUBLIC HEALTH

No unusual public health problems have occurred to date. Civilian casualties from combat action continue with most of the reported cases being treated by local medical personnel. In all reported communities, doctors and related personnel have remained in sufficient numbers to handle the civilian medical problems. Civilian hospitals are in operation in most communities but vacant beds are becoming more scarce according to reports from STOLBERG, KORNELIMUNSTER and AACHEN.

It is reported that German medical personnel are rendering excellent medical attention to the civil population. Reasonable quantities of medical supplies have been located in the pharmacies of the larger communities, but due to restriction on circulation, outlying communities have met some difficulty in obtaining drugs and dressings. Adequate stores are available for callforward by the commands for distribution to the civilian, if such should be required under current policy.

At BARDENBURG, communicable diseases reported in normal numbers consisting of diphtheria, influenza, measles and scarlet fever.

MONUMENTS AND FINE ARTS

A collection of paintings, museum pieces, furniture and other objects, was found in a hunting lodge in SCHWARZFEID about one and one-half miles south of ROETGEN. A medical unit which was occupying the lodge has been informed of the importance of the collection, which has been placed under lock and "Off Limits" signs posted.

211. CRIMEAN CONFERENCE AT YALTA, FEBRUARY 4–11, 1945[4] (EXCERPT)

(a) Protocol of Proceedings

The Crimea Conference of the Heads of the Governments of the United States of America, the United Kingdom and the Union of Soviet Socialist Republics which took place from February 4th to 11th came to the following conclusions:

I. World Organisation

It was decided:

(1) that a United Nations Conference on the proposed world organisation should be summoned for Wednesday, 25th April, 1945, and should be held in the United States of America.

(2) the Nations to be invited to this Conference should be:

(a) the United Nations as they existed on the 8th February, 1945; and

(b) such of the Associated Nations as have declared war on the common enemy by 1st March, 1945. (For this purpose by the term "Associated Nation" was meant the eight Associated Nations and Turkey.) When the Conference on World Organization is held, the delegates of the United Kingdom and United States of America will support a proposal to admit to original membership two Soviet Socialist Republics, i.e. the Ukraine and White Russia.

(3) that the United States Government on behalf of the Three Powers should consult the Government of China and the French Provisional Government in regard to decisions taken at the present Conference concerning the proposed World Organisation.

(4) that the text of the invitation to be issued to all the nations which would take part in the United Nations Conference should be as follows:

Invitation

"The Government of the United States of America, on behalf of itself and of the Governments of the United Kingdom, the Union of Soviet Socialist

Republics, and the Republic of China and of the Provisional Government of the French Republic, invite the Government of _____ to send representatives to a Conference of the United Nations to be held on 25th April, 1945, or soon thereafter, at San Francisco in the United States of America to prepare a Charter for a General International Organisation for the maintenance of international peace and security.

"The above named governments suggest that the Conference consider as affording a basis for such a Charter the Proposals for the Establishment of a General International Organisation, which were made public last October as a result of the Dumbarton Oaks Conference, and which have now been supplemented by the following provisions for Section C of Chapter VI;

C. Voting

"'1. Each member of the Security Council should have one vote.

"'2. Decisions of the Security Council on procedural matters should be made by an affirmative vote of seven members.

"'3. Decisions of the Security Council on all other matters should be made by an affirmative vote of seven members including the concurring votes of the permanent members; provided that, in decisions under Chapter VIII, Section A and under the second sentence of paragraph 1 of Chapter VIII, Section C, a party to a dispute should abstain from voting.'

"Further information as to arrangements will be transmitted subsequently.

"In the event that the Government of _____ desires in advance of the Conference to present views or comments concerning the proposals, the Government of the United States of America will be pleased to transmit such views and comments to the other participating Governments."

Territorial Trusteeship

It was agreed that the five Nations which will have permanent seats on the Security Council should consult each other prior to the United Nations Conference on the question of territorial trusteeship.

The acceptance of this recommendation is subject to its being made clear that territorial trusteeship will only apply to (a) existing mandates of the League of Nations; (b) territories detached from the enemy as a result of the present war; (c) any other territory which might voluntarily be placed under trusteeship; and (d) no discussion of actual territories is contemplated at the forthcoming United Nations Conference or in the preliminary consultations, and it will be a matter for subsequent agreement which territories within the above categories will be placed under trusteeship.

II. Declaration on Liberated Europe

The following declaration has been approved:

"The Premier of the Union of Soviet Socialist Republics, the Prime Minister of the United Kingdom and the President of the United States of America have consulted with each other in the common interests of the peoples of their countries and those of liberated Europe. They jointly declare their mutual agreement to concert during the temporary period of instability in liberated Europe the policies of their three governments in assisting the peoples liberated from the domination of Nazi Germany and the peoples of the former Axis satellite states of Europe to solve by democratic means their pressing political and economic problems.

"The establishment of order in Europe and the re-building of national economic life must be achieved by processes which will enable the liberated peoples to destroy the last vestiges of Nazism and Fascism and to create democratic institutions of their own choice. This is a principle of the Atlantic Charter—the right of all peoples to choose the form of government under which they will live—the restoration of sovereign rights and self-government to those people who have been forcibly deprived of them by the aggressor nations.

"To foster the conditions in which the liberated peoples may exercise these rights, the three governments will jointly assist the people in any European liberated state or former Axis satellite state in Europe where in their judgment conditions require (a) to establish conditions of internal peace; (b) to carry out emergency measures for the relief of distressed people; (c) to form interim governmental authorities broadly representative of all democratic elements in the population and pledge to the earliest possible establishment through free elections of governments responsive to the will of the people; and (d) to facilitate where necessary the holding of such elections.

"The three governments will consult the other United Nations and provisional authorities or other governments in Europe when matters of direct interest to them are under consideration.

"When, in the opinion of the three governments, conditions in any European liberated state or any former Axis satellite state in Europe make such action necessary, they will immediately consult together on the measures necessary to discharge the joint responsibilities set forth in this declaration.

"By this declaration we reaffirm our faith in the principles of the Atlantic Charter, our pledge in the Declaration by the United Nations, and our determination to build in cooperation with other peace-loving nations world order under law, dedicated to peace, security, freedom and general well-being of all mankind.

"In issuing this declaration, the Three Powers express the hope that the Provisional Government of the French Republic may be associated with them in the procedure suggested."

III. Dismemberment of Germany

It was agreed that Article 12 (a) of the Surrender Terms for Germany should be amended to read as follows:

"The United Kingdom, the United States of America and the Union of Soviet Socialist Republics shall possess supreme authority with respect to Germany. In the exercise of such authority they will take such steps, including the complete disarmament, demilitarisation and dismemberment of Germany as they deem requisite for future peace and security."

The study of the procedure for the dismemberment of Germany was referred to a Committee, consisting of Mr. Eden (Chairman), Mr. Winant and Mr. Gousey. This body would consider the desirability of associating with it a French representative.

IV. Zone of Occupation for the French and
Control Council for Germany

It was agreed that a zone in Germany, to be occupied by the French Forces, should be allocated to France. This zone would be formed out of the British and American zones and its extent would be settled by the British and Americans in consultation with the French Provisional Government.

It was also agreed that the French Provisional Government should be invited to become a member of the Allied Control Council for Germany.

V. Reparation

. . . .

[Approved protocol, printed following XIV.]

VI. Major War Criminals

The Conference agreed that the question of the major war criminals should be the subject of enquiry by the three Foreign Secretaries for report in due course after the close of the Conference.

VII. Poland

The following Declaration on Poland was agreed by the Conference:

"A new situation has been created in Poland as a result of her complete liberation by the Red Army. This calls for the establishment of a Polish Provisional Government which can be more broadly based than was possible before the recent liberation of (the) Western part of Poland. The Provisional Government which is now functioning in Poland should therefore be reorganized on a broader democratic basis with the inclusion of democratic leaders from Poland itself and from Poles abroad. This new Government should then be called the Polish Provisional Government of National Unity.

"M. Molotov, Mr. Harriman and Sir A. Clark Kerr are authorised as a commission to consult in the first instance in Moscow with members of the present Provisional Government and with other Polish democratic leaders from within Poland and from abroad, with a view to the reorganisation of the present Government along the above lines. This Polish Provisional Government of National Unity shall be pledged to the holding of free and unfettered elections as soon as possible on the basis of universal suffrage and secret ballot. In these elections all democratic and anti-Nazi parties shall have the right to take part and to put forward candidates.

"When a Polish Provisional Government of National Unity has been properly formed in conformity with the above, the Government of the U. S. S. R., which now maintains diplomatic relations with the present Provisional Government of Poland, and the Government of the United Kingdom and the Government of the United States of America will establish diplomatic relations with the new Polish Provisional Government of National Unity, and will exchange Ambassadors by whose reports the respective Governments will be kept informed about the situation in Poland.

"The three Heads of Government consider that the Eastern frontier of Poland should follow the Curzon Line with digressions from it in some regions of five to eight kilometres in favour of Poland. They recognise that Poland must receive substantial accessions of territory in the North and West. They feel that the opinion of the new Polish Provisional Government of National Unity should be sought in due course on the extent of these accessions and that the final delimitation of the Western frontier of Poland should thereafter await the Peace Conference."

VIII. Yugoslavia

It was agreed to recommend to Marshal Tito and to Dr. Subasic:

(a) that the Tito-Subasic Agreement should immediately be put into effect and a new Government formed on the basis of the Agreement.

(b) that as soon as the new Government has been formed it should declare:

(i) that the Anti-Fascist Assembly of National Liberation Yugoslav Skupstina who have not compromised themselves by collaboration with the enemy, thus forming a body to be known as a temporary Parliament and

(ii) that legislative acts passed by the Anti-Fascist Assembly of National Liberation (AVNOJ) will be subject to subsequent ratification by a Constituent Assembly; and that this statement should be published in the Communique of the Conference.

IX. Italo-Yugoslav Frontier
Italo-Austria Frontier

Notes on these subjects were put in by the British delegation and the American and Soviet delegations agreed to consider them and give their views later.

X. Yugoslav-Bulgarian Relations

There was an exchange of views between the Foreign Secretaries on the question of the desirability of a Yugoslav-Bulgarian pact of alliance. The question at issue was whether a state still under an armistice regime could be allowed to enter into a treaty with another state. Mr. Eden suggested that the Bulgarian and Yugoslav Governments should be informed that this could not be approved. Mr. Stettinius suggested that the British and American Ambassadors should discuss the matter further with M. Molotov in Moscow. M. Molotov agreed with the proposal of Mr. Stettinius.

XI. South Eastern Europe

The British Delegation put in notes for the consideration of their colleagues on the following subjects:

(a) the Control Commission in Bulgaria.

(b) Greek claims upon Bulgaria, more particularly with reference to reparations.

(c) Oil equipment in Rumania.

XII. Iran

Mr. Eden, Mr. Stettinius and M. Molotov exchanged views on the situation in Iran. It was agreed that this matter should be pursued through the diplomatic channel.

XIII. Meetings of the Three Foreign Secretaries

The Conference agreed that permanent machinery should be set up for consultation between the three Foreign Secretaries; they should meet as often as necessary, probably about every three or four months.

These meetings will be held in rotation in the three capitals, the first meeting being held in London.

XIV. The Montreux Convention and the Straits

It was agreed that at the next meeting of the three Foreign Secretaries to be held in London, they should consider proposals which it was understood the Soviet Government would put forward in relation to the Montreux Convention and report to their Governments. The Turkish Government should be informed at the appropriate moment.

The foregoing Protocol was approved and signed by the three Foreign Secretaries at the Crimean Conference, February 11, 1945.

> E. R. Stettinius, Jr.
> M. Molotov
> Anthony Eden

(b) Protocol on German Reparations

The Heads of the three governments agreed as follows:

1. Germany must pay in kind for the losses caused by her to the Allied nations in the course of the war. Reparations are to be received in the first instance by those countries which have borne the main burden of the war, have suffered the heaviest losses and have organized victory over the enemy.

2. Reparation in kind are to be extracted from Germany in three following forms:

(a) Removals within 2 years from the surrender of Germany or the cessation of organised resistance from the national wealth of Germany located on the territory of Germany herself as well as outside her territory (equipment, machine-tools, ships, rolling stock, German investment abroad, shares of industrial, transport and other enterprises in Germany etc.), these removals to be carried out chiefly for purpose of destroying the war potential of Germany.

(b) Annual deliveries of goods from current production for a period to be fixed.

(c) Use of German labour.

3. For the working out on the above principles of a detailed plan for exaction of reparation from Germany an Allied Reparation Commission will be set up in Moscow. It will consist of three representatives—one from the Union of Soviet Socialist Republics, one from the United Kingdom and one from the United States of America.

4. With regard to the fixing of the total sum of the reparation as well as the

distribution of it among the countries which suffered from the German aggression the Soviet and American delegations agreed as follows:

"The Moscow Reparation Commission should take in its initial studies as a basis for discussion the suggestion of the Soviet Government that the total sum of the reparation in accordance with the points (a) and (b) of the paragraph 2 should be 20 billion dollars and that 50% of it should go to the Union of Soviet Socialist Republics."

The British delegation was of the opinion that pending consideration of the reparation question by the Moscow Reparation Commission no figures of reparation should be mentioned.

The above Soviet-American proposal has been passed to the Moscow Reparation Commission as one of the proposals to be considered by the Commission.

Winston S. Churchill
Franklin D. Roosevelt
Joseph V. Stalin

212. Extracts From Roosevelt's Press and Radio Conference, Warm Springs, Georgia, April 5, 1945[5]

The President:

. . . .

It seems obvious that we will be more or less responsible for security in all the Pacific waters. As you take a look at the different places captured by us, from Guadalcanal, the north coast of New Guinea, and then the Marianas and other islands gradually to the southern Philippines, and then into Luzon and north to Iwo Jima, it seems obvious the only danger is from Japanese forces; and they must be prevented, in the same way Germany is prevented, from setting up a military force which would start off again on a chapter of aggression.

So that means the main bases have to be taken away from them. They have to be policed externally and internally. And as a part of the western Pacific situation, it is necessary to throw them out of any of their mandated ports, which they immediately violated almost as soon as they were mandated, by fortifying these islands.

. . . .

Q. Mr. President, on the question of the Japanese mandates that you say will be taken away from them, who will be controlling government in those mandates, the United States?

The President: I would say the United Nations. Or—it might be called— the world, which has been much abused now, will have a chance to prevent any more abuse.

213. Preamble to the Charter of the United Nations, June 26, 1945[6]

We the peoples of the United Nations determined

to save succeeding generations from the scourge of war, which twice in our lifetime has brought untold sorrow to mankind, and to reaffirm faith in fundamental human rights, in the dignity and worth of the human person, in the equal rights of men and women and of nations large and small, and

to establish conditions under which justice and respect for the obligations arising from treaties and other sources of international law can be maintained, and

to promote social progress and better standards of life in larger freedom, and for these ends

to practice tolerance and live together in peace with one another as good neighbors, and

to unite our strength to maintain international peace and security, and

to ensure, by the acceptance of principles and the institution of methods, that armed force shall not be used, save in the common interest, and

to employ international machinery for the promotion of the economic and social advancement of all peoples,

have resolved to combine our efforts to accomplish these aims.

Accordingly, our respective Governments, through representatives assembled in the city of San Francisco, who have exhibited their full powers found to be in good and due form, have agreed to the present Charter of the United Nations and do hereby establish an international organization to be known as the United Nations.

214. Protocol of the Proceedings of the Berlin (Potsdam) Conference[7]

Berlin, August 1, 1945

There is attached hereto the agreed protocol of the Berlin Conference.

JOSEPH V. STALIN; HARRY TRUMAN;
C. R. ATTLEE

PROTOCOL OF THE PROCEEDINGS OF THE
BERLIN CONFERENCE

The Berlin Conference of the three Heads of Government of the U. S. S. R., U. S. A., and U. K., which took place from July 17 to August 2, 1945, came to the following conclusions:

I. *Establishment of a Council of Foreign Ministers*

A. The Conference reached the following agreement for the establishment of a Council of Foreign Ministers to do the necessary preparatory work for the peace settlements:

"(1) There shall be established a Council composed of the Foreign Ministers of the United Kingdom, the Union of Soviet Socialist Republics, China, France, and the United States.

"(2) (i) The Council shall normally meet in London which shall be the permanent seat of the joint Secretariat which the Council will form. Each of the Foreign Ministers will be accompanied by a high-ranking Deputy, duly authorized to carry on the work of the Council in the absence of his Foreign Minister, and by a small staff of technical advisers.

"(ii) The first meeting of the Council shall be held in London not later than September 1st, 1945. Meetings may be held by common agreement in other capitals as may be agreed from time to time.

"(3) (i) As its immediate important task, the Council shall be authorized to draw up, with a view to their submission to the United Nations, treaties of peace with Italy, Rumania, Bulgaria, Hungary, and Finland, and to propose settlements of territorial questions outstanding on the termination of the war in Europe. The Council shall be utilized for the preparation of a peace settlement for Germany to be accepted by the Government of Germany when a government adequate for the purpose is established.

"(ii) For the discharge of each of these tasks the Council will be composed of the Members representing those States which were signatory to the terms of surrender imposed upon the enemy State concerned. For the purposes of the peace settlement for Italy, France shall be regarded as a signatory to the terms of surrender for Italy. Other Members will be invited to participate when matters directly concerning them are under discussion.

"(iii) Other matters may from time to time be referred to the Council by agreement between the Member Governments.

"(4) (i) Whenever the Council is considering a question of direct interest to a State not represented thereon, such State should be invited to send representatives to participate in the discussion and study of that question.

"(ii) The Council may adapt its procedure to the particular problems under consideration. In some cases it may hold its own preliminary discussions prior to the participation of other interested States. In other cases, the Council may convoke a formal conference of the States chiefly interested in seeking a solution of the particular problem."

B. It was agreed that the Three Governments should each address an identical invitation to the Governments of China and France to adopt this text and to join in establishing the Council. The text of the approved invitation was as follows:

COUNCIL OF FOREIGN MINISTERS: DRAFT FOR IDENTICAL IN-
VITATION TO BE SENT SEPARATELY BY EACH OF THE THREE
GOVERNMENTS TO THE GOVERNMENTS OF CHINA AND
FRANCE

"The Governments of the United Kingdom, the United States, and the
U. S. S. R. consider it necessary to begin without delay the essential preparatory work upon the peace settlements in Europe. To this end they are agreed
that there should be established a Council of the Foreign Ministers of the
Five Great Powers to prepare treaties of peace with the European enemy
States for submission to the United Nations. The Council would also be
empowered to propose settlements of outstanding territorial questions in
Europe and to consider such other matters as member Governments might
agree to refer to it.

"The text adopted by the Three Governments is as follows:
(Here insert final agreed text of the Proposal as quoted above.)

"In agreement with the Governments of the UNITED STATES AND
USSR, HIS MAJESTY'S GOVERNMENT IN THE UNITED KINGDOM
AND USSR, THE UNITED STATES GOVERNMENT, THE UNITED
KINGDOM, AND THE SOVIET GOVERNMENT extend a cordial invita-
tion to the Government of China (France) to adopt the text quoted above and
to join in setting up the Council. HIS MAJESTY'S GOVERNMENT, THE
UNITED STATES GOVERNMENT, THE SOVIET GOVERNMENT, at-
tach much importance to the participation of the CHINESE GOVERN-
MENT (FRENCH GOVERNMENT) in the proposed arrangements and
they hope to receive an early and favorable reply to this invitation."

C. It was understood that the establishment of the Council of Foreign
Ministers for the specific purposes named in the text would be without
prejudice to the agreement of the Crimea Conference that there should be
periodical consultation between the Foreign Secretaries of the United States,
the Union of Soviet Socialist Republics, and the United Kingdom.

D. The Conference also considered the position of the European Advisory Commission in the light of the Agreement to establish the Council of
Foreign Ministers. It was noted with satisfaction that the Commission had
ably discharged its principal tasks by the recommendations that it had
furnished for the terms of surrender for Germany, for the zones of occupation in Germany and Austria, and for the inter-Allied control machinery in
these countries. It was felt that further work of a detailed character for the
coordination of Allied policy for the control of Germany and Austria would
in future fall within the competence of the Control Council at Berlin and the
Allied Commission at Vienna. Accordingly, it was agreed to recommend that
the European Advisory Commission be dissolved.

II. *The Principles to Govern the Treatment of Germany in the Initial Control Period*

A. POLITICAL PRINCIPLES

1. In accordance with the Agreement on Control Machinery in Germany, supreme authority in Germany is exercised, on instructions from their respective Governments, by the Commanders-in-Chief of the armed forces of the United States of America, the United Kingdom, the Union of Soviet Socialist Republics, and the French Republic, each in his own zone of occupation, and also jointly, in matters affecting Germany as a whole, in their capacity as members of the Control Council.

2. So far as is practicable, there shall be uniformity of treatment of the German population throughout Germany.

3. The purposes of the occupation of Germany by which the Control Council shall be guided are:

(i) The complete disarmament and demilitarization of Germany and the elimination or control of all Germany industry that could be used for military production.

To these ends:

(a) All German land, naval, and air forces, the S. S., S. A., S. D., and Gestapo, with all their organizations, staffs, and institutions, including the General Staff, the Officer's Corps, Reserve Corps, military schools, war veterans' organizations and all other military and semi-military organizations, together with all clubs and associations which serve to keep alive the military tradition in Germany, shall be completely and finally abolished in such manner as permanently to prevent the revival or reorganization of German militarism and Nazism;

(b) All arms, ammunition, and implements of war and all specialized facilities for their production shall be held at the disposal of the Allies or destroyed. The maintenance and production of all aircraft and all arms, ammunition, and implements of war shall be prevented.

(ii) To convince the German people that they have suffered a total military defeat and that they cannot escape responsibility for what they have brought upon themselves, since their own ruthless warfare and the fanatical Nazi resistance have destroyed German economy and made chaos and suffering inevitable.

(iii) To destroy the National Socialist Party and its affiliated and supervised organizations, to dissolve all Nazi institutions, to ensure that they are not revived in any form, and to prevent all Nazi and militarist activity or propaganda.

(iv) To prepare for the eventual reconstruction of German political life on a democratic basis and for eventual peaceful cooperation in international life by Germany.

4. All Nazi laws which provided the basis of the Hitler regime or established discriminations on grounds of race, creed, or political opinion shall be abolished. No such discriminations, whether legal, administrative, or otherwise, shall be tolerated.

5. War criminals and those who have participated in planning or carrying out Nazi enterprises involving or resulting in atrocities of war crimes shall be arrested and brought to judgement. Nazi leaders, influential Nazi supporters, and high officials of Nazi organizations and institutions and any other persons dangerous to the occupation of its objectives shall be arrested and interned.

6. All members of the Nazi Party who have been more than nominal participants in its activities and all other persons hostile to Allied purposes shall be replaced by persons who, by their political and moral qualities, are deemed capable of assisting in developing genuine democratic institutions in Germany.

7. German education shall be so controlled as completely to eliminate Nazi and militarist doctrines and to make possible the successful development of democratic ideas.

8. The judicial system will be reorganized in accordance with the principles of democracy, of justice under law, and of equal rights for all citizens without distinction of race, nationality or religion.

9. The administration in Germany should be directed towards the decentralization of the political structure and the development of local responsibility. To this end:

(i) local self-government shall be restored throughout Germany on democratic principles and in particular through elective councils as rapidly as is consistent with military security and the purposes of military occupation;

(ii) all democratic political parties with rights of assembly and of public discussion shall be allowed and encouraged throughout Germany;

(iii) representatives and elective principles shall be introduced into regional, provincial, and state (LAND) administration as rapidly as may be justified by the successful application of these principles in local self-government;

(iv) for the time being, no central German Government shall be established. Notwithstanding this, however, certain essential central German administrative departments, headed by States Secretaries, shall be established, particularly in the fields of finance, transport, communications, foreign trade, and industry. Such departments will act under the direction of the Control Council.

10. Subject to the necessity for maintaining military security, freedom of speech, press, and religion shall be permitted, and religious institutions shall be respected. Subject likewise to the maintenance of military security, the formation of free trade unions shall be permitted.

B. ECONOMIC PRINCIPLES

11. In order to eliminate Germany's war potential, the production of arms, ammunition, and implements of war, as well as all types of aircraft and

sea-going ships shall be prohibited and prevented. Production of metals, chemicals, machinery, and other items that are directly necessary to a war economy shall be rigidly controlled and restricted to Germany's approved postwar peacetime needs to meet the objectives stated in Paragraph 15. Productive capacity not needed for permitted production shall be removed in accordance with the reparations plan recommended by the Allied Commission on Reparations and approved by the Governments concerned or if not removed shall be destroyed.

12. At the earliest practicable date, the German economy shall be decentralized for the purpose of eliminating the present excessive concentration of economic power as exemplified in particular by cartels, syndicates, trusts and other monopolistic arrangements.

13. In organizing the German economy, primary emphasis shall be given to the development of agriculture and peaceful domestic industries.

14. During the period of occupation Germany shall be treated as a single economic unit. To this end common policies shall be established in regard to:

(a) mining and industrial production and its allocation;
(b) agriculture, forestry, and fishing;
(c) wages, prices, and rationing;
(d) import and export programs for Germany as a whole;
(e) currency and banking, central taxation and customs;
(f) reparation and removal of industrial war potential;
(g) transportation and communications.

In applying these policies account shall be taken, where appropriate, of varying local conditions.

15. Allied controls shall be imposed upon the German economy but only to the extent necessary:

(a) to carry out programs of industrial disarmament, demilitarization, or reparations, and of approved exports and imports.

(b) to assure the production and maintenance of goods and services required to meet the needs of the occupying forces and displaced persons in Germany and essential to maintain in Germany average living standards not exceeding the average of the standards of living of European countries. (European countries means all European countries excluding the United Kingdom and the U. S. S. R.)

(c) to ensure in the manner determined by the Control Council the equitable distribution of essential commodities between the several zones so as to produce a balanced economy throughout Germany and reduce the need for imports.

(d) to control German industry and all economic and financial international transactions including exports and imports, with the aim of preventing Germany from developing a war potential and of achieving the other objectives named herein.

(e) to control all German public or private scientific bodies, research and experimental institutions, laboratories, et cetera, connected with economic activities.

16. In the imposition and maintenance of economic controls established by the Control Council, German administrative machinery shall be created and the German authorities shall be required to the fullest extent practicable to proclaim and assume administration of such controls. Thus it should be brought home to the German people that the responsibility for the administration of such controls and any breakdown in these controls will rest with themselves. Any German controls which may run counter to the objectives of occupation will be prohibited.

17. Measures shall be promptly taken:
(a) to effect essential repair of transport;
(b) to enlarge coal production;
(c) to maximize agricultural output; and
(d) to effect emergency repair of housing and essential utilities.

18. Appropriate steps shall be taken by the Control Council to exercise control and the power of disposition over German-owned external assets not already under control of United Nations which have taken part in the war against Germany.

19. Payment of Reparations should leave enough resources to enable the German people to subsist without external assistance. In working out the economic balance of Germany the necessary means must be provided to pay for imports approved by the Control Council in Germany. The proceeds of exports from current production and stocks shall be available in the first place for payment of such imports.

The above clause will not apply to the equipment and products referred to in paragraphs 4 (a) and 4 (b) of the Reparations Agreement.

III. *Reparations From Germany*

1. Reparation claims of the U. S. S. R. shall be met by removals from the zone of Germany occupied by the U. S. S. R., and from appropriate German external assets.

2. The U. S. S. R. undertakes to settle the reparation claims of Poland from its own share of reparations.

3. The reparation claims of the United States, the United Kingdom and other countries entitled to reparations shall be met from the Western Zones and from appropriate German external assets.

4. In addition to the reparations to be taken by the U. S. S. R. from its own zone of occupation, the U. S. S. R. shall receive additionally from the Western zones:

(a) 15 percent of such usable and complete industrial capital equipment, in the first place from the metallurgical, chemical and machine manufacturing in industries as is unnecessary for the German peace economy and should be removed from the Western Zones of Germany, in exchange for an equivalent value of food, coal, potash, zinc, timber, clay products, petroleum products, and such other commodities as may be agreed upon.

(b) 10 percent of such industrial capital equipment as is unnecessary for the German peace economy and should be removed from the Western Zones, to be transferred to the Soviet Government on reparations account without payment or exchange of any kind in return.

Removals of equipment as provided in (a) and (b) above shall be made simultaneously.

5. The amount of the equipment to be removed from the Western Zones on account of reparations must be determined within six months from now at the latest.

6. Removals of industrial capital equipment shall begin as soon as possible and shall be completed within two years from the determination specified in paragraph 5. The delivery of products covered by 4 (a) above shall begin as soon as possible and shall be made by the U. S. S. R. in agreed installments within five years of the date hereof. The determination of the industrial capital equipment unnecessary for the German peace economy and there-fore available for reparation shall be made by the Control Council under policies fixed by the Allied Commission on Reparations, with the participa-tion of France, subject to the final approval of the Zone Commander from which the equipment is to be removed.

7. Prior to the fixing of the total amount of equipment subject to removal, advance deliveries shall be made in respect to such equipment as will be determined to be eligible for delivery in accordance with the procedure set forth in the last sentence of paragraph 6.

8. The Soviet Government renounces all claims in respect of reparations to shares of German enterprises which are located in the Western Zones of Germany, as well as to German foreign assets in all countries except those specified in paragraph 9 below.

9. The Governments of the U. K. and U. S. A. renounce all claims in respect of reparations to shares of German enterprises which are located in the Eastern Zone of occupation in Germany, as well as to German foreign assets in Bulgaria, Finland, Hungary, Rumania, and Eastern Austria.

10. The Soviet Government makes no claims to gold captured by the Allied troops in Germany.

IV. *Disposal of the German Navy and Merchant Marine*

A. The following principles for the distribution of the German Navy were agreed:

(1) The total strength of the German surface navy, excluding ships sunk and those taken over from Allied Nations, but including ships under con-

struction or repair, shall be divided equally among the U. S. S. R., U. K., and
U. S. A.

(2) Ships under construction or repair mean those ships whose construction or repair may be completed within three to six months according to the type of ship. Whether such ships under construction or repair shall be completed or repaired shall be determined by the technical commission appointed by the Three Powers and referred to below, subject to the principle that their completion or repair must be achieved within the time limits above provided, without any increase of skilled employment in the German shipyards and without permitting the reopening of any German shipbuilding or connected industries. Completion date means the date when a ship is able to go out on its first trip, or, under peacetime standards, would refer to the customary date of delivery by shipyard to the Government.

(3) The larger part of the German submarine fleet shall be sunk. Not more than thirty submarines shall be preserved and divided equally between the U. S. S. R., U. K., and U. S. A. for experimental and technical purposes.

(4) All stocks of armament, ammunition, and supplies of German Navy appertaining to the vessels transferred pursuant to paragraphs (1) and (3) hereof shall be handed over to the respective powers receiving such ships.

(5) The Three Governments agree to constitute a tripartite naval commission comprising two representatives for each government, accompanied by the requisite staff, to submit agreed recommendations to the Three Governments for the allocation of specific German warships and to handle other detailed matters arising out of the agreement between the Three Governments regarding the German fleet. The Commission will hold its first meeting not later than 15th August 1945, in Berlin, which shall be its headquarters. Each Delegation on the Commission will have the right on the basis of reciprocity to inspect German warships wherever they may be located.

(6) The Three Governments agreed that transfers, including those of ships under construction or repair, shall be completed as soon as possible, but not later than 15th February, 1945. The Commission will submit fortnightly reports, including proposals for the progressive allocation of the vessels when agreed by the Commission.

B. The following principles for the distribution of the German Merchant Marine were agreed:

(1) The German Merchant Marine, surrendered to the Three Powers and wherever located, shall be divided equally among the U. S. S. R., the U. K., and the U. S. A. The actual transfers of the ships to the respective countries shall take place as soon as practicable after the end of the war against Japan. The United Kingdom and the United States will provide out of their shares of the surrendered German merchant ships appropriate amounts for other Allied States whose merchant marines have suffered heavy losses in the

common cause against Germany, except that the Soviet Union shall provide out of its share for Poland.

(2) The allocation, manning and operation of these ships during the Japanese war period shall fall under the cognizance and authority of the Combined Shipping Adjustment Board and the United Marine Authority.

(3) While actual transfer of the ships shall be delayed until after the end of the war with Japan, a Tripartite Shipping Commission shall inventory and value all available ships and recommend a specific distribution in accordance with paragraph (1).

(4) German inland and coastal ships determined to be necessary to the maintenance of the basic German peace economy by the Allied Control Council of Germany shall not be included in the shipping pool thus divided among the Three Powers.

(5) The Three Governments agree to constitute a Tripartite Merchant Marine Commission comprising two representatives for each Government, accompanied by the requisite staff, to submit agreed recommendations to the Three Governments for the allocation of specific German merchant ships and to handle other detailed matters arising out of the agreement between the Three Governments regarding the German merchant ships. The Commission will hold its first meeting not later than September 1st, 1945, in Berlin, which shall be its headquarters. Each delegation on the Commission will have the right on the basis of reciprocity to inspect the German merchant ships wherever they may be located.

V. *City of Koenigsberg and the Adjacent Area*

The Conference examined a proposal by the Soviet Government to the effect that pending the final determination of territorial questions at the peace settlement, the section of the western frontier of the Union of Soviet Socialist Republics which is adjacent to the Baltic Sea should pass from a point on the eastern shore of the Bay of Danzig to the east, north of Braunsberg Goldap, to the meeting point of the frontiers of Lithuania, the Polish Republic, and East Prussia.

The Conference has agreed in principle to the proposal of the Soviet Government concerning the ultimate transfer to the Soviet Union of the City of Koenisberg and the area adjacent to it as described above, subject to expert examination of the actual frontier.

The President of the United States and the British Prime Minister have declared that they will support the proposal of the Conference at the forth-coming peace settlement.

VI. *War Criminals*

The Three Governments have taken note of the discussions which have been proceeding in recent weeks in London between British, United States,

Soviet, and French representatives with a view to reaching an agreement on the methods of trial of those major war criminals whose crimes under the Moscow Declaration of October, 1943 have no particular geographical localisation. The Three Governments affirm their intention to bring these criminals to swift and sure justice. They hope that the negotiations in London will result in speedy agreement being reached for this purpose, and they regard it as a matter of great importance that the trial of these major criminals should begin at the earliest possible date. The first list of defendants will be published before 1st September.

VII. *Austria*

The Conference examined a proposal by the Soviet Government on the extension of the authority of the Austrian Provisional Government to all of Austria.

The Three Governments agreed that they were prepared to examine this question after the entry of the British and American forces into the city of Vienna.

It was agreed that reparations should not be exacted from Austria.

VIII. *Poland*

A. DECLARATION

We have taken note with pleasure of the agreement reached among representative Poles from Poland and abroad which has made possible the formation, in accordance with the decisions reached at the Crimea Conference, of a Polish Provisional Government of National Unity recognized by the Three Powers. The establishment by the British and the United States Governments of diplomatic relations with the Polish Provisional Government of National Unity has resulted in the withdrawal of their recognition from the former Polish Government in London, which no longer exists.

The British and United States Governments have taken measures to protect the interest of the Polish Provisional Government of National Unity and the recognized government of the Polish State in the property belonging to the Polish State located in their territories and under their control, whatever the form of this property may be. They have further taken measures to prevent alienation to third parties of such property. All proper facilities will be given to the Polish Provisional Government of National Unity for the exercise of the ordinary legal remedies for the recovery of any property belonging to the Polish State which may have been wrongfully alienated.

The Three Powers are anxious to assist the Polish Provisional Government of National Unity in facilitating the return to Poland as soon as practicable of all Poles abroad who wish to go, including members of Polish Armed Forces and the Merchant Marine. They expect that those Poles who return home shall be accorded personal and property rights on the same basis as all Polish citizens.

The Three Powers note that the Polish Provisional Government of National Unity, in accordance with the decisions of the Crimea Conference, has agreed to the holding of free and unfettered elections as soon as possible on the basis of universal suffrage and secret ballot in which all democratic and anti-Nazi parties shall have the right to take part and to put forward candidates, and that the representatives of the Allied press shall enjoy full freedom to report to the world upon developments in Poland before and during the elections.

B. WESTERN FRONTIER OF POLAND

In conformity with the agreement on Poland reached at the Crimea Conference the Three Heads of Government have sought the opinion of the Polish Provisional Government of National Unity in regard to the accession of territory in the north and west which Poland should receive. The President of the National Council of Poland and members of the Polish Provisional Government of National Unity have been received at the Conference and have fully presented their views. The Three Heads of Government reaffirm their opinion that the final delimitation of the western frontier of Poland should await the peace settlement.

The Three Heads of Government agree that, pending the final determination of Poland's western frontier, the former German territories east of a line running from the Baltic Sea immediately west of Swinamunde, and thence along the Oder River to the confluence of the western Neisse River and along the western Neisse to the Czechoslovak frontier, including that portion of East Prussia not placed under the administration of the Union of Soviet Socialist Republics in accordance with the understanding reached at this conference and including the area of the former free city of Danzig, shall be under the administration of the Polish State and for such purposes should not be considered as part of the Soviet zone of occupation in Germany.

IX. *Conclusion of Peace Treaties and Admission to the United Nations Organization*

The Three Governments consider it desirable that the present anomalous position of Italy, Bulgaria, Finland, Hungary, and Rumania should be terminated by the conclusion of Peace Treaties. They trust that the other interested Allied Governments will share these views.

For their part the Three Governments have included the preparation of a Peace Treaty for Italy as the first among the immediate important tasks to be undertaken by the new Council of Foreign Ministers. Italy was the first of the Axis Powers to break with Germany, to whose defeat she has made a material contribution, and has now joined with the Allies in the struggle against

Japan. Italy has freed herself from the Fascist regime and is making good progress towards re-establishment of a democratic government and institutions. The conclusion of such a Peace Treaty with a recognized and democratic Italian Government will make it possible for the Three Governments to fulfill their desire to support an application from Italy for membership of the United Nations.

The Three Governments have also charged the Council of Foreign Ministers with the task of preparing Peace Treaties for Bulgaria, Finland, Hungary, and Rumania. The conclusion of Peace Treaties with recognized democratic governments in these States will also enable the Three Governments to support applications from them for membership of the United Nations. The Three Governments agree to examine each separately in the near future, in the light of the conditions then prevailing, the establishment of diplomatic relations with Finland, Rumania, Bulgaria, and Hungary to the extent possible prior to the conclusion of peace treaties with those countries.

The Three Governments have no doubt that in view of the changed conditions resulting from the termination of the war in Europe, representatives of the Allied press will enjoy full freedom to report to the world upon developments in Rumania, Bulgaria, Hungary, and Finland.

As regards the admission of other States into the United Nations Organization, Article 4 of the Charter of the United Nations declares that:

1. Membership in the United Nations is open to all other peace-loving States who accept the obligations contained in the present Charter and, in the judgement of the organization, are able and willing to carry out these obligations;

2. The admission of any such State to membership in the United Nations will be effected by a decision of the General Assembly upon the recommendation of the Security Council.

The Three Governments, so far as they are concerned, will support applications for membership from those States which have remained neutral during the war and which fulfill the qualifications set out above.

The Three Governments feel bound however to make it clear that they for their part would not favor any application for membership put forward by the present Spanish Government, which, having been founded with the support of the Axis Powers, does not, in view of its origins, its nature, its record, and its close association with the aggressor States possess the qualifications necessary to justify such membership.

X. *Territorial Trusteeship*

The Conference examined a proposal by the Soviet Government on the question of trusteeship territories as defined in the decision of the Crimea Conference and in the Charter of the United Nations Organization.

After an exchange of views on this question, it was decided that the dispositions of any former Italian colonial territories was one [sic] to be decided in connection with the preparation of a peace treaty for Italy and the question of Italian colonial territory would be considered by the September Council of Ministers of Foreign Affairs.

XI. *Revised Allied Control Commission Procedure in Rumania, Bulgaria, and Hungary*

The Three Governments took note that the Soviet Representatives on the Allied Control Commissions in Rumania, Bulgaria, and Hungary, have communicated to their United Kingdom and United States colleagues proposals for improving the work of the Control Commissions, now that hostilities in Europe have ceased.

The Three Governments agreed that the revision of the procedures of the Allied Control Commissions in these countries would now be undertaken, taking into account the interests and responsibilities of the Three Governments, which together presented the terms of armistice to the respective countries, and accepting as a basis, in respect of all three countries, the Soviet Government's proposals for Hungary as annexed hereto. (Annex I.)

XII. *Orderly Transfer of German Populations*

The Three Governments, having considered the question in all its aspects, recognize that the transfer to Germany of German populations, or elements thereof, remaining in Poland, Czechoslovakia, and Hungary, will have to be undertaken. They agree that any transfers that take place should be effected in an orderly and humane manner.

Since the influx of a large number of Germans into Germany would increase the burden already resting on the occupying authorities, they consider that the Control Council in Germany should in the first instance examine the problems, with special regard to the question of the equitable distribution of these Germans among the several zones of occupation. They are accordingly instructing their respective representatives on the Control Council to report to their Governments as soon as possible the extent to which such persons have already entered Germany from Poland, Czechoslovakia, and Hungary, and to submit an estimate of the time and rate at which further transfers could be carried out having regard to the present situation in Germany.

The Czechoslovak Government, the Polish Provisional Government, and the Control Council in Hungary are at the same time being informed of the above and are being requested meanwhile to suspend further expulsions pending an examination by the Governments concerned of the report from their representatives on the Control Council.

XIII. *Oil Equipment in Rumania*

The Conference agreed to set up two bilateral commissions of experts, one to be composed of United Kingdom and Soviet Members, and one to be composed of United States and Soviet Members, to investigate the facts and examine the documents, as a basis for the settlement of questions arising from the removal of oil equipment in Rumania. It was further agreed that these experts shall begin their work within ten days, on the spot.

XIV. *Iran*

It was agreed that the Allied troops should be withdrawn immediately from Tehran, and that further stages of the withdrawal of troops from Iran should be considered at the meeting of the Council of Foreign Ministers to be held in London in September, 1945.

XV. *The International Zone of Tangier*

A proposal by the Soviet Government was examined and the following decisions reached:

Having examined the question of the Zone of Tangier, the Three Governments have agreed that this Zone, which includes the City of Tangier and the area adjacent to it, in view of its special strategic importance, shall remain international.

The question of Tangier will be discussed in the near future at a meeting in Paris of representatives of the Governments of the Union of Soviet Socialist Republics, the United States of America, the United Kingdom and France.

XVI. *The Black Sea Straits*

The Three Governments recognized that the Convention concluded at Montreux should be revised as failing to meet present-day conditions.

It was agreed that as the next step the matter should be the subject of direct conversations between each of the Three Governments and the Turkish Government.

XVII. *International Inland Waterways*

The Conference considered a proposal of the U. S. Delegation on this subject and agreed to refer it for consideration to the forthcoming meeting of the Council of Foreign Ministers in London.

XVIII. *European Inland Transport Conference*

The British and U. S. Delegations to the Conference informed the Soviet Delegation of the desire of the British and U. S. Governments to reconvene the European Inland Transport Conference and stated that they would welcome assurance that the Soviet Government would participate in the work of the reconvened conference. The Soviet Government agreed that it would participate in this conference.

XIX. *Directives to Military Commanders on Allied Control Council for Germany*

The Three Governments agreed that each would send a directive to its representative on the Control Council for Germany informing him of all decisions of the Conference affecting matters within the scope of his duties.

XX. *Use of Allied Property for Satellite Reparations of "War Trophies"*

The Proposal (Annex II) presented by the United States Delegation was accepted in principle by the conference, but the drafting of an agreement on the matter was left to be worked out through diplomatic channels.

XXI. *Military Talks*

During the Conference there were meetings between the Chiefs of Staff of the Three Governments on military matters of common interest.

ANNEX I

TEXT OF A LETTER TRANSMITTED ON JULY 12 TO THE REPRE-SENTATIVES OF THE U. S. AND U. K. GOVERNMENTS ON THE ALLIED CONTROL COMMISSION IN HUNGARY

In view of the changed situation in connection with the termination of the war against Germany, the Soviet Government finds it necessary to establish the following order of work for the Allied Control Commission in Hungary.

1. During the period up to the conclusion of peace with Hungary, the President (or Vice-President) of the ACC will regularly call conferences with the British and American representatives for the purpose of discussing the most important questions relating to the work of the ACC. The conference will be called once in ten days, or more frequently in case of need.

Directives of the ACC on questions of principle will be issued to the authorities by the President of the Allied Control Commission after agreement on these directives with the English and American representatives.

2. The British and American representatives in the ACC will take part in general conferences of heads of divisions and delegates of the ACC, convoked by the President of the ACC, which meetings will be regular in nature. The British and American representatives will also participate personally or through their representatives in appropriate instances in mixed commissions created by the President of the ACC for questions connected with the execution of the ACC of its functions.

3. Free movement by the American and British representatives in the country will be permitted provided that the ACC is previously informed of the time and route of the journeys.

4. All questions connected with permission for the entrance and exit of members of the staff of the British and American representatives in Hun-

gary will be decided on the spot by the President of the ACC within a time limit of not more than one week.

5. The bringing in and sending out by plane of mail, cargoes, and diplomatic couriers will be carried out by the British and American representatives of the ACC under arrangements and within time limits established by the ACC, or in special cases by previous coordination with the President of the ACC.

I consider it necessary to add to the above that in all other points the existing Statutes regarding the ACC in Hungary, which was confirmed on January 20, 1945, shall remain in force in the future.

ANNEX II

USE OF ALLIED PROPERTY FOR SATELLITE REPARATIONS OR "WAR TROPHIES"

1. The burden of reparation and "war trophies" should not fall on Allied nationals.

2. CAPITAL EQUIPMENT. We object to the removal of such Allied property as reparations, "war trophies", or under any other guise. Loss would accrue to Allied nationals as a result of destruction of plants and the consequent loss of markets and trading connections. Seizure of Allied property makes impossible the fulfillment by the satellite of its obligation under the armistice to restore intact the rights and interests of the Allied Nations and their Nationals.

The United States looks to the other occupying powers for the return of any equipment already removed and the cessation of removals. Where such equipment will not or cannot be returned, the U. S. will demand of the satellites adequate, effective, and prompt compensation to American nationals, and that such compensation have priority equal to that of the reparations payments.

These principles apply to all property wholly or substantially owned by Allied nationals. In the event of removals of property in which American as well as the entire Allied interest is less than substantial, the U. S. expects adequate, effective, and prompt compensation.

3. CURRENT PRODUCTION. While the U. S. does not oppose reparation out of current productions of Allied investments, the satellite must provide immediate and adequate compensation to the Allied nationals including sufficient foreign exchange or products so that they can recover reasonable foreign currency expenditures and transfer a reasonable return on their investment. Such compensation must have equal priority with reparations.

We deem it essential that the satellites not conclude treaties, agreements, or arrangements which deny to Allied nationals access, on equal terms, to their trade, raw materials, and industry, and appropriately modify any existing arrangements which may have that effect.

NOTES

Introduction

1 A good starting place is Janet Ziegler's *World War II: Books in English, 1945–1965* (Stanford, 1971); and Marty Bloomberg and Hans Weber, *World War II and Its Origins: A Select Annotated Bibliography of Books in English* (Littleton, Colo., 1975). Other sources with multilingual listings are *The Two World Wars: A Selective Bibliography* (New York, 1964); and Hans-Adolf Jacobsen, *Zur Konzeption einer Geschichte des Zweiten Weltkrieges, 1939–1945* (Frankfurt a.M., 1964). Mention should be made of new listings on World War II that appear regularly in the *Newsletter,* issued by the American Committee on the History of the Second World War (affiliated with the *Comité International d'Histoire de la Deuxième Guerre Mondiale*); the *Revue d'Histoire de la Deuxième Guerre Mondiale;* and the *Jahresbibliographie der Bibliothek für Zeitgeschichte.*

2 Roger A. Leonard, ed., *A Short Guide to Clausewitz On War* (New York, 1967), 13; and Peter Paret, *Clausewitz and the State* (New York, 1976).

3 See Basil Collier, *The Second World War* (New York, 1967); B. H. Liddell Hart, *History of the Second World War* (New York, 1971); John F. C. Fuller, *The Second World War* (London, 1949); Kurt von Tippelskirsch, *Geschichte des Zweiten Weltkrieges* (Bonn, 1956); and Henri Michel, *La seconde guerre mondiale,* 2 vols. (Paris, 1968–69).

4 See J. R. M. Butler, J. M. A. Gwywe, and John Ehrman, *Grand Strategy,* 6 vols. (London, 1956–); Hans-Adolf Jacobsen and Juergen Rohwer, eds., *Decisive Battles of World War II* (New York, 1965); *United States Army in World War II,* 71 vols. to date (Washington, 1947); *History of the Second World War: United Kingdom Civil Series; United Kingdom Medical Series; United Kingdom Military Series,* 79 vols. to date (London, 1952); S. W. Roskill, *The War at Sea, 1939–1945,* 3 vols. (London, 1954–61); and S. E. Morison, *History of United States Naval Operations in World War II,* 15 vols. (Boston, 1947–62). A still very valuable history is Winston Churchill's *The Second World War,* 6 vols. (Boston, 1948–53).

5 New York, 1958.

6 Leonard, *Clausewitz,* p. 12.

7 Theodor Schieder, *Staat und Gesellschaft im Wandel unserer Zeit* (Munich, 1958), p. 89–109; Gordon Wright, *The Ordeal of Total War* (New York, 1968), p. 233–67; and Andreas Hillgruber, *Hitlers Strategie. Politik und Kriegfuehrung, 1940–1941* (Frankfurt a.M., 1965).

8 See Bloomberg and Weber, "Individual Countries," in *World War II,* pp. 165–98; also G.A. Deborin, *Der Zweite Weltkrieg* (East Berlin, 1960); and Roberto Battaglia, *La seconda Guerra Mondiale* (Bologna, 1961).

9 See Norman Rich, *Hitler's War Aims: Ideology, the Nazi State and the Course of*

Expansion, and *The Establishment of the New Order,* 2 vols. (New York, 1973–74); Enzo Collatti, ed., *L'occupazione nazista in Europa* (Rome, 1964); David Littlejohn, *The Patriotic Traitors: A History of Collaboration in German-Occupied Europe, 1940–1945* (London, 1972); Arnold J. Toynbee and Veronica Toynbee, eds., *Hitler's Europe* (New York, 1954); Robert S. Ward, *Asia for the Asiatics? The Techniques of Japanese Occupation* (Chicago, 1945); Harry J. Benda, James K. Irikura, and Koichi Kishi, eds., *Japanese Military Administration in Indonesia: Selected Documents* (New Haven, 1965); and *Encyclopédie de la guerre, 1939–1945* (Brussels, 1977).

10 Churchill, *The Second World War,* Vol. III: *The Grand Alliance,* p. 337ff. Also see A. Russell Buchanan, *The United States and World War II* (New York, 1964); Francis L. Loewenheim, Harold D. Langley, and Manfred Jonas, eds., *Roosevelt and Churchill: Their Secret Wartime Correspondence* (London, 1975); Herbert Feis, *Churchill, Roosevelt, Stalin: The War They Waged and the Peace They Sought* (Princeton, 1957); Llewellyn Woodward, *British Foreign Policy in the Second World War,* 5 vols. (London, 1970–71); and, J. R. von Salis, *Weltgeschichte der Neuesten Zeit,* Vol. III: *Von Versailles bis Hiroshima* (Zurich, 1960).

11 Maurice Matloff, *Strategic Planning for Coalition Warfare, 1943–1944* (Washington, 1959), pp. 398, 543; and Louis L. Snyder, *The War: A Concise History, 1939–1945* (New York, 1960), p. 501ff. In addition, the British Central Statistical Office has published a *Statistical Digest of the War* (London, 1951).

12 *Geschichte des Grossen Vaterlaendischen Krieges der Sowjetunion, 1941–1945,* 6 vols. (East Berlin, 1962–68); Matthew P. Gallagher, *The Soviet History of World War II* (New York, 1963); Alexander Fischer, *Teheran, Jalta, Potsdam: Die sowjetischen Protokolle von den Kriegskonferenzen der "Grossen Drei"* (Cologne, 1973); Cyril E. Black, ed., *Rewriting Russian History,* 2nd ed. (New York, 1962); Bertram D. Wolfe, "Operation Rewrite: The Agony of Soviet Historians," in Philip E. Mosely, ed., *The Soviet Union* (New York, 1963), pp. 292–310; *Deutschland im zweiten Weltkrieg,* 2 vols.

(East Berlin, 1974–75); and P. A. Zhilin, "Policy and Strategy of the Soviet Union in the Second World War," papers presented under the auspices of the International Committee for the History of the Second World War in *Politics and Strategy in the Second World War* (Manhattan, Kansas, 1976).

13 See n. 3.

14 An example of this is Snyder's *The War: A Concise History.*

15 See Mark Arnold-Forster, *The World at War* (New York, 1974); and Peter Calvocoressi and Guy Wint, *Total War: The Story of World War II* (New York, 1972).

16 See Sadako Ogata, *Defiance in Manchuria: The Making of Japanese Foreign Policy, 1931–1932* (Berkeley, 1964); John Toland, *The Rising Sun: The Rise and Fall of the Japanese Empire, 1936–1945* (New York, 1970); George W. Baer, *The Coming of the Italian-Ethiopian War* (Cambridge, Mass., 1967); Gordon Shepherd, *The Anschluss: The Rape of Austria* (London, 1963); and Rich, *Hitler's War Aims.*

17 A. J. P. Taylor, *The Origins of the Second World War* (London, 1961); David L. Hoggan, *Der erzwungene Krieg* (Tuebingen, 1961); and a critical appraisal by H. W. Koch, "Hitler and the Origins of the Second World War: Second Thoughts on the Status of Some of the Documents," in Esmonde M. Robertson, ed., *The Origins of the Second World War* (London, 1971), pp. 158–88.

18 A. P. Thornton, *Doctrines of Imperialism* (London, 1965), pp. 209–15.

19 See Rich, *Hitler's War Aims;* F. W. Deakin, *The Brutal Friendship* (New York, 1962); and n. 9.

20 Leonard, *Clausewitz,* pp. 204–05.

21 Colonel Joseph Greene, ed. (Washington, 1943).

22 See Hans-Adolf Jacobsen, *Der Weg zur Teilung der Welt. Politik und Strategie 1939–1945* (Koblenz-Bonn, 1977).

23   See Louise W. Holborn, *War and Peace Aims of the United Nations,* 2 vols. (Boston, 1943– 48); Frederick S. Dunn, *Peace-Making and the Settlement with Japan* (Princeton, 1963); and John W. Wheeler-Bennett and Anthony J. Nicholls, *The Semblance of Peace: The Political Settlement After the Second World War* (London, 1972).

24   Thomas Hovet, Jr., *Africa in the United Nations* (London, 1963); Ruth B. Russell, *A History of the United Nations Charter* (Washington, 1958); and Ross N. Berkes and Mohinder S. Bedi, *The Diplomacy of India: Indian Foreign Policy in the United Nations* (Stanford, 1958).

25   Alexander Dallin, *The Soviet Union at the United Nations* (New York, 1962).

26   See Diane S. Clemens, *Yalta* (New York, 1970); Robert Beitzell, *The Uneasy Alliance* (New York, 1972); Herbert Feis, *From Trust to Terror: The Onset of the Cold War, 1945–1950* (New York, 1970); Arthur L. Smith, Jr., *Churchill's German Army* (Los Angeles, 1977); and John L. Gaddis, *The United States and the Origins of the Cold War, 1941–1948* (New York, 1972).

27   See Wheeler-Bennett and Nicholls, *The Semblance of Peace.*

28   George F. Kennan, *Russia and the West Under Lenin and Stalin* (Boston, 1961), p. 349. See also Gabriel Kolko, *The Politics of War: Allied Diplomacy and the World Crisis of 1943–1945* (London, 1969).

29   See Andrew Rothstein, *Soviet Foreign Policy during the Patriotic War: Documents and Materials,* 2 vols. (London, 1946–); and n. 12.

30   See Mao Tse-Tung, *Selected Works,* 5 vols. (New York, 1954– 62); Frank Trager, ed., *Marxism in Southeast Asia* (Stanford, 1960); and Stuart R. Schram, *The Political Thought of Mao Tse-Tung* (New York, 1969).

31   See Walter Millis, ed., *The Forrestal Diaries* (New York, 1951); H. Feis, *Churchill, Roosevelt, and Stalin;* Gabriel Kolko, *The Politics of War;* Lisle A. Rose, *After Yalta* (New York,

1973); and James M. Burns, *Roosevelt: The Soldier of Freedom, 1940–1945* (London, 1971).

32   *Foreign Relations of the United States* (Washington, 1963), vol. III, pp. 745– 46.

33   See John R. Deane, *The Strange Alliance: The Story of Our Efforts at Wartime Cooperation with Russia* (New York, 1947); Beitzell, *The Uneasy Alliance;* and William H. McNeill, *America, Britain and Russia: Their Cooperation and Conflict, 1941–1946* (New York, 1970).

34   See Frederick E. Morgan, *Overture to Overlord* (New York, 1950); Gordon A. Harrison, *Cross-Channel Attack* (Washington, 1951); Arthur Bryant, *Triumph in the West, 1943–1946* (London, 1958); and Samuel Elliot Morison, *The Invasion of France and Germany, 1944–1945* (Boston, 1957).

35   Burton H. Klein, *Germany's Economic Preparations for War* (Cambridge, Mass., 1959); Alan S. Milward, *The German Economy at War* (London, 1965); Jerome B. Cohen, *The Japanese War Economy, 1937–1945* (Minneapolis, 1949); Henry M. D. Parker, *Manpower: A Study of War-Time Policy and Administration* (London, 1957); Michael M. Postan, *British War Production* (London, 1952); Nikolai Voznesenski, *War Economy of the U. S. S. R. in the Period of the Great Patriotic War* (Moscow, 1948); Eliot Janeway, *The Struggle for Survival: A Chronicle of Economic Mobilization in World War II* (New Haven, 1951); Donald M. Nelson, *Arsenal of Democracy: The Story of American War Production* (New York, 1946); and W. N. Medlicott, *The Economic Blockade,* 2 vols. (London, 1952– 59).

36   Warren F. Kimball, *The Most Unsordid Act: Lend-Lease, 1939–1941* (Baltimore, 1969); and Raymond H. Dawson, *The Decision to Aid Russia, 1941* (Chapel Hill, N. C., 1959).

37   Herbert Feis, *The Atomic Bomb and the End of World War II* (Princeton, 1966); and Paul R. Baker, ed., *The Atomic Bomb* (Hinsdale, Ill., 1976).

38   See n. 11; and Wright, *The Ordeal of Total War,* p. 263ff.

39   Johannes Lepsius, Albrecht Mendels-sohn-Bartholdy, and Friedrich Thimme, eds., *Die grosse Politik des europaeischen Kabinette, 1871–1914: Sammlung der diplomatischen Akten des Auswaertigen Amtes,* 40 vols. (Berlin, 1922–26).

40   Some of the representative historians were Sidney B. Fay, Camille Bloch, Erich Brandenburg, Pierre Renouvin, Bernadotte Schmitt, Max Montegelas, G. P. Gooch, and Karl Kautsky. See also Dwight E. Lee, ed., *The Outbreak of the First World War: Who Was Responsible?* (Boston, 1958); and Fritz Fischer, *Germany's Aims in the First World War* (London, 1967).

41   The most important revisionist view presented to date is that found in Taylor's *Origins of the Second World War.* The thesis given by Taylor suggests that World War II came as a result of serious mistakes by all sides involved; however, his view has not been generally accepted. A more radical thesis has been advanced by an American historian named David L. Hoggan, who attempted to place the war's responsibility almost totally upon western statesmen. His book, *Der erzwungene Krieg,* remains little more than a curiosity and has never been published in English. The fact that the work appeared in German has been an embarrassment for German historians.

42   Robert Wolfe, ed., *Captured German and Related Records: A National Archives Conference* (Athens, Ohio, 1974).

43   David Kahn, "Secrets of the Nazi Archives," *Atlantic Monthly* (May 1969): 50–56.

Chapter I

Part 1

1   Most European references to the war use the title "The Second World War," while the United States official designation is "World War II."

2(1)   Great Britain, *Parliamentary Debates, House of Commons,* 5th ser., vol. 345, c. 2415. Hereafter *H. C. Debates.*

3(2)   *Nazi Conspiracy and Aggression* (Washington, D. C.: U. S. Government Printing Office, 1946), IV, pp. 1035–37.

4(3)   *H. C. Debates,* 5th ser., vol. 349, c. 1786–90.

5(4)   *Documents on German Foreign Policy* (Washington, D. C.: U. S. Government Printing Office, 1956), ser. D, VII, pp. 200–204. Hereafter *D. G. F. P.*

6(5)   *Foreign Relations of the United States, 1939* (Washington, D. C.: U. S. Government Printing Office, 1956), I, p. 352. Hereafter *F. R. U. S.*

7(6)   *D. G. F. P.,* D, VII, pp. 245–47.

8(7)   *Nazi Conspiracy and Aggression,* VIII, pp. 408–09.

9(8)   *D. G. F. P.,* D, VII, pp. 494–95.

10(9)   *Keesing's Contemporary Archives* (Bristol, England: Keesing's Publications, n.d.), III, pp. 3704–05. Hereafter *Keesing's.*

11(10)   *D. G. F. P.,* D, VIII,) pp. 44–45.

12(11)   *F. R. U. S., 1939,* I, pp. 428–31.

13(12)   *D. G. F. P.* D, VIII, pp. 164–65.

14(13)   *Ibid.,* p. 167.

Part 2

1(14)   *Trials of War Criminals before the Nuremberg Military Tribunals* (Washington, D. C.: U. S. Government Printing Office, 1951), X, pp. 805–06.

2(15)   *F. R. U. S., 1939,* V. pp. 36–37.

3(16)   U. S. Statutes at Large, vol. 54, pt. 1, pp. 4–6.

4(17)   *Trials of the Major War Criminals before the International Military Tribunal* (Nuremberg: United States Government, 1947), V, pp. 76–77. Hereafter *I.M.T.*

5(18) *Nazi Conspiracy and Aggression,* III, pp. 572–80.

6 On November 8, 1939, in Munich, there was a bomb attempt on Hitler's life. The official German position was that the British secret service was responsible and two British agents were arrested on the Dutch-German border at Venlo.

7(19) League of Nations, *Official Journal* (November–December 1939), pt. II: 541–42.

8(20) *British and Foreign State Papers* (London: H. M. S. O., 1940), vol. 144, p. 383.

9(21) *D. G. F. P.,* D, VIII, pp. 831–33.

10(22) *Ibid.,* IX, pp. 112-15.

11(23) *Ibid.,* pp. 300–301.

12(24) *H.C. Debates,* 5th ser., vol. 360, c. 1501–02.

Part 3

1(25) *D. G. F. P.,* D, VIII, pp. 838–45.

2(26) U. S. Congress, House, 76th Cong., 3rd Sess., 1940, pp. 6243–44.

3(27) *Keesing's,* III, p. 4087.

4(28) *D. G. F. P.,* D, IX, pp. 542–43.

5(29) *Ibid.,* p. 598.

6(30) Ibid., pp. 671–76.

7(31) *H. C. Debates,* 5th ser., vol. 362, c. 1043–52.

8(32) *D. G. F. P.,* D, X, pp. 226–29.

9(33) *The New York Times,* July 20, 1940.

10(34) *D. G. F. P.,* D, X, pp. 370–71.

11(35) *Ibid.,* pp. 372–73.

12(36) U. S., Department of State, *Bulletin* (Washington, D. C.: U. S. Government Printing Office, 1940), III, pp. 199–201.

Chapter II

Part 4

1(37) *D. G. F. P.,* D, XI, pp. 204–05.

2(38) *Ibid.,* pp. 527–31.

3(39) *Ibid.,* pp. 550–62.

4(40) *Ibid.,* pp. 899–902.

5(41) *Trials of War Criminals before the Nuremberg Military Tribunals,* X, pp. 903–04.

6(42) *D. G. F. P.,* D, XII, pp. 372–75.

7(43) *Trials of War Criminals before the Nuremberg Military Tribunals,* X, pp. 949–50.

8(44) *D. G. F. P.,* D, XII, pp. 440–42.

9(45) *Ibid.,* pp. 1070–71.

10(46) *Trials of War Criminals before the Nuremberg Military Tribunals,* X, pp. 953–54.

11(47) Hans-Adolf Jacobsen, ed., *General-oberst Halder, Kriegstagebuch* (Stuttgart: W. Kohlhammer Verlag, 1964), III, p. 3.

12(48) *Keesing's,* IV, p. 4671.

13(49) *Ibid.,* p. 4671.

14(50) *Ibid.,* p. 4681.

15(51) Jacobsen, *Halder, Kriegstagebuch,* III, pp. 38–39.

16(52) *D. G. F. P.,* D, XIII, pp. 383–84.

Part 5

1(53) *F. R. U. S., 1940,* III, pp. 18–26.

2(54) U. S., Dept. of State, *Bulletin,* IV, pp. 3–8.

3(55) *U. S. Statutes at Large,* vol. 55, pp. 31–35.

4(56) U. S. Congress, Joint Committee on the Investigation of the Pearl Harbor Attack, *Pearl Harbor Attack,* 79th Cong., 1st Sess. (Washington, D. C.: U. S. Government Printing Office, 1946), pt. 15, pp. 1485–93.

5(57) U. S., Dept. of State, *Bulletin,* IV, pp. 277–81.

6(58) *Ibid.,* pp. 443–45.

7(59) *Ibid.,* pp. 494–95.

8(60) *Ibid.,* p. 654.

9(61) *Ibid.,* V, pp. 15–16.

10(62) *League of Nations Treaty Series, 1941,* vol. 204, p. 278.

11(63) U. S., Dept. of State, *Bulletin,* V, p. 240.

12(64) *Ibid.,* pp. 134–35.

13(65) *Ibid.,* pp. 125–26.

Chapter III

Part 6

1(66) International Military Tribunal for the Far East, Proceedings 1946–1948, microfilm reel 8, frames 9879–82. Hereafter I. M. T., Far East.

2(67) *D. G. F. P.,* D, XII, pp. 219–20.

3(68) *Keesing's,* IV, p. 4574.

4(69) I. M. T., Far East, 8/10187–192.

5(70) *Ibid.,* 8/10289–290.

6(71) *Ibid.,* 8/10363–365.

7(72) *Ibid.,* 8/10373–375.

8(73) *Ibid.,* 8/8988–90.

9(74) *U. S., Dept. of State, Bulletin,* V, pp. 461–64.

10(75) *Ibid.,* p. 464.

11(76) *Ibid.,* pp. 464–66.

12(77) *Ibid.,* pp. 466–70.

13(78) *Ibid.,* p. 466.

14(79) *I. M. T., Far East,* 8/10686–688.

15(80) U. S., Dept. of State, *Bulletin,* V, p. 474.

16(81) *Keesing's,* IV, pp. 4926–27.

Part 7

1(82) U. S., *Congressional Record,* vol. 88, pt. 1, pp. 32–35.

2(83) U. S., Dept. of State, *Bulletin,* V, p. 573.

3(84) *F. R. U. S., Conferences at Washington, 1941–1942, and Casablanca, 1943,* pp. 214–17.

4(85) *F. R. U. S., Conf. at Wash. and Casablanca,* pp. 161–67.

5(86) U. S., Department of State, *A Decade of American Foreign Policy, 1941–1949* (Washington, D. C.: U. S. Government Printing Office, 1950), pp. 2–3.

6(87) *F. R. U. S., 1941,* I, pp. 192–94.

7(88) *F. R. U. S., 1942,* III, pp. 499–501.

8(89) *I. M. T.,* V, p. 219.

9(90) I. M. T., Far East, 6/7988.

10(91) *Ibid.,* 6/7990–91.

11(92) United States Strategic Bombing Survey (Pacific), Naval Analysis Division, *The Campaigns of the Pacific War* (Washington, D. C.: U. S. Government Printing Office, 1946), p. 3.

12(93) U. S. Strategic Bombing Survey (Pacific), *Interrogation of Japanese Officials,* vol. 1, pp. 422–23.

13(94) *The War Reports of General of the Army George C. Marshall, General of the Army H. H. Arnold, Fleet Admiral Ernest J. King* (New York: J. B. Lippincott, 1947), p. 79.

14(95) *Reports of General MacArthur, The Campaigns of MacArthur in the Pacific* (Washington, D. C.: U. S. Government Printing Office, 1966), vol. I, pp. 38–39.

Chapter IV

Part 8

1(96) *War Reports of Marshall, Arnold, King,* pp. 333–34.

2(97) U. S. Strategic Bombing Survey (Pacific), *Campaigns of the Pacific War,* pp. 3–4.

3(98) U. S. Strategic Bombing Survey (Pacific), *Interrogation of Japanese Officials,* vol. 2, p. 331.

4(99) *F. R. U. S., The Second Washington Conference, 1942,* pp. 449–53.

5(100) *League of Nations Treaty Series, 1942,* vol. 204, pp. 354–58.

6(101) *F. R. U. S., Second Wash. Conf., 1942,* pp. 461–62.

7(102) *Ibid.,* pp. 473–74.

8(103) *Ibid.,* pp. 475–76.

9(104) A. Bryant, *The Turn of the Tide* (London: Collins, 1957), pp. 343–46.

10(105) Operational Plan "Torch," Enclosure B, 21/8/42, RG213, *Records of the U. S. Joint Chiefs of Staff,* pp. 19796–802.

11(106) *Correspondence Between the Chairman of the Council of Ministries of the U. S. S. R. and the President of the U. S. A. and the Prime Minister of Great Britain during the Great Patriotic War of 1941–1945* (Moscow: Foreign Languages Publishing House, 1957), I, pp. 51–55. Hereafter *Correspondence* (Stalin).

12 Allied operation to invade the continent in the event of a possible Russian collapse.

13(107) B. L. Montgomery, *The Memoirs of Field Marshal, The Viscount Montgomery* (New York: World Publishing, 1958), ill. no. 15.

14(108) Snyder, *The War, A Concise History,* p. 282.

15(109) *Correspondence* (Stalin), p. 73.

16(110) *Keesing's,* IV, p. 5640.

17(111) *Ibid.,* pp. 6693–95.

18(112) *Ibid.,* pp. 6710–15.

Part 9

1(113) *F. R. U. S., Conference at Casablanca, 1943,* pp. 741–51.

2(114) *F. R. U. S., Conf. at Casablanca, 1943,* pp. 547–50.

3(115) *Ibid.,* pp. 726–28.

4(116) *Correspondence* (Stalin), pp. 94–97.

5(117) *Ibid.,* pp. 100–102.

6(118) *Ibid.,* 105–06.

7(119) *F. R. U. S., Third Washington Conference, 1943,* pp. 289–93.

8(120) *Keesing's,* V, p. 5789.

9(121) *Correspondence* (Stalin), pp. 131–32.

10(122) *Ibid.,* p. 133.

11(123) *Ibid.,* pp. 136–38.

Chapter V

Part 10

1(124) *F. R. U. S., Conferences at Washington and Quebec, 1943,* pp. 488–96.

2(125) *Records of the U. S. Joint Chiefs of Staff,* C. C. S. 334 (8–17–43), 113th Meeting, RG218.

3(126) *F. R. U. S., Conf. at Wash. and Quebec, 1943,* pp. 457–58.

4(127) *Ibid.,* pp. 1259–61.

5(128) *Ibid.,* pp. 1060–61.

6(129) U. S., Dept. of State, *Decade of American Foreign Policy,* pp. 455–56.

7(130) U. S., Department of State, *The Axis in Defeat* (Washington, D. C.: U. S. Government Printing Office, 1945), pp. 2–3.

8(131) *Nazi Conspiracy and Aggression,* VII, pp. 920–30.

9(132) *F. R. U. S., Conferences at Cairo and Teheran, 1943,* p. 652.

10(133) *Ibid.,* pp. 646–47.

Part 11

1(134) *F. R. U. S., Conf. at Wash. and Quebec, 1943,* pp. 1125–29.

2(135) *F. R. U. S., Conf. at Cairo and Teheran, 1943,* pp. 371–72.

3(136) *Ibid.,* pp. 448–49.

4(137) *Ibid.,* p. 619.

5(138) *Ibid.,* pp. 779–81.

6(139) U. S. Strategic Bombing Survey (Pacific), *Campaigns of the Pacific War,* pp. 8–9.

7(140) *Ibid.,* pp. 9–10.

8(141) *F. R. U. S., Second Quebec Conference, 1944,* pp. 442–46.

9(142) U. S. Strategic Bombing Survey (Pacific), *Interrogation of Japanese Officials,* vol. 1, pp. 60–64.

10(143) *Reports of General MacArthur,* I, p. 202.

11(144) *Ibid.,* pp. 176–77.

Part 12

1(145) *War Reports of Marshall, Arnold, King,* pp. 363–64.

2 Albert Speer, *Inside the Third Reich, Memoirs* (New York: Macmillan, 1970), p. 346.

3(146) *Keesing's,* V, pp. 6417–18.

4(147) *Ibid.,* p. 6481.

5(148) *Ibid.,* p. 6481.

6(149) *Correspondence* (Stalin), p. 222.

7(150) *Keesing's,* V, p. 6481 .

8(151) *Ibid.,* p. 6481.

9(152) *Ibid.,* p. 6479.

10(153) B. H. Liddell Hart, ed., *The Rommel Papers* (New York: Harcourt, Brace, 1953), pp. 486–87.

11(154) *Keesing's,* V, p. 6719.

12(155) U. S. Dept. of State, *Decade of American Foreign Policy,* pp. 487–90.

13(156) *Ibid.,* pp. 482–85.

14(157) *Ibid.,* pp. 494–99.

Chapter VI

Part 13

1(158) *Keesing's,* V, p. 6825.

2(159) *F. R. U. S., The Conferences at Malta and Yalta, 1945,* p. 984.

3(160) *Correspondence* (Stalin), pp. 319–20.

4(161) *Ibid.,* pp. 317–18.

5(162) *Nazi Conspiracy and Aggression,* VI, pp. 259–60.

6(163) *Ibid.,* pp. 261–63.

7(164) German Records Microfilmed at Alexandria, Va., T-77, ser. 18, reel 859, frames 5605345–5354.

8(165) *F. R. U. S., 1945,* III, pp. 778–79.

9(166) *Ibid.,* p. 779.

10(167) U. S., National Archives, *Germany Surrenders Unconditionally* (Washington, D. C.: U. S. Government Printing Office, 1945), pub. no. 46–4, pp. 32–34.

11(168) U. S., Nat. Archives, *Germany Surrenders Unconditionally,* pp. 40–41.

12(169) *War Reports of Marshall, Arnold, King,* pp. 145–47.

Part 14

1(170) *Reports of General MacArthur,* I, pp. 585–86.

2(171) *F. R. U. S., Conf. at Malta and Yalta, 1945,* pp. 395–96.

3(172) *Reports of General MacArthur,* I, pp. 601–07.

4(173) *Public Papers of the Presidents of the United States, Harry S Truman, Containing the Public Messages, Speeches, and State-*

ments of the President, April 12 to December 31, 1945 (Washington, D. C.: U. S. Government Printing Office, 1961), p. 50.

5(174) "Report to the Secretary of War," *Bulletin of the Atomic Scientists* I (May 1, 1946): 2–5.

6(175) *F. R. U. S., 1945,* I, pp. 941–42.

7(176) *F. R. U. S., The Conference of Berlin, 1945,* II, pp. 1369–70.

8(177) *F. R. U. S., Conf. of Berlin,* II, pp. 1474–76.

9(178) *Public Papers of the Presidents, Truman,* pp. 197–200.

10(179) *Reports of General MacArthur,* I, p. 708.

11(180) I. M. T., Far East, 8/11393.

12(181) *Reports of General MacArthur,* I, pp. 727–28.

13(182) *Keesing's,* V, p. 7396.

14(183) *Reports of General MacArthur,* I, plate 132.

Chapter VII

Part 15

1(184) *D. G. F. P.,* D, XIII, pp. 149–56.

2(185) *Trials of War Criminals before the Nuremberg Military Tribunals,* III, pp. 775–76.

3(186) *Ibid.,* XIII, pp. 210–17.

4(187) U. S., Dept. of State, *The Axis in Defeat,* pp. 2–3.

5(188) Royal Institute of International Affairs, *Documents on International Affairs, 1939–1946,* edited by M. Carlyle (London: Oxford University Press, 1954), II, pp. 343–44.

6(189) *Keesing's,* V, pp. 6274–78.

7(190) Dietrich Bonhoeffer, *Gesammelte Schriften* (Munich: Eberhard Bethge, 1958), I, p. 488ff., as quoted in Bundeszentrale für Politische Bildung, ed., *Germans Against Hitler* (Bonn: Press and Information Office, Federal Government of Germany, 1969), pp. 60–64.

8(191) *F. R. U. S., 1944,* I, pp. 510–12.

9(192) *Keesing's,* V, p. 6563.

10(193) *Ibid.,* p. 6563.

11(194) *Ibid.,* p. 6480.

12(195) *Ibid.,* p. 6635.

Part 16

1 On May 17, 1939, the British Government published a *Statement of Policy* as a White Paper on the Palestine problem. An independent Palestine State was envisaged within ten years. Among important points in the document were the British pledge to adhere to the Balfour Declaration of 1917, which did not contemplate that all of Palestine would become a Jewish homeland, and praise for the work of the Zionists. However, the White Paper also noted that it was not the intent of the Balfour Declaration that "... Palestine should be converted into a Jewish State against the will of the Arab population of the country." It was hoped that the proposed ten-year transitional period would provide time for the development of some shared responsibility to meet the complex problems. Meanwhile, land sales and immigration were to be restricted (75,000 Jews were to be allowed settlement between April 1939 and April 1944, with an additional 25,000 refugees later; after that there would be no more immigration without Palestine Arab consent).

2(196) *Keesing's,* V, p. 7455.

3(197) *Ibid.,* p. 7456.

4(198) Royal Institute of International Affairs, *The Middle East: A Political and Economic Survey* (London: R. I. I. A., 1950), pp. 471–74.

5(199) *F. R. U. S., 1945,* III, pp. 2–3.

6(200) *Keesing's,* V, p. 6421.

7(201) *Ibid.,* p. 6965.

8(202) *Ibid.,* p. 6966.

9(203) *Ibid.,* IV, p. 5396.

10(204) *Ibid.,* p. 5553.

11(205) *F. R. U. S., 1945,* VII, pp. 362–65.

12(206) *Keesing's,* IV, p. 5519.

13(207) *Sukarno, An Autobiography As Told to Cindy Adams* (New York: Bobbs-Merrill, 1965), p. 216.

Part 17

1(208) *F. R. U. S., 1944,* I, pp. 226–30.

2(209) *F. R. U. S., Second Quebec Conf., 1944,* pp. 101–05.

3(210) U. S. Senate Committee on the Judiciary, *Morgenthau Diary (Germany)* (Washington, D. C.: U. S. Government Printing Office, 1967), I, pp. 838–52.

4(211) U. S., Dept. of State, *Decade of American Foreign Policy,* pp. 27–34.

5(212) *F. R. U. S., 1945,* I, pp. 196–97.

6(213) U. S., Dept. of State, *Decade of American Foreign Policy,* p. 117.

7(214) U. S., Dept. of State, *Press Release No. 238,* March 27, 1947.

Glossary

Abwehr——intelligence section of the German High Command

A.E.F.——Allied Expeditionary Force

A.M.G.——American Military Government

Anvil——Allied codename for the invasion of southern France in August 1944; name changed to "Dragoon"

Arcadia——Allied codename for first Washington Conference, in 1941–1942; see Washington Conference

Argonaut——Allied codename for the Yalta Conference; see Yalta Conference

Auswärtiges Amt——German Foreign Ministry

Axis——name for cooperative activities of Germany and Italy after 1936; from a speech by Mussolini referring to the Rome-Berlin axis.

Balfour Declaration——a British promise to support the concept of a Jewish homeland in Palestine

Barbarossa——codename for the German invasion of Russia, June 22, 1941

Big Three——popular news reference to Roosevelt, Churchill, and Stalin

Biltmore Program——wartime Zionist proposal for an independent Jewish state in Palestine that controlled its own immigration policy

Blackshirts——followers of Mussolini's Fascist Party who wore blackshirts

Blitzkrieg——warfare that emphasizs speed and mobility; see "Lightning War"

Bolero——codename referring to the transfer of U.S. troops to Great Britain

Boxer (Peking) Protocol of 1901——extraordinary rights granted to foreign powers in China after the Boxer Rebellion; see "Extraterritorial rights"

Bretton Woods Conference——Allied meeting of 44 nations held in July 1944 to develop agreement on an International Monetary Fund and Bank

Cairo Conference——Churchill, Roosevelt, and Chiang Kai-shek agree on Far East war policies in November 1943

China Affair——name for Sino-Japanese war before 1941, since the conflict was not officially designated as war

Comintern——Communist International directed from Moscow; dissolved by Stalin in 1943 (Third International)

COSSAC——Chief of Staff to the Supreme Allied Commander

Curzon Line——line of demarcation from Grodno to the Carpathians proposed after World War I; it was rejected by Poland, but became the dividing line between Russia and Germany in Poland in 1939; it became the Polish-Russian frontier in 1945

"decisive theatre"——recognition of Germany and the European war as the focus of greater effort by the Allied leaders; see "Grand Strategy"

447

Dragoon——Allied codename for the invasion of southern France in 1944 shortly after the Normandy invasion (see "Overlord" and "Anvil")

EAC——European Advisory Commission

Eureka——codename for Teheran Conference; see Teheran Conference

"Extraterritorial rights"——extra rights and privileges enjoyed by the United States and Great Britain in China before World War II (formally relinquished in 1942)

Felix——German codename for planned attack upon Gibraltar; never executed

Festung Europa——descriptive term widely used by the Allies for the German defense preparations for Europe under Nazi control

Fifth Column——term from the Spanish Civil War; when a general in Franco's forces closed on Madrid with four columns, a fifth column (spies and sympathizers) aided from within

"Former Naval Person"——a name Roosevelt used for Winston Churchill in their wartime correspondence

Four Freedoms——Roosevelt speech to Congress in January 1941, proclaimed freedom of speech, worship, and from want and fear

Free Zone——that part of France left unoccupied by the Germans after the Armistice of June 1940, but occupied in November 1942; see Vichy

Freischärler——guerilla forces

G.A.F.——German Air Force; designation used in Allied reports

Gau——territorial division (largest) of the Nazi Party

Gauleiter——the ranking Nazi Party official in a *Gau;* see *Gau*

"Grand Strategy"——Anglo-American military planning that developed a blueprint for defeating Germany first and then Japan; see "decisive theatre"

Greater East Asia Co-Prosperity Sphere——Japan's name for a program launched in 1938 and aimed at military and economic control of the Far East

Gymnast——an early plan for an American assault against northwest Africa from the Atlantic; was later changed to Operation "Torch"

Husky——codeword for the Allied invasion of Sicily in July 1943

J.C.S.——Joint Chiefs of Staff; principal U.S. military advisers to the President and Secretary of Defense

Kamikaze——Japanese suicide plane manned by volunteer pilot

Ketsu-Go——Japanese defensive plan for the homelands in 1945

Kuomintang——Chinese Nationalist government headed by Chiang Kai-shek; sometimes referred to as the Chungking government

Lebensraum——living space; a word often used in reference to German territorial expansion

Leuthen——village near Breslau where Frederick the Great defeated Austria in 1757

"Lightning War"——warfare that stresses speed and motion with an emphasis on air power and mobile armor; see *Blitzkrieg*

Maginot Line——name of French fortification system along eastern border; constructed 1929–34

Manhattan Project——name given to the development of an atomic bomb in the United States during World War II

Marita——German codename for the invasion of Greece

Moltke, Helmuth von (1800–91)——German Field Marshal who headed Prussian General Staff

Montreux Convention——international agreement with Turkey regulating Straits shipping, 1936

Moscow Conference——Allied foreign ministers met in Oct.–Nov. 1943 to establish advisory councils and consider punishment for war criminals.

"new order"——name for the imposition of German rule over Europe

Octagon——codename for second Quebec Conference; see Quebec Conference

O.S.S.——Office of Strategic Services; United States intelligence unit

Overlord——Allied codename for the Allied invasion of Normandy on June 6, 1944

"Phony War"——period after Polish defeat in 1939 to German attack on Norway and Denmark on April 9, 1940; called "phony" because of lack of action by all belligerents—also called *Sitzkrieg* and Boer War

Potsdam (Berlin) Conference——Truman, Churchill, Attlee, and Stalin met in July–Aug. 1945 to develop a series of agreements on war's end

Quadrant——codename for first Quebec Conference; see Quebec Conference

Quebec Conference (first)——held August 1943; Roosevelt and Churchill decided on French invasion

Quebec Conference (second)——Roosevelt and Churchill met September 1944 for war discussions on both Europe and the Pacific

Quisling, Vidkun (1887–1945)——Norwegian traitor who hoped to make Norway a Nazi state; name has become synonymous with word traitor

Rankin——Allied codename for the preparations for an emergency European landing in the event of a premature German collapse

Reichsführer——Reich Leader in Nazi Germany

Roundup——first Allied operation planned for the invasion of France but superseded by Overlord

San Francisco Conference——Fifty Nations' Conference in April-May-June 1945, to sign U.N. Security Charter and establish Preparatory Commission for the U.N.

SD——German *Sicherheitsdienst* or Security Service

SEAC——South East Asia Command

Sea Lion——*Seelöwe*, German codename for the planned invasion of England; never executed

Sextant——Allied codeword for Cairo Conference in 1943; see Cairo Conference

Shō——Operations Plan—Japan's defense measures in 1944, consisting of plans for protecting several areas against Allied attacks

Sitzkrieg——see "Phony War"

Sledgehammer——Allied plan to attempt an immediate invasion of the Continent in the event of a possible Russian collapse in the fall of 1942

SS——*Schutzstaffel,* protective force

T.A. or Tube Alloy——codename used in Allied correspondence for the atomic bomb

Teheran Conference——Stalin, Roosevelt, Churchill meeting in Nov.-Dec. 1943; discussed aid for Tito and invasion date for France

Terminal——codename for Allied Conference at Potsdam; see Potsdam Conference

Tito-Šubašić Agreement——United Yugoslavian government; December 1944

Torch——Allied codename for the invasion of North Africa on November 8, 1942

Trident——codename for third Washington Conference in May 1943; see Washington Conference

Vichy——name of small town in unoccupied France where French government headquartered after 1940 defeat by Germany; see Free Zone

VLR——"very long range"; reference to American bomber operations against Japan

Washington Conference (first)——held in December 1941–January 1942; Roosevelt and Churchill discussed mutual war problems and placed top priority on defeating Germany first

Washington Conference (second)——Roosevelt and Churchill met in June 1942, planned North African invasion

Washington Conference (third)——met in May 1943; Allied plans discussed by Roosevelt and Churchill for Pacific and invasion of France

Weltanschaulich——ideological view

Weser Exercise or Weserübung——German codename for the attacks upon Denmark (Weser South) and Norway (Weser North) on April 9, 1940

White or Weiss——German codename for the invasion of Poland in September 1939

"Winter War"——name given to Finnish-Soviet war in the Winter of 1939–40

Yalta (Crimea) Conference——meeting of Churchill, Stalin, and Roosevelt in February 1945 that dealt with final plans to defeat Germany, a government for Poland, scheduling a U.N. Conference, and securing Soviet aid against Japan

Yellow or Gelb——German codename for the Lowlands invasion in May 1940

Maps and Charts

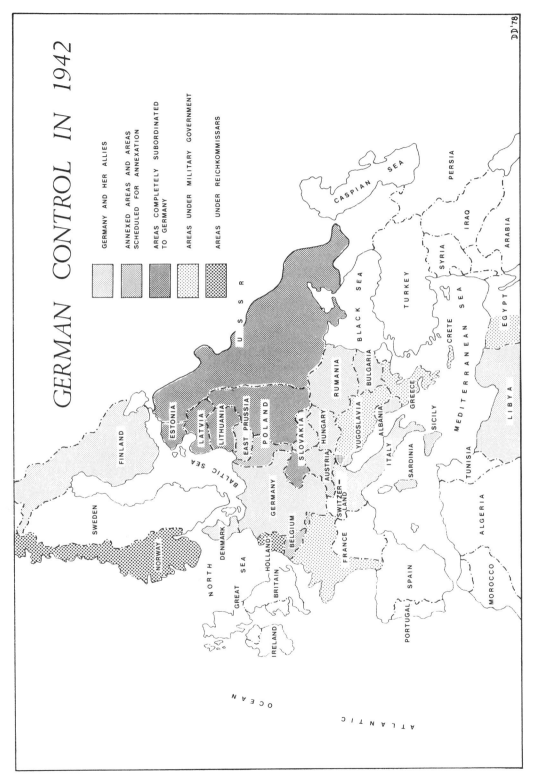

GERMAN CONTROL IN 1942

GERMANY AND HER ALLIES

ANNEXED AREAS AND AREAS
SCHEDULED FOR ANNEXATION

AREAS COMPLETELY SUBORDINATED
TO GERMANY

AREAS UNDER MILITARY GOVERNMENT

AREAS UNDER REICHKOMMISSARS

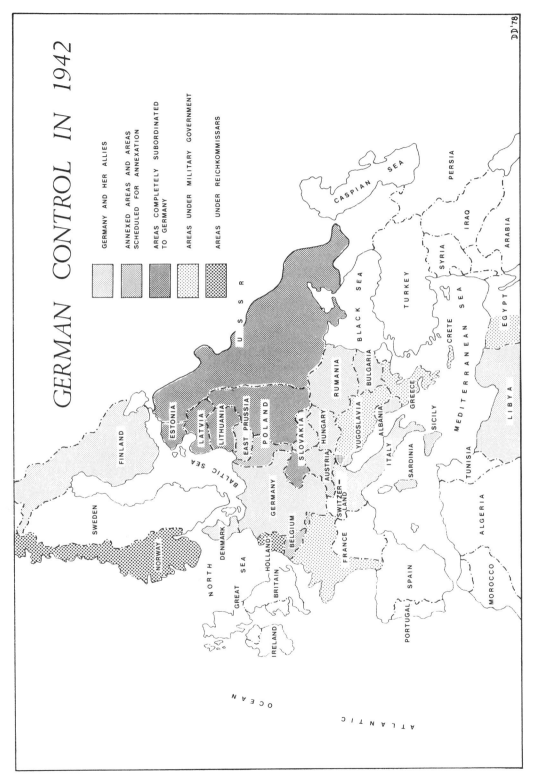

DD'78

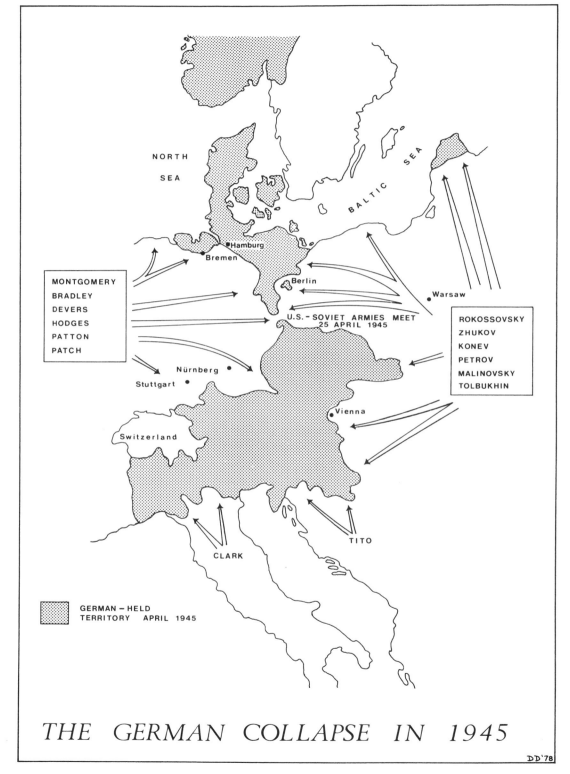

MONTGOMERY
BRADLEY
DEVERS
HODGES
PATTON
PATCH

ROKOSSOVSKY
ZHUKOV
KONEV
PETROV
MALINOVSKY
TOLBUKHIN

NORTH SEA

BALTIC SEA

Hamburg
Bremen
Berlin
Warsaw

U.S.-SOVIET ARMIES MEET
25 APRIL 1945

Nürnberg
Stuttgart

Vienna

Switzerland

TITO

CLARK

GERMAN — HELD
TERRITORY   APRIL 1945

THE GERMAN COLLAPSE IN 1945

DD'78

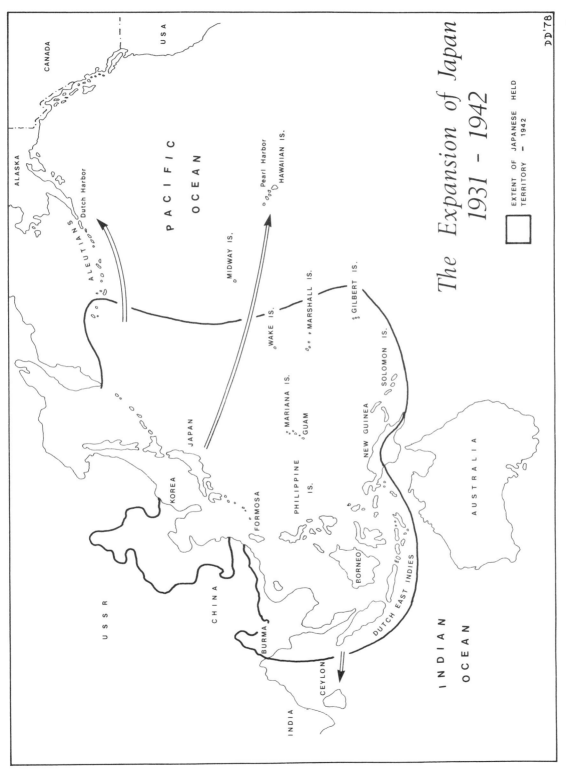

The Expansion of Japan 1931 - 1942

EXTENT OF JAPANESE HELD
TERRITORY — 1942

DD'78

455

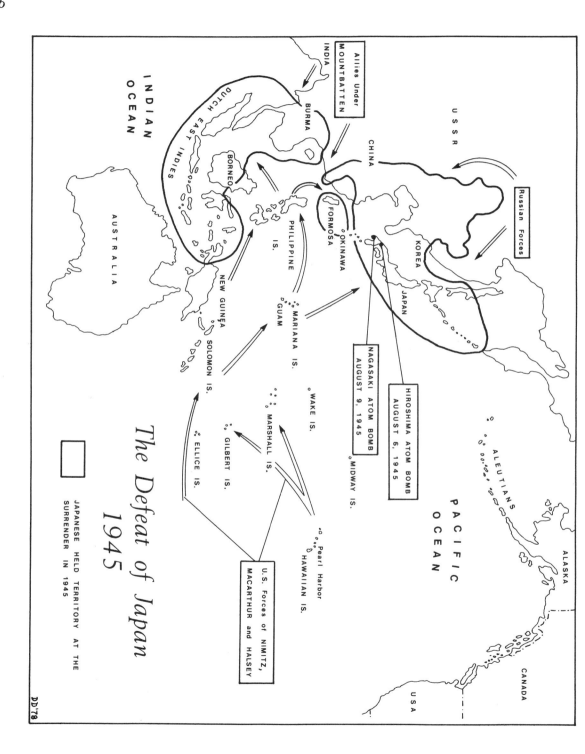

The Defeat of Japan
1945

JAPANESE HELD TERRITORY AT THE
SURRENDER IN 1945

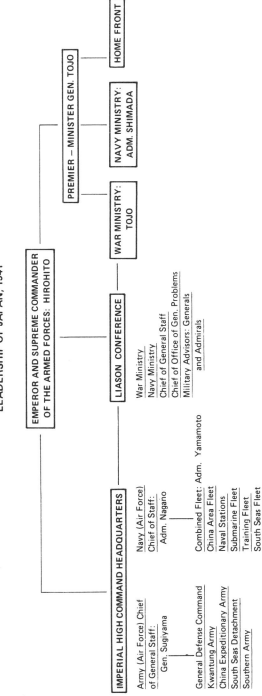

LEADERSHIP OF JAPAN, 1941

EMPEROR AND SUPREME COMMANDER
OF THE ARMED FORCES: HIROHITO

PREMIER — MINISTER GEN. TOJO

HOME FRONT

NAVY MINISTRY:
ADM. SHIMADA

WAR MINISTRY:
TOJO

LIASON CONFERENCE

War Ministry
Navy Ministry
Chief of General Staff
Chief of Office of Gen. Problems
Military Advisors: Generals
and Admirals

IMPERIAL HIGH COMMAND HEADQUARTERS

Army (Air Force) Chief
of General Staff:
Gen. Sugiyama

General Defense Command
Kwantung Army
China Expeditionary Army
South Seas Detachment
Southern Army

Navy (Air Force)
Chief of Staff:
Adm. Nagano

Combined Fleet: Adm. Yamamoto
China Area Fleet
Naval Stations
Submarine Fleet
Training Fleet
South Seas Fleet

LEADERSHIP OF THE UNITED STATES AND GREAT BRITAIN, 1944

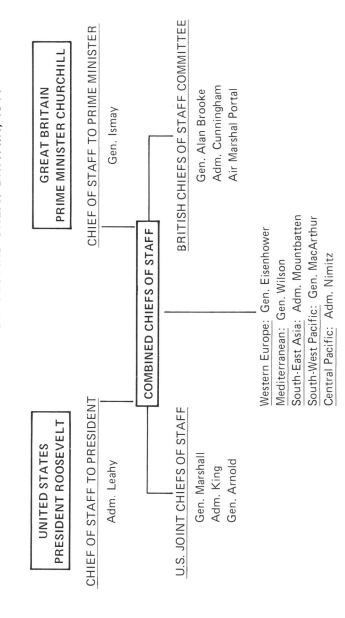

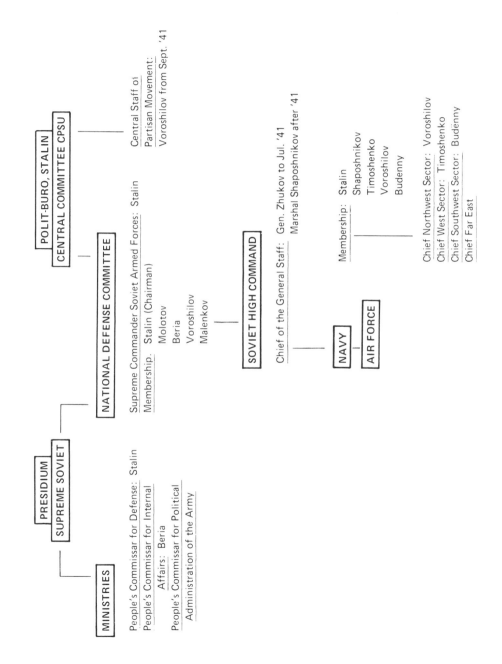

LEADERSHIP OF THE U.S.S.R., 1941

PRESIDIUM
SUPREME SOVIET

POLIT-BURO, STALIN
CENTRAL COMMITTEE CPSU

MINISTRIES

People's Commissar for Defense: Stalin
People's Commissar for Internal
   Affairs: Beria
People's Commissar for Political
   Administration of the Army

NATIONAL DEFENSE COMMITTEE

Supreme Commander Soviet Armed Forces: Stalin
Membership: Stalin (Chairman)
           Molotov
           Beria
           Voroshilov
           Malenkov

Central Staff of
Partisan Movement:
Voroshilov from Sept. '41

SOVIET HIGH COMMAND

Chief of the General Staff: Gen. Zhukov to Jul. '41
                          Marshal Shaposhnikov after '41

NAVY

AIR FORCE

Membership: Stalin
           Shaposhnikov
           Timoshenko
           Voroshilov
           Budenny

Chief Northwest Sector: Voroshilov
Chief West Sector: Timoshenko
Chief Southwest Sector: Budenny
Chief Far East

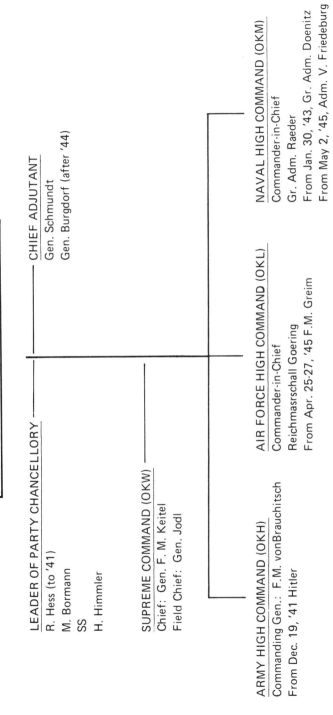

GERMAN LEADERSHIP, 1939-1945

COMMANDER-IN-CHIEF OF ARMED FORCES
AND FUEHRER AND CHANCELLOR HITLER

CHIEF ADJUTANT
Gen. Schmundt
Gen. Burgdorf (after '44)

LEADER OF PARTY CHANCELLORY
R. Hess (to '41)
M. Bormann
SS
H. Himmler

SUPREME COMMAND (OKW)
Chief: Gen. F. M. Keitel
Field Chief: Gen. Jodl

ARMY HIGH COMMAND (OKH)
Commanding Gen.: F. M. vonBrauchitsch
From Dec. 19, '41 Hitler

AIR FORCE HIGH COMMAND (OKL)
Commander-in-Chief
Reichmasrschall Goering
From Apr. 25-27, '45 F.M. Greim

NAVAL HIGH COMMAND (OKM)
Commander-in-Chief
Gr. Adm. Raeder
From Jan. 30, '43, Gr. Adm. Doenitz
From May 2, '45, Adm. V. Friedeburg

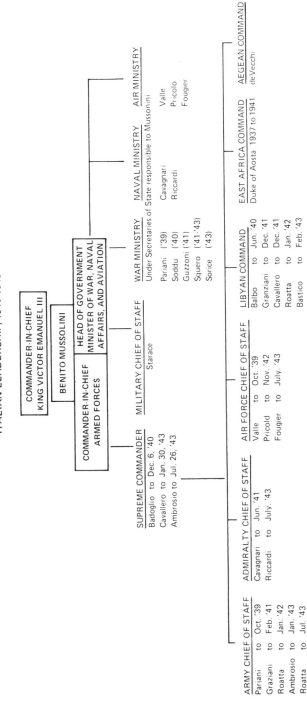

ITALIAN LEADERSHIP, 1940-1943

COMMANDER-IN-CHIEF
KING VICTOR EMANUEL III

BENITO MUSSOLINI

HEAD OF GOVERNMENT
MINISTER OF WAR, NAVAL
AFFAIRS, AND AVIATION

COMMANDER-IN-CHIEF
ARMED FORCES

MILITARY CHIEF OF STAFF
Starace

WAR MINISTRY
Under Secretaries of State responsible to Mussolini

Pariani   ('39)
Soddu   ('40)
Guzzoni   ('41)
Squero   ('41-'43)
Sorice   ('43)

NAVAL MINISTRY

Cavagnari
Riccardi

AIR MINISTRY

Valle
Pricolo
Fougier

SUPREME COMMANDER
Badoglio to Dec. 6, '40
Cavallero to Jan. 30, '43
Ambrosio to Jul. 26, '43

AIR FORCE CHIEF OF STAFF
Valle   to Oct. '39
Pricold   to Nov. '42
Fougier   to July '43

LIBYAN COMMAND
Balbo   to Jun. '40
Granziani   to Dec. '41
Cavallero   to Dec. '41
Roatta   to Jan. '42
Bastico   to Feb. '43

EAST AFRICA COMMAND
Duke of Aosta 1937 to 1941

AEGEAN COMMAND
deVecchi

ADMIRALTY CHIEF OF STAFF
Cavagnari to Jun. '41
Riccardi   to July '43

ARMY CHIEF OF STAFF
Pariani   to Oct. '39
Graziani   to Feb. '41
Roatta   to Jan. '42
Ambrosio   to Jan. '43
Roatta   to Jul. '43

Annotated Chronology

1939

9.1 The German invasion of Poland begins

9.1 France warns Germany to withdraw from Poland

9.2 Mussolini declares Italian neutrality

9.3 France and Great Britain declare war on Germany

9.17 The Soviet Union occupies eastern Poland

9.19 Russian and German troops meet at Brest Litovsk

9.23 German-Soviet Friendship Treaty concluded

9.27 Warsaw surrenders and German *Blitzkrieg* victorious in less than four weeks

9.28 The Soviet Union and Germany divide Poland

10.3 Panama Declaration states security measures for the Western Hemisphere

10.12 The Soviet Union makes territorial demands on Finland

11.3 United States Neutrality Act of 1937 amended, arms embargo repealed, adds "Cash and Carry"

11.30 The Soviet Union invades Finland for the start of the "Winter War"

12.13 British cruisers attack the German battleship *Graf Spee* near Montevideo; ship scuttled by own crew

12.14 The Soviet Union expelled from the League of Nations for the attack on Finland

1940

1.14 Admiral Mitsumasa Yonai forms new cabinet in Japan

3.12 Soviet-Finnish Peace Treaty concluded and "Winter War" is over

3.18 Hitler and Mussolini meet at the Brenner Pass and the Italian dictator expresses war readiness

3.20 Edouard Daladier resigns; Paul Reynaud forms new cabinet

3.30 Japanese-supported Wang Chung-wei government established at Nanking as Chinese puppet regime

4.9 German forces occupy Denmark and invade Norway

5.5 Norwegian exile government established in London

5.10 German invasion of Netherlands, Belgium, and Luxemburg begins

5.10 Neville Chamberlain resigns and Winston Churchill becomes new British Prime Minister; coalition cabinet formed

5.13–14 Netherlands government under Queen Wilhelmina flees to London while Dutch army surrenders to Germany

5.15 Holland occupied and French suffer defeat at Sedan

5.16   Franklin Roosevelt warns Congress of war dangers to the United States

5.28   King Leopold III of Belgium orders the end of resistance to the Germans

5.28   British forces begin evacuation from Dunkirk; losses heavy, but by June 4, some 335,000 French and British troops are rescued

6.10   Italy declares war on France and Great Britain

6.13   German forces occupy Paris and French leaders evacuate

6.16   Marshal Pétain replaces Paul Reynaud as head of the French government

6.17   Ex-Kaiser Wilhelm II congratulates Hitler on the French victory

6.22   France signs armistice with Germany at Compiegne

6.23   French National Committee in London, led by General Charles de Gaulle, announces determination to continue the war against Germany

7.3   British forces attack French fleet at Oran and Mers-el-Kebir

7.5   French government at Vichy severs relations with Great Britain

7.10   Start of the Battle of Britain and Germany plans for invasion

7.19   Hitler offers peace to Great Britain in Reichstag speech

8.4   Italian forces begin invasion of British and French Somaliland

8.17   Germany announces a total blockade for the waters around Great Britain

8.18   U.S. President Roosevelt and Canadian Premier Mackenzie King establish a joint board of defense

9.3   United States acquires bases from Great Britain in Western Hemisphere and provides 50 overage destroyers in return

9.13   Italian invasion of Egypt commences

9.22   Japanese forces enter Indochina

9.27   Japan, Italy, and Germany conclude a ten-year tripartite pact pledging mutual aid in the event of future conflicts

10.12   German troops enter Rumania to secure oil reserves

10.28   Hitler and Mussolini confer in Florence and Italian forces invade Greece

12.9   British counter-offensive against Italian forces in North Africa begins

12.18   German plan for invasion of Russia, Operation "Barbarossa," readied

1941

1.22   British forces capture Tobruk; first British drive into Libya

3.11   U.S. Congress approves Lend-Lease Act enabling the President to aid nations deemed vital to America's defense

3.25   Yugoslavia joins Rome-Berlin-Tokyo Pact

3.27   America, Britain, Canada (A,B,C) begin war strategy talks

4.6   German invasion of Yugoslavia begins; Belgrade occupied on 4.10

4.10   The United States assumes responsibility for the protection of Greenland

4.13   Japan and Soviet Russia sign a neutrality treaty

4.23   Greek resistance to Germany ends and armistice signed

5.27   The United States declares an Unlimited National Emergency

6.22   Germany launches full attack on Russia and the war assumes world dimensions

6.23   French Vichy government surrenders control of French Indochina to Japan

7.7   American forces undertake the defense of Iceland

7.12   Great Britain and Russia conclude a treaty for mutual aid

8.14   Roosevelt and Churchill issue a declaration of peace aims in the Atlantic Charter

8.25–29   Soviet and British forces establish a cooperative regime in Iran

10.17   General Hideki Tojo becomes Japanese Premier and Minister of War

11.6   The United States extends Lend-Lease to the Soviet Union

11.25   Bulgaria, Denmark, Finland, Rumania, Croatia, Slovakia, and China (Nanking) join Rome-Berlin-Tokyo alliance

12.5   German forces reach Moscow

12.7   Japan attacks Hawaii, the Philippines, Guam, Midway Island, Hong Kong, and Malaya

12.8   The United States declares war on Japan

12.11   Italy and Germany declare war on the United States

12.25   Britain surrenders Hong Kong to Japanese forces

1942

1.1   First Washington Conference ends; places first priority on defeating Germany

1.1   United Nations Declaration issued in Washington; twenty-six nations signed

1.11   Japanese forces begin the invasion of the Netherlands East Indies

1.20   "Wannsee Conference" in Berlin ("Final Solution" to the Jewish question decided)

2.15   Singapore falls to Japanese forces

4.9   The United States surrenders Bataan to Japan

4.11   Indian Nationalist Leaders demand immediate independence from Great Britain

4.18   U.S. bomber planes, led by Colonel James Doolittle, bomb Tokyo

5.6   United States surrenders Corregidor to Japanese

5.6–8   Japanese and United States forces fight the Battle of the Coral Sea; prevented Japanese invasion of Australia

5.26   The Soviet Union and Great Britain sign a twenty-year mutual aid treaty

5.26   German forces in Africa under General Rommel open second drive into Egypt; Tobruk re-captured 6.21

5.30   First 1000 Bomber raid conducted by R.A.F. against Cologne

6.4   Japanese repulsed in Battle for Midway Island; U.S. inflicts heavy losses

6.25–27   Second Washington Conference; Roosevelt and Churchill plan invasion of North Africa

8.12–15   Churchill and Stalin meet in Moscow

8.19   Unsuccessful Allied raid on Dieppe

9.16   The Battle for Stalingrad begins

10.23   General B. L. Montgomery's British Eighth Army pushes General Rommel's forces eastward at El Alamein

11.8   British and American forces land in French North Africa in massive invasion; Operation "Torch"

11.11   German troops occupy all of France

11.12   United States forces gain victory in battle for Solomon Islands

11.19-20   Soviet counter-offensive begins after Stalingrad

11.27   French navy scuttled by crews in Toulon to prevent German seizure

1943

1.11   Great Britain and the United States relinquish extraterritorial rights in China

1.14–24   Roosevelt and Churchill meet in Casablanca for conference and announce an "unconditional surrender" formula to be applied to the Axis powers

1.18   Soviet land forces close on Leningrad

1.31 German forces under Field Marshal von Paulus surrender to the Russians at Stalingrad

2.18 Goebbels calls for "total war"

4.19–5.16 Jewish uprising in the Warsaw ghetto

4.27 The Soviet Union breaks relations with the Polish government-in-exile (in London) after Katyn Massacre discovery

5.4 Generals Charles de Gaulle and Henri Giraud form French Committee of National Liberation

5.12 Roosevelt and Churchill confer in Washington on plans for a second front in Europe

5.12–13 The German Africa Corps surrenders; Rommel has long since returned to Europe

5.15 Stalin announces dissolution of Third International (Comintern)

5.24 Turning point in U-boat war: Admiral Doenitz ceases North Atlantic convoy fight

6.29 United States forces land in New Guinea

7.5 Beginning of German and Soviet battles in the Kursk salient; largest armored conflict of the war

7.10 Combined British, Canadian, and American forces invade Sicily; Allies gaining full control of the Mediterranean

7.25 Mussolini and his cabinet placed under arrest; the Duce is replaced by Marshal Pietro Badoglio, who dissolves the Fascist party

8.11–24 Allied Conference at Quebec (first) discusses war problems, second front, and possible growing alienation of Russia

9.3 The first Allied forces land in southern Italy; Oct. 1, American troops enter Naples

9.9 Italian Badoglio government accepts Allied surrender terms from General Eisenhower

9.10 German forces occupy Rome after Badoglio surrenders to Allies

9.13 Chiang Kai-shek elected President of Chinese Republic; remains commander-in-chief of the Chinese army

9.15 Mussolini, after rescue by a German force, proclaims a Republican Fascist Party for northern Italy

10.9 Marshal Tito (Josip Broz) leads Yugoslavian guerilla forces against Axis troops near Trieste

10.13 Badoglio's Italian government declares war on Germany

11.6 Soviet troops liberate Kiev

11.9 The United Nations Relief and Rehabilitation Administration (UNRRA) holds first meeting in the United States

11.22–26 First Allied Conference held at Cairo; demands Japanese unconditional surrender

11.22 American forces land in the Gilbert Islands and destroy Japanese resistance after three days of battle

11.28 Start of the Allied Conference at Teheran; Roosevelt, Churchill, and Stalin coordinate war plans

1944

3.19 German troops occupy Hungary and a pro-German government established

4.17 Japan opens a renewed offensive against China

6.4 Allied armies enter Rome

6.6 The Allies land in Normandy (Operation "Overlord") in largest invasion in history

6.13 First German flying bombs, the V-1, begin to hit England

6.15 American forces invade Saipan and first B-29 raid against Japan occurs

6.22 Beginning of the Soviet summer offensive in central Russia

7.1–15 Bretton Woods Conference establishes International Bank for post-war reconstruction

7.20 A German resistance group attempts to kill Hitler

7.23 The Soviets capture Lublin and

establish a Polish Committee of National Liberation

7.24   French forces under General Leclercq enter Paris and next day the city is liberated

8.1   Residents of Warsaw rise against the Germans, but resistance is crushed when Soviet aid is not forthcoming

8.15   Allied landings are made in southern France

8.24   Rumania surrenders to advancing Russian forces

9.4   Brussels liberated by advancing British troops

9.5   Russia declares war on Bulgaria; the government of Bulgaria surrenders on Sept. 8

9.8   First German V-2 rocket hits London

9.10   Conference at Quebec (second) finalizes plans to complete wars in Europe and the Pacific

9.12   Rumania signs an armistice with the Allies

9.12   The American First Army crosses the border into German territory

10.25   Battle of Leyte Gulf

10.28   Bulgaria signs an armistice with the Allies

12.10   France and Russia sign a twenty-year Mutual Security Alliance

12.16   German Ardennes offensive begins (Battle of the Bulge)

1945

1.1   France becomes full member of the United Nations

1.12–13   Start of major Soviet offensive against Germany

2.7–12   Yalta (Crimea) Conference attended by Roosevelt, Churchill, and Stalin; support promised for the United Nations, liberated states of Europe, and Russia agrees to enter the war against Japan after Germany's defeat

3.3   Finland declares war on Germany

3.7   The United States First Army crosses the Rhine at Remagen

3.22   Arab League created by a pact drafted in Cairo

4.12   President Roosevelt dies unexpectedly; Harry Truman becomes the new American President

4.25   Beginning of United Nations Conference in San Francisco, representatives of 50 nations meet to draft the U.N. Charter

4.25   Russian and American forces meet at Torgau on the Elbe

4.28   Mussolini caught and executed by Italian partisans as he attempts escape to Switzerland

4.30   Adolf Hitler commits suicide in Berlin; Admiral Karl Doenitz appointed his successor

5.7   Doenitz's government signs formal surrender at Reims signalling Germany's total defeat; surrender ratified two days later in Berlin

7.10–19   American attacks against Japanese home islands increase in intensity

7.16   The United States explodes an atomic bomb in a secret test at Alamogordo, New Mexico

7.17   Start of the Potsdam Conference (Berlin) with participation by Great Britain, Russia, and the United States; decisions reached on treatment of Germany; meeting ended 8.2

8.6   First atomic bomb dropped by the United States on the Japanese city of Hiroshima; over 50,000 people killed

8.8   The Soviet Union declares war on Japan, and Russian forces enter Manchuria

8.9   Second atomic bomb dropped by the United States on the Japanese city of Nagasaki

8.28–9.2   United States forces land in Japan; terms of surrender signed on board U.S.S. *Missouri*

9.2   Japan signs formal terms of surrender in Tokyo

10.24   The United Nations comes into official existence with ratification of its Charter by 29 nations; headquarters to be located in the United States

Photographs

1. Signing of the Russo-German non-aggression treaty, Aug. 23, 1939. Molotov seated, von Ribbentrop in middle, Stalin on right.

2. Execution of a young Pole by the German SS, 1939.

3. British searchlights probe the skies over London for German planes during the Battle for Britain, 1940.

4. Roosevelt and Churchill aboard the cruiser *Augusta* during the signing of the Atlantic Charter, Aug. 1941.

5. Rommel directs his first offensive into Egypt beginning March 1941.

6. The destruction at Pearl Harbor after Japan's attack of Dec. 7, 1941.

7. The face of a captured Russian soldier; somewhere on the eastern front, 1942.

8. American troops leave for England aboard the *Queen Mary*, 1943.

9. U.S. Maj. Gen. D. H. Connolly presides over transfer of Lend-Lease supplies to the U.S.S.R. in Teheran, 1943.

10. An important part of Allied propaganda was delivered by leaflets; compare texts of the authentic Safe Conduct leaflet (left) with the altered German copy on right, 1944.

11. Allied leaders meet at the Yalta Conference in Feb. 1945. Eden facing camera, Molotov and Stalin directly above, Churchill lower left.

12. American B-17s bombing Dresden, Feb. 1945.

13. Hitler effigy decorates Rhine bridge, Apr. 1945.

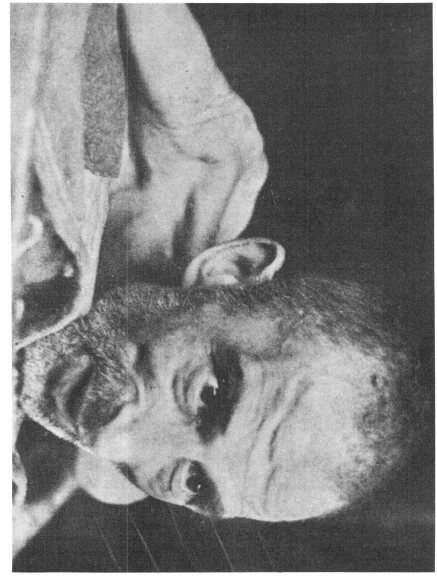

14. A survivor of Germany's death camps, Apr. 1945.

15. Russian forces enter Vienna, Apr. 1945.

16. American and Russian soldiers meet at Torgau on the Elbe, Apr. 25, 1945.

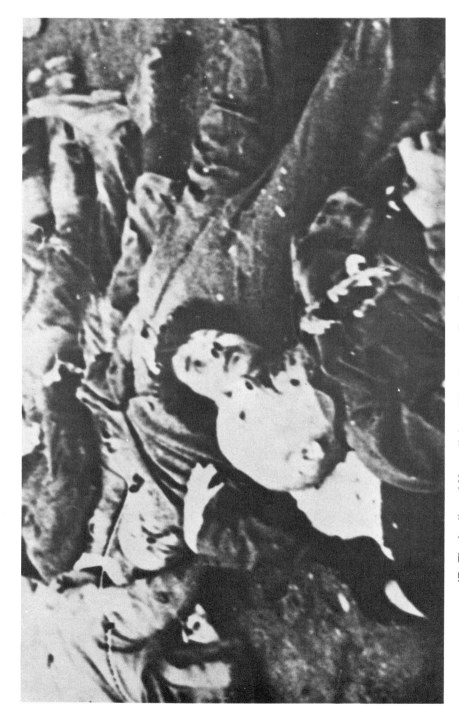

17. The bodies of Mussolini and his mistress Clara Petacci in Milan, Apr. 29, 1945.

18. Red soldiers raise their flag over the ruins of the German Reichstag in Berlin, Apr. 1945.

19. **An American soldier receives jubilant welcome from Czech girls in Pilsen, May 1945.**

20. Japanese forces surrender to Great Britain in Burma, 1945.

21. The atomic blast over Nagasaki, Aug. 9, 1945.

22. War crimes trial at Nuremberg, 1945–46. Front row left Goering, Hess, von Ribbentrop, Keitel; top row left Doenitz, Seyss-Inquart, von Schirach, Sauckel; Speer standing.

Index

Events are listed chronologically under main headings.

A

ABC-1 (American, British, Canadian staff conversations), Mar. 1941, 126, 127, 141–145, 186

Admiralty Islands, 287, 295

Adriatic, 94, 110, 367

Aegean, 100, 204, 247

Africa (*see also* Operation Torch), 4. 8, 66, 94, 98, 128, 134, 196, 226, 239, 309

Aitape, 295

Alaska, 194, 195, 224, 248

Albania, 21, 94, 108–109, 114, 247, 361, 367

Aleutian Islands, 187, 211, 214, 217, 248, 290

Alexander, Harold, British field marshal, 234, 237, 238, 264, 308

Algeria, 227

Algiers, 228ff., 252

Allied (*see also* Combined Chiefs of Staff)
Combined Planning Staff, 263ff.
Control Commission, 315, 421, 432, 434
report on Russian front, Aug. 1943, 273
Declaration on Iran, Dec. 1943, 283–284
Declaration on German Atrocities, Nov. 1943, 364–365
Armistice with Rumania, Sept. 1944, 313–314
Armistice with Bulgaria, Oct. 1944, 314
Armistice with Hungary, Jan. 1945, 314–315
plans for Germany after defeat (*see* Morgenthau Plan, European Advisory Commission, Yalta Conference, Potsdam Conference, Strang memorandum)
invasion of France (*see also* Operation Overlord), 377ff.
occupation reports on Germany, 408–412
Reparation Commission, 417

America-Britain
Grand Strategy, 186, 193–195
strategy for 1943, 243–249, 273–274

Anglo-American assistance to the Soviet Union, Aug. 1941, 155–156

Anglo-Soviet alliance, May 1942, 219–221

Ankara, treaty of, 95

Anson, 129

Antonescu, Ion, Rumanian general, 96, 357
"Order of the Day," June 22, 1941, 118

Antonov, Soviet general, 322–323

Antwerp, 266

Apamama, 294

Aquitania, 201

Arab League Pact, Mar. 22, 1945, 380, 385–390

Arabia, 390–391

Arabian Sea, 38–39

"Arcadia" (*see also* Washington conferences), 186

Ardennes (*see also* Battle of the Bulge), 305, 333

Argentina, 35

Arima, Japanese admiral, 298

Ark Royal, 79

Arnold, Henry, American air general, 197, 199, 211
first war report of Jan. 4, 1944, 213–214
statement on Allied air attack of May 12, 1944, 305

Asia, 4, 8, 133, 134, 136, 145, 159ff., 192, 211, 212, 241, 289

"Associated Powers," 142

Atlantic (North, Central, South). 38, 65, 81, 127, 129, 130, 133, 134, 187, 206, 232, 241, 353, 366

Atlantic Charter, Aug. 14, 1941, 8, 9, 127, 156–157, 186, 201, 203, 241, 284, 399, 414

Atomic bomb
"A Report to the (U.S.) Secretary of War,"

493

H